FISCAL POLICY FOR
ECONOMIC GROWTH IN LATIN AMERICA

JOINT TAX PROGRAM

ORGANIZATION OF AMERICAN STATES
INTER-AMERICAN DEVELOPMENT BANK
ECONOMIC COMMISSION FOR LATIN AMERICA

FISCAL POLICY
FOR ECONOMIC GROWTH
IN LATIN AMERICA

Papers and Proceedings of a Conference on Fiscal Policy.

held in Santiago, Chile, December, 1962

Published for THE JOINT TAX PROGRAM

by THE JOHNS HOPKINS PRESS

Baltimore, Maryland

JOINT TAX PROGRAM

Alvaro Magaña	(OAS)
James A. Lynn	(IDB)
Pedro Mendive	(ECLA)

Foreword

The present volume contains the papers, proceedings and final report of a Conference on Fiscal Policy for Economic Growth in Latin America which was held in Santiago, Chile, 5—14 December, 1962, under the auspices of the Joint Tax Program of the Organization of American States, the Inter-American Development Bank, and the United Nations Economic Commission for Latin America.

Approximately seventy experts in tax and fiscal matters attended this Conference. The meeting allowed a free, and at times vigorous, exchange of views between academicians and high government officials charged with administrative responsibilities in many of the areas discussed. The discussion was aided by the fact that all who attended the Conference did so in their personal capacity and not as spokesmen or representatives of any institution or government. The Conference evoked a broader and deeper analysis of the technical and practical issues of fiscal policy and tax reform than had heretofore been undertaken in Latin America.

The present volume may be considered a survey of the general features of the tax reform measures required by the Latin American countries as one of the keys to accelerate their development process, following the basic principles of the Act of Bogotá and the Charter of Punta del Este.

Opinions expressed by authors, discussants, and participants are their exclusive responsibility and do not necessarily coincide with those of the organizations sponsoring the Conference. A Spanish version was published by the Pan American Union in 1964 under the title *Reforma Tributaria para América Latina: II Problemas de Política Fiscal.*

The Directors of the Joint Tax Program wish to thank Mr. Marto Ballesteros, Chief of the Public Finance Unit of the Department of Economic Affairs, Organization of American States, for his assistance in reviewing and editing, for publication in this volume, the papers and proceedings of the Santiago Tax Conference.

Contents

1

Fiscal Policy in Latin America's Economic Development

by Victor L. Urquidi*

INTRODUCTION

It has never been so urgently necessary as it is today for the Latin American countries to define and harmonize the fiscal and financial policies of their governments. The commitments embodied in the Charter of Punta del Este go beyond the mere enunciation of the desirability of a development policy: they imply more rapid economic development until an annual per capita rate of growth of the product amounting to at least 2.5 per cent has been reached and maintained, the attainment of a high level of social well-being, and a more equitable distribution of national income. As the Latin American countries are to move toward these goals, the governments and the various private sectors, together with foreign and international official agencies and foreign private opinion, will have to pay increasing attention to the aims and implications of fiscal policy as an essential factor in the accelerated growth and structural transformation of the Latin American economies.

This contention assumes that it is incumbent upon the governments to play a decisive part in the task of quickening development and pursuing new social aims, even though the scope and methods deemed appropriate for each country must be observed. But the private sectors affected by and contributing toward fiscal policy should, no less than the government itself, assume a fundamental re-

sponsibility for economic and social development. The success of development policy and, ultimately, of the programs and plans drawn up is just as dependent on the level and composition of private investment and on the efficacy of production and distribution activities in the private sectors as it is on their public counterparts.

Accordingly, the first thing to realize is that fiscal policy is not merely a government concern or one which only governments should formulate but is a matter which should be understood and appreciated by the public generally.

A technical meeting such as that now being held is only a first step. In this, as in many other economic fields, there has been a failure to adapt or transform general ideas that are applicable everywhere or in the more developed countries with a view to transplanting them to the less developed areas, particularly Latin America, where institutional, political, and human characteristics differ from those of the countries in which the technical concepts of finance and growth originated. Fiscal policy, even in the isolated or fragmentary way in which it is applied in Latin America, reflects a state of affairs quite distinct from that implicit in the models furnished by the developed countries. Yet no theory of fiscal policy in Latin America has been formulated, no doubt largely because those called upon to study it seem, in the majority of cases, to be shackled by traditional basic concepts or fall into rather academic theorizing. Without

*Adviser to the Ministry of Finance and Public Credit, Mexico City, Mexico.

1

attempting to justify the unsound aspects of Latin American fiscal policies, let alone the complete absence of policy we sometimes meet with, we must not find fault with the heterodoxy of Latin American fiscal policies simply because they are different. Current fiscal policy may, however, be criticized as irrational or incompatible with development aims, even assuming that it has some *raison d'être*.

In these circumstances, and in view of the problems of achieving economic development and securing social justice that are of paramount concern to the Latin American governments today, the public finance expert has a responsibility in three fields: more accurate understanding of the real situation, pure research, and practical recommendations to governments. It is equally essential that ideas on fiscal policy be disseminated and discussed in professional circles and—with the help of suitable machinery—in the private sectors. The universities, the national and international research institutes and centers, and the relevant official agencies have within their reach the possibility of collaborating with private industrial and commercial organizations in studying and assessing each country's requirements in the way of fiscal policy for its economic development. The private sector, in particular, insofar as it is able to rise above the mere consideration of its business or group interests and to pay due heed to the complex relations between the public and private sector that are implicit in economic development, is undoubtedly capable, with proper guidance, of collaborating actively and effectively in furthering fiscal policy and perfecting its instruments.

THE OVER-ALL CONCEPT OF FISCAL POLICY

In keeping with the foregoing, it will be useful to try to define the sphere of action that fiscal policy can or should embrace in Latin America today.

The sphere of fiscal policy may be taken to be the whole body of measures relating to the tax systems, public expenditure, contracting of internal and external debt by the state, and the operations and financial situation of the autonomous and semipublic agencies and bodies, through the medium of which the amount and distribution of investment and public consumption as components of national expenditure are determined and the amount and composition of private investment and consumption are influenced directly or indirectly.

In some ways, this definition may be too broad; for instance, if the operations of state enterprises that usually act as if they were private industrial or commercial firms are regarded as coming within the orbit of fiscal policy. But it may also be regarded as a little too narrow if we consider that many other measures taken by the state and semipublic agencies—and even events and actions of a purely political nature—affect public income and expenditure and the decisions of the private sector with respect to its own investment or its consumption pattern. In common with all definitions, the definition of the scope of fiscal policy will naturally not be satisfactory by every standard, but it can be used as a basis for considering the main elements of a fiscal policy designed to help economic development and, more particularly, for determining the effectiveness of the instruments that could be used by the public sector to achieve the goals established.

The proposed definition implies that the influence of fiscal policy on economic and social development depends essentially on what each country conceives to be the role of the state. To the extent that it is recognized, as it is in most Latin American countries, that the state should be responsible for creating the infrastructure for development by means of direct basic investment in different economic and social fields—irrigation, roads and ports, schools, hospitals, housing, and even for some agricultural, industrial, and distribution activities (machinery-distribution centers, production of fertilizers, steel material, manufacturing, generation of electric energy, and marketing of foodstuffs or of certain export goods)—the direct influence of fiscal policy may be considerable. In this case, the public sector will appropriate a large proportion of private revenue by means of taxation and other instruments and then transfer it to other hands, creating new revenue through investment and other types of expenditure. In some instances, the concept of the state's responsibility for development goes even further and includes, for example, petroleum production, rail transport, banking, insurance, etc.

But even if it is assumed that in any particular country the idea prevails that the state should have as little as possible to do with infrastructure matters and that it should only exceptionally undertake activities directly related to production or distribution, still the fiscal policy, although less effective as regards the participation of the public sector in national income and expenditure, will be just as significant and important as in the previous case, since it will be responsible for guiding the multifarious decisions taken with respect to private investment and consumption, reconciling them with national economic development aims, and adapting their tempo and distribution to the requirements implicit in those aims.

It may even be said that if it is thought preferable for the bulk of investment to be made by the private sector and for the state not to undertake industrial, commercial, or distribution activities, fiscal policy should be defined with even greater precision and with an increased awareness of its repercussions. As long as the state plays a very important part in national investment and consumption and absorbs a large proportion of national income, fiscal policy will tend to become a policy for the optimum distribution of expenditure and, from the operative point of view, will require above all the application of satisfactory criteria and the establishment of co-ordination mechanisms in the public sector that will enable the state to act with greater efficiency. But where the direct contribution made by the state is small, the basic tenets of

fiscal policy should be amplified to include the many ways in which—through incentives and banking and monetary regulations as well as legislative and administrative measures in the agricultural, industrial, public utilities, and other sectors, and even trade policy instruments—private decisions can be so guided as to contribute toward the attainment of development targets acceptable to the community.

According to quantitative data available, at the present time most of the Latin American countries are, in practice, closer to the second than to the first extreme. There are few countries where the public sector represents more than 15 per cent of national expenditure, where public investment exceeds 33 per cent of total gross investment, or where tax revenue is over 12 per cent of the gross product. Consequently, a fiscal policy formulated as a harmonious and consistent whole and defined with proper clarity is, in most cases, of supreme importance to programs for the accelerated economic development of Latin America, since the behavior of the private sector will largely condition the results achieved.

In discussing fiscal policy as a whole, it should be pointed out, however obvious it may seem, that it is not confined either to the tax measures adopted by a country's central or federal government or to the parallel consideration of the distribution of the central government's expenditure, with greater or lesser emphasis on the proportion allotted to investment and financing to raise national production capacity. The repercussions of taxation and expenditures should be considered jointly in relation to the economic sectors that each affects, but the concept of fiscal policy should also include the influence and significance of budget deficits or surpluses and the ways in which the former can be remedied or the latter utilized. There has been a tendency to regard an unbalanced budget as a monetary policy and central bank problem or as a strictly "financial" matter, but it should be increasingly realized that this type of deficit or surplus is essentially a component of national expenditure or saving and that its economic repercussions—i.e., its repercussions on the flow of income and on the balance of payments—are as important as its monetary aspects, if not more so.

Fiscal policy also covers the state, provincial, and municipal governments as well as the federal or central districts in which some Latin American countries have their capital cities. The relative importance of taxation, expenditure, and borrowing in the provinces or states, the central district, and the municipalities is conditioned by a number of factors; and although these may be of minor importance in some countries, they should nonetheless be co-ordinated with fiscal policy as a whole. Any inconsistencies in the measures adopted by the central government and a provincial government may affect the rate of private investment adversely or militate against certain categories of productive investment.

What is less obvious—or, even if admitted in theory, has been put into practice only in exceptional cases—is the extension of the field of fiscal policy to embrace autonomous or semipublic agencies and enterprises that are wholly or partially owned by the state, including state banks. The incorporation of a wide range of semipublic organizations and institutions poses a number of practical problems, some of which bristle with juridical and administrative difficulties. There are agencies whose purpose is to make a certain kind of investment and to which the revenue from a specific tax is assigned, as well as a capital subsidy deriving from the budget. Such agencies are simply an offshoot of the government with administrative autonomy, and in a consolidation of accounts they would necessarily form part of the total income and expenditure of the public sector. But if a given agency also provides a service and receives a rate or payment for that service, it is a moot point whether its income and expenditure should be considered in gross or net form. The answer depends on the extent to which the service in question resembles the service that would normally be provided by the government. The further it departs from this, the

more reason there is for considering only net current revenue and the increment in its depreciation reserves (net and gross savings) and gross physical investment effected by the agency as components in the public sector's account, and not the agency's total income and expenditure.

It is generally agreed that state agencies that operate as if they were industrial, commercial, or transport firms or that are actually corporations constituted in accordance with the commercial legislation in force form an intrinsic part of the public sector, but only their savings and investment accounts, and not their current accounts, are thus treated. In an over-all concept of fiscal policy, however, an enterprise's entire income and expenditure should be included, (i.e., its gross effect on the flow of national income and expenditure), since even when an enterprise enjoys a considerable amount of independence its policy is, in the final analysis, determined by the decisions that its owner—in other words, the state—takes through the executive (and frequently with the vigorous intervention of the legislative as well). The total economic effect of the income and expenditure administered by the state can be assessed only if the whole of the public sector's accounts are consolidated at the gross level (excluding transfers within the sector itself).

Similarly, fiscal policy, in the widest sense of the term, can be applied through the changes in the net income of semipublic enterprises. This is quite clear in the case of transport or electric-power enterprises whose rates can be fixed more or less as the state decides, either to cover the cost of the service and provide a margin for investment or as a way of subsidizing the private sector without fully defraying the costs.

This is less obvious, but equally true, in the case of state enterprises that compete with private firms in the production of goods and services. The sales price of goods produced by state industrial enterprises is to a certain extent determined by this competition; but as semimonopolistic situations are such a common occurrence, the state can fix prices (through the public enterprise concerned) at higher than normal levels, sometimes in conjunction with its private "competitors" and nearly always with the aid of tariff protection or other methods of import control. In such cases, part of the sales price—or, to put it another way, part of the net profit of the state enterprise—is in actuality a tax. That is to say, fiscal policy really acts through the medium of the commercial or industrial operations of the semipublic enterprises and agencies. To be even more precise, it should be stressed that it does not operate solely through price policy but also through costs particularly the wages and prices paid for the physical inputs supplied by other enterprises in the public sector. Theoretically, at least, and provided that the state had real control over the numerous semipublic enterprises, it would be possible to manipulate the prices of inputs and of the goods and services produced in such a way as to ensure that net income would derive mainly from activities in which it was thought necessary to link up the state directly with investment programs.

A case that merits special consideration is that of social security institutions and insurance and pension funds. In some countries, the tripartite nature of the contribution to such institutions makes it doubtful whether they can strictly be considered as part of the public sector. However, in view of the significance of social security systems for the community as a whole, they should operate as part of that sector, since the contributions made by workers and employers are analogous to a tax assigned to a specific purpose, and the current surplus of income over expenditure (after the transfer of funds from the central government to the institutions in question has been taken into account) is often one of the principal sources of saving in the public sector. Moreover, investment in hospitals and welfare and housing centers by social security organizations often acts as a substitute for the investment that should be directly effected by the state. In practice, fiscal policy extends to the social security systems.

Another factor in fiscal policy that is not always fully recognized concerns the contracting of debt by the different branches of the public sector. The internal or external indebtedness of the central government or of provincial or municipal governments presents no problem. In this respect, financial policy—the administration of the floating or funded debt and of the rate of interest—may be conceived as an integral part of fiscal policy, since to a certain extent the creation of debt is an alternative to taxation as a method of absorbing the savings of the private sector. On determining the scope of fiscal policy, the same problem recurs when financial transactions in the subdivision of semipublic agencies and enterprises come to be considered. To be consistent with the theory that has been put forward, debts contracted by semipublic enterprises should be treated as an aspect of fiscal policy, with the possible exception of short-term commitments (for less than a year) entered into purely for the purposes of current or cash operations.

The activities of government banks constitute another case that is hard to fit into fiscal policy proper. Strictly speaking, the idea that the state has authority over the financial resources—including the income and expenditure—of the different subdivisions of the public sector means that the debit and credit transactions of state banks cannot be excluded. They are financial intermediaries which, insofar as they act and, what is more, achieve their aims, carry out a very important part of the government policy of channeling private savings toward specific investment targets in the private sector itself or even in the semipublic sector. Although, in the case of state financial intermediaries, integration in the consolidated account of the public sector is simply a question of their net income (savings) and their direct physical investment, for the purposes of an over-all concept of fiscal and financial policy a thorough analysis and quantitative assessment would have to be made of the sources of their liabilities and the distribution of their assets, since these can undoubtedly exert a considerable influence on economic development.

In most of the Latin American countries, there is some official mechanism designed to facilitate the marketing of crops, guarantee minimum rural prices, absorb production surpluses, and regulate supplies and stabilize prices of food in urban areas. Such operations are not customarily regarded as forming part of fiscal policy, but in fact they accord with the general concept of it perfectly well. The regulating agency is part of the public sector; its purchases require the support of tax resources or of an allocation against bank credit channeled through the public sector or deriving therefrom. Guarantee prices may act as a subsidy to the agricultural sector if the agency sells at lower prices or incurs losses or, conversely, may represent a tax on the farmer when, for example, they are established at a level below that of external market prices or in any situation in which the regulating agency is a leading purchaser. The stabilization of prices at the consumer level is frequently practiced as a means of subsidizing consumption for the broad masses of the population in large urban centers. Last, losses incurred by the regulating agency affect the central government's budget and financial policy, while its profits, if any, go to swell the public sector's revenue.

In countries where control mechanisms with differential exchange rates exist, the exchange operations of the central bank also come within the sphere of fiscal policy insofar as the differences exceed the normal sale and purchase margins. Many Latin American countries have relied on exchange profits as the equivalent of a source of taxation, and differential exchange rates are considered to constitute export or import duties by virtue of their effects.

To sum up, the conclusion may be reached that the legitimate field of fiscal policy is extremely broad, although in practice it is clearly difficult not only to arrive at the figures whereby the policy in question can be expressed in quantitative terms but also to overcome the administrative, legal, and political obstacles to the unification of fiscal and financial policy under a single authority.

FISCAL AND FINANCIAL PLANNING

If development policy is recognized as consisting of a body of public and private decisions calculated to affect the amount and composition of aggregate demand and in particular to raise the proportion of expenditure devoted to productive investment, and if, moreover, this policy can be given expression within the framework of a medium- or long-term plan or program—which implies the adoption of quantitative targets—the need for an over-all financing plan whereby the aims in question can be achieved becomes obvious. Thus, the fiscal and financial policy of the public sector constitutes the cornerstone of an over-all plan for the financing of development not only through the way in which it finds expression in the income, expenditure, and debt situation of the public sector itself but also through the influence it may exert on the private sector. It is therefore desirable that in Latin America the scope of fiscal policy should be recognized; means of unifying it should be studied, and the best ways of putting it into practice should be determined in the light of each country's structure and conditions.

Before embarking on a consideration of the objectives of fiscal policy and the principal forms it may assume in its various fields of action, it may be useful to explore briefly the problem of the mechanisms for the formulation and definition of a fiscal policy plan.

At first sight, this might seem a relatively minor problem, given the weight and authority that must necessarily be carried in such a matter by the minister for finance. It often happens, however, that policy as regards expenditure is not determined by the supreme financial authority but results, because of the complexity of the functions of the state in Latin America and the different crosscurrents of authority, from decisions adopted without sufficient co-ordination at the sectoral level by various administrative departments and autonomous agencies. Financing of the public sector's expenditure is, in effect, subordinated to expenditure programs which are not always prepared in conformity with an over-all plan, and the general practice is to secure financial resources piecemeal, internal or external sources being tapped independently without reference to the financing of other programs or to other aspects of government financing. These practices go hand in hand with inefficient utilization of the financial resources available within the public sector itself, for want of information and of intercommunication among the various components of the semipublic sector. While it is not suggested that all these components should become communicating vessels, it would certainly be a significant improvement if there were more fluidity in the use of the savings generated in the public sector so that those public agencies which needed them might have access to them before drawing upon outside sources.

With these ends in view and with due regard to the other aspects of fiscal policy, it seems strongly advisable that in every Latin American country financial co-ordination mechanisms should be established at the highest level, particularly if development plans or programs are adopted in which central planning agencies participate. Only by means of a study of the possibilities for the generation and satisfactory channeling of domestic savings, combined with consideration of the expediency and the terms of external borrowing, can it be decided whether a specific public and private investment plan is feasible. The presentation of an investment plan without an extremely precise formulation of the corresponding fiscal and financial plan does not afford sufficient guarantee of success in attaining the proposed development targets.

Taking into consideration the various forms assumed by planning in the Latin American countries, the machinery for adopting decisions will not be complete until it includes some means of submitting to the joint consideration of a committee presided over by the minister for finance not only the manifold aspects of tax and expenditure policy at all governmental levels but also the financing patterns of semipublic agencies and enterprises (including social security services), together with the amounts involved, and the operations of the official banking system and of the agencies responsible for regulating supplies and prices. If no formal mechanism can be established for such purposes, the minister for finance should at least have all the relevant information at his disposal, punctually presented in systematic and well-ordered fashion, so that the central government can make known, through the appropriate channels, the principles to be followed and exercise the necessary supervision. Where constitutional or legal obstacles exist, the provisions concerned should be revised in order to facilitate the essential task of co-ordination.

OBJECTIVES AND INSTRUMENTS OF FISCAL POLICY

One of the fundamental objectives of fiscal policy as an instrument of development is to create sufficient public savings to cope with the estimated volume of public investment and to collect, by means of internal and external borrowing, such additional resources as it may be prudent to obtain from private savings or from foreign savings. Another basic aim consists in absorbing from the private economy, by the most equitable and efficacious means, the income required to cover the provision of those public services which the community regards as indispensable or desirable. A third objective consists in the manipulation of various tax, expenditure, exchange, price- or rate-fixing, and other instruments in such a way as to provide the private sector with sufficient incentives to generate the volume of savings required for economic development and to effect the corresponding investments.

The foregoing basic objectives may be associated with others, in respect of which fiscal policy may play a useful role without necessarily being the best or the most decisive instrument. One of these is the modification or compensation of short-term fluctuations in the economy, a problem particularly apt to arise in Latin America in those countries whose exports consist of a few commodities for which the external markets are unstable and domestic demand is not dynamic or substantial enough to offset a decline in demand abroad. In such cases, fiscal policy, properly co-ordinated with monetary and credit policy, may act as a stabilizing element both on the side of expenditure and on that of easing the tax burden and may even, if monetary conditions permit, help to absorb the real resources diverted by the fluctuation of external demand.

Fiscal policy alone, however, without the support of other aspects of government policy, could not assume responsibility for stabilization without neglecting objectives of more fundamental importance. For example, in situations where the balance of payments is weak, an expansionist policy of fiscal origin has often led to the intensification of inflationary trends and to the propagation of the inflation process beyond the bounds of expediency, thus jeopardizing economic development. It cannot, therefore, be said to constitute an adequate instrument with which to counter a short-term decline in exports. An upward fluctuation is almost the only circumstance in which it can be efficacious as a means of absorbing income and restricting domestic demand so as to prevent excessive expansion. But in both these cases, fiscal policy may better be described as accessory to monetary policy.

Another aim in which fiscal policy can co-operate, without being the most appropriate instrument, is the improvement of income distribution. The need for a more equitable distribution, accepted without question in the more developed countries, is still a subject of controversy in Latin America, the focal point of the discussion being the contention upheld by some that the unequal distribution of income is desirable as a means of promoting the private savings needed to make increased investment possible. This argument has lost a great deal of its force since it has been recognized that there is, as a rule, no connection between the decision to invest and the

prior formation of savings. Moreover, a breakdown of the consumption function by income levels demonstrates that a markedly inequitable income distribution implies only underconsumption and dissaving at the lowest extreme and luxury consumption (largely of imported goods and services) at the highest. But irrespective of the controversy which is still being waged, the Charter of Punta del Este establishes, *inter alia,* a commitment to achieve a more equitable distribution of national income, and to this end all instruments of economic policy must be applied in ways compatible with more rapid development.

Some care is required, however, in measuring the possible effect of fiscal policy as an agent of income redistribution. A more progressive income tax and the various forms of taxation on net wealth and on luxury private expenditure do not really reduce the disparities between levels of personal income before tax. Such incomes may continue to be generated just as unequally as before in consequence of a country's agrarian, commercial, and industrial structure. All that taxation thus achieved would be to redistribute income through the expenditure of the public sector, and that only if the composition of the expenditure in question were such as to place the emphasis on outlays representing services (or production of goods) which would mean an increase in the real consumption and the welfare of the lower-income sectors. None of this is impossible, but it would contribute little unless the state and the community as a whole took action in other fields so as to raise the productivity and the real income of agricultural and industrial workers. Progressive taxation alone might even reduce incentives to private investment; and if this latter were not to expand, the ensuing delay in absorption of labor force increments might greatly slow up the adjustment of income distribution.

The sole purpose of the foregoing remarks is to point out that the improvement of income distribution must be tackled at the root of the problem, i.e., the sources of income itself and the relations between capital and labor which determine the distribution of the product. Fiscal policy, through taxation and expenditure as well as through its links with monetary policy, can make a valuable contribution to the redistribution of income, but this process is not one of its primary objectives. It must be stressed that the fundamental aim of fiscal policy—striking as is the importance of its distributive and social aspects—should be that of building up the public savings required to finance the public investment necessary for economic development, influencing the rate and structure of private investment and consumption in directions consistent with the over-all and sectoral development targets, and procuring the resources needed by the state for the expansion of its current expenditure.

Fiscal policy may be said to operate in four principal areas of action, in which the results achieved play a decisive part in the success of development programs or plans: taxation, public expenditure, the economic efficiency of semipublic production agencies and enterprises, and internal borrowing. On the precision and consistency of the action taken in these fields will depend not only the volume of external debt contracting that a country may need for its development but also the possibility of making effective use of the foreign resources available. Within each area of action, recourse may be had to different instruments and procedures for channeling fiscal policy, and some consideration of these is called for, even though it must be relatively brief.

Taxation

The term "tax reform" should be taken to refer not only to the establishment of new and heavier taxes—an interpretation prevalent today among quite a number of technical experts as well as the general public—but also to a true reconstruction of the tax system, which may involve new taxes but may at the same time imply the elimination or reduction of others.

It cannot be definitively asserted that tax systems in Latin America invariably evolve from complexity to simplicity (perhaps the intricacies introduced in some countries in recent years far outdo anything that financiers in colonial times could have imagined), but there is certainly a tendency to rely more on direct than on indirect taxes—at least in central government taxation—and especially on income tax. If a tax structure is to be efficacious, it must be adapted to the country's institutional life, viewed both in retrospect and in its current patterns, and it must also adequately serve the ends pursued. As one of the instruments of a fiscal policy designed to expedite economic development and implement specific social principles, the tax system may lend itself to the furtherance of that policy's objectives, as described above, but it cannot safeguard its efficacy by dissociating itself from the political and institutional environment. Consequently, efficient fiscal and administrative technique must be combined with sound political judgment if a tax reform is to be anything more than a mental exercise.

This point has a particular bearing on the question of whether effort should be directed in specific circumstances toward completing or strengthening income tax or, for a time, toward improving and rationalizing the various taxes on production, consumption, and transactions (including import duties). Unquestionably, income tax, carried to the height of theoretical perfection as a system designed to tax enterprises and individuals progressively and in conformity with their total economic capacity, is the most equitable, effective, and stable form of taxation and, as long as its rates are not excessively high, the least discouraging to economic activity. But any change in the prevalent form of income tax must be based on the existing situation, including the psychological climate and the atmosphere of the relations between tax authorities and taxpayers produced by the application of the prevailing system. It is no easy matter to make radical alterations in a tax system, any more than to increase the efficiency of fiscal administration. And in countries where there is a good deal of illiteracy, a high proportion of nonwage-earning agricultural and urban population, and a wide dispersion of activity among small production units whose accounting procedures are only rudimentary, the income tax burden is concentrated in practice on a small proportion of the economically active population and a limited number of agricultural, commercial, or industrial enterprises. Even if income tax is wisely conceived and well administered, its yield is restricted by the narrowness of the tax base itself and lacks sufficient elasticity.

Due allowance being made for these limitations, if the real possibilities of each individual country are taken into account, there are undoubtedly vast areas within which the Latin American income tax systems can evolve in the direction of higher yields and greater equity. Perhaps the first step should be a careful revision of many juridical theories which may be unnecessarily cramping the concept of taxable income, especially in relation to individuals, or which in one way or another tend to protect the economic capacity of persons in the higher income brackets or to lessen the effect of progressive rates. The points which should be elucidated and reviewed in the interest of more equitable taxation include, for example, the ideas of imputed or potential income from rents, equity or inequity in respect of family exemptions or allowances at various income levels, retroactivity in taxation on capital gains accruing from immovable property, income deriving from common property in the case of married couples, and so forth. Not far removed from these problems is the question of whether the object of taxation should be income, no matter how it is generated, or work, property, capital, professional activity, etc.—conceptions of taxability which still survive in legislation and above all in the minds of those specialists who cling to tradition. The more progress is made toward the notion of taxing income as such and the farther legislation moves away from the idea of taxation on the source of income, the more likely is the adoption of equitable and efficacious systems.

In most of the Latin American countries, the income tax system is schedular, partly owing to the tradition of regarding the source of income as taxable rather than income itself; the adoption of a consolidated personal income tax gives rise to apparent and real difficulties. Unless the schedular system is a mere administrative device for withholding tax at the source and constitutes only a preliminary step toward the half-yearly or yearly computation of tax liability on the basis of total personal income, it has a serious drawback in that it precludes the equitable application of family allowances and leaves room for inequitable taxation on different sources of income through different progressive scales or rates. The establishment of an over-all surtax on accrued personal income does not entirely solve the problem and does considerably complicate tax administration and the task of the taxpayer himself. It seems essential that an attempt should be made to simplify income tax, in the sense of making a single rate applicable to consolidated personal income and requiring returns from all those persons whose income level exceeds a specified and relatively low figure.

Owing to the structure of agricultural and industrial property which characterizes most of the Latin American countries, personal income deriving therefrom—rents, dividends on shares, interest on loans, yield of securities, royalties, etc.—is concentrated in the hands of a few, in forms not easily identifiable. The well-known shortcomings of the registers of both rural and urban real estate and the practice of authorizing issues of bearer shares and securities are no doubt serious obstacles to the effective application of income tax, but methods of tackling this problem can be devised, and, in particular, the deficiencies and omissions can be reduced as the tax system as a whole becomes more equitable and a keener sense of fiscal responsibility is created.

Improvement of the income tax system, which could mean a considerable increase in government revenue in many Latin American countries, should also aim at preventing any reduction of incentives to investments. This can be achieved by adopting rates that do not rise in an excessively sharp curve, with an average maximum rate of not more than about 35 to 40 per cent at very high income levels. Public resistance to progressive scales is often the result of the lack of clarity with which they are presented. A tax cannot be called very heavy merely because, for example, the marginal rate amounts to 50 per cent, unless it is also known at what income level this tax applies, what is the progressivity at the other levels, what exemptions and family allowances are established, and what other taxes have to be absorbed by the economic capacity of persons in the high-income groups (such as the net wealth tax, specific property taxes, taxes on particular forms of expenditure, etc.). When reference is made in the United States to a 90 per cent tax on personal income, it is usually not explained that this is a marginal rate, that even at fairly high income levels the average rate does not exceed 65 per cent, and that at all rates the taxable income may be considerably less than that earned by the taxpayer by reason of deductions, so that the average rate applicable to the total income is even lower. Similar observations might be made with respect to the rates of income tax in Latin American countries so as to make clear the real effect of the rates. However, it would be preferable, instead of providing such explanations, to present the rates to the public as average rates instead of marginal rates; this would be easier to understand and would facilitate the taxpayer's mental calculations. In any case, for most taxpayers at the intermediate income levels and even for those just inside the higher brackets, an average rate of 30 to 40 per cent might well militate against any desire to invest or to undertake activities that involve risk. Until income tax systems can be improved, the effective application of a moderate maximum rate would seem preferable to the application of very high rates with inefficient administration and incomplete coverage.

However, investment incentives may be more important in relation to taxes on earnings or profits than to taxes on personal income, and it may be that this important aspect of tax policy has been neglected in Latin America. There are, in fact, various types of exemptions, mainly in the form of deductions from the net taxable income of enterprises, either because of the type of activity engaged in (new or essential industries, industries located in particular areas, etc.) or because of special concessions, the creation of reinvestment reserves, etc.; or the exemption may consist in not applying the tax on profits or the tax corresponding to a particular schedule. But it does not appear that there has been a proper rationalization of the existing system of tax exemption with respect to its effects on investment, and in most cases it would be difficult to determine whether the profits tax exemptions granted have constituted a factor that determined or positively affected industrial investment or whether such investments were made because of the other elements that influence the investor's judgment.

It may well be that in many cases the exemptions amount to nothing more—particularly if they are long maintained—than a largely unjustified subsidy, which ensures neither the continuation of the enterprise's investments, an increase in its productivity, nor even reasonably efficient operation. Accelerated depreciation, whose use as an incentive is fairly recent even in the industrial countries, has the advantage of being accorded in respect of investments already made and not of possible future investments subject to various contingencies; consequently it represents a stimulus which, according to the depreciation rates allowed and the period for which the deductions concerned may be made, can be highly effective. In addition, it is a more positive instrument, since it can be applied in different ways in different branches of industry and thus be adapted to the growth projections in industrial development plans and programs. Although this is not the place to enter into more detailed consideration of accelerated depreciation, it may not be amiss to say that it would be useful to make a careful study of the experience of countries in other areas where it has been applied, as well as of the more limited experience that is being obtained in Latin America, with a view to applying this technique on a broader scale as a tax incentive in the place of others that have thus far proved less reliable.

In the tax field, income tax, besides providing a more equitable system, is recognized as also providing a more stable source of government revenue than the traditional taxes on foreign trade and internal transactions. As trade and industry develop, together with a stronger trend toward the conducting of economic activities by corporations, the eventual result, if a firm and rational course is pursued, will be that the taxes on profits and on personal income will represent the largest and most reliable source of government revenue. But zeal for modernization and improvement should not lead to neglect of indirect taxation in the form of taxes on production and consumption, foreign trade, and other types of transaction.

The export tax, which is looked at askance in traditional public finance and has only recently been revived in other underdeveloped areas, cannot be properly regarded as indirect taxation, being in some measure a substitute for income tax as applied to primary activity; it has been particularly useful where there has been a need to impose taxes promptly on the windfall profits for exporters resulting from a currency devaluation or an unforeseen and abrupt increase in international prices. It has also served to maintain a reasonable sales price within the country, below the external price, when an export item such as cotton is also an important raw material for domestic industry. As a tax collection device, it has on occasion proved extremely effective—probably more effective than income tax would have been, considering the delay necessarily involved in income tax collection. However, the export tax is clearly a clumsy and inequitable device as a permanent method of taxing export revenue, since it does not differentiate between the various levels of productivity and efficiency normally reflected in costs and is shifted back to the weakest link in the chain of production and distribution, so that it nearly always affects the agricultural worker either through his wages or through the local

price of his product. As with other taxes on transactions, the arguments for or against the export tax have greater or lesser validity in practice according to the rate of the tax; the lower the rate, the less serious the disadvantages of this form of taxation.

It must be pointed out that other taxes on transactions, whether specific taxes on production or consumption or general taxes in the form of sales taxes or taxes on gross revenue, should be regarded above all as a source of government revenue. This means that they should be at a sufficiently low level, in ad valorem terms, not to discourage production or mass-consumption patterns but sufficiently high to make a substantial contribution to tax revenue. It is true that there are important points to be borne in mind in connection with indirect taxes as regards their possible regressive character, their impact on the real income of large sections of the population, and their effect on production. However, regressivity cannot be properly determined without at the same time considering the structure of public expenditure; for example, a government that devotes a high proportion of its budget to providing free education may be increasing the incomes of the bulk of the taxpayers by a greater proportion that that represented by the incidence of consumption or production taxes on their nominal incomes. It must be admitted that in this field the prime need is not so much for theoretical studies as for empirical studies aimed at applying this form of taxation on sounder lines. In countries that have passed through or are still passing through periods of violent inflation, and to the extent that this contributes to a continuing budget deficit, increases in indirect taxes may be less regressive than the inflation rate itself.

In Latin America, it is above all indirect taxation that has lacked any more or less clearly defined policy. This type of taxation dates from colonial times and still appears, especially when imposed as local and provincial taxes, in forms that may hinder internal trade and, in the final analysis, agricultural and industrial development. Some countries have replaced a multiplicity of specific taxes by general taxes on sales or gross revenue, sometimes shared with the provinces and municipalities, and this trend seems to have much to recommend it from the standpoint both of the economic effects and of fair apportioning of the tax burden. It is more equitable that a man should pay even a modest amount on the basis of what he consumes, whatever the type of consumption, than that he should be exempt from taxation merely because he does not share certain tastes or habits as a consumer, although he still benefits from the services provided by the government.

However, no government should neglect the opportunities that exist, even in conjunction with the trend to establish general sales or gross revenue taxes, to establish special rates for particular types of consumption that are associated with the high-income groups or that are subject to more pronounced income elasticity. Perhaps the simplest form of applying specific taxes at a higher rate on these types of consumption would be to establish the charges in the form of multiples of the amount of the general sales tax, applicable to particular types of transaction; this would avoid the need to establish taxes on each article or service sold and simplify the work of the business enterprise that has to act as the tax collector by adding on the tax. Many financial experts have indicated that special taxes on forms of consumption by the higher-income groups would not only represent an addition to tax revenue that might be considerable but would constitute an equitable supplement to income tax and counteract possible evasion through expenditures made out of unreported income.

Import duties, traditionally an important source of public revenue, now seem to be at a stage where it becomes increasingly difficult to rationalize them from the revenue standpoint. As industrialization progresses in Latin America and tariff protection is extended to cover intermediate goods and even capital goods, import duties, if they are to become more effective as a protectionist device, must become less effective as a revenue instrument. Moreover, in many countries industrial development is effected with the aid of exemptions from import duties, which further diminishes their fiscal value. It would seem that the development of the tax systems in Latin America will have to be on the lines of a gradual decrease in the revenue aspect of import duties.

Tariff protection as such is also, of course, an element in fiscal policy, since it has the aim of encouraging investment in specific activities and safeguarding internal levels of production and employment that in areas of relatively low-productivity levels, such as Latin America, might be difficult to sustain in the face of foreign competition. Despite the many arguments advanced against tariff protection (and other forms of import control) and the no doubt well-founded assertions that in many cases tariffs are excessive, it does not seem likely that tariff protection can be dispensed within Latin America's industrial development plans (except for the intra-area free trade agreements).

This is another subject that cannot be given extended treatment here. However, it may be pointed out that with the structural changes that are likely to take place in the industry of all these countries, it will become more and more difficult to apply the tariff policy, since the protection accorded to given industries will constitute an additional cost burden, and even a hindrance, to other industries which the government is also anxious to establish or develop.

A special type of taxation that in some countries amounts to an important, or even the most important, source of public revenue is that applied to the profits and activities of foreign investment in primary commodities. In recent years, there has been a trend toward seeking agreements with the foreign firms concerned with a view to a comprehensive type of taxation, through taxes on profits, production, etc., representing a given proportion of the total earnings, possibly even exceeding 50 per cent. This type of taxation may be justified from a number of angles, both economic and political; but two points stand out: first, that the extraction of raw materials involves a drain on natural resources calculated to weaken the country's future economic capacity and, second, that such activities have often involved an inordinately rapid distortion of the economic structure that has made it more difficult to develop other economic sectors. Additional taxation of these foreign investments thus merits support as a form of compensation for these adverse effects and can be an important element in fiscal policy if it is used, in particular, to advance economic development programs through public investment in the infrastructure and the financing of expanded national investment in agriculture and industry.

The manipulation of exchange systems through multiple rates of exchange has also served as a source of public revenue in many Latin American countries. In the last analysis, varying rates of exchange act as export and import taxes, although this is not always the reason for establishing them. Where they do exist, the profits or earnings of the exchange fund should be included in general government revenue.

One of the notable defects of the tax systems in Latin America is the low taxation of rural and urban property because of the lack of cadastral surveys and weaknesses in the methods of valuation. Here is not only a very considerable potential source of revenue which may be particularly valuable for provincial and municipal governments (and indirectly for central or federal government), but this type of tax could constitute a device which, applied with administrative efficiency and at differential rates, could stimulate the redistribution of agricultural property and limit, or make more burdensome, the ownership of vast holdings in rural and even in urban areas.

It emerges from the foregoing that if taxation in Latin America is to be an instrument of the first importance in fiscal policy, as seems to be necessary, the moment has come to make a careful evaluation of the tax systems, do away with obstacles created by legal or administrative tradition, simplify the various taxes and make them more comprehensible to the general public, achieve a better understanding of the need to pay taxes on an equitable basis and according to capacity to pay, and introduce into the fiscal structure technical improvements that will make it possible to effect a considerable increase in the revenue collected and ensure that investment decisions in the private sector will have favorable economic effects.

Public Expenditure

Tax reforms will be difficult to justify unless at the same time the governments of Latin America formulate and carry out public expenditure policies that are more in line with the aims of development and welfare that they have undertaken to achieve. Government expenditure is nothing more than a reflection of carefully formed plans and projects expressed in the form of the annual budget; if such plans and projects do not exist or are drawn up in an incomplete or vague fashion, public expenditure will reflect the fact. As part of fiscal policy and in accordance with its other aspects, public expenditure must be in line with investment requirements in the public sector, with the extension and improvement of the educational, agricultural, health, and other services as well as the administrative and defense services, and with the policy of transferring funds to the private sector (in the form of subsidies, etc.), and all this must be done within the framework of over-all and sectoral targets.

Consequently, the only way of rationalizing public expenditure is to prepare long-term plans, based on projections of the investments needed in the public sector and of current expenditure requirements, especially those that increase the population's productive capacity. Program budgeting, widely known for a number of years but applied only on a very limited scale in Latin America, appears to be the most suitable instrument for ensuring that public expenditure becomes more effective. One obstacle to this method is that administrative traditions or legal provisions will have to be modified. Another is that the staff responsible for directing the formulation of the budget lack training; but this can be remedied.

No general a priori criterion can be laid down governing the desirable scope of a government's expenditure, whether in the form of current expenditure or investment. It can be determined only in the light of all the annual plans or programs for investment and expenditure in the public sector and of the growth requirements and short-term considerations that may make it advisable to provide a stimulus in a greater or lesser degree to particular programs. Nevertheless, whatever the volume of expenditure and in view of the tendency for government expenditure to expand, it is essential that the productivity of public administration in Latin America should increase—an aim not incompatible with an improvement in the pay scales and a relative limitation of the volume of public employment.

Efficiency of the Semipublic Sector

The considerable expansion of the semipublic sector in Latin America is attributable largely to the need that has grown up over the years to deal with specific problems, sometimes during a period of crisis, by methods different from those traditional in the public administration. Another reason is that it has been considered in the national interest, for a number of reasons, that the state should dominate a basic sector in the country's present or future production, such as, for example, petroleum, steel, electric power, and so forth. In most of these countries, the public services, often short of capital, have passed from foreign private ownership to the public sector, for example, the railways, telephone companies, and others. But under the development programs of the last few years, the state has also undertaken investments in a number of industries, either directly or through corporations or financial institutions which are likewise state-owned, generally with the aim of providing a stimulus and assuming the risks that private enterprise has not always been able to accept.

The needs in the way of new investment in the semipublic sector and replacement of capital that has been used up are tending to increase and to constitute a considerable proportion of the total for the public sector. The investment programs formulated are an important instrument of a fiscal policy intended to promote and accelerate economic and social development. The problem posed by investment in the semipublic sector is financing. In this respect, four types of semipublic bodies can be distinguished: those with social purposes, enterprises providing public services or producing goods and services which are politically sensitive, institutes that regulate supplies, and enterprises engaged in production on the same lines as private firms.

Semipublic bodies with social purposes may be of various kinds, but two important examples may be given: institutes for housing and for social security. The former, in their initial stages, require capital backing which must nearly always come out of the government budget and may be supplemented by internal and external credit. Insofar as they perform their activities with social efficiency —that is to say, by meeting the vital need for public housing—there is little likelihood of adequate recovery of their investment so as to make a revolving fund out of their capital. Consequently, they create a financing problem which may become serious for the public sector as a whole, since for the most part they will have to be subsidized for many years. This is a factor which must be taken into account in public expenditure programs and in considering the urgency of tax reforms.

Social security institutes, on the other hand, are normally organs which contribute very largely to public sector savings, owing to the accumulation of reserves which the security system makes necessary. This accumulation takes place, even with the continual expansion of their services, by virtue of the fact that in most countries the number of insured persons increases rapidly and industrial and commercial development itself constitutes a continuous source of growth. Some social security systems provide for investment of part of their surplus resources in housing programs, based on guaranteed recovery, and others allow variable proportions of investment for purposes of public health and welfare. There is possibly a tendency, derived from the very abundance of the income of social security institutes, to effect investments which may not always have a very high national priority, and this can be corrected only to the extent that social security finances are integrated into a country's general fiscal policy in order to place social security savings at the disposal of the public sector as a whole, with the required guarantees and yields and by means of the mechanisms of credit, debt issue, etc., most suitable in each case. Immobilization of social security savings or their inadequate use may represent a considerable real cost in the light of other less suitable forms of financing to which governments must often resort.

Public service enterprises, subject to rate fixing and at the same time to considerable expansion requirements nearly always essential to over-all development programs, are faced in Latin America with difficult internal financing problems which at times actually delay the utilization of external credit. The reluctance of governments to adjust electricity and transport rates, for example, has reduced the operating yields of the enterprises concerned, even those which have been nationalized. In terms of the public sector as a whole, this means that the net savings generated by these services is insufficient and that other sources of public funds, including borrowing, must come to the aid of expanding enterprises, at the risk of postponing very high-priority investment programs. The main reason for avoiding a readjustment of public service rates is political: the fear of creating discontent among the users. Even if this is considered a good reason in the case of private concerns, which might be charged with concealed profits or an attitude not in keeping with the aims of national development, in the case of nationalized enterprises it is a rather weak argument,

because what the user does not pay directly as the price for the service he receives he will end up by paying indirectly through taxation or inflation.

If electric-power or transport services were used mainly by persons of low income and not, as is in fact the case, by commercial or industrial enterprises or by users who can afford to pay, a policy of rate subsidies in these services might be justified. But in view of the structure of the demand for power and transport and because of its inelasticity, the rates for electricity can be established in such a way as to fall progressively most heavily on the users with the largest consumption or who can best afford to pay, thus making it possible to subsidize a certain class of users as a matter of social policy. In the case of transport, it is feasible, even if some sensibilities are wounded, to provide different services according to the category of users, as in fact is done in the railways of many countries, instead of subsidizing even those users who can well afford to pay. There would seem to be an urgent need in Latin America for a reconsideration of all the problems of the public service enterprises with a view to formulating, within the over-all framework of the public sector's income and expenditure and in the face of development needs, rate and financial policies more in line with the over-all fiscal policy.

The institutes which regulate the supplies of staple foodstuffs constitute a problem similar to that of the housing institutes, in the sense that they can hardly expect to recover their investment or a substantial part of their expenditure. That is to say, they do not make a positive contribution to the public sector savings, even though they perform economic, social, and at times political functions of the highest importance. These institutes, moreover, make the implementation of monetary policy difficult insofar as—in many countries, at any rate—their funds do not derive from the budget but from credits made available by the central bank which, if not subsequently recovered, may constitute fiscal indebtedness. The need to regulate supplies stems from the unsatisfactory conditions in which much of Latin America's agriculture is still carried out and from the inelasticity of production. Therefore, the fiscal drain which they represent can be stopped only to the extent that the agrarian and agricultural improvement programs undertaken by the Latin American countries are achieved, a question which it is not practicable to examine in this paper. All that need be stressed is that the operations of the commodity agencies are at the moment the Achilles' heel of fiscal policy as a whole.

Last, semipublic enterprises for the production of goods and services and similar to private enterprises are potentially bright spots in the firmament of the public sector insofar as it is assumed that their operations will secure a volume of net income adequate to meet part of their requirements for additional investment. Where the semipublic industrial enterprises make large profits and are not faced with immediate investment needs, this contribution to public savings should be available to other branches of the public sector, either as credit or financial investment. Within the public sector, there is no reason based on fiscal policy to prevent cross-financing among the industrial or other enterprises comprising the sector, providing that the result is effective use of the total resources of the enterprises and assistance in achieving the over-all objectives of development programs and financial policy. The progress made in this direction will depend on the effectiveness of the co-ordination machinery which a government can set up.

It is assumed—though as a rule there are no adequate studies to prove it—that semipublic industrial enterprises are less efficient, or operate at higher cost, than similar enterprises in the private sector. While private enterprises have a pecuniary incentive and are liable to criticism by the shareholder, public enterprises should at least be spurred on by the desire to serve the community in the most productive way possible, not to make enormous profits but to provide services and products at low cost, to create financial reserves for future expansion, and to add to the over-all resources of the public sector. That is to say, government enterprises should not indulge in waste or luxuries which may in the end have repercussions on other aspects of fiscal policy; hence the establishment or strengthening, as the case may be, of the machinery needed for public supervision of their functioning and financial operations is highly recommended.

Internal Contracting of Debts

The forms in which the public sector contracts debts are no less important in fiscal policy than taxation, the structure of expenditure, or the operations of semipublic enterprises. In view of what has happened in the past with respect to public finances in Latin America, there can hardly be said to have been a deliberate policy of internal borrowing; rather this has occurred as an expedient to meet the public expenditure required for every type of government program. There has been contracting of debts for specific development purposes through investments in infrastructure but also for the mere purpose of defraying current administrative expenses or of covering losses in the semipublic sector. Inflationary situations have been both the cause and the effect of deficit financing, and, in general, indebtedness has considerably exceeded the possibilities of absorption by the capital market, particularly the placement of securities against the private sector's available savings.

For the purposes of a broad and general consideration of the problems of fiscal policy as attempted here, it seems unnecessary to enter into details on the possible characteristics of different internal debts contracted by the public sector; it seems better to concentrate on a problem closely related to monetary policy: the limits of internal public contracting of debts.

On the assumption of considerable fluidity as regards financial resources within the public sector and of a general program of investment and utilization of public savings being established, the problem of the internal borrowing that might be necessary would be simplified if the government issued a single type of long-term debenture and allocated the funds to the different parts of the public sector according to their needs. This would be preferable to allowing each public body— state, department, province, or municipality— to issue bonds under different conditions as regards maturity, interest, security, etc. The capital markets of Latin America are still too undeveloped to permit this type of differentiation, and in the end the only effect would be to impair generally the credit of the public sector.

Even if the internal debt issues were unified, there would still remain the problem of determining the absorptive capacity of the capital market. While this problem does not seem to have been carefully studied, experience in Latin America shows that this capacity is relatively limited and that open competition between the government and private enterprise for the scanty private funds available would not be advisable. There are, on the other hand, segments of the capital market to which the public sector could easily turn, such as insurance companies, the reserve funds of public sector agencies, savings and pension funds, etc. However, greater possibilities are offered by the banking system in countries where credit control regulations have been established which ensure placement of part of the resources of banks in government bonds. In this case, the limits—that is to say, the proportion which must be invested in public sector bonds—are set by the regulations themselves and by the monetary policy. A flexible monetary policy can, within moderate limits, "create" within the banking system a growing market of internal debt issues, provided that selective regulation of credit is maintained. On the other hand, a rigid or excessively stabilizing monetary policy would be an obstacle to prudent borrowing by the public sector.

These remarks should be construed not as a preference for either monetary policy but as an indication of the connection there might be between fiscal and monetary policy through

internal borrowing which, along with the other factors—taxes, expenditure, and savings in the rest of the public sector—could facilitate financing of development without impeding the success of monetary policy. It is, no doubt, important that the public sector should revive internal borrowing as a deliberate instrument of financing among the measures aimed at rationalizing development programs.

FISCAL POLICY AND EXTERNAL FINANCING

A fiscal policy directed principally toward facilitating economic development and, accordingly, formulated and executed in such a way as to increase public investment and modify its composition is at once the best guarantee that savings brought in from abroad, in the form of direct loans or investment, will contribute positively and effectively to the achievement of the development targets. While external financial and technical cooperation is essential for carrying out more intensive development programs in Latin America, foreign capital can never replace internal savings or obviate the need to use the latter as effectively as possible. Economic development must rest, as has been repeatedly stated, on internal effort, much of which must be financial.

External borrowing is subject to one general and several specific limitations. The general limitation is the borrowing country's future capacity to pay. In view of the external demand conditions facing Latin America along with other underdeveloped areas, and presupposing a slow growth of exports of most primary products, optimum use of such foreign exchange as is obtainable requires that most of it should be used to pay for imports essential to economic development and only within safe limits for amortizing and paying interest or dividends on foreign debts and investment. If, in order to service foreign capital, a country has to restrict imports of capital or intermediate goods considered essential, the advisable limit of borrowing will have been exceeded. In determining this limit, some part is played not only by the export prospects for goods and services but also by the success of the development program with respect to the substitution of imports produced by the increase in internal production capacity in relation to the growth of over-all demand. In order to broaden the margin of external borrowing, dynamic import substitution must in turn be based on a coherent public and private investment program and also, of course, on the proper and effective use of internal savings; this means, in the final analysis, that there is a link between the possibilities for contracting debts and fiscal policy.

This relationship is found also in the fact that external borrowing is subject to specific limitations. Notwithstanding the fact that it might be advisable for foreign credit given in support of development programs to consist of a general financing of the deficit in the balance of payments current account, composed partly of long-term and partly of medium- or short-term credit, the fact is that there is no international machinery which allows this type of financing at the moment and that the policy of international financial agencies and various government loan offices tends to be to finance specific projects and, at best, sectoral or regional programs of limited scope. Only in very exceptional cases have credits been granted for balance of payments purposes or to refinance the external floating debt (apart from those of the International Monetary Fund).

The comprehensive way in which the major part of the additional imports required by Western Europe for its postwar reconstruction was financed has been given scant attention in considering the external financing provided for in the Punta del Este Charter. So long as the policy of financing only specific projects prevails, the prospects of using external credit may be limited by lack of internal financial resources in the project concerned from the outset or allocated to it. For example, an autonomous agency or a semipublic enterprise without sufficient means of its own to finance part of its expansion program will not be able to obtain the necessary external credit or will be able to use only part of the amount contracted for. External credit is granted only for the purpose of financing the import costs of the project or, exceptionally, part of the internal costs. Its use will, therefore, be conditioned, in fact, by an important aspect of fiscal policy previously mentioned, i.e., the capacity of the semipublic sector to generate sufficient net income. If lack of such capacity is made up for by a government budget allocation or through internal credit, the problem will remain unchanged as regards the fact that external capital can be used only if fiscal policy as a whole is adequate.

Foreign private investment, as a factor contributing to the development of industry and of Latin America's natural resources, may also be limited by certain shortcomings in fiscal policy. The most obvious shortcoming is the prevailing fiscal system, whether devised specifically to enable the recipient country to participate in the profits of enterprises engaged in the development of primary products or the general system insofar as it may discriminate against foreign capital or contain unduly harsh provisions. But the policy developed over the past few years of combining foreign capital with domestic capital in a given proportion may also have some influence. Among the many factors which may limit or hinder the investment of domestic capital in subsidiary enterprises financed with foreign capital or in association with such capital are the methods and rates of taxation of personal income, or the lack of specific incentives to purchase shares in this type of concern which, it is said, offer at times a smaller margin of profit than the domestic investor is accustomed to. This is mentioned merely to show once again that the relationship between fiscal policy and the use of external financial resources is important.

Last, it should be remembered that programs of international financial co-operation in Latin America are not mere unilateral offers but form part of the set of objectives and procedures considered in the Punta del Este Charter; these include undertakings on the part of Latin American governments to speed up structural changes in the economic and social field. Consequently, as far as fiscal

policy as a whole is an instrument for recasting the internal structure and tends to increase productive capacity and to retain in Latin America the savings generated and use it for the benefit of development programs, external financial co-operation could no doubt be more extensive and more prompt.

Comment

FELIPE PAZOS*

Victor Urquidi's paper clearly, systematically, and comprehensively states the problems of fiscal policy in Latin America, thus admirably fulfilling the function assigned to it of serving as an introduction to the discussions of this conference and as background and general frame of reference for the other papers, which analyze the various instruments and some of the aspects of fiscal policy.

Following a strictly logical order, Mr. Urquidi defines the sphere of action of fiscal policy, examines the manner of formulating and implementing it, lists its objectives, and then proceeds to analyze the efficacy of its various means and instruments. These include not only taxation and expenditures of the national government, the provinces, and the municipalities but also the operations of social security funds, agricultural price-stabilization agencies, other semipublic agencies, government enterprises, and the mechanisms of financial intermediaries and money creation. I am in entire accord with the author's over-all treatment of these activities and mechanisms, which are intimately interrelated and whose functions could not be well understood if studied separately. My only reservation, which is entirely one of terminology, is whether we should call the technique of over-all management of these instruments "fiscal policy" or whether it would be better to refer to it as

*Member of the Panel of Nine, Alliance for Progress, Washington, D.C.

"financial policy" or "fiscal and financial policy." But the name is not important; what *is* important is that the author is completely correct in studying the instruments as forming part of one system.

I consider Mr. Urquidi's paper to be the best over-all study that I have read on the problems of fiscal and financial policy in Latin America, and I agree with most of his reasoning and recommendations. I could devote a good part of these comments to support the theories with which I agree, but in so doing I would not be making good use of the space available, since I would not shed much additional light on the author's arguments or strengthen them significantly. I shall therefore concentrate on the points upon which I differ with Mr. Urquidi, or rather, the single basic point of difference, which is one only of degree, although important and with various ramifications.

The theory with which I differ is contained in the following statements, which are taken from various parts of the work:

Another aim in which fiscal policy can co-operate, without being the most appropriate instrument, is the improvement of income distribution. . . . Fiscal policy . . . can make a valuable contribution to the redistribution of income, but this process is not one of its primary objectives. . . . Progressive taxation alone might even reduce incentives to private investment. . . . Even if income tax is wisely conceived and well administered, its yield is restricted by the narrowness of the tax base

itself. . . . Improvement of the income tax system . . . should also aim at preventing any reduction of incentives to investments. This can be achieved by adopting rates that do not rise in an excessively sharp curve, with an average maximum rate of not more than about 35 to 40 per cent at very high income levels. . . . For most taxpayers at the intermediate income levels and even for those just inside the higher brackets, an average rate of 30 to 40 per cent might well militate against any desire to invest or to undertake activities that involve risk. . . . The improvement of income distribution must be tackled at the root of the problem, i.e., the sources of income itself and the relations between capital and labor which determine the distribution of the product.

I should explain that some days prior to reading the work that I am now commenting upon, I was re-examining the instruments and policies that our countries might use to achieve a significant improvement in the distribution of income, and I had arrived at the conclusion (tentative and subject to revision, but firmly believed) that in Latin America's present circumstances the only instrument for redistributing income and expenditures that can bring about significant improvement within a short time and without seriously upsetting the economy of our countries is fiscal policy. Moreover, I concluded that fiscal policy, in any case, is a necessary complement to other measures and steps.

I reached that conclusion after studying the following policies of a nonfiscal nature: (a) promulgation of laws or decrees increasing wages; (b) promulgation of laws or decrees establishing minimum wages; (c) strengthening of workers' organizations; (d) intensification of competition between producing and distributing enterprises with reduction of the degree of monopoly; (e) payment of subsidies to foods and/or other essential goods and services, as, for example, urban transportation; (f) promotion of technology in agriculture, in order to increase food production and reduce its cost; (g) agrarian reform; and (h) increase in the productivity of labor within the development process.

The first of the policies mentioned has no effect other than to cause prices to rise if total consumer expenditures and business investments are not reduced but increase proportionately, as generally happens, and if what Kalecki calls the degree of monopoly is not reduced either. The second, regarding minimum wages, is probably effective in some sectors if used moderately, but it would tend to produce the same effects as the first of the measures considered or to cause disturbances and distortions, including an increase in unemployment, if the minimum wages were set too high.

The strengthening of labor organizations, especially in agriculture, is a basic measure for sound social policy, but its efficacy is limited as long as the organizations strengthened, like the present ones, have to wage an uphill battle against the unemployed and underemployed who offer to work at any wage, against low productivity, and against the high price of food and other essential consumer goods. In the countries that are on or beyond the edge of what Joan Robinson calls the inflationary barrier, strengthening labor unions would help the workers to better protect their real wages but not to increase them substantially, for the reasons noted in connection with wage increases imposed by law.

The fourth policy listed—that is, to intensify competition through measures to combat monopolistic practices—is very difficult to carry out successfully in countries such as ours, where the markets are so limited. Here, the obvious solution is to speed up the progress of the Latin American Free Trade Association. The fifth policy was included among the nonfiscal policies in error, because it is obviously fiscal. Those listed under letters f, g, and h do not rapidly affect distribution of income.

If the foregoing analysis is correct—and I wish that it were not—to abandon the fiscal instrument for the purpose of appreciably redistributing the national expenditure in favor of the poorer classes means that the frightful disparities in living standards prevailing among our peoples will continue for the foreseeable future. And I ask myself: must we passively resign ourselves to contemplating them?

Having said this, we can go on to study the possibilities for redistribution by means of fiscal policy in Latin America. The estimates of distribution of income made in our countries indicate that this is more unequal than in the industrial nations. In the United States, England, Canada, and Japan, 10 per cent of the highest-income families receive about 30 per cent of the total monetary income,[1] whereas in Mexico in 1957 that figure was 46.7 per cent, according to the excellent study made by Ifigenia M. de Navarrete,[2] and in Venezuela in 1958, about 45 per cent, according to the careful estimates of Carl Shoup in his report on the fiscal system of that country.[3] Although the authors themselves admit that these last two figures are not based on fully trustworthy data, they must be approximately correct, because we come to more or less similar figures if we make a rough estimate of the distribution of income on the basis of the distribution of population between rural and urban, differences in income between agricultural and nonagricultural workers, and the two following hypotheses that cannot be far removed from fact: (a) that income from property makes up about 40 per cent of national income and (b) that the bulk of property is owned by 10 per cent of the population. Making that same rough estimate for other countries of our hemisphere, we find that the case of Mexico and Venezuela is not the exception but the rule with reference to distribution of income.

The greater knowledge about the distribution of income in our countries should make us revise our former concept, still maintained by Mr. Urquidi, regarding the narrowness of the income tax base in the Latin American economies. The great concentration of income in the upper 10 per cent of the population—one and a half times greater than in the industrial countries—provides an excellent basis for the income tax and for the tax system in general. As Kaldor says, "The taxation potential of the semideveloped countries of Latin America . . . must be fully as large as that of the highly developed countries, although their actual tax revenue is typically only one-third or one-half as large."[4]

The 45 per cent of personal income earned by the upper decile must equal between 35 and 40 per cent of the gross domestic product. In Table 1–1, which has been prepared to show the numerical relationship between the various items of income before and after payment of taxes, we have assumed that this income equals 37 per cent of the gross domestic product. Consequently, if, as Harberger suggests,[5] the income tax should take 20 per cent of the income of that tenth of the population, the amount collected would equal 7 per cent of the gross domestic product and not 2 per cent, which is the assumption we make in the table, although this probably exceeds the average of our countries by a good deal. If taxes on luxury items were to take 20 per cent of the income of that upper-income segment of the population, after payment of income tax, the amount collected would equal 6 per cent of the gross domestic product, or 2 per cent more than is assumed in the table. With only these two items, not counting the possible yield from a more effective collection of the income tax, we would be making an effective redistribution of the benefits from the expenditure by the upper decile to the other deciles—mostly, probably, to the lower two or three—by an amount equal to 7 per cent of the gross domestic product. And how much could be accomplished through the proper investment and

[1] United States, Department of Commerce, *Statistical Abstract of the United States* (Washington, D.C.: 1962), and Irving B. Kravis, "International Differences in the Distribution of Income," *The Review of Economics and Statistics* (November, 1960).

[2] See Ifigenia M. de Navarrete, *La distribución del ingreso y el desarrollo económico de México* (México: Escuela Nacional de Economía, 1960).

[3] Carl S. Shoup *et al.*, *The Fiscal System of Venezuela* (Baltimore: The Johns Hopkins Press, 1959).

[4] See his paper, "The Role of Taxation in Economic Development," in this volume.

[5] See his paper elsewhere in this volume.

TABLE 1–1: Gross Income before and after Payment of Taxes in a Hypothetical Latin American Country

	Availability of gross income before payment of taxes (in percentages of GDP at factor cost)		Availability of gross income after payment of direct taxes (in percentages of GDP at factor cost)		Expenditure (in percentages of GDP at market prices)	
Individuals:						
Highest decile	37		35		31	
Nine other deciles	47	84	45	80	43	74
Domestic companies:						
Undistributed profits and taxes withheld	5		4		4	
Depreciation reserves	3	8	3	7	3	7
Foreign companies:						
Profits sent abroad and taxes withheld	7		4		4	
Depreciation reserves	3	10	3	7	3	7
Government		—		6		12
Gross domestic product[a]		100		100		100

[a]At factor cost in the first two columns and at market prices in the third.

administration of 7 per cent of the gross product!

Nevertheless, we must ask what effects this redistribution will have on the highest 10 per cent. The classic answer is that it will reduce the amount of investment, for two reasons: (a) because the group will have fewer funds to invest and (b) because it will have less inducement to invest. Mr. Urquidi is not greatly concerned with the first reason, for, as he says very correctly, "This argument has lost a great deal of its face since it has been recognized that there is, as a rule, no connection between the decision to invest and the prior formation of savings." To this it might be added that there is every indication that personal savings represent a relatively small fraction of total private savings in the Latin American countries. Most of the private savings are accumulated by companies. Furthermore, the bulk of personal savings is invested directly or indirectly in building, and not in industrial, agricultural, or mining enterprises. And yet it might be objected that the upper decile does not actually save 7 per cent of the gross domestic product but probably not more than 4 or 5 per cent (which is reduced by 2 or 3 per cent by dissaving on the part of the lower segment of that decile and of the remaining deciles). And perhaps there is some reason for fear regarding the first impact of that redistribution. It is possible and even probable that personal savings may be reduced during the first year or two; but after that time, consumption should readjust itself and savings should again climb to their original or perhaps even to a higher level because, feeling that they are less well-to-do, many individuals with a high income may decide to increase their savings in order to recover the amount of revenue and personal security that they had previously. Reactions in this regard differ among different people, and the net collective effect on savings is as difficult to predict as the net collective effect on savings of a change in interest rate.

The other possible negative consequence of a significantly progressive tax, the decline in investment because of a reduction of incentives, which is feared by Mr. Urquidi, does not disturb me excessively, for a number of reasons. First, the bulk of real and directly productive investment is made by companies, which should not be burdened with a progressive tax but with a proportional tax that is not very high (let us say, 30 per cent); and the existence of a high tax on personal income promotes an increase of savings by business because it discourages the distribution of profits. Second, individuals in the higher-income groups, where the discouraging effect might be felt, are as much motivated by power, pride, rivalry, and creativity as by mere profit, or more so; and they would continue, as they have continued in the United States and Canada and in other countries where high incomes are heavily taxed, the struggle to make their businesses bigger, more efficient, and more powerful than their rivals. The game will continue with the same or greater intensity, even though the absolute size of the prizes to be won is limited. And third, in limiting gains, the amount of losses is also limited, and the investor will not be so fearful of undertaking risks. From the psychological point of view, an individual for whom

each marginal peso is worth only 40 centavos is more likely to put his money in a risky investment than another whose marginal peso is worth 100 centavos.

Having examined the potential yield from taxes on income and luxury consumption and the various arguments for and against these taxes, we may now approach the question more clearly and precisely. For me, the problem can be stated in the following terms: should we or should we not advise the governments of the Latin American countries to raise the taxes of individuals in the upper decile of the income scale, so that the increase in government revenue may equal 5 to 10 per cent of the gross domestic product?

In his paper, Victor Urquidi answers this question with caution and reserve, whereas my answer is an emphatic, categoric "yes."

Comment

ANÍBAL PINTO*

1. The document presented by Mr. Urquidi covers a wide field of fiscal matters, and I must begin by saying that I agree with his observations and suggestions. Therefore, rather than indulge in a critical discussion or analysis of his opinions, I shall deal at greater length with certain points that appear to be of primary importance.

2. First of all, I wish to draw attention to Mr. Urquidi's reference to the vast sphere of action and to the machinery under governmental authority in our countries.

Latin America is not fully aware of the magnitude of the resources and the diversity of instruments available to government authorities. The participation of public expenditures in the national gross product, which is

*Director of the ECLA/BNDE Economic Development Center, Rio de Janeiro, Brazil.

the index most frequently used, gives an inadequate idea of the real situation. In order to appreciate this more fully, it should be borne in mind—even though it is obvious—that in a large number of countries the governments more or less completely control foreign trade transactions, the monetary system, public utilities, certain basic industries, social security systems, salary and wage negotiations, and the like. Nevertheless, opinions or impressions in our countries insist on emphasizing the limitations on government action and demanding new powers, new laws, new agencies—all of this, naturally, in the circles that request, or agree to, the presence of the government as a strategic element in economic development.

Naturally, in many cases it may be necessary to expand official powers and instruments, but I think it would be difficult not to agree with the general assumption that, as a rule, governments utilize the great potential at their disposal in a very unsatisfactory manner.

One of the main reasons for this lies in the so-called "process of accretion" in the public sector, that is, the proliferation of widely divergent agencies that have been added to the traditional administrative structure without being integrated into a coherent whole. This evolution has been observed in many places to a certain degree, but in Latin America it appears to have assumed a particularly pronounced character, for the foliage of new governmental units has grown with unusual rapidity, while the old central machinery has remained practically unchanged.

There is also a lesser but significant fact which could be called a "legalistic deviation"; this is the quite widespread tendency, having deep cultural roots, to believe that legal documents and their administrative products are the same thing as an effective attack on, and solution of, the problems that we face.

These two elements have brought about a kind of variation of "Parkinson's Law," which expresses itself, among other things, in the constant appearance of new agencies designed to meet old problems without implying that existing agencies having the same responsibilities will be terminated or absorbed. Moreover, it has not been uncommon to see the consolidation of important administrative and economic enclaves: small states within the state that determine their own policies, stubbornly resist all higher discipline, and frequently follow a policy of absorption with respect to the establishment of higher-than-average income levels.

However, these circumstances do not tell the whole story, and they are not self-explanatory.

In the main, this disuse or underutilization of the possibilities of a potentially powerful state is due, in my opinion, to two factors: on the one hand, the lack of a definite policy regarding the responsibilities of governments and, on the other, their relations with private enterprise.

In this respect, it should be frankly recognized that government participation is still interpreted in many influential circles as a mere *de facto* or emergency condition and not as a normal and essential peculiarity in the conditions of Latin American economic development: for example, the customary repetition of statements about "free initiative" and "free enterprise," together with the rejection of and opposition to the establishment of a clear and legitimate framework for the varied public duties. It is true that oral and doctrinary postures have not prevented extensive participation by the government, but there can be no doubt that they have prevented the rationalization of this participation by creating or arousing antagonisms that are frequently artificial and by preventing the achievement of a kind of "peaceful coexistence" between the public and private sectors. Actually, the entire blame for this situation does not lie with those who have a fictitious or transplanted picture of the problem. Part of the blame lies with the "interventionists" who, in addition to being remiss in clearly defining the terms of the matter, have helped to invest this advance of public responsibility with a casual, sporadic, and emergency character, not to mention the many contradictions in decisions taken from day to day.

In addition to the lack of political definition regarding responsibilities of the government and its relations with the private sector, which is partly a reflection of the "balance of power" in each country, is the other fact that can explain the low output of large governmental machinery. We refer to the evidence which is increasingly proved in practice and is borne out by the tax studies at this meeting: that it is very difficult to adopt criteria and to take decisions in specific fields and situations without a general view of the objectives sought. In the absence of a framework of economic policy in which to fit resolutions, it is almost impossible to get away from generalizations and academic references, and the only road open is that to disconnected action and the hope that what one hand does is not undone by the other.

In short, I wish to repeat that the possibilities of a successful handling of public institutions and machinery seem to depend mainly on the political definition adopted in each country with respect to the public scope of action and responsibilities and relations with the private sector as well as the establishment of the aims and means chosen in the context of global planning.

3. In dealing with other aspects of the foregoing general question, Mr. Urquidi refers to various problems affecting enterprises that are controlled by the government. I wish to add a few comments to those contained in that document.

It would be superfluous to insist on the importance that has been acquired by productive units under government tutelage, and I wish only to add my personal opinion that this importance will tend to increase in the future. I do not hold this opinion because of doctrinary leanings but because the more complex and demanding phase of development faced by our countries will make public initiative indispensable, whether isolated or in close collaboration with the private sector. On the other hand, those who believe that the government should finance and organize productive enterprises in order to turn them over to private interests forget an important fact that seems to be in conflict with the new patterns of social justice that are being raised as a banner today. We refer to the fact that, in these cases, it is the savings and effort of the community, coupled with the government's technique and stimulus, that make it possible to develop these activities, and it does not seem logical, to say the least, that after the community has assumed all the risks and obligations they should be transformed into sources of individual profit.

Many familiar problems arise in connection with public or mixed enterprises that still require study. One of them, referring to the standards of efficiency for the operation of such enterprises, has so far fluctuated between two equally unsatisfactory points of view: on the one hand, that of persons who believe that these enterprises should be regulated by the same standards that govern private entities and, on the other, that of persons

who reject private efficiency indexes but as a rule have been unable to produce any others that are better suited to their specific nature and that will permit economic rationalization of their efforts. One very noticeable result during this period of lack of orientation in this field is the large deficit incurred by certain public enterprises, which is reflected in indiscriminate subsidies that accentuate the inequality of incomes by their effects on a regressive tax structure.

Admitting that private indexes such as rates of return on, or equilibrium of, financial operations are unsatisfactory in most cases, except as indirect means of reference, one of the first measures in solving these problems, as Mr. Urquidi points out, is to bring out the real social content of decisions taken with respect to these enterprises—for example, in matters of rates—by permitting the public to choose between the subsidies they may hide and the taxes that will have to be paid to finance them. In this respect, I wish to call attention to the skepticism or indifference that is common in our countries regarding the possibilities for bringing about the basic, understandable, and educational informing of public opinion. My conviction is that this attitude is unfounded and that there is no reason why the public sector cannot utilize, or why it should underestimate, the possibilities for persuasion that are so widely used by private interests.

It should also be recalled that the dissemination and application of the techniques of program-budgeting provide a genuine possibility of checking, from a realistic point of view, on the greater or lesser efficiency of the productive units of the public sector. In this respect, the seminar on budget classification and administration held by the Economic Commission for Latin America last September was another step forward.

However, it is well known that not only technical difficulties affect the efficiency of that sensitive and basic area of governmental activity. One primary aspect is the dependency of those enterprises on political administration. It would be very easy to quote a few fundamental truths here; for example, that the "politicizing" of these enterprises has always had a bad effect and that, on the other hand, when those enterprises have succeeded in resisting the most powerful political pressures, they have proved that there is no incompatibility between good administration and public ownership.

The difficulty is that technical administrative autonomy and adherence to the criteria established by the economic policy of the government must be balanced at a point that cannot be fixed precisely. Neither closed compartments within the government itself nor branches of the political apparatus are solutions to the problem. However, even if clear solutions may not be proposed, it would be useful and interesting, on the other hand, to study a few typical cases in Latin America in order to derive some guidance on the problem, bearing in mind that it is also a source of concern in the industrialized countries.

4. With respect to another topic examined in Victor Urquidi's paper—the tax problem, which is the principal subject of the meeting—I wish to say that the time has passed for formal discussions and academic presentations on the nature, advantages, and disadvantages of particular taxes. There is no lack of documents and discussion on the matter. *What is of timely interest today is to establish a few general guidelines that may be refined and adapted to the particular conditions of each Latin American country.* I wish to point out the following.

a) A majority of opinion is agreed that income tax—it is to be hoped, of an over-all nature—should have a more important place in tax structures, following the trend of the industrialized countries. However, there is also a general awareness of the administrative and other difficulties involved in carrying out this development, some of which are deeply rooted in the structure of the underdeveloped economies. A reasonable method to overcome this problem, and one that has received some acceptance, is to concentrate use of that tax instrument on the small minority *that is really wealthy,* that is—in order to establish some measure—on those who have net incomes at least ten times higher than the average.

b) The foregoing implies that other taxes must make a relatively more significant contribution than is the case in the industrialized countries. Outstanding among these, because of their obvious progressive bias and certain characteristics of the accumulation process in economies and societies such as ours, are the taxes imposed on wealth and on different types of fixed assets, particularly land and buildings. It is mainly a question of increasing the participation of such taxes, which as a rule is very small at present, in order to have a broader basis and one of easier administrative control for progressive taxation.

c) It appears obvious that anything that may be achieved in this respect will not minimize the role of consumption taxes to any great extent. The principal task is to associate this purpose with the no less important aim of preventing an accentuation of the regressivity in the distribution of income. In this point, it is clear that thought should be given to another and dependent form of tax classification, bearing in mind its social incidence. The problems in this respect are obvious and cannot be cleared altogether, but there is a fundamental factor that may be taken as a guide: the fact that in a region that has such a low average income and an even lower income among the large masses of population, the consumption standard of the latter is reduced to groups and types of expenditures that are not hard to define. Taking due note of these expenditures, and keeping in mind the possible effects of a progressive structure of public expenditures, it may be considered that nearly all the indirect taxes will have *some* progressive impact or, at least, will not be regressive to any great extent. The really complicated point is that such a policy will also affect the interests of the average- and higher-salaried groups and, possibly, those having more power for political negotiation, for example, through taxation of consumer durables. In any case, the orientation is quite clear.

5. As Victor Urquidi points out and as other documents attest, the impact of taxes is closely connected, so far as the final incidence of fiscal operations is concerned, with the nature of expenditures. I wish to state, in this respect, that the prevailing trend toward a greater increase of transfer expenditures for social security appears to be disadvantageous with respect to the other main possibility, namely, a preference for "collective welfare" expenditures such as those for education and health, which are much more equalitarian and have greater effect on the conditions that influence the distribution of income and the real income of the population.

6. Pursuing the problem of expenditures discussed in the papers, I wish to recall that a serious obstacle in solving the problem is the unwillingness to accept the desirability and the reality of the trend toward a continuing increase in public expenditures. This trend is really motivated by three elements: population growth, rate of urbanization, and government responsibility in basic investments and in semipublic investments. It can, therefore, be accepted as a reasonable hypothesis that expenditures will increase in real terms at least at a higher rate than population growth. Naturally, this will depend on the correlative increase in the national product; but this, in turn, will depend greatly on those expenditures, provided they are distributed rationally.

7. Finally, I wish to make two objections to Victor Urquidi's statement with respect to the possibilities of fiscal instruments in the distribution of income and compensatory policy. I believe, furthermore, that Mr. Urquidi did not have time in his summary to express all his thoughts in this respect.

Regarding the first problem—the role of fiscal instruments in the redistribution of income—I agree with Mr. Urquidi that the situation in our countries does not make it possible to attribute the same significance to these mediums that they have in the developed countries. Actually, any action in this field must be much broader and deeper, embracing the determinants of the "original distribution" of income. However, fiscal responsibility is very important in the over-all strategy, and in order to make an evaluation I think it is essential to have a clearer understanding of the various possibilities and forms of redistribution through fiscal channels than can be imagined. I would call the first "direct monetary distribution," and it would be based on taking income away from the high-income groups and giving it to the low-income groups in any way that would raise their monetary income. The second would consist of taking income away from the wealthy in order that the government could finance the provision of goods and services to needy sectors; for example, by giving them food, clothing, and the like. The third would consist of taking income away from the wealthy in order that the government could use it to create conditions that are basic factors in determining the distribution of income; for example, distribution of property, educational opportunities, and the like.

With regard to my other objection, I also agree that a compensatory policy faces many difficulties in our countries and that it would scarcely have the possibilities that exist in the industrialized countries. But no one could think that it would be better not to resort to this policy when a depressive situation in the foreign sector develops, fearing the problems it might pose, instead of allowing the restrictive effects that characterized the gold standard system in the past to take place. On the contrary, in spite of all its difficulties, a defense of the level of activity, employment, and income will not only alleviate the difficulties to some extent but also create a condition more favorable than depression to sustain or further the process of economic development. Furthermore, it should be kept in mind that, aside from any academic discussion, probably no Latin American government could accept the old passage through the purgatory of deflation without the considerable risk of ceasing to be a government within a very short time.

Discussion

MR. URQUIDI said that the fundamental problem of fiscal policy in Latin America today was the lack of prior definition of development policy. However fiscal policy was defined and irrespective of whether it was assigned a broader or narrower scope, it was very difficult to carry out a consistent and rational fiscal and financial policy until such time as governments, political forces, and private sectors agreed on a minimum development plan or program establishing sectoral targets and recognizing the work that both the public and private sectors must carry out to achieve it.

The formulation of adequate development programs had not made much headway in Latin America, and the implementation of important aspects of development policy was deficient. In those circumstances, many of the measures that formed part of fiscal policy were proposed or adopted without a clear understanding of the purposes they were intended to achieve or of their probable effects. Most of them were adopted, rather, to meet pressing financial or public expenditure needs or for the purpose of promoting or restricting some form of private activity.

However, there was an increasingly clear feeling that the trend toward development programing would have to be accompanied by a reshuffling of ideas on financing and on the use of different fiscal instruments and that any public or private investment plan must be in keeping with a fiscal and financial plan formulated with the utmost possible precision.

Fiscal policy could not be more precise than development plans; but that did not prevent evaluating it in terms of the targets that today were accepted as essential components of any development policy in Latin America, namely, the need to increase the relative volume of public and private investment and to change its sectoral composition, to increase the public sector's current expenditure to provide essential services for economic develop-

ment, and to improve the distribution of income. Fiscal policies could and should adhere to these aims, at any rate in a very general way.

In order to do so, efficient methods should be adopted for the formulation and control of fiscal policy. In that connection, it should be stressed that the financial administration of a country needed a unified command: the minister for finance should be in a position to co-ordinate taxation, expenditure, and borrowing policies at all levels of government as well as the financial and price or tariff policies of the semipublic sector, including social security, state banks, and the agencies responsible for regulating supplies.

Fiscal policy was the whole body of measures relating to the tax system, public expenditure, contracting of internal and external debt by the state, and the financial operations and situation of the autonomous and semipublic agencies and bodies, through the medium of which the amount and distribution of public investment and consumption as components of national expenditure were determined and the volume and composition of private investment and consumption were directly or indirectly influenced. The definition implied that the influence of fiscal policy on economic and social development depended in essence on what each country conceived to be the role of the state. Paradoxically enough, even if it were assumed that in any given country the idea prevailed that the state should have as little as possible to do with matters of infrastructure and that it should only exceptionally undertake activities directly related to production or distribution, fiscal policy would be just as significant and important as in cases where the state played a substantial part in the creation of the infrastructure of development or in the establishment of agricultural, industrial, or distribution enterprises, since it was responsible for guiding the multifarious decisions taken with respect to private investment and consumption, reconciling them with national economic development aims, and adapting their tempo and distribution to the requirements implicit in the aims in question.

At the time of speaking, most of the Latin American countries were closer to the first than to the second extreme. There were few countries where the public sector accounted for more than 15 per cent of national expenditure, where public investment exceeded 33 per cent of total gross investment, or where tax revenue represented over 12 per cent of the gross product. Consequently, a fiscal policy conceived as a harmonious and consistent whole and defined with proper clarity was, in such cases, of supreme importance to programs for the accelerated economic development of Latin America, since the behavior of the private sector would largely condition the results achieved.

The over-all concept of fiscal policy was not confined to the tax measures adopted by a country's central or federal government but also covered the sphere of state or provincial and municipal authorities. Any incongruities between the measures adopted by a central government and a provincial authority, for example, might adversely affect the rate of private investment and exert an unfavorable influence on specific categories of productive investment. Similarly, the field of fiscal policy had to be extended to embrace autonomous or semipublic agencies and enterprises that were wholly or partially owned by the state, including official banks. If the tariffs or prices charged by such bodies were high, their effect was the same as that of a tax; if, on the other hand, they were low, they really represented a subsidy to the groups or sectors making use of the goods or services concerned.

Another special case that merited separate consideration was that of social security institutions, insurance and pension funds, etc. In some countries, the tripartite nature of the contributions to such institutions made it doubtful whether they could, strictly speaking, be regarded as belonging to the public sector. However, in view of the significance of social security systems for the community as a whole, it was necessary that they should operate as part of that sector, since the contributions made by workers and employers were analogous to a tax assigned to a specific purpose, and the current surplus of income over expenditure (after the transfer of funds from the central government to the institutions in question had been taken into account) was often one of the principal sources of saving in the public sector; moreover, investment in hospitals, welfare centers, and housing by social security agencies frequently acted as a substitute for the investment that should be directly effected by the state.

Another factor in fiscal policy that was not always fully recognized was the contracting of debt by the different branches of the public sector. The internal or external indebtedness of the central government or of a provincial or municipal authority presented no problem, but difficulties did arise in relation to financial transactions in the subdivision constituted by semipublic agencies and enterprises. To be consistent with the theory hitherto sustained, debts contracted by semipublic enterprises should be treated as an aspect of fiscal policy, with the possible exception of short-term commitments (for less than a year) entered into purely for the purposes of current or cash operations.

Fiscal policy should also be taken to include exchange measures and the activities of central banks as well as the control mechanisms established by the state to facilitate the marketing of crops, guarantee minimum rural prices, absorb production surpluses, and regulate supplies and stabilize prices of food in urban areas.

To sum up, the legitimate field of fiscal policy was extremely broad, although in practice it was clearly difficult not only to arrive at the figures whereby the policy in question could be expressed in quantitative terms but also to overcome the administrative, legal, and political obstacles to the unification of fiscal and financial policy under a single authority.

With regard to the objectives of fiscal policy, those directly linked to economic development were of more importance than those of a social nature and were three in number: (*a*) to create sufficient public savings to cope with the estimated volume of public investment and to collect, by means of internal and external borrowing, such additional resources as it might be prudent to obtain from private or foreign savings; (*b*) to absorb from the private economy, by the most equitable and efficacious means, the income required to cover the provision of those public services which the community regarded as indispensable or desirable; and (*c*) to manipulate various tax, expenditure, exchange, price- or rate-fixing, and other instruments in such a way as to provide the private sector with sufficient incentives to generate the volume of savings required for economic development and to effect its proper share of investment.

The foregoing basic objectives might be supplemented by others, in respect of which fiscal policy could play a useful role without necessarily being the best or the most decisive instrument. One of them was the modification or compensation of short-term fluctuations in the economy. In that case, fiscal policy alone, without the support of other aspects of government policy, could not assume responsibility for stabilization without neglecting objectives of more fundamental importance.

Another aim in which fiscal policy could co-operate, without being the most appropriate instrument, was the improvement of income distribution. But a more progressive income tax and the various forms of taxation on net wealth and on luxury private expenditure did not really reduce the disparities between levels of personal income. Such incomes might continue to be generated just as unequally as before, in consequence of a country's agrarian, commercial, and industrial structure.

Where taxation was concerned, a tendency had been observable in Latin America in recent years to rely more on direct than on indirect taxes, at least in central government taxation, especially income tax. If a tax structure was to be efficacious, it had to be in line with a country's institutional life, viewed both in retrospect and in its current patterns, and it also had to be properly in keeping with the ends pursued. Consequently, efficient fiscal and administrative technique must be combined with sound political judgment if a tax reform was to be anything more than a mental exercise and was to have the backing of the taxpayer. In that connection, perhaps the first step ought to be a careful revision of many juridical theories which might be unnecessarily cramping the concept of taxable income, especially in relation to individuals, or which in one way or another tended to lessen the effect of progressive rates. The points which should be elucidated and reviewed included the ideas of imputed or potential income from rents; equity or inequity in respect of family exemptions or allowances at various income levels; retroactivity in taxation on capital gains accruing from immovable property; and income deriving from common property in the case of married couples.

In most of the Latin American countries, the income tax system was schedular, with the resulting serious drawback that it precluded the equitable application of family allowances and left room for inequitable taxation on income from different sources through different progressive or proportional rates. It seemed essential that an attempt should be made to simplify income tax, in the sense of making a single rate applicable to consolidated personal income and requiring returns from all persons whose income level exceeded a specified and relatively low figure. Nor should efforts to improve the income tax system overlook incentives to investment, which could be safeguarded by the adoption of scales that were not overprogressive and whose average maximum rate did not exceed about 35 to 40 per cent at very high income levels.

The problem of incentives to investment might be more significant, however, in relation to taxes on the gains or profits of enterprises than in relation to taxes on personal income, and that important aspect of tax policy had possibly been neglected in Latin

America. Although there were various types of reliefs, the existing system of tax exemptions had not been properly rationalized with respect to its effects on investment. Accelerated depreciation had the advantage, in relation to exemptions, of being accorded in respect of investments already made and not of possible future investments subject to various contingencies. In addition, it was a more positive instrument, since it could be applied in different ways to different branches of industry and could thus be adapted to the growth projections incorporated in industrial development plans or programs.

Zeal for modernization and improvement of the fiscal system should not lead to neglect of indirect taxation. The export tax was in some measure a substitute for income tax as applied to primary activities and had been particularly useful where the need had arisen to impose taxes promptly on the windfall profits accruing to exporters from a currency devaluation or an unexpected and abrupt increase in international prices. But it was a clumsy and inequitable device, since it did not differentiate between the various levels of productivity and efficiency normally reflected in costs and was shifted back to the weakest link in the chain of production and distribution, almost always reaching the agricultural worker. Other taxes on transactions should be regarded primarily as a source of government revenue, which meant that they should be sufficiently low, in ad valorem terms, not to discourage production or mass-consumption patterns but sufficiently high to make a substantial contribution to tax revenue.

However, no government should neglect the opportunities that existed—even in conjunction with the trend toward imposing general sales or gross income taxes—for establishing special rates in respect of particular types of consumption that were associated with the higher-income groups or were subject to more pronounced income elasticity. Such taxes, besides representing an addition to fiscal revenue that might be considerable, constituted an equitable supplement to personal income tax and forestalled evasion by expenditure out of unreported income.

Import duties were becoming increasingly difficult to rationalize from the revenue standpoint. As industrialization progressed in Latin America and the scope of tariff protection was extended, import duties, if they were to be effective as a protectionist device, would have to become less effective as a revenue instrument.

A special type of taxation that in some countries amounted to an important or even the principal source of public revenue was that applied to the profits and activities of foreign investment in primary commodities. Such taxes could be justified not only from the political standpoint but also on economic grounds. In that connection, two arguments stood out: (a) the extraction of primary commodities implied a drain on natural resources calculated to weaken the country's future economic capacity, and (b) such activities had often involved an inordinately rapid distortion of the economic structure which had made it more difficult to develop other sectors of the economy. Additional taxation on the foreign investments concerned would offset those negative factors and would be an important element in fiscal policy if it were used to support economic development programs through public investment in the infrastructure and through the financing of expanded domestic investment in agriculture and industry.

Tax reforms would be difficult to justify unless at the same time the governments of Latin America formulated and carried out public expenditure policies that were more in line with the development and welfare aims they had undertaken to achieve. The technique of program budgeting, as yet applied only on a limited scale in Latin America, appeared to be the most suitable instrument for ensuring that public expenditure became more effective. By its means the government budget could be reconciled with development plans, but its adoption entailed special training of budget office personnel and administrative or legal reforms.

Some semipublic bodies had difficulty in financing their own investment, but others were possible sources of savings or revenue for the treasury. They should at least be spurred on by the desire to serve the community as productively as possible and should aim not at unduly large profits but at providing low-cost goods and services, creating financial reserves for future expansion, and adding to the over-all resources of the public sector.

With regard to internal contracting of debts, it was important to consider a problem closely related to monetary policy: that of the limits of such borrowing. Capital markets in Latin America had not much absorption capacity, and it would be inexpedient for the government to compete in them with the private sector. However, it could create, within the banking system, a growing market of internal debt issues, provided that selective credit controls were maintained.

External borrowing was subject to one general and several specific limitations. The general limitation consisted in the borrowing country's future capacity to pay. In determining it, some part was played not only by export prospects for goods and services but also by the success of the development program with respect to import substitution resulting from an increase in domestic production capacity in relation to the growth of aggregate demand. If the margin of external borrowing was to be broadened, dynamic import substitution would, in its turn, have to be based on a coherent public and private investment program and, of course, on the complete and efficient utilization of domestic savings; in other words, there was a link between the possibilities for contracting debts and fiscal policy. Specific limitations included the credit patterns followed by the international agencies and the inadequate capacity of fiscal policy to attract foreign private investment.

The enumeration of all the foregoing important aspects of fiscal policy clearly showed that fuller and better studies on the subject were required. Some recommendation might

emerge from the meeting on the need for such studies to be carried out and for the private sectors to co-operate in the working out of fiscal policy.

MR. PAZOS said that Mr. Urquidi's paper on "Fiscal Policy in Latin America's Economic Development" was the best over-all study on the subject that he had read and that he fully endorsed most of its arguments and recommendations. There was one point, however, on which he was not in agreement, namely, the secondary role assigned by Mr. Urquidi to fiscal policy as an instrument of income redistribution.

Before reading the paper under discussion, he had reviewed the instruments and policies which the Latin American countries could use to improve income distribution, and he firmly believed that in existing circumstances the only instrument whereby that aim could be achieved over the short term, without causing serious distortions in the Latin American economies, was fiscal policy.

He had arrived at that conclusion after careful consideration of a number of non-fiscal measures (a) promulgation of legislation to raise wages; (b) promulgation of legislation on minimum wages; (c) strengthening of workers' organizations; (d) intensification of competition between the producer and distributor enterprises (limitation of monopolies); (e) payment of subsidies for foodstuffs and/or other essential goods and services; (f) promomotion of technical advances in the agricultural sector, in order to expand food production and reduce costs; (g) agrarian reform; and (h) improvement of the productivity of labor as part of the development process.

Generally speaking, the first three measures did not have the effect of increasing the real income of wage earners, because as a rule the prices of essential goods rose accordingly. The fourth was difficult to put into effect in countries with markets as restricted as those of Latin America. The fifth was really an aspect of fiscal policy and had been mistakenly associated with the rest; and the remaining three failed to influence income distribution rapidly enough.

If the foregoing analysis was sound and if the fiscal instrument was rejected as a means of appreciably redistributing domestic expenditure in favor of the lower-income brackets, the appalling disparities in standards of living that were prevalent among the Latin American peoples would be indefinitely perpetuated.

In the context of the possibilities of fiscal policy as an instrument of redistribution of income, he compared income distribution in the industrial countries with the situation in Latin America. There was a good deal more inequality in the Latin American countries than in the highly industrialized group, for whereas in Canada, Japan, the United Kingdom, and the United States 10 per cent of the households in the higher income brackets received about 30 per cent of monetary income, in Mexico the corresponding figure had been as high as 46.7 per cent in 1957, while in Venezuela it had amounted to about 45 per cent in 1958. Although those were only approximate figures, very similar results were obtained when other methods of calculation —also approximate—were adopted. The application of such methods to other Latin American countries showed that there, too, income distribution was much the same as in Mexico and Venezuela.

As fuller information was currently available on income distribution in the Latin American countries, the time had come to modify earlier ideas, still upheld by Mr. Urquidi, as to the narrowness of the tax base for income tax in the economies of the region. The great concentration of income in the hands of the top decile of the population afforded a splendid basis for income tax and for the tax system as a whole. On the assumption that 45 per cent of the personal income accruing to the highest decile was equivalent to 37 per cent of gross domestic production and that income tax took 20 per cent, the revenue thus obtained would amount to 7 per cent of the gross domestic product, instead of the 2 per cent postulated, a figure which in any case was probably higher than the average for the Latin American countries.

Moreover, if taxes on luxury consumption, after payment of income tax, took 20 per cent of the income of this upper stratum of the population, the corresponding revenue would be equivalent to 6 per cent of the gross domestic product, which again would be a figure in excess of that assumed. By means of those two items, the benefits of the expenditure of the top decile could be effectively redistributed among the remainder of the population to an amount equivalent to 7 per cent of the gross domestic product.

However, the possible effects of such a redistribution on the top decile would have to be taken into account. The assumption was that the volume of investment would decrease as a result of diminished resources and a reduction of the incentives to invest. As far as the first of those factors was concerned, it was currently recognized that (as Mr. Urquidi himself had acknowledged) the decision to invest had no connection with prior formation of savings and that probably personal savings represented a relatively small fraction of private saving in the Latin American countries. Even so, it was possible that private saving might decline at first as a result of redistribution, but in all probability consumption would be readjusted after a year or two and the level of saving would rise as high as or even higher than before.

With respect to the reduction of investment incentives and the decrease in investment which Mr. Urquidi feared might result, he thought that was unlikely to happen, for several reasons: first, because the bulk of real and directly productive investment was effected by corporations—which should be taxed at a uniform and not unduly high rate and should not be subject to progressive taxation —and saving on their part would increase, inasmuch as a high personal income tax discouraged the distribution of profits; secondly, because the action of the higher-income groups was not prompted solely by desire for profit but by other motives, and they would continue to invest in order to keep their establishments ahead of their competitors; and thirdly, because the limitation of their gains also limited the investors' fear of risks.

In view of all the arguments he had put forward, he thought it might be suggested to the Latin American countries that they should tax persons in the highest-income decile of the population more heavily in order to increase fiscal revenue by the equivalent of 5 to 10 per cent of the gross domestic product.

MR. PINTO agreed in general with the observations made by Mr. Urquidi but said he would like to enlarge upon one or two points that he considered to be particularly important.

The first concerned the scope of the state's sphere of action in Latin America and the nature of the instruments it employed. The region was not yet fully aware of the scale and variety of the resources and instruments at the disposal of its governments and tended to assess them according to the share of public expenditure in the gross national product, which did not give a true picture of the situation. It was thought in some circles that the state had a limited field of action, but in many Latin American countries the governments had almost complete authority over foreign trade, the monetary system, public utilities, some basic industries, the social security systems, and wage and salary negotiations. In fact, the state had a great potential at its disposal which was often not used to its full extent.

Its failure to make use of it was largely due to the constant addition of new agencies to the public sector, which simply overlaid the traditional administrative machinery without replacing or being assimilated into it. The ensuing duplication of work and responsibilities could be found in other parts of the world but was particularly marked in Latin America.

A minor but still significant factor was the widespread tendency to regard legal provisions and their administrative corollaries as substitutes for practical solutions.

The inability to make good use of the resources and mechanisms at the state's disposal was, however, not attributable to those factors alone. He himself thought that the main reasons were twofold. First was the fact that the state's responsibilities and, by extension, its relations with the private sector were not clearly defined in terms of policy. In many influential circles, the participation of the state was still looked upon as proper for emergencies only instead of as a normal and indispensable part of the economic development process. There was a tendency to take full advantage of such concepts as "free enterprise," while ignoring the public responsibilities involved therein. The divorce between words and deeds had not prevented the state from acting, but it had undoubtedly hampered the rationalization of its activities and created antagonism between the public and private sectors. The second reason was the difficulty of adopting criteria and taking decisions in particular sectors or situations in the absence of an integrated economic policy and an over-all picture of the aims pursued.

With reference to Mr. Urquidi's remarks on the problems besetting public enterprises, he first wished to lay stress on the increasing importance of state-administered productive enterprises which, in view of the more complex and exacting stage of development that the Latin American countries were entering upon, would make government action, either in isolation or in close association with the private sector, indispensable.

One question that still remained to be clarified concerned the criteria by which the efficiency of public or semipublic enterprises was to be determined. He considered it equally unsatisfactory that the latter should be governed by the same standards as private firms or that they should discard the yardsticks used by private firms before devising others that would be more suited to their particular functions. One measure of efficiency that should be used was the technique of program budgeting, which needed to be more generally taught and applied.

A prerequisite for solving the problem was, as Mr. Urquidi had pointed out, to make the general public aware of the purpose and social implications of the work of state enterprises so as to convince it that what was received as a subsidy was paid out in the form of taxes.

But the problems involved were not merely technical. They also derived from the balance that had to be struck between the need for public enterprises to preserve their autonomy in technical and administrative matters while adhering to the policy laid down by the government. No definite line of demarcation could be drawn, but it would be helpful to study specific cases in Latin America so as to establish some basic criteria for future action.

With regard to another point—that of taxes themselves—he considered that the time for weighing the relative merits and demerits of different types of taxes was past. What needed to be done was to lay down some general guidelines that could be adapted to the requirements of individual countries. In that respect, he stressed three considerations. First, one way of resolving the conflict between the prevailing belief that income tax should play a more important part in Latin American tax systems and the administrative difficulties involved was to levy it particularly on the wealthy minority, e.g., on persons with a net income at least ten times the average figure. Second, other taxes, such as those levied on net wealth and various types of fixed assets, particularly real estate, should make a greater contribution than in the industrialized countries. In doing so, they would help to widen the tax base and to facilitate tax administration. Third, the importance of excise taxes should be maintained without enhancing the regressive nature of income distribution. Some other way of classifying excise taxes should therefore be devised that would take into account their social implications. It would be difficult to do so, except for the fact that the pattern of consumption in the lower- and intermediate-income groups in Latin America was fairly easy to determine. Provided that that pattern was respected and the possible repercussions of a progressive public expenditure policy allowed for, virtually all indirect taxes would be progressive to some extent.

With respect to the final results of fiscal policy, he pointed out that the tendency to increase transfers of funds for social security purposes was unfavorable in comparison with the alternative of increasing expenditure on education and health which, apart from being intrinsically more equitable, was more apt to raise the real income of the population.

Last, he had two objections to make to Mr. Urquidi's observations on the role of fiscal mechanisms in income distribution and compensatory policy. On the first point, he agreed that such mechanisms could not have the same significance in Latin America as in more developed countries. Although any endeavor to change income distribution would have to go beyond fiscal policy, the latter would have an important part to play. In order to determine its responsibility, it was essential to understand the different ways in which fiscal policy could bring about a redistribution. One was to take income away from the higher-income groups and transfer it to the less well-off. Another was for the state to tax the wealthy and use the revenue to provide goods and services for the poorer classes, and a third was to use the same source of revenue to influence the factors that underlie income distribution.

He agreed that compensatory policy faced many difficulties in Latin America but should nonetheless be resorted to when foreign trade was declining, to maintain the levels of employment and income and to prevent the rate of economic development from slackening.

Mr. Cosciani, commending both the document on the subject under discussion presented by Mr. Urquidi and the author's verbal comments on the paper at the previous meeting, agreed with him regarding the need to co-ordinate fiscal and financial policy in its different sectors and at the highest administrative level. He wondered, in that respect, whether the best and most logical way of securing such co-ordination might not be through over-all economic planning and whether it might not be advisable to attempt such co-ordination at the international level.

With regard to the effect of fiscal policy on

the distribution of national revenue, he also agreed with Mr. Urquidi that it could be achieved only if fiscal policy was preceded by structural reforms. Although Mr. Pazos was skeptical about the efficacy of such reforms, there was surely no doubt that they constituted a prerequisite for investment, which was only feasible in an atmosphere of peace and social security; a progressive income tax was an effective instrument to achieve that.

With regard to Mr. Urquidi's remarks on public enterprises, he thought it wrong to generalize on the prices of services in relation to cost; instead, in some cases the use of prices which were fundamentally consumer subsidies might be justified. The opinions of Mr. Urquidi and Mr. Pazos regarding the limitations of fiscal policy or alternative measures to achieve redistribution of income struck him as overpessimistic, and he did not share them entirely.

Mr. NAHARRO agreed with Mr. Urquidi regarding the necessity of planning and co-ordinating fiscal policy with the other economic activities of the country as well as on the difficulties that involved. He wondered what the co-ordinating or planning agency should be; as so-called planning boards did not usually have executive powers, a political-administrative machinery capable of achieving such co-ordination effectively would have to be found. He also agreed with the author on the advisability of obtaining the co-operation of the private sector in regard to fiscal policy, to the extent that the latter constituted an instrument or tool of development. Aside from the indirect forms of co-operation obtainable through the parliamentary system and the influence of public opinion, he wondered how it would be possible to enlist the co-operation of the public and private sectors in that field by direct means.

In addition to the foregoing general remarks, he would like to make special reference to certain other matters dealt with by Mr. Urquidi. He wondered, for example, whether it would not be advisable, for tax purposes, to distinguish between income derived from capital and from work, when such a distinction, in kind and quality, might further the redistribution of income. With regard to rates for essential public services provided by independent enterprises, he pointed out the danger of resorting to the system of price differentials, although he recognized that they might be useful for the redistribution of resources and for economic development if made to favor the more promising sectors. It might be preferable to replace such a system by a system of subsidies which do not produce distortions in relative prices.

Mr. HERSCHEL drew attention to the importance of making a distinction between the theoretical and practical aspects of fiscal policy and of ensuring efficient co-ordination of public and private interest in that field; he agreed with Mr. Urquidi on those points. On the other hand, he disagreed with him regarding the proportion of the public sector's participation in domestic expenditure and the gross national product, at least as far as Argentina was concerned. With regard to tax incentives, in his country they did not constitute the main factors in investment decisions. Customs duties played an important part in the fiscal revenue of some Latin American countries.

Mr. CASAS emphasized that the objectives of fiscal policy could not be different from those of economic policy, which were to obtain an optimum level of productivity and income, to ensure economic stability, and to secure a more equitable income distribution. The three aims were interdependent. In connection with the third objective, a redistribution of wealth and income should be such as to ensure an increase in productivity. Failure to understand that had led to a somewhat inaccurate approach to the development of fiscal policy. Fiscal policy could be used to achieve a redistribution of wealth and income by correcting existing inequities and preventing those which might arise in the future. Existing inequities could be corrected through intervention by the state in the form of an imposition of a progressive tax or an increase in direct taxes. Fiscal policy was an especially important factor in enabling the government to create conditions beneficial to the private sector and therefore had an essential part to play in creating the conditions required for economic development.

MR. VEGA observed that, in Mr. Urquidi's view, the primary objective of fiscal policy was to secure increased revenue for the government rather than to redistribute wealth and income. The latter objective, however, should not be disregarded. As to which should come first, it was rather a question of timing and methods than of priorities. Fiscal policy alone as a means of ensuring a redistribution of wealth and income was not very effective. Such redistribution could be better achieved through agrarian reform, which was an instrument not merely for redistributing land but also for securing a more equitable distribution of wealth and income. Public expenditure was also an instrument for securing redistribution of income, although its main aim was to provide more infrastructure works, primarily benefiting those able to invest.

He did not agree with Mr. Urquidi's view that it would be preferable to present tax rates to the public as average rates instead of marginal rates. It would be difficult to collect enough revenue to finance the budget merely from the use of average rates. To use the latter would be to abandon progressive taxes in favor of proportional taxes. Nor could he support Mr. Urquidi's contention that investment incentives could best be sought through accelerated depreciation rather than tax concessions. He felt that the latter were preferable.

MR. DESCARTES felt that Mr. Urquidi's concepts of economic development programming were both useful and effective, and he was in agreement with the main points made, particularly with respect to the broad scope of fiscal policy. Care should be exercised, however, with respect to the responsibility of ministries charged with specific objectives of fiscal policy, on the one hand, and the position of economic planners on the other. Both were essential to effective action. He fully agreed with Mr. Urquidi regarding the

important part that should be played by the minister for finance in this area.

While he supported Mr. Urquidi's position with respect to the primary objective of fiscal policy—namely, economic development—he felt that the importance of income redistribution should not be minimized. Both were essential to development, and they did not conflict.

Another important factor was the income tax and the need to educate the public on the benefits to be derived therefrom. That could best be done through advisory committees in which the private sector was represented. Such committees had produced good results in Puerto Rico as a means of ensuring public understanding of some tax programs.

With regard to autonomous agencies, he felt that they should be self-supporting and that public utility rates, e.g., in the electric-power industry, could be lowered in some cases to ensure social benefits without destroying the aim of economic self-sufficiency of the rate structure as a whole. He stressed the danger of adjustments made for social purposes but felt that they could be effected with moderation and common sense, bearing in mind that the over-all rate should cover costs.

He further stated that a good public accounting system was important to the economic development process, and he supported program budgeting.

Lastly, he shared the concern expressed by Mr. Pinto regarding the proliferation of government agencies and legal machinery. Attention should be paid to those points, and an attempt should be made to remedy existing deficiencies.

MR. KALDOR said that he was sure that Mr. Urquidi was largely in agreement on the main issues with those who had commented on his paper and would undoubtedly subscribe to two beliefs held by those present: first, that the share of income from property in the national income was too high in Latin American countries and larger than in other areas; and second, that as a result of defects in tax legislation and administration, property incomes did not bear their fair share of the tax burden. He himself agreed with Mr. Urquidi that the redistribution of income from the rich to the poor was not the primary objective of taxation, which must be to collect revenue and in so doing to transfer resources from unproductive to productive use. However, that could not be done without drawing the large mass of income from property into the tax net. The share of the national income paid in taxation could not be increased unless a government could reach the large proportion of income received from property, for example, the 46.7 per cent referred to by Mrs. de Navarrete as accruing to the top 10 per cent bracket in Mexico, on which little tax was paid. The aim must be to make a larger proportion of the national resources available for productive purposes, whether for recurrent items such as public services or non-recurrent items such as savings. Even though the objective of taxation was not to redistribute income, it was very probable that that would be its effect.

Referring to pages 9 and 10 of Mr. Urquidi's paper, he said that he must disagree, from the standpoint of economic theory, with the views expressed there. The share of income to property in the form of profits depended largely on the levels of consumption by property owners. An increase in taxation yield would improve the balance between public revenue and expenditure; taxation of property, if it reduced the propensity to consume from property income, would also change the respective shares of national production going to labor and capital before taxes. It was no mere coincidence that in countries where there was effective taxation of property income, such as the Scandinavian countries, the United States, and the United Kingdom, the share of income going to profits before taxes was lower than in countries where property income was not taxed because of defects in the tax system. In other words, in the latter countries the share of the national income going to labor was reduced because of the high propensity to consume of property owners, which increased the share

of profits in output. He could not, therefore, agree with Mr. Urquidi that progressive taxation did not tackle the root of the problem of the share of production accruing to different social classes.

MR. JARACH, while agreeing with Mr. Urquidi that the primary objective of fiscal policy was to increase revenue, could not support the contention that taxation could not lead to income redistribution. He shared Mr. Pinto's view that redistribution depended on the use made of public expenditure. Moreover, economic development should not be confused with investment, since among its aims were the creation and maintenance of essential services in education, public health, and housing, all of which led to conditions of social stability conducive to economic development. Income redistribution might not only be an objective per se; it was at the same time a prerequisite of economic growth. Furthermore, it could break up the dynastic concentration of wealth so that the wealth could be used for productive purposes.

MR. DESAI, referring to Mr. Urquidi's paper, said that he preferred Mr. Kaldor's definition of the aim of fiscal policy as adjusting government spending to government objectives and obtaining the necessary funds. Although, as Mr. Urquidi had said, fiscal policy touched closely on such other matters as monetary policy, public enterprises, and so forth, the definition of fiscal policy should not be made so broad as to include all those areas of economic policy. There was a tendency to attempt to relate fiscal data with the national accounts, although the latter had developed on the basis of premises somewhat different from those relevant to economic analysis of the process of economic development. Mr. Urquidi's presentation had led to the idea that government investment was the prime means of effecting economic development, whereas in fact all government expenditure, current or capital, could be directed toward development, and there were instances of greater misuse of resources by a government in investment than in current expenditure. He also thought it would be an academic exercise to try to indicate priorities in expenditure, since most government budgets reflected national priorities, which varied from country to country. In most countries, the defense budget was already accepted as a given datum in allocating government expenditure.

MR. PIEDRABUENA stressed the need for a clear-cut definition of fiscal policy to provide guidance to those responsible for its practical application.

On the question of taxation, care should be exercised regarding the amount of the taxes imposed. Mr. Urquidi's level of 15 per cent as representing the public sector's share of national expenditure had in many cases been exceeded in Latin America. The question was how that 15 per cent was distributed. Moreover, a higher percentage might have unproductive results. The regressive nature of the tax system was demonstrated by the fact that while workers received 40 per cent of the national income, they paid more than 40 per cent of the taxes.

He agreed with Mr. Pinto that the ends and means of fiscal policy should be co-ordinated. However, what was needed was a system of priorities regarding the ends of fiscal policy.

MRS. DE NAVARRETE said that fiscal policy must be viewed as an integral whole within the general framework of economic development. Its aim must be to increase national production, leading to better distribution. By way of illustration, she referred to her own experiences in underdeveloped areas in the south of Mexico. Investment in infrastructure, however essential, was not enough in itself and must be accompanied by other forms of investment, including social investment, that would make it possible to develop such areas by providing the necessary housing, education, and industrial training without which industry could not flourish.

MR. FERNÁNDEZ felt that in fiscal policy emphasis should be placed on economic development, since the aim of economic development was mainly to increase productivity and over-all consumption. However, there was no point in increasing production unless

a market existed which could absorb the increase. That market could be created through income redistribution. Lack of such redistribution could, as in the case of Chile, result in devaluation of the currency and inflationary conditions.

MR. HART said that he hoped the interest of the conference in a sophisticated type of fiscal policy would not in any way prejudice the taking of practical steps to improve the present situation. The fact was that present fiscal policies in Latin America were inadequate because tax revenue did not match expenditure. Some of the gap could be filled by more efficient administration and better collection. He referred to his experience with the Chilean tax system and suggested that there was sometimes a link between unrealistic rates and inefficient application of the taxes and that administrative reform might require some adjustment of rates. He also pointed out that some forms of government expenditure could amount to a regressive redistribution of income, such as the provision of free higher education if only those in the upper income levels were able to enter the universities, or expenditure that benefited car owners, if they represented only those in the higher income levels. He agreed with Mr. Pinto that public enterprises might be sold to private firms, provided that a fair price was paid, and that public enterprises should not receive disproportionate subsidies. A national price policy could solve many such problems. He agreed with Mr. Kaldor that tax revenue must be increased by progressive taxes on property income. He supported Mr. Urquidi's view that public understanding was an important factor and thought that the essentials should be explained to the public in a simplified form, particularly the salient fact that the revenue now obtained from taxation was insufficient.

MR. GNAZZO agreed with other speakers that the basic aim of fiscal policy must be to collect funds first for current expenditure and secondly for economic development. However, fiscal policy was also an instrument for the redistribution not so much of wealth as of income. Further, it could reduce the structural rigidities that led to an inequitable distribution of income. The principle aim should be to co-ordinate fiscal policy with general economic policy; all the elements concerned should be co-ordinated as part of a single whole, without giving priority to the various components.

Mr. CAZAL thought that three main points had emerged from the discussion: that it was important to establish the aims of fiscal policy, that there must be full co-operation among the bodies responsible for executing fiscal policy, and that due emphasis must be given to the participation of the private sector. In some countries, confusion arose because the aims of fiscal policy, not being clearly defined, were either not known to the public or even were not clearly apprehended by the officials concerned. Though the ultimate aims of fiscal policy of various countries were likely to be similar, the intermediate aims might well vary according to the stage of development and particular problems of the country concerned. The first step should be to define both the ultimate and intermediate aims of fiscal policy; the second, to establish an order of priorities for the allocation of resources; and the third, to ensure that all concerned fully understood the aims and priorities.

Mr. LESSA said that although the point had not been raised in any of the documents before the conference, he thought it particularly important to consider what might be called the preconditions for the application of fiscal policy in relation to development. In Brazil, for example, the institutional stucture inherited from the past was one appropriate to nineteenth-century Europe, and any government action regarding taxation involved a cumbersome and lengthy process of discussion. In many other Latin American countries, any tax amendment was subject to lengthy discussions by legislative bodies and in various committees, which constituted a serious obstacle to tax reform. The scope and use of the fiscal instrument might be greatly increased by certain institutional reforms that would remove such obstacles.

Mr. URQUIDI expressed his appreciation of the favorable opinions voiced by Mr. Pazos and Mr. Pinto in commenting on his paper and also thanked the other speakers who had participated in the debate. He called attention to the fact that various aspects dealt with in the paper, such as the contracting of debts, taxing of foreign enterprises, regulating agencies, etc., had not been discussed. The omission confirmed his opinion that the manner in which fiscal policy was usually approached and envisaged was unsatisfactory and indicated the need for a deeper analysis. Actually, he was in agreement with most of the comments made in the course of the debate by the various speakers.

Referring in particular to the questions raised by Mr. Naharro, he reaffirmed his view that the financial authority should at all times take part in any matters calculated to affect fiscal and financial policy. The necessary planning and co-ordination should be the responsibility of a commission including the minister for finance and endowed with quasi-executive powers, subject only to the approval of the President of the Republic. Functionally, such a commission would divide up its work among as many specialized subcommissions as might be necessary. The most efficient way of ensuring co-operation from the private sector would appear to be not by having it represented in planning committees and subcommittees but through special consulative agencies.

With regard to price of services supplied by semipublic agencies, he was opposed to the policy of subsidies, which would ultimately hit the consumer. He did not believe there should be any distinction, for tax purposes, between earned and unearned income; such a system, far from ensuring the requisite fair treatment (as witness the case of the poor *rentier*) would discourage savings and investment. The problem lay rather in establishing a consolidated personal income tax.

Since the lack of savings and capitalization was characteristic of developing countries, it was essential for them to have recourse to tax incentives, one of which was accelerated amortization; such an incentive would be particularly effective in the case of enterprises with long-term output.

When he said he preferred average rates rather than marginal rates, he had not meant that such rates should be proportional; he had merely referred to the manner in which they were expressed: they should be progressive to the extent that the degree of progressivity of the tax was compatible with the promotion of investments.

He stressed that fiscal policy should assign priority to the economic objective as such; he did not feel as pessimistic as some participants believed he was or as optimistic as Mr. Pazos appeared to be with regard to the redistributive effects of fiscal policy, which in any event could be obtained more rapidly by other measures. The creation of public savings for investment in the public sector was a fundamentally important aim in Latin American countries; therefore that aim should be kept separate from current expenses, and it was also desirable to manage fiscal policy in such a way as to encourage private savings and investment.

When he expressed reservation regarding the redistributive effects that could be achieved through fiscal policy, he had been referring always to income and not to wealth, as he had no doubts about the possibility of its redistribution. However, it should not be forgotten that a redistributive policy could discourage investment. In that respect, and provided it did not adversely affect investment capacity, he agreed with Mr. Kaldor regarding the advisability of reducing the consumption propensity of the wealthier classes.

Finally, with regard to the policy of compensating short-term fluctuations by declining external prices, he felt that it should not be supported or reinforced by fiscal measures such as tax exemptions or reductions, because such measures were liable to cause budget deficits with the well-known inflationary consequences. Monetary policy was more useful for correcting such fluctuations and should be supported by international measures aimed at stabilizing income in the form of foreign exchange from exports of primary products.

2

Fiscal Capacity of Developing Economies

by Rajanikant Desai*

ISSUES OF TAX POLICY

Requirements of economic growth have compelled the governments of developing economies to entice a large proportion of resources away from consumption and much of it away from the private sector in order to invest it in economic and social infrastructure for growth. The task is rendered difficult because per capita incomes are low and the average propensity to consume remains high. Evaluating fiscal capacity or potential of developing economies, therefore, has to be preceded by a common agreement on policy issues, since these issues call for a shift in emphasis from the principles traditionally accepted in economic discussions relating to taxation.

Canons of Taxation

The principal reason for all tax levies is, of course, the need of the government to secure resources to implement its "functions of state." In the context of the developing countries—Africa, Asia, Latin America—taxation problems have to be viewed not only in relation to the functions of law, order, and literacy directly undertaken by the government but in relation to the programs of economic growth promotion under the aegis of both government and private sectors. The relative mix of the two sectors may vary from one country to another, but the growth objective remains common to all of them. To the ex-

tent that co-operation of the private sector is sought—not only as entrepreneurs and employers, but also as wage earners and farmers—the question of incentives becomes relevant to the discussion of taxation problems. In other words, account has to be taken of the effects of specific tax measures and of the tax system as a whole on the direction and efficiency of capital investment and of individual efforts. Finally, problems of taxation, more than of any other field of economic discussion, are affected by considerations of equity. The government is called upon to collect revenue (and reallocate spendable incomes) in such fashion as to mitigate inequality, realistically assumed to be a concomitant of the prevailing institutional arrangements for sharing (and inheriting) incomes and wealth. Evaluation of a fiscal system, therefore, contains a blend of three considerations: revenue (i.e., transfer of resources to the government), incentives (largely for the private sector), and equity (in sharing the "burden" of taxes and also the benefits of public spending).

The three aspects, conceptually distinct, are obviously interdependent. Revenue measures may affect adversely the incentives to work and to invest. Concentration on incentives or extensive relief for low-income groups, on the other hand, by reducing public revenues may actually hurt the poor themselves if such giveways hamper growth by decreasing government spending on economic or social overheads. There cannot be, therefore, any absolute rules prescribing an optimum for the mix of revenue, incentives, and equity in framing or evaluating a fiscal pattern or sys-

*Fiscal and Financial Branch, Department of Economic and Social Affairs, United Nations.

tem. A teleological and pragmatic approach is required. Growth being the prime concern of economic policy, economic efficiency in the use of resources must provide the guiding principle in such an approach.

Revenue versus Incentives

The lagging behind of fiscal performance in relation to fiscal potentials in most developing economies would suggest, however, that increasing the fiscal yield constitutes the principal direction of tax reform. If that is the case, what importance should be given to the related questions of incentives and equity?

The question of incentives is phrased in two forms: it is a plea for a low average rate of taxation, taking all taxes together, and it is a plea for generous but specific incentives irrespective of whether the average level of taxation is high or low.

The plea for a low average rate of taxation is advanced more generally in those developed countries where the private sector is the major provider of economic growth. It is argued there that the established tax levels are high; they dampen private sector incentives to produce, save, and invest; and they are thus injurious to growth.

In the context of developing economies, however, this view has meaning only if the average level of taxation impinges on subsistence or, at the most, on the basic amenities of life. On the other hand, in these countries revenue is essential to provide the needed resources for government investment in infrastructure or other public activities which constitute a prerequisite for activating private investment and economic expansion.

The alternative of leaving these resources in private hands raises the question of how much they would contribute to growth. The propensity to consume is inordinately high in some countries of Asia, and more generally of Latin America, where the "demonstration effect" with respect to consumption is significant and inflation has discouraged savings. The outflow of capital from the latter region, especially to the United States, is of substan-

tial importance. And the relatively low level of private domestic investment is often channeled into "investment" in luxury buildings and the like. The "discouragement" of too little taxation provides perhaps a more general instance of the misuse of resources in developing economies than the "disincentive" influence of too much of it.

As to specific incentives, a gamut of these has been evolved in order to encourage the private sector to save and invest in *new and necessary* ventures, as several of the investment promotion laws describe them. The concessions aim at reducing the cost of capital goods through relief from excise or import taxes or at increasing the profitability (or, conversely, reducing the period for recouping initial investment and thus the initial risk of investment) through income tax concessions. While these incentives were widely welcomed and generously implemented in the fifties, a doubt seems to be emerging with regard to their efficacy and the desirability of suffering the revenue loss which they entail. As the 1960 survey of the Economic Commission for Asia and the Far East (ECAFE) puts it:

Tax incentives are rather a delicate instrument of economic policy; they can be effective only if the general climate is favourable to private investment. Tax liability is only one of several factors taken into account in arriving at investment decisions; although it is an important consideration, it is not necessarily the most important one. If the concessions are to be effective, they have to be co-ordinated with other factors having a bearing on private investment. The most powerful incentive for private investment in the postwar period has perhaps been provided by the aggregate effect of fiscal policy on the level of effective demand in the economy and by the assurance that the demand will continue to expand and that competing products from abroad will be shut off by protective tariffs.[1]

Indeed, general tax stimuli seem to be no longer advisable, once industrialization has

---

[1] United Nations, Economic Commission for Asia and the Far East, *Economic Survey of Asia and the Far East,* 1960, p. 99.

passed beyond the initial stage.[2] By exempting the new, growing, and sheltered industries from paying taxes, governments have suffered revenue losses which can hardly be justified if account is taken of how well these industries have done, as judged by their capital appreciation in the stock markets of their countries. General concessions, such as broad tax holidays, ought to be replaced by more limited and selective directional incentives, such as investment and depreciation allowances geared closely to reinvestment.[3]

Revenue versus Equity

If more revenue is to be obtained in poor countries, what importance should be given to the question of equity in apportioning the tax burden among the different groups of taxpayers? This question, also, must be approached from the standpoint of efficient utilization of the resources of a developing economy for growth. It is obvious that if all the resources over and above those necessary to maintain subsistence living—the "economic surplus" of the community—were to accrue to or remain with those with relatively low incomes, they would tend to be almost exhausted in further consumption. Undoubtedly, augmented consumption levels are in themselves the object of economic development, and by reacting favorably on sanitation and health they would in turn enhance economic productivity. But beyond a certain basic need for individual action, collective measures for public health and education undertaken by the government are more economical, efficient, and effective. Whether the economic surplus accruing to those with high incomes should be left with them will similarly depend on the use to which the high-income groups are putting the resources at their disposal. If

the presumption is that they behave as *rentiers* and use their incomes (or accumulated or inherited wealth) for luxury living, then again the government should collect these incomes to build up the necessary capital for economic growth. Such a society would, therefore, call for heavy taxation both of the low- and high-income groups. It would be a society in which the attempt of the government might well be to obtain most, if not all, of the economic surplus.

If, on the other hand, those with high incomes save—in the sense of abstaining from consumption—and invest in productive endeavor or could be made to do so by judiciously selective government action, including incentives, then taxation of the rich becomes a subject for delicate handling. Although considerations of equity may demand a sharply progressive taxation of high incomes, those of economic growth may dictate otherwise. The compromise to be favored is the one which would secure the largest proportion of the economic surplus to be devoted to activities which would promote growth in the community, that is, the public and private sectors taken together.

It is in this area that governments of several developing economies seem to be caught on the horns of a dilemma. Democratic and often socialistic in their orientation, their legislators consider it a political mandate to reduce inequalities of income and wealth in their societies. In doing so, they increase the potentialities for consumption at the expense of those for saving (and investment). By legislating for a low revenue yield (or a high volume of income transfers to the private sector), they expose their governments to two alternatives: giving up programs which would have helped economic growth, or pursuing them under conditions of inflation, which again is a highly inequitable way of obtaining resources.

The question of equity, therefore, has to be seen from a new angle. Even from the point of view of those with low incomes, economic growth is the best guarantee for relief from poverty. They are going to be hurt if the economy stagnates. Second, inflation is also

---

[2] A special problem of the Central American Common Market is the competitive race to grant costly and wasteful concessions to attract industries to be located in the territory of one country rather than that of its neighbor. A special treaty has now unified tax incentive laws to overcome this problem.

[3] See United Nations, *The Promotion of the International Flow of Private Capital* (February 26, 1960) (E/3325), pars. 146–59.

likely to injure them, since their bargaining power is weaker than that of the well-off. In underdeveloped countries, their best hope, therefore, lies in avoiding both stagnation and inflation, even if this means submitting to higher levels of taxation. Equity would, of course, suggest a sharp progression in taxing those with high incomes. But the latter may have to be rewarded *if* (and only on that condition) the necessary impetus and effort for growth could be secured from them in return. While, therefore, taxation of the low-income groups becomes almost mandatory, taxation of the well-off, approached from the standpoint of economic growth, requires a particularly discriminate and pragmatic handling.

A minor conundrum may be removed in concluding this discussion of equity. In many instances of tax advice, considerable attention is given to equity aspects of single taxes. It is true that if every tax in a fiscal system is equitable, the system as a whole is equitable. But a similar result can be obtained also by a combination of taxes, some borne primarily or wholly by the poor and others by the rich. It is not the equity of every single tax that is important. What is relevant is the equity of the tax system as a whole.

Even the question of the aggregate tax system has to be related to the distributional consequences of aggregate government spending which is normally biased in favor of the low-income groups. Thus, it is the equity of the whole gamut of government operations which is relevant. In any case, seeking equity through government operations—and further still, equality through government legislation —has complex ramifications for economic growth. An adequate discussion of these ramifications would be beyond the scope of an inquiry directed primarily to problems of fiscal policy. Here it would suffice if it is recognized that considerations of equity may have to take second place to those of economic productivity in devising for developing economies fiscal systems which are geared to growth.

Of course, it is not inconceivable that governments may fritter away resources (for instance, in inflated payrolls, military adventures, or luxurious government buildings) which, left in private hands, could have been utilized in economic activities conducive to growth. If the governments are to enjoin and enforce upon the citizens the need to refrain from unnecessary consumption or ostentation, the governments, in their turn, owe to these citizens the same utmost economy and growth-oriented use of resources. Frivolous spending becomes as much a habit with governments as with individuals. Measures for tax reform, therefore, cannot be advocated in dissociation from concern with the purposes and pattern of government spending.

AGGREGATE FISCAL CAPACITY

Upper Limits of Fiscal Capacity

Theoretically, the whole national income over and above the subsistence-level existence for the community (or even more, if capital levy is brought into the picture) can be channeled into the state coffers. Such a level of taxation has been conceived of in the context of centrally planned economies, where all entrepreneurial activity is taken over by the state and where the state enforces rigorous savings on its citizens for rapid capital formation. In practice, even in the centrally planned economies of the world, resource control of this magnitude has hardly endured, although attempts have been made at various times to reach almost such a level.

In mainland China, for instance, the state collected for "the state-owned economy" as much as 33.2 per cent of the country's "net material income" in 1957, shared in the 64 per cent of the income which went to "joint state-private economy" and "co-operative (collective) economy," and left only 2.8 per cent at the free disposal of the "individual economy."[4] Considering the low absolute level of the national income of the country, it is conceivable that almost all income above sub-

---

[4] Peoples' Republic of China, State Statistical Bureau, *Ten Great Years* (Peking, 1960), p. 42.

sistence levels must have gone to defray the costs of national investment (all investment having been nationalized) and other government expenditure.

The economic upper limit of taxation may, as a rule, be considered to be set at that level beyond which taxation would tend to reduce the (potential) rate of economic growth. This economic upper limit has, however, got to be distinguished from the political upper limit of taxation, which may lie below or above the economic limit. In the case of mainland China, the political limit may have gone beyond the economic limit, since, following an economic setback, the government was subsequently compelled to relax the extent of its control over resources. Even in free-enterprise economies, in an extreme emergency such as war, the government may, for a short period, stretch its "long arm" beyond the economic limit. This may also happen in countries where the government's zeal for redistribution of economic power through the employment of fiscal mechanisms may be pushed to a point where it retards growth.

In practice, it is more usual to find that the political upper limit of taxation remains substantially below the economic upper limit of taxation. Taxation, beyond a certain limit and in specific areas of economic activity, may evoke so strong a political opposition that such reform has to be treated as impracticable. Closely allied to the political factors are the institutional arrangements of a society— institutions such as those of ownership of property, systems of family and inheritance, etc. Institutions get so entrenched that it may be almost impossible, in the short run, to alter their pattern. In other words, the discussion of tax policy has to reckon with the limiting constraint of what may be described as the political and institutional milieu of the society under consideration. Even if it may be permissible to ignore these factors in considering taxable capacity from the standpoint of economic theory, in any discussion of economic policy it is prudent (and realistic) to acknowledge the existence of this restraint upon fiscal reform, at least over the short run.

Recognition of the political and social barrier, however, does not mean the acceptance *in toto* of existing political alignments or of a given institutional structure; all potentialities of change and improvement must be explored. Nor does it preclude the possibility of a difference of opinion as to where the political limit stands or as to the prospect of bringing about institutional changes. It should, however, be feasible to obtain a more or less general agreement on the criteria for measuring fiscal capacity within a given institutional pattern or within a projected change in it, even if this change has to be considered as an exogeneous element representing the political or social will of the community.

Determinants of Fiscal Capacity

In principle, the capacity of a country to raise taxes would be a function of the absolute level of *per capita national income*. The higher this absolute level of per capita income, the greater the size of the economic surplus and, therefore, the capacity of the community to spare resources for common functions.

Given the absolute level, the *distribution of national income* becomes relevant, since those with high incomes have proportionately greater capacity to contribute to the fisc than those with low incomes.

Empirically, however, it is found that tax performance has varied largely with the institutional and economic facilities for tax collection. Thus, a community with a higher ratio of foreign trade to national incomes usually collects a larger proportion of the national income as revenue than another at a similar level of national income but with greater domestic orientation of its economy. Primarily institutional factors—such as the relative significance of the monetary sector as compared with the nonmonetary sector in the economy, of the corporate sector as against unincorporated enterprises, of plantations as against peasant farms—seem to have had a determining influence on the proportion of aggregate national resources governments have been able to collect in revenue. In other words, if the institutional pattern of a society provides a number of *accessible tax bases,* it vastly augments its fiscal potential.

Finally, taxable capacity is related to the *competence and integrity of the civil service* of the country. The widespread evasion of taxes and corruption of public officials in several underdeveloped countries point toward potential which could be realized even without altering the substantive structure of the tax systems.

Fiscal Capacity and National Income

As noted above, the linking of fiscal capacity to national income stems from the concept of economic surplus, which represents the proportion of total output in excess of the amount required for subsistence. This surplus is what is available for additional consumption and investment (in functional terms) and for distribution between the private and public agencies (in sectoral terms). In a low-income, centrally planned economy where all investment is nationalized, in attempting to attain a rapid rate of growth little allowance is made to augment consumption (in the private sector). The fiscal performance of such an economy, therefore, tends to encompass almost the whole of the economic surplus. In economies at the other end, where the private sector is counted on to contribute a substantial proportion to national investment, the government, due to economic and political reasons, has to allow some proportion of the economic surplus to remain with its citizens for augmenting their average levels of consumption over and above bare subsistence and for private investment. Where precisely the line is drawn between these two extremes is a matter of an implicit or explicit political decision. It does, however, remain true that the larger the size of the economic surplus, the higher the fiscal potential.

The lower per capita income of the developing economies would thus normally indicate a lower ratio of fiscal potential to national income. There are, however, considerations which suggest that, as a norm, the developing countries may rather approximate or exceed the proportions of national income actually attained by advanced countries. In the first instance, the distribution of incomes in the newly developing countries is generally more unequal than in the advanced countries—a fact which favors a higher tax potential. What is more important, however, is the significance of this inequality for economic growth. In many developing countries, the rich tend to use their wealth (and inordinately high incomes) to a great extent for purposes inconsistent with raising economic productivity of the communities. The second main reason, partly following from the first, is that governments of the developing economies are called upon to assume responsibility for a relatively larger proportion of national investment than in the advanced countries. Since, therefore, more of the economic surplus is needed for investment and more of the needed investment is to be made by the public sector, the proportion of the economic surplus required to be channeled to the government in the developing countries is larger than in the advanced countries. Thus, on the one hand, the size of the economic surplus tends to be small in the developing economies because of their lower per capita incomes; on the other hand, a larger proportion of it has to be made potentially available to the state to undertake the tasks of development. Nevertheless, the wide discrepancies between the absolute levels of per capita national incomes of the developing and the advanced countries would continue to be reflected in the absolute volumes of per capita fiscal yields.

Again, whatever the average ratio of tax potential to a given level of national income, it should be possible to increase this ratio with a rise in the national income. In other words, it should be possible to secure higher proportions from marginal rises in national income. The tax system as a whole could be progressive in relation to the rise in the level of the national income. And still, in several countries (particularly in Mexico and Central America), while the national income has increased, the ratio of revenues to national income has tended to stagnate or even fall.

Fiscal Performance

In advanced private-enterprise economies, revenues obtained seem to vary from one-fifth to one-third of the net national income. In the less developed countries, the ratio of government revenue to net national income falls within a wider range; for instance, from 7 to 27 per cent in Latin America (see Table 2–1). Similar discrepancies can also be observed in Asia. The fiscal products in the centrally planned economies run much higher.[5]

The ratios in Table 2–1 could serve only as rough indicators since, as stated in the notes to the table, the coverage of total government revenue, as given by official statistics, varies from country to country and since the estimates of national income also differ widely in coverage and reliability. Despite these limitations, the statistics suggest that tax performance is not really related to the level of the national income. The revenues in Venezuela, Argentina, Brazil, and Ecuador in Latin

America or Ceylon and Taiwan (22 to 23 per cent of national income in 1958) in Asia correspond with the levels reached in several advanced countries. And this does not necessarily mean that their potentials have even been fully exploited. Thus, for instance, the high level of Venezuelan revenues is derived primarily from taxation of petroleum. The oil companies pay substantial amounts directly in income taxes and royalties. If this direct contribution of petroleum industry is excluded, the rest of the Venezuelan economy, accounting for about three-fourths of the national income, contributed some 12 per cent; here there may be scope for further expansion of revenues. Or taking into consideration the major tax groups as given in Table 2–2, with the aforementioned exception of Venezuela, no country in Latin America seems to have collected more than 5 per cent of its national income from taxes on income in 1959. There is, therefore, room for enlarging the scope of income taxes even in those countries which altogether collect a substantial proportion of national income for government revenue.

The high-revenue countries thus still permit a margin for further increase in revenues, and there is no reason why this margin should not be further exploited. But in this case it

[5]In the Soviet Union and Poland, for instance. government revenue was 53 per cent of net material income in 1959. *Revue de Législation et de Science Financière* (January, 1962), pp. 33–34.

TABLE 2–1: Latin American Countries: Government Revenues in Percentages of Estimated Net National Incomes 1959[a]

Countries with a high level of tax revenue		Countries with a medium level of tax revenue		Countries with a low level of tax revenue	
Venezuela	27.0	Peru	19.5	Panama	15.0
Argentina	24.0	Chile	18.0	Mexico	14.0
Brazil	23.5	Costa Rica	16.0	Colombia	14.0
Ecuador	22.0	Guatemala	16.0	El Salvador	13.5
				Honduras	11.0
				Bolivia	7.0[b]

SOURCE: Compiled from national publications.
NOTES: Government revenues include all current receipts —from taxes, sales and charges, surplus of government enterprises, etc.—of central and local governments (except in Bolivia, Peru, and some Central American countries, where local revenue is of minor importance). Certain earmarked taxes for quasi-governmental funds and enterprises have not been included insofar as they do not appear in available official statistics; the omitted revenue from taxes may be quite important in countries such as Colombia, for instance. Capital receipts are excluded. Social security or pension contributions are also excluded. The gross receipts of the social security systems are quite significant in Chile (14 per cent of national income) and Argentina (8 per cent) and only somewhat less so in Brazil (6 per cent), Ecuador (4 per cent), and Mexico (3 per cent). The net revenue contribution to the social security taxes, however, is considerably lower than these gross levels, from which government contributions and benefit payments to the private sector have to be deducted.
[a]Except Argentina (1960), Bolivia (1958), and Peru (1956).
[b]Per cent of gross national product. Tax revenue in real terms increased by about 50 per cent during 1958–61.

TABLE 2–2: Latin American Countries: Sources of Government Revenues, 1959 (*Per cent of net national income*)

Country	Total revenue	Export taxes	Import taxes	Internal transaction taxes^a	Income taxes	Property taxes^b	Other receipts^c
Venezuela	27.0	9.7^d	3.8	2.0	10.0	—	1.5
Argentina^e	24.0	2.8^d	2.8	6.1	4.4	2.0	5.9
Brazil	23.5	0.1	1.3	10.5	3.3	0.5	7.8
Ecuador	22.0	1.3	5.4	3.7	1.8	0.6	9.2
Peru^f	19.5	2.5	4.4	4.0	3.8	—	4.8
Chile	18.0	2.1	2.6	6.0	3.1	1.5	2.7
Costa Rica	16.0	3.1	9.0	1.1	1.8	0.6	0.4
Mexico	14.0	1.1	1.6	2.3	3.4	1.6	4.0
Colombia	14.0	1.2^g	1.9	1.6	4.8^h	1.2	3.3
El Salvador^i	13.5	2.8	4.8	2.3	1.2	—	2.4
Honduras	11.0	0.5	5.0	2.5	1.7	—	1.3
Bolivia^i	7.0	0.2	3.6	2.2	0.6	—	0.4

SOURCE: Compiled from national publications.
COVERAGE: See *Notes* to Table 2–1.

^aCommodity and sales taxes (including turnover taxes), insofar as they could be determined or estimated. Other indirect taxes such as those on property transfers, stamp taxes, etc., are excluded. Sales taxes in some countries also apply to export sales, and these may account for a significant part of sales tax revenue (this would appear to be the case in Brazil especially). Where the revenue corresponding to export sales could be determined, as in Argentina, it has been included under export taxes.
^bTaxes on urban and rural property, insofar as they could be determined or estimated, and where they represent a significant amount. In some countries, however, taxation of urban property is effected through municipal fees, and revenue would be included under other receipts.
^c"Other" taxes, fees for government services, profits of public enterprises, income from government property, etc. These receipts have been so grouped because they could not be properly itemized for most countries.
^dIncluding oil royalties (Venezuela) and internal tax on export sales (Argentina).
^e1960.
^f1956.
^gIncluding government receipts from exchange differential transactions.
^hIncluding patrimony tax.
^i1958.

is a matter of concern that, after such a high proportion of national income is gathered into government hands, in a few cases (through fortuitous circumstances) an excessive proportion of it is applied to nondevelopmental expenditures. Venezuela and Brazil, with 27 and 24 per cent of their national incomes collected in revenue, spent almost 20 per cent of national income as current expenditure.[6] Here there is some scope for pruning nondevelopmental expenditure, since the amount saved from being so spent is tantamount to an equivalent gain in revenue which could be utilized for growth. A rational allocation of government expenditure promises as fruitful a reserve of growth resources as an expansion in revenue in almost all developing economies, but this comment applies particularly to those countries which already collect a high proportion of national income as government revenue.

The problem of fiscal expansion per se is acute for countries which collect 15 per cent or less of their net national incomes in revenue. This situation is typical of Asia and Africa, but less so of Latin America, even though five[7] out of a total of fourteen countries listed in Table 2–1 fell into this category in 1959. Bolivia provides a striking example of low revenues: in 1958, it collected only 7 per cent of its gross national product as government revenue, mostly from taxes on consumption on imported or domestically produced items, while other sources yielded insignificant amounts. Such a situation suggests the questions: Are there ways and means for Bolivia to double the proportion of its national income which it collected for revenue in 1958? Can the medium-level countries raise their proportions to bring them into the 20 to

[6]A classification of government expenditure into current and capital is extremely unsatisfactory in this regard since a considerable proportion of current expenditure is developmental and a sizable volume of capital expenditure may consist of monumental frivolity.

[7]Colombia has been excluded, since earmarked taxes would significantly raise its ratio of total revenues to national income in Table 2–1.

25 per cent range? The answers, as outlined in the annex to this paper, can be provided only by analysis in terms of national studies, taking into account the data (on income distribution, consumption and saving patterns, distribution of existing tax burdens) available and the specific alignment of political and economic forces in each country. In a global or regional approach such as the one necessarily employed in the main body of the paper, it would be more fruitful to consider the subject of fiscal expansion by major tax groups and review in broad terms the potentialities for growth each of these groups offers to serve the purposes of economic development.

AVENUES OF FISCAL EXPANSION

Taxation of Foreign Trade

The revenue potential of the foreign trade sector is determined by the size of the sector, the relative productivity of export enterprises, the structure of imports, and the ease of tax collection. The importance of these factors varies substantially in the different economies of Latin America. In general, however, activities directly connected with foreign trade have typically provided a significant proportion of revenue in these countries.

The export segment of this important sector, however, has tended to experience violent short-term fluctuations and relative stagnation on a long-term basis. Income inelasticity of demand for primary products and technological changes making for economy in the use of raw materials have made the market for primary commodities soft in the postwar period, with the exception of the short-lived boom during the Korean War. The world prices of a great number of the most important export commodities of Latin America[8]

[8]Coffee represents 45 per cent or more of the value of total exports from Brazil, Colombia, Costa Rica, El Salvador, and Guatemala; copper, 70 per cent of the exports from Chile; tin ore, 65 per cent of the exports from Bolivia; bananas, 47 and 37 per cent of the exports from Honduras and Costa Rica, respectively; and petroleum, 92 per cent of the exports from Venezuela.

have tended to decline during the last decade. This softness in the world markets for primary commodities has affected revenue not only from export taxes but also from taxes on imports, incomes, etc. Export taxes have suffered directly and often sharply where sliding scales of duty were in operation. The attempts made by countries exporting primary products to improve their long-term position, by curtailing supplies or by entering into commodity agreements in order to maintain prices, have not as yet been wholly successful, even though they have appeared to give temporary relief.

The ensuing balance of payments difficulties have also tended to restrict imports in volume and in terms of the type of goods imported. Essential consumer goods and capital items, received either as aid or paid for by exports, are admitted duty-free or bear low rates of duty. Such imports take the lion's share of the total. Imports of amenities and luxuries with high revenue potentials are being edged out. The replacement of revenue tariffs by protective tariffs has also made for a reduction in yields.

These trends, the outcome partly of export difficulties and partly of domestic-oriented economic growth, seem to suggest a continuing decline in the still predominant importance of taxation on the foreign sector in the revenue systems of most economies of Latin America. International trade, however, is large in relation to national income in these economies. The productivity of the export sector is distinctively higher than the productivity of the domestic sector, and imports may still provide a fruitful tax resource. Foreign trade is conducted primarily through a few points of entry or exit by land or sea. The imposition of taxes on foreign trade enables governments to collect revenues efficiently and cheaply. Finally, considerable experience has gone into developing fiscal administration of the customs, and major efforts are under way to overcome the still considerable threat of smuggling. Such accessibility to taxation is an asset which need not be frittered away by governments desiring to raise their revenue.

Revenue from the export sector can be obtained either from customs duties, from direct income taxation on exporting enterprises, from sales taxes, or from royalties. Revenue may also be obtained from differential charges on foreign exchange transactions or through a wide variety of government trading organizations. These mediums of tax collection are not mutually exclusive, but their accessibility and relative importance vary with the degree of economic and administrative development of the economy, with the structure of the export sector and with the institutional pattern of the country.

Since customs duties are easy and economical to collect, export duties have played and still play a significant role in less-developed export economies. Costa Rica, El Salvador, and Peru, for example, obtain some 2.5 per cent or more of their national income as revenue from export duties. Honduras and Bolivia, on the other hand, obtain less than 0.5 per cent.

An alternative means of taxing the export sector is direct income taxation on exporting enterprises. This type of taxation is significant in all the large and more developed economies of Latin America. Chile, for example, has no export duties but obtains a substantial part of its total revenue from direct taxation on a few large copper-exporting corporations.

Sales taxes on exported commodities are of importance in the revenue systems of some countries, for example, Brazil and Argentina. Royalties from the petroleum industry constitute the main part of the revenue system of Venezuela. They contribute almost one-third of the aggregate fiscal income of the country. Revenue from foreign exchange transactions was of substantial importance in several countries of Latin America during the decade after World War II. This kind of "taxation," which has been abandoned recently in many countries in the course of their attempts to rationalize their exchange systems, is still of importance in Brazil and Colombia and, to a lesser degree, in Venezuela.

Government revenue from the export sector of Latin America is thus obtained from a wide variety of alternative tax bases. The revenue yields from this sector, however, vary considerably among the different countries. Venezuela obtains some 15 per cent of national income as revenue; Argentina, Brazil, Peru, and Costa Rica, over 3 per cent; and Bolivia and Honduras, for example, about 1 per cent or less. Government mines, accounting for some 75 per cent of the mineral production of Bolivia, run at a loss, which means that almost half of the export sector fails to contribute any revenue. This partly explains the low ratio (only 0.2 per cent) of

TABLE 2–3: Central American Economies: Comparative Taxation of the Export Sector, 1959

Country	Value of exports (per cent of national income)	Value of main export articles (per cent of value of total export)	Income taxes[a]	Revenue from export taxes	Total
			(per cent of net national income)		
Costa Rica	22	Coffee 50 Bananas 37	1.8	3.1	4.9
El Salvador	23	Coffee 71 Cotton 13	1.2	2.8	4.0
Honduras	23	Bananas 47 Coffee 19 Lumber 10	1.7	0.5	2.2

SOURCE: Compiled from United Nations, *Statistical Yearbook*, (1961) and *Yearbook of International Trade Statistics*, 1960, and national publications.
[a]It has not been feasible to estimate from available statistics the revenue obtained from export enterprises under the income tax. It is assumed, however, that the proportion of the contribution of the export industries to total revenue from income taxes does not vary to any significant degree in the three economies.

revenue from export taxation to national income in that country.

Although the demand for Latin American exports has in general become soft, some countries have succeeded in obtaining considerably higher revenues than others in a roughly equivalent situation. The size and structure of the export sector of Costa Rica, El Salvador, and Honduras, for example, are similar. The fiscal income from the export sector of Costa Rica, however, is higher than that of El Salvador and more than double that of Honduras, where the large banana companies enjoy an old legal concession which forbids the government to impose new taxes on banana exports. There are also similar discrepancies in the ratios of revenue from export taxation among countries with comparable export structure, which suggests that the export sectors of the low-ratio countries in these groups may constitute fiscal resources of considerable importance. The type of tax which is most adequate for and accessible to a given country or the magnitude of revenue gain will, of course, depend on its special situation.

Import duties and excise or sales taxes on domestically retained articles are alternative means of taxing the import sector. All Latin American countries obtain fiscal incomes from import duties. Their relative importance, however, differs substantially, from about 1 to some 9 per cent of national income. Costa Rica and Honduras, for example, receive about half of their total revenues from import duties, El Salvador and Guatemala about one-third, and Argentina, Brazil, Colombia, Mexico, and Venezuela about one-tenth. Argentina, Brazil, and Chile, on the other hand, obtain some 6 to 10 per cent of national income from taxes on internal transactions, while the less-advanced economies of Central America only receive some 1 to 2.5 per cent. With the domestic orientation of economic development, an increase in revenue from internal taxes at the expense of import taxes is to be expected. First, as soon as domestic production reaches a sizable proportion of total supply, major reliance has to be placed on internal taxes. These then become an instrument of taxation for both imports and domestically produced goods. Second, the process of industrial development is accompanied by protective (and prohibitive) tariffs, with adverse implications on the yields from import duties.

The continuing balance of payments difficulties and the change in the structure of imports suggest a decline in revenues from taxation of imports. Strengthening of import taxation, however, seems possible and can be recommended on economic grounds. Since the poor have to be taxed, customs duties on imported necessities would be a convenient way of collecting such revenue. It may also be worth considering whether the general exemptions of duty on imports of capital goods should be reviewed. In countries or industries where the cost of capital goods is not an important barrier to investment and where foreign exchange and domestic capital are available to entrepreneurs at prices which are low in relation to their basic scarcity, import taxation could be used to bring the prices of capital goods nearer their true economic values (or costs). If government revenues are intended to be spent on growth promotion, such taxation of necessities and capital imports, kept within limits, may be consistent with economic advancement.

Government trading monopolies, marketing boards, and bulk-purchasing or selling arrangements may also secure for the government a sizable volume of revenues. The successful marketing of rice in Burma and of cocoa in Ghana in the fifties provides good instances of government policies serving a dual purpose: revenues were augmented at the same time as domestic price stability was maintained. A contrary example is provided by Ceylon, where the price of rice for domestic consumption was maintained for a number of years at lower than world prices through production and import subsidies entailing a substantial volume of net spending by the government.

The choice between import duties and taxes on internal transactions would depend basi-

TABLE 2–4: Latin American Countries: Revenue from Commodity Taxes, 1955

	Import duties		Taxes on internal transactions	
Country	Per cent of net national income	Per cent of total revenue	Per cent of net national income	Per cent of total revenue
At low level of self-sufficiency				
Bolivia[a]	3.6	51	2.2	31
Costa Rica	9.0	56	1.1	7
El Salvador[a]	4.8	36	2.3	17
At medium level of self-sufficiency				
Colombia	1.9	14	1.6	11
Ecuador	5.4	25	3.7	17
Peru[b]	4.4	22	4.0	18
At high level of self-sufficiency				
Argentina[c]	2.8	12	6.1[d]	26
Brazil	1.3	6	10.5[d]	45
Mexico	1.6	12	2.3	16

SOURCE: Compiled from national publications.   [d]Including sales taxes on export commodities.
[a]1958.   [b]1956.   [c]1960.

cally on the degree of self-sufficiency of the economy concerned. Countries with a low level of self-sufficiency would continue to rely primarily on import duties levied on the large volume of their needs obtained through imports. In countries with a medium level of self-sufficiency, expansion of the fiscal system may require enlargement of the scope of both import duties and internal taxes. But the latter group of taxes will be more productively deployed in the more industrialized countries such as Argentina, Brazil, and Mexico, for reasons already mentioned.

Taxation of Internal Transactions

Taxes on internal transactions—excise taxes, sales taxes, license fees, etc.—constitute the second major group in the fiscal systems of most of the Latin American countries. These taxes are, in general, mainly intended to procure revenue but may also be used for the purpose of curtailing consumption and saving on imports. For revenue purposes, the most suitable items are those which have a low price elasticity and high income elasticity of demand. On the other hand, objectives of direct curtailment of consumption and import saving, if achieved, would not be particularly revenue-yielding. The items selected will have to possess a high price elasticity and a low income elasticity so that when prices are raised consumption will be reduced more than proportionately, or when incomes go up consumption will not rise *pari passu* with incomes. In either case, taxation is likely to secure the major requirements for economic growth—viz., the enlargement of the proportion of economic surplus which can be enticed away from consumption and toward saving or investment—assuming, of course, that the amount transferred to the government would be spent on purposes conducive to growth.

Among the group of consumption taxes, those on alcohol and tobacco have been the mainstay of fiscal systems almost everywhere in the developing economies. In countries where smoking or drinking is almost universal, they siphon off a substantial amount for revenue, although in a regressive fashion.

But in countries where these habits are confined to a small group, as in some African and Asian countries, the yield is small, and heavy taxation of a few while others are let off introduces an ethical judgment which may be difficult to uphold. From the economic standpoint, it cannot be argued that teetotalers or nonsmokers *ipso facto* make more productive use of incomes left in their hands.

Expansion of the yield from excise taxes calls not only for an increase in the existing rates of such taxes on the traditional items—tobacco, liquor, gasoline, entertainments—but for introduction of new commodities to the list of items already taxed. Since the low-income and even the middle-income groups remain exempt from taxes on income, levying taxes at relatively low rates on necessities such as sugar, matches, and fuel would not seriously pinch the individual family, but through their almost universal application such taxes could collect a sizable amount in revenues for the government. Luxury spending of the well-off can also be tackled directly by the heavy taxation of commodities and services favored by the rich—automobiles, domestic appliances, jewelry, luxury apartments, travel—particularly of those which specifically serve ostentatious purposes or use up scarce foreign exchange. Commodities such as textiles could be taxed more flexibly to take in and discriminate among several classes of taxpayers.

In order to obtain revenue from general spending, as distinct from spending on individual commodities, sales or turnover taxes are being increasingly favored by governments of the developing economies. These taxes could also be used as effective counter-inflationary measures. In advanced countries, sales taxes provide an additional means of taxing the well-off, since further steepening of income taxes is considered as disincentive. Sales taxes have the advantage over income taxes in that they can catch incomes which may have avoided or evaded income taxes and spending from accumulated wealth. In the developing economies, however, they provide a means of primarily getting at the low- and middle-income groups, who generally escape income taxation altogether and whose spending tends to be tax-sensitive. They still permit differentiation of tax burden according to income levels through the media of rate differentials, basic exemptions, etc.

The pricing policy of public enterprise involves basically the same issues as those related to taxes on internal transactions. It is more than common to find most of these undertakings operated at a loss to the government except where they are specifically operated as fiscal monopolies. The reasons for this loss operation are varied (and a prominent one is operating inefficiency), but one of the most common factors is undoubtedly that consumers of government services or of products of government enterprises expect these services and products to be provided cheap, if not free. As a result, the enterprises become vehicles of large-scale subsidization of employees and consumers. They should serve instead as sources of government revenue, since they offer an ideal base for tax collection. Indeed, it is greatly to be desired that public opinion in the developing economies be brought to recognize that standards of amenity in public services of the advanced countries could only follow and not precede the growth in national economic productivity.

In the meanwhile, the government's major task is to raise savings, and one effective way governments can do this is by providing government services at profit. A good example of revenue productivity of public enterprises is provided by the railways of India.[9] Government ownership of enterprises, by permitting "monopoly profits"—the wide gap between costs of production and the prices charged to consumers—has provided the centrally planned economies with their major source of resources for growth. Socialist orientation of economic policies in the developing economies elsewhere seems to lead to general giveaways, causing a diminution in the wherewithals for

[9] The railway budget is introduced separately in the Parliament of India. This practice makes it quite clear that an essential part of railway finances is revenue collection.

growth. The demands for medium- or short-term benefits by the citizens of the developing economies are here clearly in conflict with their long-term interests either as workers or as consumers.

It may be concluded, therefore, that taxes on internal transactions (including amounts collected through public enterprises) have a legitimate function to perform within the fiscal systems of developing economies and afford a very important source of additional revenue for many developing countries. The evidence available from Table 2–2 shows that many Latin American countries can capture at least an additional 5 per cent of national income through these taxes and that, in the case of those countries which rely more heavily on import duties, this ratio could be further increased as import duties decline in importance, due to the factors mentioned in the preceding section.

Taxation of Incomes

Taxation of incomes, with built-in features such as exemption limits, allowances, dependency credits, progressive rates, and differential treatment of individuals and corporate units, satisfies almost all the broad requirements of fiscal policy. In many ways, it is the fiscal instrument par excellence from the standpoint of economic growth. It promises revenue yields progressively related to the growth in the national product and a substantial volume of unexploited revenue potential in view of its inadequate development. At the same time, it permits delicate refinement to suit both general and specific growth objectives.

Although many developing countries had introduced income taxation even before the war and most others have taken steps since to add it to their fiscal arsenal, it does not cover a substantial portion of the incomes earned, nor is it a mass tax, in the advanced countries. In fact, it touches only a fringe of the total population. In India in 1957/58, after some seventy years of continuous existence, "99 per cent of the population and about 93 per cent of the potentially taxable income in the country remained outside the purview of the income tax system."[10] The situation is similar in other countries of Asia and Latin America.

TABLE 2–5: Latin American Countries: Coverage of Income Taxation

Country	Income tax revenue (per cent of national income)[a]	Number of returns[b] (per cent of urban population)	Number of taxpayers[b,c] (per cent of urban population)
Venezuela	10.0	3.0	2.0
Colombia	4.8	n.a.	5.7
Argentina	4.4	6.9	2.9.
Peru	3.8	n.a.	n.a.
Mexico	3.4	n.a.	n.a.
Brazil	3.3	5.0	2.8.
Chile	3.1	n.a.	1.3[d]
Costa Rica	1.8	9.7	5.4
Ecuador	1.8	n.a.	2.9
Honduras	1.7	8.8	3.9
El Salvador	1.2	n.a.	1.1
Bolivia	0.6	n.a.	n.a.

SOURCE: Compiled from national publications. Urban population for 1960 is given in the *Statistical Supplement* to the *Economic Bulletin for Latin America,* Vol. VI.
[a]For 1959, except as indicated in footnotes to Table 2–2.
[b]1957 (Colombia and Venezuela), 1958 (Ecuador and Honduras), 1959 (Argentina and Costa Rica), and 1960 (Brazil and El Salvador).
[c]Individuals and companies.
[d]Complementary tax only.
[e]Excluding persons who derive income solely from salaries and whose income tax liability is completely covered by the withholding system (in Brazil, only up to a certain level of income).

In interpreting Table 2–5, the relative importance of the export sector and the differences in the tax treatment of this sector must be taken into account. In Venezuela and Chile, for instance, income taxes on oil and copper companies accounted for 72 and 50 per cent, respectively, of the total revenue from income taxes in 1959. In Costa Rica, on the other hand, the low ratio of income tax revenue, notwithstanding its relatively high ratio of taxpayers, is partly explained by the fact that the export sector is taxed largely through export taxes, which amounted to 3.1

[10]United Nations, ECAFE, *Economic Survey of Asia and the Far East 1960,* p. 94.

per cent of national income in 1959. Apart from this, the available data show that taxes on business enterprises, including withholding taxes on dividends or profits remitted abroad, as a rule account for 75 per cent or more of income tax revenues. The noncorporate sector, however, is not of minor importance in this field. In Argentina (1959) and Colombia (1957), taxes paid by individuals (including proprietors of businesses), as distinct from corporations or "juridical persons," accounted for 57 and 40 per cent, respectively, of income tax revenues.

The major direction in extending the scope of income taxes in the developing countries seems to be downward toward the base of the social pyramid. "Any effort in a poor country to raise savings at the expense of consumption will have to obtain these from the poor; the standard of minimum taxable capacity might have to be placed at a lower level. As for there being no taxable capacity in the low-income groups owing to the incidence of indirect taxation, there is no clear evidence."[11] In Asia, personal incomes up to a multiple of ten to twenty times the average per capita income remain altogether exempt from income taxes, whereas the corresponding multiple is one to three in most advanced countries. The coverage problem is more acute in Asia than in Latin America, where schedular taxes (many of which have no exemptions) make a difference, the incidence of indirect taxes on the lower-income groups is greater, and the situation with regard to tax exemption coefficients is somewhat mixed. In countries such as Brazil, Chile, or Peru, the exemption coefficients (based on a family unit of husband, wife, and three children) are more or less similar to those in Asia, whereas the coefficients in other countries, particularly in Argentina, Colombia, Ecuador, and Mexico, correspond more closely with those in the advanced countries. No doubt, the absolute level of per capita income is, in general, relevant in choosing the exemption level. And

since per capita income remains low in the developing countries, the exemption coefficient has to be relatively high. Moreover, relative circumstances of the specific economy will have to be considered in determining the exemption coefficient. The major factors to be taken into account are the income distribution (importance of the middle class, for instance), the extent to which lower-income groups need to be taxed, and the ways and means that are and could be devised to take in these groups by means of the more economically administered commodity or sales taxes.

Another area promising a fruitful exploration of revenue potential is expansion of the coverage of the tax base, viz., "taxable income." In some countries of Asia where the land tax is in operation, agricultural income used to be exempt from income taxation. Similarly, in both Asia and Latin America capital gains, which constitute an important proportion of the total incomes of the well-off, either are tax exempt or receive preferential treatment. Capital gains are not taxed, on the principle that it is the income and not the source of income which should be taxed. But from an economic standpoint, or even that of the taxpayer himself, capital gains constitute income, like any other income from property. Basically, therefore, capital gains (including especially gains for transactions in land) ought to be taxed; but whether, because of their long-term and irregular nature, they should be taxed on a different basis from personal incomes is a matter which requires further consideration and which permits a difference of opinion. In any case, so long as capital gains remain tax exempt or receive a preferential treatment, conversion of taxable incomes into capital gains will constitute a major avenue for tax avoidance. Other loopholes available to the well-off to avoid paying income and wealth taxes consist of undistributed profits in closely-held companies, earnings retained in trusts, incomes earned from capital holdings abroad, gifts given during the lifetime of the donor to escape death duties, and the widely preva-

[11]United Nations, ECAFE, *Economic Survey of Asia and the Far East, 1960*, p. 95.

lent "tax deductible" expense accounts and "perquisites" which hardly merit description as economically useful expenses or as "expenses that are wholly, exclusively, and unavoidably incurred" in earning the income.

"All these loopholes have been so universally exploited that there is a considerable amount of truth in the popular aphorism that taxable income is the only luxury the rich cannot afford."[12] And all these loopholes available to those with high incomes have coexisted with very high marginal rates—75 per cent and above—for the upper brackets of assessed taxable income. Henry C. Simons, before the war, described such coexistence as a "subtle kind of moral and political dishonesty . . . a grand scheme of deception, whereby enormous surtaxes are voted in exchange for promises that they will not be made effective. Thus, politicians may point with pride to the rates, while quietly reminding their wealthy constituents of the loopholes."[13]

In the developing economies, the income tax system is not that much a product of deception. Largely copied from the models prevalent in the advanced countries, it has been made even more blunt in the course of its adaptation to the conditions (rather than requirements) of the developing economies. It has let off the lower- and middle-income groups altogether by high exemption limits and a considerable portion of the incomes of the well-off by retaining the loopholes in the tax systems of the advanced countries. The developing countries have had the further disadvantage of poor administrative systems which have tolerated, and by doing so encouraged, outright tax evasion. While they have adopted tax rates which approximate those of the advanced countries, they have not attained the level of enforcement prevalent in the advanced countries necessary to make such rates effective. The high rates have only increased the premium on evasion

without attaching any commensurate risk. Even in an administratively well-endowed country like India, tax evasion in 1955/56 was estimated by Nicholas Kaldor to be of the order of three-quarters of the incomes assessed to tax and the volume of revenue lost about one and a half times as much as the revenue obtained.[14] In Argentina, the central bank estimated underreporting of 50 per cent in 1952 and 60 per cent in 1957. The income assessed to complementary tax in Chile was estimated to have been underreported by 65 per cent in 1956. Tax evasion in other developing economies may be of the same order of magnitude. In countries where foreign trade and foreign capital constitute a large element in the economy, a considerable amount of revenue (and foreign exchange) may be lost through accounting malpractices such as padding of invoices, fictitious charges for commissions, and the use of tax havens for the sole purpose of reducing tax liabilities in both the capital exporting and the capital importing countries.

It may be concluded, therefore, that there is at present a considerable margin for increasing revenues from the income tax, even in the case of those countries which have reached relatively high levels of yield from income taxation. The potential of this fiscal base will grow substantially in importance with the economic advancement of the countries concerned and through improvement of the administrative systems and application of stiffer penalties to tax evaders in order to close the great gap of unreported incomes. But this is not enough. In those instances (particularly schedular taxes) where income tax rates have been prescribed at very high levels on the assumption that a major portion of incomes will in fact evade reporting, these high rates will have to be scaled down to the intended "effective" levels as a precondition to any serious effort to achieve complete income

[12]United Nations, ECAFE, *Economic Survey of Asia and the Far East, 1960*, p. 96.
[13]*Personal Income Taxation* (Chicago: The University of Chicago Press, 1938), p. 219.

[14]The Central Board of Revenue of the Government of India estimated that income evading income tax was about 30 per cent of the income assessed to tax. Even so, revenue loss might well have exceeded one-half of the revenue received.

disclosure. The full task of correcting tax evasion is assuredly not easy, and it may be quite a long way ahead before major increases in revenue are obtained, but it is a real possibility. In addition, more revenue may be obtained if the income tax is extended downward to cover the middle and lower incomes, but this will depend on the extent to which consumption taxes can be employed to take in these groups.

Taxation Associated with Benefits

Although, in principle, it would be unwise to tie down revenue to providing direct benefits to specific taxpayers, such taxes could be used effectively to supplement the revenue system, since they employ a form more acceptable to the taxpayers. Social security taxes, for instance, provide an example of an essentially regressive type of income taxation which is still acceptable to the low-income groups because of eligibility for benefits. This form of taxation is relatively well developed in several Latin American countries, as indicated in the notes to Table 2–1. The nationalized life insurance scheme of India also serves a somewhat similar purpose. Several countries, for instance, Brazil and Colombia, have experimented with compulsory savings schemes. The gambling instinct has also been turned to advantage in obtaining revenue through taxes on lotteries (and bonds) and on parimutuel betting, which exist in several countries of Asia and Latin America.

In any case, to the extent that the amount collected as social security taxes, life insurance premiums, compulsory savings, or receipts from the sale of lottery tickets exceeds the amount given out as current benefits or repayments, the net receipts of the government constitute an additional fiscal resource which could be put to developmental use. Furthermore, insofar as social security coverage extends to hospitals and other health services, it replaces direct government expenditure on these services and is thus equivalent to a gain in revenue. In other words, through the social security system a major part of the provision of these services can be placed on a self-sustaining basis whereby the strain on general government revenue is reduced and resources are freed for alternative use.

Taxation of Agriculture

The process of economic growth in developing economies requires that some part of the population move away from land and the remaining population produce enough over and above its own subsistence to provide food and raw materials for the nonagricultural sectors. Price inducements often fail to attract increased "surpluses" from the agricultural sector as the phenomenon commonly described by economists as the "backward-sloping supply curve" comes into operation. These conditions are more likely to be encountered in countries with small farm units and subsistence cultivation. Taxation of consumer commodities also fails to bring out this surplus, since a large portion of the sector remains outside the monetary economy. It is, therefore, essential to tax cultivation, which may be a device not only to increase revenue but also to induce larger agricultural output and which may, incidentally, lead to further monetization of the economy.

The traditional tax on agriculture, the annual land tax, is operating in many developing countries, but its yield and impact are being eroded by the rise in prices and the lagging process of valuation. On the other hand, economic growth almost invariably tends to turn the real terms of trade in favor of agriculture and to increase land values, excepting, of course, the special difficulties of export agriculture. It would, therefore, seem rational to revitalize agricultural taxes and impose betterment levies, although these taxes appear to evoke substantial resistance on the part of farmers who have come to appreciate the economic value of their political strength.

The situation in Latin America, however, differs from the one described above, which applies basically to Asia. First, the traditional land tax can be and is of less importance in Latin America. The ratios of property tax revenues to national income in Table 2–2 cover the taxes on both urban and rural property; although exact figures could not be generally obtained, indications are that a major portion of those revenues is from urban property taxes. In Chile, for example, agricultural land tax accounted for only 5 per cent of the total property tax revenues in 1958. Second, export agriculture and the reliance on export taxes (and internal sales taxes) to raise revenue from this sector are more important elements in Latin American countries. Third, a number of countries rely on income taxes to include (rather than exclude) agriculture, although it appears that the use of the income tax in this field has been only partially effective. In Brazil, for example, official statistics show that agriculture accounted for only 1 per cent of total taxable income of individuals and juridical persons (excluding incomes subject exclusively to the withholding tax). This extremely low ratio could be attributed largely to the fact that in Brazil, as in other Latin American countries, a large proportion of agricultural taxpayers are assessed on the basis of imputed income, which is derived as a percentage of the valuation of the property, which in turn is usually both underassessed and out of date.

However, the most characteristic difference of Latin American from Asian agriculture is the sharply unequal distribution of land. The latifundia with over a thousand hectares each, take up two-thirds of the cultivated area, although they number only 2 per cent of total landholdings. At the other end of the scale, the minifundia, almost three-fourths of the total number of holdings, cover only 4 per cent of the area under cultivation.[15] There are, therefore, good economic, social, and administrative reasons to deploy the fiscal instrument as one of the weapons in a broad program of land reform. The often absentee large landowners tend to keep their holdings partially or fully idle or inefficiently cultivated, since land is held by them mainly for reasons of prestige or speculation. The heavy concentration of property in a few hands makes it more necessary and at the same time relatively easy to devise fiscal measures. In doing so, technical factors of assessment and collection do not present an insuperable obstacle, as is often assumed. A land tax, progressive (or even punitive), based on the potential productivity or market value of land, would force the rich landowners to cultivate their lands more efficiently in order to pay the taxes or to part with some of their holdings to lower their marginal rates of taxes.[16]

Problems of Administration[17]

The expansion in the scope of the revenue system thus calls for an increase in taxpayer coverage and in the number of items constituting the tax base. Implementation of such a reform would undoubtedly make further demands on the administrative machinery. However, there is considerable scope for rationalizing the existing administrative structure, even if it is conceded that the structure is both weak and strained.

First, there is room for legislative simplification of the tax system. Assessment would be simplified if two or more taxes operating on the same tax base could be amalgamated into one. It is not unusual to find the same commodity paying a number of separate taxes. Moreover, some of the imported finesse (particularly in the income tax systems) may be quite unrelated to the situation of the developing economies and could be abandoned. Last, almost all tax systems carry deadwood in the form of antiquated taxes which absorb

---

[15]In Guatemala, 516 farms (0.15 per cent of all farms) represent 41 per cent of the agricultural land. In Ecuador, 705 units (0.17 per cent) include 37 per cent of the farm land. Half the farm land in Brazil is in the hands of 1.6 per cent of the owners, and in Nicaragua 362 owners have control over fully one-third of the agricultural acreage. Albert O. Hirschmann (ed.), *Latin American Issues* (New York: The Twentieth Century Fund, 1961), pp. 163–65.

[16]For a fuller discussion of tax policies in relation to land reform, see United Nations, *Progress in Land Reform. Third Report of the ECOSOC* (April 5, 1962—mimeographed) (E/3603), chap. 5, sec. A.

[17]Problems of administration have been already dealt with at the preceding Conference on Tax Administration at Buenos Aires in October, 1961.

administrative resources quite out of proportion to their yields.

The second aspect of simplification would consist of measures to secure economy in the use of administrative resources. Taxation of the low-income groups does not call for approaching or assessing every taxpayer, as would be the case with a poll tax. A few necessities taxed at the source may suffice. The middle-income-group employees and industrial workers could be covered by payroll deductions and by commodity taxes again levied, as far as possible, at the source. Multiple-stage sales taxes could be replaced by single-stage taxes levied once and for all at the manufacturing or wholesale stage. The small traders and professions could be assessed on their gross turnover, both for the collection of sales and income taxes. Keeping accounts could also be simplified for the taxpayers. The government could prescribe standard simplified bookkeeping models and distribute this material and tax tables for ready reckoning to taxpayers, once a certain level of literacy was reached.[18] They could then be switched to a system of self-assessment under oath. Finally, the work load of revenue offices could be considerably lightened by the use of accounting machines and modernization of other office equipment.

The administrative resources released by these and similar steps could then be employed to service the new or extended measures described above and to check evasion. Tax evasion would greatly decrease if the governments could be stricter than they are with tax evaders and corrupt officials and prescribe deterrent punishment for the evasion exposed. At the moment, the discoveries of evasion are infrequent and the penalties lenient. This encourages the taxpayers to evade paying taxes in the hope that evasion will not be discovered at all or, if caught, they will be let off lightly. The ordinary legal courts and procedures for civil suits should be re-

placed, where constitutionally possible, by special economic courts and legal machinery tailored to the specific problem of economic crimes such as tax evasion, black-market transactions, etc. The operations of company accountants and tax lawyers could also be supervised more intensively.[19]

Rationalization of tax administration is a comprehensive subject in itself. In considering issues of tax policy, it would suffice if it is recognized that such rationalization is feasible and if achieved could release perhaps the most important reserve of untapped fiscal potential. However, if administrative facilities are a real handicap in the short run, it is possible, as noted, for governments to increase their revenue from a number of alternative tax bases. The design of the tax system in that event may be guided, at least in part, by the principle of giving priority to those taxes which are easy to collect and difficult to avoid or evade. An examplary case for reform is provided by the income tax on business units in Brazil, where almost 85,000 (31 per cent) business taxpayers were assessed to income tax on a presumptive basis to yield only 1.5 per cent of the total yield from this tax. Land taxes in India also require an administrative machinery out of proportion to their yields. In such cases, administrative machinery could be thoroughly overhauled, legislation revised, or such taxes eliminated altogether in favor of alternative tax bases. In the long run, however, fiscal administration has to be developed to match the complexity of the fiscal system as it expands and gets more refined in its application. Only then does tax reform become a potent instrument of economic growth.

CONCLUSION

To sum up, fiscal upper limits, whatever they are and wherever they exist, either in economic or political terms, are at some dis-

[18]Illiteracy, on the other hand, is not as big a handicap as it is usually made out to be. In India, the *ryotwari* land tax, coming down the ages, is in many ways nothing but a gross income tax paid largely by illiterate peasants.

[19]See Karl Lachmann's "Comments" on the paper by Oliver Oldman on "Controlling Income Tax Evasion" at the Buenos Aires Conference, the proceedings of which will appear in *Problems of Tax Administration in Latin America* (Baltimore: The Johns Hopkins Press, 1965).

tance still in relation to the current tax performance of the developing economies. There are both the need and scope for further taxation of the low-income groups by means of taxes on consumption commodities, whether imported or domestically produced. The middle-income groups, at present mostly covered by commodity taxes, could be further reached by expanding the taxpayer coverage of the income taxes, by sales taxes, and by making new commodities subject to excise and customs duties. The well-off could also be made to pay through a more progressive land and urban property tax, heavy taxation of luxury articles of consumption, more effective expansion of the concept of income subject to income tax, plugging of loopholes for tax avoidance, and rigorous measures to deter tax evasion. There are also other alternative or complementary avenues which could be explored. Finally, there is broad scope for improving the efficiency of tax administration all round and the effectiveness of penalties against evaders to secure larger yields from existing and new taxes.

In recommending these measures, greater attention has been given to their revenue-yielding capacity than to provision of incentives. A lower priority has also been assigned to considerations of equity, since in the developing economies the poor have to be forced and the well-off permitted to save. Undertaxation of the poor and overtaxation of the rich are easily the fallacies into which these governments may stumble in their concern for equality and equity, although, for the moment, there is undertaxation of both these groups. On their part, governments have to expose themselves to the same scrutiny of the purposes and efficiency of their spending as of those in the private sector, from the standpoint of attaining an optimum utilization of national resources for economic growth.

ANNEX

Estimation of National Fiscal Capacity

Having reviewed the current tax performance and explored the potentialities for reve-

nue of the major tax groups, the next step is to translate these broad recommendations on tax policies into a specific and quantitative assessment of national fiscal potentials. The latter task calls for a set of economic data which are at present only inadequately available. As already noticed, it calls for fiscal techniques which may be simultaneously less refined and more delicate than those in force in the advanced countries. Some of these techniques have been suggested in many country studies and reports but remain largely untried. Finally, it requires working out *ad hoc* adjustments to fit variant institutional situations, since in this regard the developing economies remain further apart than the advanced ones. In other words, there cannot be a general method. Fiscal potential has to be estimated for each economy in terms of its specific conditions.

Still, it would be useful to summarize a few steps in the process. The first step would be to ascertain what constitutes the economic surplus of the community. If it is a very poor economy, almost all the surplus above subsistence levels would constitute the economic surplus which has to be utilized for growth. If it is a more advanced economy, a level of living correspondingly above subsistence levels will have to be allowed for in determining the surplus.

There is, however, another concept which has been used in centrally planned economies and may be more suitable for fiscal analysis. In these economies, since the public sector theoretically controls all output, it may determine what proportion of the total output should be devoted to nonpublic consumption —the salable output—and what proportion it will retain for governmental implementation of collective consumption needs and national capital formation. The latter proportion is known as the nonsalable output. Although the term *nonsalable* is clearly inapplicable, the economic planner of a developing free-enterprise economy may also make an assessment of the proportion corresponding to the nonsalable output of the centrally planned economy, viz., the proportion which is required to be devoted to national (public and private sector) capital formation and governmental current needs, with a certain growth rate in mind.

Having decided on the magnitude of the economic surplus or the nonsalable output (the two are not the same thing), the second major decision that the planner takes into account is the extent to which growth resources should remain in private hands. This decision will depend not only on criteria of economic efficiency but also on the political and social philosophy of the community.

In any case, once the decisions are made on the magnitude of nonsalable output and the part of it which has to be retained in the private sector, the fiscal target is set. The target for government revenue thus consists of all national output which is not required to be retained in the private sector for maintaining essential or accepted levels of consumption and the requirements for growth.

The magnitude of such output to be mobilized by the government would, of course, depend on the size of total output (that is, the size of per capita national income), on its distribution, and on the dynamism of the private sector. The higher the per capita national income and the more unequal its distribution, the greater the resources that could be devoted to collective consumption and growth. Finally, political philosophies apart, the more dynamic the private sector, the lesser the burden on the government to provide directly for economic growth.

Having set the fiscal target, the next step is to determine who is to pay the taxes and through what mode or means revenues will be gathered.

Since all taxes ultimately bear upon the citizens in one way or another, it would be useful, at the outset, to have a broad idea of existing tax burdens. In assessing these burdens, the following information is required:

1. The size and distribution of personal incomes.

2. Spending, saving, and investing patterns of major income groups.

3. The proportion of incomes paid out to defray existing income and commodity taxes.

Such data are, of course, inadequately available. But for administrative purposes, it is not difficult to obtain them. The facilities of censuses and national sample surveys could be effectively used for this purpose, as has been done in India.

It may also be necessary to study the distribution of national income in other forms: by economic activity (farming, industry—small and large—professions, etc.) and by economic organization (monetary and nonmonetary sectors, unincorporated and corporate sectors, domestic and foreign trade sectors, private and government sectors, etc.). Comprehensive information may be sought on the size of these sectors—the incomes, commodities, or transactions they comprise—and on the burden of existing taxes.

Another study would concern the supply and demand elasticities of commodities, and some judgment might have to be formed independent of the market criteria as to what commodities constitute necessities, amenities, or luxuries. Information is also required as to the number of hands or stages of manufacture a commodity passes through before it is finally consumed by citizens or exported or used up in the process of manufacturing. Is the commodity produced and/or consumed by large units, or is it produced and/or consumed by diffused small units?

Such a microeconomic study of incomes (distributed by persons and economic sectors) and commodities, and of existing taxes on these, would thus supplement the macroeconomic evaluation of the national fiscal potentials. Of course, since the incidence of some taxes would remain quite diffuse and of others more or less precise, any assessment of existing or projected tax burden is likely to remain arbitrary. However, if the estimates were broken down into a crisscross detail in terms of persons, economic sectors, and commodities, it would be possible to make an assessment of acceptable accuracy to form the basis for governmental policy and action in the fiscal field. The microeconomic analysis would not only bring to view the myriad minor streams which together constitute the national aggregate potential but also reveal a number of accessible tax bases.

Since all tax potentials have to be not only theoretically assessed but realized in practice, the question of accessible tax bases is of particular importance. Bearing in mind the policy issues outlined in the paper, the problem of fiscal expansion can be approached from the standpoint of tax administration, since in almost all underdeveloped economies administration remains a scarce and valuable factor. Which taxes are the most productive of revenue vis-à-vis their cost of collection in terms of administrative resources? Which of the new tax bases can be easily administered? Which of the existing ones have been already well developed, and which of them permit of further expansion? Is it not possible to abandon unremunerative taxes? Is it not possible to simplify the present legislation or administration? How does each of the tax bases, when exploited, react on personal incomes, on types of economic activity or organization, or on demand and supply schedules of commodities? What is the scope of government undertakings? Can they not be run efficiently to yield profits? Do they permit of a change in wage and price policies?

These and many other questions can be asked. But, as is obvious, there cannot be a definitive answer. So far as the answer can be given in general terms, it has been attempted in the main body of this paper. In any given economy, the answer will depend on its specific economic situation and on its alignment of political, economic, and social forces. A fiscal planner will be called upon to make judgments at every step on matters both within and beyond the realm of economic calculation. But his judgments would be more sound if he were to start out with a broad agreement on policy issues on the lines described in the paper and the type of economic and statistical data described in this Annex.

Discussion

MR. DESAI referred to the previous afternoon's discussion, in which there had been almost complete agreement that economic development was the prime objective of fiscal policy. That was also the basic assumption in his paper. The questions he wished to ask concerned the ways in which fiscal instruments could be used to attain such development and the extent to which they could be so used. In exploring those questions, he had taken it for granted that fiscal performance in underdeveloped countries fell far short of its potential level. He regretted that the role of tax advisers on measures of reform could not be discussed separately, since it was clear from Mr. Schlesinger's paper that their views differed considerably, and it would have been interesting to ascertain the reasons for their disagreement.

The first point he had tried to bring out in his paper was the great importance of revenue for fiscal policy. He had then reviewed the capacity of governments to obtain revenue, which had two ceilings: the economic and the political. Neither seemed to have been reached in the developing countries.

The three main policy issues were revenue, incentives, and equity, of which the first was the most important. With respect to the question of incentives, opinion was gaining ground that they had been used too liberally, since they were apt to lose the government a great deal of revenue, particularly from the industrial sector, and it had not been proved that they played a decisive part in ensuring the success of new industries. The whole question should be reassessed. With regard to the third aspect, he felt that the need for every tax to be equitable had been overstressed. It was more important to have an equitable tax system as a whole, or further still an equitable government tax-*cum*-expenditure policy.

He disagreed with Mr. Urquidi on the importance attaching to considerations of equity in planning economic development objectives. The assignment of first priority to the redistribution of income was apt to impede the achievement of economic growth and could therefore not be regarded as wholly desirable.

His treatment of the question of fiscal capacity had been exploratory and derived from the need for a more precise quantitative criteric n than the general idea of obtaining more revenue. He pointed out that the political and economic upper limits of fiscal capacity were not necessarily commensurate. In rather poor economies, the ceiling was fixed by the balance that remained over and above subsistence levels. The political limit might be higher, as in the centrally planned economies or in other economies during an emergency such as a war. In the short run, the political limits were the determining factor; but over the long run, opposition to institutional changes could be overcome and public opinion educated.

It was thought in principle that fiscal capacity was essentially determined by the absolute level of per capita national income. Income distribution was also a factor, especially when it tended to be unequal, in view of the great potential of the wealthy groups as a source of revenue. In practice, however, tax performance was largely dependent on the technical facilities for tax collection and on the efficiency and integrity of the public administration. That was a particularly important point for the underdeveloped countries, where capable administrators remained an extremely scarce factor.

His view of the relationship between fiscal capacity and national income was rather pragmatic, since he did not consider that the economic surplus should inevitably accrue to governments but should go to those who would make the best use of it, and there were specific cases in which governments had frittered away the resources at their disposal.

There was no real reason why the ratio between revenue and income should be lower in less developed countries because, owing to the inequality of income distribution and the fact that the private sectors often used resources in a less productive way, the governments had greater responsibilities than in the more advanced countries and therefore needed a larger proportion of the national income.

He pointed out that fiscal yield as a proportion of national income varied greatly in the different Latin American countries, and no one level could be taken as a definite yardstick. For instance, a critical level of 15 per cent had been mentioned, but that was exceeded by at least eight countries in the region. What could not be denied, however, was the existence of a potential capacity for raising more revenue in each one.

The question of fiscal policy could be viewed in different ways, according to the conditions obtaining in particular countries. When a national revenue represented a fairly large proportion of national income, the government's expenditure policy required more scrutiny. When the proportion was low, the question was primarily one of obtaining more revenue.

He then reviewed certain broad categories of taxes, which should ideally be considered in relation to the political, economic, and institutional structure of each Latin American country. Export taxes were becoming less useful than they had been because of the increasingly vulnerable state of the primary commodity markets. Import taxes, on the other hand, could be made to yield more revenue, although that would not be so if present trends continued. He suggested that one way of helping underdeveloped countries to progress was to tax the lower-income groups by means of small levies on imported staples, which would undoubtedly yield a considerable amount of revenue. One type of tax that should be discussed was the levy on capital goods, which were currently made available to entrepreneurs in underdeveloped countries at preferential rates of exchange. If government revenue was to be spent on the promotion of economic growth, the taxation of capital imports might be consonant with economic advancement. The preferential treatment of new or developing industries was also another aspect that should be re-examined. What was important was to make use of the existing sources of collecting revenue. Since the customs administration had been efficiently developed in Latin American countries, particular stress should be laid on exploiting the revenue potential of import taxes.

With respect to excise taxes, Mr. Urquidi had rightly pointed out that they might be gradually developed to replace import taxes as a source of revenue. His main doubts with respect to progressive indirect taxes concerned the possibility of tax evasion on the part of the wealthier groups—which could be dealt with by the choice of commodities with a fairly inelastic demand for the application of punitive tax rates—and the fact that most of the items subject to heavy taxation were imported and might therefore have to be restricted because of balance of payments considerations. Income tax offered a large field for future exploitation. There were two aspects that required consideration: first, the expansion of the coverage to include more groups and, second, the tightening up of the concept of taxable income and sealing of loopholes for evasion. Other types of taxes were acceptable since they could be associated with benefits, i.e., social security systems and government lotteries.

Inasmuch as agricultural taxes were to be discussed as a separate item, he would merely point out that their application posed very different problems in Asia and in Latin America because of the sharp disparities in land ownership in the latter. Land taxes were probably easier to apply than other types, provided they did not meet with undue political opposition from landowners, and he hoped that the practicability of the different kinds would be considered at the conference when the subject of agricultural taxation came up for specific discussion.

Finally, the improvement and simplification of tax legislation and administration should also be taken into account as an additional source of revenue.

MR. HARBERGER agreed with Mr. Desai that the cases in which tax exemption was granted to particular industries in Latin America required revision. It was justifiable to accord exemptions and subsidies to those activities which deserved encouragement because the resulting social benefits were different from and greater than the private advantages reaped. But in many countries exemptions had been established without clear proof that they were really necessary. A case in point was Chile, where special treatment was granted to the small- and medium-scale mining companies, although investment in that sector had not increased thereby, whereas a few private individuals had amassed inordinately large fortunes.

He differed from Mr. Desai with regard to the significance of indirect taxation, although he agreed that if a high tax was levied on very precisely specified goods and their substitutes were tax-free, the former were simply ousted by the latter and the tax produced a very low yield.

Given that the income elasticity of luxury goods was higher than unity and the income elasticity of other consumer goods was usually very close to unity, so that an average income elasticity approximating to unity could be assumed, 50 per cent of goods had an income elasticity in excess of unity; and if those goods could be taxed, an element of progressiveness would be introduced in that part of the tax system which might compound for direct taxation when the latter proved difficult to apply.

MR. PINTO congratulated Mr. Desai on his sound interpretation of the concept of tax capacity, which had usually been a sort of futile and ineffectual figment of the imagination because it had been estimated on the basis of abstract and unrealistic figures which took no account of the conditions in which the analysis had meaning. It was impossible to talk of tax capacity without due regard to the purpose of taxation. Thus, several basic factors of tax capacity had to be taken into consideration, such as: (a) the nature of expenditure; (*b*) the source of funds; (*c*) tax collection capacity, which was, in his opinion (at any rate in Latin America) limited over the short term; and (*d*) political capacity to appropriate resources of which the state thought it would be able to make better use than the private sector. If a more realistic approach to tax capacity were adopted, great progress could be made in that field.

MR. HERSCHEL expressed the view that it was necessary to analyze the distribution of tax potential or the tax burden over the various areas of a given country. He endorsed the opinion of other speakers that empirical studies should be carried out to ascertain the degree of efficacy, if any, of the incentives provided.

Another interesting subject for study would be the evolution of tax revenue as income levels rose. In Latin America, specialists in the field were concerned with the problem of the inflexibility of the tax system when taxable or real income increased—an inflexibility attributable to evasion, exemptions, and deductions.

MR. NÚÑEZ felt that all the speakers who had referred to incentives had judged them very harshly and that the matter merited more careful analysis, since there had been cases in which the desired effect had apparently been produced. Perhaps too little imagination had been exercised in their application for the purpose of encouraging an activity or suppressing it and in the use of the fiscal system to bring about changes in income distribution.

The most striking feature of Latin America's tax systems was what Mr. Desai had so felicitously described as the statistical jungle, namely, the proliferation of low-yield taxes which had developed because they constituted a means of procuring funds without giving rise to serious concern on the counts of equity or incentives.

The public sector had to weigh the merits of the alternative methods of obtaining revenue, and the decision as to which ones it would adopt was affected by what Mr. Desai called the political upper limit of tax capacity,

apparently referring to the whole series of powerful factors involved.

Mr. Desai had been right in describing the progressivity of income tax as a farce; it was disturbing to think that all the countries were its victims, and it was therefore desirable to seek ways and means of ridding income tax of the stigma.

MR. NAHARRO wondered what value attached to the estimate of an average income elasticity of consumer goods approximating unity, to which Mr. Harberger had referred. If that assumption was realistic, at least 50 per cent of consumer goods would surely have an income elasticity higher than unity; and that would invalidate the traditional notion of what constituted a luxury article. However, in considering the revenue yielded by progressive indirect taxation on the consumer goods in question, another variable would have to be taken into account, namely, the volume of actual spending. Even if income elasticity were high, the volume of expenditure might not equal it, and the progressiveness of a tax on consumer goods would be justifiable from the standpoint of equity but might mean little from that of the transfer of sums on any substantial scale to the treasury.

MR. BACA, referring to the allusion in Mr. Desai's paper (footnote 2) to the competitive race by the Central American countries to attract industries, said that the problem no longer existed, as the countries concerned had recently signed an agreement to standardize the incentives accorded to new industries.

MR. HART said that in Table 2–2 of the same document the situation existing in Chile was not accurately presented; no figure appeared under the head of export taxes, whereas actually 50 per cent of the figure for income tax revenue was constituted by taxation applied to foreign companies engaged in export activities.

MR. KALDOR doubted whether indirect taxes on luxury goods could be applied in such a way as to be the equivalent of a progressive tax. The income elasticity of a consumer good could relate only to a specific income, and it became very difficult to ensure progressiveness, because there was no way of equating the goods consumed with income levels. That did not affect the social need to tax luxury consumption but merely implied that progressive income taxes were much easier to adjust to the individual taxpayer's capacity to pay. Those indirect taxes which were really progressive—for example, on domestic help, living space, etc.—would be politically unacceptable.

MR. GOODE agreed that there was no group of indirect taxes which could be efficaciously applied to obtain the same results as might be derived from a progressive program of taxation on income, net wealth, or total expenditure. But it was unfair to compare indirect with direct taxes on the assumption that the operation and administration of the latter would be flawless, and indirect taxes should not be discarded altogether, even if they did no more than reduce the degree of progressiveness of the tax system as a whole.

MR. URQUIDI was in agreement with the general tenor of Mr. Desai's remarks, especially with respect to the political upper limits of taxation. For instance, when such expressions as "taxing the poor" were employed, he thought it advisable that even in technical meetings heed should be taken of the unnecessary opposition which might be aroused by the very terms in which such measures were couched.

With regard to the need to institute severe penalties for evasion and official corruption, he attached more importance to the private sector's willingness to accept taxation. A milder policy of fiscal education would be more fruitful than punitive methods.

MR. PREST felt that Table 2–1 of Mr. Desai's paper was inconsistent with the discussion in the actual text, since it referred to the proportions of national income represented by tax revenue and not to the proportion of the economic surplus. Nor did it give a very realistic picture of the revenue of the public sector, since in many instances it failed to include transfer payments.

With respect to the need for a tax system sensitive to variations in national income, he thought that difficulties would arise in two fields: (a) incentives; and (b) the situation of a country whose fiscal revenue depended largely on the export sector, when abrupt fluctuations in export prices were registered.

MR. LEWIS thought it was essential not only to calculate total tax capacity but also to ascertain in which fields it was least efficiently utilized. In Latin America, apparently, the real estate sector was the one in which the level of tax collection was relatively lowest.

MR. DESAI, replying to the comments, did not quite understand whether Mr. Pinto agreed with him or not. To call tax capacity a figment of the imagination was doubtless correct if any claim was made to define its limits with absolute precision. But an estimate was useful, even if computing it was a purely academic exercise, since without it there would be a risk of formulating unco-ordinated tax recommendations for want of an integrated framework into which they could be fitted.

In the discussion on indirect taxes, the differences of opinion were not fundamental but related rather to ways of defining luxury consumption. Nobody called the usefulness of such taxes in question, especially if progressive income tax had a ceiling. But no general rule could be laid down for indirect taxation, since all kinds of problems arose in connection with substitution, the need to restrict imports, administrative difficulties, and so forth which would affect its application in each country.

He differed from the opinion put forward by Mr. Núñez, since in his experience the apparent success of tax incentives in the establishment of new industries had been mainly due to other concomitant factors.

The point elucidated by Mr. Baca had already been incorporated in the English version of the document.

Mr. Urquidi's objections did not seem to him valid. He could not see why it was politically undesirable to refer to taxation of the low-income groups. It might be that such a possibility had not yet arisen in Latin America because of the extreme inequality of income distribution, but sooner or later the relevant decision would have to be adopted. Taxation of the low-income groups, besides teaching them fiscal discipline, served other ends. In the first place, the expenditure of the well-to-do was much easier to control and guide into appropriate channels than the spending of the lower income brackets. Again, as national income rose, the proportion contributed by the various sectors would increase, and the day was bound to come when, in order to further economic development, the government would be compelled explicitly to require certain sacrifices of the whole population, including the low-income groups.

3

The Role of Taxation in Economic Development

by Nicholas Kaldor*

FISCAL ASPECTS OF DEVELOPMENT POLICY

Problems of taxation, in connection with economic development, are generally discussed from two different points of view which involve quite distinct and often conflicting considerations: the point of view of *incentives* and the point of view of *resources*. Those who believe that it is the lack of adequate incentives which is mainly responsible for insufficient growth and investment are mainly concerned with improving the tax system from an incentive point of view through the granting of additional concessions of various kinds, with less regard to the unfavorable effects on the public revenue. Those who believe that insufficient growth and investment is mainly a consequence of a lack of resources are chiefly concerned with increasing the resources available for investment through additional taxation, even at the cost of worsening its disincentive effects.

In my opinion, a great deal of the prevailing concern with incentives is misplaced, except in particular cases, such as in the matter of tax concessions granted to foreigners which *may* increase the inflow of capital from abroad.[1] It is limitation of resources, and not inadequate incentives, which limits the pace of economic development. Indeed, the importance of public revenue from the point of view of accelerated economic development

could hardly be exaggerated. Irrespective of the prevailing ideology or the political color of particular governments, the economic and cultural development of a country requires the efficient and steadily expanding provision of a whole host of nonrevenue-yielding services—education, health, communications systems, etc., commonly known as "infrastructure"—which require to be financed out of government revenue. In addition, taxation (or other compulsory levies) provides the most appropriate instrument for increasing savings for capital formation out of domestic sources.[2]

The only feature that is common to most underdeveloped countries is the shortage of revenue which makes it impossible for them to provide essential public services on the required scale. The common assumption is that these countries are unable to lift themselves out of their predicament because of their very poverty. No doubt the "taxation potential" of a poor country—the proportion of its gross national product that can be diverted to public purposes without setting up intolerable political and social pressures—is generally lower, and in many cases appre-

*King's College, Cambridge, England.
[1]See below, p. 73.

[2]The only alternative is inflation, which by comparison is a clumsy and ineffective instrument for mobilizing resources, since a large part of the "enforced" reduction in the consumption of the mass of the population brought about by the rise in prices in relation to incomes is wasted in the increased luxury consumption of the profit-earning classes. Also, it is difficult to conceive of inflation as more than a temporary instrument for mobilizing resources: once wages rise in consequence of the rise in prices, the rate of price inflation is accelerated without securing any further savings.

ciably lower, than that of a rich country. But more important, in my view, is the low "co-efficient of utilization" of that potential—due to bad tax laws, bad tax administration, or both—which in turn is only partly to be explained by lack of knowledge, understanding, or of administrative competence: it is also the result of resistance by powerful pressure groups who block the way to effective tax reform. Accelerated development in all such cases is predominantly a political issue; expert advice can point the way, but overcoming resistance to more effective policies for mobilizing resources must depend on the collective will, operating through political institutions.

The inadequacy of public revenue has two important consequences. It forces undue economies precisely in those fields of public expenditure (like health and education) which are more easily sacrificed in the short run but are the most important from the point of view of long-run development. It also yields persistent budgetary deficits which force the monetary authorities to follow highly restrictive credit policies (to protect the balance of payments and to limit the pace of inflation), which in turn has highly undesirable effects on the pace of economic growth without fully compensating for the effects of the weakness in the state of public finances on the stability of the currency.

Many underdeveloped countries suffer not only from lack of revenue but also from an irrational scale of priorities in the allocation of public funds. Too much may be spent on the (real or fancied) needs of defense or for ostentatious purposes of various kinds, such as public buildings and ornaments, lavish diplomatic missions, etc. There is nothing much to be said about all this, beyond noting the fact; and for the rest of this paper we shall consider the problem entirely from the revenue side: what determines a country's taxation potential, and how can that potential be more fully exploited?

The taxation potential of a country, as defined above, is obviously greatly dependent on (a) real income per head, (b) the degree of inequality in the distribution of income, (c) the sectoral distribution of the national income and the social and institutional setting in which the output of particular sectors is procured, (d) the administrative competence (and so forth) of the tax-gathering organs of the government.

It is a commonplace to say that taxes can be paid only out of the economic surplus: the excess of production over the minimum subsistence needs of the population. Moreover, insofar as such surplus is not consumed by the people to whom it accrues but is saved and invested, it can be made available for the purposes of public expenditure only at the cost of reducing the rate of capital accumulation of the community. This is bound to react adversely on the country's economic development except insofar as investment is diverted from inessential or "luxury" purposes (such as luxury housing) to purposes important for development. It would be more correct to say, therefore, that the taxation potential of a country depends on the *excess of its actual consumption over the minimum essential consumption of the population* and of its investment which serves the needs of future luxury consumption.

In practice, however, the "minimum essential consumption" of a community cannot be defined or measured; it is not just a matter of the biological requirements of subsistence (which themselves vary greatly with climate and location) but of social conventions and habits and the actual standard of living to which the bulk of the population of any particular community has become accustomed. Since governments ultimately depend on the consent of the people whom they govern, it is impossible as a matter of policy to compress, by means of taxation, the actual standard of living *of the mass of the population* outside fairly narrow limits,[3] though in a

[3] If this were not so, the taxation potential would vary enormously with the actual level of real income per head. Supposing this potential were 10 per cent in a country with an income per head of $60 a year, it would be no less than 82 per cent in a country whose income per head is $300 a year. Yet even the richest countries with incomes per head of over $1,000 a year find it very difficult to raise more than 30 to 35 per cent of their gross national product in taxation.

progressive country, with a rising income per head, it is always possible to raise the taxation potential over a period by slowing down the rate of increase in consumption.

It can happen, on the other hand, that the amount of food or other necessities produced in a country is limited, not by the availability of natural resources (land) or by knowledge or ability, but by the customary way of life of the agricultural population, who prefer a maximum of leisure and a minimum of material income and therefore work just hard enough to cover their immediate and traditional needs. In such circumstances, additional taxes levied on them would tend to make them work harder and produce more, i.e., to reduce their leisure rather than their standards of material consumption. Taxation would then act as an incentive to produce more (as opposed to forcing the people concerned to consume less), and this may not encounter the same kind of resistance, particularly if the increase in taxation is a gradual one. From this point of view, the countries of Africa— where, in general, shortage of land is not a critical factor in agricultural production—are more favorably placed than the underdeveloped countries of Asia.

Excluding, however, the case where taxation may itself serve as an instrument for increasing real income per head, the taxation potential of a country will be strongly dependent on the prevailing inequality in the distribution of the national income, which in turn is closely linked to the relative importance of incomes derived from property, as against income derived from work, and to the degree of concentration in the ownership of property. As between two countries with the same real income per head, the accustomed standard of living of the bulk of the population will evidently be lower, and the share of unnecessary or luxury consumption larger, in the country in which a larger share of total incomes accrues to a minority of wealthy individuals.[4]

From this point of view, the underdeveloped countries of different regions of the globe (or even individual countries within the same region) show the widest differences. At one end of the scale, a country such as India, with one of the lowest incomes per head of population, has a high ratio of property income in total income (a ratio that is comparable to that of the country with the highest income per head, the United States) and in consequence has a relatively high taxation potential in relation to real income per head.[5] At the other end of the scale, there are some underdeveloped countries (particularly in Africa) in which incomes derived from property ownership are relatively insignificant and in which a wealthy property-owning class can hardly be said to exist.

The share of the national income of underdeveloped countries accruing to property is largely dependent on the pressure of population on the land and the prevailing system of landownership. In the relatively overpopulated countries of the Middle East and Asia, a considerable share of income accrues (or has accrued, until recently) to a wealthy landowning class who not only pre-empt an undue share of the national resources for their personal ends but whose very existence bars the way to the development of a more efficient agriculture. Even in countries where the ratio of population to natural resources is relatively favorable (as in many of the countries of Latin America) and where the fertile or accessible land is firmly held by feudal absentee owners, incomes derived from the ownership (as distinct from cultivation) of land account for a considerable share of incomes produced.

[4]This is not to suggest that either the inequality of incomes or the inequality in standards of consumption could be eliminated by taxation. It is not possible or expedient to prevent the owner of the successful business from enjoying the fruits of his success during his lifetime, any more than it is possible to prevent scarce talent from earning its high reward in a socialist state. But clearly not all forms of economic privilege fulfill any positive social function—absentee landlords, for example —and the experience of Western Europe and North America has shown that the consumption of the entrepreneurial class can be reduced within wide limits by means of progressive taxation without interfering either with incentives or with the means of continued growth and accumulation. (It is consumption, rather than savings out of profits, which shows wide differences between countries, according to the nature of their tax systems.)

[5]Although the "coefficient of utilization" of that potential appears to be rather low.

This results in a high ratio of resources being devoted to unnecessary consumption. The same is true of countries in the earlier stages of industrialization, where fortunes made in the course of industrial development virtually escape taxation and where, in consequence, a much higher share of the profits earned in industry and commerce are devoted to personal consumption.[6] In view of this, expressed as a proportion of gross national product, the taxation potential of the semideveloped countries of Latin America (with incomes per head of $200 to $300 a year) must be fully as large as that of the highly developed countries, although their actual tax revenue is typically only one-third or one-half as large.[7]

There are some underdeveloped countries which, while they lack a domestic property-owning class, have important foreign enterprises in their territory (for the exploitation of valuable minerals or the product of plantations), so that a considerable share of their

[6]In a study of Chile some years ago, I found the following percentage allocation of the gross national product between various categories of expenditure:

Chile: *Allocation of Gross National Product in 1953 by Categories of Expenditure, in Percentages*

Gross Domestic Investment (Public and Private)		12
of which		
Gross fixed capital formation	9	
Increase in stocks	3	
Government Current Expenditure		11
Personal Consumption		77
of which		
Wage and salary earners (69 per cent of active population)	37	
Self-employed (31 per cent of active population)	18	
Recipients of profits, interest, and rent	22	
Total		100

The total share of property in GNP was 34 per cent, of which direct and indirect taxation took a little over 12 per cent (i.e., 4.5 per cent of GNP) and about one-fifth (or 7.5 per cent of GNP) was saved. If an effective system of taxation had existed which compressed property owners' consumption by one-half, this would have released resources sufficient to double government current expenditure, or alternatively to increase gross fixed capital formation by 125 per cent.

In the highly industrialized countries of the United States and the United Kingdom, the share of GNP accruing in the form of gross profits, interest, and rent is much smaller (less than 25 per cent in 1953) and the proportion paid in taxation much greater. Property owners' consumption accounted for only about 7.5 per cent of GNP in the United Kingdom in 1953, as against Chile's 22 per cent.

[7]Tax revenue accounts for 9 per cent of the gross national product of Mexico, 14 per cent of Chile, 10 per cent of Brazil, 16 per cent of Venezuela (excluding oil royalties).

gross *domestic* product accrues to nonresidents. Since the right of a country to tax all income arising within its jurisdiction is now firmly established, this provides a source of taxation that is essentially similar to that of a wealthy domestic property-owning class. There is a danger, however, that owing to the comparative ease with which this source can be tapped (by means of export duties or taxes on income and profits) such taxation may be carried to the point where it inhibits the development of export industries which may be vital to the development of the economy.[8] On the other hand, many underdeveloped countries have recently been competing with one another in according all kinds of tax privileges and immunities to newly established foreign enterprises in an attempt to attract foreign capital to their own territory, with adverse consequences on their ability to collect revenue. Although it can be argued plausibly that an underdeveloped country gains from the inflow of foreign capital even if the income accruing from the investments is left untaxed (owing to the wage and salary incomes generated as a result and the increased export earnings), it is an uncertain matter how far the total flow of capital investment from the developed to the underdeveloped areas is enhanced in consequence of such policies; and if it is not, such "beggar-my-neighbor" policies of stimulating development deprive the underdeveloped countries of revenue, without any compensating benefit.[9]

Underdeveloped countries differ also as regards the relative magnitude of the "non-monetized" or subsistence sector and the "monetized" or market exchange sector, as well as the nature of the prevailing type of enterprise in each. The most appropriate forms of taxation will differ as between an economy where commercial and manufacturing activities are carried on by small traders and one where they are concentrated in the

[8]It is said, for example, that the excessive taxation of the foreign-owned copper mines of Chile was largely responsible for the decline in the share of Chile in the world copper market.

[9]This point is further discussed below, p. 80.

hands of large-scale business enterprises. Similarly, the prevailing forms of land tenure, the nature of social and family relationships, the extent of economic inequality, etc., call for differing methods of taxation of the subsistence sector. The general tendency in most underdeveloped countries is to throw a disproportionate share of the burden of taxation on the monetized or market sector and an insufficient amount on subsistence agriculture. The reasons for this are partly administrative and partly political: taxes levied on the agricultural community are far more difficult to assess and collect and are socially and politically unpopular because they appear unjust; the people in the subsistence sector are always much poorer individually than the people in the market sector. Yet for reasons set out a few paragraphs below, it is the taxation of the agricultural sector that has a vital role to play in accelerating economic development; the disproportionate taxation of the monetized or market sector tends to retard economic progress by reducing both the source and the incentives to accumulation.

The general conclusion is that the efficient utilization of the taxation potential of an underdeveloped country raises problems which vary with the circumstances of each country, though certain features may be common to all of them. The term "underdeveloped countries" covers a wide variety of different situations, and it would be more appropriate to group the different underdeveloped countries into three or four separate classes, but for the fact that any attempt at such a classification would raise as many new problems as it solves. From the point of view of taxation and taxable capacity, the extent and importance of a domestic landowning class, the nature of enterprise in the secondary and tertiary sectors, the role and importance of foreign enterprise, and finally the competence and integrity of tax administration are the main issues.

In the remaining sections of this paper we shall consider separately the issues raised by (a) the taxation of the agricultural sector; (b) the role of indirect (commodity) taxation; (c) direct taxation on income and capital; (d)

the taxation of foreign enterprises and of foreign income; (e) compulsory savings; and and (f) problems of tax administration.

THE TAXATION OF THE AGRICULTURAL SECTOR

The most important common feature of underdeveloped countries is that a high proportion of the total population is occupied in the so-called "primary" or subsistence agricultural sector; indeed, the proportion of the population engaged in the provision of food supplies for domestic use is the best available index of the stage of economic development of a country. In the poorest and most backward economies it reaches 80 to 90 per cent; in the relatively poor but semideveloped economies it is around 40 to 60 per cent; in the highly developed areas it is 10 per cent or less. This means that as development proceeds, the proportion of the working population engaged in producing food for domestic consumption is steadily reduced and the proportion engaged in manufacturing, commerce, and services is steadily increased. In order to make this possible, the proportion of food produced on the land which is *not* consumed by the food producers must steadily increase; this in turn inevitably implies that each family engaged in food production should sell a steadily larger part of its output for consumption outside the agricultural sector. Unless this happens, it is impossible for the nonagricultural sector to expand so as to occupy an increasing proportion of the community's manpower. Such an expansion of the "agricultural surplus" cannot be relied on to arise automatically as part of the over-all process of growth in the economy. Economic incentives do not operate in the same way in the subsistence sector as in the case of industry and commerce. A shortage of food is not likely to call forth increased production; a rise in the price of locally produced food may even lead to a *decrease* of the amounts which are offered for sale, since it may cause the agricultural families to reduce their amount of work (or increase their own consumption) if their own needs for things which can be procured only with money can now be satisfied in exchange for a smaller quantity of foodstuffs. But since, on account of the nature of food as a primary necessity, a very large part (and if necessary, an increasing part) of the urban' worker's income is spent on food, it is the supply of foodstuffs to the nonagricultural sectors which limits the effective demand for the products of the nonagricultural sectors. Hence, it is the growth of the demand for labor outside agriculture which is limited by the proportion of food production which goes to the market (as against the food consumed by the food producers themselves), and not the other way round.

It follows that the taxation of agriculture, by one means or another, has a critical role to play in the acceleration of economic development, since it is only *the imposition of compulsory levies on the agricultural sector itself* which enlarges the supply of "savings," in the required sense for economic development. Countries as different in their social institutions or economic circumstances as Japan and Soviet Russia have been similar in their dependence on heavy agricultural taxation (in the case of Japan, through a land tax; in the case of Soviet Russia, through a system of compulsory deliveries at low prices) for financing their economic development.

An annual tax on land, expressed as a percentage of the value of the produce per acre, is one of the most ancient forms of taxation both in Europe and in Asia. Up to the beginning of this century, the land tax still provided the principal source of revenue in the countries of the Middle East, in India, and in many other areas (in Europe its relative importance had been declining for a century or so as a result of the diminished relative importance of agriculture in the total national income). Since that time, however, political pressures, combined with monetary changes, have succeeded almost everywhere in eroding the weight of this tax almost completely, and its rehabilitation now faces heavy political and administrative obstacles. Yet there can be little doubt that with heavier agricultural taxation the rate of development

of all these countries could be much accelerated.

The main political objection to this tax is that it is socially unjust in its incidence since (taking needs into account) it hits the poor farming families far more heavily than the rich. However, it would be possible to avoid its antisocial features by making it a progressive tax varying with the total size of family holdings. Since in most countries that are relatively overpopulated and in which land is scarce the distribution of the ownership of land is very uneven (with something like one-half of the available land being owned by 10 per cent or less of the agricultural families in typical cases), it is quite possible to exempt the very small farmer from this tax altogether and yet collect adequate revenue by making its incidence progressive on the owners of the larger holdings. Nevertheless, a progressive land tax naturally raises the most fierce resentment in all countries where a landowning class exists, and to my knowledge, it has not yet been put into practice anywhere.

Another objection frequently made against a land tax is that it requires relatively frequent periodic reassessment of each individual holding, a task which is extremely costly and difficult to perform. It would be possible, however, to assess the potential fertility of individual pieces of land *in relation to the national or regional average* on the basis of more or less permanent criteria (such as average annual rainfall, irrigation, slope and inclination of the land, porousness or other qualities of the soil, etc.); and once this work of evaluation of "potential relative fertility" is accomplished, it need not be repeated at frequent intervals. On the other hand, the actual tax liability could be changed year by year by estimating the average value of output per acre for the country or region as a whole[10] and multiplying this by the coefficient which

[10] One way of doing this is by making an estimate of the total output of foodstuffs for the country or region and then dividing it by the estimate of the number of cultivable acres in that region. Once statistical estimates had been made for a sufficient number of years, the average value of the produce per acre could be calculated as a moving average of, say, the past five years. In years of drought, the tax could be remitted altogether either on a local or a national scale, as the case may be.

relates the fertility of any particular acre to the national average.

It would be technically feasible, therefore, to revive the ancient land tax in a way that would make it both more effective and more in keeping with present-day conceptions of equity (a) by a system which assesses the potential yield of any particular piece of land, not in terms of the actual value of output, but in relation to the yield of the *average* land in any particular region; (b) by making the tax a progressive one, the effective rates of taxation of which vary with the total value of landholdings of the family unit. Such a tax would preserve the merit of the ancient land taxes in that it would be a tax on the potential output rather than on the actual output of any piece of land, meaning by "potential output" the *output which the land would yield if it were managed with average efficiency.* Thus, the inefficient farmer whose production is less than the average for the region and for the type of land concerned would be penalized, whereas the efficient farmer would be correspondingly encouraged. Such a tax on potential output is far superior in its economic consequences to any tax based on actual income or profit; and it is technically feasible to impose it in the case of agriculture (where the nature and quality of land provides a measurable yardstick) in a way which is not feasible for other types of economic activity. It would thus give the maximum incentive for efficient farmers to improve their land and expand their output; it should also greatly encourage the transfer of landownership from inefficient to efficient hands and thereby raise the average productivity of land nearer to that obtained by the best-managed farms.[11]

Another important advantage of a tax on these lines is that it would operate as a potent instrument of land reform, and its efficiency in this respect could be enhanced to any desired extent by increasing the rate of progression of the tax. It could be made to operate so as to induce the owners of large estates—particularly when the tax schedule is expressed in terms of *effective* rates rather than *marginal* rates—to sell part of their holding in order to bring themselves into a lower tax bracket, thereby making the distribution of landownership more equal and at the same time creating a freer market in land. In many countries, agricultural stagnation is largely the result of absentee ownership and of the unwillingness of existing owners to part with any of their possessions, even if they are incapable of putting their land to good use. By making the land market more fluid, a progressive land tax would enhance the chances of able and energetic cultivators to get hold of the land.

In some underdeveloped regions—as, for example, in most areas of Africa—the traditional social customs and the prevailing system of land tenure, among other factors, have made the establishment of a system of an annual land tax hitherto impossible. Instead, resort has often been had to an inferior substitute, the poll tax, which is levied generally on the basis of the number of adult males in each region. The great advantage of the poll tax is the ease of assessment; and in countries where there is not much economic inequality in the rural areas this tax is not so obnoxious as it would be in older, overpopulated countries where a high degree of economic inequality prevails. Nevertheless, a poll tax can never fulfill the same functions as a land tax based on the *potential* fertility of land. A poll tax, unlike a land tax, does not give the same incentives to improve cultivation; it does not make for greater fluidity in the ownership and/or occupation of the land. And because it can take into account economic inequality, not only a land tax is capable of yielding a much larger revenue than a poll tax, but it should also be politically more acceptable.

The importance for economic development of an efficient system of taxation of the agricultural or subsistence sector of the community cannot be overestimated. In the ab-

[11]A tax reform on these lines would, of course, be the more efficacious in raising agricultural productivity if it were combined with other measures for improving agricultural productivity: e.g., the provision of cheap credit facilities, the institution of agricultural extension services, etc.

sence of a direct tax on the subsistence sector —whether in the form of a land tax or a poll tax—this sector can be taxed only indirectly through taxes on commodities which are bought by the agricultural sector. However, such methods of indirect taxation can never fulfill the same function; they do not provide the same incentives for increased production or an increase in marketable supplies and may even tend to retard the development of the rural regions. Since, moreover, it is impossible to differentiate in indirect taxation among various classes of consumers, and since only a small part of the real income of the subsistence sector may be absorbed by the consumption of products bought for money, the scope for such indirect methods of taxing the subsistence sector is strictly limited.

TAXES ON COMMODITIES OR TRANSACTIONS

Although commodity taxes are not an adequate method for taxing the agricultural sector, they are bound to be one of the principal methods of taxing the economy at large and one of the chief sources of government revenue. As a method of taxing the monetized or exchange sector, they are superior to direct taxes wherever the economy consists largely of small enterprises, with few employees in each; in these circumstances, income tax is not a convenient or efficient instrument for taxing either the profits of the employer or (through the P.A.Y.E., or deduction-at-source method) the wages and salaries of employees. To assess and collect taxes on commodities which pass through the frontier is relatively simple, particularly where imports and exports pass through a port. And, to an extent not always realized, such taxes may fall partly on the profits of *producers* or *suppliers* (domestic or foreign) and not only on the *consumers* of the taxed commodities.

Thus, in the case of commodities imported for domestic consumption, where particular imports are under the control of a single company or a limited number of companies (either because the bulk of the local market is controlled by a single great merchant house or because the imports are controlled by worldwide concerns, as with oil and petrol), the price to the domestic consumers may tend to be fixed at the "optimum monopoly" price, so that it may not pay the importer to pass on the full incidence of the tax to the local buyer. In this case, the import duty is partly a method of taxing the profits of the importer (which is often a foreign company) and only in part a method of taxing the domestic consumer.

Similarly, in the case of exports of minerals or plantation products, an export duty may be a more effective method of taxing the profits of producing companies than an income tax, particularly where the local operating company is a subsidiary of a foreign company which is also its trading partner, so that the profits shown by the local company may be arbitrary. The danger is, however, that once the export duties are imposed, the exigencies of revenue lead them to be fixed at excessive levels, with the result that the development of export industries is inhibited.[12]

Though it is possible to vary the rate of commodity taxes according to the degree of luxuriousness of the commodity, thereby introducing a certain progression into the tax system, the revenue potentialities of taxes on luxurious goods are limited, since total imports may be small and consumption may be substantially reduced by heavy taxation. To get maximum revenue, it is necessary to tax articles of mass consumption—cotton cloth, sugar, flour, beer, tobacco, kerosene, etc.— and this raises all the political difficulties associated with a reduction in accustomed standards of living of the mass of the population. Yet this is a peculiar feature, not of such taxes alone, but of taxation in general. It is impossible to increase the amounts raised in taxation suddenly or substantially without

---

[12]The expansion of the Ceylon tea industry is said to have been severely hampered through excessive taxation by means of export duties.

public resistance—whatever form the taxation takes—though, of course, any community is more ready to accept sacrifices, the more it is convinced of their necessity.

There is finally a *general tax on sales* or on *turnover* levied either at the retail stage, at the wholesale stage, or at all stages of production and distribution. Varying forms of such taxes are a common feature of numerous countries, both developed and underdeveloped. The objections commonly made against such taxes are that they cause a great deal of distortion (particularly when the tax is levied at all the successive stages), that they may encourage the creation of vertical combinations, and that they are difficult to enforce. When the degree of evasion is large, it is productive of inefficiencies as well as of inequities in the tax system.

There is, however, one variant of such a tax which has much to recommend it, since it is capable of providing a firm base for the administration of the whole tax system, and this is the *value added tax,* i.e., a tax on the sales minus the purchases (on fuel and materials or possibly also of capital expenditure items) of each enterprise. Such a tax has already proved successful in some countries (e.g., France and Brazil), and its introduction is now under consideration by a number of European countries. A value added tax is really a tax on the gross income generated by each enterprise (in the form of profits, interest, rent, wages, and salaries), and for that reason it could be treated as a species of direct tax as well as a streamlined form of a sales tax. Apart from the fact that it avoids the distorting features of the general sales tax, it is a more favorable tax, in its economic effects, than a corporation profits tax and could also be regarded as a partial substitute for the latter. It must be remembered that from a macroeconomic point of view there is not much difference in the over-all incidence of the value added tax and of the corporation tax: both tend to be "shifted" equally if either is introduced in substitution for the other, leaving the total amount of profits in the economy, after tax, the same in the two

cases. But the distribution of after tax profits, as among individual enterprises, is very different. A value added tax of equivalent yield would improve the position of those enterprises who paid most of the profits tax, and it would worsen the position of those who, under the profits tax, paid little or nothing. In other words, it would alter the distribution of profits as between efficient and inefficient units; it would increase the reward for efficiency and penalize inefficiency. The prevailing system of a high rate of profits tax combined with numerous exemptions—for depreciation, promotional expenditure, past losses, etc.—is really a tax on marginal profits, and it has the effect of shielding inefficient units from competition and thereby limiting the growth of the efficient units. Hence, the substitution of a value added tax for a profits tax (even if only a partial one) would have the same effect as a strengthening of the degree of price competition: it would tend to improve the allocative efficiency of the economy.

However, the most important advantage of a value added tax probably lies in its *self-reinforcing character,* assuming the tax is universally applied to enterprises of all kinds and is appropriately administered. The tax could be defined as a tax on the receipts from sales less such expenditures (in the appropriate categories) as are properly certified by vouchers made out by the seller of goods and which must include the tax code number of the seller. Provided that the rate of tax is not too low (say, of the order of 10 to 15 per cent rather than 2 to 3 per cent), so that it is to the interest of each taxpayer to claim all exemptions for purchases, it would be simple, with the aid of modern electronic computers, to build up an independent source of comprehensive information on the total volume of sales of every enterprise (and of the total income of all kinds generated by them) from the information supplied by the purchasing enterprises. This would provide a proper framework for the administration of all direct taxes (and not only the value added tax). Moreover, it could have the great advantage, from the point of view of general economic planning, of providing an up-to-date transaction matrix (a continuing input/output table) for the whole economy, which in turn would form an invaluable basis for the calculation of the whole set of national accounts.[13]

DIRECT TAXES ON
INCOME AND CAPITAL

The importance which progressive direct taxes on income and capital should have in the tax system necessarily varies with the stage of economic and social development. The experience of a wide variety of countries shows that taxes on income or profits can be successfully imposed only on large-scale enterprises or on the employees of such enterprises. In many undeveloped areas, the bulk of income tax revenue comes from a few large business firms and from government employees. The extension of the tax to small traders, artisans, or professional persons meets with serious administrative difficulties, as there is no way of ascertaining income where no proper books are kept or no regular accounts are prepared or audited. It has often been suggested that a more promising form of bringing small and medium traders within the scope of direct taxation would be by means of a tax assessed on the value of their property—a net wealth tax—since property (whether in the form of land and buildings, plant and equipment, or stock in trade) is more difficult to conceal than income. However, in the few underdeveloped countries where graduated taxes on net wealth have been introduced (such as India and Ceylon), they operate with a large exemption limit and are intended as an additional form of taxation on wealthy individuals, not as a tax on small and medium business, so that there is no

actual experience to show how successful such a tax would be in practice.

In semideveloped countries which possess large-scale enterprises engaged in industry and commerce and where a wealthy domestic capitalized class exists, progressive taxes on income and wealth are potentially very important both for mitigating the growing economic inequalities among different classes (and the political and social tensions which are attendant on this) and for reducing the share of national resources devoted to socially unnecessary luxury consumption.[14]

There is hardly any semideveloped country, however, where an efficient system of personal taxation can be said to exist (with the exception of taxes on salaries and wages). In most countries of Latin America, for example, though nominal tax rates mount to fairly high levels—levels comparable to those in the United States or the United Kingdom— the proportion of large incomes effectively paid in taxation (according to all available evidence) is considerably lower than that of small or medium incomes. This is partly due to defective tax legislation; for example, many countries follow the so-called "cedular" system of income taxation, which imposes a separate tax on different sources of income (and which leaves important sources entirely untaxed) instead of a single comprehensive tax on all income, as in the United States or

---

[13]For this purpose, each enterprise must be provided with a tax code number consisting of three elements: the first indicating the tax office or district, the second the nature of the business (on some standard industrial classification), and the third the actual number in the tax register of the district concerned.

[14]This objective cannot be attained by a graduated system of commodity taxation alone. Since the same commodities are bought by people of very different wealth— the richer people buying more *kinds* of goods and services and not just more "luxurious" goods—and since many of the things on which the rich spend money cannot be effectively taxed (domestic service, foreign travel, antiques, etc.), the spending power of the wealthy classes can never be tapped by means of commodity taxes to anywhere near the same extent as by means of progressive taxes on income or wealth.

It is sometimes argued that in underdeveloped countries the "luxury consumption" of the rich is largely spent on services (i.e., domestic servants, etc.), increasing the volume of employment and thereby performing an important social function. This view overlooks, however, that it is the supply of wage goods (particularly food) which sets a limit to the total volume of employment that can be offered outside the agricultural sector without creating inflation; if more people are taken into unproductive employment, there is less room for productive employment. The mere existence of surplus labor in a community does not imply, therefore, that such luxury consumption is harmless or that it does not involve the use of scarce resources.

Western Europe. In part it is due to prevailing legal institutions permitting anonymity in the ownership of wealth (mostly on account of the prevailing system of "bearer shares" in the case of companies or the system of "banami" in India), which prevents any effective taxation on incomes derived from capital or on wealth (either in the form of inheritance taxes or of annual taxes on capital). It is also due to sheer inefficiency (and to an unknown extent, perhaps, also of corruption) in administration, which prevents the existing provisions from being effectively enforced even to the limited extent to which existing systems of tax laws would permit.

In the context of Latin America, the most important reform is undoubtedly the creation of a single uniform tax on the total income of individuals from all sources, based on a comprehensive notion of income which embraces all such gains or benefits which increase an individual's potential net worth over a period. Some Latin American countries already levy, in addition to the cedular tax, a supplementary tax—the "global complementary tax"—on the aggregate income of individuals. As the evolution of the British income tax has shown, however, it is not necessary to levy two separate taxes in order to have an effective progressive tax on total income. It is possible to merge the existing cedular system (while preserving its administrative advantages) into a single comprehensive tax by making provisional assessments under each schedule (with the maximum use of the deduction-at-source system) and adjusting the final liability on the basis of the over-all return. Whichever method is used, however, there is no justification for retaining different tax schedules and rates of progression for the different sources of income, except insofar as it is desired to differentiate between incomes from work and incomes from property; but this latter objective could be secured better through a supplementary tax on net wealth, discussed a few paragraphs below. With regard to the profits of companies, on the other hand, it is best to follow the United States system of a separate corporation profits tax levied at a flat rate which is separate from the income tax liability of shareholders on the dividends distributed to them.

Effective income tax reform in Latin American countries has, in my opinion, four major requirements.

a) The first is that the tax should be made comprehensive. It should encompass capital gains as well as income which takes the form of dividend interest, etc. It should extend to income from land and houses, including the imputed rent of owner-occupiers. It should avoid exemptions, such as interest on government bonds or on mortgages, which at present undermine its effectiveness in so many countries.

b) The second requirement is that it should treat the family, rather than the individual, as the basic economic unit for purposes of personal taxation. This means that the income of husband and wife and minor children should be aggregated for tax purposes (as is the case in France), but there should be generous personal allowances which differentiate the effective burden according to the size of the family. It is a matter for consideration whether this is best done by the adoption of the French "quotient system" (which divides total income according to the number of adult units and taxes each separately) or by some variant of this which sets a minimum and a maximum to the tax allowance for each member of the family.

c) The third requirement is that, as far as possible, tax should be deducted at source on each particular kind of income at some standard rate (which is preferably the maximum rate), any excess deductions being repayable when the final liability is computed. To protect the interests of the taxpayer, it is advisable that the government should pay interest on excess deductions for the whole period during which the taxpayer is out of pocket.

d) The fourth, and perhaps the most important, requirement is that the rate schedule should be both simple and moderate. There is no point in starting to levy tax at a very small rate: 10 per cent should be regarded as the minimum chargeable rate for the excess of income above the exempted amount; and there is no point in having too many steps. I think the schedule should provide for no more than six to eight separate income brackets, any incomes in excess of a certain level being charged at a uniform rate. The rate of tax on the successive levels of income should rise by steps of 5 per cent to a maximum of 40 to 45 per cent. It is an essential precondition of an effective and loophole-free system that the maximum rate of tax should not be an immoderate one; marginal rates of over 50 per cent militate against the introduction of effective tax reform. Where normal tax rates mount to very high levels (to 80 or 90 per cent in a number of cases), it is in practice impossible to extend the tax to all forms of income (as for example, to capital gains) or to get rid of the numerous exemptions. It is also impossible to secure the compliance of the taxpayer and to administer the tax laws effectively (high tax rates are often no more than an excuse for maintaining an inefficient system), and the amount of revenue lost to the state through a defective tax system is likely to be many times the revenue actually collected from individuals who are subject to the high marginal rates of tax.

It would go far beyond the scope of this paper to consider these requirements in more detail—the more so since the detailed requirements of tax reform vary considerably with the circumstances of each particular country. I am convinced, however, as a result of studying the problem in a number of countries,[15] that in all countries which have attained the stage of development at which the need for an effective system of direct personal taxation arises, there are no insuperable technical or administrative obstacles to its introduction, provided the need is adequately recognized and the opposition from vested interests to

the necessary legal and institutional reform can be overcome.[16]

Apart from a tax levied on the income of individuals and of companies, an effective system of direct taxation also requires that there should be taxes levied on personal wealth which could be administered conjointly with the income tax. Such a tax should be levied in two different forms. The first is a relatively small annual tax on the net wealth of the individual (as now administered in a number of European countries and in India and Ceylon), which is the most appropriate method of tapping the additional taxable capacity inherent in the possession of wealth as such. Clearly, as between different individuals who have the same income, the man who possesses property as well as income is better off and has a higher taxable capacity than the man who has no property. Since different individuals possess disposable wealth and money income in widely differing proportions, a tax assessed on net wealth which is additional to income tax is a much fairer method of allowing for such differences than the alternative method of charging income derived from property (the so-called unearned income) at a higher rate than income from work. Also, it has been the experience of many countries that a combined system which levies an annual tax both on wealth and on income improves the efficiency of the tax administration considerably, since it makes

[15]Two of these studies have been published. See India, Ministry of Finance, *Indian Tax Reform, Report of a Survey* (New Delhi: 1956) and *Suggestions for a Comprehensive Reform of Direct Taxation*. Sessional Paper IV—1960 (Colombo, Ceylon: Government Publication Bureau).

[16]The most important of the necessary legal reforms is the abolition of the widely prevalent system of anonymity in mobile property (i.e., bonds, obligations, or ordinary shares). So long as wealth can retreat into complete anonymity by the simple act of transferring the ownership of physical assets to legal entities, the titles to which are in the form of bearer shares, it is impossible to impose an effective and comprehensive system of income taxation or to have an effective wealth tax or inheritance tax. Whereas dividends can be taxed through some form of "coupon tax," the taxation of the gains made on the sale of securities is, in practice, impossible; and so is the effective taxation of gains on the sale of real property, since the owners of real property are also free to conceal their wealth through the device of owning property through holding companies. It would be possible to gain most of the advantages of a system of registered securities (such as obtains in the United Kingdom or the United States) by a provision compelling the holders of securities to keep them permanently deposited with certain designated banks which would keep an up-to-date register of all depositors and would thus record the changes in the ownership of all securities.

evasion and concealment more difficult than a system which levies tax either on income alone or on wealth alone. Here, again, an effective system requires that such an annual tax on wealth should be levied at moderate rates (starting at 0.5 per cent per annum, with a total exemption for property under 10,000 to 20,000 U.S. dollars) and that the maximum rate should not exceed 1.5 or at most 2 per cent per annum.

The other form of taxation on wealth arises in connection with the gratuitous transfer of property from one generation of owners to the next. This generally takes the form of an inheritance tax which is levied in connection with the passing of property at death, though a number of countries recognize that gifts *inter vivos* form an easy method of inheritance tax avoidance and levy a complementary tax on *inter vivos* transfers (usually called the gift tax) as well. The ideal system would be to levy a single tax on all gratuitous transfers, payable by the individual recipient of the gift, bequest, or inheritance and levied on a progressive scale, depending not on the size of the individual gift or legacy but on the total wealth (including the gift or legacy in question) of the donee. Most countries recognize the need for inheritance taxes as a means of counteracting the tendency of an increasing concentration of wealth through the accumulation of successive generations. A system which levies the tax according to the wealth of the recipient, rather than the wealth of the donor, is evidently fairer and is more conducive to the promotion of a wider distribution of ownership. However, its administration raises greater difficulties; and it can be recommended as a feasible proposition only to those countries which are prepared to maintain a comprehensive record of the personal balance sheets of all wealthy individuals. This is, in any case, necessary for the effective taxation of incomes derived from property (including the taxation of capital gains) and for an annual tax on net wealth, as well as for a tax on gratuitous transfers.

Apart from taxes on income, some Latin American countries impose considerable payroll taxes in connection with their social security systems. These raise difficult problems of their own which cannot be gone into here. It should, however, be pointed out that wide differences in the social security taxes of different countries (in the same way as wide differences in the systems of income and profit taxation) can be a potent source of distortion in the allocation of resources between countries; and if the countries of Latin America move toward economic integration in an analogous way to the countries of the European Economic Community, it would be highly desirable to introduce greater uniformity in their systems of social security taxes as well as in their systems of taxation of income and profits.

TAXATION OF FOREIGN ENTERPRISES AND OF FOREIGN INCOME

The tax treatment of foreign enterprises and of foreign investment raises two distinct problems to underdeveloped countries. The first concerns the question of how far underdeveloped countries should go in the offer of special concessions—in the form of immunity from taxation, etc.—in order to attract foreign capital and enterprise to their country. The second relates to the most appropriate method of taxing the profits of foreign enterprises when they are not exempt. Both questions raise difficult problems as a result of developments which have occurred since World War II.

Foreign investment, in its various forms, holds out the best hope of accelerated development to many underdeveloped countries; it may be indispensable at critical stages of development when industrialization gives rise to greatly enlarged imports of equipment and materials but before there is any corresponding increase in export availabilities to pay for these. Foreign enterprise may be indispensable also in imparting the know-how necessary for the efficient development of local industries. Moreover, in the case of many countries the production and export of valuable minerals found in their area holds out the only hope of generating the economic surplus which is a necessary precondition for their internal development. For many countries, the production of minerals for export forms a considerable share of their gross national product and is the principal source of their public revenue. It is evidently in the interest of underdeveloped countries that the production of such minerals be developed and that this should be followed up by the development of processing facilities which gives rise to industrial development; it is better to export aluminum than crude bauxite, or refined copper than copper ore; it is better for oil-producing areas to have their own oil refineries so as to export their oil in refined form. Most underdeveloped countries have neither the money nor the know-how to undertake such developments on their own; moreover, the marketing of many of these commodities is closely controlled by large international concerns.

On the other hand, it is broadly true that the amount of investment which the large international concerns are ready to undertake both in mining and in processing depends on their over-all view of the requirements of the world market and their estimate of the annual growth of world consumption. It is therefore a priori unlikely that any special concessions (in the form of tax holidays, etc.) granted by the producing countries are likely to have any appreciable effect on the *total* flow of international investment. They can have important effects, however, on its allocation: since most basic minerals are to be found in many different regions, it is naturally in the interest of international capital to develop them in those countries which offer the most favorable prospects, both from the point of view of production cost and also from the point of view of the tax treatment of the resulting gains. But this in turn tends to bring about an unhealthy competition in the offer of special concessions to foreign capital. Whereas any *particular* country will normally stand to gain by the offer of such tax conces-

sions, if the concessions offered are relative to the existing tax treatment of foreign enterprises in competing countries, the very fact that the various countries are in competition with one another for getting a larger slice of such investments will cause any new concession offered by one country to be copied by the others, so that in the end they are all deprived of the prospect of obtaining their due share from these developments without benefiting any one of them: the competing concessions will largely cancel out each other.

The situation is basically different when the concessions offered to foreign enterprise serve the purpose of developing domestic industries largely catering for the internal market. In such cases, tax concessions may well have the effect of increasing the *total* flow of international investment; some particular project of developing a local textile mill, a cement factory, or an assembly plant may appear sufficiently attractive with tax concessions when it would not be attractive without.

This question of how far underdeveloped countries *as a group* should go in offering privileged tax treatment to foreign investment (or for that matter, to domestic enterprise) is therefore a complex one which cannot in general be answered one way or another. In cases where the concessions serve the purpose of increasing the aggregate flow of investment, it is clearly to their interest to forgo additional tax revenue, even for a considerable number of years, since their rate of economic development may be greatly enhanced as a result. But in other cases it is not; and in view of the haphazard multiplication of tax privileges of various kinds in recent years, there is a clear case for international discussions, possibly leading to conventions or agreements that would eliminate the element of unhealthy competition which undoubtedly exists at present. It is to the interest of underdeveloped countries as a group that the tax treatment—both the scope and the rates of taxation of enterprise and of the nature and extent of tax holidays, etc., granted—should, as far as possible, be uniform and that individual countries should not offer additional concessions except in agreement with the others.

The second important issue concerns the manner in which the profits of foreign enterprises engaged in production for exports (or in the import trade) are to be taxed. The most satisfactory method is a tax on the profits arising from local operations. An export duty, as we have noted, can be a potent form of taxation, but it is not a satisfactory substitute for taxation on the basis of profits: if the export duty is heavy, it may have an inhibiting effect on development; if it is light, it cannot secure adequate revenue. Taxes based on profits are less discouraging to the foreign investor, precisely because their burden depends on the gains actually made; if the operations turn out to be unsuccessful (either because there were unexpected costs in local operations or because the market conditions are unfavorable), the entrepreneurs are relieved of them.[17]

The problem with profit taxation, on the other hand, is to ascertain the true profit in all those cases where the resident operating companies are merely branches or subsidiaries of international concerns whose trading operations are not at "arm's length," since they sell to (or buy from) nonresident companies belonging to the same group. The prices in such transactions are, in fact, internal accounting prices of the concerns; it is well known that an international concern operating through a chain of subsidiaries can easily shift its profit from one place to another by changing the price which the subsidiaries (or associated companies) charge to one another. So long as profits are everywhere subject to tax and so long as the rates of taxation are not too different, the incentive for such profit-shifting will not be strong, particularly when the rates of taxation are heavier in the countries where the parent companies are situated than in the underdeveloped countries where the branches and subsidiaries operate. But

since the war, international companies have made increasing use of the so-called tax havens: they have established holding companies or subsidiaries in territories where the profits are not subject to tax (or only at nominal rates) or in countries which do not bring into charge the profits earned in the overseas operations of their resident companies.[18] The result has been that an increasing proportion of the profits made by such concerns have been siphoned into such tax havens, thus depriving both the producing and the consuming countries of revenue.[19]

Thus the profits made in the extraction and processing of minerals may be understated by invoicing exports at unduly low prices. The profits made in the importation and local distribution of foreign commodities or services may be understated by invoicing imports at unduly high prices.[20]

Sooner or later, the arbitrary allocation of profits in the production or distribution of commodities which enter into international trade will make it necessary for countries to look beyond the accounts of the local companies and, if necessary, to impute profits to them based on an appropriate share of the total world profits of the companies which operate local branches or subsidiaries. Here, again, there is a fruitful field for international

---

[17]It is for this reason that export duties, in many cases, are fixed in terms of some sliding scale, the incidence of which varies with the prices actually realized in relation to some average.

[18]For a description of the facilities offered by such tax haven countries, see Gibbons, *Tax Factors in Basing International Business Abroad* (Cambridge, Massachusetts, Harvard Law School, International Program in Taxation, 1957).

[19]This problem is not peculiar to underdeveloped countries but affects the parent companies as well, as is shown by the current efforts of the United States administration to get United States tax legislation amended so as to bring the profits of foreign subsidiaries and associated companies within the scope of the United States corporation tax.

[20]In the case of the international oil industry, the tendency has been to fix the price structure in such a way that the profits arising from the whole complex of international operations are concentrated on the production of crude oil and not in the refining and distribution of oil products. The reasons for this are partly to be sought in tax considerations (since the royalties paid to the governments of the oil-producing countries qualify as a tax offset in the "parent" countries) and are partly political and strategic. But the result has been that the oil-producing areas obtained more revenue than could have been obtained if a free competitive market had existed, whereas the oil-consuming countries (both developed and underdeveloped) have been deprived of revenue (other than in the form of import duties or excise taxes).

co-operation. If it were possible to get agreements among the various countries on how they should handle such problems, they could be dealt with far more effectively than if each country tried to act in isolation.

A related problem, which is perhaps best considered here and which has considerable importance for Latin American countries, is the question of the taxation of income received by residents from abroad. The majority of Latin American countries leave such income untaxed at present (though they are subject to withholding taxes paid in the foreign country where the income originates). On the other hand, the prevailing practice in most countries with a developed global income tax is to tax both the foreign income of residents and the income which originates in the country and accrues to nonresidents; but in the majority of cases (and as a result of the numerous double taxation agreements concluded since the war) the tax which is levied on the income in the country of origin is allowed as a credit against the domestic tax liability of the recipient of the income.

There is undoubtedly a strong case on grounds of equity for extending the liability to income taxation to income received from abroad, and it is known that the residents of many Latin American countries own very substantial amounts of capital abroad. Indeed, one of the frequent arguments against an effective tax reform is that it would "drive" capital abroad, to the detriment of the economy. The difficulty is the practical one of compelling residents to declare their foreign assets and the income received from these. The effective solution of this problem requires the co-operation of the governments of those foreign countries where the assets are held. Some countries already provide such information on a mutual basis under international tax treaties, and such countries could no doubt be induced to provide the same service to Latin American governments as well. The question should also be explored how far it would be possible to follow the British system, under which all foreign nominative securities (outside the Sterling Area) must be registered

not in the owners' own name but in a "recognised marking name" (in the name of one of the local financial institutions) who deduct income tax at source from the dividends, etc., paid to the individual owner. If the co-operation of the United States and of some European countries could be obtained in disclosing to particular Latin American governments the assets owned in the respective foreign territories by Latin American nationals, the countries should be in a position to ensure a fair degree of compliance with such a provision.

COMPULSORY SAVINGS

A relatively new form of raising internal resources for development purposes, which has been introduced recently in a number of countries (e.g., Turkey, Ghana, British Guiana, Brazil, and some others), is compulsory savings. This obliges individuals and businesses to apply a certain percentage of their income to the purchase of interest-bearing but nonnegotiable bonds which are repayable (together with accrued interest) after five, seven, or ten years. The scheme is usually administered in connection with income tax or (as in the case of Ghana) in connection with the purchase of cash crops by a marketing board. The advantage of the scheme, as against straightforward taxation, is that as people are merely asked to postpone their consumption and not forgo it altogether, considerations of equity do not require the same kind of differentiation or graduation as is the case with income tax, and in consequence more substantial amounts can be raised at relatively modest rates. Thus the compulsory levy is generally imposed on wage and salary earners at a flat rate of 3 or 5 per cent on the *whole* of income, though the obligation extends only to people whose incomes are above certain minimum levels. There may be a similar obligation on businesses and professional persons, generally with a higher rate of contribution.

It is possible to combine such a scheme

with a lottery scheme (like the "premium bonds" in the United Kingdom), which might make it more attractive to the majority, who are given a chance to win large cash prizes even before bonds are due for redemption. But the lottery element makes the administration of this scheme far more complicated; also, it has been found in some cases that there was a great deal of moral opposition (by the churches, trade unions, and farmers' organizations) to compulsory lottery.

It is possible also (though this requires far more administrative preparation) to make the scheme into a universal contributory pensions scheme, drawn up on an actuarial basis whereby the repayment of the compulsory loan takes the form of a pension upon retirement, graduated according to the amount of the contributions made during working life. A compulsory savings scheme which results in a universal old age pensions scheme is likely to be far more popular than a scheme where the contributors are supplied with non-negotiable bonds repayable after a fixed number of years.

A scheme of this kind is appropriate only to underdeveloped countries which have already attained a stage of development which makes it possible to bring a considerable section of the population within the scope of direct taxation—or where there is a major cash crop (such as cocoa in Ghana) which is purchased by a central marketing board at fixed prices.

THE PROBLEM OF
TAX ADMINISTRATION

It cannot be emphasized too strongly that the efficacy of the tax system is not just a matter of appropriate tax laws but of the efficiency and integrity of tax administration. In many underdeveloped countries, the low revenue yield of taxation can be attributed only to the fact that the tax provisions are not properly enforced, either on account of the inability of the administration to cope with them or on account of straightforward corruption in the administration. No system of tax laws, however carefully conceived, is

proof against collusion between the tax administrators and the taxpayers; an efficient administration consisting of persons of high integrity is the most important requirement for exploiting the taxation potential of a country.[21]

One important condition for this is that the government departments concerned with the administration of taxes should not be overburdened, and this in turn requires that complicated taxes should be avoided unless there is an administration able to cope with them. Yet in many countries there are hundreds of different taxes with a negligible yield—the cumulative result of the gradual accretion of imposts which have long since lost their justification but have never been formally withdrawn—the administration of which is a great deal more costly than the amounts collected. Indeed, there is no other field where bureaucracy can be so cumbrous and absurd as in the administration of taxes; and in many countries there will need to be an infusion of a new spirit, which makes it possible to apply modern techniques of business administration, before any major reform can be accomplished.

Many underdeveloped countries suffer both from an insufficiency of staff and from the relatively low grading of the staff of the tax administration departments. Persons of ability and integrity can be found for these jobs only if sufficient recognition is given to the importance of the tasks which they are asked to perform, and this should be fully reflected in their status, pay, prospects of promotion, etc. Any additional outlay incurred in improving the status and pay of the officials of the revenue department is likely to yield a very high return in terms of increased revenue.

[21]There is a glaring discrepancy in most underdeveloped countries between the amount of incomes of various types as computed by the method of national output statistics and the incomes declared in tax returns or computed on the basis of tax receipts. In the "developed" countries, the national income estimates based on the "income" and the "output" method of computation are more easily reconciled and do not reveal such glaring differences. It is probably not exaggerated to say that the typical underdeveloped country collects in direct taxation no more than one-fifth or possibly only one-tenth of what is due.

Comment

FEDERICO J. HERSCHEL*

INTRODUCTION

Professor Kaldor has presented a very comprehensive outline of what the tax policy should be in a developing country. Therefore it becomes difficult to criticize or enlarge upon it. For this reason, aside from making a few remarks in that direction,[22] I feel that it would be advisable to dwell on two more aspects of this matter, namely:

a) Certain instances of concrete experience having to do with some of the questions discussed by Mr. Kaldor. In this paper, I shall refer above all to Argentine experience.

b) Mr. Kaldor has summarized what might be called the present state of knowledge in the field of taxation. Therefore, what he offers is recommendations, although they are formulated in a summary manner. I believe, however, that we should also give thought to the introduction of new forms of taxation and to pointing out, in general, the possibility of bringing new methods into this field. His book on an expenditure tax was an example of this kind of thinking. It is my understanding that the purpose of this conference is essentially to formulate principles that may serve as guides to practical policy. However, it seems to me opportune that a meeting attended by so many experts in the field should also recommend that theoretical studies and empirical research be carried out for the purpose of developing new lines of thought that can be applied later in the concrete tasks confronting the countries of this hemisphere.

*Faculty of Economic Sciences, University of Buenos Aires, Buenos Aires, Argentina.
[22]I should like to thank Messrs. J. J. Santiere, S. Itzcovich, and Jorge Macón for the important comments and suggestions I received from them.

FISCAL POLICY AND DEVELOPMENT POLICY

Although Mr. Kaldor may have mentioned this indirectly or implicitly, I feel that it is advisable to point out clearly the aims of development policy and, therefore, of fiscal policy. At a time when the term "economic and social development" is being used more and more, it seems to me appropriate to clarify, for the record, that an equitable distribution of income is one of the aims of a development policy; in the instances—perhaps less frequent than is usually supposed—in which this objective may clash with that of development itself, the need of making a choice becomes apparent. The result will depend on the circumstances in each case. Often it might seem advisable to lean toward the side of growth since, in the final analysis, that will also make possible an improvement in the standard of living of the lower-income groups. However, in my opinion it is imperative to be clearly aware of the social cost that is at stake.

In speaking of public expenditures, Mr. Kaldor briefly mentions undesirable scales of priority. I believe that there is a question of even greater scope involved, one that affects not only the expenditures of the public sector but also its revenues. In short, tax policy may bring about discrimination among social groups, factors of production, industrial sectors, goods produced, and regions of a country. This differentiation may or may not be efficient, and it may have a greater or lesser effect, but it will always be there; even a supposedly neutral policy influences it, since by favoring the free play of the existing economic forces it may make it difficult to bring about the necessary structural changes in the underdeveloped countries.

How can a clear idea be obtained of what this policy of discrimination should be in the context of taxation, and what priorities should be established in the context of public expenditures? I believe that only a development plan can be a truly adequate instrument for this purpose. In countries in which a plan of this kind has not been prepared, the question has arisen as to the extent to which fiscal policy can be an instrument of short-term policy. I believe that these two purposes do not in any way exclude each other. As a short-term policy, the most obvious reforms should be adopted, either because there is a taxation potential of which advantage has not been taken or because certain changes can be introduced that will better take into account the taxable capacity. Once the plan has been formulated, the more basic reforms would be adopted.

If this development plan is the fruit of co-operation among all the economic sectors of a country, as is true of the economic plans of France and the Netherlands, it can be hoped that this will to some extent reduce the resistance of the pressure groups, or at least of those that are not opposed to change. The political strategy should supplement merely economic considerations in this field. There is no doubt of the fact that when it is necessary to increase tax rates the affected groups will always offer resistance, as has been shown by experience in Argentina and other countries.

PUBLIC EXPENDITURES
AND TAX POLICY

It is plain that the government has a basic role to play in the development process. This, therefore, gives rise to the need for increasing amounts of resources. For this policy to be effective, however, it is necessary that the priorities of the development plan be taken into consideration and that at least an acceptable degree of efficiency be achieved in the provision of services.

The basic services that the government should provide were mentioned by Mr. Kaldor merely by way of example. Therefore, it may not be proper to seek to expand the list. However, because of the importance the subject has for many countries, I shall do so, as I desire to cite the case of certain enterprises or activities that should be initiated by the government and that cannot be financed, in the first stages, entirely from income received from the sale of their products, thus making necessary an increase in public resources.

The disproportionate burden of certain "unproductive" expenditures of the government is indisputable. However, I should like to add two basic points with respect to the use of the funds that are collected. First, we cannot hide the fact that there is an inefficient and costly bureaucracy in many Latin American countries. While the adversaries of the government's playing an active role in economic affairs use this as an easy weapon for fighting against the necessary intervention of the government in many fields and for opposing planning, those of us who believe in the fundamental role of the government often pass over this very obvious fact, with the result that frequently the government influence comes to nought and the ground is prepared for a return to forms that have been superseded by better ones in almost all countries of the world. Some of the observations made by Mr. Kaldor with respect to the staff of collecting agencies are, therefore, applicable to a much larger field. I should like to add only one observation: here, too, the easy solutions are not usually the most successful ones. That is to say, a massive or general reduction in the "salaries" item of administration frequently reduces the number of precisely those persons of greatest ability who are working in the government, so that the efficiency of the government machinery deteriorates even more. If, on the other hand, the number of low-salaried persons is reduced, social consequences will ensue, the cost of which may be higher than the amount that can be saved in achieving greater efficiency by reducing the amount of disguised unemployment.

THE PROBLEM OF INCENTIVES

In general, I share Mr. Kaldor's opinion that too much importance has been given to incentives. I believe, however, that this problem should be studied in greater detail. First, it would be desirable to define the term "incentive" more precisely. Often Latin American countries have given exemptions or tax allowances of various kinds that are difficult to justify as incentives to sectors or activities that contribute to economic development. Despite all the difficulties inherent in this problem of terminology alone, I feel that it is advisable to restrict the use of this word. But what is a real problem is the fact that the large number of exemptions—in some cases difficult to justify—has contributed to the inflexibility of the Latin American tax systems.

With respect to the incentives that can be justified because of their contribution to development, the following problems should be discussed.

a) Are they really efficient means of promoting the sectors or activities it is desired to encourage?

b) Among the possible instruments of taxation, which one would be most efficient?

c) Is it advisable for the incentives to be applied on a general scale (for example, to the entire manufacturing sector), or is it preferable to make them specific (apply them to a specific subsector, for example)?

With respect to the first problem, I believe that, in general, tax exemptions do not play a significant role in the determination of investment. A survey made in Argentina of 119 industrial enterprises confirms this general impression, as can be seen in Table 3–1. To the extent that this observation may be generalized, Mr. Kaldor's recommendation acquires even greater weight, since not only is it possible to produce a loss in tax revenues, but it is also possible that an incentive may be given to something that does not clearly respond to a tax stimulus.[23]

With the foregoing limitations—that is to say, the relative effectiveness of incentives—it may be pointed out that the influence of each tax instrument will depend on the particular characteristics of each country and of the economic sector or activity that it is desired to encourage and, above all, on the particular features of the respective system of taxation itself. As an example, some conclusions that emerged from the aforesaid survey made in Argentina are shown in Table 3–2.

Finally, it should be pointed out that to the extent that tax incentives are able to be of influence, it would be advisable to limit them to those economic sectors or actions that can contribute most to economic growth and on which the aforesaid exemptions can exert the most influence. If the field of incentives is limited in this way, there will be no incompatibility between the incentives and the increasing revenue needs of the public sector.

Until now we have spoken only of incen-

TABLE 3–1: Survey on Tax Incentives in Argentina: Factors That Have Most Influenced the Decision to Invest in the Past Five Years

	Percentage
1. Consumer market	20
2. Facilities for obtaining external funds	14
3. Availability of internal funds	13
4. Foreign-exchange concessions and/or exemption from customs duties for the importation of machinery and raw materials	12
5. Monetary stability	8
6. Availability of raw materials	6
7. Tax exemptions	6
8. Availability of labor	5
9. Availability of other production resources (transportation, roads, power, etc.)	5
10. System of anonymity of stockownership	4
11. Other factors	7

SOURCE: Consejo Federal de Inversiones, *Política fiscal en la República Argentina* (in press). (Study made by the Economic Research Center of the T. Di Tella Institute.)

[23]For example, this is what happened in connection with the investment exemptions that were given in Argentina, inasmuch as the investments that were made took advantage of the tax benefits granted, but the benefits were not "responsible for" the investments themselves.

As regards the influence of the tax factor in general on investments, there is the well-known study by J. Keith Butters, "Tributació, incentivos y capacidad financiera," in *Lecturas sobre política fiscal* (Madrid: 1959). With respect to the specific problem of incentives, see E. Cary Brown, "Tax Incentives for Investment," *American Economic Review—Papers and Proceedings* (May, 1962).

TABLE 3–2: Survey on Tax Incentives in Argentina
The tax system might be able to encourage future investment by:

	Percentage
1. Reducing the rate of taxes on consumer goods (luxury goods, etc.)	24
2. Avoiding the superimposition of national, provincial, and municipal taxes	17
3. Exempting from taxation profits used for the formation of reserves	12
4. Reducing income tax rates	8
5. Exempting the production of a plant from payment of the profits tax for a certain number of years	7
6. Exempting the production of a new plant from payment of consumption taxes for a certain number of years	6
7. Permitting periodic revaluation of assets	6
8. Simplifying the legislation in general	5
9. Allowing systems of accelerated depreciation	5
10. Reducing rates of other taxes	4
11. Exempting the production of a new plant from other taxes for a certain number of years	1
12. Other types of incentives	5

SOURCE: Consejo Federal de Inversiones, *Política fiscal en la República Argentina* (in press).
NOTE: The question was asked in connection with each enterprise surveyed.

tives, but is this the only way in which the allocation of economic resources can be influenced?

To a certain extent, the problem may be attacked in two ways: either by providing incentives to those activities or groups that are desirable for economic development or by discouraging those that appear to be less desirable. From a theoretical point of view, both approaches are only two ways of looking at the same problem; in practice, however, this is not so. If, when there is a basic or normal rate, an activity is encouraged[24] by means of tax reductions, the tax reduction may be taken advantage of, although the encouragement may come from other factors (not taxes). However, if a surcharge or higher tax rate (or other form of tax discouragement) is introduced, at least more funds will be collected if the activity itself is not discouraged.

[24]This may be extended to exemptions or surcharges applying to certain economic sectors, activities, or regions.

INFLATION AS A TAX

With respect to inflation, I am in agreement with Mr. Kaldor in that, in the long run, it is not a very efficient way of financing; however, it is so widely used that I believe it would be more advisable to be realistic about it and to point out the cases and the extent to which inflationary finance resources may be utilized. This desideratum is, perhaps, Utopian, if we recall the very contradictory conclusions reached on the problem of inflation and its influence on growth. I believe that the effect of inflation may vary according to the use that is made of it.[25] The effect of inflation will clearly be one thing if the currency issued or the credit granted has been used to finance public investment in infrastructure and another thing if it has been utilized to increase expenditures in an inefficient bureaucracy. It is common to argue that inflation may have different effects, depending on its rate. However, it would be much more meaningful to establish criteria that may serve to determine at what point inflation becomes dangerous. As an example, I should like to mention Professor Higgins' thinking along this line, as he expressed it in Buenos Aires approximately one year ago. According to him, inflationary periods should be interrupted by periods of stabilization, to create certainties for speculative movements.

The way in which the instrument of inflation is used—or, in other words, the new allocation of resources—is of special significance, of course, from the moment when that greater forced saving is accompanied by a reduction in the voluntary saving (when, in Mr. Kaldor's words, inflation can no longer be used as a temporary tool). That is to say, from this time on only the attainment of the

[25]Generally speaking, Argentina and Brazil are pointed out as examples of countries that had a large amount of inflation, but with the difference that in Brazil there was an appreciable increase in the national product. I believe that it is significant in this connection to point out that in the 1947–55 period the per capita investment by the central government increased by 81 per cent in Brazil but by only 6 per cent in Argentina. These figures have been taken from United Nations, Economic Commission for Latin America. *Estudio económico de América Latina, 1955*, p. 125.

best distribution of economic resources through this means can justify the use of inflation as an active tool. From the strictly fiscal point of view, moreover, two basic facts should be taken into account. First, inflation affects government expenditures to a greater or lesser degree, irrespective of whether inflation has been generated by the public sector itself or is the result of the structural imbalances characteristic of underdeveloped countries. In the second place, inflation may affect tax revenues negatively. This is true not only of the taxes based on a fixed monetary evaluation (such as usually happens with real estate taxes) but frequently also of those taxes that in developed countries are characterized by their automatic flexibility, such as income taxes, and that in the Latin American countries are relatively inflexible.[26]

THE TAXATION POTENTIAL

I do not believe that the problem of the taxation potential can be separated from the use that the government makes of the taxes collected.

By way of example, let us imagine an extreme case in which the government collects an amount that affects the "subsistence mini-

mum" but at the same time provides certain essential services or products. This is not, of course, an entirely theoretical example. Actually, other things being equal, it is not the same thing for a particular increase in the tax pressure to be used to finance a nationalized public health service as it is for it to be used for larger defense expenditures. With respect to tax evasion, it should be pointed out that the inadequate provision of essential services has created resistance on the part of the taxpayers of many Latin American countries, a situation that is not totally incomprehensible.

The reduction in consumption that Mr. Kaldor mentions is not only difficult to obtain in practice but may also be undesirable, because it may create an insufficiency of effective demand that may cause a reduction in the real product, unless an effort is made to compensate for the lower consumption by greater investment. Although it is clear that the latter is the purpose of reducing consumption, it must be kept in mind that greater capital formation is not automatically achieved.

PARTICULAR FEATURES OF CERTAIN TAXES

It is said that taxation—in certain cases, and especially in agriculture—may contribute to increasing the real income. In this respect, it is interesting to cite the bill presented in Uruguay that is designed to place heavier taxes on inefficient production and lighter ones on production that is efficient. I do not know what the practical result of this type of taxation will be. However, while the result of indirectly encouraging productive investment is uncertain, doubtless it is worth while to give thought to the possibility of providing incentives to increase production by following Baumol's proposal.[27] I know that it is difficult

[26]Thus, for example, in a study made in Chile the following coefficients of flexibility were determined:

Flexibility of the Tax System

Year	Total	Income tax	Property tax	Taxes on transactions, goods, and services
1950	0.0397189	0.0198101	0.0165187	0.0033901
1951	0.0654399	0.0126148	0.0032086	0.0496164
1952	0.0225777	0.0140675	0.0019269	0.0065834
1953	0.0147004	0.0116113	0.0015747	0.0015144
1954	0.0198196	0.0131517	0.0018373	0.0048305
1955	0.0289407	0.0066092	0.0047926	0.0175389
1956	0.0323948	0.0160272	0.0008156	0.0155520
1957	0.0313229	0.0101395	0.0093388	0.0118446
1958	0.0196613	0.0068098	0.0050821	0.0077694

Source: Chile, Office of Tax Studies, *El sistema tributario chileno* (Santiago, Chile: 1960), p. 56.

[27]Baumol's proposal consisted in the following: An additional tax would be established that would affect the producers, but this tax would be combined with deductions that would vary with the percentage increase in the product over that of the previous year. For this purpose, the value of the production would be calculated at constant prices. William J. Baumol, *Business Behavior, Value, and Growth* (New York: Macmillan), pp. 151 ff.

enough to do this in agriculture, and if we should desire to extend the principle and apply it to other sectors, the problem would be greater. However, I believe that this is one of the new forms of taxation to which we should give thought if we want taxes to provide resources for the public sector while at the same time, we desire to achieve something more than a return to traditional finance theory, where the main purpose of taxes was to raise public revenues.

As regards agriculture, Argentina provides an interesting case. Generally speaking, in Argentina, as in other Latin American countries, most of the production is not the result of the cultivation of the land by small farmers. There is rather a predominance of large holdings, which are usually in the hands of a small number of persons. Although all the provinces have progressive land taxes, the real significance of these taxes has been greatly reduced as a result of a failure to adjust old appraisals (this is true of the majority of provinces).

It should be added that special exemptions have recently been granted to the agricultural sector, with the probable result that greater capitalization of agriculture will not be obtained but that, in large measure, this step will serve to increase luxury consumption.

With respect to consumption taxes, the possibility of translating these to the producer or to the foreign seller seems remote to me if we take into account the fact that, in general, the developing countries, considered individually, are confronted by selling prices over which they have no influence. This situation may change if common market agreements are consolidated and broadened.

The problems related to customs duties (and their equivalents) are considered only tangentially and, to a certain extent, as a special means of taxing consumption. I believe, however, that customs duties, foreign exchange surcharges, and multiple rates of exchange should be analyzed from the point of view of the balance of payments and of the relation of the latter to economic develop-

ment. We might fall into the easy alternative of isolating the taxes on foreign trade from the other fiscal problems, but I do not believe that this would be desirable, considering how largely the Latin American countries depend on foreign trade taxation.[28] In other words, the criteria that tend to utilize customs duties as a protective tool must be co-ordinated with those governing fiscal requirements. There may also arise here a clear conflict between the objective of development and the fiscal

[28]The proportion of income obtained from foreign trade (including import duties) in Mexico, Colombia, and Chile in 1956 was 34, 15, and 27 per cent, respectively. In Venezuela and El Salvador, the respective figures were even higher: 87 and 56 per cent (United Nations, Economic Commission for Latin America, *Inflación y crecimiento: Resumen de la experiencia en América Latina* [E/CN.12/563], p. 73). In turn, in the 1953–54 period, foreign trade taxation amounted to 66 per cent in Costa Rica, 65 per cent in El Salvador, and 67 per cent in Nicaragua. It should be remembered that these figures include import and export duties. With respect to the question discussed in the text, the effect of import duties becomes even more meaningful, since it is by means of these duties that the discriminatory policy referred to can be carried out. The following table for 1953 or 1953–54 shows the importance of import duties in the tax structure:

Country	Import duties in relation to ordinary revenues (percentage)
Argentina	2
Brazil	10
Chile	13
Colombia	16
Costa Rica	52
Ecuador	36
El Salvador	38
Guatemala	38
Honduras	50
Mexico	14
Nicaragua	61
Peru	20
Venezuela	14

SOURCE: United Nations, ECLA, *Estudio económico de América Latina, 1955.*

In Argentina, the proportion of customs duties (including foreign exchange surcharges) in relation to the total tax revenue in recent years was as follows:

Fiscal Year	Customs duties as a percentage of total tax revenues
1957/58	8.5
1958/59	16.6
1959/60	12.6

SOURCE: Consejo Federal de Inversiones, *Política fiscal en la República Argentina* (in press).

objective, and I believe priority should be given to the first, which tends to aggravate further the problem of domestic financing.

Even though the countries having low per capita income cannot escape the need of imposing taxes on certain popularly consumed articles if we have as our ultimate purpose not merely an increase in revenue but some form of distribution of income that is considered appropriate, I believe that insofar as possible we should search for means of progressive taxation, even within the field of indirect taxes, that is, we should tax commodities which, even though they are not in the luxury class, are not absolute essentials, such as flour and sugar. The expenditure tax, which is so strongly proposed by Mr. Kaldor, is naturally the ideal example, with all its well-known practical difficulties.[29]

But should we not consider the advisability of making greater use of the system of "indicators" by means of which some of the elements of the sales tax could be incorporated, although indirectly, into the income tax structure?

If we analyze the structure of indirect taxes from the point of view of the distribution of the tax burden, an important problem arises: when the taxes do not directly affect sales to the final consumer but affect only the intermediate goods, it is not easy to evaluate, even approximately, the final burden that results. In other words, it is possible that it will result in a merely theoretical evaluation of the tax burden, without taking into account the real situation.

In Table 3–3, these differences are evaluated for Argentina, within the limits that a shortage of statistical information imposes on this type of estimate.

The imposition of a sales tax at the retail level may offer some difficulty in practical application, but against this, consideration

[29]There are various problems that should be settled in case it is desired to introduce this tax into the Latin American countries. To name only one, no South American country, with the exception of Colombia, has both an income tax and a net wealth tax. Cf. *El papel del impuesto al gasto en la economía de los países latinoamericanos.*

TABLE 3–3: Argentina: Comparison between the Incidence of Indirect Taxes (Net of Subsidies) Considered as Inputs and by Unit of Final Demand

Sector	As technical coefficient	Coefficient by unit of final demand
1. Agriculture	−0.020941	−0.003096
2. Stock raising	0.016148	0.025437
3. Deposits, quarries, and mines	0.026161	0.059144
4. Foodstuffs, beverages, and other packing plant products	0.040123	0.081538
5. Tobacco	0.510875	0.529090
6. Textiles	0.058707	0.107184
7. Clothing	0.043801	0.101701
8. Lumber and other forest products	0.059789	0.108034
9. Paper, cardboard, and newsprint	0.059336	0.098828
10. Chemical products	0.101431	0.151207
11. Fuels, lubricants, and other petroleum derivatives	0.263146	0.301386
12. Manufactured rubber	0.133132	0.177440
13. Leather and leather goods	0.055221	0.117216
14. Rock, glass, ceramics	0.073192	0.124014
15. Metals and metal goods	0.063573	0.106531
16. Vehicles and machinery, excluding electrical	0.081845	0.117198
17. Electrical appliances and machinery	0.046199	0.088216
18. Other industries	0.113270	0.158691
19. Construction	0.030226	0.079944
20. Transportation, communications, and trade	0.035505	0.064756
21. Electricity and sanitation works	−0.028472	0.047125
22. Personal and financial services	0.069209	0.081176
23. Housing	0.007704	0.017914

SOURCE: Consejo Federal de Inversiones, *Política fiscal en la República Argentina* (in press).

must be given to the distortion that might be introduced into the tax system if the imposition of the tax should go back to stages apart from the final sale.

With respect to direct taxes, Argentina is an example of a country where the existence of bearer shares and a special so-called "anonymity" system has hindered the effective application not only of the income tax but also of the taxation of gifts. This development, which has now been changed in part, is all the more deplorable because even with bearer shares a system was previously arrived at whereby the stockholder was identified for the sole purpose of seeing that the income tax was paid.

With respect to the conditions required for establishing a complete income tax system, it is of basic importance that consideration be given to the drain that might be produced by the flight of capital abroad. (This problem, of course, leads directly to repercussions in the sphere of foreign exchange, but this is not the place to discuss that matter.) Suffice it to mention that, in spite of the drawbacks that this might cause in other respects, quantitative control of foreign exchange would facilitate control of the tax rates. These problems are mentioned by Mr. Kaldor. Ideally, of course, it would be desirable to be able to impose a tax on the total income of the residents of a country. But until this can be achieved, it is of basic importance that the system of taxation not encourage the flight of funds, either because dividends paid abroad are taxed at a lower rate than those paid within the country or because the stocks that are held abroad escape individual identification for purposes of the income tax.

There is one topic that should, in my opinion, be analyzed because it also belongs to the tax aspect of a development policy. I refer to the regional problems of tax policy (of course, the geographical distribution of public expenditures is an even weightier problem). In the first place, an effort should be made to have the system of taxation help to bring about balanced growth in a country, with all the limitations and reservations inherent in this idea. This geographical distribution of the tax burden, moreover, is clearly justified from the point of view of the just distribution of income, as applied in a geographical context.

To what extent are there conflicts, in those countries that have a federal structure of government, with respect to obtaining a uniform fiscal policy with regard to the problem of the tax burden? As an example, the data in Table 3–4 provide an estimate of the tax burden imposed upon the various provinces of Argentina.

TABLE 3–4: Tax Burden on Argentine Provinces

Province (in decreasing order of per capita income)	Per capita income (1950 pesos)	Per capita tax collections (1950 pesos)	Tax burden (percent-age)
Federal Capital	6,134.3	1,396.3	0.2276
Santa Cruz	6,091.2	1,164.0	0.1911
Chubut	3,814.0	863.0	0.2263
Tierra del Fuego	3,115.9	760.9	0.2442
Río Negro	2,950.0	983.6	0.3334
Buenos Aires	2,840.7	598.9	0.2198
Mendoza	2,654.6	569.1	0.2144
Santa Fé	2,521.3	502.5	0.1993
Jujuy	2,147.9	343.2	0.1598
Córdoba	2,130.1	426.0	0.2000
La Pampa	2,096.2	347.5	0.1658
Tucumán	2,092.9	381.8	0.1824
Neuquén	1,978.8	473.1	0.2391
Formosa	1,967.5	314.0	0.1596
Salta	1,905.7	323.2	0.1696
Chaco	1,845.8	310.4	0.1682
San Juan	1,821.1	387.8	0.2129
Entre Ríos	1,697.7	267.2	0.1574
San Luis	1,539.7	256.2	0.1664
Misiones	1,173.6	224.9	0.1916
La Rioja	1,156.4	187.6	0.1622
Catamarca	1,038.7	196.7	0.1894
Corrientes	1,033.1	224.2	0.2170
Santiago del Estero	943.7	172.9	0.1832

SOURCE: Consejo Federal de Inversiones, *Política fiscal en la República Argentina* (in press).

Comment

RODRIGO NÚÑEZ*

It is truly an honor for any economist to have the opportunity to comment on the work of Professor Kaldor. But for a poor "under-developed" farmer like myself, this is an un-

*General Planning and Administrative Authority, Panama.

dertaking of gigantic proportions. However, there is an advantage in endeavoring to comment on the work of a person of the caliber and prestige of Mr. Kaldor: one may be harsh in his criticism without endangering the author's stature. I propose to make full use of this advantage. I propose, in the first place, to explain what I believe are the main lessons we can learn from Mr. Kaldor's paper. Then I intend to criticize five points in Mr. Kaldor's work in which I believe there are omissions or errors. Last, I shall take advantage of this opportunity to discuss the strategy of tax reform.

The most important lesson we can learn from Mr. Kaldor is, in my opinion, to be found in his section on "Direct Taxes on Income and Capital." He states: "In the context of Latin America, the most important reform is undoubtedly the creation of a single uniform tax on the total income of individuals from all sources, based on a comprehensive notion of income which embraces all such gains or benefits which increase an individual's potential net worth over a period." This is a very true and important conclusion. The most important tax reform would be the establishment of a system that is not in existence at present, namely, a really progressive tax on total income. Practically everything else is of minor importance. The sooner this basic premise is accepted, the sooner we shall be able to differentiate between real reform and all the meaningless talk that we have been asked to swallow as though it were reform.

As Mr. Kaldor states, a tax on wealth and a tax on inheritances and gifts are important supplements to a basic tax of this kind. Taken as a whole, such taxes include the essential factors of what we are seeking in the new concept of Latin American tax systems.

Mr. Kaldor also gives us to understand that although income, wealth, inheritance, and gift taxes are the keystone of all tax reform, it is not possible, for many reasons, to limit ourselves to these taxes, and he provides us with a number of enlightening points on the need for taxes on the agricultural sector and for indirect taxes, especially on imports. His remarks on the taxation of foreign enterprises are also valid, particularly in citing this as a field in which international co-operation, or at least co-operation at the inter-American level, might be able to make a contribution. Something has already been done at this latter level. Last, Mr. Kaldor mentions the need for an efficient and honest administration of

the tax structure. This is also an important admonition, although neither the space given to it nor the place where it is mentioned is indicative of the importance of the matter of administration. We know that the criticisms that are levied at the administration of the tax system soon become a potent enemy of reform. It is easy enough to speak of a deficient and corrupt administration as the cause of everything that is wrong with taxation. This is a good excuse: why change the tax structure so long as its administration is not efficient? And in carrying on the search for proper administration, which is always made with "good intentions," we shall spend years without achieving any real reform.

Just as Mr. Kaldor touched upon these problems, he could also have touched upon many other specific problems of greater or lesser importance. *I should like to give the emphasis that Mr. Kaldor did not wish to give to the fact that the fundamental thing in tax reform in Latin America is and must be the establishment of an effective, comprehensive, and progressive income tax, supplemented by a tax on wealth and a tax on inheritances and gifts.*

I should now like to devote myself to an analysis of what, in my opinion, Mr. Kaldor is forgetting and of what I believe are errors in his study. These points involve: the almost total omission of the role of a tax system in the redistribution of income and wealth; the slight emphasis given to the tax system as a complex of incentives; inflation as a tax experience in Latin America; the problem of the cost of taxes and the taxation of the agricultural sector.

I was frankly surprised that Mr. Kaldor looked upon the problems of taxation only from the points of view of incentives and resources. It is possible that my surprise is the result of the myopia that has been a common weakness in Latin America recently, owing to the emphasis that has been placed on the redistribution of income and wealth, especially in the Act of Bogota and the Charter of Punta del Este. Naturally, we preferred to disguise this basic concern with redistribution with the cloak we have called social development, because this sounds less cutting and less revolutionary.

Even a most superficial observation of the Latin American countries shows tremendous differences in the distribution of income and wealth. An indisputable fact of life in many countries is that a large percentage of the people live on the border line of what we consider to be mere existence, whereas a small percentage have extremely high incomes and therefore a large untapped capacity to pay taxes. It is economically justifiable that the latter group be compelled to contribute more to economic development because their incomes and wealth are often used for conspicuous consumption and for the kind of investments that have low social priority. And I should add that even if it were not economically justified, a drastic redistribution of income and wealth *is politically mandatory in Latin America today*. Although blood is not being shed in all of Latin America, we are at the dawn of a social revolution that requires not only a larger income but a better distribution of that income, as well. The effort to achieve tax reform in accordance with aims of the Alliance for Progress can be understood only if it leads us to the birth of economic democracy. Latin American tax systems require reforms in terms of providing the necessary resources for government action as well as in terms of providing an efficient system of incentives. But the most evident characteristic of the present Latin American systems is the scramble to obtain funds from any place from which they can be obtained with least difficulty, without giving any consideration whatsoever to the most elementary principles of justice.

I do not believe that Mr. Kaldor's forgetting the distributive aspects is due to his believing that the tax system cannot be or has not been a powerful weapon for achieving a substantial redistribution of income and wealth. There is theoretical and historic evidence of the power of tax reform in the distribution of the national product.

I was also surprised to see the simple man-

ner in which Mr. Kaldor discusses the role of the tax structure in the creation of an efficient system of incentives. Perhaps this surprise is the result of another case of myopia, arising this time from my occupation as planner. But, again, it seems to me that the realistic history of the Latin American countries is replete with lessons (to my way of thinking, on how *not* to use fiscal incentives) that show the tremendous reaction to tax incentives. Of all the weapons at the disposal of a government for directing, leading, or guiding the economy, it seems to me that none is so powerful as tax incentives. Here we surely have a potential tool that is just as efficient for influencing the use of resources as are prices, precisely because it is the (only) "real price control." This is a sphere that deserves to be more deeply explored when we discuss the role of taxation in economic development. I do not feel that I should do more than point this out in these comments.

Leaving aside the functions of distribution and incentives in the tax system, Mr. Kaldor passes even more rapidly over the problem of the utilization of public funds in spite of the fact that, in order to justify the emphasis on the tax structure as a means of obtaining resources for the promotion of development, it is necessary to be really convinced that development is promoted by transferring resources from the private sector to the government. Since I am a biased student of what is happening in Panama, I cannot avoid reacting violently to this premise. It seems difficult to me to accept as dogma that it is desirable to enlarge the public sector. Clearly, this is not the time to consider the desirable size of the public sector, since that would lead us to a study of the functions of government, of the relative efficiency of the public and private sectors, and of the income elasticity of the demand for various services, etc. The only thing that should be done here is to caution that consideration should be given to determining whether or not it is desirable to enlarge the public sector, especially since its present size varies so greatly from one Latin American country to another. There are some countries where government activities account for a large part of the national product, but there are others in which the public sector constitutes a very small part of economic activity.

Also, it does not appear to me that the relation between an increase in government revenue and an increase in expenditures for the promotion of economic development is so simple or so direct as Mr. Kaldor supposes. The pressures that have customarily sought to increase government consumption instead of investment are similar to those that we find in other countries of the hemisphere. Indeed, we have on various occasions heard of the necessity for self-help in connection with government investments. This is the solution that is adopted in an effort to change the marginal propensity to consume of the Latin American governments. It is an incentive to invest more, because otherwise the public sector would not be performing its function as a promoter of development. There is evidence to show that in the government sector there are high marginal propensities to consume, undoubtedly higher than those of the private sector. The governments that undertake substantial public investment programs are rare, indeed. In Panama, for example, over the long term, the government sector seems to show a marginal propensity to consume higher than one.

Even accepting, for purposes of analysis, the thesis that the outstanding problem is that which Mr. Kaldor sets forth—namely, what determines a country's taxation potential, and how can that potential be more fully exploited —it appears to me that he overlooks Latin American experience. Recent experience in the field of taxation in Latin America indicates that one of the most important features is the inflationary process by means of which the governments have acquired a large part of their resources. It is not sufficient, therefore, to place a note at the foot of the page stating that this is a "clumsy" method and ineffective for mobilizing resources. We must not fail to give very careful thought to this possible tax resource, in view of the fact that Brazil has obtained 44 per cent of real government consumption and 5.4 per cent of its gross domestic product through inflation; Chile, 40 per cent of government consumption and 3.8 per cent of the gross domestic product; Argentina, 65 per cent of government consumption and 8.7 per cent of the gross domestic product; and Mexico, 22 per cent of government resources and 1.1 per cent of the gross domestic product.[30]

Nor do I believe that this inflationary process can be called nothing more than a temporary effort, as this is not in keeping with the long inflationary experience of this hemisphere. Actually, what impresses me most in the history of Latin American inflation is the fact that the people who are responsible for monetary policy have ignored the persistent anti-inflationary sermons that abound in the professional literature in the two decades of inflationary experience and that have even come to exert strong pressure on some of the hemisphere's governments. Inflation has even been identified, with classic Puritanism, with all that is evil.

Nor do I believe that a transfer that has cost only 2.5 per cent per unit transferred in Brazil, 10 per cent in Chile, 13 per cent in Argentina, and 0.5 per cent in Mexico can be called "clumsy."

This brings us to a basic point in Mr. Kaldor's theoretical structure, namely, the fact that the cost is forgotten. If we choose to forget, as he does, the problems of redistribution and incentives in order to concentrate our analysis on the transfer of resources to the governments, we do not have purely a problem of defining and utilizing the taxation potential. There are alternatives, and we must, therefore, make choices. This brings us to what does not appear to be of much importance to Mr. Kaldor—the cost of the alternatives. The problem that thus arises is the common one of minimizing (or maximizing): how to obtain the desired amount of government resources at the lowest possible cost.

I should now like to analyze the matter of taxes on the agricultural sector. It seems

[30]Rodrigo Núñez, *Costos de eficiencia de la inflación* (Guatemala, Guatemala: 1960). IV Reunión de Técnicos de Banco Centrales.

to me completely erroneous to identify the agricultural sector with a subsistence agriculture. A large part of the agricultural sector in Latin America is commercial. Therefore, economic incentives influence it in the same way as they do other sectors of the economy. The conclusion that Mr. Kaldor reaches that "it is the growth of the demand for labor outside agriculture which is limited by the proportion of food production which goes to the market" also seems doubtful to me. The most I can accept is that this is true of a closed economy in which there are no new investment and no technological changes. This is not the situation of the Latin American economies. It is hard for me to understand how the imposition of compulsory taxes on the agricultural sector will produce savings and not cause a substantial reduction in the production of this sector, as happened in Argentina and Chile.

Even if we accept the analytical framework set up by Mr. Kaldor, it seems to me we would have to decide how to impose a tax on the agricultural sector. Again, this decision would be subject to the cost of each unit of resources obtained through the various means of taxation.

In my opinion, a land tax based on potential fertility, even if estimated in terms relative to the region, has two essential features: it is a tax on pure economic rent, and it is a tax on a certain type of wealth. In the part that is a tax on pure economic rent, it is a good tax because it causes no distortions of any kind. It may be objected to only in terms of definition, justice, and collection costs. There are many difficulties in defining economic rent operationally enough to enable a tax law to be drawn up and applied. It suffices to consider that for a tax to be placed on pure economic rent, it is necessary to differentiate between the land itself and the improvements on it. Moreover, the tax should fall only on the nonreproducible part of the land, that is to say, what Ricardo called the original and indestructible powers of the soil. Perhaps this should also include the value resulting from the growth of communities

and the establishment of communication routes. Obviously, it is much more difficult to place a tax of this kind on the "relative potential" of these qualities in specific parcels of land. But as soon as the tax ceases to fall only on nonreproducible property, it affects the utilization of the factors of production that make up the costs. The amount of these costs will depend on the elasticities of substitution, and the ideas about their magnitude are based on impressions rather than on solid empirical evidence.

Aside from problems of definition, the tax on the pure economic rent of land may be attacked as unjust because at the start it has effects in terms of redistribution of wealth that would be discriminatory. Landowners will pay, regardless of their total wealth, and those who are not landowners will not pay. For the purposes of this analysis, there is no substantial difference between establishing this tax on the flow of incomes over a period of time and establishing it on the capitalized value of these incomes.

Moreover, because of the soil studies that must be made, the problem of clearing title to property, and other factors that must be considered such as average rainfall, the amount of supplementary capital, etc., it is a very expensive tax to administer. The more closely it is desired to assure that the tax is imposed on the pure potential economic rent of a parcel of land, the more expensive the administration will be. In my country, for example, we would have to begin with a clarification of every title. Then there would have to be soil studies and the examination of capital improvements such as irrigation works, erosion controls, etc. Although it is true that these studies would, perhaps, have to be made only once, the cost of collecting the data would be relatively high.

That part of the tax which is purely a tax on a class of wealth has characteristics of unfairness that are much less defensible, although the problem of definition and the collection costs are less than in the case of the pure economic rent. However, the tax would have substitution effects that would involve costs because of the distortions that it would create in the utilization of resources. While it is true that there would be incentives for one farmer to produce more per unit of land than the other farmers, an incentive would be created to use less land and more complementary factors. This is a serious problem, especially where there is a shortage of capital. It is also clear that there would be an incentive to reduce the average of the region and not to utilize marginal land or land that is barely superior to marginal.

Mr. Kaldor, further, presents two alternatives for taxing the agricultural sector. In addition to the tax on the potential of the land, he considers a capitation or poll tax and a group of indirect taxes on goods purchased by the agricultural sector. Until there is a more efficient way of taxing the pure economic rent of land, the most attractive thing, it seems to me, is to include under the tax on wealth all the wealth that is utilized in the agricultural sector. We would lose the opportunity to tax the pure economic rent of the land; but, solely on the basis of the impression that today almost all of what is called land is reproducible, I believe that this is a small loss. We would, however, have incentives for efficient agricultural production, and, moreover, we would eliminate the injustice of discriminating among classes of wealth. It seems to me that this would not be a more difficult tax to administer, and it would probably be cheaper than a tax on the relative potential of the land.

I should like to end my comments with a few observations on something that Mr. Kaldor did not mention: the strategy of tax reform.

The strategy that is being used to introduce tax reform in Latin America—its form and its meaning—is what is actually hindering progress. Let there be no doubt about the fact that the assemblies or congresses of most countries are not anxiously awaiting tax reform bills. On the contrary, any bill that has as its purpose the redistribution of income and wealth, any reform that affects the *status quo*, carries with it a large number of protests from landowners, industrialists, and commercial interests. The pressures exerted against tax reform are tremendous, particularly with the use of advertising and paid services. In view of these circumstances, the technical expert cannot maintain an impartial attitude concerned only with the "science" of tax policy. Probably the most important thing is the support given to reform bills. These bills should be defended and explained and must be fought for. And if the technical experts are not ready to take on the burden of this task, their projects will become nothing more than interesting reading for posterity. If this is what it means to be a technical expert, I prefer not to be one.

To do justice to Mr. Kaldor, I must admit that perhaps the strategy of tax reform does not fall, strictly speaking, within his terms of reference. However, I could not ignore it, because although it is necessary to know what reforms we must carry out in Latin America, it is also essential to know the way in which they should be carried out.

Discussion

MR. KALDOR referred to the first two paragraphs of his paper and explained that he had wished to dismiss the question of incentives as relatively unimportant, compared with the main question of revenue. However, he did not wish to give the impression that he believed there was any necessary conflict between the incentive and revenue aspects of taxation. Taxation had both incentive and disincentive aspects, and the form in which taxation was imposed would determine which aspect dominated. Economists distinguished between the income effects of taxation and the substitution effects, the former being recognized as constituting an incentive and the latter a disincentive. The relative importance of those two factors depended on the relationship of the effective tax burden to marginal rates; high marginal rates constituted a disincentive, and a high effective tax burden an incentive. Various exemptions introduced into the tax system to improve the incentive effect by narrowing the effective tax base often had the opposite effect: the effective burden was decreased, and the marginal and nominal rates were increased to offset the loss of revenue. That represented the vicious process, referred to in several of the papers before the conference, of taxing more and more on less and less. In some systems, the incentive effect of taxation might predominate, and some of the conference papers emphasized the incentive effect that an agricultural tax could have, compared with the disincentive effect of the lack of such taxation. The main disincentive effects of taxation related to its effects not so much on individual action as on the allocative efficiency of the economy; high marginal rates of profit taxation combined with a large number of exemptions had the effect of shielding inefficient enterprises and penalizing efficiency. The result was a reduction in the efficacy of competitive forces in the market.

Besides, it would be incongruous to argue that heavier taxation would have a disincentive effect in the context of Latin American countries which suffered from continuous inflation; if heavy taxation acted as a disincentive, it would lead to deflation, which could be resolved by easy-money policies which stimulate investment. Economists were well aware that low taxation, in conjunction with the tight monetary policy necessitated by such taxation in order to counteract the inflation it led to, was the very opposite of a true incentive to development. The effect was to transfer to consumption resources that should be available for investment. The opposite

formula of high taxation and an easier monetary policy would stimulate business investment and development. One special aspect of that subject was the question of whether foreign investment could be attracted by special concessions, but he wondered whether that might not result merely in the transferring of foreign capital to one underdeveloped country instead of another rather than attracting a greater total flow of foreign capital.

He believed there was general agreement on the fact that the main need was for more revenue, although not on what that revenue was needed for. He could not agree with Mr. Urquidi that the main object of fiscal policy was to generate more savings for public investment; that was to put the case too narrowly, if public investment was taken in its ordinary sense of nonrecurrent expenditure for the creation of physical assets such as factories, roads, schools, or hospitals. That was only one aspect of the fiscal program; the first need was to provide recurrent expenditure on public services on a wider scale. Experts attached special importance to the quality and quantity of education. Whatever figures were produced to show that Latin American countries spent a certain percentage of their budget or their gross national product on education, the fact remained that it was not enough. More and better educational facilities were essential to a faster growth rate; they would provide more efficient administrators and managers, more skilled workers, and a higher literacy level and would improve the incentives and intelligence of the workers in agriculture and industry. Good governments were those that provided socially useful services, of the infrastructure type, on a wide scale; bad governments provided such services only in insufficient quantity and quality, and that lack was the main obstacle to a faster growth rate of the whole economy.

Public savings through budgetary surpluses were also an important means of securing private investment. If taxation and revenue were extensive enough to provide a budget surplus, expansionist financial and monetary policies could be adopted that would stimulate private investment. More revenue to establish the proper climate for rapid progress was the essential precondition for accelerated development. An economic setting could then be established for expanded investment instead of a perpetual application of economic brakes in order to deal with problems of inflation and balance of payments.

He believed that the conference would also agree that the additional revenue must be sought where the money was available, namely, in the top 10 per cent bracket that at present, for a number of reasons, largely escaped taxation in Latin America. Something like 40 to 50 per cent of the national income went to those in that bracket, and if that income paid only 20 per cent in taxes, in addition to the 5 or 6 per cent now being paid, the resulting revenue would represent about 8 to 10 per cent of the gross national product.

He had identified three areas where radical reforms were needed: the first was agricultural taxation, dealt with separately because of its separate problems; the second was personal direct taxation on income and wealth; and the third was business taxation. One of the main objects of agricultural taxation in Latin America must be to secure a better use of resources by getting the land transferred to those who could make the best use of it. Land reform was not the only method to secure that end; progressive taxation could induce those who failed to use the land properly to give it up. Competitive forces did not operate in agriculture as they did in industry and commerce, and an inefficient landowner could hold onto his land without risk of bankruptcy through competition with the more efficient. Consequently, competitive forces must be brought into play by the introduction of a progressive land tax, which would both increase agricultural efficiency and constitute an important source of revenue. He was glad to see the same line of thought in two other conference papers. He himself had drafted such a land tax scheme for the Turkish government early in 1962; it had been rejected because of strong opposition by

landed interests, but he was happy to see that the Chilean government had adopted a very similar scheme, although it was not yet in force.

With respect to income and wealth taxation, he drew attention to the four major requirements he had listed in his paper and said that he would welcome comments on those points. He believed that a really efficient system of progressive taxation of personal income and wealth must be fully integrated; both those elements must be included. There must be a system, jointly administered, for the taxation of income, capital gains, and net wealth (in the form of an annual tax) by means of a scheme of comprehensive returns. Such a system would be largely self-reinforcing, whereas taxation on any one of those elements alone would not.

He regretted that no separate treatment had been accorded to the taxation of foreign enterprises; it was a complicated issue, with a number of important aspects that deserved full discussion.

There was one aspect of tax reform to which he particularly wished to draw attention: the value added tax. It could be regarded either as a streamlined form of sales tax or as a substitute for a business profits tax and could not be classified exclusively as either a direct or indirect tax. It amounted to a tax on business sales minus purchases of fuel and materials; in other words, a tax on gross income, or on gross profits plus the interest, rents, wages, and salaries generated by each enterprise. That was the same as sales minus purchases, except for the value of the change in stocks. One of the reasons for his wishing to draw attention to the idea of such a tax was that serious consideration was being given by various experts in Europe (including the United Kingdom) to introducing a value added tax in full or partial substitution of a tax on business profits. The tax had great advantages, particularly for Latin America. In the first place, it was fairer in its economic effects and incidence than a sales tax, the weight of which varied, in terms of gross income, with the ratio of gross to net output.

The ratio of value added to sales might vary from 10 per cent to as much as 80 per cent in various enterprises. Second, the cumulative burden of the sales tax varied according to the number of times the article changed hands before the final purchase; that led to distortions that were avoided with the value added tax. In addition, the self-reinforcing nature of the tax could provide a firm framework for the administration of other taxation, if correctly operated.

If the tax was not too low (the rate should be of the order of 10 to 15 per cent rather than 2 to 3 per cent), it would be in the interest of each taxpayer to claim all exemptions for purchases. If the purchases were certified by vouchers that included a tax code number, it would be simple, with the aid of electronic computers, to build up an independent source of comprehensive information on the total volume of sales of an enterprise, provided that the tax was comprehensive and universal and did not exempt a substantial number of sectors. Moreover, it would be a great advantage, from the standpoint of economic planning, to have really reliable current statistics on the transaction matrix that would constitute an up-to-date input/output table. He would recommend a system with three sets of numbers, the first for the tax district or office, the second for the nature of the business (on the basis of some standard industrial classification), and the third for the number on the tax file in the district concerned. With that system, it would be a simple matter to keep a current record of the sales of each taxpayer on the basis of the purchases of others, and underreporting would be made very difficult. Moreover, a reliable indication of the gross income of each enterprise would be very useful from the standpoint of other taxes levied. Collusion among businesses would have to be very widespread to defeat the self-reinforcing feature of the value added tax.

As regards other economic effects, the over-all incidence of the value added tax was not very different from that of a corporation profits tax which yielded the same revenue.

Both would be partly transferred. The gross profit element in the value added tax was very high; in the United Kingdom it was about a third, and it might be as high as one-half in Latin America. The value added tax made it possible to cut out all irrational exemptions, and instead of taxing the net profit, as at present, the tax would be on the gross profit, at a conveniently low rate. Thus the total incidence, as between profit earners and wage earners, would be much the same. But the distribution of the tax burden as between various enterprises would be very different from the profits tax. The value added tax would relieve the businesses that pay most of the profits tax and would tax those who at present pay nothing; it would relieve the efficient units and penalize the inefficient. Whereas high marginal rates, in conjunction with many exceptions, shielded the inefficient and limited the scope of growth of the efficient, the value added tax, if imposed in partial substitution of the profits tax, would thus improve the allocative efficiency of the economy; it would have the effect of strengthening the forces of competition.

The creation of an efficient tax system was not difficult, regarded as a purely technical problem. The papers submitted to the present conference, as well as the discussion thus far, showed that experts would have no great difficulty in reaching agreement on the various issues. Unfortunately, fiscal reform was not a purely technical matter and depended mainly, not on expert advice, but on the balance of political forces. It would affect the economic interests of the most powerful sectors of society, and some believed that consequently it could not be effected without a revolution. Since revolution was unlikely to aim merely at progressive taxation or land reform, it was in the long-term interest of the propertied classes to avoid it by accepting such reforms, even though that weakened their economic position in the immediate future. In the United Kingdom, the ruling classes had succeeded in maintaining much of their former position by displaying such enlightened self-interest, but he doubted whether the same attitude would be displayed in Latin America. Tax experts must pursue their pedestrian task of explaining the technical precondition of an efficient tax system to ministers for finance, but they would have to bear in mind that theirs was perhaps the least important part of the task in hand.

Mr. HERSCHEL said he would base his comments on Mr. Kaldor's paper mainly on actual experience in Argentina. But, first of all, he would like to say that he was in complete agreement with what Mr. Kaldor had said in the last part of his verbal statement at the present meeting as to the role of experts in tax and fiscal reform, since it was a true reflection of the situation in Latin America. Introducing his comments on Mr. Kaldor's paper, he touched on public expenditure, the incentive problem, inflation as a tax resource, the tax potential, and certain specific aspects of particular taxes, indicating where he agreed or disagreed not only with Mr. Kaldor's paper but also with the views of other speakers who had referred to those points at earlier meetings.

Mr. NÚÑEZ introduced his comments on the paper on the role of taxation in economic development. He expressed his agreement with many of the points made by Mr. Kaldor and dealt in some detail with other points that he considered had been overlooked or were incorrect, including the almost complete omission of the tax system's function in redistributing income and wealth, the lack of emphasis on the question of incentives, the relationship between inflation and the tax system, the problem of tax administration costs, and taxes on agriculture. He also expressed views on the strategy of tax reform, which was not mentioned in Mr. Kaldor's paper, although it had been dealt with in his statement at the beginning of the present meeting.

Mr. URQUIDI said he feared that some of the recommendations made by Mr. Kaldor in his paper, particularly the establishment of a tax on agriculture, could not be carried out in Latin America. There would also be practical difficulties in taxing family rather than individual income, because family in the economic sense was not easy to define. A tax on wealth would give rise to alarm, and its introduction would involve an administrative operation which might be out of proportion to the revenue yielded.

With respect to the value added tax, which Mr. Kaldor proposed as a substitute for the income tax, he felt that its practical effect would be to tax not only profits but also the payroll. Such a tax, in his view, was both inapplicable and discriminatory, particularly against enterprises which employed a large amount of labor. It would run counter to the objective of generating large-scale employment of labor in countries in the process of development, which was precisely the position of the Latin American countries.

Referring to Mr. Kaldor's suggestion that tax incentives should be abolished in favor of tax reduction, he asked whether Mr. Kaldor meant the specific incentive of accelerated depreciation or whether he referred to incentives in general.

With regard to the much-discussed question of the objectives of fiscal policy, to which Mr. Kaldor had referred directly, he observed that in his own paper he had not expressed any preference for public savings as against current expenditure. However, the budget surplus to which Mr. Kaldor had attached such great importance as an instrument of investment by the public sector was not very different from public savings.

Mr. NAHARRO expressed general agreement with Mr. Kaldor's statement. However, without prejudice to a fuller discussion of the topic when his own paper relating to taxes on production and consumption was taken up by the conference, he shared Mr. Urquidi's pessimism with respect to the value added tax. However, his position in the matter was only slightly at variance with Mr. Kaldor's, since he agreed that a value added tax was similar to a tax on gross product. It was a tax area in which direct and indirect taxation appeared to overlap. However, the substitution of one tax for another implied a change of attitude as to what a tax system should be. To offset the advantages of the value added tax, there were also disadvantages, some of them of the utmost importance. Not only would its application involve a heavy administrative task but it might upset the price system by producing a vertical concentration of productive enterprises aimed at concealing added values and reducing the sphere of free competition. In support of his contention, he referred to the "tax on the volume of sales" applied in Spain in 1927. In spite of the fact that the tax administration was quite efficient, the tax base could not be established, so that the tax had been a total failure, even though all that had been attempted was to assess gross income.

With respect to some of the additional advantages attributed to the tax on added value, he feared that Mr. Kaldor's statement was not altogether clear to him, but he failed to understand how a transaction matrix could constitute an input/output table, since a transaction was not quite the same as an input.

To sum up, while he was not completely opposed to the value added tax, he felt that its application would be dangerous and inadvisable in Latin America.

MR. FERNÁNDEZ said that the statements made by the previous speakers had confirmed his view that problems of fiscal policy, whether in general or in the more restricted framework being discussed at the current meeting, could be solved only if supported by other measures related to that policy. The aims of tax policy were twofold: to channel resources and to redistribute income. In his opinion, the two aims were not mutually exclusive. Income redistribution in favor of the lower-income groups benefited economic development, since it reduced imports of nonessential items and thus curtailed the flight of currency.

He considered of utmost value Mr. Kaldor's recommendation that there should be a progressive tax on income, supplemented by a tax on business profits. On the other hand, as far as Latin America was concerned, the worst form of taxation would be a tax on the cost of production. He was therefore opposed to a value added tax, since it taxed the cost of a product before it reached its final stage.

MR. JARACH was gratified to note that most of the points made by Mr. Kaldor coincided with the views he himself had expressed in the paper he had prepared for the conference, which was to be discussed at a later stage. That was particularly true of Mr. Kaldor's position on such questions as the role of property taxes, inheritance taxes, and the taxation of agricultural land. On the question of incentives, he felt that in the matter of fiscal policy for development, undue importance was attached to incentives in the form of tax concessions and rebates which jeopardized the basic aim of maintaining fiscal revenue and providing the essential services and infrastructures of development. Preference should be given to taxes containing automatic incentives by encouraging increased output and discouraging unproductive ownership.

The question had been raised as to how far views of tax experts and the results of tax conferences could actually lead to tax reforms. He took the optimistic view that recommendations generally agreed upon by tax experts served a useful purpose and could be used as a potent argument to combat the widely publicized views of the vested interests opposed to tax reform which based their stand on pseudo doctrines.

MR. BACA observed that the countries of Central America had had some success in the use of tax incentives. However, it should be clearly understood that such incentives were a temporary measure and should be provided to new industries only. He pointed out that when capital exporting countries failed to take account of income tax exemptions granted for the purpose of promoting industry, such exemptions were rendered ineffective and constituted merely a gift by the country granting them to the capital exporting country.

With respect to the value added tax, he felt that it could not be a substitute for a tax on gross profits because it became a tax on consumption to the extent that it could be transferred. Moreover, if it was not transferred it discriminated against industries with smaller profits.

He did not think that a general tax on sales

could be readily applied in Latin America unless collected at the producer level.

MR. GNAZZO felt that the question of the effects of taxation had given rise to some uncertainty during the discussions. A tax on luxury goods, for instance, might not be of much practical value if it affected only a very small percentage of the population. On the contrary, it might create dislocations in the supply-and-demand position by encouraging the illegal entry of luxury items. Export taxes, on the other hand, might create balance of trade problems. A tax on agricultural land, however, could produce practical results. In Latin America, agriculture could play an essential role in reducing existing bottlenecks in the economies of the countries concerned. In view of the low world market prices for primary products, improved productivity could do much to better conditions. Improved agricultural productivity could be achieved through the taxation of unproductive agricultural sectors.

The recommendation in favor of a value added tax should not be rejected out of hand since some elements might be usefully studied for possible application in Latin America.

MR. VEGA said that several of Mr. Kaldor's tax recommendations were already being applied in his own country, Ecuador, particularly with respect to the social aims of fiscal policy, such as to provide increased educational, public health, and other services. Consideration had also been given to adoption of the technique of value added in the sales tax. Other aspects of the tax should, nevertheless, be studied. An effective tax on agricultural land, of the type suggested by Mr. Kaldor, would be difficult to impose under present conditions in Latin America and would have to be preceded by a lengthy process of education and persuasion.

MR. PIEDRABUENA, referring to Mr. Kaldor's views on incentives, believed that in Chile such incentives would have to be rationalized, established on a traditional basis, and applied in a manner which distinguished between business and personal income.

Mr. Prest's comments might be supple-

mented by Mr. Kaldor's alternative suggestion of partially replacing the corporation profits tax by a value added tax; the sales tax could thus be suppressed. The value added tax afforded sectoral control. The difference between the two types of tax was that the value added tax put a premium on efficiency and penalized inefficiency. Consequently, such a tax could take the place of the excess profits tax, which actually penalized efficiency.

In his opinion, the transition from a sales tax to a value added tax should not be difficult; as an alternative, provision had been made in Chile to exempt industrial inputs, thus avoiding verticality, since the entrepreneur was allowed to deduct his purchases and taxes.

Referring to tax evasion, he observed that it existed in fact and could not be overlooked; but means should be devised to endeavor to reduce it to a minimum.

He thanked Mr. Kaldor for mentioning the tax reform act recently approved in Chile, and explained that assessments would be made on the basis of the potential value of the current use of land.

He did not believe that the tax on wealth was just; in his opinion, it had been established to compensate for administrative inefficiency; he could not only conceive of such a tax as a comparative test, i.e., it would serve as a minimum but could not be added to income tax, except in the case of inheritance.

MR. LESSA said that while there was a consensus in the conference that economic development was the final objective of fiscal policy, there were differences of approach as to the manner of applying tax revenue to achieve it. Mr. Urquidi favored spending on infrastructure to change the productive functions of a community and establish its stock of capital, while Mr. Kaldor assigned more importance to social needs—education, health, etc.—as improving a country's working capital. He personally agreed with the former, since it had often been seen in Latin America that, owing to deficiencies in the structure of production, labor left the country or had to be absorbed by the public administration, which, as a result, became excessively swollen.

With regard to agricultural taxes, a system similar to that favored by Mr. Kaldor had been tried in Brazil but had failed, owing to the difficulty of administering it. While taxation might be a help in agrarian reform, it could also be self-defeating, as when an entrepreneur, instead of selling his land, decided to capitalize his productive unit by adopting a more advanced technology, which was reflected in a lowering of the man-land ratio. In such cases, labor was ousted from the land and could not find work in the cities, thus aggravating unemployment, which was serious enough anyway in Latin America, owing to the rapid growth of the population. In Brazil, for instance, the industrial sector, which had a 9 per cent annual rate of growth, had not been able to absorb even half the population growth.

With regard to the suggestion of establishing a tax on value added, such a system had been established in Brazil in 1957 and had been yielding 30 per cent of the total tax collections for the federal government. It would be a good idea to introduce the system in Latin America to correct the regressive nature of the sales tax, which was particularly unfair when there were differences in the degree of development of different regions of the same country, as in Brazil.

MR. COSCIANI said that taxes on sales, purchases, and value added were all of the same nature in that they were transferred to the final consumer. The value added tax offered certain advantages, and he found it curious that Mr. Naharro assigned to it the effect of encouraging monopolies, since it was a tax neutral in its effect. However, he agreed with Mr. Naharro that the application of such a tax implied that all business firms kept books recording all sales and purchases and that small firms would be able to evade it.

Referring to taxes on capital gains, he asked Mr. Kaldor whether his suggestions referred to supplementing the income tax or whether they were inspired by the desire to punish speculation. In the latter case, it would be necessary to introduce an index of speculation in applying it in Latin America, bearing in mind the period over which the capital gains had taken place and the percentage of the total capital they represented.

MR. GOODE wished to make a few comments on Mr. Kaldor's suggestion of a value added tax. If it were to be levied on the value of an enterprise's sales or receipts minus its purchases of raw materials, without any deduction for capital outlay, he feared that it might have an unfortunate effect on investment, since the enterprise would have to pay tax twice over.

Regarded as a partial replacement for profits tax, he doubted whether it could be applied over a larger area than the latter since it was not suitable for agriculture, small enterprises, or the professions.

He doubted whether the self-reinforcing features of the value added tax would be as effective as Mr. Kaldor claimed. Even with the aid of electronic computers, he thought that tax collection would remain a problem, and enforcement would undoubtedly entail much field work.

MR. HART believed that attention should be paid to the possibility of integrating or supplementing the various taxes and cited as an example the case of taxes on net wealth and income; if both existed, an income tax could be applied without any discrimination. If only income tax were applied, a distinction would have to be made between income derived from work and income from property.

He noticed that Mr. Kaldor had not mentioned net wealth taxes in regard to agriculture; possibly taxes on potential income combined both wealth and income aspects.

The value added tax offered possibilities of integrating or supplementing it with sales or production taxes. One of the advantages of such a tax was its simplicity, which was defeated when exemptions were introduced, as in the case of foodstuffs. On the other hand, its introduction demanded a rather high minimum level of administration, and there was a danger of failure if it were applied before it reached that minimum stage. A strong point in its favor was that it implied a conflict of interests between taxpayers.

MR. DESCARTES said that, in general, he agreed with Mr. Kaldor's opinion, but he had certain reservations. Mr. Kaldor's views seemed to be directed toward long-term objectives.

He supported the idea of a nonschedular tax on total income, based on reasonable rates. He had some reservations regarding the tax on value added. With reference to taxes on wealth, he was concerned about their effect on economic development. As for the use of development funds, it was extremely difficult to choose between direct development purposes and traditional government expenditure—on health and education, for example. Nevertheless, he did not believe that there was a clear-cut conflict. Each country could and should decide what was best for it. The ideal would be to finance both; but if there was a shortage of funds, something had to be sacrificed. Under certain conditions, the building of a factory or the capitalization of an autonomous entity providing electric power might be more useful than an increase in expenditure on public health. He agreed that education was vital to economic development and that it would be difficult to sacrifice it for the sake of other ends.

MR. PREST said that the main point he wished to make had already been made by Mr. Goode. There were three ways of applying the value added tax: without any deduction for depreciation of capital goods, with some allowance made for depreciation, or with a deduction for purchases of capital goods, the last being equivalent to a tax on consumption.

In comparing the sales and the value added tax, Mr. Kaldor had stated that the sales tax was less neutral. That depended on the particular way in which each tax was used. There was no difference, for instance, between a sales tax applied at one stage only and a value added tax of the third type.

Mr. Kaldor's idea should be contrasted with the suggestion put forward in a recent book by Professor Baumol, of Princeton University,

that firms should be given subsidies according to the value added from one year to the next.

With respect to the question of incentives for private enterprises, he thought that some more definite and quantitative answers might be obtained if the subject were approached from the standpoint of the enterprises themselves rather than from that of fiscal policy. According to Mr. Kaldor, the crux of the matter was not whether incentives produced a surplus for the government but whether the development of national income and expenditure produced a surplus, which was the optimum condition for the encouragement of private enterprise. In practical political terms, he himself thought that such a condition existed in a country where the controlling social and economic classes were able to adapt themselves to economic development.

MR. KALDOR wished to reply to the comments that had been made point by point rather than according to the order of speakers, as many of them had dealt with the same aspect.

It had been charged that he neglected the redistributive functions of taxation. On the contrary, he felt he held very strong views about them, as witnessed by his work in Mexico, Ceylon, and British Guiana. He considered that progressive taxation was redistributive in a double sense: first, because, if effective, it reduced available income for consumption; and second, because the compression of luxury consumption diminished any inequalities that existed before tax. It was not only that profits generated luxury spending; luxury spending also increased the volume of profits. If the share of national resources claimed by the wealthy classes were reduced by progressive taxation, their income before taxation would also be reduced.

With respect to the criticisms of his treatment of inflation by Mr. Herschel and other speakers, he did not wish to say that he opposed inflation in all circumstances but was nevertheless convinced that it was a clumsy and inefficient instrument for mobilizing resources, since when prices rose in relation to income more money was transferred to the profit-earning classes, who used it for luxury spending instead of for investment. Thus part of the enforced reduction in consumption of the masses of the population was wasted in the higher consumption of the recipients of profits. Inflation was also socially unjust in that it enhanced the regressive structure of taxation.

With regard to Mr. Núñez' contention that land taxes were difficult to apply, he referred him to the example of Chile. It had been said that he exaggerated the critical role of agricultural surpluses as a determinant of economic development, but in underdeveloped and predominantly agricultural countries the difficulty of developing new industries to the point where they could compete successfully with the manufacturing capacity of highly advanced countries had to be taken into account. The lack of an agricultural surplus could not, therefore, be compensated for by imports, which were paid for by the export of manufactures. Doubt had also been cast on whether a progressive land tax could stimulate productivity. He would like to leave that point open for discussion at a later meeting.

With reference to the charge that his ideas were not practical, he asked whether that meant that they were unrealizable from a technical point of view or would be likely to arouse opposition among powerful interests. If the latter, he felt very strongly that it was the duty of economists, and indeed of experts in any field, to consider the public interest and not to bow to political considerations.

As regards the concept of family taxation, i.e., the integration of the unearned income of husband, wife, and minors, he referred Mr. Urquidi to his report on tax reform to the Mexican government, where the idea had been developed in detail. There was no reason to doubt its efficacy, since it was being successfully applied in many European countries, India, and Ceylon.

It had been said that he had not made the order of priority for his plan for tax reform sufficiently clear. In his opinion, measures to enhance the integrity and efficiency of the tax administration should take precedence over all other considerations, since they formed the cornerstone of successful tax reform.

With respect to his suggestion of a value added tax, Mr. Urquidi had said that it would not serve for small enterprises which did not keep proper accounts. He himself thought that if enterprises could be taxed in other ways, there was no reason why a value added tax should not be equally successful, particularly as it was simpler and more practical than sales taxes. He disagreed with Mr. Naharro that it would tend to distort the price system and resource allocation, as it was a completely neutral tax, being simply a sales tax with the element of duplication removed. As Mr. Prest had said, it was comparable to a comprehensive single-stage sales tax. He further disagreed with Mr. Naharro that the tax tended to stimulate the formation of monopolies; but where economies of scale were present, it did promote the development of larger and more efficient enterprises and eliminated inefficient units with little competitive power.

With reference to some remarks by Mr. Piedrabuena and Mr. Hart, he agreed that the value added tax had to be judged in relation to the tax it supplanted or complemented. It was best to look upon it as a substitute for the sales tax and partial replacement for the corporate profits tax. In answer to Mr. Goode, he thought that the value added tax was as applicable to retail trade as the sales tax. He agreed that the self-reinforcing features of the tax could be effective only if its coverage was comprehensive.

Mr. Urquidi and other speakers had criticized his neglect of the question of incentives in taxation. He was fully aware of their importance, particularly when the objectives aimed at had been made clear beforehand, but he did not consider that they were a salient factor in economic development and deplored their haphazard application, which often left loopholes for tax evasion.

What he did disagree with was the idea that heavier taxation acted as a disincentive. On the contrary, its stimulating effects were apt to outweigh its potentiality as a deterrent. It was also likely to produce more revenue for investment instead of for consumption.

In answer to a point raised by Mr. Naharro, he agreed that direct taxes were more equitable than indirect taxes in that they were levied on a person's actual capacity to pay. But since indirect taxes were intended primarily as instruments for collecting revenue and the criterion that should be applied was one of economic efficiency, the question of equity was less valid in relation to taxes on enterprises than in relation to taxes on persons.

Since the value added tax was intended to produce revenue rather than equity, he thought that it should be universal, without excluding foodstuffs, as had been suggested. Any adverse effects it might have on distribution could be counteracted by the introduction of subsidies at one stage or another. He insisted on the importance of a single uniform rate for the value added tax.

4

Issues of Tax Reform for Latin America

by Arnold C. Harberger*

INTRODUCTION

I should like to begin this paper with a statement of its scope and objectives. The topic assigned to me is a general one which could easily be interpreted to cover a hodge-podge of separate, essentially unrelated issues. I do not want this paper to be such a pot-pourri; yet at the same time I do want to meet the requirements of the title by covering more than one or two limited issues of tax reform. In drawing the line between very narrow focus, on the one hand, and "complete coverage," on the other, I shall deal briefly with two matters connected with the general philosophy with which tax problems are approached and shall then concentrate on two substantive areas which appear to me as likely candidates for tax reform in Latin America. The two matters of general philosophy are (a) the problems and goals of tax planning in Latin America and (b) alternative views of the role which elimination or reduction of tax evasion can play in meeting the future tax needs of Latin American countries. The two substantive areas for tax reform that I shall consider explicitly are (c) possibilities for the development or expansion of progressive excise tax structures and (d) possibilities for improving and rationalizing the taxation of income from capital.

I should like also to point out in this introduction that it is virtually impossible to discuss issues of tax reform without at the

same time making a series of value judgments, either explicitly or by implication. I have tried to base the discussion which follows on value premises which are widely held: that a tax system should be progressive, that it should not interfere significantly with the achievement of an efficient allocation of resources, that it should not artificially direct investment into low-productivity uses, that it should provide adequate revenue to meet expected levels of government expenditure without chronic resort to inflationary financing, and that it should, on equity grounds, tax income from capital somewhat more heavily than income from labor. I have also argued that a tax system should be so designed as to minimize the injustices resulting from the differential capacities of different groups to evade particular taxes. Those readers who object to some or all of these premises are likely, on this account, to disagree with some of the conclusions drawn from the analysis which follows. I can only at this point express my hope that most readers will find the premises sufficiently congenial to provide a reasonable basis for a discussion of issues of tax reform.

SOME ISSUES OF GENERAL PHILOSOPHY

Given that the demands of economic development and social improvement will almost certainly require that an increasing fraction of the national income be channeled through

*Department of Economics, University of Chicago.

the public sector, the tax authorities should develop a planning mechanism by which they attempt to foresee and provide for the necessary increases in revenue. It seems obvious that adequate tax planning should be part of any over-all, co-ordinated development policy; indeed, tax planning would probably be one of the most rudimentary and least difficult parts of such a policy. Yet many Latin American countries have conspicuously failed in the past to levy taxes sufficient to cover their existing levels of government expenditure. Adequate public sector support for future growth will require substantially increased expenditure even in such traditional areas of public sector activity as education, road building, and public utilities. Increases in health and welfare expenditures are also likely in the future as governments take increasing interest in the welfare of the poorer classes. If these added tasks of the public sector are to be accomplished without disrupting the economies of the countries concerned, there must occur a drastic improvement in the capacities of many governments to raise revenue. What I have here called tax planning—the sorting out of alternative ways of achieving needed revenue increases and the decision in advance as to which ways appear most acceptable—is simply the first step toward obtaining such a drastic improvement.

Given that unforeseen contingencies are likely to arise, requiring on occasion rapid increases in tax receipts, the tax-planning authorities should maintain a series of specific plans as to how they would suggest raising given amounts of extraordinary revenue within given periods of time. In addition to the budget instability which might come from natural disasters, etc., many Latin American countries face potential instability due, on the one hand, to the variability of the international prices of their principal exports and, on the other hand, to the tendency for public sector wage levels to move in brusque and discontinuous jumps and in response to circumstances and pressures that cannot always be foreseen. If periodic budgetary crises are to be surmounted, the tax authorities must have available to them, in moments of crisis, acceptable ways of capturing such short-run increases in revenue as the situation appears to require. This can be done only on the basis of a reasonable amount of advance planning.

Up to a certain point, evasion must be accepted as a continuing phenomenon. Some taxes are more susceptible to evasion than others, and some groups can more easily evade any given tax than others. The maintenance of adequate tax equity is accordingly more likely if each individual's or group's tax burden is distributed among a number of taxes with distinct tax bases rather than concentrated heavily on particular taxes which some groups may have an extraordinary capacity to evade. This classical principle of taxation is well observed in the regressive components of most existing tax structures but inadequately observed in their proportional and progressive components.

This should not be taken to condone laxity in tax administration or to suggest that much existing evasion cannot be eliminated. It should be taken instead to suggest that 100 per cent compliance is an absurd goal for tax planning and that the design of a tax system, even with the best administration, should recognize that the capacity for evasion will differ significantly among groups.

It should also be recognized that such gains in yields as can be achieved by improved administration are likely to accrue only slowly through time. The idea that improved administration will provide funds to meet an immediate crisis or contingency is surely erroneous; yet this is, in fact, the ground on which the opposition to many proposed increases in taxation in Latin America rests its case. To consider the reduction of evasion as a means for providing short-run increases in revenue is itself a gross evasion of responsibility. It is probably also true that the demands for increased revenue which will arise in the next decade or so in Latin America will substantially exceed the additional revenue that can be obtained through improved administration within this longer period.

THE CASE FOR A PROGRESSIVE EXCISE TAX STRUCTURE

A progressive structure of excise taxes has much to recommend it as a way of meeting part of the foreseeable increase in revenue needs while at the same time reducing the relative importance of inequities due to evasion. Increasing the rates of personal income taxation would yield added revenue, but attempting to meet the entire burden of increased taxation in this way would augment the inequity between those who are able and willing to evade this tax and those who comply with their full obligations. Increasing the regressive component of the tax structure would, on the other hand, result in an unjust division of the burden of added taxation among income groups.

A progressive structure of excise taxes is also an almost ideal basis for meeting unexpected contingencies. The rates of these taxes may be raised or lowered on short notice, and the administration of these changes is comparatively simple. Moreover, if the excise tax structure is reasonably progressive, a just sharing of the burden of meeting contingencies can be reasonably assured by an across-the-board percentage adjustment of rates in the excise tax structure as a whole. Up to now, in Latin America, contingencies have typically been met by increases in the regressive components of the tax structure (cigarettes, sales tax, etc.) or by inflationary finance.

The case for progressive excise taxation is a good one, but the well-known arguments favoring nondiscriminatory (e.g., income) as against discriminatory (e.g., excise) taxes remain valid. The benefits of progressive excise taxation in terms of equity, administrative feasibility, and aptness for meeting contingencies are bought at a cost in terms of the distortion of individual choices among commodities. This cost increases with the rate of tax and with the substitutability of products which are taxed (or taxed at high rates) for products which are not taxed (or taxed at low rates). In the design of a progressive excise

tax structure, care should accordingly be taken to avoid excessively high rates of tax and the effort should be made to tax products which are close substitutes for each other at similar rates. As a rough approximation, it may be stated that tax rates higher than the 30 to 40 per cent range should be subject to careful scrutiny, as there is a presumption that beyond this range indirect taxes can impose substantial costs by artificially destorting the choices confronting individual consumers.

It is recognized that the Latin American countries have for a long time had progressive import duties. These were levied not for the purpose of protecting domestic industries but for the dual purpose of restraining the use of foreign exchange for luxury consumption and of obtaining a just distribution of the total tax burden. The second of these objectives corresponds well with the arguments made above; indeed the correspondence is complete in the case where imports are the only source of supply of the goods included in the progressive tariff structure. However, when domestic production of goods suitable for luxury taxation exists, a progressive import-tariff structure on these same goods yields less revenue (due to the substitution of domestic for imported goods) and serves less well than before the purpose of achieving progressiveness and equity in the tax structure. Latin American countries have been slow to place excise taxes on locally produced luxury consumption goods. This may not have been an important step to take in a period when there was little or no local production of these goods, but today, with luxury consumer goods production growing in virtually every Latin American country, and large in magnitude in several, it merits the most serious consideration.

Special attention should be given to the taxation of automobiles. It is implicit in what has already been said that in those countries where there is local production of automobiles, this production should be subject to excise taxation, though not, of course, necessarily at the same rates as the tariffs applying to imported cars. But a tax on locally produced cars, together with an import duty on cars imported through commercial channels, leaves out a source of supply which has been quite important in many Latin American countries: namely, those cars which are imported duty-free by foreign diplomats or other functionaries or by returning nationals fulfilling certain requirements. These privileged groups receive, in effect—as personal capital gains—large sums that might otherwise have accrued as tax revenues to the government. There are a number of ways of coping with this unfortunate state of affairs. One which I find particularly appealing, and which fits well in an over-all scheme of progressive excise taxation, is a system of progressive license or use taxes on automobiles. To illustrate, the annual license tax for a new Cadillac might be $1,000; for a 10-year-old Cadillac it might be $200; that for a new Jeep might be $200; and that for a 10-year-old Jeep might be $20. Such a system could be made much more neatly progressive than any prevailing system of import duties on automobiles, and it would at the same time greatly limit the extent of capital gains which the privileged groups mentioned above would be able to extract from the Latin American countries.[1]

THE SPECIAL TAXATION OF INCOME FROM CAPITAL

I entitle this section "The Special Taxation of Income from Capital" because I mean to isolate for consideration those taxes or tax provisions whose tax base is either the amount of capital, the income from capital, or parts thereof, in particular sectors or activities, or generally. A tax striking all value added in the economy at an equal rate hits both the income from labor and the income from capital; it is therefore not a special tax on

[1]This proposal does not preclude a simultaneous direct attack upon the problem of capital gains by the privileged groups, such as requiring that cars imported duty-free either be re-exported or, at the option of the owner, be sold to the government of the host country at their original purchase price or at their original purchase price minus a reasonable charge for depreciation.

income from capital in the sense in which I am using the term. Likewise, a progressive personal income tax which takes the same amount from all individuals of given income, regardless of whether that income came from capital or from labor, is not a special tax on income from capital. On the other hand, a tax on corporation income, in cases where income received as interest, dividends, and possibly as capital gains is additionally taxable as the personal income of the recipient, is clearly a special tax on the income from capital. So also is a property tax, in cases where the income of the property owner is additionally taxable under the personal income tax law. I shall also consider in this section special treatments, whether favorable (exemptions) or unfavorable (surtaxes or special additional taxes), falling on property or on the income from property in specific sectors or industries. This set of distinctions is simple to make for countries with a unified personal income tax structure, but some adjustments of the basic data are required before it can be applied to countries where "category taxes" are in force. For example, in a country where the category rate for wages and salaries is 10 per cent and the category rate for corporate profits is 50 per cent, the analysis of this section would treat the system as consisting of a basic tax rate of 10 per cent plus a special tax of 40 per cent on corporate profits. A more complex system with a category rate of 10 per cent for wages and salaries received by persons, of 20 per cent for dividend income of persons, and a 50 per cent rate for corporation income would be treated in this analysis as consisting of a basic tax rate of 10 per cent and a special tax rate for corporation income of between 40 and 50 per cent (the precise rate depending on the fraction of profits paid out in dividends). Actual systems are still more complex than this, and the required adjustments would necessarily vary from case to case, but the basic principle for adjustment is simple: one only has to find the total tax paid out of income from capital in each line of activity (and perhaps by type of capital), estimate the amount by which total tax receipts would fall if the recipients of income from capital had received the same sums as additional labor income, and express this difference as a percentage of the income from capital in the activity (or of the type) involved. The result is the rate of special taxation of income from capital in that line of activity or of that type.

The principal argument for the special taxation of income from capital runs in terms of equity. A man receiving a given income as the fruit of his own labor "deserves" it more than a man receiving the same income as the return to his capital. This argument is particularly strong where inheritance and/or gift taxes are low or ill enforced, for then the income received from capital will in large measure be income coming from assets which were built up by people other than the income recipient himself and which were transferred to him without the prepayment of a tax reflecting the recipient's less meritorious claim to income from them.

The argument above could be used to justify special taxes on income from capital at rates which were progressive according to the amount of income from capital received by an individual or according to the amount of property owned by an individual. The equity argument does not, however, easily justify rates of taxation of income from capital according to the sector or activity in which the income is generated or according to the type of claim (stocks, bonds, etc.) which the ultimate income receivers may own. Given that, in practice, most "special" taxes on the income from capital take a certain percentage of the affected income or (what amounts to much the same thing) a certain percentage of the value of the affected capital, we may conclude that equity considerations would be well met if tax rates were designed so as to take roughly the same fraction of income from capital of all types and in all activities or alternatively to take each year roughly the same fraction of the value of capital of each type and in each activity.

Considerations of resource allocation argue even more forcefully than considerations of equity for the application of equal rates of special taxation to the income from capital in all sectors. Even in poorly organized capital markets, there exists a strong tendency toward the equalization of the net (after tax) rates of return on capital of different types and in different activities. For a variety of reasons (risk differentials, inadequate information, indivisibilities, legally protected monopoly positions, dynamic change in the conditions of technology and of demand), actual equalization of net rates of return is never achieved in the real world. But it remains true that investment decision makers prefer a 20 per cent net rate of return to one of 10 per cent and that unless they are unaware of the differential or are otherwise prohibited from exercising their preference, they will tend to concentrate new allocations of funds and resources in the high-return sector, driving down the rate of return there and simultaneously tending to raise the rate of return in the low-yielding sector. Where the rate of tax on income from capital is the same in all sectors, this tendency is an exceedingly healthy one from the standpoint of economic efficiency and the promotion of economic growth. The contribution of a unit of capital to the national income can (with some qualifications) be measured by its gross-of-tax rate of return. If, in the above example, the tax rate applying to income from capital were 33-1/3 per cent, the contribution of additional capital to the annual national income would be roughly 30 per cent of the value of the capital in the high-return sector and roughly 15 per cent of the value of the capital in the low-return sector. Concentration of new allocations of capital in the high-return sector would accordingly tend to enhance the rate of economic growth. And such concentration is the natural consequence of the preference of investment decision makers for high rates of return.

Suppose, however, that in the sector with a 30 per cent gross-of-tax rate of return a tax amounting to half the income from capital is levied and that in the sector with a 15 per cent rate of return no tax at all is applied.

Then the net rate of return will be 15 per cent in both sectors, and there will be no tendency to concentrate new investment in the high-return sector. The presence of differential rates of taxation (here 50 per cent and zero per cent, respectively) produces and tends to maintain an inefficient pattern of resource use and reduces the contribution of capital investment to economic growth. There is a strong presumption that virtually any pattern of taxation which strikes the income from capital at different rates in different sectors or activities will have similar effects. Desirable results in terms of economic efficiency and economic growth are produced when there is a tendency to equalize gross-of-tax rates of return, while the natural operation of market forces tends to equalize net-of-tax rates of return. When the rates of tax applying in all activities are the same, the market forces are harnessed to promote the objectives of efficiency and growth. When different rates of tax apply in different sectors or activities, the natural operation of market forces tends to frustrate the achievement of maximal efficiency and growth.

I appreciate that the discussion above may sound a bit too idealized for direct application to the situations of many Latin American countries. Market imperfections there may be too big to warrant great reliance on the effectiveness of the tendency for equalization of net rates of return. Accordingly, in this paragraph, I discuss the policies which would be desirable for the achievement of the objectives of efficiency and growth in the presence of substantial capital market imperfections. These objectives clearly demand the concentration of new investment in areas with a high (gross-of-tax) rate of return. If capital does not flow naturally into such areas, it is a reasonable objective of tax policy to attempt to induce such a flow. This could be achieved by taxing the income from capital more heavily in sectors and areas with low rates of return and less heavily in sectors and areas with high rates of return. But this is precisely the opposite pattern of discrimination from that which prevails in most Latin American

countries. The sectors in which capital is taxed at low effective rates (e.g., real estate and agriculture) are precisely the sectors in which capital has relatively low marginal productivity, while the sectors in which capital is taxed at high effective rates (e.g., industry) are precisely the sectors of relatively high marginal productivity. Thus, the prevailing tax systems discriminate in the opposite way from that which would presumably be required to correct for capital market imperfections.

Imperfections in the labor market appear to work in the same direction as imperfections in the capital market. The use of the gross-of-tax rate of return to capital as a measure of the social marginal productivity of capital in a sector is correct when the wages paid by the sector reflect the alternative productivity of the labor it employs. If a sector pays wages which are higher than the alternative productivity of its labor, the social rate of return on the capital employed in that sector will exceed the gross-of-tax rate of return perceived by the enterprises in that sector; and if a sector pays wages which are lower than the alternative productivity of its labor, its social rate of return on capital will be less than the gross-of-tax rate of return which it perceives. I believe I am correct in stating that in every Latin American country the agricultural, service, and construction sectors have relatively low wage scales, whereas the industrial and mining sectors have relatively high wage scales. I believe, moreover, that these differentials persist even after differences in capacities and skills are taken into account. That is, agriculture, the service industries, and construction pay less for *equivalent* labor than do manufacturing and mining. I conclude, therefore, that the social rate of return on capital is likely to be lower than (or at most equal to) the perceived gross-of-tax rate of return to capital in agriculture, services, and construction, whereas the social rate of return almost certainly exceeds the perceived gross-of-tax rate of return in industry and mining. The pattern of taxes on income from capital which would tend to correct for these labor market imperfections would entail rates of tax on the income from capital in agriculture and real estate which were higher than the rates applying to income from capital in manufacturing and mining. Once again, the prevailing tax structures create incentives in precisely the opposite direction from what would be required to correct for existing market imperfections.

Granted (a) that the estimation of the degree (as distinct from the direction) of market imperfections and the design of a tax structure to offset them would be exceedingly difficult tasks; (b) that the move to a system of equal taxation of income from capital in all sectors would itself entail a major and fundamental reform of existing tax structures; and (c) that the gradual elimination of imperfections in the labor and capital markets, itself a desirable goal of economic policy, would render a pattern of equal, nondiscriminatory taxation preferable to a discriminatory system—I propose as a proximate and long-term goal of tax reform in Latin America the special taxation, at roughly equal rates, of all income from capital, regardless of type or source. By "special" taxation I mean, to reiterate, that after the payment of special taxes, all net income from capital accruing to individuals would be fully taxable as personal income to them. In still other words, the policy I propose is a policy of conscious but nondiscriminatory double taxation of all income from capital.

Before turning to problems connected with the implementation of this proposal, let me suggest the possible orders of magnitude of its yield. It is conservative to estimate that in most Latin American countries somewhere between 30 and 40 per cent of the national income accrues to capital. It is unlikely that in any Latin American country capital earns (before taxes) less than 30 per cent of the national income; on the other hand, it is highly likely that in at least a few Latin American countries capital's return (before taxes) amounts to more than 40 per cent of the national income. The potential yield of a tax which took 20 per cent of all income

from capital would (conservatively) lie between 6 and 8 per cent of the national income; and the potential yield of a tax which took 30 per cent of all income from capital would likely be between 9 and 12 per cent of the national income. Thus, without resort to "exorbitant" rates of tax, this proposed reform could by itself overcome the chronic fiscal disequilibrium of many Latin American countries and at the same time provide the fiscal base for an expanding contribution of the public sector to economic and social development.

In dealing with problems of implementation, I shall discuss (a) the taxation of income from owners' equity in the corporate sector, (b) the taxation of income from owners' equity in the noncorporate sector, (c) the treatment of interest payments, (d) possible special provisions relating to income from agriculture, (e) possible special provisions relating to income from real estate, and (f) problems connected with valuation of capital. In order to give some flavor of realism to the discussion, and because at certain points the relative magnitudes of different tax rates become a matter of some importance, I shall assume that the goal of policy is to take, by means of special taxes, something like 30 per cent of all income from capital. Needless to say, the order in which the various provisions are discussed below does not reflect their order of priority or importance.

The special taxation of income from corporate equity capital is already an established part of virtually all national tax systems. The vehicle by which this is accomplished is the corporation income tax. To achieve this part of the over-all objective would require nothing more than the imposition of a 30 per cent rate of tax on all corporate income. The most important way in which current practice in Latin America fails to meet this goal lies in the frequent exemption of income in particular lines of activity from the corporation income tax. Such exemptions are often claimed to promote economic development because they help corporations in new lines of activity over their difficult early years.

There is a grain of truth in this assertion, but it should be noted (*a*) that the most difficult early years are those in which the corporations in question sustain losses—years in which they would have no taxable income in any case; and (*b*) that with a moderate (e.g., 30 per cent) rate of tax even a new corporation is not grossly penalized when its investments begin to bear fruit and produce net income. Against the dubious claims made in favor of exemptions, we must weigh the following facts: (*a*) although exemptions are easy to grant, they appear to be considerably more difficult to remove; (*b*) in the short run, at least, exemptions tend to create within the corporate sector certain islands of privilege, wherein abnormally high private returns to capital can be earned even though the social returns to capital are not abnormally high and may be abnormally low; (*c*) in the long run, at least, exemptions tend to attract excessive amounts of capital to the affected industries, thus promoting an inefficient allocation of the economy's scarce capital resources. I conclude that the nondiscriminatory treatment of income from corporate equity capital is an important part of a program aimed at achieving the nondiscriminatory taxation of all income from capital.

Countries with a category tax system are in a good position to adopt the measures required to capture the desired fraction of the return to capital in unincorporated enterprises, for in these countries some special tax on the income of unincorporated enterprises typically already exists. Countries without a category tax system would do well, in this respect at least, to adopt similar measures. If we take for granted that a tax on the income of unincorporated enterprises does exist or will be imposed, we may confront the real difficulty facing the taxation of income from capital in this area: namely, the difficulty of apportioning the income of an unincorporated enterprise between "return to proprietors' labor" and "return to capital." It is fruitless, I believe, to hope for a precise method of apportionment, given the number and the variety of types of unincorporated enterprises

in any country and given the difficulties of administrative control over their record keeping. I would therefore propose, as a second-best solution, the introduction of a progressive special tax on the income of this broad class of enterprises. It is to be presumed that the contribution of proprietors' labor to the total income of the enterprise will tend to be larger in those enterprises with small total incomes and smaller in those with large total incomes. One might think of a minimum rate of special taxation of 10 per cent (applying to enterprises with low total incomes and presuming, implicitly, that some two-thirds of the total income of these enterprises is due to proprietors' labor) and of a maximum rate of around 25 per cent (applying to enterprises with high total incomes and presuming, implicitly, that only one-sixth of the total income of these enterprises is due to proprietors' labor), with appropriate gradations in between. The rate of special tax applied to the total income of unincorporated enterprises should in no case exceed the rate applied to corporate income, because the income of unincorporated enterprises invariably includes some return to the labor of proprietors. If the proposed progressive tax were to be adopted, it would be necessary to take some measures to prevent tax avoidance by the artificial splitting up of enterprises. One step in this direction might be a requirement that all unincorporated enterprises owned by a single tax-paying unit (person or family) be treated for tax purposes as a single enterprise.

The interest paid by an enterprise on bank loans, other loans, or bonds is just as much a part of the income from capital generated by that enterprise as the profits accruing in it. One simple way of assuring that interest payments would be subject to the special tax on income from capital would be to disallow their deduction as a cost in computing the income (corporate or noncorporate) subject to special taxation. This simple device has much to recommend it. My only reason for considering alternative measures stems from my confidence that some of the main recipients of interest payments (banks and other financial intermediaries) are more reliable taxpayers (in the sense of being less prone or able to evade or avoid their tax liabilities) than some of the entities that pay interest to them. In short, it may be administratively simpler for the government to capture the tax "due" to it on the interest paid by enterprises by taxing that interest when it is received by banks and other financial intermediaries than by taxing it at the source of payment. Likewise, in a country in which interest payments on industrial bonds are significant and in which bond issues must be publicly registered, the tax on bond interest might be made payable to the fiscal authorities at the time of each periodic interest payment.[2]

If in line with this proposal, interest paid to banks and financial intermediaries and possibly interest paid on bonds are subject to distinct tax treatment, there are two alternatives for the treatment of other interest payments. The first is to allow the deduction, for purposes of computing income subject to the taxes on corporate and unincorporated enterprises, only of such interest costs as were paid to banks and financial intermediaries or on bonds. Other interest payments would not be deductible and hence would automatically be taxable at ordinary income tax rates. Alternatively, other interest payments could be made deductible, but a special tax could be levied on such interest payments

(other than those on bank loans, bonds, etc.) for which deduction was claimed. The rate of tax applicable to these other interest deductions could in no case be greater than the rate of tax applicable to corporate or noncorporate income (else no enterprise would claim deductions, and the system would reduce to that discussed under the first alternative).

Under any system of taxing interest payments, it would be necessary to accord special treatment to financial intermediaries. If the interest paid by enterprises to banks is subject to a special tax, the interest paid by banks to their depositors should not also be subject to a special tax.

There is no strong argument for treating the return to capital in agriculture differently from the return to capital in other activities. Corporations operating within agriculture could easily be subjected to the same tax treatment as other corporations, and ordinary (unincorporated) farms could be treated in the same way as other unincorporated enterprises. The difficulties of assessing farm income are great, however, and they have led some countries to impute farm income on the basis of the value of the property. This same procedure can be used for approximating farm income within a system, such as that proposed in this paper, designed to strike all income from capital with special taxes at roughly equivalent rates. If, for example, the annual income from agricultural property was imputed to be 7 per cent of the value of the property, the special tax on the annual return to capital in agriculture could be set at, say, 2 per cent of the value of the property. It is important to realize here that the value of the property assessed should include not only the value of the land but also the value of all improvements, equipment, and inventories. For example, the value of irrigation canals, barns, machinery, orchards, vineyards, and livestock should be included in the capital sum on the basis of which income from property is imputed. And unless an additional special tax is levied on the imputed income from residential housing in rural areas,

[2] If interest paid to financial intermediaries and interest paid on bonds were to be taxed separately, as suggested here, an issue arises as to whether the tax should be paid by the borrowing enterprise, in addition to the contractual interest, or whether the tax should fall on the recipient. This issue is not a serious one as far as the long-run results of the tax are concerned, for the long-run results depend only on the existence of the tax and not on which group is nominally liable for its payment. In the short run, however, there are real differences in incidence, depending on which group is nominally liable. The appropriate policy on this issue would depend on whether it was deemed important that the special tax on interest payments have its full impact in the short run and whether one group or the other seemed a more likely subject for bearing the short-run impact of the tax, from the standpoint of the general policy of the country concerned. The long-term effect could be achieved without having any special short-term impact on either group, simply by making the tax on bank (bond) interest payments payable only on the interest on loans made (or bonds issued) after the law became effective.

the value of residences should also be included in the total from which income is imputed. It is also important to realize that the special tax we are discussing here is not a substitute for the personal income tax. If income subject to personal tax is also imputed, then, using the same figures as in the above example, 5 per cent of the value of the property (7 per cent imputed yield less 2 per cent paid in special tax) would be the annual imputed income from property on the basis of which personal income tax would be levied.

In the case of residential housing, the income obtained from rented properties could be treated in just the same way as other return to capital and taxed at the rates of special taxation applicable to the (corporate or unincorporated) enterprises concerned. The income from owner-occupied houses would, however, have to be imputed; or, what amounts to essentially the same thing, the special tax, at least on owner-occupied residences, would have to be expressed as a percentage of the value of the property. Administrative considerations might dictate giving the same treatment to all residences, whether or not they are owner-occupied. In this latter case, an annual tax of, say, 2 per cent of the value of the property might be levied on all residences. If this were done, however, it would not be correct to subject interest payments on mortgages to an additional tax.[3]

As in the case of other forms of income from capital, the income (actual or imputed) from residential property should be subject to personal income taxation in addition to the special taxation just considered. Rental income is everywhere subject to personal income tax-

ation, so we need not discuss it further here. The imputed income from owner-occupied residences, however, is not subject to personal income taxation in many countries; the purpose of this paragraph is to emphasize that it should be. The failure to tax imputed income on owner-occupied residences introduces an extraordinarily regressive component into a country's tax system. The poor owner-occupier, whose marginal personal income tax rate is zero, receives no benefit from the exemption of imputed income. The middle-class owner-occupier, whose marginal personal tax rate is, say, 20 per cent, receives a benefit equal to 20 per cent of the rental value of his dwelling as a result of the exemption of imputed income. The wealthy owner-occupier, whose marginal personal tax rate is, say, 50 per cent, receives a benefit equal to half the rental value of his dwelling. Not only is the exemption of imputed rental income inequitable; it also creates artificial incentives for investment in luxury housing, an area where (precisely because of the exemption) the marginal productivity of capital is likely to be low and also where investment is unlikely to carry with it the beneficial external effects (associated with improved techniques and possibly with transfers of labor from sectors of low to sectors of high marginal productivity) that might be expected normally, for example, from investment in industrial capital equipment.

If taxes are to be levied, or income imputed, on the basis of the value of agricultural and/or residential properties, it is important that assessment procedures be adopted which estimate the true economic value of property with reasonable accuracy. Assessment procedures have been notably weak in most Latin American countries and are badly in need of reform. The economist's answer to the assessment problem is simple and essentially foolproof: allow each property owner to declare the value of his own property, make these declared values a matter of public record, and require that an owner sell his property to any bidder who is willing to pay, say, 20 per cent more than the declared value.

[3] This same proviso holds in the case (discussed in the paragraph above) in which the special tax on income from property in agriculture is based on the value of the property rather than on the actual income received. Where the tax is on actual income and interest payments are deductible in the computation of income subject to tax, there *should* be—according to the principle of roughly equal special taxation of all income from capital—a special tax on interest payments. Where interest payments are not deductible in computing the income subject to special taxation, or where that income is imputed on the basis of the value of the property, there *should not* be a special tax on interest payments.

This simple scheme is self-enforcing, allows no scope for corruption, has negligible costs of administration, and creates incentives, in addition to those already present in the market, for each property to be put to that use in which it has the highest economic productivity. The beauty of this scheme, so evident to economists, is not, however, appreciated by lawyers, who object strongly to the idea of requiring the sale of properties, possibly against the will of their owners. The economist can retort here that if owners value their property at the price at which they would be willing to sell, they should not be unwilling to sell at a price 20 per cent higher. But there are also other ways of accommodating the objections of the lawyers. Perhaps the simplest way is to create, within the office in charge of property assessments, strong incentives against underassessment— penalizing assessment officers whenever properties assessed by them sell for prices substantially above the assessed value and rewarding assessment officers with "good" records (i.e., whose assessed values turn out to be reasonably close to the actual sales prices of those properties which are sold). Within a framework which stimulates high assessed values, the interests of the property owner can be protected by permitting him to make a bona fide offer of sale and to use as the assessed value in this case a figure 20 per cent below his offer price. Under this procedure, a property owner is never required to be in the position of being *forced* to sell, although he may *voluntarily* place himself in that position if he considers the value put on his property by the assessing officers to be too high. Regardless of which of the two assessment schemes outlined above is adopted, it would be important for assessed values and/or the offer prices placed on their properties by owners to be linked to a price index, so as to avoid the possibility of owners' being required to sell their properties simply because inflation had rendered unrepresentative prices which, when they were initially set, reflected fairly accurately the true market values of the properties in question.

CONCLUSION

I believe that the proposals outlined in this paper would provide the basis for tax systems sufficiently robust to meet the demands of the next decade in most Latin American countries. Where more than 30 per cent of the national income accrues to capital, it should not be excessively difficult to capture 6 per cent of the national income through the special taxation of income from capital. If a serious effort is made to develop a system of progressive excise taxation, it should be possible to capture an additional 6 per cent of the national income as revenue from this source (this could be accomplished, for example, by taxing one group of commodities accounting for 10 per cent of the national income at a rate of 30 per cent, by taxing another group of commodities accounting for 10 per cent of the national income at a rate of 20 per cent, and by taxing a third group of commodities accounting for 10 per cent of the national income at a rate of 10 per cent). In addition to these taxes, it should not be difficult to obtain a yield equal to a further 6 per cent of the national income from the personal income tax. With 6 per cent of the national income being taken in special taxes on the return to capital, and allowing something like 4 per cent of the national income for corporate saving and the return to capital owned by government, we can estimate that some 90 per cent of the national income would accrue as income of persons after the special taxation of return to capital. Two-thirds of this amount could be exempted entirely and the remainder taxed at progressive rates averaging out to 20 per cent, and the yield would still be 6 per cent of the national income. Thus, without resort to excessively high rates of taxation, it should be possible to garner something like 18 per cent of the national income out of the two sets of taxes treated in this paper, plus the personal income tax. Moreover, these components of the tax structure would definitely be progressive. Additional revenue would still be obtainable from import duties, from taxes (as in

Chile) or exchange profits (as in Brazil) on certain export commodities, from social security taxes. And side by side with a genuinely progressive set of taxes such as those discussed above, some resort to broad-based taxes on sales or value added could be had without introducing serious injustices into the total tax structure. In short, the reforms suggested in this paper can contribute substantially to improve the equity of tax structures, to provide for required secular increases in revenue, and to create the possibility for a rapid and equitable response of the tax system to unforeseen contingencies.

Comment

CARLOS MATUS*

GENERAL CRITICISM

First of all, I want to say that there are more points in Mr. Harberger's paper that I disagree with than that I agree with, which makes my task as a critic easy. As a second initial and general observation, I should like to mention that it is evident from Mr. Harberger's paper that he has made an effort to understand the problems of Latin America and that, in so doing, he has abandoned certain traditional and profoundly unrealistic concepts held by some schools of thought in the United States. I am particularly gratified not to find in his work any recommendation for a single tax on imports, regardless of the type of products involved. Nevertheless, the traditional has been set aside only to a relative extent, since his arguments in favor of not discriminating in taxes on income from capital have a pronounced classical flavor and could have unexpected consequences in tax matters.

Mr. Harberger begins by saying that he does not want his work to be potpourri. His paper, however, leads us through a number of topics, some of which are commented upon perhaps too generally and others of which are described in great detail. It seems to me that the work is somewhat uneven and that it lacks a general organic statement as to the characteristics that tax reforms in Latin America should have and the possibilities of accomplishing them simultaneously. The absence of this general framework makes for some confusion and raises a number of questions in the mind of the reader. If Mr. Harberger *separately* analyzes excise taxes and taxes on income from capital as the most essential areas for tax reform, does that mean that a combination of taxes necessarily forms a *tax system?* Why does he not even mention the concept of a *tax system?*

I believe that in this respect the paper has a basic defect, because the only way to avoid having to cover such a number of miscellaneous topics as those included in the broad subject dealt with by Mr. Harberger is to approach it from the standpoint of the basic elements that should characterize the Latin American tax systems. If Mr. Harberger had done this, it would have been possible to integrate the analysis of progressive excise and income from capital taxes, their interrelation with other taxes making up the system, and the way in which the various taxes contribute to the general objectives of the tax system, the planning of development, etc.

Mr. Harberger's initial statements on a "general philosophy" are in this respect completely insufficient. We should not be sur-

*Latin American Institute for Economic and Social Planning, Santiago, Chile.

prised, therefore, that one page of the work is devoted to the treatment of the tax on automobiles in connection with eliminating capital gains for diplomats and only two pages to general statements on the characteristics of a tax reform.

I certainly understand that to prepare the work using the approach that I suggest requires more effort and also more time to allow experiences and ideas to mature. But I also believe that for a seminar this effort is worth while. I cannot deny that Mr. Harberger's paper gives me the impression of having been written in a hurry.

Having made these general remarks, I now go on to comment upon specific aspects of the work and shall end by analyzing the general elements that in my opinion should characterize Latin American tax systems and stating some of my misgivings regarding the subject.

THE VALUE JUDGMENTS MADE IN MR. HARBERGER'S ANALYSIS

The value judgments that make up the basis of the work appear to me to be flimsy. In the first place, the classification of elements is not presented on a single, homogeneous plane. This is the case of the requirement of non-interference with the allocation resources and preventing the tax system from channeling investment toward low-yielding activities. Both are part of the same general problem of resource allocation. The same is true of the requirements of progressivity and of discrimination against income from capital. Both are aspects of the same general objective, which is to redistribute income.

In the second place, it seems to me that some of the statements do not have a sound economic foundation; such is the case with the requirement that pertains to resource allocation and the one involving the level of tax receipts. It seems to me contradictory to propose that the tax system not interfere with the allocation of resources when one of the functions of this system is precisely to change

the resource allocation dictated by market forces to make it conform to that envisaged by development plans. Some economists may disagree with the social criteria for resource allocation set forth in the plans, but this is not an insurmountable technical difficulty that should necessarily lead us to prefer faithful adherence to the market forces. This is especially true in the underdeveloped countries in which the allocation of resources determined by market forces is strongly influenced by a very bad distribution of income, a disorganized market dominated by privileged minorities, heavy unemployment and underemployment of the labor force, inefficient and often interested regulation of certain economic activities, serious balance of payments problems, etc. Within this framework, market forces do not reflect consumer preferences or the social rate of return of investments; they are simply the result of the concentration in a few hands of income, wealth, and power, the inseparable trinity that keeps Latin America stagnant. For these reasons, I cannot agree with the negative tone of the proposal. In my opinion, one of the functions of the tax system is precisely to interfere with the allocation of resources dictated by market forces.

I also reject the proposal regarding the level of tax receipts, to the effect that they should be sufficient to meet expenditures. But I reject it for somewhat sophisticated reasons. I believe that the function of taxes is not to finance public expenditures but to free physical resources that the government may wish to demand, to the extent necessary to preserve stability. I realize that this raises a question of interpretation; and what I want to avoid—and I am sure that Mr. Harberger will agree with me—is to make it appear inadvertently that a tax system is required to collect an amount of revenue equal to that of expenditures; conditions for stability are much more complicated than that.

Finally, it seems to me that the coverage of the paper is incomplete. Among the most important subjects omitted are the elasticity of the tax system, the issues of tempering the internal effects of foreign trade fluctuations and orienting the conduct of the private sector to bring it in line with the objectives and goals of the plan, and the organic tenor that should characterize a tax "system."

Under "Some Issues of General Philosophy," Mr. Harberger expands his thoughts and adds new general ideas on tax reform, with which I agree on the whole. I particularly regret that the second paragraph is so short, because a number of important problems are concealed there. I agree with Mr. Harberger's conclusion that a reasonable amount of advance planning in handling the tax system will contribute toward its stability. I am not sure, however, that my reasons for reaching that conclusion are the same as those of Mr. Harberger. For one thing, his explanation for the trend toward instability in the underdeveloped countries seems to me extraordinarily naïve. Referring only to the budget, let us say that the Latin American tax systems are "automatic destabilizers," since tax revenues are very inflexible and public expenses tend to grow at least at the same rate as income at current prices. In these circumstances, any increase in money income automatically provokes a budget deficit, which cannot be easily made up by changes in the tax rates. To this must be added the fluctuations in foreign trade that may erratically aggravate or lessen such trends. In an estimate that I made for Chile, using the 1940–50 period as base, we came to the conclusion that for each 10 per cent of increase in national income, tax revenues rose only 7.4 per cent and public expenses 11 per cent. The low elasticity of the tax system was a determining factor in the formation of budgetary deficits "induced" by the inflationary process itself. Nevertheless, the elasticity of a tax system depends on the tax structure itself (progressiveness, lag in payments of taxes, system of deductions and minimum exemptions, existence of specific taxes, system of property assessment, etc.) as well as on elements outside the tax system. Unfortunately, on the one hand, the outside elements that affect the elasticity of the system are more important than those inside; on the other hand, they generally represent inevitable changes in the economic structure within the development process. For example, imports of capital goods increase in importance in relation to consumer goods in a development plan, and since capital goods are taxed less, taxes on imports tend to be inelastic, unless imports increase at a sufficiently more rapid rate than income. The same tendency toward inelasticity occurs when variations in the exchange rate lag behind the price level. It is also characteristic for wages to pay lower taxes than profits; hence a growing participation of wages in the national income makes for inelasticity in the system. There are certainly some favorable trends, such as the diminishing participation of agriculture in total income, agriculture being taxed at very low rates, but these favorable factors are weak.

In conclusion, we may say that to organize an elastic tax structure does not necessarily tend to make revenues adequately elastic, since changes in the structure and composition of income are not elements that can be managed for purposes of tax elasticity.

Tax planning is essential. Naturally, that does not mean that tax planning will solve the problem of instability, whose causes are structural. It is a matter, rather, of ensuring that over a long period there will be an adequate accumulation of government savings to finance investment goals. The problem of stability greatly exceeds the possibilities of the tax structure in underdeveloped countries.

THE PROGRESSIVE EXCISE TAX

I am especially sympathetic toward progressive excise taxes and therefore agree that it is important to have them in our tax systems. Nevertheless, I do not believe that this type of tax can serve as a basis for the redistributive action of the tax system, unless it were a general tax on expenditures, accompanied by a very efficient administration free of group interests. To be progressive, excise taxes must be placed on luxury goods and services; but if excise taxes are to serve to redistribute income effectively, those goods and services must also be price-inelastic. We know that high-income groups have the ability, ingenuity, and power to solve such simple problems: they substitute entertainment abroad for domestic entertainment and foreign goods—brought back following such pleasure trips—for domestic goods.

Moreover, the concept of luxury to which the concept of progressiveness is linked depends not only on the type or quality of the goods or service in question but also on the quantity demanded by one individual. The consumption of one kilo of meat a week by a typical family may be necessary consumption, but not 10 kilos. How do we introduce the quantitative concept of luxury into a system of individual excise taxes? This is the advantage of Mr. Kaldor's expenditure tax, from the standpoint of its redistributive effect, because it not only distinguishes between types of goods but also between *levels of consumption*.

In any case, I do not attribute great importance to the redistributive effect of some taxes or even the tax system as a whole. I believe that the tax system is inefficient to bear the principal burden of income redistribution if we also want it to reach other complex objectives. The policy of redistributing income in underdeveloped countries is fundamentally one of redistributing property, a wage policy, a price policy, and a policy of credit and public expenditures.

Mr. Harberger's paper contains one sentence that impressed me: "The benefits of progressive excise taxation in terms of equity, administrative feasibility, and aptness for meeting contingencies are bought at a cost in terms of the distortion of individual choices among commodities." From this, Mr. Harberger concludes that in order to limit these losses, tax rates must not exceed 30 or 40 per cent. This is the most surprising statement in the whole paper, especially since it is one of the first. What is Mr. Harberger's concept of efficient allocation of resources that allows him to state that levying high taxes on luxury

goods and services will unfavorably change the allocation of resources and result in a loss to the economy? In this respect, my opinion is exactly the opposite, since by definition progressive excise taxation tends to discourage superfluous activities and to free resources to produce goods and services for wage earners. Mr. Harberger's mention of substitute goods seems to me totally irrelevant, since an *effective substitute* of a luxury good or service is by definition also a luxury good and should be taxed at the same rate as the thing replaced. If the substitute is ineffective—a night club for a movie theater, for example—I see no reason to look upon a greater investment in movie theaters at the expense of night clubs as a loss to society. In any case, it is a loss greatly resembling a gain in terms of the welfare of the majority of the population.

In one paragraph, Mr Harberger discusses automobiles belonging to diplomats and other international functionaries. Here I must congratulate Mr. Harberger, both for his sense of humor in presenting his proposal before so large a number of interested persons and for the efficacy of his solution. I do not know why, but this paragraph reminds me of the tax inspector who was invited out to dinner and, finding no way in which to please his host, took the occasion to estimate his presumed income on the basis of his standard of living and to present him with the tax bill while coffee was being served.

TAXATION OF INCOME FROM CAPITAL

Mr. Harberger proposes a special taxation of income from capital. This kind of taxation exists in one form or another in almost all the Latin American countries, so that this part of the paper is a rationalization of tax conditions as they exist in the area. There are some important things to point out, however. In the first place, it is evident that Mr. Harberger felt more at home in this subject, since he devoted almost two-thirds of his paper to it. Secondly, there are a number of statements and ideas that require special comment, whether favorable or unfavorable.

In this part, it is once again brought to the reader's attention that Mr. Harberger is averse to the idea of discriminatory taxation by sectors on grounds of an efficient allocation of resources. It seems that this is a principle to which the author is strongly attached. In this part, however, it is evident that his convictions lead him to the point where his recommendations are obviously incompatible with the common sense drawn from reality. The entire analysis is far removed from reality and excessively academic, although oversimplified and occasionally contradictory.

Mr. Harberger starts by saying that even in the most poorly organized markets there is a strong tendency toward the equalization of the net (after tax) rates of return on capital in different activities. The first thing that is surprising here is the phrase "after tax," since if we are talking about a tax on income from capital that does not discriminate between activities, the relative return before or after taxes will be the same. Or is it that rates of return tend to become equal precisely through tax discrimination? The phrase is confusing, and I must confess that I do not fully understand its scope. With reference to the tendency toward equalization of rates of return, it seems to me that this will require perfect competition, or something like it, if such equalization is to be achieved. Of course, an investor prefers a return of 20 per cent to one of 10 per cent, if it is in his power to get it. The choice to which Mr. Harberger refers is more commonly made, I believe, in determining the characteristics of a single project rather than of deciding between alternative projects; at least, this is the case in our countries. I do not think that this tendency to equalize rates of return exists at every stage of the development process, at least to any significant degree. From this tendency, Mr. Harberger deduces some normative principles. The whole analysis seems weak to me, however, since it rests on the concept of the "market rate of return."

At one point, the following statement is made: "Concentration of new allocations of capital in the high-return sector would accordingly tend to enhance the rate of economic growth. And such concentration is the natural consequence of the preference of investment decision makers for high rates of return." It seems to me that the experts in economic development will find it difficult to accept this statement. It is not necessary to point out once again that there is no reason for a high rate of commercial return to coincide—and it usually does not coincide in our countries—with high social returns. Of course, we could increase the national product by cutting down on shoe production and establishing more roulette and gambling casinos, since the return on capital, measured in commercial profits, is greater in the latter activity. But who would dare call such a change economic development? The only thing it shows is that the concept of national product is inadequate to measure the changes in the development or growth of a country. Frankly, for reasons that I have already mentioned, I have no respect for market forces as determinants of the allocation of resources, whereas Mr. Harberger's entire study of taxation of income from capital indicates that he himself has an excessive respect for them. We can thus understand his saying, "Desirable results in terms of economic efficiency and economic growth are produced when there is a tendency to equalize gross-of-tax rates of return, while the natural operation of market forces tends to equalize net-of-tax rates of return."

His next paragraph begins with an encouraging sentence, in which Mr. Harberger recognizes the idealized treatment he has given the subject and the pronounced imperfections of the market. Nevertheless, the whole paragraph is confusing, since Mr. Harberger does not define his concept of gross-of-tax rate of return. At the beginning, it seems that Mr. Harberger was going to amend his previous statements in the light of market imperfections. This notion is dispelled, however, upon reading the following: "Accordingly, in this paragraph, I discuss the policies which would be desirable for the achievement of the objectives of efficiency and growth in the presence of substantial capital market imperfections. These objectives clearly demand the concentration of new investment in areas with a high (gross-of-tax) rate of return. . . . This could be achieved by taxing the income from capital more heavily in sectors and areas with low rates of return and less heavily in sectors and areas with high rates of return." Mr. Harberger complains that this is not actually done, since agriculture is taxed at lower rates than industry. Carrying the matter to an extreme and applying Mr. Harberger's criteria, Chile would have to levy lower taxes on its copper industry and higher ones on agriculture and national industry. Fortunately, Latin American governments do not listen to economists! Mr. Harberger's normative principle means that for the sake of resource allocation according to market forces, we must negatively redistribute income under circumstances where it is precisely the very bad distribution of income that entirely invalidates the allocation according to market forces. Ironies of orthodoxy!

In any case, it is hard for me to understand the meaning of the discrimination proposed by the author, because if there is a difference in the rates of return between agriculture and industry, according to Mr. Harberger the discrepancy would tend to disappear naturally, since "even in poorly organized capital markets, there exists a strong tendency toward . . . equalization." These are his own words.

In summary, the only thing upon which I can agree with Mr. Harberger is that, for reasons of equity, income from capital must be taxed at higher rates than income from labor. I do doubt whether this value judgment accepted by Mr. Harberger is consistent with his own analysis of the market forces.

Mr. Harberger also deals with specific aspects of taxation of income from capital. Generally, I agree with his statements and do not care to comment upon them so as not to get too involved in details. There is, however, one point that should be discussed, since it has been proposed by many economists for some time. This has to do with making realistic assessments of real property. Here there seems to be a tendency to look for ingenious, apparently simple solutions, but solutions that are not very practical. The idea is suggested—and Mr. Harberger supports it—that the property owner declare the commercial value of his own property for tax purposes and be required to sell it to any bidder who is willing to pay 20 per cent more than its declared value. Fearing that he might otherwise have to sell it, the owner would be forced to set an evaluation on his property that was more in keeping with the market price.

Mr. Harberger recognizes that lawyers are not sympathetic to the idea. It is true that the legal mind is ill equipped for analyzing economic problems, but in this case I think the lawyers are right.

In the first place, I do not believe that anyone can be compelled to sell his property *to another individual,* even when his price is reasonable. The government has the right to expropriate for the benefit of the community, but the individual cannot have the right to expropriate for his own benefit. If anyone is interested in making a purchase against the will of the owner, it must be because he is gaining some advantage.

In the second place, the commercial value of a piece of property need not coincide with its value to the owner. Family memories and other intangible values that a property may possess have no market price, and no one should be compelled to pay taxes on them.

In the third place, the system lends itself to many abuses, especially in the case of agricultural property, by making purchase bids when long-run investments are beginning to bear fruit.

Fourth, the owner would feel insecure in his farming activity, since he would be exposed to the whim of any neighbor who wanted to purchase the land.

In the fifth and last place, under the system proposed, if the property owner cheats the government through a low assessment this benefits, not the community, but some other owner.

I believe that there are more efficient methods for correctly assessing property, which are also less costly in terms of equity.

The alternative system proposed by Mr. Harberger—that is, of rewarding assessment officers whose assessments approximate actual sales prices, and vice versa—is not practical either, since an assessment cannot be made by just one official but requires a committee, and generally the owner affected has several resources for appeal. In the final analysis, it is a court of appeals that fixes an assessment, and it would be absurd to reward or punish a court financially.

It seems much more simple to correct assessments by means of sale prices, if these are accurately known. (Sale prices are consistently falsified in real estate deeds as a means of evading the tax on property transfer.)

I do not believe that direct and realistic assessments should not be sought. In any case, what is important is for the tax system to operate as a whole, in the sense that a taxpayer evading a property tax will have to pay an excessive tax on something else.

THE REQUIREMENTS OF A TAX REFORM

To give some cohesiveness to these comments, I should like to close by summarizing my own viewpoints on the requirements that should be met by tax reform in our countries. These requirements have to do with both techniques and tax administration and are as follows. (a) Tax reform must contribute toward the redistribution of income; (b) it must have a reasonable revenue elasticity; (c) it must contribute toward mitigating internal repercussions resulting from fluctuations in exports; (d) it must maximize the restrictive effect on demand for each peso collected and be capable of curtailing demand to the degree desired (this implies fulfillment of the fiscal objectives with the least tax pressure); (e) it must orient private behavior toward the objectives and goals of development plans; and (f) it must organize a technically and administratively organic system.

Now I shall briefly discuss each of these requirements.

a) *Contribution of the Tax System toward Redistribution of Income.* I have already said that I have little confidence that the tax system can attain such a great number of objectives simultaneously and harmoniously. For that reason, I believe that, generally speaking, the tax system in underdeveloped countries tends to be ineffective for redistributing income and that decided recourse should be had to policies of direct redistribution of property, of elimination of monopolistic power, of measures improving wages, prices, and profit-sharing for workers.

In any case, the tax system can contribute to the redistribution of income through progressive excise taxes and taxes on income and property, proper handling of customs duties, and taxes on inheritance and on property transfer in general. I believe that the over-all tax system, together with the policies already mentioned, can make a positive contribution to the redistribution of income, but I do not believe that the burden of redistribution can be basically fiscal nor much less that it can rest on a few taxes.

b) *Adequate Revenue Elasticity of the Tax System.* The tax system should be rid of all elements that contribute to its rigidity. Nevertheless, we should be prepared to make advance plans for changes in the system that will become necessary as income grows and changes in structure, since, for the reasons given at the beginning of this commentary, it is probable that those changes, which are normal in development, tend to cause taxes to increase more slowly than national income.

c) *Contribution of the Tax System toward Mitigating the Fluctuations of Foreign Trade.* This aspect has been greatly neglected in the Latin American tax systems, wherein a defeatist attitude has prevailed with respect to the inevitability of foreign trade fluctuations. Personally, I think that taxes can play a role in moderating these fluctuations, in connection with the capacity of the Latin American countries to import. For example, those countries whose sources of export are in the hands

of foreign firms can unload part of the fluctuations on the profits that those firms send
abroad. The use of average prices and volumes of production over a certain number of
years to determine taxable profits of foreign
exporting firms could substantially help to
stabilize the capacity to import of some Latin
American countries.

d) *To Maximize the Restrictive Effect on
Demand per Peso of Tax Collected.* It is well
known that the different taxes making up a
tax system have differing restrictive effects.
Thus, for example, a peso of taxes levied on
the profits of national firms reduces private
consumption less than a peso of taxes on personal income. A tax on luxury imports may
even tend to increase the private consumption
of national products, etc.

Therefore, within certain restrictions of tax
structure, in order to attain other objectives
such as redistribution of income, providing
incentives, etc., the minimum tax level that
will produce the desired restriction on demand
can be determined. The tax burden and the
social cost of fulfilling the objectives of the
plan are thus minimized.

e) *Orientation of Private Behavior toward
the Objectives of the Plan.* The tax system
must help to change normal private behavior
to make it coincide with that stipulated in the
plan. Here we fall headlong into the complex
problem of incentives. I want to be frank by
saying that I do not have much faith, either,
in the effectiveness of the tax instrument in
reaching these objectives conscientiously. The
complications in the administration of incentives are very great, and the effects of these
incentives tend to be minor in the underdeveloped countries, where tax rates are low.
I refer fundamentally to incentives to firms,
since incentives to change decisions of consumers with respect to the structure of consumption do not present major difficulties.

Let us take an example: the investment
made by firms. Let us suppose that we want
to encourage investment in certain activities
and that we establish a mechanism whereby
firms can add to their costs x per cent of the
increase in investment from one year to the

next. The first difficulty for the tax administration consists in appropriately defining investment so as not to encourage investments
in luxury activities and to verify that those
investments are made. But additional complications arise immediately if we want to handle
incentives conscientiously. Why give that
benefit to industries that do not fully use their
productive capacity? It is evident that we
should deny them the benefit, since otherwise
we would be encouraging the underutilization
of productive capacity. Therefore, the administration must define the concept of underutilization, measure it, and verify it, in order
to administer the incentives.

In summary, I believe that in these aspects
credit policy should play a more important
role than it has up to now, in order to alleviate somewhat the many responsibilities of the
tax system. In any case, the over-all tax system must indicate clearly what action is expected from the private sector and what objectives are sought with that action.

f) *The System Should Be Organic from the
Technical and Administrative Standpoint.*
This, I believe, is the primary condition of a
real tax reform. The tax system cannot be an
aggregate of miscellaneous taxes, in which the
objectives of some taxes are canceled out by
the effects of others and in which the administration of one tax is totally independent of
the rest. All taxes must be consistent in their
economic effects, and their administration
must be self-reinforcing, in order to make tax
fraud more difficult.

It has always seemed to me that the tax
report on India by Mr. Kaldor is one of the
greatest contributions to an understanding of
what a "tax system" is. I know that his proposals have met with difficulties in India and
Ceylon, but I think that the germ of the idea
will flourish when the technical level of tax administration is improved and certain changes
in the political structure take place.

For my part, I only want to present a few
ideas for the transition stage, to give the Latin
American tax mechanisms some semblance of
organic structure, without entering into the

complexities of a refined mechanism of self-control.

Unfortunately for the taxpayers, the great majority of the taxes of a system are interdependent. For example, the revenue from the personal income tax depends on the yield of real estate tax, since the latter may be deducte d in calculating taxable income; social security payments affect the yield of the tax on profits; taxation of distributed profits affects the income tax, etc. For the economy as a whole, we could establish an interdependence matrix of taxes that would be very useful for estimating the effect of changes in tax rates. We could also establish such a matrix for the individual taxpayer as a means of verifying the accuracy of his declarations and checking on any discrepancies.

One example may clarify the problem. When employers have to declare and pay social security contributions, they tend to understate the payroll in order to reduce the tax thereon; on the other hand, in making their declaration for purposes of taxes on profits they try to overstate their costs. These are contradictory tendencies. If presentation of a receipt for social security contributions were required, this would be sufficient to eliminate one source of evasion. Tax systems are frequently plagued with these contradictions. A solution of this type could be found to the problem of assessing real property through a suitable capital gains tax, which could serve as a basis for adjusting assessments back for a reasonable number of years. Naturally, the smart taxpayer will always find that it is more advantageous to him to concentrate his fraud in one kind of tax, even if this means that his other taxes will be higher, since his over-all tax liability will thereby be reduced. But also an intelligent tax administration can organize matters in such a way as to concentrate administrative control on those taxes that offer the highest rewards in terms of fraud. It is essentially like a problem in game theory.

Discussion

Mr. Harberger said that the first part of his paper could be summed up in five main points.

1. Latin American countries require strong tax increases because the development programs they are undertaking demand heavy fiscal expenditures.

2. Latin American countries should have the means to face unforeseen contingencies, such as the fluctuation of government revenues due to changes in the international prices of export products, and such as sudden rises in wages and salaries.

3. However important reducing evasion might be, it would not produce all the funds required by those countries in the next decade.

4. To obtain a fair distribution of the tax burden, it would be necessary to have recourse to several taxes. Although the income tax can be much improved, there will remain different possibilities of evasion for different community groups, and it will be necessary to have recourse to other taxes in order to strengthen the progressive effect of income tax.

5. One way of achieving greater progressivity in the over-all tax system was to apply taxes to groups of luxury or semiluxury goods. In Latin America, a start had been made in that direction through import duties, but as the countries now tend to produce such goods themselves, thought would have to be given to taxing them, even when they were locally manufactured. In this connection, and as a matter of secondary importance, he mentioned the possibilities of augmenting fiscal revenue by the modifica-

tion of diplomatic privileges for automobile imports.

Mr. Harberger next referred to taxes on income from capital, which he felt should not be applied solely to corporation profits but should be extended to income from capital in unincorporated enterprises, interest, agricultural activities, and income derived from urban property, without prejudice to applying the personal income tax concurrently. The difficulties in taxing unincorporated enterprises could be solved by means of schedular taxes such as those already existing in many Latin American countries. The taxing of interest paid to banks and other financial intermediaries would not be very difficult because these institutions use efficient accounting methods and are not in a position to evade taxes. In taxing urban and rural property, recourse might be had to a system of self-assessment, whereby the owners would be obliged to sell to anyone ready to pay, for instance, 20 per cent above the value declared.

Mr. Ross read the comments made by Mr. Matus.

Mr. Urquidi said that many of the points made by Mr. Harberger were excellent, especially with reference to the need for planning taxes to meet contingencies. However, he disagreed with the restriction on consumption of domestically produced luxury goods, since it might have adverse effects on employment and industrial activity, and consequently on fiscal revenue.

In his view, Mr. Harberger's reference to duty-free imports of automobiles by diplomatic missions was hardly correct, as the yield obtained from a tax on such transactions would not justify the difficulties that would arise.

With regard to taxation of income from capital, he believed that the idea of levying property taxes should be more generally adopted; that was no novelty in Latin America, since they were in use in a number of countries in the region.

Referring to the suggestion made by Mr. Harberger of instituting the compulsory sale of property when the owner received an offer of purchase at a certain percentage above the value of his assessment, he believed it would not be feasible. There were other means of establishing gradually a system of honest assessment which were far more practicable than the method proposed by Mr. Harberger. For example, in Mexico, assessment by a bank, duly certified by a notary public, was required.

Mr. Prest referred to Mr. Harberger's comments on progressive excise taxes. With respect to substitution effects, he wished to draw attention to the possibility of such an effect in relation to the demand for leisure, or the supply of work. Secondly, he said that on the basis of twenty years' experience of progressive excise taxes in the United Kingdom, they could not be regarded as very successful; it was difficult to ensure that comparable goods were taxed at comparable rates, and rates were now being consolidated in order to avoid irrational discrimination. Last, European experience with a common market had shown that the different structures of progressive excise taxes in different countries led to problems in establishing a common market; such problems were not insoluble, but they should be given careful consideration before establishing such taxes if they did not already exist.

Mrs. de Navarrete, referring specifically to the tax on income from capital, reminded the meeting that it already existed in many countries, including Mexico. After explaining in detail how the tax operated in that country and pointing out that its rapidly progressive rates climbed to as much as 40 per cent, she said she was not in favor of *ad rem* taxation. What was urgently necessary, in her view, was a personal and progressive tax on capital. If applied to agriculture, the tax proposed by Mr. Harberger would have a discouraging effect, inasmuch as it would hinder capital formation. The author of the panel paper, in estimating the probable income from the taxes he suggested, had not taken into account evasion in respect of capital as a factor reducing the tax base. On the other points raised in the panel paper, she supported Mr. Harberger's views.

MR. NAHARRO said he was in general agreement with Mr. Harberger's excellent paper, and endorsed the proposal respecting a tax on capital, however difficult it might be to apply. However, he asked Mr. Harberger to make clear his solution to the problems arising in connection with taxation of interest received as profits by banks which were already taxed when paid by the borrower. Similar cases might arise in connection with other financial intermediaries, subsidiary companies in relation to the head office, investment trusts, etc. While those problems of double taxation were not insoluble, they were complicated, and Mr. Harberger's comments on that point were most useful.

MR. HART referred to the question of whether corporations should be subject to a tax on income from capital at the same rate as unincorporated companies. Although a tax on the net activity of a corporation corresponded to the concept of a tax on capital income, the same was not true for unincorporated companies, where to some extent the profit represented the remuneration of the entrepreneur's labor, the labor element being proportionately larger in the smaller companies. He referred to experience in Chile in relation to the possibility of taxing the two categories of enterprise at different rates. Moreover, it was difficult to establish a net income consisting of interest if the current inflation rate was higher than the nominal interest rate.

MR. RIOFRÍO thought that all the papers presented to the conference were of high quality, though he disagreed with them on a few points. What caused him most concern with regard to the work of experts was the lack of continuity and even the incompatibility of their ideas, since the outcome might be bewilderment and misgivings among those who were anxious to follow their advice. To support his contention, he cited several cases that had arisen in Ecuador.

With regard to the tax on income from capital, in his opinion, income, by its very nature, was always net, and he would be loath to tax gross income. He also saw difficulties in connection with the multiplicity of taxes on the same source and the problem of determining where progressiveness in indirect taxation began. He thought the best thing was to avoid every kind of discrimination by establishing a global tax on capital and a further supplementary tax which might play some part in the redistributive function proper to fiscal policy. He asked Mr. Harberger what level of progessivity he would recommend for the taxes on consumption suggested in his paper.

MR. DESCARTES, referring to the assessment of agricultural and residential properties, said that he viewed with some misgiving a system of assessment or collection which appeared to be oversimplified. He felt that assessment of property raised numerous problems and hoped that they would be discussed in connection with the taxation of agriculture.

MR. GNAZZO took it that what Mr. Harberger meant by a tax on corporate profits was a tax on the capital profits of an enterprise. He wondered whether a distinction could be made between the profits of an enterprise and those of a shareholder. Some enterprises were owned by a single shareholder. He would therefore ask Mr. Harberger whether it might be better to consider corporate profits as the capital profits of shareholders and to tax them at the time the profits were distributed.

MR. DARDÓN, referring to the question of the assessment of property for tax purposes, agreed with Mr. Harberger's proposal of self-assessment based on the declaration of the property owner. The question of a statutory provision, however, required further discussion. The solution must necessarily vary from country to country.

MR. COSCIANI believed that the organic, progressive tax on consumption proposed by Mr. Harberger had several disadvantages. One of them was that, as the propensity to consume was less in the groups with higher income from capital, the rate formally applicable to the tax would not correspond to the rate actually charged. An ordinary tax on net wealth seemed to him to be preferable and simpler.

MR. NÚÑEZ referred to Mr. Harberger's position that income from capital should be taxed at a higher rate than income from labor. He understood a capital profits tax to mean a progressive personal tax on capital profits. Such a tax would be easier to collect than a tax on wealth, particularly if based on a progressive rate. There would be some advantage to combining the progressive tax on capital profits with the income tax.

Mr. Harberger's proposed method of assessing property was interesting, and he had recommended its adoption in Panama. However, the Panamanian government had preferred to tax property on the basis of the size of the holdings.

MR. GOODE supported the idea that there should be an effort to increase substantially the taxes paid in most Latin American countries on urban residential property, as well as on agricultural land. Referring to Mr. Harberger's paper, he said that he distrusted the proposal that property should be assessed on the basis of a simple assessment of the value of his property by the owner himself. Moreover, the idea of obliging the owner to sell his property if offered 20 per cent above that assessed value would introduce the constitutional problem of forced sale. In addition, it might leave room for corruption, or for sharp practice on the part of those who had easy access to information about, for example, the building of a road that would lead to an increase in the value of certain properties. Again, there might be no likely buyers for a property that was unusually large or valuable, or at least none outside the social circle in which the owner moved, where social restraints would operate to prevent an attempt to force a sale, whereas there would be a much larger market for small properties.

With respect to the adjustment of established values, he doubted very much whether a general price index would be appropriate for the purpose, especially for agricultural property, in view of the instability of agri-cultural prices. He sympathized with Mr. Harberger's aim, but could not agree with his views about achieving that aim. Property valuation was a technical problem that the Latin American countries would have to deal with by getting technical assistance and advice from the various public and private agencies that specialized in that field. It would be a lengthy and costly task, but it was urgent and important, and the only true solution of the problem of getting a correct assessment of taxes on property.

MR. KALDOR suggested an amendment to Mr. Harberger's proposal regarding self-assessment of property values by the owner, which might meet some of Mr. Goode's objections. The scheme might be more acceptable if the owner always had the option of retaining his property if he revalued it above the offer made; for example, if an offer was made to buy the property at the owner's valuation plus 20 per cent, the owner could retain it if he raised his valuation by 25 per cent. That would lead to a correct valuation on the basis of a kind of auction, without involving forced sales. Mr. Harberger's original proposal might lead to certain difficulties; for example, an owner who was particularly attached to his property might overvalue it through fear of losing it, which would lead to resentment against the system.

As for Mr. Goode's suggestion about the difficulty of finding buyers for large properties, it was quite likely that a syndicate could be found as a buyer if there was the chance of a large profit. If no one came forward, that would mean that the market value of the property was in fact lower than the valuation plus 20 per cent, and that the valuation was approximately correct. The question of self-assessment had been discussed in public finance circles in the United Kingdom for the past fifty years, and the view had long been held that expert valuation was to be preferred; but that view was now changing. However good the expert advice, there would be strong pressure for undervaluation unless the tax administration was entirely free of corruption. No country had found an ideal method of adjusting assessed values. In Latin America, assessed values represented less than 1 per cent of current market values; but even in highly developed countries the situation was not satisfactory. In the United Kingdom, assessed values represented about 10 to 30 per cent of market values; and in the United States, where there was no shortage of experts, assessed values in some states were entirely out of line with current values. Whatever expert system was used, values would be out of date within a few years; but if Mr. Harberger's system, amended as suggested, were adopted, assessed values would continue to rise as inflation or other factors led to a continued rise in market values.

MR. HARBERGER, replying to the comments made on his paper, did not think there was any great discrepancy between Mr. Matus' views and his own, since both were in favor of recommending a progressive tax on consumption and felt that capital should be taxed more heavily than labor. The difference in their views would appear to stem rather from their basic outlook, since Mr. Matus had little use for market forces, while he himself had somewhat more respect for them; hence his favorable attitude toward an equal rate of tax on all income derived from capital, whatever its origin, although he admitted the possibility of levying higher taxes on the less productive sectors in order to channel capital toward uses with higher productivity.

In view of the lack of flexibility of current tax systems, and so long as it subsisted, recourse should be had to establishing new taxes or increasing existing ones. Improved administration by itself would not be adequate to solve Latin America's fiscal problems.

As to whether the budget should be balanced or not, he was inclined to say no, provided the size of the deficit—which depended on a number of circumstances—was not unduly large, as unfortunately was the case in many Latin American countries.

With regard to Mr. Urquidi's observations, he recognized that every tax had inherent in

it a possible unemployment effect, but efforts should be made to ensure that the tax system as a whole was designed to produce the desired yield from taxes with the least possible unemployment. The tax on income from capital outlined in his paper was intended to be double taxation, as in the case of corporations. Regarding assessments, he recognized likewise that it was difficult to reach a consensus on the subject; however, it was extremely important to obtain a system of assessment which ensured that assessments were reasonably in line with the real value of the property. With respect to cars owned by diplomats, he insisted that the loss of revenue could not be regarded as inconsiderable, recognizing that the capital gains now derived therefrom by private parties could be captured by the fiscal authorities. Moreover, the question of principle involved should be looked into. That remark was also valid for the observations made by Mr. Descartes and Mr. Dardón.

While it was true that the progressive tax could discourage the desire to work, as Mr. Prest had pointed out, he did not feel there was cause for concern, provided the rates were moderate. The progressive indirect tax system that he personally recommended for Latin American countries was based on his belief that substantial increases in revenue would be required during the next decade. With regard to the attempt being made to establish a common market and its influence on the tax system, he believed that tax rates on the same goods in any country should be the same, regardless of whether the goods were produced in that country or by one of its common market partners.

Concerning Mrs. de Navarrete's views, he believed that systematizing of taxes on income from capital was desirable. It was true that he had not taken tax evasion into account in the rough calculations made in his paper, since these figures were meant solely to illustrate possible orders of magnitude.

It was not easy to reply to the doubts voiced by Mr. Naharro. While he would like to think about them at greater length and recognized that they still needed an answer, he could say at once that he did not feel it was wrong to levy taxes on the interest obtained by banks in addition to their own income from capital, since under his proposal a bank would merely act as tax collector for the taxes due to the government on the interest paid by that bank's clients.

Mr. Hart's observation was not without some foundation. However, if it were possible to tax income from capital in the case of small firms at lower rates than larger enterprises, the unfavorable effects of the proposed tax would not be so great.

Although he agreed that Mr. Riofrío's scruples were laudable, the aim he had in mind in proposing in his paper that gross income should be taxed was precisely double taxation. To establish progressivity in taxes on consumption, he would recommend that surveys of families be made for different income levels in order to classify goods into different groups according to their income elasticities. Depending on the degree to which they were luxury goods, they would be taxed at varying rates: 30, 20, or 10 per cent.

When Mr. Gnazzo made a distinction between corporation income and the income accruing to their shareholders, he was possibly thinking of a single income tax and not of double taxation of the type proposed in Mr. Harberger's paper.

He agreed with Mr. Cosciani that the propensity to consume declined proportionately with the rise in capital income, but that would not prevent the establishment of a truly progressive system of indirect taxes as he himself had proposed. Moreover, the system he proposed could quite easily be supplemented by the net wealth tax.

Reverting to the system of self-assessment, he insisted that despite all its drawbacks it was fairer than the system based on area only, as mentioned by Mr. Núñez.

In the reply to Mr. Goode and Mr. Kaldor, he feared that if owners were allowed to retain properties on which a bid had been made, simply by paying a penalty, the system of self-assessment would be much weaker than under the method he had proposed. But provided the penalties in question were high enough to be effective deterrents to those who would like to understate the values of their properties, he would have no objection to make, since in that case they would not affect the substance of his suggestion.

5

Public Expenditures
and Economic Development

by *John H. Adler**

NEED FOR A RATIONAL
EXPENDITURE POLICY

The analyses of and proposals for the improvement of the fiscal policies of the Latin American countries tend to focus primarily on public revenue policies, particularly on problems of taxation. This is as it should be; but the preoccupation with taxes should not make us forget that rational public expenditure policies are also of great importance.

They are important for a variety of reasons. First, at the risk of saying the obvious, one must start with the simple proposition that taxes are justified by the expenditures they finance. A fiscal policy which does not pay enough attention to the public expenditure side is inadequate and incomplete. This is particularly true in the case of developing countries, because government expenditures play an important role in the development process. The resources in the hands of the government are limited, and the need for government expenditures to promote and stimulate economic development is great. Thus, a

careful scrutiny of the composition of public expenditures is essential.

Second, there is undoubtedly a close connection between the effective use of government funds and the willingness to pay taxes. In many Latin American countries, the vociferous resistance of the public to tax increases is based in part on charges of inefficiency and wastefulness of public expenditures. Incompetence and graft are also advanced as arguments against an increase in the scope of government operations. The low level of compliance with tax laws likewise is frequently blamed on the deficiencies in public spending policies, the argument being that the taxpayers feel justified in their practices of evasion because "their" money, if paid to the government, would only be wasted.

It would clearly be wrong to assert that the unwillingness to pay taxes, the opposition to an expansion of government activities, and tax evasion were due entirely to faulty expenditure policies and deficiencies in public administration. But there is some connection between these factors. The inefficiency of the public administration and the wastefulness of public expenditures make the public more willing to condone tax evasion and more readily persuaded that the level of public revenue and expenditure should be kept low.

Third, the pattern of public expenditures must be taken into account to determine the

*I wish to acknowledge the valuable help of Messrs. Marinus van der Mel and Sylvain Plasschaert of the Economic Staff of the International Bank for Reconstruction and Development, who prepared and selected much of the material on which the paper is based. But neither they nor the bank is to be held responsible for the content of the paper and the points of view expressed in it.

Mr. Adler is Director, Economic Development Institute, International Bank for Reconstruction and Development, Washington, D.C.

135

appropriateness of the revenue structure. The system of government revenue and expenditure may be viewed as two phases of a scheme redistributing income among the various sectors and income groups of the economy. The public revenue takes resources away from the taxpayers or, more exactly, those units of the economy on whom the burden of taxation comes to rest after a complex shifting process. The benefits of public expenditure, on the other hand, accrue to various sectors and income groups, mainly in kind, in the form of services provided free of charge, but in some instances also in the form of money receipts (doles, subsidies, etc.). It is the differences between the value of benefits accruing to particular income groups or sectors and the burden which the tax structure imposes on them which bring about a redistribution of income.

As a result of political and social forces, this redistribution will in general result in an increase in the income of the lower-income groups and a decrease of the income of higher-income groups. This is bound to be the case, even if one assumes that the benefits of certain government expenditures—such as the benefits of expenditures on defense and of expenditures for the protection of private property—accrue to the individual members of the economy proportionately to their income, for there are many categories of expenditures which inevitably bring larger benefits to the members of the lower-income groups than to the members of high income brackets. They include such expenditures as those for orphan homes and relief expenditures in general; but expenditures on education (which the members of the lowest-income group presumably could not afford), hospitals, health services, etc., fall also in this category.[1]

The redistributive effects of public expenditure are important because within certain institutional limits the authorities have a choice as to the extent to which they want to rely on the revenue structure, on the one hand, and on the expenditure structure, on the other, to bring about that degree of redistribution of income which is considered politically and socially desirable. It is conceivable (though admittedly unlikely) that a government derives its revenues from a tax structure which imposes a burden proportionate to income and combines this inequitable method of taxation with a pattern of expenditures which provides large sums for the services from which the lower-income groups benefit more than the members of the higher-income brackets, thus bringing about a more equitable distribution of income.

It is, of course, impossible to decide in general terms what constitutes the "right" degree of redistribution and to what extent government should rely on the revenue structure and on the expenditure structure, respectively, to bring it about.[2] But several relevant comments can be made. The first is the presumption (or hypothesis?) that the need—on social and political grounds—for redistribution varies inversely with the rate of economic growth. In other words, it seems plausible to argue that an "initial" degree of income inequality is tolerable as long as the

[1]Exceptions to the general proposition that the fiscal structure will bring about a (somewhat) more equal income distribution are, of course, possible and under certain conditions even likely. For example, when social security benefits are provided to only a small group of the population (as is the case in some Latin American countries), income redistribution due to state subsidies may work the wrong way. The International Labour Organisation has commented on this as follows: "If the development of social security slows down and is restricted for a long period to those classes of workers that are easiest to enroll and have the highest wage levels, this may lead to the paradoxical situation that the state is in effect subsidizing social coverage for classes of workers who are privileged by definition, at a time when its resources will not suffice to give a reasonable minimum standard of protection to the classes that are most in need of it." (United Nations, International Labour Organisation, "Gradual Extension of Social Security Schemes in Latin American Countries," *International Labour Review* [Geneva: September, 1958], p. 23). Another type of exception, this time on the revenue side, is the possible effect of a system of schedular income taxes common in Latin America. Taxes of this type do not have a clear "vertical" redistribution effect. Because of rate structures, gaps in the taxable income basis, and differential tax evasion possibilities in the various social or professional groups, some sort of "horizontal" redistribution among those groups may result.

[2]One factor which complicates the issues is that the credit system also brings about a redistribution in the command over resources. The redistributive effect of the credit system is here intentionally disregarded.

members of the lower-income groups have the feeling that their level of living is perceptibly increasing. Conversely, the pressures for redistribution are likely to be high in an economy which is stagnating, or appears to stagnate, because economic growth is so slow as to be hardly felt. It is, of course, impossible to say even within wide margins what a "perceptible" rate of income growth is or what degree of income inequality will be tolerated at what rate of income growth. But the experience of the Latin American countries in the postwar period seems to confirm the general proposition that continued income inequality is tolerable in a period of high economic growth. The experience of Mexico for most of the postwar period and also of Brazil prior to 1957–58 may be interpreted to suggest that a growth in per capita income of 2.5 per cent per year (or even 2 per cent per year), which doubles income in twenty-eight years, or within one generation, and is more or less evenly distributed among all income groups would constitute a "perceptible" growth rate and would permit a continuation of the existing degree of income inequality.

There is, however, need for reliance on the fiscal structure to bring about a correction of the income distribution if income growth is heavily concentrated. In the case of Mexico, for example, the share of the lowest two deciles of the population declined between 1950 and 1957 from 6.1 per cent of total personal income to 4.4 per cent.[3] Under such conditions, political and social pressures may result from the deterioration of the relative standing of an income group, even if per capita income increases.[4] This is the more important because inequality by income groups is made worse by growing regional disparities (e.g., the Northeast of Brazil com-

pared with the industrial areas of Rio and São Paolo, the South Pacific area of Mexico against the Federal District and the North Pacific region) or ethnic-cultural cleavages (the Peruvian highlands against the high-growth central areas).

With a lower rate of economic growth and, *a fortiori,* with stagnating per capita income, the redistributive effects of the fiscal system become increasingly important. It is in this case that the choice between the revenue structure and the expenditure structure as the mechanism for redistribution becomes particularly relevant. The reason for this is obvious: an increase in the rate of economic growth may call, *inter alia,* for a revenue structure permitting a high rate of private capital formation, and this in turn would seem to make it necessary to limit the tax burden imposed on the income of the well-to-do entrepreneurial class (which presumably is responsible for the bulk of private savings). In a situation like this, it appears essential to limit the progressiveness of the tax structure and to supplement its redistributive effects by a pattern of expenditures which brings greater benefits to the lower-income groups than to the higher.[5] This means that social expenditures, and particularly expenditures for education (which, as is pointed out below, also have important development effects aside from the redistribution effects emphasized here), acquire a high priority rating.

FORMULATING EXPENDITURE POLICIES

Public expenditure policy, in its quantitative and qualitative aspects, is reflected and recorded in the government's budget. Therefore, any systematic discussion of public ex-

[3] Ifigenia de Navarrete, *La distribución del ingreso y el desarrollo económico de México* (México: Escuela Nacional de Economía, 1960), p. 95.

[4] Cf. J. W. Elder, "Land Consolidation in Uttar Pradesh," *Economic Development and Cultural Change* (October, 1962), pp. 36–37. Members of the lower-income groups objected to consolidation measures because their relative position deteriorated, although their situation improved in absolute terms.

[5] This does not imply that moderate tax rates on high-income groups *assure* a high rate of capital formation. In most instances, it may be preferable to grant tax concessions on invested income only, rather than "spare" entrepreneurial income as a whole. But such a system of tax exemptions and incentives, if effective, also reduces the tax burden on the well-to-do.

penditures must start with an account of the process of budget preparation. When speaking about "the budget," most people, including politicians, mean the administrative or "conventional" budget. In this budget, expenditures are classified according to the administrative units, such as departments responsible for the implementation of the activities for which public funds are appropriated. In countries with a democratic form of government, the administrative budget is an essential instrument to delineate the spheres of influence of the executive and legislative branches of government. The appropriation process enables the legislature to set the level and determine the composition of governmental outlays. The appropriation procedure, together with the activities of special control organs, such as the court of accounts, provides the framework within which the legislature assures that the appropriated sums are expended "legally," i.e., within the limits and for the objectives prescribed in the budget.

The administrative budget, geared primarily to this particular political and legal control function, performs a useful role and indeed an indispensable one. It is not sufficient, however, to assure the co-ordination of public sector operations with the development efforts of the economy as a whole, whether these efforts take place within the framework of a development plan or program or not. Its limitations have become more obvious in recent times as government budgets have grown in size and complexity and attempts have been made to remedy these deficiencies.

Traditional budget procedures suffer from two major difficulties. First, their coverage is usually incomplete. The normal budget does not cover all public sector operations—not even those carried out by the central government. The operations of autonomous and semi-autonomous agencies are almost inevitably—as it were, by definition—excluded. To be sure, in virtually all countries there exist autonomous or semi-autonomous agencies whose operations are not recorded in the budget, although they fall clearly within the perimeter of the public sector. In developing countries, however, the number of public entities outside the public budget is usually large, and their activities are of major importance in determining the direction and pace of the development process. In Latin America, in particular, autonomous agencies are numerous, and their role in the development process is great. In some countries, the tendency to create autonomous agencies has obviously gone too far. The outstanding case is that of Ecuador, where, according to one source, not less than eight hundred autonomous agencies have been counted.[6]

Decentralization of public sector activities has merit and is justifiable in some cases. But the proliferation of autonomous agencies is objectionable, the more so when the increase in their numbers indicates merely the failure of the regular departmental machinery to cope with the problem of public administration in a developing economy. As one observer of the Latin American scene observed, "The widespread attempt to solve [the problem of public administration] by the creation one after another of new organizations, autonomous or nearly so, could contribute to the solution of particular administrative problems, but represented *in toto* a series of makeshifts instead of a fundamental reform of the organization and methods of the public service, such as was needed in the new situation" (generated by the new and complex tasks confronting governments).[7]

Where responsibility for public sector activities is spread over many centers of decision, it becomes very difficult, not to say impossible, to frame a consistent policy for the public sector as a whole. This is especially true with regard to capital investment. Unless steps are taken to co-ordinate public investment activities with one another and

---

[6] United Nations, Secretariat, Economic Commission for Latin America, *La experiencia de algunos países de América del Sur en materia de reforma presupuestaria* (Santiago, Chile: September 3–14, 1962) (E/CN.12 BRW.2/L.10).

[7] Dudley Seers, "Inflation and Growth: A Summary of Experience in Latin America," *Economic Bulletin for Latin America*, Vol. VII, No. 1 (February, 1962) (United Nations, Economic Commission for Latin America).

with those of the private sector, one cannot expect public investment resources to be properly allocated.[8] Therefore measures must be taken to provide decision makers with a comprehensive picture of public sector operations. This does not imply that all details of all autonomous agencies should be included in the budget. But it should be possible to learn from the budget what funds are used to subsidize the operations of the autonomous agencies and to finance their investments and what use is being made of these agencies' own resources (i.e., depreciation funds and net earnings).

Another drawback of conventional budgeting is its emphasis on the cost aspect of government expenditures. The administrative budget shows the cost to government of acquiring goods and services. It does not relate this cost to the results achieved, that is to the benefits which the economy derives from public expenditures. In recent years, new methods of budget classification have been devised which are particularly useful for developing countries. They can be of great help in developing countries in the formulation of public expenditure policy. They may also serve to show the way for the modernization and rationalization of public administration. A number of Latin American countries have already changed the presentation of their budgets, and others have started with reform plans. But much remains to be done.[9]

The budget reform follows various lines and has various primary objectives. The functional budget and the performance budget are devices of particular usefulness for the improvement of public expenditure policies and for the preparation of public expenditure plans as part of a development program.[10]

The functional budget provides a basis for a rational choice among competing objectives of public expenditure. It classifies public expenditure by specific governmental function, such as defense, health, education, promotion of agriculture, etc.[11] This procedure is clearly superior to the classification of expenditure by different administrative units. For example, if school construction is entrusted to the ministry of public works, the functional budget will still show it under education. This makes it possible for the government to measure all outlays on education against other expenditure.

Performance budgeting is more than a classification device. It constitutes a new approach to budget formulation and budget execution. Its main objective is to provide a mechanism for measuring the benefit of the various items of public expenditures and to relate benefits to costs incurred. It can also be used to set targets for the various functions to be performed by the same administrative unit in a budget period.

The functional budget indicates the maximum cost that can be incurred in financing the activities pertaining to a particular function of government. When allocating money between, say, primary education and vocational training, policy makers already have some ideas about the comparative benefit to be derived for society as a whole from these outlays. They may be based to some extent on an objective analysis of such variables as the projected population growth, regional imbalances in the provision of educational facilities, and other factors.

All allocational decisions imply some sort of a cost-benefit notion, although the assessment of prospective benefits may have been arrived at in an intuitive way and purely political considerations may also have influenced the decisions. But the functional budget can do no more than indicate *ex post*

---

[8] It may be noted in this connection that the widespread practice of earmarking taxes for the use of particular agencies or for special purposes increases the danger of misallocation.

[9] United Nations, ECLA, *La experiencia de algunos países.*

[10] The "economic" budget classification is only indirectly relevant in this context. Its chief objective of classifying all public receipts and expenditures as current, capital, or transfer operations is necessary for the preparation of national accounts. Only insofar as national accounts serve as a basis for decisions regarding public

sector operations is the economic budget a tool of expenditure policy.

[11] See the scheme suggested in United Nations, *Manual for Economic and Functional Classification of Government Transactions* (New York) (Sales No. 58.XVI.2) Table 25.

facto whether the maximum amount of the projected costs has been exceeded. It does not provide any means to detect whether the projected benefits have in fact materialized, assuming that they have been expressed in terms of an objective unit of measurement, such as the additional number of children that would go to school as a result of the training of teachers.

In the preparation of the performance budget, however, the relation of benefits to cost can be carried considerably further. Performance budgeting presupposes an explicit determination of the objective to be attained by an outlay and thereby involves almost inevitably some cost-benefit calculations, based either on past performance or some other relevant information.

Performance budgeting becomes, of course, virtually indispensable if the budget, or a part of the budget, forms a part of a development program. In a mixed economy, the hard core of a development program is a program of public expenditures, chiefly to finance capital projects but also to pay for "supporting" activities (e.g., research, training, education). The program objectives are stated in terms of specific targets and projects, and thus it becomes the goal of the budget, or of a series of budgets, to provide funds to reach these targets and to carry out these projects.[12]

THE MARKS OF A RATIONAL PATTERN OF PUBLIC EXPENDITURES

What is the present pattern of public expenditures of the Latin American countries, and how does it compare with what one might consider an "ideal" pattern of public expenditures? On at least two grounds, answers to these two interrelated questions are difficult. In the first place, the data, based almost entirely on an administrative classification of expenditures, do not provide an accurate pattern of the composition of government expenditures. This makes an appraisal of the performance of particular countries difficult and an intercountry comparsion virtually impossible.

The second reason for finding it difficult to provide anything approximating a comprehensive answer to the two questions raised is, of course, the difficulty of conceiving what would constitute an "ideal" expenditure pattern for a particular country or for a "typical" country in Latin America.

We must, therefore, limit ourselves to a number of specific comments on certain aspects of the patterns of expenditure as they emerge from a variety of data. In the absence of any "ideal" pattern, it may be useful to single out those expenditure categories which most, if not all, economists would consider as desirable expenditures, in the sense that they are likely to enhance the development process. They are (*a*) public capital formation, (*b*) expenditures for education, (*c*) expenditures for public health, and (*d*) other "development-related" expenditures. Against these, we may then set expenditures which on the same a priori grounds may be considered as having a low priority. These categories might include defense expenditures, expenditures for internal security, and general administrative expenditures, although many exceptions to this general "rule," particularly for various types of administrative expenditures, come to mind immediately.

The Level of Expenditures

Before commenting on certain categories of government expenditures, a few words about the level of total government expenditures seem necessary. Few observers of the Latin American scene would take issue with the general proposition that governments have an important role to play in the present state of Latin American economic growth. Readily available data (which, however, may not be quite accurate) suggest that in recent

---

[12]Performance budgeting, particularly within the framework of a development program, may also have important side effects. It may permit an evaluation of administrative arrangements and improvements in the allocation of functions to be performed by various departments of governments and at various levels of government.

years government expenditures of the Latin American countries averaged 13 per cent of the gross national product. These figures exclude expenditures of government enterprises and those of state and local authorities, which, however, are unimportant (except for Brazil, in whose data they are included). The share of government expenditures in the national product does not seem to have changed appreciably in the decade of the 1950's, although for particular countries significant changes have taken place, with government expenditures of some countries showing sharp increases in the share of the national product (e.g., Venezuela) and others showing quite significant decreases (e.g., El Salvador).

It would be erroneous, however, to conclude from the stability of the government's share in the national product, or from the fact that the concentration around the mean is fairly pronounced, that this level of expenditures is about "right." As Table 5–1 shows, there is no simple relation between the rate of economic growth, on the one hand, and public expenditures, on the other. Even if the rate of capital formation is taken into account, no obvious relation between the

three statistics can be established. Nevertheless, it may be argued that, other things being equal, an increase in government expenditures (financed, of course, from noninflationary sources, i.e., chiefly tax revenue) would assist the growth process, provided the increase in expenditure would go for such "desirable" purposes as those indicated above.

The intercountry comparison may permit, however, a negative conclusion. The very low share of public expenditures in the gross national product of countries which have experienced little or no growth in recent years (i.e., Bolivia, Paraguay, Haiti) suggests that a low level of public expenditure, which corresponds to an equally low or perhaps even lower share in public receipts, does not appear to be conducive to economic development. The data also convey the impression, however, that a low level of public expenditure does not necessarily interfere with growth (e.g., Colombia, Mexico).

Public Sector Capital Formation

The data at hand permit somewhat firmer conclusions regarding the contributions which government savings can make to total capital formation and thereby to the rate of economic growth. It is clearly not an accident that in the countries shown in Table 5–2 a high level of government saving is associated with a high level of gross domestic capital formation and net domestic savings. The importance of this conclusion is reinforced by a cross reference with the figures shown in Table 5–1, since all countries with a high rate of gross domestic capital formation, except Argentina, also show a rather high rate of growth in domestic product. A further conclusion, more in the nature of a speculation than based on quantitative evidence, is that government saving does not appear to conflict with private saving. It may also be observed in Table 5–2 that for the median countries shown there government saving accounts for 40 per cent of net domestic saving. This is to say that public capital formation plays an important role in total capital formation.

TABLE 5–1: Growth of Output, Capital Formation, and Public Expenditure, 1950–1959, in Selected Latin American Countries

Country	Rate of growth in gross domestic product (per cent per annum)	Gross domestic capital formation (per cent of GDP)	Central government expenditure (per cent of GNP[a])
Venezuela	8	27	21
Mexico	6	16	8
Brazil	6	16	10
Costa Rica	6	20	13
Panama	6	12	15
Guatemala	5	12	15
Ecuador	5	14	12
Colombia	5	18	8
Chile	4	10	17
Honduras	4	15	10
Argentina	2	20	13

SOURCE: For rates of growth and capital formation: United Nations, *World Economic Survey, 1960*, Table 2.1. For details pertaining to particular countries, see notes to Table 2.1. For government expenditure, Pan American Union, based on official data.

[a]Average of 1953, 1957, and 1960. Government enterprises are excluded.

TABLE 5–2: Sources of Financing of Capital Formation, 1950–1959, in Selected Latin American Countries (*Expressed as per cent of GDP*)

	Gross domestic capital formation 1	Total gross saving 2	Depreciation 3	Total net saving 4=2−3	Foreign saving 5	Net domestic saving 6=4−5	Government saving 7	Total private saving 8=9+10	Corporate saving 9	Household saving 10
Venezuela	27	27	8	19	3	16	10	6	3	3
Argentina	20	20	10	10	2	8	n.a.	n.a.	n.a.	n.a.
Costa Rica	20	20	5	15	4	11	4	7	3	4
Colombia	18	18	9	9	—	9	4	5	1	3
Brazil	16	16	5	11	1	10	3	7	4	3
Ecuador	14	14	5	9	1	8	4	5	2	3
Honduras	15	15	5	10	2	8	2	7	1	6
Panama	12	12	6	6	6	−1	1	−1	2	−3
Guatemala	12	12	4	8	2	6	n.a.	n.a.	n.a.	n.a.
Chile	10	10	7	3	2	1	2	−2	n.a.	n.a.

SOURCE: United Nations, *World Economic Survey, 1960*, Tables 2.1, 2.2, and 2.3.
N.B. Figures may not add because of rounding.
      For details pertaining to particular countries, see notes to tables.

In many Latin American countries, the importance of the public sector in the national economy is understated by the share of total expenditure in the national product, since the expenditure figures exclude the operations of state enterprises. The share of expenditures of state-owned enterprises in Latin America varies greatly from country to country, and even order-of-magnitude figures are difficult to come by. It is well known, however, that in most Latin American countries railway transportation is now almost everywhere a public sector operation and that a large share of power generation is in the public sector. Since, aside from the construction of highways, public buildings, and a certain proportion of housing, most public investment expenditures are devoted to the expansion of transportation and power enterprises and of some state-owned manufacturing and mining facilities, the financial policies of these enterprises are of paramount importance for the level of capital formation in the public sector. They also determine to what extent governments must make use of tax proceeds or other current revenues to finance investment.

Price Policy of State Enterprises

Most persons familiar with the crucial role of social overhead capital in the development process and of the high income elasticity of the demand for the services of public utilities agree that the financial policies of the state enterprises operating in the utilities sector must be such as to generate from their own operations a substantial part of the resources necessary to finance their expansion. Otherwise, these financial requirements, even if met in part by loans on conventional or nonconventional terms from abroad, are likely to become a heavy burden on the budget. Unlike the situation prevailing in advanced countries, the governments of Latin American countries cannot rely on the domestic capital market to finance a significant part of these capital requirements but are forced to resort to financing through the budget.

Under these conditions, it is inevitable that the users of the services provided by utilities will be made to pay for their "full" cost, including an adequate return on the total capital invested in those enterprises. If the return on capital is set high enough so as to reflect the opportunity cost of capital rather than conventional rates and if depreciation charges are based on replacement rather than on original cost (particularly if the latter are distorted by changes in exchange rates), then the gross earnings of state enterprises can make a substantial contribution toward meeting investment cost. Under the conditions prevailing in most Latin American countries, rate policies based on these objectives are not likely to encounter any significant economic difficulties, since the demand for these services is likely to show little response to price changes. The prices at which the services of public enterprises are sold are hardly ever a crucial element in the cost of production to users of these services. Moreover, in view of the high capital intensity of public utilities facilities, any increase in the demand for these services induced by low prices leads to an inefficient allocation of scarce capital resources, which should be avoided.

These arguments for a policy of full-cost pricing of public power and transportation enterprises are subject to certain qualifications. The possibility of transitional periods during which full costs are not being met must be recognized. Whether temporary losses can be avoided depends chiefly on the minimum economic size of installations relative to the size of the market. In some circumstances, the competition of railway charges with the prices of other methods of transportation becomes important. It may even be necessary to take account of certain strategic, political, or social considerations and deviate sometimes from the principle of full-cost pricing, but these cases should be considered as exceptions requiring special justification and not as the rule.

The application of the principle of full-cost pricing of the services of public enterprises should be extended also to road transportation, for which, from the point of view of the availability of financial resources and on equity grounds, the case for financing part of the facilities by means of user charges is equally strong. The principle implies that all road expenditures, including the average annual expenditures on new construction made on the network of roads and highways, should be covered by the yield of charges imposed on the users of the road system. These charges are in the first instance gasoline taxes, fees for motor vehicle and drivers' licenses, and import duties and other fiscal levies imposed on motor vehicles. In some instances, the increase in property tax revenues resulting from increases in the value of property made more accessible and thus more productive by new roads may also be included in the "gross return" of the road system.

In the case of roads, it may also be impossible to adhere in practice to this general principle on grounds of equity and political and social considerations, and deviations from the general rule may have to be made. Moreover, in many instances the benefit of road construction and improvements may accrue to persons other than the users of motor transportation, such as users of animal-drawn vehicles, for whom it would be difficult to devise proper user taxes. But it must be clearly recognized that the general principle of rational resources allocation demands also in the case of free transport services rendered by the government that the ground rules of full-cost pricing be adhered to.

The appropriate pricing of road services is of particular importance when road transportation competes directly with railroad transportation, a condition becoming more and more frequent in Latin American countries. Because in many circumstances road transportation is more economical than railway transportation, a partial replacement of railway by road transport is inevitable in many Latin American countries, just as in most other countries in the world. But it would be clearly to the disadvantage of the countries of Latin America if they had to meet the rapidly growing demand for road facilities and at the same time incur the burden of meeting the deficits of railways which cannot compete with subsidized road transport. This is what they have to do if the charges on road transportation facilities are too low.

The record of the Latin American countries in adopting financial and pricing policies for government-owned utilities and other state enterprises is spotty, to say the least. The record is poor for publicly owned railways, whose operations and financial position have been suffering from a variety of causes. The most important of them undoubtedly has been the reluctance of governments to increase railway charges sufficiently to come even close to the full-cost pricing principle. In a number of countries, revenues have been inadequate even to meet operating expenditures. Subsidies to railways have imposed heavy burdens on the treasuries of a number of countries, including Argentina, Brazil, Chile, and Mexico. In Argentina, the railway deficit has been responsible for the major part of the over-all deficit and may thus be considered one of the chief causes of the monetary and balance of payments difficulties besetting the country.

The financial history of Peru offers an example of an unfortunate combination of low gasoline taxes and wholly inadequate road facilities. Because of the low price of gasoline, it pays to make use of road transportation even on very poor roads. The bad roads, in turn, shorten the useful life of motor vehicles and make large imports of spare parts necessary, thus imposing a burden on the balance of payments. In 1959, the price of gasoline was raised, but it is doubtful whether the increased revenue is sufficient to cover the average annual cost of roads.

In Mexico, the financial situation of road transportation was similar several years ago. Gasoline prices were low, and roads were poor. A side effect of this situation was that the earnings of the government petroleum monopoly (Pemex) were low and insufficient to provide funds for a level of exploratory work adequate to assure the continued expansion of oil production. Three years ago, the prices of oil products were raised, and the financial position of Pemex has improved accordingly.

The financial record of publicly owned power companies in Latin America is better than that of railways because the need for earnings sufficiently high to provide funds for expansion has been generally recognized. Power rates have been raised in several countries at the insistence of the International Bank. The records of such state enterprises as Endesa in Chile and the rate policy adopted last year by the Mexican authorities at the request of the Comisión Federal de Electricidad, which has accepted the principle of full-cost pricing, show that sound financial policies of state enterprises are possible and can make important contributions to the soundness of the government's financial position.

Expenditures for Education

Education is an objective of economic development as well as a means of attaining a high rate of growth. Therefore it is generally considered a high-priority objective of government expenditure. The allocation of a high proportion of public expenditure for education is essential if illiteracy, one of the most meaningful measures of backwardness, is to be eliminated. It is one of the disconcerting aspects of the development process of Latin America that illiteracy is still widespread in the entire hemisphere, with the degree of illiteracy showing a rough correlation to per capita income. The importance of education has been recognized by the political leaders of Latin America. The Punta del Este declaration of 1961 calls for the elimination of illiteracy in this decade.

Unfortunately, so far only insufficient thought has been given to the financial implications of such a policy commitment. Moreover, there is a wide range of views as to what constitutes the type of education most conducive to the development ambitions of Latin America. The subject matter content of secondary education, in particular, is a highly controversial topic, with the firmness of convictions of those taking part in the controversy presumably adversely correlated with our knowledge and relevant experience.

It must be considered as a significant accomplishment that for Latin America as a whole the proportion of total public expenditures allocated to education has increased considerably in recent years (Table 5–3). The increase is in part the result of a conscious effort of the authorities to provide educational facilities for a larger proportion of the population. It also reflects the increase

TABLE 5–3: Public Expenditures on Education as Per Cent of Total Central Government Expenditures

	1938	1939	1940	1953	1955	1956	1957	1958	1959	1960	1961	1962	Year ending
Argentina	16.2	n.a.	n.a.	9.6	n.a.	n.a.	8.7	9.9	8.9	8.5	n.a.	n.a.	Oct. 31
Bolivia	n.a.	n.a.	n.a.	23.4	24.9	33.4	17.0	n.a.	n.a.	n.a.	23.6	n.a.	Dec. 31
Brazil (Federal Government)ᵃ	5.6	n.a.	n.a.	10.2	n.a.	n.a.	8.8	9.8	10.7	13.0	13.8	n.a.	Dec. 31
Brazil (States and Federal District)	n.a.	n.a.	11.6	14.5	13.7	13.5	14.4	13.7	13.9	n.a.	n.a.	n.a.	Dec. 31
Chile	n.a.	n.a.	11.5	15.5	n.a.	n.a.	15.5	16.6	17.3	13.2	15.7	n.a.	Dec. 31
Colombia	n.a.	9.6	n.a.	5.4	n.a.	n.a.	n.a.	9.3	8.7	9.1	11.5	14.4	Dec. 31
Costa Rica	14.0	n.a.	n.a.	n.a.	n.a.	19.3	21.4	23.6	26.2	26.5	27.8	n.a.	Dec. 31
Ecuador	n.a.	n.a.	n.a.	13.7	n.a.	n.a.	10.8	12.4	11.5	11.0	10.7	12.9	Dec. 31
El Salvador	14.3ᵇ	n.a.	n.a.	12.3	n.a.	13.5	14.5	14.7	17.1	16.5	n.a.	n.a.	Dec. 31
Haiti	n.a.	6.9	n.a.	10.5	n.a.	n.a.	n.a.	10.6	9.9	10.5	10.6	10.2	Sep. 30
Honduras	n.a.	5.9	n.a.	11.3	12.1	10.3	11.1	n.a.	17.8	18.1	n.a.	n.a.	Dec. 31
Mexico	n.a.	11.1	n.a.	n.a.	n.a.	10.8	10.7	11.1	13.2	19.4	20.2	n.a.	Dec. 31
Panama	n.a.	n.a.	n.a.	22.6	n.a.	19.0	22.8	21.0	20.4	21.2	18.6	n.a.	Dec. 31
Peru	n.a.	n.a.	n.a.	7.1	6.3	7.4	7.3	9.8	10.6	n.a.	n.a.	n.a.	Dec. 31
Venezuela	n.a.	n.a.	n.a.	n.a.	n.a.	7.2	6.2	4.5	8.0	9.4	9.0	11.7	June 30

SOURCE: United Nations *Statistical Yearbook, 1961.*

ᵃIncludes "Health."
ᵇIncludes "Other Social Services."

TABLE 5–4: Literacy, Education, Health, and Defense Expenditures in Selected Latin American Countries

	Literacy indexᵃ		Government expenditures onᵇ		
	Rural	Urban	Education	Health	Defense
			(as per cent of GNP)		
Argentina	80	93	1.5	0.4	2.6
Brazil	42	80	2.3	0.4	2.8
Chile	71	92	2.7	1.6	2.5
Colombia	51	80	0.7	0.5	1.2
Costa Rica	76	93	3.3	0.3	0.5
Ecuador	49	86	1.4	0.3	2.3
Guatemala	22	75	n.a.	n.a.	1.5
Honduras	34	78	1.2	1.1	1.3
Mexico	49	82	1.3	0.5	0.8
Panama	65	95	3.4	3.4	0.0
Peru	35	89	1.6	0.8	3.2
Venezuela	40	76	2.0	n.a.	2.5

SOURCE: For Literacy Index: United Nations, *Demographic Aspects of Urbanization in Latin America, 1958,* Table 23. For Government Expenditures: Derived from United Nations, *Statistical Yearbooks,* and United Nations, *National Account Statistics.*

ᵃBased on 1950 census, except for Argentina (1947), Chile (1952), Colombia (1951). For definition of index and other explanations, see Source.
ᵇAverage 1958–60; for some countries one year is missing. Central government only, except for Brazil.

in the rate of population growth which has brought about a disproportionately large increase in the number of persons of school age.

The first two columns of Table 5–4 give an indication of the degree of literacy which prevailed in twelve Latin American countries approximately ten years ago. For the continent as a whole, some improvement has pre-sumably taken place since. But as recent reports indicate, the provision of educational facilities in many Latin American countries, particularly in rural areas, is still deplorably inadequate.[13]

In Table 5–4, an attempt has been made

[13]Cf: Inter-American Development Bank, *Social Progress Trust Fund, First Annual Report* (Washington, D.C.). Sections on education.

to relate public expenditures on education to the degree of literacy. The impression which emerges from the comparison is that, wide variations notwithstanding, literacy is at least in part a function of the proportion of the gross national product devoted to education. The table shows that, with the exception of one country in which special conditions prevail (Argentina), the literacy is lowest in countries which devote less than 2 per cent of the national product for education. The table also conveys the impression that in order to satisfy minimum educational standards in Latin America, an allocation of at least 3 per cent of the gross national product for education is necessary. This figure does not take account of the increased needs of higher education and the additional outlays which are necessary to improve secondary education in line with the growing complexity and increasing specialization of a society in the process of industrialization.

Table 5–4 reveals another fact which is at least symbolically meaningful: the two countries which devote more than 3 per cent of the gross national product to public education (Costa Rica and Panama) also have the lowest proportion of their gross national product allocated for defense purposes. This does not mean, of course, that the allocations for education compete only with allocations for defense. But it does bring out that expenditures for priority objectives generally compete with the use of public funds for lower-priority purposes.

Expenditure on education has been singled out as high-priority expenditure for two additional reasons. The category of education expenditure—to which might be added expenditure on public health—constitutes an example of the type of expenditure which is probably related directly to the willingness to pay taxes. In areas in which schools are inadequate, an increase in taxes is in all likelihood easier to bring about if the explicit objective of the tax increase is an expansion of educational services. This holds true also for expenditure on health services such as the operation of hospitals and clinics.

The close connection between certain types of expenditures and the willingness to pay taxes or, more appropriately, to accept tax increases brings out another aspect of the fiscal structure typical for Latin American countries. Chiefly for historical reasons, Latin American countries make little use of local taxation as a means of financing government services. There is undoubtedly scope for an increase in local taxation, because local taxation is par excellence the suitable means of exploiting the close connection between increases in public services and the willingness to pay taxes.

Defense Expenditures

Except for Panama and Costa Rica, all countries shown in Table 5–4 spend more than 1 per cent of the gross national product on defense, and half of them spend more than 2.3 per cent. In seven of the countries listed, defense expenditure exceeds the expenditure for education.

Economists tread on unfamiliar and dangerous ground if they question the priority rating of defense expenditures for developing countries, particularly in times in which advanced countries find it necessary to devote a considerable proportion of their national product to defense purposes. But it is disconcerting, to say the least, to find that the size of the armies of all Latin American countries (excluding Cuba) is about 600,000 men and that defense involves total outlays substantially in excess of a billion dollars a year. Probably the worst aspect of Latin American defense expenditures, however, is what might be called the "military demonstration" effect, i.e., the fact that, for instance, the purchase of a naval vessel by one country leads immediately to a similar purchase by a neighboring country. On occasion, thoughtful pleas have been made for a curtailment of defense expenditures by Latin American countries and particularly for a limitation of the inter-American armaments race resulting from the military demonstration effect. But such pleas have had no effect so far.

The low priority rating given to defense expenditures appears to disregard the fact that military forces are necessary not only to defend a country but also to supplement on a stand-by basis, so to speak, police authorities responsible for maintaining law and order. This is not the case, however, since the expenditures for this internal security function would normally involve only a small fraction of the total outlays now incurred under the heading of defense.

General Administration

The functional breakdown of public expenditures for most Latin American countries shows by far the largest amounts under the heading of general administration. This classification includes an amorphous mass of government activities, ranging all the way from the very essential class of tax and customs administration and economic planning, on the one hand, to such items as doormen and office servants in public buildings and gardeners of public parks, on the other. There is little that can be said in general terms about the priority rating which one would accord the various services subsumed under the heading of general administration from an economic point of view. But observations in many Latin American countries suggest that the number of persons engaged in less essential or unessential activities, such as doormen, guards, and office attendants, is large and in many cases excessive and reflects the impact of nepotism and political patronage rather than real needs for services.

Reports prepared by public administration experts indicate also that in many Latin American countries the efficiency of the low- and middle-level government employees is poor. These observations are frequently combined with the suggestion that the salary scales in the public service are too low to attract competent personnel and that the low salaries, together with the low standing of government employees in the respect of the community, perpetuate the prevalent combination of inefficiency and excessive numbers of employees. Efficiency in public service is difficult to measure, but the low level of salaries paid to government employees is easily proved by comparisons with salaries prevailing in the private sector for jobs of the same type. It has been pointed out, however, that these comparisons are not conclusive, because the work performance and work discipline of employees in the private sector is much higher than in the public sector. This difference is partly borne out, it is claimed, by the fact that many public employees supplement their income by additional jobs, on a part-time or even a full-time basis, in the private sector.

It is, of course, easy to see how this situation can be changed and improved. What is necessary is a decrease in the number of persons employed in government and an increase in salaries high enough to make government service attractive for better-qualified personnel. But it must be recognized that it will take much time and continuous effort to bring about an improvement.

It is doubtful whether a reduction of the number of government employees will lead to a reduction in government expenditures. It may well be that the increase in salary scales necessary to attract better people into the public service will cost more than can be saved by reducing the number of employees. But the changes suggested here are nevertheless essential if government is to function properly. Moreover, it would not make the financial position of governments worse, because it would also have a favorable effect on the public's willingness to pay taxes.

Comment

JORGE MÉNDEZ*

Mr. Adler is an excellent representative, in the International Bank, of the growing interest within that agency in a policy of over-all development for the underdeveloped countries. He has followed very closely the efforts that have been made in this direction in Chile and other Latin American countries, and, along with Gerald Alter, who has done the same for my country, he has personally and professionally associated himself with those efforts on the basis of recommending that external aid, which is more than ever necessary today, be directed toward supplementing domestic efforts intended to assure a gradual but comprehensive and solid solution of the problems that hinder growth and that the amount and continuity of the aid be dependent on the domestic economic policy's being organized around organic concepts of stabilization with development. We Latin Americans cannot help being enthusiastic about this view of the problems and the prospects of our economic and social development that is apparently establishing itself so firmly in the International Bank.

Colombia has introduced a system of planning that seeks precisely the aims that the bank is interested in: to act on the whole of the economy in such a way that a rate of growth may be achieved that will be progressively accelerated, but under conditions of stability; that little by little this growth will be made free of the excessive fluctuations of international trade; and that certain especially acute social problems will be attacked with a criterion that takes into consideration at the same time the urgency of a solution and the general interest of increasing the productive capacity of the country. In this national effort, we have had very promising and important results in certain aspects. In others, we have

*National Council for Economic Policy and Planning, Bogotá, Colombia.

had to face, and are now facing, serious problems. Some of those problems have arisen from the very complexity of the development process, once the attempt is made to break away somewhat from the passive and resigned molds that were traditional with us. Other problems arise from the technical weakness that is naturally present at the beginning of an over-all system of development programing.

These first experiences, some of them negative, are, fortunately, leaving in our country a healthy national conviction that has strongly prevailed: that the most important thing in a process of intensive programing of development is to persevere in it. Its greatest value lies in its persistent and systematic continuity. We are paying a price, a tax, for the fact that we have decided to work for our intensive development, and that price, that tax, is much less than we would have had to pay for inaction, systematic disorganization, and resignation in the face of a stagnation of development.

Mr. Adler's theme touches on one of the key points in the idea of programing. I should like to comment on certain concepts outlined in his paper, in the light of what we in Colombia have tried to do, with a system of budgetary management and a Public Investment Plan that in the last two years have been formally connected with the over-all programing.

It is in fact true that fiscal policy, above all in Latin America, has been studied principally in relation to what it signifies as a procedure for obtaining resources for the government, that is to say, in relation to the problems that the tax system may originate or prevent or in relation to the monetary effects (inflationary or deflationary) that may be produced by certain fiscal practices. But public expenditure as an active agent of development and in the attainment of certain social purposes has received relatively little study. At times it would appear that public expenditure and budgetary deficits have so justly and deservedly acquired a bad reputation in the inflationary process that afflicts most of our countries that it would be useless to try to ascribe a noble and constructive mission to them. Mr. Adler's paper shows that the topic of the active role of expenditures, of the necessity for selecting them carefully and assigning them specific functions in the development process, is a primary one and deserves very special attention, because it is true that public expenditure began to be considered as a strategic factor in anticyclical policy several years ago. But the systematic formulation of a theory of the role of government expenditures in the process of development and of redistribution of income remains to be perfected.

This gap is particularly evident if one takes into account the scope of the role of the government in a country at a relatively low stage of development, which is inevitably of more decisive effect, although probably of smaller relative magnitude, than is the case in the industrialized countries. In the latter, public expenditures as a percentage of the gross national product are generally more than in the relatively underdeveloped countries. But this relationship, which might seem to mean that in the rich countries the government is more powerful, is deceptive. In the rich countries, the subtraction in favor of the government of a major share of individual income is easier and leaves very large purchasing power and capacity to invest in the hands of the private sector. In the poor countries, in contrast, the part of the national product that the government reserves to itself represents marginally much more of a hardship for the individuals. And, moreover, the degree of urgency of the expenditures that are made with such revenues and their capacity fundamentally to change the conditions under which development is carried out are much greater. Government resources are much scarcer in the relatively underdeveloped countries, in relation to the needs to be met, and therefore require much greater care in their distribution

and much more forethought regarding the role to be assigned to them. Development cannot be achieved unless infrastructure capital is available in the form of means of transportation, electric-power plants, etc., the educational services are being developed, and the basic administrative agencies and offices function adequately in the fields of justice, property registry, authorizations and stimuli in the economic field, etc. At the same time, some profound problems that arise from the very poverty of the country must be attacked systematically and preferentially. Almost none of the foregoing can be done by private initiative, and, in addition, private initiative needs the stimulus and the environment created by the action of the state. The usual criticisms by many private sectors against state intervention in national affairs, although correct in some cases, generally ignore the fact that the purpose of such intervention is to create a strong and progressive national economy in which private initiative can find a wider field for expansion and a more just social environment for its survival.

The adoption of a system of over-all programing of development, in which it must be assumed that the resources anticipated are distributed in a way that will lead to a maximum increase (within reasonable limits) in production and to a fairer distribution of income, and in which a public investment plan is an integral part of a general program of development, seems to me the best way to attempt to attain the three objectives of a public expenditure policy that stand out in Mr. Adler's paper. Those objectives are:

a) To assure that the resources the state has available will play the most important role possible for development and social welfare.

b) To assure that taxes will be paid by the private sector with the conviction that the group as a whole will be benefited.

c) To assure that the redistribution of income that is generated by public expenditure will be both just and conducive to that level of private saving and investment that the economy requires.

In fact, the methodology used in a general program of development enables one to pursue these aims consciously. A program should begin by knowing as profoundly as possible what the needs of the economy are and what resources can be made available by adequate mobilization. In this examination or diagnosis, the basic needs for investment will emerge. Some of the lines of action can and should be undertaken by private initiative, which will need only a suitable framework of stimuli for carrying them out. In the face of this role of private initiative, and interdependently with it, one can deduce the role of the state. It will be possible to decide, even though at the beginning only in an approximate degree, what should be the over-all distribution of resources in which the expenditures of the state are justified because, for example, their marginal utility, either in the purely economic sense or in the social sense, is at least as great as that which would result from an expenditure of the same resources in the private sector. This concept, whose perfection would undoubtedly imply the utilization of a technique of linear programing or of the bases of judgment for public expenditure that are found, for example, in the works of Professor Musgrave, is outlined and practiced in a general program of development, no matter how early its stage of operation and technical detail. The participation of the public sector in total expenditures of the economy, in fact, is calculated—taking into account the need for leaving the private sector sufficient purchasing power to attend to basic consumer needs and to devote savings of its own to investment—in sufficient amount to meet the anticipations of the program. In this way, it must be assumed, at least in theory, that neither will public expenditure demand resources beyond the limits where necessary private investment would begin to be endangered nor will the private expenditures prevent the carrying out of the investments and operating expenditures of the public sector that are necessary for the state to fulfill the mission that has been assigned to it in the program. A continuing series of adjustments, in view of the total

capacity for growth, can be expected over a period of time.

In the same way, the distribution of the expenditures of the public sector among the various fields must be assumed to be determined, in a development program, on the basis of distributing the revenues that have been considered possible and desirable, in accordance with an investment plan for the public sector, among the various fields in which the state should perform functions. The resources will be sufficient, in most fields, for meeting only part of the needs. The success of the process of distribution will depend on adequate decisions having been made as to the extent to which the needs should be met in each of those different fields and on the proper carrying out of the operative phase of those decisions.

In Colombia, a four-year public investment plan entered into operation in 1961, within the framework of a general program of development. The general government sector was analyzed and projections made for it for the next ten-year period, and from that first approximation there emerged the magnitude of resources that could be made available for that sector within the anticipations of the program as well as the assumed levels that should be attained with regard to public savings, transfers from the private sector to the public sector, the level of the tax burden, etc. The public sector, thus included within the framework of the general program, was then subjected to a special analysis, which began by projecting the compulsory or operating expenditures, leaving a quantity of savings that, added to the anticipated amounts of external aid and domestic credit, could be utilized in the investment plan.

In its first phase, all the expenditures of the national budget and those of the autonomous national institutes were included, but, in contrast, those of the regional corporations, departments, municipalities, and certain mixed legal entities were excluded. Clearly the purpose was to proceed gradually to include in the plan all the expenditures of the general government. This process of enlarging the scope of the plan has been carried out. In 1962, additional entities were included, among them the Cauca Valley Corporation.

Therefore, machinery has begun to be available that already covers a very large percentage of public expenditure and that serves as co-ordinator of the investment plans of the government. Any decision to undertake works, to continue others at a given rate, or to seek new sources of financing must take into account a general table that shows the relations between certain works and others, in view of total availabilities, and in which the significance of taking care of certain areas before others can be rated with over-all criteria.

It is natural, as was indicated above, that the degree of perfection with which criteria of priority can be used cannot be so complete now as will be possible later. In the first place, it is not easy to establish criteria of priority with sufficient knowledge of cause, and this requires detailed studies of each sector, which at the beginning are available only in part. In the second place, one must start from a basis that includes irreversible facts, such as works that cannot be suddenly abandoned, even though they may not be of high priority, and that covers certain executing agencies that will need some time to perfect their operating capacity. In Colombia, therefore, the public investment plan, although it has already firmly introduced criteria of priority, still needs much more detailed work before what could be called a well-formulated schedule of priorities will be in operation. It is undeniable, in any case, that the plan has already had very important effects in behalf of accelerated development of the economy: the total amount of investments made has practically doubled in the course of these years, and it has been possible to face a number of needs for action with greater forethought and awareness. Budgetary problems of a financial nature—the appearance of fiscal deficits, for example—have delayed the over-all advance of the plans and have partly cracked public confidence in them.

To the extent that it is possible to perfect the system of priorities and to overcome the financial problems that the intensive investment effort naturally brings with it, the systematic application of a plan of public expenditures, within the framework of a general program of development, appears to correspond in optimum fashion to the postulates included in Mr. Adler's paper in regard to the quality the expenditures of the government should have.

It is appropriate to add some brief comments on two specific points that appear in Mr. Adler's paper. The first is the statement that redistribution of income is more urgent and desirable in an underdeveloped economy that is not growing than in an underdeveloped economy that has managed to assure a perceptible rate of growth. Mr. Adler seems to think that growth—that the increase in opportunities growth brings with it—can be sufficient to keep the masses of the people happy and contented. I do not think so. I would rather think the opposite: for one thing, that more or less intensive redistribution becomes nearly impossible and is self-defeating in an economy that is not growing. There appears, then, a kind of vicious circle, in which a real chance of redistribution can come only from the assurance of having a rapid rate of growth. In the second place, it is not true, to my way of thinking, that growth in itself alleviates the expectations of the poorest classes of society. On occasion it may increase them and create dangerous social frustrations. In certain countries, it has been noted that growth is produced around more or less extensive social groups (a middle class) that, however, tend to form privileged groups in turn, without the process of developments substantially improving the lot of the great nucleuses of population that for one reason or another remain outside the central process of growth.

In any case, it is well worth while to elaborate this subject much further. It is one of the most significant and difficult topics of the theory of development.

The second point on which I should like to make a very brief comment is that of the use of the method of program-budgeting. In Colombia, this system was introduced in 1960 as a first-line auxiliary tool for the correct carrying out of the budget and for being able to judge the operational validity of the public investment plan. Until now, the result has been barely satisfactory. Much more co-ordination between the work done by the National Bureau of the Budget and the General Accounting Office of the Republic, on the one hand, and the planning agencies, on the other, would have been needed. Nevertheless, the system exists, and it can be improved. The National Planning Council is organizing an *ad hoc* committee, made up of representatives of planning and of the Ministry of Finance, which will be responsible for following step by step all those aspects of the carrying out of the budget that have to do with the attainment of the goals of the plan. Until now, the relations between the two spheres, of planning and carrying out of the budget, have been too infrequent. Planning maintains supervision of the process of achievements by the various executing agencies, but the policy on supplying funds is decided by the Bureau of the Budget, and the two aspects of the question frequently may not coincide, especially when there is danger of a fiscal deficit.

Discussion

MR. VAN DER MEL introduced Mr. Adler's paper on public expenditures and economic development. The first part of the paper dealt with the need for a rational expenditure policy, since appropriate expenditures were the basic justification for the levying of taxes and there was a close connection between the effective use of government funds and the willingness to pay taxes. The structure of revenue should be determined in close relation to the structure of expenditure, since the fiscal machinery, in the wider sense, aimed at redistributing income. The need for redistribution of income was more strongly felt in a stagnant economy than in a country where there was a considerable growth rate shared by the low-income brackets, but such redistribution might be better achieved through expenditure policies than revenue policies, to guard against too great a reduction of incentives to saving and investment in the private sector.

The paper went on to deal with the budgetary process, touching on the drawbacks of the conventional administrative budget and the advantages of the functional budget and of performance budgeting, which made it possible to relate benefits to costs incurred.

A related point was the need to have consolidated data and co-ordination of spending policies for the public sector as a whole, especially when expenditure was spread over many ministries, autonomous agencies, public enterprises, etc.

The comments on the level of public expenditures had to be somewhat tentative because of the lack of comparability of the data available. Table 5–1 seemed to show that there was no simple relation between the rate of economic growth and the rate of public expenditures expressed as a percentage of the gross national product. It could not be established whether the growth rate would have been higher if public expenditures had been higher. The decisive point seemed to be the quality of government expenditure.

The second half of the paper dealt with certain important categories of public expenditure and touched on public sector capital formation, on the need for full-cost pricing of public services and enterprises, and on education, defense, and general administration. In connection with its lending operations, the World Bank had on numerous occasions been confronted with problems of pricing of public enterprises and had been able to exercise some influence for good. In general, the situation appeared somewhat better, although least with respect to railways. Subsidies, where unavoidable, should be regarded as exceptions requiring special justification. The proportion of total public expenditure allocated to education appeared to have increased in recent years, but the additional facilities provided were to a considerable extent absorbed by the population increase. Literacy ratios for 1950 were shown, but none were yet available for 1960. There appeared to be some relation between the literacy rate and the proportion of the gross national product spent on education. Expenditure on such social services as education and health seemed directly related to the willingness to pay taxes; that could be exploited, particularly by increasing local taxes, little used in Latin America as a means of financing government services. Although defense expenditure was an area where experts must tread warily, they had a duty to draw attention to the element of waste involved from the standpoint of economic development in a substantial portion of expenditure under that head in Latin America. Although data on general administration were not susceptible to detailed analysis on a comparative basis, it seemed clear that Latin American government services included a large number of superfluous posts, that efficiency at the low and middle levels was poor, and that there was an urgent need for better pay scales and status for government employees in general.

MR. MÉNDEZ said he would confine himself for the time being to making some general comments on Mr. Adler's paper, which he would enlarge upon in a written paper that he intended to present later to the conference.

As Mr. Adler had stressed, too little attention had been paid in the past to analyzing the structure of public expenditure as a function of development, particularly from the practical standpoint. In his opinion, that was the salient point in Mr. Adler's paper.

He considered that prior over-all development planning was essential, whether fiscal expenditure for investment purposes was regarded as a complementary function of the private sector, whether such expenditure was expected to have a redistributive effect, or whether the end pursued was to secure the backing of public opinion for economic development plans.

From that standpoint, the basic questions posed by fiscal expenditure were to what extent the state could act in pursuance of overall development aims without prejudicing the private sector and how public expenditure could be systematically distributed. The development program itself would answer those queries and would set the limits for state intervention.

Admittedly it was impossible for the criteria that determined the order of priority for expenditure to be altogether perfect, and it was not always easy to carry out the necessary structural reforms. It was equally true that an intensive investment plan would inevitably lead to higher recurrent expenditure than had been envisaged and that investment outlays that had already begun to be made could not always be broken off abruptly when the plan was initiated. All those considerations would act as so many further obstacles to investment policy. Despite the difficulties, however, it was always desirable to establish a plan and endeavor to keep to it.

Turning to some specific points made by Mr. Adler in his paper, he said he did not agree that the redistributive function of fiscal policy should be applied chiefly in the less developed countries with a stagnant economy; it might tend to aggravate the situation of those countries in some cases, whereas the opposite might occur in others. It was likewise possible that the redistributive effects of fiscal policy were more urgently needed in developing countries where the economy was not stagnant. He did not think that a general formula could be advocated which failed to take into account the individual features of each case.

With respect to the prices of public services, he thought all price policies should be an integral part of the respective expenditure policy. Only in that way would it be possible to avert the dangerous distortions from which development programs were apt to suffer.

In conclusion, he wished to stress again that the chief merit of Mr. Adler's paper was that it opened up a fundamentally important avenue of economic development which had hitherto been insufficiently explored.

MR. NAHARRO wished to stress one point with respect to expenditure on education. Whatever the volume of expenditure on education, it seemed to be the general practice in Latin America that when that volume of expenditure was allocated in the form of specific payments, very little went to pay teachers who taught high-level graduates who constituted an important factor in development. Hence, experts were "produced" who were of lower quality than would have been the case if the production factor constituted by "professors" could devote all their efforts to teaching, which could be done only if they were well paid, instead of having to do other work.

MR. LEWIS felt that one aspect of the question of public expenditure should be emphasized. In discussing such matters as reforms in the tax structure and tax administration, participants had thought in terms of timing, of what was actually being done at the government level and in legislative bodies. The same realistic approach might well be taken to the question of public expenditure and budgetary procedures by thinking in terms of what was being done currently, how many civil servants were needed and how long it would take to train them, what budgetary procedures should be introduced, and what political decisions were needed to enable the necessary legislation to be passed.

MR. MONTERROSO, referring to Mr. Adler's example of Peru as a country offering an unfortunate combination of low gasoline taxes and wholly inadequate road facilities, observed that road facilities were also inadequate in some countries which imposed a high tax on gasoline. That was due to the fact that the income from gasoline taxes was not specifically used to improve the highway network but went into a general fund. He wondered whether it might be desirable in Latin America to apply income from certain taxes to specific purposes, perhaps on a percentage basis.

MR. DARDÓN, speaking on the question of the price of public services, observed that prices were not always directly related to costs and that costs were usually inflated because of top-heavy bureaucratic administration. The problem might be solved partly by providing for the participation of the private sector, e.g., by transferring some public services to the private sector.

MR. DESAI felt that Mr. Adler's paper had failed to tackle the real issues. The question of public expenditure could not be viewed on the same basis as tax policy. The functional distribution of expenditure was a matter, not for bureaucrats, but for legislators. Decisions on national priorities were the prerogative of the legislature and of ministers of finance.

He thought that there was still a considerable misunderstanding of the development process itself. First, the national accounts, when developed, were subject to major errors, since the problems of imputations were serious and largely affected the estimates computed for the developing economies. The nature of the processes of economic development was also complex. In connection with his work with the Economic Commission for Asia and the Far East, one conclusion reached was that the process of economic growth depended on many things, of which capital investment was not always the major factor. Even for countries of Western Europe, that appeared to be so. The multivariate analysis made by the European Economic Community, which had selected three variables, viz., capital input, labor input, and all other elements excluding capital and labor inputs, gave the surprising outcome that growth was most closely related with the balance factor other than capital and labor inputs. Economic growth was a complex process which could not be viewed in terms either of investment activity alone or of any other single area. The human factor must be taken into account. That point should be particularly stressed, especially in Latin America.

Expenditure policy could not be applied in terms where investment was treated as a major element and such questions as education were treated as a side issue. Priorities in public expenditure depended on specific conditions in each country. The major question was what could be done to make expenditure effective in terms of the objectives sought, and in that field more needed to be done by way of fiscal research.

MR. URQUIDI was in general agreement with the points made by Mr. Adler, particularly the emphasis he had placed on the redistributive effects of expenditure. He supported Mr. Desai's views on the question of public expenditure priorities. The Latin American countries had to undertake considerable social expenditure which also had economic consequences. Lastly, he supported Mr. Adler's view that program-budgeting techniques should be extended.

MR. JATAR-DOTTI regretted that the important question of public expenditure and economic development was being disposed of at a single meeting. The point he wished to make was that the contribution of the public sector in stimulating economic development could not be measured solely in terms of the coefficient of real investment. It should be measured by the increase in economic efficiency determined by public expenditure. The question was rather what the participation of the public sector was in capital formation. If a government purchased a piece of land, it would contribute to economic development only if that land was made available to a large number of people who would thus be given employment.

MR. MONTERROSO could not agree that, with respect to income redistribution, public expenditure was more important than the collection of revenue. He felt that the fiscal authorities should endeavor to improve national income both by a progressive tax system and by an increase in transfer expenditure, i.e., by considering at all times both sides of the medal: income and expenditure.

MR. VEGA agreed in general with the views expressed by Mr. Adler and, in particular,

with the points made by Mr. Desai and Mr. Jatar-Dotti. With respect to Mr. Méndez' comments, he hoped that recommendations on the planning of public expenditure would ensure that budgetary provision was made for the completion of long-range programs. The division of the budget into functions did not ensure efficiency, even if allocations were made on a percentage basis. For example, if the construction of a highway cost $10 million and budgetary expenditure was spread over fifty years with an annual allocation of $200,000, that did not constitute efficient public expenditure.

MR. NÚÑEZ felt that the discussion so far had shown that very little was known about the effects of public expenditure. He recommended that an appraisal of those effects should be made.

MR. VAN DER MEL considered Mr. Méndez' comments an amplification of what Mr. Adler had stated in his paper rather than a criticism of the recommendations made. He fully subscribed to Mr. Méndez' view that planning was desirable, that it raised a number of difficulties, and that it should be adaptable to changing circumstances. He further agreed on the desirability of income redistribution through fiscal machinery and the need for taking into account the individual features of each case. With respect to pricing policies, it was an important factor with regard to public enterprises, and the aim should be full-cost pricing, allowing for certain exceptions. While the difficulties were clear, the point was worth restating.

On the question raised by Mr. Naharro, he felt that the nature of expenditure on education was important. There would still be much to learn in the field of the economics of education. The International Bank recognized the increasing importance of education in the context of economic development and believed that in the present circumstances more should be done in that field. Lack of data made it difficult to come forward with tangible suggestions. More study and research were needed as to the type of education which gave the best results in terms of economic development.

Replying to Mr. Lewis, he agreed that it would be desirable, in the context of the efforts being made to improve fiscal policy in Latin America, to devote attention to expenditure policies.

On the point raised by Mr. Monterroso—the question whether it was preferable to have a unitary budget or to allocate specific taxes to specific uses—he felt that the problem should be viewed realistically and that a flexible approach to the problem of assigned revenue should be adopted.

The problems raised by Mr. Dardón could be attributed to inefficient administration. However, in a number of cases it was difficult or undesirable to transfer public services to the private sector.

He felt that some of the misgivings expressed by Mr. Desai were the result of misunderstanding due to the rather general nature of Mr. Adler's paper.

With respect to the functional distribution of expenditure, he agreed that the ultimate decision rested with the legislature. However, it was the task of civil servants and experts to submit sensible recommendations to the legislators. On that point, all that Mr. Adler's paper sought to emphasize was the usefulness of a functional classification of expenditure.

On the question of the economic development process itself, he agreed that statistical data might be inaccurate. However, a paper on public expenditure had to provide some figures, however limited, rather than none at all. After all, statistical data did provide some order of magnitude.

The question of the forces behind economic development raised many problems, and he agreed that oversimplification should be avoided. It should, nevertheless, be borne in mind that capital output ratios drew attention to other underlying factors.

He did not agree with Mr. Desai that the question of education had been minimized in Mr. Adler's paper. He could assure Mr. Desai that the author was fully aware of the importance of education.

With respect to the role of technicians in establishing public expenditure priorities, he agreed that it was limited but repeated that the views of experts should be made available.

He fully supported Mr. Desai's plea for further research on fiscal problems.

Replying to Mr. Urquidi, he felt that public expenditure on specific items must necessarily vary from country to country. Some countries in Latin America, as Mr. Urquidi had pointed out, were committed to substantial expenditure in certain fields.

He agreed with Mr. Jatar-Dotti that high investment figures did not automatically lead to a high growth rate.

In conclusion, he shared the views expressed by Mr. Vega and Mr. Núñez.

6

Personal Income Tax in Latin America

by Richard Goode*

The personal income tax is widely regarded as one of the best forms of taxation. The net income of natural persons is a broad measure of capacity to contribute to the support of the state, and, although admittedly an incomplete measure, it is often considered the most nearly adequate single basis of taxation. Like other direct taxes, the income tax permits allowances to be made for the family responsibilities and other personal circumstances of taxpayers, and it is adapted to the use of graduated rates. A progressive income tax is a prime method of "demanding more from those who have most" and of reducing excessive inequality.[1] An elastic yield, which responds both to the growth of real output and to inflationary increases in money incomes, is another characteristic of a well-enforced income tax that is highly convenient for governments.

A personal income tax is now levied in nineteen of the twenty Latin American republics, but in some of the countries important categories of income are not subject to the tax. In most Latin American countries the tax is a minor source of revenue, and nowhere in the area is it a powerful instrument for modifying the distribution of income and wealth. Compliance and administration are often reported to be incomplete and erratic. These conditions are not peculiar to Latin America. Indeed, there are only a few countries of the world in which the personal income tax is the largest source of revenue, and in some of these it is an object of sharp criticism.

Can the personal income tax be made more effective in Latin America? Should its scope and yield be diminished or expanded? What guidelines can be suggested for the design of an income tax that is suitable for Latin American conditions?

ECONOMIC ISSUES

One school of thought holds that income taxes and other forms of progressive taxation should be minimized or wholly avoided in less developed countries because these taxes have especially adverse effects on saving, enterprise, and work. The industrialized countries of Europe and North America, it is pointed out, did not begin to impose heavy income taxes until they had accumulated a large capital stock and had gone far toward the establishment of modern economies. In Great Britain, to be sure, the income tax was in effect during most of the nineteenth century, but usually the rate was low and the graduated surtax was not introduced until 1910. The personal income tax dates from 1913 in the United States and from 1917 in France. The U.S.S.R., a late-comer to industrialization, has not followed the trend toward heavy income taxes.

*Opinions and interpretations are my own and do not necessarily reflect the views of officers or other staff members of the Brookings Institution.

Mr. Goode is with The Brookings Institution, Washington, D.C.

[1] These objectives are stated in the Declaration to the Peoples of America made in conjunction with the Charter of Punta del Este. Pan American Union, *Alliance for Progress* (Washington, D.C.: 1961) (Official Documents Emanating from the Special Meeting . . . Held in Punta del Este, Uruguay, from August 5 to 17, 1961).

Soviet income tax rates have always been low, relative to consumption tax rates and to income tax rates in many other countries. A program for virtual elimination of the income tax over a five-year period was announced in 1960 but was suspended in 1962[2]

The hypothesis that earlier adoption of heavy income taxes would have retarded economic progress in the countries that are now industrialized cannot be decisively refuted. But the evidence on which it is based is weak and does not support the implication that income taxation and prosperity are incompatible. The heaviest users of the income tax are countries with incomes per head that rank toward the top of the international array. It is not evident that the income tax has slowed economic growth in these countries.

A long-standing objection to progressive income taxes is that they curtail saving. This objection is especially pertinent in developing countries, which need to build up their capital stock at a rapid rate. It raises a number of issues that have not been resolved. The debate cannot be fully reviewed here, but a few comments may be in order.

First, the contention that progressive taxes reduce saving more than proportional or regressive taxes is based on the assumption that the fraction of a small, permanent change in income that will be reflected in saving rises with the size of income. Although this assumption is plausible, statistical evidence for it is sparse in the industrialized countries and even more meager in the less developed countries. Many observers have suggested that high savings ratios are less characteristic of those with large incomes in the underdeveloped countries than in countries with a long capitalist tradition. There are lavish spenders among the rich everywhere, but the groups who are especially inclined to that style of life usually make up a much greater proportion of those with large incomes in the underdeveloped countries than in the countries with

a long capitalistic tradition. Many scholars now believe that, even in the latter countries, the relation between income size and personal saving propensities, and hence the influence of tax progressivity on the national saving ratio, have been greatly exaggerated in the past.

Second, conditions such as the security of property, the prospective rate of inflation, and investment opportunities may have much more influence on personal saving than the form of taxation. Third, saving by corporations is likely to be strategically important and to grow with economic development; hence, the taxation of corporations may affect private saving more than the taxation of individuals. Finally, a small change in the size of the fiscal deficit or in the proportion of government outlays which take the form of investment may have a greater impact on the national saving ratio than a drastic revision of the tax structure.

Another line of criticism of the income tax is that it blunts incentives to innovate and to make the many adjustments that are necessary to speed economic growth. Economic theorists sometimes make essentially the same point by saying that the tax impairs the usefulness of commodity prices, profits, and wages as guides for the allocation of resources. So long as economic activity is left largely in private hands, reliance must be placed primarily on monetary rewards as inducements to carry out the many small changes which in the aggregate can transform the economy. It would be shortsighted to destroy this system by either direct controls on prices and wages or excessive taxation. But the income tax is not the only kind of tax that reduces profits and wages. Excise taxes on production or export taxes that cannot be passed on to customers may be more burdensome and more discouraging to enterprise than taxes on net income. Taxes on items that are bought by salaried persons and wage earners reduce the real value of compensation and, in a world in which the significance of changes in the purchasing power of money is widely appreciated, may provoke the same kind of reactions as income taxes.

[2] N. S. Khrushchev, *Raising the Soviet Standard of Living*, Report to the U.S.S.R. Supreme Soviet (New York: Crosscurrents Press, 1960), pp. 19–33, 96–99; *Washington Post and Times-Herald*, September 25, 1962.

Aside from the greater visibility of the income tax, the economic difference between it and indirect taxes is due mainly to the graduated rates that are usual in the income tax. The rates of personal income tax and supplementary taxes that are imposed on increments of income reach high levels in a few of the Latin American countries. In certain circumstances, the top rates of tax are so high that a person who complies with the law will have little monetary inducement to undertake activities that will enlarge his income. Unless this situation reflects a deliberate decision to limit the size of personal incomes—which seldom seems to be the case—it is a self-defeating use of the tax machinery. A real danger of the personal income tax is that it lends itself to excessive progression. It is reckless to impose tax rates that nullify incentives without setting up another system for guiding the economy. Often the applicability of the high statutory tax rates is limited by evasion and by special exemptions. This involves its own complications and distortions.

But the fact that the income tax may be abused is an argument for moderation, not for abandonment of the tax. On economic grounds, the personal income tax seems to merit a favorable report, if not as enthusiastic a recommendation as was occasionally given it in the past.

CONDITIONS FOR SUCCESSFUL INCOME TAXATION

Like certain kinds of modern technology, the income tax requires for its efficient operation a trained staff and a favorable social and economic environment, for the assessment and collection of the income tax is far more complex than the application of most indirect taxes and certain elementary forms of direct taxation. The complexities cannot be avoided because they arise from the nature of the income tax—from the fact that net income is an elusive concept that in many cases can be measured only on the basis of fairly elaborate compilations of information interpreted with the guidance of accounting and legal conventions. The income tax requires not only skill on the part of administrators but a high degree of co-operation on the part of taxpayers.

Summary of Prerequisites

The prerequisites of successful use of the personal income tax as a major revenue source range all the way from prosaic matters of bookkeeping to fundamentals of political attitudes and social values. One list summarizes these conditions as follows:

1. The existence of a predominantly monetary economy;
2. A high standard of literacy among taxpayers;
3. Prevalence of accounting records that are honestly and reliably maintained;
4. A high degree of voluntary compliance on the part of taxpayers;
5. A political system in which the rich are not dominant; and
6. Honest and efficient administration.[3]

Many variations of the statement of necessity conditions are possible.[4]

An important point to recognize is that in the absence of conditions such as these the income tax is liable to lose its characteristic advantages. The difficulty is not merely that the tax will be somewhat less efficient than the treatises make it seem but that in practice it will degenerate into an unequal levy bearing little resemblance to the theoretical ideal. Exorbitant taxes will be collected from the honest and the unlucky, while others pay little or nothing.

Writing in mid-nineteenth-century England, John Stuart Mill expressed the opinion that a fairly assessed income tax "would be, in point of justice, the least exceptionable of all

[3]Richard Goode, "Reconstruction of Foreign Tax Systems," *Proceedings of the 44th Annual Conference on Taxation, 1951* (Sacramento: National Tax Association, 1952), pp. 213–15.
[4]See, for example, Motokazu Kimura, *Conditions for Direct Taxation and Other Essays* (Tokyo: Science Council of Japan, Economic Series No. 17, 1958), pp. 17–20, and Sei Fujita, "Political Ceiling on Income Taxation," *Public Finance* (The Hague), Vol. 16 (1961), pp. 183–200.

taxes." But he thought that, in practice, the tax was apt to be so badly assessed that it should "be reserved as an extraordinary resource for great national emergencies, in which the necessity of a large additional revenue overrules all objections."[5]

Mill's comments sound familiar. They will bear quotation at some length.

. . . no amount of inquisitorial power which would be tolerated by a people the most disposed to submit to it, could enable the revenue officers to assess the tax from actual knowledge of the circumstances of contributors. Rents, salaries, annuities, and all fixed incomes, can be exactly ascertained. But the variable gains of professions, and still more the profits of business, which the person interested cannot always himself exactly ascertain, can still less be estimated with any approach to fairness by a tax-collector. The main reliance must be placed, and always has been placed, on the returns made by the person himself. No production of accounts is of much avail, except against the more flagrant cases of falsehood; and even against these the check is very imperfect. . . . The tax, therefore, on whatever principles of equality it may be imposed, is in practice unequal in one of the worst ways, falling heaviest on the most conscientious. The unscrupulous succeed in evading a great proportion of what they should pay; even persons of integrity in their ordinary transactions are tempted to palter with their consciences, at least to the extent of deciding in their own favour all points on which the smallest doubt or discussion could arise: while the strictly veracious may be made to pay more than the state intended, by the powers of arbitrary assessment necessarily intrusted to the Commisioners, as the last defence against the taxpayer's power of concealment.[6]

Considerations such as these have led a few experts to recommend that the underdeveloped countries dispense with the personal income tax or impose only a token tax. But

they may be better interpreted as an indication of problems to be solved and a warning against overly ambitious tax plans. It is worth remembering that Mill's advice was not heeded in Great Britain and that the British tax developed into what is widely regarded as a model of fair and complete compliance with the statutory requirements. The British development took place over a long period of time during which the income tax applied to only a limited group of taxpayers and without graduated rates and many other refinements.

Modern conditions do not require the less developed countries to repeat the slow evolution of the British tax and perhaps do not allow them to do so. It is still true, however, that we learn by doing and that the income tax can be perfected only by giving administrators and the public experience over a period of time with a tax that is modest enough to allow reasonably satisfactory assessment and collection.

The Latin American republics no doubt differ considerably in the extent to which they are now prepared to make effective use of the personal income tax. Some of them can apply efficiently no more than a rudimentary tax, whereas others have already gone far beyond that stage. It is not realistic to expect that many countries in the area will soon be in a position to administer a mass income tax applying to the majority of income recipients. Where these taxes exist, they appeared only after much effort had gone into the elaboration of a more narrowly based tax. In the United States as recently as 1939, only about 5 per cent of the population were subject to the personal income tax (including taxpayers and their spouses and dependents), compared with about three-fourths of the population in recent years.

Administrative Procedures and Aids

Constructive experience with income taxation depends on the use of appropriate administrative procedures and aids. This is not the place for an extended discussion of adminis-

[5]*Principles of Political Economy*, Bk. V, Chap. iii, Sec. 5, ed. by W. J. Ashley (London: Longmans, Green, 1929), pp. 829, 831. Ashley's notes indicates no change in this language after the first (1848) edition.
[6]Mill, *Principles of Political Economy*, pp. 830–31. Ashlev's notes indicate no change in this passage after the first edition.

tration, inasmuch as that was the subject of the Buenos Aires conference of 1961. Mention may be made, nevertheless, of a few requisites of good administration, most of which apply to all taxes but are especially important for the income tax.[7] These include codified tax legislation of reasonable completeness; official, published regulations providing details concerning the application of the law; and carefully designed forms with accompanying instructions for taxpayers. It is essential that administrative personnel be chosen on the basis of qualifications, given specific training, paid adequately, required to give full time to their work, and held to high standards of probity. The administration should be given ample powers of investigation and enforcement. The staff should be provided with operational manuals, office equipment, suitable office space, and funds for necessary travel. Elaborate procedures and equipment often are not the most efficient.

The most troublesome administrative problems relate to the assessment of tax against self-employed professional persons, independent businessmen, and prosperous agriculturists. These difficulties are not new, as is shown by the quotation from Mill, and they are not peculiar to Latin America; they are encountered in all countries. There are no easy solutions, but three kinds of procedures deserve mention even in a brief treatment. Efforts should be devoted first to building up a roster of persons who are presumed to have enough income to be subject to tax. A variety of sources of information can be exploited by ingenious officials. These include lists of persons holding professional licenses, members of professional associations, chambers of commerce, and the like; holders of import and export permits; and occupants of commercial and industrial buildings. Newspapers should not be overlooked as sources of names of prospective taxpayers. Information of this

kind can be used by the administration, of course, only if it maintains an up-to-date filing system and roster of taxpayers. The administration should probably have authority to require any person to file an income tax return on demand even though he maintains that he does not meet the usual filing requirements. Needless to say, this authority should not be used indiscriminately.

A second set of procedures relates to the use of collateral sources of information in the examination of tax returns. The sources that suggest themselves immediately are information that is already available to the government in connection with the assessment of land taxes, stamp taxes, customs duties, excise taxes, and *patentes* and from applications for import and export licenses or foreign exchange allocations.

A third set of possibilities, which are more debatable and concerning which experience is more limited, involves the assessment of income tax on the basis of presumptions or indirect evidence. There is a long history of taxes on items that were regarded as indicia of superior economic and social status. These include taxes on windows, carriages, horses, and the employment of menservants. The possibility under consideration now is the somewhat different one that certain external evidence be used to establish a minimum liability for personal income tax. The item most often suggested and one which has been used at times in Belgium, Greece, Switzerland, and other countries is the value of a person's residence. The rationale is that occupants of residences with a certain annual rental value have a certain average income. If the income reported on the tax return is far out of line with this ratio, it is assumed that there has been fraud or a mistake or that, for some reason, the individual has had a bad year. The first question to be asked about such a presumptive assessment is whether it is indeed consistent with experience: does the assumed ratio conform to the actual average, and how much dispersion is there among individuals? Second, how much easier is it to obtain reliable information about the item on

---

[7]Several of these points were developed by Joseph P. Crockett in a paper entitled "Common Obstacles to Effective Tax Administration in Latin America," prepared for the Pan American Union and presented to the Buenos Aires Conference of 1961.

which the presumptive assessment is based than about income itself? There is the obvious danger that the income tax will degenerate into a tax on house occupancy or whatever item serves as the usual basis of presumptive assessments. If this is likely to happen, would it not be simpler and more candid to start with a tax on the indicator instead of a tax that is nominally on net income? Clearly, there are objections; nevertheless, the possibility of greater reliance on presumptive assessments derived from indirect evidence seems to merit further exploration. A formal provision for presumptive assessments is not necessary to permit supplementary use of the indirect evidence that would enter into a presumptive formula. Occasional use is already being made of such evidence in many countries, particularly in cases of suspected fraud.

SOME QUESTIONS OF TAX DESIGN

A successful income tax must be adapted to local conditions, which vary significantly among countries. Hence no one set of provisions will be suitable for all countries, and it is useless to try to draw up a single "model" income tax law for Latin America. Certain questions of tax design, nevertheless, arise so frequently in the drafting of a new income tax or the appraisal of an existing tax that a few comments are appropriate.

Global Tax versus Schedular Taxes

The first question is whether personal income should be taxed under a global tax assessed on the aggregate of an individual's income from all sources or by means of several schedular taxes on different kinds of income. The schedular system was formerly usual on the continent of Europe and in Latin America, whereas a unitary tax was levied in the United Kingdom, the British Commonwealth, and the United States. The situation was somewhat obscured by the fact that the British tax was nominally schedular,

although in practice it was equivalent to a unitary tax. Most of the countries that started with a schedular system have added a supplementary tax on the aggregate income of the individual, usually called the "global complementary tax" in Latin America. Mexico took this action in 1961. The Argentine tax, like the British, is formally schedular, but income is aggregated and is subject to a single rate schedule except that the tax free minimum is larger for earned income than for investment income. Unitary taxes exist in Colombia and Central America.

The reason for the adoption of a global complementary tax or for preferring a unitary tax is easy to discern. The philosophy of the personal income tax requires that account be taken of the taxpayer's individual circumstances; this is possible only if income from all sources is aggregated. Another way of stating the same proposition is that the income tax is commonly regarded as a tax on persons rather than on things or income flows.

Aggregation is significant because of three features of income taxes: (1) personal exemptions, (2) personal deductions from taxable income, and (3) graduated rates. With personal exemptions and graduated rates, failure to aggregate income gives an obvious advantage to persons who receive income from more than one source. These individuals obtain multiple benefits from the personal exemptions and from the low rates applicable to the first part of taxable income. Personal deductions for items such as medical expenses cannot readily be fitted into a pure schedular system because it is not clear under which schedule the deductions should be allowed. Personal exemptions and deductions pertain to the individual and his special circumstances and not to wages, profits, and interest as such. Similarly, the rationalization for progressive taxation turns on an appraisal of personal sacrifice or of the political desirability of lessening economic inequality. In either case, the relevant matter is the size of the total income of an individual or a family.

That this line of reasoning or similar considerations have gained wide acceptance is suggested by the spread of global complementary taxes. The question arises whether there is any real advantage to a combination of schedular taxes and a global tax, or is the combination a cumbersome heritage from the past that should be dropped in favor of a unitary tax at the first convenient opportunity?

An advantage that is claimed for the schedular arrangement is that it is better adapted than a unitary tax is to collection at source by means of withholding. It is true that collection at source is simple for a pure schedular tax that incorporates neither personal exemptions nor graduated rates, because the amount withheld can be treated as the final tax liability and no individual return need be made. Once personal exemptions or graduated rates are introduced into the schedular tax, however, a final return is needed to determine whether too little or too much tax has been withheld. A crude kind of personal exemption can be allowed for wages without a year-end return by requiring employers to withhold tax only on payments to individual workers in excess of a stated amount per pay period. But this lends itself to abuse, and it discriminates against workers who are employed only part of the year and in favor of those who hold two or more jobs simultaneously. In Latin America, personal exemptions are generally provided in schedular taxes on salaries and wages but not always in taxes on investment income. The omission of personal exemptions for investment income simplifies administration less than might be supposed; information on amounts received by individuals is still needed to check compliance with the global complementary tax. Denial of personal exemptions for investment income, moreover, seems inequitable and inconsistent with the objective of fostering a wide dispersion of security holdings and savings accounts. Withholding, of course, is perfectly feasible under a unitary tax, as is shown by the experience of many countries.

A second advantage often claimed for the combination of schedular taxes and global complementary tax is that it allows different tax rates to be applied to different kinds of income. One basis for differentiation is the presumed completeness of tax enforcement. Thus, higher rates may be recommended for profits and income from independent professional practice than for salaries and wages, interest, and rent on the grounds that the former are likely to be less fully reported than the latter. Differential rates, it is alleged, will give more nearly equal taxation than a nominally uniform rate. This is true, however, only if there is a roughly uniform degree of evasion for each kind of income, a most unlikely condition. Furthermore, the whole argument serves as an excuse for continued and growing evasion and makes it hard for either the public or tax administrators to take seriously legal requirements for complete reporting of income. The mentality underlying the notion of effective uniformity through different degrees of cheating compensated by differential tax rates is incompatible with a strong income tax.

Are there good reasons for aiming at differentiation of *effective* tax rates on various forms of income? One motive for differentiation might be the desire to regulate the economy by placing high tax rates on activities that the government wishes to discourage and low rates on activities that it wishes to stimulate. Schedular systems, however, do not seem to be designed for this purpose, and it is hard to see how they could be. Regulation of the economy calls for more detailed specifications and more variations than can be feasibly reflected in a schedular income tax. Special deductions and exemptions under a unitary tax seem to be more flexible instruments.

Another kind of differentiation is between income from personal effort—so-called earned income—and property income. Many national systems impose lower taxes on earned income than on property income, and the distinction has been endorsed by eminent theorists. It can be justified on the grounds that earned income is less permanent than property income because it depends on the health and life of the recipient. Also, earned income is defined on a less nearly "net" basis than property income because allowances are not made for certain costs of acquiring earned income, such as educational expenses and special occupational expenses. More fundamentally, it seems intuitively evident that income is an incomplete measure of taxable capacity. A person with an income of $8,000 and property of $100,000 is surely better off than one with an income of $8,000 and no property. In a relevant sense, the former has more taxable capacity. The additional capacity of propertied individuals can be tapped by imposing a higher tax rate on property income than on earned income, or by a property tax or wealth tax, or perhaps by a combination of the two methods.

Preferential taxation of earned income under the income tax may be achieved by application of a separate rate schedule or by excluding part of earnings from the income that is assessed to tax. Such differentiation is not commonly thought of as an example of a schedular system and in fact is found in countries that are usually said to have unitary taxes. Nevertheless, it is similar to a combination system with two schedular taxes and a global complementary tax.

To sum up, a combination of schedular taxes and a global complementary tax seems to have no great advantages or disadvantages in comparison with a unitary tax. Differences between rates and exemptions for the schedules, however, should be critically examined.

Capital Gains and Losses

The treatment of capital gains and losses under a personal income tax is a subject on which opinion and practice differ widely. Capital gains and losses are profits and losses realized on transactions in real estate, securities, and other investments as distinguished from profits and losses on sales of a merchant's or dealer's stock in trade. One tradition, long followed in the United Kingdom and in several Latin American countries, is to leave capital gains quite free of income tax and to allow no deductions for capital losses. Exceptions are sometimes made, however. For example, in Brazil gains on real estate are

taxed at a special rate, and in the United Kingdom short-term gains of a speculative character were brought within the scope of the regular income tax in 1962. Another approach, adopted in the United States and in certain Latin American countries, is to tax capital gains, but at rates lower than those applicable to ordinary income, and to allow only limited deductions of capital losses against ordinary income.

The arguments about whether capital gains are really income are too lengthy to review here. Much of the debate about the economic effects of capital gains taxation has only limited relevance for the present discussion because it concerns securities markets at a more advanced stage of development than obtains in Latin America.

Whatever one's opinions on the classical issues relating to taxation of capital gains, it seems that one can agree that there are special reasons for taxing them in Latin America. First, the absence of capital gains taxes enhances the attractiveness of speculation in land and urban real estate compared with investments that are socially more productive. Many observers have noted an unwholesome preference for speculation over sound investment in different parts of Latin America. Second, a tax on capital gains helps somewhat to redress the inequities of inflation because it reduces the gains of those who have been most successful in taking advantage of inflationary conditions. This characteristic is desirable in countries that have experienced moderate inflations, but most countries that have undergone more extreme inflations have considered it advisable to make provisions for revaluation of assets or other abatement of capital gains tax. Third, capital gains are more widespread in a society that is undergoing rapid economic change than in a preindustrial community. To the extent that Latin America succeeds in speeding progress, it will create conditions favorable to the realization of capital gains. Fourth, it is extremely difficult to distinguish sharply between ordinary investment income and capital gains. Often ordinary income can be deliberately converted into capital gains. Facilities for such conversion are now less elaborate in Latin America than in certain other parts of the world, but ingenious schemes for tax avoidance will be stimulated by the existence of a wide difference between the tax payable on capital gains and on ordinary income. Finally, the taxation of capital gains helps satisfy demands for social justice. Failure to tax capital gains will benefit mainly the rich and may add to political unrest.

The taxation of capital gains involves administrative problems relating to the discovery of sales and sales proceeds and the verification of taxpayers' representations about the original cost of capital assets. These problems cannot be wholly avoided by excluding capital gains from the tax base because an alert administration will scrutinize many transactions to determine whether they are nontaxable sales of capital assets or the realization of taxable income.

Income from Foreign Sources

A subject that has attracted considerable attention recently is the taxation of income from foreign sources. Although reliable statistics are not available, it is alleged that Latin American investors hold large amounts of capital in Europe and the United States in the form of bank accounts and securities.[8] It has been alleged that the outflow of capital has been encouraged by the fact that in several of the Latin American republics income from foreign sources is not subject to local taxation.

Investment abroad by Latin Americans no doubt is stimulated by more fundamental influences than the opportunity of escaping income tax at home. In fact, foreign taxes on interest and dividends sometimes exceed the tax that would be imposed by the investor's home country. Nevertheless, it is questionable

policy for a country that is trying to mobilize resources for development to offer more favorable tax treatment to citizens who invest abroad than to those who invest at home. And, even if the capital outflow of the past has not been due to tax considerations, a modification of the tax system might help discourage further outflow and help induce repatriation of funds now held abroad.

The common Latin American practice of excluding from the tax base income received by citizens or residents from foreign sources may derive from the schedular approach. Countries with a history of schedular taxation tend to follow the principle of taxing income at the place of origin, whereas countries with unitary taxes incline toward the place of residence of the recipient.[9] These are logical applications of the two philosophies; the schedular system looks at the income stream, and the unitary system looks at the person. But more important may be the fact that several of the countries with unitary systems—including the United States, the United Kingdom, and the Netherlands—are capital exporters, whereas the Latin American countries are capital importers. If only one jurisdictional principle is to be followed, the place of origin is relatively favorable to capital importing countries, and the place of receipt is preferable for capital exporting countries. The Latin American countries would strike a poor bargain if they agreed with other countries that all income should be taxed only at the place of residence of the recipient.

It is unnecessary, however, to choose one principle or the other. Countries are free to adopt both principles and to tax both the income that originates within their borders and that which is received from foreign sources by persons who reside within their territory. Most of the capital exporting countries do this. A country can also use the test of citizenship, as the United States and Mexico do, and tax its nationals even though they reside abroad and receive their income from foreign

---

[8] Estimates ranging from $5 billion to $15 billion were presented to a subcommittee of the U.S. Congressional Joint Economic Committee in 1962. United States, Congress, Joint Economic Committee, Report of Subcommittee on Inter-American Economic Relationships, *Economic Developments in South America*, 87th Cong., 2d Sess., July, 1962, p. 1.

[9] Martin Norr, "Jurisdiction to Tax and International Income," *Tax Law Review* (New York), Vol. 17 (March, 1962) pp. 433–37.

sources. An expansive interpretation of national taxing power is not prevented by international law because, as one authority summarizes the position, "No rules of international law exist to limit the extent of any country's tax jurisdiction."[10]

But is it practicable to extend the income tax to interest and dividends from bank accounts and securities held abroad? How can the revenue administration obtain information on the portion of this income that is credited to investors' foreign balances and not remitted to them? If reliance must be placed solely on the declarations of investors, an attempt to tax foreign source income is likely to degenerate into an extreme case of penalization of scrupulous people.

The taxing country, however, may be able to obtain assistance from the source country under a general arrangement for the latter country to provide information on income paid to nationals of the taxing country or credited to accounts held by them. Banks and other payers or agents are ordinarily required to report these items to the authorities of their country. Tax treaties often contain provisions for the exchange of such information between countries. The Latin American republics, however, do not have a network of tax treaties under which they could obtain information, and the negotiation of separate treaties undoubtedly would be a slow process. Even without treaties, the countries in which flight capital is commonly held could provide information on a unilateral basis if their administrative agencies were empowered to do so, by legislation where necessary. The Latin American countries might wish to consider the advisability of requesting the United States and several of the European countries to make information available to them on a unilateral basis. Of course, such a request should be presented only if plans have been formulated for making good use of the information.

Few governments will wish to treat their own citizens more severely than other permanent residents. Hence, a government that decides to tax citizens on income from foreign sources will usually apply the same rule to aliens who are permanent residents. Although this is equitable, it may have the disadvantage for less developed countries of discouraging foreign businessmen and technicians from staying in the country. The situation is different from that which prevails with respect to income earned locally. Aliens who are ready to pay tax on income that they earn in a country in which they are temporarily working may not be reconciled to taxation on investment income that they receive abroad and never expect to bring to the host country. Furthermore, any double taxation that results in such a case is not likely to be alleviated by tax credits or other unilateral measures. Under United States law, for example, a United States citizen who resides abroad would still be subject to full United States taxation on income from investments in the United States, and he could not credit against his United States liability any tax paid to another country on the same income because the United States foreign tax credit applies only to taxes on income from abroad.

The problem would not arise if the Latin American country granted a credit for income taxes paid to other countries on income from abroad. A foreign tax credit is clearly desirable for countries that wish to encourage their nationals to invest abroad, but it is much less attractive to countries that would prefer to discourage capital outflow.

Another approach that may be better adapted to Latin American interests is to apply a liberal rule for determining how long an alien may remain in the country before he is considered a permanent resident and hence subject to local taxation on income from foreign sources. In view of the gains that accrue to less developed countries from the activities of foreign businessmen and technicians, and the advantages of having these people stay long enough to become familiar with local conditions, a sojourn of five years or more might be allowed before

[10]Norr, "Jurisdiction to Tax and International Income," p. 431.

residence was deemed established for tax purposes. Each government will have to decide for itself how to balance the factors of equity and expediency.

Imputed Rental Income

An income item that merits special mention is the imputed rental value of owner-occupied dwellings. Although not received in monetary form, imputed rent is part of economic income because a dwelling yields services which are salable and which would have to be bought by the owner if not obtained from his property. The purchase of a dwelling is an investment, regardless of whether one expects to occupy it or to rent it. In several Latin American countries, particularly those with rapid inflation, owner-occupied houses and apartments have been popular investments for the middle classes and the rich.

Omission of the imputed rent of owner-occupied dwellings from the income tax base results in inequities between owners and tenants and between investors in dwellings and in other assets. It encourages a form of investment that is often thought to be relatively overextended in Latin American cities and socially less productive than other kinds of capital formation. These considerations indicate that it would be desirable to include imputed rent in taxable income if it is feasible to do so.

Many countries, including some in Latin America, have attempted to apply the income tax to imputed rent. On the whole, experience has not been encouraging, primarily because assessments have been erratic and have failed to keep pace with rising rental values. Dissatisfaction became so acute in the United Kingdom that the Chancellor of the Exchequer in his budget speech of April, 1962, promised to eliminate the tax on imputed rent.

An income tax administration, harassed by more pressing problems, is not likely to be able to develop satisfactory assessments of imputed rent unless it receives substantial assistance from other agencies. When a reasonably equitable property tax is being applied

to owner-occupied dwellings, the income tax administration can assess imputed rent on the basis of the valuations made for purposes of the property tax and may even be in a position to co-operate in the valuation process. Where property tax is levied on capital value, imputed rent can be presumed to equal a stated fraction of that value. The owner-occupant, however, should be allowed a deduction for interest paid on any indebtedness relating to the property; that is, he should be taxed only on the imputed return on his equity.

In summary, it seems that the inclusion of imputed rent in taxable income is well justified in principle but in practice is linked to a property tax on urban real estate. There are few places in Latin America that now have property taxes that would provide a satisfactory basis for the assessment of imputed rent under the income tax.

Personal Exemptions and Allowances

The level of personal exemptions and allowances determines the number of persons who are legally liable for income tax, and it is an important factor in the progressivity of effective tax rates. The tendency in Latin America is to allow personal exemptions that are lower than those granted in most of the industrialized countries, if converted at the going exchange rate, but substantially greater in relation to national income per head than the exemptions in the industrialized countries.[11] Thus, for example, in Colombia in 1960 the exemptions for a family consisting of husband, wife, and two children totaled 7,000 pesos—equivalent, at the free exchange rate, to approximately U.S. $1,000 and equal to about 4.5 times the per capita national income. In contrast, the personal exemptions for a family of four in the United States amount to U.S. $2,400, which is only a little more than the per capita national income of 1960. These relations do not always hold, however. The Uruguayan income tax law in-

[11] United Nations, Economic Commission for Latin America, *Economic Survey of Latin America, 1955* (1956), pp. 142–44.

troduced in 1960, for example, provided initial exemptions much greater in terms of United States dollars than those allowed in the United States.

A principle that is often suggested is that the income tax exemptions should cover at least the amount necessary to provide a minimum standard of living. When interpreted as a socially acceptable minimum rather than a bare physiological subsistence, the figure must be regarded as variable with circumstances. The social minimum depends on the resources of the community. Surely, it is wrong to designate as the minimum a figure that is above the median income of the community and hence beyond the reach of the majority of the population. Such a figure may indicate a minimum level of aspirations, but the tax system must be adapted to current conditions. Considerations such as these underlie the comparisons that are often made between personal exemptions and national income per capita. Less commonly recognized, but also valid, is the proposition that the acceptable minimum of private consumption depends also on the urgency of the state's need for revenue.

But governments do not in fact leave free of tax a socially acceptable minimum of consumption. Often they impose heavy excise taxes and customs duties on commodities that are consumed by the poorest families and thus tax these families more heavily in relation to income than many who are above the social minimum. In the foreseeable future, it does not seem likely that governments can and will eliminate indirect taxes, although it may be possible to dispense with particular taxes that strike the poor with especial severity.

In setting income tax exemptions, then, it is necessary to have regard for other taxes. Segments of the population which are not subject to income tax nevertheless contribute to the support of government through the payment of indirect taxes. This observation has prompted different experts to draw opposite conclusions. One view is that reduction of income tax exemptions below the level that is commonly considered the social minimum is defensible because the poor will in any case have to pay taxes and will be more fairly taxed under the income tax than under excises and customs duties. The indicated policy is that indirect taxes be partly replaced by an income tax with low exemptions. The other view is that income tax exemptions may appropriately be set well above the social minimum because this simplifies administration and still does not leave free of all taxation those who are exempt from income tax.

The administrative considerations should probably prevail in most of the Latin American countries at the present time. It is not feasible to bring exemptions down to a level as low in relation to per capita national income or the socially acceptable minimum as the ratios obtaining in many of the industrialized countries. An attempt to do so is likely to cause a breakdown of administration or to lead to conditions in which the income tax is so unequally applied that it loses its supposed advantages. There may be countries in which the personal exemptions could be increased advantageously. Prudence demands, however, that increases be enacted only when a strong case can be made for them.

A specific method of determining personal exemptions is to begin by asking how many income tax assessments the administration can efficiently handle and then to set the exemptions at a level estimated to produce about that number of taxpayers. A danger is that this approach will give too little weight to the possibility of increasing the capacity of the administrative machinery. With fixed exemptions, however, population and income growth and, in many cases, rising prices will increase over time the number of taxpayers and the demands placed on the machinery. If realistic goals for improvement are set, determination of exemption levels mainly on the basis of administrative efficiency has much to commend it.

Tax Rates

Critical comments on personal income tax rates must be limited to rather vague generalizations. One of these is that beginning rates are often so low that the liability of many taxpayers is too small to cover the expense of collection. In setting rates, it is well to bear in mind that under the usual system the tax applies only to income above the exemption level. If, for example, the personal exemption is $1,000 and the beginning rate is 10 per cent, the tax on an income of $1,200 is $20, or an effective rate of 1.7 per cent. There will, of course, always be some returns for which the tax is very small, but a fairly high beginning rate will decrease the number of these. As a means of holding down the administrative work load, it may be desirable to disregard tax liability when it is below some minimum figure.

As already noted, there is a danger that rates at the upper end of the scale will be too high. There is a strong presumption that the top rates of income tax that are appropriate for Latin America in present conditions are considerably lower than the highest rates now imposed in the United Kingdom, the United States, Canada, and a number of other high-income countries. Indeed, many critics believe that the top rates are excessive in the latter countries. No general rule can be laid down concerning the appropriate numerical value of the maximum rate.

Taxable Unit

The impact of progressive tax rates is greatly influenced by the definition of the taxable unit, a technical matter that is often overlooked. The main questions are whether the incomes of husbands and wives are aggregated or taxed separately and whether the rates applicable to aggregated income of the spouses are the same as those on separate incomes or incomes of single persons. When incomes of husbands and wives are combined and assessed at regular tax rates, the degree of effective tax progressivity is much greater than when spouses are taxed separately on their separate incomes or are taxed at preferential rates on combined incomes. The relative taxation of married persons and single persons is, of course, also affected.

Practices differ greatly, and general property law, including the community property system, is often not controlling for tax purposes.[12] Some countries allow separate taxation of earned income of husbands and wives but aggregate all property income (Venezuela) or all income from property held under community property arrangements (Argentina and Brazil). In the United States all income is usually aggregated, but the rate brackets for joint returns of husbands and wives are twice as wide as those for single persons. France carries this system further by aggregating the incomes of husbands, wives, and minor children; dividing by the number of persons in the family, with children counting as half units; and determining the final tax as the sum of the separate taxes on the apportioned income.

No attempt will be made here to evaluate the considerations of social policy and administrative convenience that enter into the choice of the taxable unit. The main reason for alluding to the subject is to stress the need for taking it into account in comparing tax rates in different countries and in estimating revenue yields and effects on income distribution.

Special Exemptions and Deductions

In discussions of social and economic policy, the idea often occurs that desirable behavior can be induced by tax exemption or other favorable tax provisions. A wide variety of such plans have been proposed, and many have been adopted. In the income tax field, common schemes call for tax exemption (or exclusion from taxable income) for profits of new enterprises, dividends and interest from shares or bonds of private corporations carrying on especially important activities, interest on government bonds, and interest on savings accounts. Other measures include the deduction from taxable income of amounts paid in life insurance premiums and investments in

[12]See the papers by Oliver Oldman and Ralph Temple, "Tax Legislation Applicable to Women," United Nations, Economic and Social Council, Commission on the Status of Women (E/CH.6/344, January 26, 1959) and "Comparative Analysis of the Taxation of Married Persons," *Stanford Law Review*, Vol. 12 (May, 1960), pp. 585–605.

designated securities. There are also proposals for deducting all saving from taxable income.

These measures cannot be described and appraised in detail here. Nevertheless, a few general comments may be appropriate. First and most fundamental, a tax exemption or deduction merely removes a possible barrier; it does not create incentives where they were not present before. An income tax exemption will not entice people to invest in enterprises that offer no prospect of profit. When a profit is confidently expected but is considered too low, after subtraction of income tax, to be attractive, an exemption may be effective. Deductions of amounts invested may be more powerful because the tax saving due to a deduction can transform an expected return from a zero or negative figure to a positive amount. Still, the principle is the same; the prospective return must be attractive, compared with other opportunities, when enhanced by the tax saving.

Second, exemptions and deductions are more effective in influencing the form of investment and saving than in affecting their total volume. For example, tax exemption for interest on savings accounts is more likely to encourage an increase in the proportion of saving placed in these accounts than to raise total saving. This is true because, for the individual, the choice between forms in which savings may be held is of less moment than the choice between saving and consumption. The recognition of this characteristic points to a real cost of the special schemes. When they are most successful in stimulating particular forms of saving and investment, they are most potent in diverting resources from other uses. The net gain is not the gross yield of the favored saving and investment but only the difference, if any, between its social product and that of the activities that are displaced.

Third, another offset which should not be neglected arises from the sacrifice of government revenue. Nearly always this leads to higher taxes on other sectors, more inflation, or smaller government expenditures, any of which may be detrimental to progress. A pop-ular argument is that the tax exemptions do not really cost any revenue because they stimulate additional production and thus increase the yield of existing taxes. Although this can occur, the contention that it will do so in a particular case should be viewed with skepticism. The reaction must be very strong to compensate for the revenue loss. With representative Latin American tax systems, the *net* increase in gross national product would have to be some five to eight times the initial value of the tax exemption or deduction in order to generate automatically a fully offsetting growth of revenue.

Fourth, the value of a tax exemption and its cost depend on the effective tax rate. When income tax rates are low or the tax is widely evaded, a tax exemption or deduction is not a powerful instrument.

And, fifth, special tax incentives, if conscientiously administered, usually involve more complications than expected. The main difficulties relate to proper identification of the favored activities, which always requires fine distinctions between eligible and ineligible transactions. Too liberal an interpretation will add to the revenue cost while dissipating the incentive value of comparatively favorable taxation of well-defined activities. Problems of choice would be minimized if all saving were exempt from income tax. However, most governments do not consider all forms of saving equally desirable and hence would not wish to relinquish an opportunity for influencing the channels into which saving flows. Great administrative difficulties would be encountered, moreover, in auditing taxpayers' statements of net saving.[13]

These rather negative comments should not be read as a condemnation of all special tax deductions and exemptions. Sometimes they are useful. It seems, however, that their merits are more often exaggerated than understated. A critical examination of existing provisions as well as new proposals might serve as a corrective for excessive enthusiasm.

[13]Richard Goode, "Taxation of Saving and Consumption in Underdeveloped Countries," *National Tax Journal* (December, 1961), pp. 305–22.

CONCLUSION

This brief review shows the complexity of the personal income tax and also its versatility. When levying this tax, the state attempts to exact a contribution which is adjusted to the circumstances of individual citizens, which takes more from the prosperous than from the poor, and which automatically grows with national production. It would be naïve to expect that these advantages can be easily attained. They will be missed if the income tax is very unequally or erratically applied. Then it may be worse than cruder and simpler measures.

The separate decisions of an overwhelming majority of countries in all parts of the world show that the personal income tax is widely considered an essential constituent of a mod-ern revenue system. Its acceptance has been promoted by the social and political forces that have stimulated demands for democracy and economic progress.

Conditions that influence the operation of an income tax vary greatly among the Latin American republics. In some countries, a prolonged period of experience with a tax of severely limited scope and yield may be necessary to lay the foundation for a more ambitious law. In other countries, important forward steps seem feasible now. Everywhere, restraint is indicated in order to avoid excessive rates and overly exacting refinements. With sustained thought and effort, the personal income tax throughout Latin America can, in time, be made more just, productive, and flexible.

Comment

IFIGENIA M. DE NAVARRETTE*

I wish, first of all, to congratulate Professor Goode on his very pertinent, suggestive paper. My comments are not at all intended to dispute his opinions but merely to add certain views that I consider important in relation to that part of the study in which he states: "In most Latin American countries the [personal income] tax is a minor source of revenue, and nowhere in the area is it a powerful instrument for modifying the distribution of income and wealth." Therefore, I shall endeavor to avoid the important matter of the corporation income tax, although I shall have to refer to the tax on unincorporated businesses, which are very common in Latin America. Moreover, the profits tax is the part of the income tax that has developed most in Latin America. In Mexico, for example, it provides 75 per cent of income tax revenues (the total of which constitutes 35 per cent of all federal taxes) and between 2 and 2.5 per cent of the national income; however, there remain important problems of administration and tax evasion in medium and small businesses. The rates for this tax have also attained high levels, for they are steeply progressive and can be as high as 39 per cent of the profits, plus 4 or 5 per cent more if the excess-profits tax is included.[14] In addition, the tax on distributable profits is objective and proportional, and many tax experts consider it as an additional tax on corporate profits and not as a tax on the owners of the business, since it is neither personal nor progressive, as we shall see later.

In contrast, what can be considered as a personal income tax in Mexico takes scarcely 0.5 to 1 per cent of the national income, whereas in the United States it takes 17 per

*National School of Economics, University of Mexico, Mexico City, Mexico.

[14]Excess profits are considered to be profits in excess of 15 per cent of capital employed.

TABLE 6–1: Direct and Indirect Taxes of Certain Countries (*Per cent of national income*)

		1960				
	National per capita income	Total income of the govt.[a]	Indirect taxes[b]	Income tax		
Countries				Total	Business	Individuals
Colombia	231	14.6	8.0	5.7	2.5	3.2
Chile	502	28.3	12.7	14.8	7.2	7.6
Mexico[c]	275	15.8	9.4	3.5	2.5	1.0
Peru[d]	112	16.1	6.8	9.3	5.4	3.9
United States	2,289	33.7	11.3	22.3	5.4	16.9
Canada	1,528	35.4	17.2	15.3	5.4	9.9
Great Britain	1,084	37.2	16.8	17.9	3.5	14.4
Japan	341	26.4	12.0	12.6	5.4	7.2

[a]Includes: Central government, local governments, social security, profits, earnings, and interest from property and superavits of government enterprises.

[b]Includes all kinds of taxes on goods and services as well as taxes on the ownership of property, including real property.

[c]In the case of Mexico, income of the federal government, federal agencies, municipalities, social security, and superavits of government enterprises were taken into consideration. The taxes on exports and on metallurgical ore production were classified as indirect taxes; included in taxes on business were the tax on excess profits, royalties, interest, and dividends; and in personal taxes only Schedules IV, V, and contributions by those covered by social security.

[d]For the year 1959.

SOURCE: United Nations, *Yearbook of National Statistics, 1961, Statistical Yearbook, 1961, Demographic Yearbook, 1961.* Banco de México, *Annual Report.*

cent; in the Netherlands, 20 per cent; in Chile, 8 per cent; and in Colombia, 3 per cent. (See Table 6–1.)

There is another point I should like to clear up first, and that is the schedular or unitary nature of the income tax. If a schedular division is used for administrative purposes owing to the greater ease of collecting it at the source, as in Great Britain and other countries, it is not conceptually different from the unitary tax, since both taxes achieve the same purpose. However, if the schedular tax applies different rates and procedures for the different income sources and therefore does not reflect the economic capacity of individuals, it becomes a form of direct taxation that discriminates against those who are subject to the schedules having the highest rates and the most effective collection control. If to these conditions is added a standard global rate (as happened in Mexico in 1962), the differences and inequities are increased instead of being eliminated, and the economic capacity of individuals is not taxed equitably. Obviously, in this case it cannot be said that there is a personal income tax, and the task of the fiscal policy will be to move toward

the unitary concept (with or without schedules) as soon as possible. It is even desirable that those countries that now have a schedular tax retain that tax structure for administrative purposes. In that event, the problem boils down to standardizing rates and procedures so that *persons having the same economic capacity have the same tax burden* and the tax burden increases progressively as the income level rises.[15]

In what follows, I shall try to confine my comments to the limitations found in an underdeveloped country in establishing and operating an income tax effectively, in order to analyze certain objections and see if the reasons used to justify its lack of development have some real basis that cannot be overcome. I shall classify the objections into three groups: theoretical or economic, technical or administrative, and political, even though at

[15]This does not mean that certain income, such as that derived from work, cannot receive a limited preferential treatment or that there do not exist general systems of exemptions and incentives for investment (in the profits tax) that lighten the tax burden for economic activities that merit a special stimulus (accelerated depreciation, investment credits, exemptions, reinvestment of profits, etc.).

times the difficulties are complex and involve more than one aspect at the same time.

ECONOMIC OBJECTIONS

1. It is said that the so-called perfection of the income tax as a measure of economic capacity has been exaggerated; that the countries that have adopted excessively progressive rates and strict conditions in their concept of taxable income want to reduce the former and be more liberal in the latter; that, if a government is to tax the economic capacity of the individual more equitably, direct progressive taxes on wealth, net assets, capital gains, and personal expenditures must be added. It is argued that since it is obvious that in the Latin American countries the degree of economic development and the level of public administration could not support a comprehensive system of direct taxation, it is vain to urge a very strict personal tax at the present time. To increase revenues, it will be preferable to continue the present tax structure, despite its imperfections, and to concentrate on improving tax administration. In addition, in those countries where the personal income tax has developed considerably, it is now being realized that direct taxation has its limits, and that indirect taxation also has certain advantages when one wants to finance a large public expenditure.[16]

I agree with Mr. Goode that such criticism does not apply to the Latin American countries because, although it is true that it would be very difficult to establish a comprehensive system of progressive direct taxation, the personal income tax is still the most important fiscal mechanism a democratic government has in a capitalist economy. This tax reduces the disparity in income distribution that accompanies rapid capitalization; it has great flexibility from the standpoint of fluctuations and growth in economic activity; and it

brings to the government substantial resources from individuals with larger incomes, which permits financing the increasing expenditures for economic and social development. These advantages are powerful arguments for making the effective establishment of the personal tax a primary objective of the fiscal policy of underdeveloped countries. Such a goal should not mean abandoning or lessening indirect taxation, since fiscal reform in Latin America should include the technical and administrative improvement of the entire tax system. Also, although the public expenditure needs in Latin America are large, they do not require as high average levels as in the developed countries, which have a heavy military budget. From the standpoint of yield, excessively steep progressive rates merely constitute a deliberate form of cutting down personal income considered to be excessive, since they provide only a very small part of the revenue, as shown in the case of the United States and other countries.[17]

2. It is argued that, at the beginning of their industrialization, the developed countries did not have high progressive taxes. However, neither did these countries have the degree of government intervention that is now necessary to promote development, nor did they think about financing development plans. The development promoted by economic policy and public investment requires that the government have a larger porportion of resources than the liberal governments of the nineteenth century needed. The social conscience of the times also requires larger current expenditures and more transfers and investments of a social character. Moreover, it is recognized that such expenditures contribute to the increased productivity of the population and hence to an increase in the rate of economic growth.

I agree with Mr. Goode that the negative effect of the tax on the level of personal

[16]See an analysis of the way direct and indirect taxes affect saving and comsumption in Richard Goode, "Taxation of Saving and Consumption in Underdeveloped Countries," pp. 305–22.

[17]It is estimated that in the United States the marginal rates of over 50 per cent yield only 2 per cent of the total personal income tax. See Committee for Economic Development, *Growth and Taxes, Steps for 1961*, p. 12.

saving has been exaggerated. I admit that, at any given time, a society may have a consumption function according to which, on the average, families save more as they move up in the income scale. However, the following factors must be taken into account.

a) At the present time, families are spending a greater proportion of their real income on perishable goods and durable goods. As for durable goods, families "invest" a large part of their income in housing, cultural and recreation materials, and other goods that last for a long time and are readily available to large groups of the population. This means that "family savings" (interpreted as that part of income not consumed within a certain period of time) are assuming very different forms from those that existed previously. Opportunities for spending are much greater, as is natural when a society prospers.

b) National saving is composed of savings of consumers, enterprises, the government, and foreign sources. I agree with Mr. Goode that the corporation tax can have a greater impact on national saving than the personal tax, because the personal tax has decreased in importance as a source of financing national investment and because, in contrast, the importance of corporation and government savings has increased.

3. The criticism that taxes reduce incentives to work and invest is more applicable to the profits tax, although its supposed incidence is an important point in this argument. Actually it is high rates that can cause the greatest discouragement, despite the fact that there are several methods of counteracting them (exemptions, accelerated depreciation, subsidies, investment credits, and, of course, tax evasion). I agree with Mr. Goode that if we desire to promote economic growth, the income tax should be used moderately.

ADMINISTRATIVE OBJECTIONS

Administrative procedures are so important in the application of the income tax that they may emasculate the theoretical ideal.

It seems to me that in underdeveloped countries, the nature of income and the occupational structure of the population receiving it should be analyzed in order to reach useful conclusions aimed at establishing an efficient, equitable administration of the personal tax. For the sole purpose of pointing out certain difficulties that arise in the application of the tax, I shall analyze certain problems relating to taxpayer control, dividing the economically active population into three groups:

1. Nonagricultural wage earners.
2. Population engaged in agriculture:
    a) Independent or self-employed farmers;
    b) Farm laborers.
3. Nonagricultural entrepreneurs and property owners.

Persons belonging to more than one group (wage earners with income from property; property owners receiving wages or a salary; independent workers who also receive wages, etc.) may be considered as belonging to the group from which their main income is derived.

Not all the economically active population may be subject to the personal income tax in Latin America. The extent to which it is, depends on the minimum taxable income. If it is established at very high levels in ratio to the average per capita (or per paid worker) income, a large part of the population will escape the tax, and therefore the administrative task will be eased, but the revenue will decrease. It is estimated that in Mexico in 1960, two-thirds of the paid working force received an income below the minimum taxable, which was 500 pesos a month, the equivalent of 1.7 times the average income. (See Table 6–2.) According to these figures, workers who received an income below the minimum taxable in relation to the total paid workers were: nonagricultural wage earners and salary workers, 18 per cent; day laborers, 16 per cent; independent farmers, 22 per cent; nonagricultural entrepreneurs, 7 per cent. In other words, at this relatively low level the personal tax would

TABLE 6–2: Mexico: Structure of the Economically Active Population (*Thousands of workers*)

Sectors	1960 Population by thousands	Per cent	Workers with monthly incomes Less than $500	Workers with monthly incomes More than $500	Percentage of total of salaried workers Less than $500	Percentage of total of salaried workers More than $500
Total population	35,232	100.0				
Economically active	12,014	34.0				
Unpaid workers and unemployed	1,514	12.6				
Paid workers	10,500	100.0	6,639	3,434	63.3	32.6
1. Nonagricultural wage and salary workers	4,000	38.1	1,875	2,125	17.9	20.2
2. Farmers	5,000	47.6			38.3	5.2
a) Salaried	1,810	17.2	1,685	125	16.0	1.2
b) Not salaried	2,763	26.3	2,337	426	22.3	4.0
c) Unspecified	427	4.1	—	—	—	—
3. Nonagricultural entrepreneurs	1,500	14.3	742	758	7.1	7.2

SOURCE: Economically active population: Nacional Financiera, Department of Economic Research.
The distribution between salaried and nonsalaried workers was estimated on the basis of the relative importance of each group in the agricultural sector and the nonagricultural sector in 1950.
Monthly income: estimate by the author based on various statistics provided by the Bank of Mexico, Nacional Financiera, Social Security, Department of Industry and Commerce, Department of Surveys, and the Ministry of Finance.

apply to only 37 per cent of the total paid workers. If the exempted income were fixed at a higher level, a larger part of the population would escape and a large part of the revenue would be sacrificed. The distribution of the workers by income level clearly shows that a compromise system must be sought that makes it possible to apply to most of the population a personal income tax of a simple structure with low rates, to perfect the tax administration, and to increase the rates gradually as the income level of the taxpayers rises.

1. *Nonagricultural wage earners and salaried employees.* This is the group that can be most easily taxed, because its members receive a fixed income, easily controllable by a system of withholding at the source (by a schedular or unitary tax structure). It should be started by controlling the employers, who are a small group, and requiring them to keep records on their workers. Administrative control is facilitated if there is a social security system, for in that case the various deductions can be combined. If the coverage of the two systems is different, the social security information can be used to check on the tax information. However, it is very diffi-

cult to put into operation a system of deductions at very low income levels because the administration cost would be greater than the revenue; furthermore, in complicating the administration, more productive taxpayers might be neglected. If deductions are not allowed in order to facilitate the administration (as is done in Mexico), the principle of tax equity suffers. In the interest of efficient administration, it is preferable to establish a reduced tax at low income levels and to increase the tax burden gradually; but, at the same time, the lack of a system of deductions to render comparable the situation of taxpayers with different family responsibilities will be felt. On the other hand, at the higher income levels deductions lose their importance as a means of lightening the actual tax burden. Consequently, it is in the middle-income group of families that the problem of an excessive tax burden may exist. Again, an effort will have to be made to find a compromise solution making it possible to obtain ample revenue and still retain the principles of equity of the personal tax. For example, a system of standard deductions open to taxpayers with certain family dependents may be established. Another solution would be to use the system of deductions for those levels at which rates begin to be rapidly progressive, thus permitting taxpayers to choose, within certain limits, either low rates with no deductions or higher rates with a right to deductions from gross income. Another characteristic of this group of taxpayers is the need to lump together the earnings of those who have more than one job. In a way, such persons have greater expenses and difficulties than they would have if they worked for only one employer, and yet they are generally subject to the progressive rates on their total earnings. However it may be, the principal problem of this group is deductions and not the control of the taxpayers or the actual collection of the tax. It is estimated that in Mexico wages and salaries constitute 34 per cent of the national income and that from 5 to 10 per cent could be collected by direct taxes (including social security contributions).

2. *Farm workers.* In the agricultural sector, account must be taken of the prerequisites enumerated by Mr. Goode, namely: a monetary economy, literacy, accounting records, voluntary compliance, honest administration, and a situation in which the rich are not dominant—conditions which are lacking in the agricultural sectors of most underdeveloped countries. Moreover, this sector constitutes the majority of the economically active population. In Mexico, agriculture, stock raising, forestry, and fishing occupy 53 per cent of the economically active population and 48 per cent of the paid workers, but about four-fifths of the latter group receive less than the minimum taxable income. In general, this group has a low taxable capacity, with the exception of those who grow export crops. Most of the workers receive very low wages, except in the most prosperous areas. Likewise, it is more complicated to exercise control over farm employers than urban employers for the reasons mentioned earlier. In this group, instead of the income tax, the export tax has been used successfully. It taxes promptly and efficiently the profits derived from agricultural products for the international market, the chief source of taxable capacity in this sector. We all know the advantages and disadvantages of an ad valorem tax on exports; and although it is recognized as an important fiscal instrument in an underdeveloped country, I believe, for reasons of equity, that it should not be used as a substitute for the income tax but as a complement to it.

The group of self-employed entrepreneurs made up of farmers, small businessmen, craftsmen, and small manufacturers can be taxed by a dual system of income taxes consisting of (*a*) a simple system, without deductions, with low, proportional rates on the gross income for low income levels and (*b*) a tax on net income (rapidly progressive, reaching an average rate of, let us say, 40 to 50 per cent) for large-scale farmers and independent entrepreneurs who can be more readily controlled because they are very well known in small towns and the various regions. The objective will be to reduce the first group of taxpayers, who are subject to an imperfect tax for the sake of administrative convenience.[18] It is particularly difficult to determine the net income of farmers and small businessmen because they also use their products for family consumption and keep no record of it. If family consumption is not included in taxable income and monetary income alone is taxed, this group will be in a preferential situation. There is in addition another problem: What is an appropriate method for integrating the profits tax and the personal income tax? A technical solution might be to tax independent workers as a business and then credit the tax paid against their personal tax liability. However, such a solution could be used for only a small number of taxpayers in the middle- and higher-income groups.

In Mexico, the net agricultural income ac-

---

[18]For this group of taxpayers, the value added tax proposed by Professor Kaldor at the conference could also be adopted. The taxpayers would have to keep a record of their income and their purchases: the tax would be applicable to the balance, deducting all income (wages, rent, interest) on which tax had already been paid.

counts for approximately 22 per cent of the national income, and it would be difficult to obtain 1 per cent of this amount by a personal income tax. In 1960, the tax on agricultural profits represented 0.09 per cent of the agricultural income.

3. *Nonagricultural entrepreneurs and property owners.* The concept of net income and deductions is understood from the fiscal standpoint as it refers to independent entrepreneurs who obtain large incomes, such as professional people, artists, and people who carry out a technical or artistic activity, but the administrative control of this group is one of the most difficult, and it requires ingenuity and astuteness on the part of the fiscal officials to see that such taxpayers pay taxes according to their economic capacity. There is also a certain number of prosperous family enterprises that for some reason still prefer to operate as such and to which the same statements apply.

The largest group of taxpayers is the one consisting of people who derive their income from earnings from their property, including dividends, interest, royalties, rent, operation of concessions, patent, etc. In this group, a distinction should also be made between small and large property owners. Control over the small property owner is not so difficult as control over farmers because the degree of wealth concentration in urban areas is greater than that of income. The small property owners are not very important, either in number or in the concentration of their economic power. Generally, they are a handful of individuals who are well known in their community, whose education is above the average, and who can keep adequate accounting records. However, in small towns (and in the countryside), it will be difficult to provide a check on the usurer.

Frequently in a schedular system the beginning rates on income from capital are much higher than those on income from labor; and the small *rentier* may bear a heavier tax burden than other persons with equal economic capacity who derive their income from other sources. I concur with Mr. Goode's opinion that the small property owners should also receive fair tax treatment. In addition, distribution of ownership and the formation of voluntary saving should be encouraged.

The problem of greatest fiscal and economic importance is to establish a tax, suitable in concept and administratively effective, on the large property owners who constitute a socially privileged group in most Latin American countries owing to their tremendous economic and political power. Moreover, the anonymous form of ownership, a system that is very widespread in Latin America, makes tax control of the property owners even more difficult. Many times the practical solution has been to fix proportional rates that are withheld at the source (if progressive rates exist, generally they are not applied) without regard for the personal economic capacity of the property owner. In Mexico, in order to promote the development of financial capitalism, the earnings from almost all fixed-income private and public bonds were exempted from the income tax until recently. They are now taxed at a very low proportional rate (between 2 and 5 per cent) when their yield is more than 8 per cent a year. (See Table 6–3 and Graph 6–1.) In the case of income from capital to which progressive rates are applied, the tax is too high for the small investor and too low for the big investor, to the detriment of the revenue, since ownership of securities tends to be concentrated in the high-income groups. The absence of a progressive tax on dividends is due in part to a mistaken concept of double taxation. Some influential persons still believe that a tax on dividends taxes the same source twice and that the profits tax is already quite high; and even the experts who admit that two different taxes are involved consider (tacitly, and at times, explicitly) that, since in Latin America most companies organized as corporations are actually partnerships, if their owners pay the profits tax, they should not be liable for the personal tax, because that would be an excessive tax burden on a single taxpayer.

TABLE 6-3: Average Income Tax Rates, 1962 (Percentages of taxable income)

					SCHEDULE					
Annual taxable income (pesos)	I and II Business and industrial profits	III Farm profits	IV Wages	V° Professional persons	VI Interest on securities	VI Other interests	VII^b Dividends	VIII^c Rent and royalties	VIII, Section II^a Rent from urban real property	IX Royalties from government concessions
2,000	—	—	—	3.0	2–5	10.0	15.0	10.0	—	20.0
6,000	3.9	2.4	0.9	3.6	2–5	11.1	15.0	11.1	—	21.1
12,000	5.9	3.4	1.6	4.4	2–5	12.3	15.0	12.3	3.5	22.3
24,000	8.0	4.7	2.8	5.8	2–5	13.9	15.0	13.8	3.5	23.8
36,000	9.4	5.6	3.9	6.9	2–5	15.1	15.0	15.1	3.5	25.1
48,000	10.5	6.3	5.0	7.9	2–5	16.1	15.0	16.1	3.5	26.1
60,000	11.4	6.9	6.0	8.7	2–5	17.0	15.0	17.0	3.5	27.0
72,000	12.2	7.4	6.8	9.5	2–5	17.8	15.0	17.8	3.5	27.8
84,000	12.9	7.9	7.6	10.2	2–5	18.6	15.0	18.6	3.5	28.6
96,000	13.5	8.4	8.4	10.9	2–5	19.2	15.0	19.2	3.5	29.2
108,000	14.2	8.8	9.0	11.5	2–5	19.7	15.0	19.7	3.5	29.8
120,000	14.7	9.2	9.7	12.0	2–5	20.3	15.0	20.3	3.5	30.3
150,000	15.8	10.0	11.3	13.3	2–5	21.4	15.0	21.4	3.5	31.4
180,000	16.8	10.8	12.9	14.3	2–5	22.5	15.0	22.5	3.5	32.5
210,000	17.8	11.5	14.2	15.3	2–5	23.4	15.0	23.4	3.5	33.3
240,000	18.6	12.1	15.8	16.2	2–5	24.1	15.0	24.1	3.5	34.1
300,000	19.9	13.0	18.1	17.6	2–5	25.4	15.0	25.4	3.5	35.3
360,000	21.0	13.9	21.2	18.9	2–5	26.4	15.0	26.4	3.5	36.4
420,000	22.0	14.7	23.6	20.1	2–5	27.4	15.0	27.3	3.5	37.2
480,000	22.9	15.3	24.9	21.0	2–5	28.4	15.0	28.4	3.5	37.9
1,000,000	27.1	18.5	37.3	25.8	2–5	36.1	15.0	36.1	3.5	41.4
10,000,000	37.4	24.3	49.9	32.3	2–5	48.6	15.0	48.6	3.5	53.1

aRate applicable to the net income.
bThe rate may be 20 per cent if the taxpayers own bearer shares and do not disclose their name (Article 154 of the Law).
cExcept Section II.

GRAPH 6-1: Average Income Tax Rates

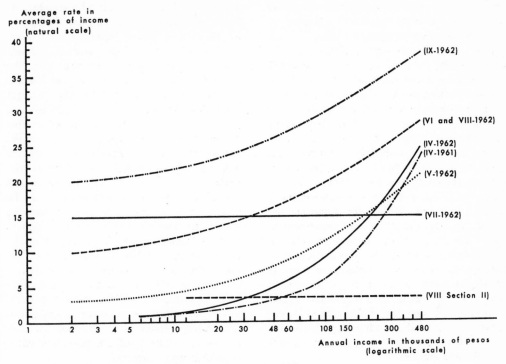

NOTE: This graph was kindly supplied by Mr. Victor Urquidi.

There is no doubt that in Latin America, with the exception of foreign companies and a small number of domestic companies, the corporation is rather a kind of legal organization that does not mean distribution of ownership nor a separation between ownership and management of the company. In general, corporations and limited liability companies belong to a few individuals, bound by close family ties, and frequently the other stockholders are purely nominal, only for purposes of complying with the law. However, the concept of double taxation no longer has the negative connotation it used to have. High rates are the same as applying to the same source low taxes two or more times. The important thing with respect to profits is to know what part of the annual income flow is going to be absorbed by the government. Once the proportion has been determined (in the developed countries, it exceeds 50 per cent), a

decision has to be made regarding at what stage, and the manner in which, the revenue will be obtained. I consider it inconsistent to impose high tax rates on a business, which is the source of productive activity and investment, and to tax lightly and deficiently the income received by the owner of the business, inasmuch as he belongs to a privileged class and tends to indulge in excessive luxury consumption that is often antisocial. To accelerate economic development, it would seem more desirable to follow the opposite course, that is to say, to tax business more lightly (although it will be necessary to seek some means to avoid reducing the tax burden of foreign companies, since their owners do not reside in the country), or else to soften, with general fiscal incentives, the taxes of companies that invest and at the same time apply to the income received by the owners a strict, progressive personal tax. A more moderate global rate on profits would have the advantage of letting the market determine the efficiency of the business. However, if tax incentives are applied in a special way, judging each case on its merits, there is the danger that it will be the government administrators who will decide, on discriminatory bases, who deserves to enjoy a reduction of his tax burden.

There is even less justification for preferential treatment of other kinds of income from capital because they are income currents that were not previously taxed. This is the case of interest, royalties, fees for technical services, rent, etc. If the taxpayer is a large property owner, it is not difficult to determine his actual income, for it is only necessary to apply the external indicia recommended by Mr. Goode, although the complications of anonymous ownership continue to exist. It would be highly desirable to put an end to this kind of fiscal and economic screen which, in my opinion, offers serious social disadvantages and no advantage. However, strong political pressures are opposing it with considerable success.

POLITICAL OBJECTIONS

The uneven distribution of income in the Latin American countries is a fact. Although the standard of living of large segments of the population has been improved, a small group has been able to obtain substantial improvements and receives a large part of the personal income. This is the group of big and medium businessmen, certain professional people, both salaried and independent, technical experts, artists, and real property owners, stockholders, bondholders, and owners of other forms of capital. It is estimated that in Mexico 1.5 per cent of the economically active population is made up of property owners who receive 42 per cent of the national income[19] and that 5 per cent of the families receive between 37 and 40

[19]About one-half of the property owners have incomes below the minimum taxable level. (See Table 6–1.)

per cent of the personal income. This is the group that has additional taxable capacity. Modern governments have increased responsibilities and require, in order to fulfill them, a substantial part of the national income, perhaps no less than 20 per cent, since the countries where social services and benefits are more or less satisfactory take a larger proportion. On the other hand, business and private saving also have an important role to play in the area's progress. Therefore, the government should harmonize fiscal interests with favorable treatment for all those who undertake an activity or are willing to risk capital or postpone consumption. For the success of a development fiscal policy, the income tax should permit the government to share in business profits and cut part of the income received by the privileged class. The most important short-term fiscal reform is uniform, progressive taxation of income derived from capital, which, owing to a number of theoretical, administrative, and political factors, remains in a privileged situation if compared with the direct taxes applied to wage and salary workers.

It appears paradoxical that in Latin America it has been possible to impose high progressive rates on business profits when, at the same time, high-income groups have, owing to the economic power they hold, so successfully opposed the application and effective operation of the personal tax. The explanation may lie in the supposed incidence of the former tax: the companies affected consider that they are shifting the tax to the consumer. The Mexican Employers Association itself so declared. It is well to mention the surveys conducted by the United States and British tax commissions, in which businessmen stated that they were shifting the tax because they took it into account in figuring their net after-tax earnings. There is a debate that has not yet ended nor been clarified concerning the shifting and incidence of the tax. There is no doubt that, because of taxes, a businessman tends to demand a larger return for his part in production and that he will exert effort to obtain it; but whether or not he obtains it will depend on other factors that operate only over the long term. Most fiscal experts agree that, in the short run, it is difficult to pass on the tax and that it is absorbed out of profits, which would probably be higher without the tax. Nevertheless, as a result of this illusion of the entrepreneurs, they seem willing to accept high profits taxes and oppose progressive personal taxes.

Another reason for the paradox is the fact that it is possible to decrease the profits tax burden by using subsidies, exemptions, tax credits, and other tax incentives. These measures could not be applied to the personal tax. Both administrators and taxpayers should keep in mind the disadvantages that result from tax discrimination: on the one hand, it has an unfavorable effect on the revenue collected; on the other, the political handling of taxes and exemptions becomes irritating and demoralizing to the taxpayer.

In Mexico, the schedular tax is not merely an administrative measure. In theory, it continues to be a schedular tax with different treatment for different types of income, and it is too complex in structure. There are now nine schedules, sixteen rates, and two surtaxes. The rates for low levels of certain in-

comes from capital are too high, and although at the present time these cases are of little practical importance, they may come to be important. These include the wage earner who has a few shares of stock on whose return he must pay a tax of 15 per cent. In contrast, the large property owner, who should be subject to a higher rate, pays the same or less if he receives an income from sources that are not taxed so heavily. Within the framework of the Alliance for Progress, there is no room for such discrimination. However, it is feared that drastic reforms in the concept of the income tax may alter the country's financial structure (transfer of assets, sale of securities, capital flight, etc.).

In the future, more urgent fiscal reforms will center on the income tax and an effort will be made to overcome the difficulties involved in its establishment. In my opinion, the fiscal reform should be aimed chiefly at taxing progressively and efficiently the personal income obtained by entrepreneurs and owners of capital. A great effort should also be made to improve the administrative apparatus so that the actual revenue collected approaches the potential amount and equal treatment is given to all taxpayers having the same economic capacity.

Comment

Alfonso Moisés Beatriz*
and Ulises Flores**

The author of the document on which we are commenting decribes very thoughtfully the chief characteristics of the phenomenon, the personal income tax, in Latin America

*Salvadorian Association of Industrialists, San Salvador, El Salvador.
**Doctor of Jurisprudence and Social Sciences, San Salvador, El Salvador.

and the fundamental aspects that should be examined in considering the possibilities of making of it a suitable instrument for the equitable distribution of the tax burden and the attainment of other fiscal policy objectives.

We express below some ideas which reflect our personal observations regarding tax administration in Latin America, especially in El Salvador and the other Central American countries.

REASONS WHY THE INCOME TAX IS OF LITTLE IMPORTANCE IN LATIN AMERICAN COUNTRIES

Mr. Goode states that in most Latin American countries the income tax is a minor source of revenue and that nowhere in the area is it used as a powerful instrument for modifying the distribution of income and wealth.

Further on in his article, the author lists six prerequisites to success of the income tax in any society. An examination of these prerequisites against the backdrop of the social and economic characteristics of most of the Latin American republics leads us to the conclusion that Mr. Goode has stated very accurately the reasons why the income tax has met with little success in Latin America.

Parallel to these causes, we wish to point out another one of similar importance which, because it stems from the actual situation of the levels of per capita income, is, in our opinion, also an obstacle to making the income tax a source of major government revenue. We believe that, in view of the pronounced progressivity of the income tax, its application is easier and less debatable, from the standpoint of economic development, when most of the population receives substantial incomes. Only in that case can one consider a general income tax, a tax that reaches the majority.

When such conditions do not exist in a given country, the tax is applied to such a small number of the population that it loses one of its fundamental characteristics: its general application.

In Latin America, this situation is seen all too frequently. Most of the population, especially in Central America and northern South America, receive an annual per capita income of no more than 200 dollars. This means that, generally speaking, in Latin America, with the existing level of per capita income, there can be no thought of a general income tax, which fact decreases the possibility of using it as an effective instrument of economic policy.

Although it is a repetition of what has already been said on other occasions, especially at the Conference on Tax Administration held in Buenos Aires last year, we must also state that the acceptance of the system of government in a country is an important factor in the voluntary compliance of the taxpayers with their obligations. These conditions can never be established by tax administrators or tax theorists. The reasons for this situation go deeper, but students of tax matters must point out their contribution to an attitude of indifference or resistance to compliance with tax obligations.

A TAX TO MEET OUR SITUATION

Pragmatic consideration of these facts leads us to conclude that we must consider forms of taxation that are in line with our economic and social situation, even though such forms may not be in accord with the traditional structure adopted by other countries.

Mr. Goode has enumerated the prerequisites for the efficient administration and application of an income tax. These prerequisites are present in their entirety in the highly developed countries; in most Latin American countries, however, they are absent or exist in only a rudimentary form. Therefore a complex income tax system aimed at general application, productivity, and sufficient flexibility to be adapted to the individual circumstances of the taxpayer so as to achieve a high degree of tax justice could not be applicable to the Latin American situation. That is why we suggest that, bearing in mind the various degrees of development in the Latin American countries, simple systems be applied and that they be gradually improved as development conditions permit the application of more refined and more complex forms of taxation that are more consistent with the principles of equity.

We believe that every effort should be made to determine what the characteristics of the social and economic structure of our countries are and to seek the income tax structure best suited to those characteristics. Simply adopting the complex tax forms that have been successful in the highly developed countries is the wrong approach to our tax problems.

We repeat that we must seek simple tax forms consistent with our social, economic, and administrative structure and with the class of taxpayers found in Latin America. Frequently, the simple income tax systems that have been proposed for Latin America are scorned by those who are used to complex tax forms in the developed countries. We ought to prepare ourselves to answer such criticism with the conviction that a developing country should have a tax system in line with its characteristics.

HIGH TAXES AND THE ACCELERATED RATE OF CAPITALIZATION

It has frequently been said that high income taxes prevent the rapid formation of private capital because it is thought that the marginal propensity to save is higher in the group of high income taxpayers who are the ones most affected by progressive taxes. On the other hand, it is recognized that a tax system that gives preferential treatment to investment in certain economic activities will permit, more or less satisfactorily, the transformation of our rudimentary economic systems, directing the economy toward new forms that are more suitable to economic development. A fiscal policy that employs taxation as a means to channel investment requires high taxes in order to be effective. To influence the economic behavior of the taxpayer, low taxes are inadequate. Therefore, even if the theory that high taxes discourage saving and investment is valid, we must recognize that substantial tax exemptions will be an effective means for channeling investment toward certain sectors of economic activity that are considered desirable for the country's development.

In speaking of the urgent need for the developing countries to accumulate capital, we must mention the desirability of promoting the establishment of corporations. Although Mr. Goode's paper about which we are commenting is limited to an analysis of the personal income tax, this kind of tax cannot be separated from the corporation tax if we are to influence the Latin American investor's method of operation.

TAXATION OF WAGES

Mr. Goode has given special attention to the possibility that if the requisites for a social and economic environment favorable to the income tax do not exist, such a tax might not only be inefficient but might in practice degenerate into an unequal tax that would levy high taxes on the honest and the unlucky, while others would pay little or nothing. One of the harmful results of establishing income tax systems that are not consistent with the characteristics of the economy of a country is the obvious unfairness with which the tax is applied to some taxpayers with respect to others. An example of this is the heavy burden constituted by this tax for wage earners in certain Latin American countries. This inequality arises not because of higher rates on wages than on income obtained from other activities—for example, from business, agriculture, or indusry—but because in practice taxpayers who receive their income from these sources, owing to the circumstances stated earlier, are not reached with the same effectiveness and efficiency achieved by the tax administration in taxing wages, where the withholding system is frequently applied.

These ideas make us view favorably the adoption, in countries where the tax administration is defective, of systems that establish preferential treatment for income derived from wages, through the recognized systems being used in certain countries, such as taxing only partially the income derived from that source.

PROGRESSIVE TAX ON NET WEALTH

A few Latin American countries are applying with relative success, but very good intentions, a progressive tax on net wealth, aimed at reducing the inequality referred to in the preceding point, or because they feel that the property owner has a greater tax capacity than one who obtains income solely by his personal effort. We believe, in particular, that the progressive tax on net wealth is to be recommended for those countries whose characteristics are the least desirable and least suitable for the establishment of an efficient income tax system. Of course, the net wealth tax involves the problem of an accurate evaluation of the assets; however, it seems easier to evaluate property fairly than to determine income correctly.

In speaking of the schedular tax, Mr. Goode maintains that the "rationalization for progressive taxation turns on an appraisal of personal sacrifice or of the political desirability of lessening economic inequality" and that "in either case, the relevant matter is the size of the total income of an individual or a family." In our opinion, it is not sufficient to consider the amount of the income as the only element in appraising taxable capacity. This is acknowledged by Professor Goode when he states further on that income is not a complete measure for determining that capacity. It is necessary to consider the precarious condition of income derived from work, especially in most Latin American countries, where, unlike many countries of Europe and North America, there are no effective social security benefits to compensate for the uncertainty of the income derived from personal services.

Consequently, a system that combines a personal income tax with a progressive property tax will achieve two things in Latin America: more equitable taxation and the possibility of redistributing wealth.

CAPITAL GAINS AND LOSSES

Mr. Goode clearly analyzes the old problem of taxes on capital gains in developing countries. He concludes that they should be taxed in Latin America for various special reasons, which he enumerates in his paper.

Some of these reasons are more economic than fiscal because he feels that this kind of taxation can favor considerably a policy intended to reduce the attractiveness of speculation in real estate and to channel investment toward sectors that are more productive socially.

Other reasons enumerated by Mr. Goode are to comply with principles of fiscal justice, as, for example, to tax profits obtained because of inflationary conditions, and the evidence that the absence of a capital gains tax benefits chiefly the rich.

In our opinion, there is no doubt whatever that it is both desirable and advisable for Latin American countries to tax capital gains. We think that if certain capital gains to which we shall refer were excluded from the application of this tax, no valid objection could be raised that a strong, progressive tax would decrease the possibility of saving and investment. On the contrary, it would be an effective instrument for achieving an economic policy combating purely speculative investments that do not contribute to an increase in the national income. Also, the establishment of such a tax is highly equitable, because there is nothing to justify the exemption from the income tax of gains that are not derived from the personal efforts of those receiving them, while it is applied to the earnings that should be considered strictly a product of the effort or intelligence of the taxpayers. There is no reason whatever for taxing the latter income and excluding the former. Often, especially in developing countries, capital gains are the product of factors totally independent of the effort of the taxpayer and are due largely to demographic pressure, the general economic growth, and, in short, to a host of factors that cannot be attributed to the person receiving the capital gain in particular.

However, capital gains obtained from the sale of securities should be mentioned for exclusion from the field of application of this tax. We wish to stress the fact that our countries need to increase their capitalization rate, and every measure intended to promote savings, by the poor as well as the rich, will further the attainment of this goal, so necessary to the development of our economies. Many countries are making efforts to create a stock market in order to stimulate investment by small savers and permit them to participate in the benefits brought by accelerated economic growth. That is why we feel that gains obtained from the sale of securities should be exempt from capital gains taxation; this, instead of impeding saving and investment, will promote their growth and channel investments toward activities of this kind, in view of the favorable treatment, as opposed to another type of investment that will be punished by the capital gains tax.

Some authors have stated that the capital gains tax should be an independent tax, the amount of which would depend on the tax-paying capacity of the one receiving the income. This consideration is based on the contention that this kind of tax is an instrument intended not so much to produce revenue for the treasury as to serve effectively in a policy to combat speculation and channel investment toward productive activities.

Many advantages besides the ones mentioned would be obtained by the establishment of the capital gains tax. One of the effects—which, although secondary, should not be ignored—is that it would aid effectively in the correct determination of other taxes on property, such as land tax and wealth taxes, gift taxes, and inheritance taxes. If the buyer had a special interest in having the true purchase price stated in the deed, the elements for the determination of the other taxes on the property would undoubtedly be improved.

Finally, it should be stated that the introduction of this new tax in the Latin American countries that do not yet have it should be done carefully in order to prevent the serious consequences that could result from the levying of a new tax, owing to inexperience or lack of foresight. At any rate, it must be concluded that the levying of this tax will contribute effectively to upholding the principle embodied in the Charter of Punta del Este that those who have most should pay most, without thereby harming the levels of desirable investment.

INCOME FROM FOREIGN SOURCES

While considering the possibility that certain problems may arise in its application, Mr. Goode recommends that the income tax be extended to income from foreign sources.

The objectives pursued are two: to prevent the flight of Latin American capital and induce the repatriation of funds now held abroad, and to produce increased revenue.

There is no denying the right of a country to tax the income received by its nationals or residents, regardless of the location of the source. However, it appears that most Latin American countries do not apply the income tax to such income because they consider it fundamentally impractical.

Actually, there is no doubt that the incentives for Latin American investment abroad are not precisely to avoid the income tax in their country of origin, since, in general, the taxes on such activities abroad are higher than those in the investor's country of origin. Undoubtedly, the reasons for this behavior by the investor are different. This is not the place to mention them, but a remark to that effect should be made. In any case, we think that to extend the income tax to these earnings will not encourage the repatriation of the funds now held abroad, if the fundamental reasons behind the investor's action are not related to the tax, and especially if the investor is given, as is usual in such cases, a deduction or credit for the tax paid in the country of origin of the income.

It has also seemed to be impractical up to now to apply this idea as a means of increasing government revenue. Although it is feasible to conclude agreements with the countries where this kind of investment is made, it is also true that in most cases some principle will operate to eliminate or decrease the double taxation; and since, in general, the countries where this income is received have a higher tax than is levied in the Latin American countries, it is to be suspected that the Latin American countries will have nothing left but the cost of an unproductive administration.

IMPUTED RENTAL INCOME

Mr. Goode believes that the principle of including the imputed rent for the house in which the owner resides in taxable income is justified, although he believes that the experience of the Latin American countries in this practice is not very encouraging.

Following the commonly accepted principle of taxing most the one who has most, it is, from any standpoint, justifiable to tax this type of imputed income. Basically, in Latin America, where homeowners are frequently the wealthy, such taxation is completely fair.

Actually, not only from the standpoint of tax justice but from that of the attainment of the principles of economic policy, this tax may be an effective instrument for discouraging investment in property that is not very socially productive. If we consider the experience of certain Latin American countries in periods of economic prosperity, we shall see that a large part of the increase was invested in the construction of high-cost, sometimes excessively luxurious, homes to the detriment of other investment sectors that would have been eminently desirable from the standpoint of economic development. For that reason, despite the difficulties of determining the amount of this imputed income accurately, it appears desirable to include it in the income tax.

PERSONAL EXEMPTIONS

Mr. Goode quite rightly criticizes the liberal exemption policy in most Latin American countries.

It is true that the administrative capacity establishes a reasonable limit on the number of taxpayers subject to the tax. However, there are fundamental reasons that lead one to believe that the personal exemption should be reduced to more realistic levels. One of them is based on the need to make the composition of government revenue more progressive. In general, such revenue in the Latin American countries comes mostly from indirect taxes levied on all the inhabitants of a country, regardless of their taxable capacity. If we wish to change this situation in order to make the direct tax the chief source of fiscal resources, knowing that this type of taxation will permit us to achieve not only a fairer distribution of the tax burden but a more flexible and effective fiscal policy owing to the broadening of the tax base, we must realize that a high personal exemption will constitute an unjustified advantage for many, since it restricts the ability of the administration to apply a tax that has generally been considered an adequate measure of the tax-paying capacity. Any increase in personal exemptions is an injustice for those who pay indirect taxes—an injustice that must be eliminated gradually, but firmly and surely.

Tax relief for many of those who come under the high personal exemption is not justified, considering the urgent need to decrease the tax burden of the poor. Such relief is unfair in view of the obvious priority of the low-income groups.

We have stated that the success of the income tax as an instrument of fiscal policy will depend to a large extent on its general application. Consequently, broadening the tax base and reducing personal exemptions to reasonable limits will make it a more general tax. The success of economic policy measures sought through this tax will depend on how many taxpayers are affected by it.

It should also be considered that, owing

to the social composition of most Latin American countries, ample facilities should be given for exemptions for family depend-ents, especially if the personal exemption is low, since in Latin America families are not always organized according to the civil law.

Discussion

Mr. Goode introduced his paper. The practical question was how the personal income tax could be made more effective in Latin America. It was a form of tax that was based broadly on capacity to contribute; it could reduce excessive inequality; and it could provide an elastic yield responsive to increases in real output and inflationary increases in money incomes. Although the tax had been criticized as tending to curtail savings, the evidence to support that contention was not persuasive: moreover high savings ratios were possibly less characteristic of high incomes in underdeveloped countries than in countries with a long capitalist tradition. Moreover, other factors, such as the security of property, the prospective rates of inflation, investment opportunities, the taxation of corporations, fiscal deficits, and government investment, might all have a greater impact on the national saving ratio than the taxation of individuals. It was true that the income tax lent itself to excessive progression, but that was an argument against abuse of the tax, not against the tax itself. There was no scientific method of forecasting the reaction of individuals to progressive taxation, but he agreed with Mr. Harberger that if rates were moderate and there was due regard for certain aspects such as the definition of net income, adequate allowance for capital consumption, etc., there was not much danger of an adverse effect on incentives to work or invest.

However, the income tax was likely to lose its characteristics in the absence of certain preconditions, which include a predominantly monetary economy, a high literacy rate, accounting records that were predominantly honest and reliable, extensive voluntary compliance by taxpayers, a political system not dominated by the rich, and an honest and efficient administration. The last condition was as essential as the others, but perhaps easier to bring about in the short run. In the light of those requirements, Latin American countries differed considerably in the extent to which they were equipped to make effective use of the personal income tax.

With respect to tax design, he thought it was now widely recognized that a global tax had substantial advantages over a schedular form of tax; the two might be used jointly, but a schedular tax alone was likely to operate unfairly and ineffectively.

There were a number of reasons for taxing capital gains as a form of income; not only was it correct in principle, but it restricted speculation.

In several Latin American countries, income from foreign sources was not subject to domestic taxation because the tax principle invoked was taxation of income at the place of origin instead of the place of residence of the recipient. There was no reason why countries should not tax both income generated within their borders and income received from foreign sources by residents. Even in the absence of tax treaties providing for exchange of information on income paid or credited to nationals of the taxing country, foreign countries might be willing to provide such information on a unilateral basis, provided there was a serious intention of using the information to good purpose.

Omission of the imputed rent of owner-occupied dwellings from the income tax base resulted in inequities between owners and tenants and between investors in dwellings and in other assets and encouraged a relatively less productive type of capital formation. However, in practice there were few countries in Latin America with property valuations that would provide a satisfactory basis for assessment of imputed rent under the income tax.

With respect to personal exemptions and allowances, administrative considerations should probably prevail in most Latin American countries at present. It would not be possible to bring exemptions down to a level as low, in relation to per capita national income or the socially acceptable minimum, as the ratios prevailing in more industrialized countries.

In setting rates, it was preferable to establish a fairly high beginning rate in order to reduce the number of payments too small to cover the cost of collection. Upper rates should not be too high, and in Latin America appropriate rates would be considerably lower than in such countries as the United Kingdom or the United States. If the incomes of husbands and wives were not aggregated, the tax would be less progressive than it appeared.

There was no doubt that the personal income tax deserved a substantial place in the revenue system of Latin America, but the considerable advantages of such a tax could not be obtained without sustained thought and effort. Above all, there must be restraint in order to avoid excessive rates and over-refinements.

MRS. DE NAVARRETE, presenting her comments, said that she was in general agreement with the paper and would confine herself to the question of the establishment and effectiveness of a personal income tax in underdeveloped countries. The objections against such a tax could be classified as theoretical or economic, administrative or practical, and political; and she laid special stress on the administrative type, examining the case of nonagricultural wage earners, agricultural taxpayers, and nonagricultural entrepreneurs, pointing particularly to the low real capacity of the agricultural taxpayers, at any rate in Mexico. She believed it self-defeating to impose high rates on enterprises and low rates on the income received by their owners, who usually formed part of a privileged social class though the enterprise itself performed the productive work. She therefore believed that the tax burden on enterprises should be reduced, provided foreign firms whose owners did not reside in the country did not receive the same treatment. She was opposed to granting preferential treatment to income derived from capital not previously taxed (interest, royalties, fees for technical services, rents, etc.); she was also opposed to imputed house rentals being included in the taxable base, although it might be taken into account in calculating national income.

She considered that, in the future, the most pressing tax reforms would revolve around the income tax and that they should tax personal income derived from capital in a progressive and efficient manner. A great effort should also be made to improve the administrative machinery so that taxes actually collected would come as near as possible to what was expected and all taxpayers in similar situations would receive equal treatment.

MR. FLORES, introducing the written comments on Mr. Goode's paper which he and Mr. Moisés Beatriz had presented jointly, said that Mr. Goode had accurately analyzed the causes of the relatively unsuccessful imposition of the personal income tax in Latin America. A pragmatic consideration of conditions in Latin American countries must lead to the conclusion that forms of taxation had to be adopted in those countries which were adapted to their economic and social environment, even if that meant a departure from the traditional tax structure. Moreover, the simpler the income tax imposed, the better. The social, economic, and administrative structure in Latin America and the type of taxpayers in the countries concerned precluded the application of complicated forms of taxation such as those used in the more developed countries. Preferential tax treatment should be granted in favor of investment in specific economic activities as a means of directing the economy toward more advanced systems conducive to economic development.

MR. MOISÉS BEATRIZ, continuing the presentation of the joint paper, observed that a progressive tax on net wealth was being applied with some success in a few Latin American countries. Such a tax was to be recommended in countries where conditions were least suitable for an effective income tax.

With respect to capital gains and losses, he had no hesitation in supporting the application of a tax on capital gains in Latin America. Provided that capital gains were taxed, the tax would combat purely speculative investment which did not contribute to national income and would channel investments into productive activities. He would exempt capital gains derived from the sale of securities so as to attract investment by persons with small savings and allow them to share in the benefits of increased economic development. Care should be taken in imposing a capital gains tax in order to avoid the unfortunate consequences which might result from lack of experience or foresight.

He felt that extension of the income tax to income from foreign sources would, in most cases, fail to prevent the flight of Latin American capital or to increase fiscal revenue but would only result in an unproductive rise in administrative costs.

He supported the taxation of the imputed rental from owner-occupied dwellings because it was, in fact, a rental whose exemption would be regressive and because it was an economic fact in Latin America that the owner of a dwelling was a privileged person.

MR. NAHARRO, intimating that he was in general agreement with the paper, went on to refer to the twofold possibility of considering income tax from the point of view either of strictly collecting revenue or of providing a system of incentives to guide economic development in a specific direction. Without prejudice to the idea of directing it over the long term with an eye to its yield, in order not to distort the revenue producing aims inherent in it, the income tax might be used as a short-term instrument to promote de-

velopment by means of a suitable system of rebates and exemptions. In that regard, he favored total exemption of certain forms of savings, limiting the taxable base to the income spent, despite Mr. Goode's objections to such exemption since it was admitted that savings were not forthcoming in sufficient quantities for development. Precisely, to ensure that they reached the desired level, it would be advisable to create additional incentives in favor of savings invested in capital formation helpful to economic development.

MR. JARACH, referring to what Mr. Goode had said about the taxation of income from foreign sources, pointed out that the main reasons for the attitude of Latin American countries had been a reaction against the position of the capital exporting countries, which had based the tax on the place of residence of the recipient instead of on the place of origin of the income, and the position of the capital importing countries themselves, which wished the tax to be based on the source and origin of the income. The situation had now changed for Latin America, in that while capital for investment was being sought, domestic capital tended to leave the country because of inflation or other reasons, and consequently a new approach was required. In some Latin American countries, a solution had been sought by basing the tax on the place of residence; but under that criterion nationals were taxed while foreigners were exempt, which was obviously unfair.

Another point he would like Mr. Goode to clarify was the question of tax havens against a progressive income tax provided by holding companies, which might purport to represent investment by foreigners when they did not. There was a need for international co-operation to prevent such an asylum from taxes on income and wealth.

Although there was a case for taxing imputed income from owner-occupied houses, it was necessary to guard against loopholes enabling taxpayers to report tax losses in this connection that could be offset against other income.

Although he had been living in a Latin

American country for many years, he supported the views of those outside Latin America who did not have much faith in tax incentives. One important reason was that the incentive effect was sometimes more apparent than real; if the reduction in government revenue led to a budget deficit and consequent inflation, the result was to transfer the burden to other classes, and the total effect was disincentive. Another argument not mentioned by Mr. Goode was that the tax reductions tended to affect income taxed at high marginal rates, rather than the average levels, and were hence regressive.

MR. VIDAL said that, in his opinion, the desirability of an income tax with limited progressive rates had been sufficiently well established, and he wondered whether it might be possible for legislation to take into account a system of periodic adjustment of such rates in relation to currency devaluation, in order to prevent rates from remaining stagnant, to the detriment of the taxpayer, as was the case in his country. Regarding the unitary or schedular system he agreed with the general feeling in favor of the former, although he believed that some decision would have to be taken on the matter of including the sale of bearer securities as personal income. With regard to taxation of income from domestic investment abroad, he said that such income was taxed in his country, but, in his opinion, the flight of capital was not strictly a tax problem; he recalled that there had been some suggestions made in that connection at the meeting of the Latin American Center for Monetary Studies (CEMLA) in Mexico.

He agreed with Mrs. de Navarrete regarding imputed rentals which in practice were distorted in an ad valorem assessment of dwellings. Yachts, race horses, etc., were in the same situation, not being taken as income. They were capital investments, and until fair standards were available, they should be subject to the appropriate taxation as property. Moreover, in the case of dwellings—which usually paid land tax—they should not be doubly taxed with income tax, particularly if the income was fictitious.

Referring to tax incentives, he agreed with Mr. Naharro regarding exemption of income from savings, but only where they were invested in industry, housing, etc., in a manner determined in advance by the state. Individuals, i.e., private activity, should above all be given the opportunity of helping in the task of economic development. The state should step in only when they did not do so, levying a tax on over-all personal income, in compliance with its social responsibilities.

MR. KALDOR agreed with most of the proposals made by Mr. Goode with respect to the personal income tax. The tax should be comprehensive, free of loopholes, broadly based, and should include capital gains, which would be taxed as income. The tax rates should be moderate. That applied equally to the developed and underdeveloped countries. High marginal rates (in some cases as high as 90 per cent) made the tax virtually impossible to administer and thus shielded persons in the higher income brackets, as had been the case in the United Kingdom and the United States.

Mr. Goode had perhaps not dealt sufficiently with the basic requirements of an effective personal income tax in Latin America as it related to income from capital. Wages and salaries presented no problem, since evasion was most apt to be engaged in by persons with income from capital. Such income would be difficult to tap unless the tax administration had full knowledge of the total wealth owned by individuals. As long as income could be concealed through such systems as bearer shares in corporations, a capital gains tax would be difficult to apply. The Latin American countries should create a system by which the total assets owned by a taxpayer were known and their value could be reasonably ascertained. That might be achieved through requiring a declaration of wealth from individuals, as was done for corporations. Such a declaration would include an annual declaration of purchases and sales of capital assets, properly assessed at their market value.

If a distinction had to be made between income from labor and from property, it could not be done by levying two different schedular rates on income, but only by applying an annual tax on net wealth combined with a tax on personal income. Property holders should be taxed on the basis of their asset holdings as well as on their income from property. A combined tax on net wealth and income would facilitate the keeping of records of individual capital assets and of changes in such assets and would be a means of preventing evasion. The problem in Latin America was not only to institute tax reform in order to tax income now excluded from taxation but also to include existing income which escaped the tax net.

He agreed with Mr. Goode that the imputed rental value of owner-occupied dwellings should be part of taxable income. It had been so considered in the United Kingdom, but the tax on the imputed rental value of homes in that country was about to be abolished because there seemed to be an irrational feeling about that particular tax.

MR. HARBERGER observed that the Latin American countries could be among the world's leaders in tax reform. They could not only apply what was being done in other areas but also point the way. That was particularly true of the taxation of capital gains, which should be taxed as income at the same rate as the personal income tax. It had been argued that to do so would be unfair where the capital gains were obtained in a single year. That objection could be overcome by a simple averaging device.

He wished to emphasize the importance of maintaining a broad base for the personal income tax. A narrow base would require high rates, whereas the rates could be lower if the tax base were broader.

He disagreed with some of the points made by the commentators on Mr. Goode's paper. Mrs. de Navarrete, for instance, had objected to the imputed rental from owner-occupied dwellings being considered as income for tax

purposes. He did not see why a person living in his own home should be favored over someone living in a rented dwelling. He agreed, however, that imputed income from other sources was similar in nature to the imputed rental income from owner-occupied dwellings and that tax legislation would have to draw an arbitrary line between those forms of imputed income which would be taxed and those forms which would not.

Mr. Flores and Mr. Moisés Beatriz advocated exemption from the capital gains tax of income from the sale of securities. He could not support that view. There were two types of capital gains. On the one hand, there were gains from changes in relative market supply and demand, i.e., from increases in the relative price of some goods. Those might be considered accidental gains. On the other hand, capital gains might be deemed to be normal in the case of corporations which reinvested their profits, and it would accordingly be wrong to exempt increases in the value of their securities from the capital-gains tax.

He did not share Mr. Naharro's views with respect to incentives to savings, which were not very responsive to the rate of interest. All tax incentives that make investment more attractive have the effect of raising the rate of interest, but savings would not be considerably reduced if there were no tax incentives. Moreover, if governments could invest their additional tax revenue either directly in the public sector or in the private sector by purchasing shares, they would be contributing to an increase in total national savings more than by granting tax incentives.

MR. PIEDRABUENA felt that the suggested system of first raising the income tax and then admitting a system of exemptions under the heading of tax incentives to promote certain types of investments was contradictory. In his opinion, it was preferable to establish moderate rates of a general nature really likely to be complied with and to suppress all exemptions in personal income tax; however, he would not advocate the same procedure for corporate income tax. In any event, if such exemptions were admitted, it should be compulsory to declare exempted income, in order not to destroy the progressivity of the tax. It was not easy to agree on a definition of personal income or to determine its scope. As to casual capital gains, they should be incorporated into income without prejudice to the possibility of making allowances based on the number of years that had elapsed since the investment was made. The introduction of imputed rental could give rise to great injustice.

MR. LESSA said the redistributive effect of the income tax had to be balanced against the incentive effect. If the state was to act as the executor of development policy, it must have some means of influencing the private sector and ensuring that investment was directed to development ends. However, incentives could be established on a progressive basis, with lower exemptions for the higher income brackets. Exemptions should be allowed only for investment in development, and failure to meet the requirements of development planning should be punished by withdrawal of the exemptions.

MR. HERSCHEL was of the opinion that the advantages mentioned by Mr. Goode did not really exist, in view of the seemingly inevitable lack of flexibility of the income tax patterns which Mr. Goode attributed to the tax. With regard to exemptions, like Mr. Jarach he had no faith in the results of a policy of tax incentives, which in any event would make the taxable base narrower.

MR. MONTERROSO agreed in general with the opinions set forth by Mr. Goode in his paper, except on a few points; for example, where imputed rentals on dwellings were concerned, a matter on which he shared the objection raised by Mrs. de Navarrete. The social need for promoting the construction of housing, which was generally accepted and in itself constituted sufficient argument against Mr. Goode's view, should be taken into account. While it was true that there appeared to be too many luxury dwellings in Latin America, it should not be forgotten that they were also subject to the real estate tax. How-

ever, the inclusion of imputed rental based on a percentage of the cadastral value of the dwellings was acceptable, provided that no rebate was allowed for maintenance costs and that nonluxury dwellings were exempted.

With regard to income of foreign enterprises, if the intention was to promote the investment of foreign capital, it would be ineffective not to tax such income in the country where it was obtained if the country of origin of the enterprises concerned allowed the deduction of taxes paid there.

MR. JATAR-DOTTI, referring to a tax on imputed income from owner-occupied dwellings, agreed with Mr. Kaldor that such a tax would not be very useful in a country which already applied an effective tax on wealth, although it was essential, even if defective, where wealth was not effectively taxed. In that connection, he felt strongly that luxury housing should be reduced in Latin America, since it did not contribute to economic development.

With regard to capital gains, some participants had argued that a tax on capital gains should be applied on a broad base to include income from securities. In Venezuela, the tax was confined to the revaluation of real property and did not cover income from shares and bonds.

He agreed with Mr. Goode that there were certain risks to granting tax exemptions and deductions but felt, as did Mr. Goode, that the possibility of providing for such exemptions and deductions should not be rejected out of hand. They might, for instance, be applied to income which was reinvested and might also be useful to encourage savings.

MR. RIOFRÍO recalled the theoretical and legislative background of presumptive income, which he felt had more and greater disadvantages than advantages, and family income. In regard to casual capital gains, he called attention to the wasting effect of inflation upon them. He believed that income from foreign sources should be taxed not at the place of domicile but at the source.

MR. DESCARTES agreed with Mr. Goode and Mrs. de Navarrete on the importance of establishing a tax on personal income in Latin American countries based on relatively moderate rates of taxation. Such a tax was essential in Latin America, even if applied within a narrow range. He supported Mr. Kaldor's suggestion of an annual declaration of wealth but observed that even the more developed countries had found it virtually impossible to institute such a method. However, he agreed that an attempt to require an annual declaration of wealth should be made by the Latin American countries.

With respect to Mr. Goode's suggestion concerning imputed rental from owner-occupied dwellings, he thought that the Latin American countries would do better to concentrate on other more positive aspects of the personal income tax.

The question of the taxation of foreign enterprises, he thought, should be dealt with through treaties between the countries concerned.

With regard to tax incentives, he felt that the solution applied in Puerto Rico, in view of its special position in the American market, could only partly serve as a model for Latin America as a whole. Even in Puerto Rico, incentives had had to be granted and an aggressive campaign undertaken to seek out industrialists and to offer them tax incentives. The field of tax incentives was a difficult and dangerous one for Latin America and should be entered into with extreme caution.

MR. CASAS referred particularly to income from the agricultural sector, which had certain peculiar characteristics, and to the disadvantages of granting preferential treatment to that sector for tax purposes. In support of his views, he mentioned the experience of Colombia, where investments in agriculture were used as a form of evasion. With regard to the relative advantages or disadvantages of the schedular as compared with the global system, he pointed out that in the recent Colombian tax reform the latter had been preferred because of its simplicity and its traditional roots. However, the schedular system might well be acceptable so as to reduce personal exemptions. Taxing of presumptive income had given satisfactory results in Colombia, although it should be recognized that the revaluation of real estate and perhaps the tax on capital gains which accompanied it helped to obtain such results.

MR. GNAZZO thought that the conference should state its position clearly in regard to personal income tax. There was a tendency for the participants to give undue importance to administrative problems and to overlook the fact that the essential aim was to define personal income tax as an instrument of fiscal policy. Mr. Goode, for instance, had mentioned several prerequisites for the successful application of the tax, which fell into the same vicious circle in that they could not be applied for want of suitable administrative machinery. He agreed with Mr. Naharro that the prime objective of income tax was to promote economic development. The conference should therefore decide in favor of a solution in absolute terms which would state clearly whether income tax was an appropriate instrument for Latin America or whether others should be sought.

With respect to the imputed rental of owner-occupied dwellings, under Uruguayan law the portion of such rental over and above 30 per cent of the nontaxable personal or household minimum was deemed to constitute income. The rent payer, in turn, could deduct as expenses up to 30 per cent of the nontaxable minimum.

MR. BACA concurred with the fundamental points made by Mr. Goode and congratulated him on his understanding of the real situation in the region, which he appeared to have grasped more clearly than other non-Latin American writers. Taxable income should be fixed at a higher minimum level than in the more developed countries and at rates that did not exceed 50 or 60 per cent.

Foreign experts often recommended a taxable minimum of 200 per cent of per capita income, forgetting that in Latin America the annual average was 200 dollars and that if taxation was based on 400 dollars it would mean whittling away what was a bare subsistence level. They also tended to forget that the purchasing power of money was much greater in the more developed countries than in Latin America, particularly insofar as services such as health and education were concerned. He believed that the minimum taxable income limit ought to be fixed between 500 and 600 per cent of per capita income; he had therefore been surprised to hear that in Mexico, according to Mrs. de Navarrete, the monthly limit was 500 Mexican pesos (40 dollars). In Costa Rica the treasury had found that it was unprofitable to tax income in the lower brackets, although the monthly minimum had been set at 63 dollars.

He disagreed with Mr. Goode on the treatment of foreign investment, because the Latin American countries were not exporters of capital. The effect of the system in force, whereby capital could enter Latin America tax free, was to make a gift to the treasury of the country exporting the capital. What was needed in such cases was an over-all solution, not bilateral or temporary agreements.

Mr. Vega referred to two specific points that had been raised by Mr. Goode: (a) the imputed rental of owner-occupied property and (b) incentives. The former was obviously taxable income, and where it had been exempted from taxation, the reasons had been of a social and not a fiscal nature. His impression was that Mr. Goode was in favor of allowing a deduction for the unpaid balance of debt on housing. To him that seemed unfair, since the same argument would warrant that income from capital loaned and invested in an industry should be exempt from taxation.

With respect to incentives, there were many possibilities, but in the case of income tax they should be applied *ex post facto* and should consist in tax rebates on savings used for investment instead of for consumption. Capital formation in the country concerned would thus be promoted, and there would be no risk of an inordinately large proportion of savings being channeled into the infrastructure projects for which the public sector was properly responsible; on the contrary,

productive undertakings would be encouraged.

Mr. Matus said that Mr. Goode's paper was an excellent synthesis of the problem and it was therefore difficult to disagree with him. However, it could not be said that the income tax in Latin America was elastic. On the contrary, it was very inelastic on account of inflation and the fact that there was a time lag between the dates when the tax liability was incurred and when it was payable. He thought that an attempt to increase elasticity might result in a loss of equity, since tax administration was defective.

In his view, there were flaws in Mr. Goode's argument in relation to the effects of progressivity on savings. It was true that the coefficient of consumption remained relatively constant when income rose over the years, but that bore no relation to the purposes of the analysis. What mattered for the effect of progressivity on savings was that the savings coefficients were very different at various income levels and therefore progressivity affected savings. However, the effects of progressivity were not very important. Moreover, no importance would attach to a decrease in the savings of the sector, since it was the level of total savings that mattered. The vital point was that the progressiveness of the tax system should be reasonable.

In connection with the use of incentives, he felt that no clear-cut assertions could be made, since it depended on the level of taxation, its importance among all the factors which affected the decisions of economic units, the type of reaction sought, the economic unit whose behavior was to be changed, the influence of extra-economic factors, and the administrative capacity to handle them. It was easy to change the structure of consumption through incentives or penalties. On the other hand, it was difficult to control the level of private investment consciously and to subject it to the specific aims of the plan. It was precisely because of administrative difficulties that he viewed certain types of incentives with skepticism.

He did not agree with Mrs. de Navarrete's

contention that taxation of the lower-income groups was a useful source of revenue, since, in his opinion, various alternative patterns of taxation would have to be applied in the case of low incomes.

MR. GOODE said that he would confine himself to commenting on the most important points that had been raised during the discussion.

With respect to the question of tax incentives, he said that it was apparent from the observations that had been made that the Latin American countries had more confidence in the ability of incentives to stimulate development than was the case in some of the more developed countries. Without exploring the reasons for the difference in opinion, he would point out that in the United States the public finance experts had less confidence in tax incentives than business groups or the public in general, probably because they could see more clearly the difficulty of devising a sound plan and administering it. In addition, as one speaker had pointed out, it was necessary to determine the area to which tax incentives might appropriately be applied, which involved the definition of a new firm and a new industry, etc. Nor should it be thought that a system of incentives was the easiest way to promote development. From his own observation, it had often failed to give good results. In fact, they were more effective in influencing the allocation of resources among different uses than in increasing the over-all amount of investment or savings. It should be realized that if one form of investment was encouraged over another, the social gain achieved was simply the difference between the product gained from the favored activity and the product that would have been obtained from the activity it had supplanted.

As regards the question of income from foreign sources, he had not alleged that the flight of capital from Latin America to other regions was attributable to tax considerations alone. It was, however, anomalous that countries needing revenue and capital formation should give better treatment to those who invested their capital abroad rather than at home. He had taken what was perhaps an opportunistic standpoint in urging Latin America to tax income from capital at its place of origin and place of receipt in common with a number of capital exporting countries. Although the majority of the participants did not seem to agree with him, he hoped that they would give further consideration to his suggestion.

He did not attach as much importance to the question of imputed rent of owner-occupied property as some of the other participants. But he did feel that property of that kind was tantamount to a source of income for the owner and, if not taxed, would lead to inequity between owners and tenants. He agreed that all consumer durables should in principle receive the same treatment as houses but did not consider this feasible. He did not feel that the argument should be extended to include cash balances, as Mrs. de Navarrete had suggested, since such balances were presumably held in order to take advantage of investment opportunities, and if investment income was taxed upon accrual, the effect would be the same as taxing the gains accruing to the holder of a cash balance.

With respect to the interesting suggestion of tax exemptions for savers to stimulate investment, he would be loath to offer full exemption because of the possible repercussions on income distribution and because it was more equitable to tax income than consumption. A stronger case could be made for selective exemptions, but it would be difficult to decide what type of saving should be promoted or to determine the net increase in saving obtained thereby from one year to the next.

As regards taxation of net wealth, he would not go into details, since the subject would be thoroughly discussed at the forthcoming meeting. He would merely say that the idea was attractive and that it would be desirable to have complete information on a person's net wealth as a check on the accuracy of assessment for income tax. He feared, however, that it would be extremely difficult to obtain satisfactory balance sheets from the taxpayer.

He thought that capital gains should be taxed at the same rate as other types of income, provided that an allowance was made for the fact that often gains realized in a single year had accrued over several years. In view of the difficulty of referring to tax returns for past years, he suggested that capital gains might be taxed in full in the year in which realized but that the tax rate might be that applicable to an increment of ordinary income equal to a third or a fifth of the capital gain. This would be equivalent to prorating the gain over three to five years.

With respect to price level changes, he did not think that allowance should be made for changes in the value of money from year to year, but he admitted that countries suffering from great inflation might find revaluation socially expedient.

Finally, he was convinced that a well-administered income tax, incorporating prompt collection through withholding at source, would have elasticity of yield, although it had been pointed out at the meeting that the elasticity of the tax had in fact been low in some of the Latin American countries.

Mr. Rapoport explained that in Argentina the system of declaring net wealth in tax returns was already in force.

7

Taxes on Net Wealth, Inheritances, and Gifts

by Dino Jarach*

OBJECTIVES OF FISCAL POLICY

The evaluation of a tax structure within the framework of fiscal policy should be undertaken through an analytical study to establish, on the one hand, the aims and objectives of the policy and to ascertain, on the other hand, whether or not the effects of the taxes under consideration appear well adapted to the achievement of those aims. Using this approach, I shall make in this paper an inquiry into the position of the net wealth tax as a fiscal policy measure, with particular reference to developing countries, and more specifically to Latin American countries.

Accordingly, I proceed to sketch in outline the possible aims of fiscal policy. I wish to make it clear, however, that the presentation of no standard position is involved here, but merely a recognition of principles which are generally accepted in these critical times and which, broadly speaking, exert a determining influence on the objectives of fiscal policy in most modern states.

1. To be classed as a primary purpose of fiscal policy is the framing of the public sector of the economy in such fashion that it conforms with the objectives assigned to it, as distinguished from objectives of the private sector. In other words, the primary object of

*Faculty of Economic Sciences, University of Buenos Aires, Argentina.

a fiscal policy lies in the framing of public finances to constitute a system of economy different from the economy of the market or private sector for the output of services which political, economic, and social circumstances of a given country at a given time assign to action of the state. This first objective should comprise the providing of public services in the traditional sense of the term; the carrying out of an investment program by the state, and the creation and operation of enterprises regarded as falling within the state's competence for the reasons stated above.

In their relation to this fundamental purpose, the taxes adopted as sources of revenue should possess the traditional characteristics of productivity and elasticity, that is, they should provide the state with an adequate source of revenue to meet changing needs, either automatically or through modifications in rate.

2. The measures to procure revenue by taxation should adhere to criteria of justice and equity conforming with the political standards prevailing in each country and in each period.

While principles of equity as applied to equal, proportional, or minimum sacrifice are regarded as arbitrary and baseless—and the same is also true of the different, if not contrary, view that taxes should be evaluated by reference to the benefit principle—it must be acknowledged, nonetheless, that for concrete decisions in each country at any given time the deliberative bodies are influenced by determined principles of justice and equity more in accord with a given conscience than with rigid scientific criteria. Consequently, an adaptation of the instruments of taxation to the prevailing ideas of justice or equity should be regarded as falling within the objectives of fiscal policy.

3. To influence the distribution of wealth or the achievement of a redistribution in conformity with the views and scope of prevailing political ideas has been regarded for decades as a possible objective of fiscal policy. Without partisan alignment in favor of or in position to tax neutrality or its effectiveness as a medium of redistribution, it must be recognized as a general proposition that to influence the distribution or redistribution of national income is an existing or accepted objective of fiscal policy.

4. Commonly accepted as an objective of fiscal policy is an influence on a program of stabilization, i.e., the elimination of fluctuations in the economy. For this aim, taxes should be sufficiently flexible to counteract inflationary tendencies and not to affect purchasing power and spending in periods of depression.

5. Finally, an accepted objective of fiscal policy is to promote a country's economic development or growth.

With respect to taxes, the objective is twofold. On the one hand, taxes as such should allow to the state a flow of revenue enabling it to advance economic development by its own activities. In this respect the objective of fiscal policy under examination coincides precisely with the primary aim mentioned in paragraph 1, since the principle, in essence, is merely to assure a solid revenue structure for the public sector. On the other hand, this objective carries with it the adoption of measures such as exemptions or reductions in fiscal charges and taxes or the creation of a system of incentives designed to stimulate investment in the private sector.

It is evident that in many cases the two aspects can be contradictory, and it can even happen that a fiscal policy tending to promote development in the private sector materially weakens the public treasury itself, failing not only to achieve economic development but also to provide the traditional public services and so failing to take care of economic stability by losing control over inflationary tendencies.

DIFFERENT FORMS OF PROPERTY TAXATION

The taxation of property can assume different forms.

1. That of a global tax on the net wealth of individuals, of an ordinary or periodic character, that is, an annual tax.

2. Taxes of greater or lesser coverage on different kinds of real and movable property. This form includes a tax with elements of a personal nature, whereby all property of a certain type belonging to a given taxpayer is grouped for taxation.

3. Taxes on the net assets of enterprises and companies, without regard to the owner or to partners or stockholders to whom the equity interest belongs.

4. Taxes on the transfer of property for a valuable consideration.

5. Taxes on the transfer of property by gift or death, in the two forms of a tax on the total amount of the decedent's estate and a tax on each inheritance or bequest, legacy or gift, received by each heir or beneficiary.

These different forms of property taxation, which do not include property taxes of an extraordinary nature, or, as usually called, capital levies, have an interrelation among themselves in spite of their structural differences and diverse economic effects.

Thus, an annual tax on the total wealth of individuals can be replaced, with a degree of approximation, by partial taxes on certain forms of property, such replacement being supported by practical reasons of fiscal administration rather than by theoretical principles and in spite of the different effects that the two forms of taxation may have.

Taxes on the transfer of property for a valuable consideration can replace or complement the periodic taxation of wealth, and it is even possible to establish statistically an equivalence between the two forms of taxation which, however, does not imply an absolute similarity in effects or in the achievement of the same objectives of fiscal policy.

Finally, the taxes on gifts and estates can be regarded as alternatives to periodic taxes on wealth, general or partial, and the equivalence can be statistically established more precisely than in the previous case. Even in this case, however, the effects of the taxes are different, and they do not lend themselves in the same way to achieving the objectives of fiscal policy.

TAX ON THE NET WEALTH OF INDIVIDUALS

The net wealth of an individual could be regarded, on first sight, as an indicator of personal income, because of the correlation that in general exists between net wealth and income. Therefore a net wealth tax could be regarded as an alternative for the income tax.

A closer examination, however, indicates that this is not so. No perfect correlation exists between wealth and total income of the individual. The divergent aspects are essentially as follows:

1. There is no uniformity in the distribution of assets and of incomes among the various categories or brackets in which the property owners and income recipients can respectively be grouped.

Statistical studies, made by Professor Benini[1] and accepted by other authors, have led to the conclusion that there exists a correlation between the distribution of incomes and the distribution of wealth that can be summarized in this basic formula: as income increases at a geometric rate of two, corresponding assets increase at a geometric rate of three.

In spite of this, as Cosciani[2] has observed, and even overlooking the inaccuracies and criticism of the form in which Benini enunciates his law,[3] the law has some meaning as general statistical evidence, and to this extent it is valid for the average of income- and wealth-holders. But for the individual and even for groups within a society, substantial variations can exist, i.e., individuals with greater income and lesser wealth, or others with greater wealth and lesser income, or finally in proportions differing from those of the relation cited above.

2. There are forms of property which do not produce income, and in this connection it is pertinent to distinguish between the hypothesis of a physical or legal impossibility to produce and that of a voluntary forgoing of productive use. There are other properties which do produce benefits but not in money, and the measure of the value of such benefits is not precise. Finally, there are properties which produce very small income, for all kinds of reasons.

This simple analysis leads to the following conclusions: Wealth is not a suitable instrument for effecting the taxation of income, and income is not a means for reaching wealth by taxation.

The taxation of wealth must be regarded as a separate fiscal measure. It may complement the taxation of income and also attain better certain objectives which are envisaged in, but only imperfectly achieved by, income taxation.

[1]R. Benini, "Principi di Statistica Metodologica," *Biblioteca dell'Economista*, Serie V, Vol. XVIII (Turin: UTET, 1906), pp. 188–91 and 333; "La Finanza in Regime Corporativo Fascista," *Atti del II Covengo di Studi Sindacali e Corporativi*, Vol. 1 (Roma: Tipografia del Senato, 1932); "Lezioni di Economia Politica" (Bologna: Zanichelli, 1936), special part, Cap. V, Tit. I, Sec. I c; "A Proposito della Correlazione tra Redditi Totali e Patrimonii," *Rivista di Diritto Finanziario e Scienza delle Finanze* I (1939), 264 ff.

[2]C. Cosciani, *L'Imposta Ordinaria sul Patrimonio nella Teoria Finanziaria* (Urbino: STEU, 1940); "Possibili Orientamenti dell'Imposta Ordinaria sul Patrimonio," *Rapporto della Commissione Economica del Ministero per la Costituente* (Roma: Istituto Poligrafo dello Stato, 1946), Vol. V, Part I, p. 308; *Istituzioni di Scienza delle Finanza* (Turin: UTET, 1961), Chap. V, pp. 247–48.

[3]See E. Vanoni, "Chiose alle Nuove Imposte sul Patrimonio e sull'Entrata," *Rivista di Diritto Finanziario e Scienza delle Finanze*, I (1940), 28.

Personal wealth, conceived as the net value of an individual's assets and liabilities, serves as an alternative to global income for the determination of the degree of the owner's wealth, and thus of his taxable capacity, in accordance with prevailing social values concerning the imposition of taxes.

There is, furthermore, a case for using wealth as a yardstick for the measure of the economic well-being of the individual, inasmuch as the ownership of property in itself enables him to enjoy a capacity to spend; the ownership of pre-existing wealth can relieve him of the necessity of saving a part of his current income as a reserve for the future and permit him to consume his income in its entirety. Also, as has been repeatedly observed, the possession of wealth and the income which it produces or can produce leaves the individual with intact working powers which he can devote to increasing his economic potential.

It has been argued that taxation of wealth precedes taxation of income and is better suited to a less developed stage of the economy and of financial institutions. This argument is valid only when applied to taxes *in rem* on certain kinds of property, especially real estate, but must be rejected with respect to a personal and global tax on the individual's wealth. Structurally, this tax involves the same difficulties that are well known in enforcement of the income tax; for example, adequate investigation of all assets owned by the taxpayer and also of his liabilities.

Besides these, there are other specific difficulties, of which the most important is the valuation of the properties. It is true that actual income can be difficult to determine, but for this there are objective bases and other elements furnished by a market economy. The use of presumption is reduced to a minimum. This does not happen in the case of the wealth tax, where all assets must be the object of an appraisal.

The need to value assets, which of itself involves difficulties and the possibility of varying subjective criteria, has, as its end

result, the use of heterogeneous standards of value applied to different components of wealth.

Another difficulty springs from the modern tendency to convert real estate and tangible property into movable and intangible property by transferring it as paid-in capital to companies in exchange for shares of participating interests. Direct ownership of the real estate is thus lost. This tendency gives rise not only to valuation problems but also to questions of tax jurisdiction and to fiscal evasion.

Hence arise the complexity of the tax and the regulatory and administrative aspects designed to overcome the difficulties outlined.

SHIFTING AND EFFECTS OF THE TAX

Because of its general and personal character, the tax on individual net wealth cannot be shifted. In certain cases, however, where markets are imperfectly competitive—for example, mortgage notes—a shift could take place. Also, under certain hypothetical conditions, there could be a shift of the tax on leased real estate to the lessee. This possibility is sometimes prevented by protective legislation in favor of tenants.

In the case of sole proprietorships, partnerships, and family corporations, some shift could be effected under imperfect competition in the market. But in such a case the shift is made difficult by the competition of the large corporations, which can hardly shift a tax falling on the shareholder's net wealth.

It should be pointed out in this connection that if the individual net wealth tax does not apply to shares held, but in lieu thereof a tax is imposed on the net assets of corporations, this substitute tax might be shifted, and besides, the transfer of the tax or the net assets of sole proprietorships and partnerships would be facilitated.

In general, owing to the lack of untaxed investments providing alternatives to the owners of properties, the tax in large part is not shifted. In particular, there is no possibility of shift in the case of one's own dwelling, property in use, money, and credit.

With regard to securities, the possibility of shift must be excluded. Rather there is to be assumed the possibility of a reduction in the interest rate because of the incentive to dispose of cash and invest it in securities.

The meager possibilities of shifting an individual net wealth tax warrants a study of the ultimate effect on consumption and savings, it being assumed as a premise that the tax is in fact paid by the legal owners of the properties.

If decisions on the use of income for consumption or for saving depended exclusively on the tax borne by the taxpayer in one or the other case, it would be evident that the net wealth tax encourages consumption and discourages saving, inasmuch as the net wealth tax would fall only on saved income which is converted into a capital asset of the taxpayer. It seems doubtful, however, that such decisions are reached because of tax incidence. A preference for consumption motivated by the net wealth tax may be regarded as probable in the case of the tax as applied to the low-income groups of individuals, who may consider the slender margin of benefit from saving over the sacrifice of renouncing consumption as neutralized by the tax.

For medium- and higher-income groups, the decision to save does not depend on that subjective calculation but rather on the fact that their income exceeds expenditures for consumption, as required by their social status. It is possible, however, that in slightly developed countries a tax on wealth may accentuate the preference for consumption in taxpayers of medium income, particularly in outlays for parties, shows, summer resorts, trips, and the like.

This preference will be given effect along with another form of consumption: the acquisition of durable goods which fall within the scope of the wealth tax. It is hardly to be expected, however, that the wealth tax will promote a preference for consumption to be compared with that for the acquisition of durable goods of importance, such as housing, which provides benefits of longer duration, status, and other advantages of weight in an individual's decision. Of course, I am passing over in silence a number of other subjective motives springing from the individual's character and inclinations which may slant in other directions his use of income.

To the degree to which the wealth tax applies to individuals without periodic income from their property, there will be a tendency to pay the tax out of previously accumulated savings, and hence capital formation can be more severely affected than it is by the income tax. Nonetheless, it can be said that only in rare instances does wealth consist solely or preponderantly of assets which do not produce income. On the other hand, while the tax applies to assets which do not produce cash income, it can be paid wholly or partly with income derived from other assets.

In comparsion with the wealth tax, the income tax will have a greater effect on capital formation if the rates are steeply progressive.

On the other hand, under the existing structure of the economy, it is very often not the individual who voluntarily makes the decisions to save and to invest. To a great extent, savings and investments are due to decisions of large companies and principally through the judgment of their directors who are uninfluenced or only slightly influenced by the individual views of the shareholders about the consequences of the tax on net wealth. Only in sole proprietorships or family enterprises can the net wealth tax influence the decisions of the enterprise, inasmuch as the assets of the individual and of the enterprise are here merged into one.

Consequently, the net wealth tax cannot be regarded as discouraging savings and investments except insofar as it applies to a small amount of property consisting principally of the assets of an individual proprietorship or of a family enterprise.

It should be kept in mind, however, that the net wealth tax can also be progressive, and in a sense this is always so (although the nominal rate is proportional) in accordance with the distribution of wealth in relation to the distribution of income under the above-mentioned law of Benini.

Insofar as the wealth tax applies to the assets of enterprises which have not begun to yield profits, it discourages investment, and in greater degree the longer the period of preparation or of nonprofitable activity. With the income tax, the reverse is true. Hence it follows that, if viewed as an incentive to economic development, the wealth tax, whether falling on real or movable property, should not fall on an enterprise during the early years of its organization and operations.

For the same reason, the wealth tax is more burdensome for the marginal enterprise than is the income tax, but this disadvantage can be obviated by appropriately phrased exemptions.

The wealth tax constitutes an incentive to replace safe investments having a low yield and a high degree of liquidity by others of greater risk, less liquidity, and increased return. For example, in the absence of exemptions, the wealth tax can lead to a preference for the securities of commercial firms over those of government issue. Among commercial securities, preference will be given to common shares over preferred shares or to shares in general over debentures.

Property, as a measure of taxable capacity, connotes essentially a potential wealth which may or may not be real. Therefore, a tax on an individual's global property is equivalent to a tax on his potential or abstract net income but not on his income in fact.

From this basic principle there flow many of the consequences and peculiar characteristics of the net wealth tax and also the factors that may be decisive in the election of this taxing instrument instead of the income tax, or vice versa.

1. The taxpayer who holds assets which are wholly unproductive but are capable of productive use is induced to use them for production or to sell them in order to neutralize in this way the tax incidence. The owner of uncultivated lands is induced to cultivate them, or if this is not possible, to dispose of them in whole or in part and make a profitable use of the money received from their sale. The owner of money or inactive funds has an incentive to invest them.

In other words, the taxation of wealth, for the very reason that it falls upon potential rather than actual income, accomplishes the principle termed "productivist" by the Italian school,[4] whereby taxpayers who keep their capital productive are rewarded and those who hold funds inactive or properties unproductive or underproductive are penalized. It also tends to discourage the hoarding of money and so stimulates investment.

2. While the income tax falls in the same way upon the profits of enterprises subject to differing degrees of risk, and even upon risk premiums and so on elements of cost, the wealth tax does not discriminate against the more risky enterprise because the capital value of an enterprise is computed by capitalizing income net of the risk factor.

Consequently the wealth tax is neutral with respect to the more venturesome enterprises and permits entrepreneurs to direct their activities to new products without suffering tax consequences.[5]

3. The individual net wealth tax corrects distortions as to which the income tax is neutral, due to noneconomic preferences resulting from traditions, attractions, or antipathies toward certain classes of investments. The income tax falls only on certain income actually derived in money from those investments. The wealth tax, on the contrary, falls on the capitalized value of income actually received and also on income represented by psychological elements, positive or negative, stemming from these noneconomic predilec-

[4]Its best expositor is L. Einaudi, "La Terra e l'Imposta," *Annali di Economia dell'Università Bocconi* (Milan: 1924; new edition: Turin: Einaudi, 1942). By the same author: *Miti e Paradossi della Giustizia Tributaria* 3d ed. (Turin: Einaudi, 1959), chap. X.
[5]Cf. Cosciani, *Istituzioni*, pp. 210 ff. and the full bibliography cited by him.

tions. Thus, it discourages investments in which the irrational factor is postive and encourages others in which the psychological income is negative.[6]

4. The wealth tax is less of a burden in those regions of the same country in which a relative scarcity of available capital brings with it a higher rate of return, for in such areas the taxable value of capital assets is less in comparison with others to which capital flows in greater volume.[7]

5. The wealth tax makes it possible to reach indirectly capital gains through the appraisal of property at market price to the extent that the appraisal reflects prospective future gains because of rises in market values.[8]

Of course, this is an indirect and less exact way of taxing capital gains than that provided by a tax on income defined to include such gains or by a special tax on them, but it does have the advantage of automatically eliminating the problems stemming from the difference in character between capital gains and other types of income and, indeed, between short-term and long-term capital gains, which differences, as is well known, render very difficult their inclusion in the framework of an income tax; or, if they are subjected to a separate tax, then the tax is a departure from a personal tax.

6. The wealth tax makes a complete distinction between earned and unearned income.

Obviously, the imposition of the wealth tax without a concomitant income tax would be equivalent to a total exemption of income earned by the performance of personal services. In combination with an income tax, the wealth tax would admit of a distinction impossible to achieve by the income tax alone. For, however diversified the income tax may be according to the nature of its sources—labor, capital, or both combined in different degrees—the differentiations can be reduced to two or three distinct rates or to the deduc-

tion of different amounts as exempt minima or as additional deductions, as the case may be. It is well known, furthermore, that these diversifications complicate the mechanics of the income tax and are particularly at variance with the character of a unitary tax on global income but can be better adapted to a schedular tax system.

The application of the wealth tax in combination with the income tax allows a gradual and continuous distinction to be made. No matter how small the capital used in producing the income along with personal services, the wealth tax can reach it, thus providing a different tax treatment for the income from labor only and accentuating the difference as the amount of capital used increases with a corresponding decrease in the labor factor.[9]

7. The income tax reaches nonmonetary income with difficulty and in very limited instances. In general, the taxing schemes of the different countries extend to the taxation of presumed income from the occupancy of one's own dwelling, but not of parks, gardens, automobiles, yachts, art galleries and collections, jewels, and furniture. The net wealth tax falls on the income from all these assets and eliminates the difficult problems in making estimations such as the owner-occupied dwelling presents and the evasions so common in this field.[10] Nonetheless, there is no avoiding the possibility that assets may be concealed and escape tax. Means to suppress or diminish these evasions lie outside the scope of this paper.

The tax on properties which produce nonmonetary income are significant not only as a possible means of completing the income tax but also as a means of subjecting to tax personal property, that is, a taxpayer's nonproductive assets. This is of particular importance in underdeveloped countries as a way to disocurage the holding of such property and to favor productive investments.

[6]Cosciani, Istituzioni, p. 216.
[7]Ibid., p. 217.
[8]Ibid.

[9]E. Vanoni, "Chiose alle Nuove Imposte sul Patrimonio e sull'Estrata," pp. 30–31.
[10]F. Due, Government Finance, An Economic Analysis, rev. ed. (Homewood, Ill.: Richard D. Irwin, 1959), Chap. 21.

8. The application of the global tax on wealth, in combination with the income tax, accentuates the progressivity of the income tax, since normally wealth is concentrated in the hands of those who receive medium and high incomes.

In this connection, it is pertinent to observe that the wealth tax in itself, even when at proportional rates, is progressive with respect to income; and Benini's law does not need to be rigorously certain for this to be true. The progressivity of the personal global net wealth tax can be accentuated if minimum property exemptions are granted, and to a greater degree, if a progressive rate scale is adopted.

9. The global wealth tax is an instrument to prevent fiscal evasion, especially in the field of income and inheritance taxes.

It has been noted that the wealth tax reaches subjective, nonmonetary income. Besides this, to itemize all elements of a taxpayer's property facilitates a control over and a more precise determination of the sources of income and provides an advance listing of the assets that will be transferred without consideration by death or gift.

Then, too, to itemize the properties and to exercise an annual control over them facilitates a determination of capital gains stemming out of the changes in the property items of each taxpayer.

With the characteristics and effects of the individual net worth tax thus established, an evaluation of it can now be made with respect to the objectives of fiscal policy which I enumerated at the beginning.

1. As for the primary purpose of fiscal policy, the net wealth tax is an appropriate instrument with which to supply abundant revenue to the state, but it lacks flexibility.

The technical characteristic of this tax, which requires an appraisal of almost all elements of property, militates against the possibility of annual adjustments in valuations and tends to promote acceptance of valuations as more or less constant for certain periods of time.

A frequently accepted view is that property valuations, especially of business assets, should be the original value, and hence no adjustments should be made in the light of rising prices and increased budgetary needs. This gives little elasticity to the tax, and to adapt it to changing requirements would demand complex technical work or a continuous modification of details.

The necessity of exempting small assets, especially those consisting of property for personal use, would further complicate the picture. From this point of view, it seems logical to conclude that the wealth tax cannot play a principal role in fiscal policy but only a secondary or complementary one.

In other words, to meet greater fiscal needs, it would seem preferable to fill out the tax system by the creation of a net wealth tax rather than to count on an increase in the income tax. On the other hand, introduction of the net wealth tax is advisable provided— and only provided—that an income tax is already in force and that a system of personal declarations and requisite inspection machinery have been adequately developed.

2. From considerations of justice or equity, the wealth tax satisfies the principle of taxpayer capacity as a valuation of wealth for political purposes, conformant to modern ideas of social justice.

From this point of view, its principal function is undoubtedly to permit more efficiently a discriminatory treatment between earned and unearned incomes and to take, as an index of wealth, the more substantial properties for use even when they do not produce income; at the same time it permits discriminatory treatment against the holders of unutilized properties and properties held for enjoyment and in favor of properties subject to business risks.

3. To accentuate the progressivity of the tax system and to make it progressive by nature, this tax takes into account the distribution of wealth and exercises a redistributive function, the scope of which can be appraised only through a complete acquaintance with fiscal policy, inclusive of the expenditure side of the public budget.

4. As a means of fiscal policy in the field of stabilization, the wealth tax should be unfavorably judged. In times of depression or business recession, the net wealth tax will weigh heavily on enterprises which lose money or produce no profits, in sharp contrast with the income tax, which automatically gives relief to enterprises in such condition.

5. As for fiscal policy in its role for development of the economy, I have already indicated that this role can be examined in two aspects: on the one hand, as a means of strengthening the revenue system of the public sector, and on the other hand, as a means of furnishing, through the instrument of taxation a system of incentives which encourage investment and capital formation in the private sector.

I have stated that the two objectives could prove to be in conflict. In fact, incentives in fiscal legislation are implemented principally through deductions and exemptions. On the one hand, these diminish the revenue of sectors fully able to pay, and so the financial structure of the state is weakened.

It is evident that in theory the diminutions of revenue caused by exemptions could be compensated by other receipts, for example, by consumption taxes. But this involves other problems and runs into difficulties that perhaps cannot be overcome. The consequence could be the state's neglect of essential services which constitute the basis of economic development in the private sector, as, for example, public education, health, transportation and roads, or the necessity of providing these services through means that would bring on inflation.

On the other hand, the exemptions accorded to the business sector also impinge on the common social conscience, inasmuch as they produce an impression of tax inequity which frees those who have a greater taxable capacity and unloads the fiscal burdens on lower-income sectors.[11]

Within the framework of a fiscal policy for development, the wealth tax has the virtue of embodying incentives through tax mechanisms without need for recourse to exemptions or exclusions.

I have previously pointed out the effects that in the Italian financial school are termed "productivist," being a tendency to favor productive investments instead of unproductive assets; the utilization of uncultivated lands or their sale to others who could devote them to cultivation and an application by the seller of proceeds to new income-producing investments; a neutrality and hence a furthering of investments involving risk, in contrast to the income tax which discriminates against these; discrimination against the traditional type of investment which produces little income and of those in property for personal use, and discrimination in favor of productive investments; discrimination against liquid assets, particularly against cash holdings, and encouragement for investment of the money; a greater use of savings for the acquisition of securities, especially shares.

This activity favorable to the objectives of economic development by the private sector does not jeopardize the public treasury nor represent a violation of ideals of equity in the distribution of the tax burden.

It is not my wish to pose as an apologist for the wealth tax, but I believe in the merits of that fiscal instrument because it has in its favor the possibility of promoting a majority of the recognized objectives of fiscal policy, provided, of course, that collection machinery and administrative capacity overcome difficul-

---

[11] I presented these views at a conference held July 13, 1962, at the Instituto de Desarrollo Económico y Social of Buenos Aires. I point out with satisfaction that they coincide completely with the views presented by Kaldor in his work, "The Role of Taxation in Economic Development," for the Conference on Fiscal Policy at Santiago, Chile, paragraph 2.

I point out furthermore that these views are confirmed, in my opinion, by the important actual experience of recent developments in Argentina, where a series of tax incentives such as a revaluation of assets, largely tax free, and liberal deductions for new investments have led to a decrease in revenue, causing a substantial fiscal deficit. All the disadvantages indicated in the text have been proved: inequitable distribution of the tax burden with the consequent popular reaction; well-known falling off of essential public services; and finally inflation, so that incentives for the private sector, in their fiscal aspect, resulted in an inflation which has seriously compromised the very objectives of economic development.

ties of a practical nature from which they may suffer.

EXPERIENCES WITH THE WEALTH TAX

In most countries of Europe in which the individual wealth tax is part of the tax system, it has the nature of a complementary tax—*Ergänzungssteuer*—and its fundamental purpose is to make a distinction between earned and unearned income.

Only in some cantons of Switzerland does the wealth tax serve as a substitute for the income tax. In those cantons the tax system comprises a wealth tax to reach unearned income and an income tax applying to earned income.

There is no net wealth tax in the United States, despite current criticisms of the system of property taxes which do not have the characteristics of a net wealth tax even in those states where it comprises in theory property of all kinds, real and movable, tangible and intangible.

There are examples of the net wealth tax in Central America—in El Salvador and in Nicaragua—but difficulties in collection and the modest proceeds realized have led to repeal and the substitution of a real estate tax.[12]

Colombia has in force a net wealth tax as complementary to the income tax and co-ordinated with an excess profits tax. The tax is progressive and is designed to make a distinction between earned and unearned income, as is stated in the congressional reports on the bill.[13]

Very recently Argentina enacted an individual net wealth tax to finance the servicing of a loan contracted in August, 1962. The duration of the tax is for the period of re-quired servicing, that is, until the loan has been paid off. The rate is 2 mills, and it is particularly worthy of mention that corporate shares are exempt, while the corporation itself is subjected to a wealth tax at the same rate on its net assets.

Despite the moderate rate and absence of progression, the tax has met with extraordinary resistance by all groups representing business interests. They have not hesitated to define it as a "capital tax" and to regard it as a dangerous precedent. These arguments, enriched with such slogans as "The fiscal nuisance" or "The fiscal voraciousness," do not admit of discussion.

REAL ESTATE TAXES

While the net wealth tax is found in the tax systems of only a few countries, and very exceptionally in Latin America, real estate taxes on both rural and urban land, in contrast, are traditional there. Hence, a rapid evaluation of the characteristics and effects of these taxes in relation to fiscal policy and as compared with wealth taxes is in order.

From a structural viewpoint, real estate taxes reflect only in a rudimentary and indirect way the taxable capacity of those subject to them, essentially for the following reasons: the tax falls on the value of the property independently of the indebtedness to which it is subject, and it excludes the rest of the taxpayer's wealth.

From the viewpoint of incidence, the tax is not shifted when real estate occupied by the owner is involved and, perhaps in accordance with classical theory, when rural land is involved and when the tax is measured exactly by the net land rent. A shift is often possible, however, in the case of rented urban real estate; it is normal in the case of the tax falling on industrial or commercial business properties and is possible in the case of the tax falling on agricultural enterprises operated by the proprietor or lessee. Since this is so, the same possible effects cannot be assumed

[12]United Nations, *Tax Policy and Economic Development in Central America* (E/CN.12/486), Chap. V, pp. 66 ff.

[13]H. Agudelo Villa, *Memoria de Hacienda,* presented to the National Congress of 1961: Annex II, "Tax Reform" (Bogotá, 1961), pp. 25–26.

for the real estate tax as have been indicated for the wealth tax.

A further differentiation with respect to the effects of this tax must be attributed to the possibility of the phenomenon termed amortization or capitalization, whereby tax on real estate affects the owner through a decrease of the asset value of his property when the tax is created or increased, while owners who acquire the property thereafter pay a price net of the capitalized amount of tax and hence do not suffer its incidence.

With respect to real estate taxes, the serious problem of appraisal is always present and, as a result of that, the inelasticity of the tax yield. Along with wealth taxes, however, real estate taxes are characterized by falling on potential, not actual, income, and they constitute an automatic system of incentives for the utilization and improvement of farm land.

There is also the possibility—and indeed it has been tried—of adopting progressive taxes on real estate by the simple form of a progressive rate table according to the valuation of each parcel or in the more perfected form of a progressive rate table applying to the total valuation of all tracts of a single taxpayer.[14] A tax of this kind has, as an effect, the creation of a tendency to divide up real estate. Attempts to evade the tax by the organization of companies, and especially corporations, for each tract can be prevented by the adoption of a progressive tax on the real estate of these companies.

The urban real estate tax on vacant lots has, as an effect, the promotion of sales and a fall in prices, provided the tax is high enough. It also falls indirectly on capital gains. The rigidity of valuations, however, especially in periods of a rapid price rise or under inflationary conditions, neutralizes this effect.[15]

In the same order, and by the same criteria, I shall now make an inquiry into whether or not the real estate tax is suitable for the several objectives of fiscal policy.

1. The real estate tax can furnish for the state an abundance of revenue. In almost all countries, and especially in Latin America, where taxes of this kind are usually imposed, a dwindling down of the proceeds of this tax and a drop in its relative importance in the fiscal picture over a period of time is very common. Technical difficulties and political resistance obstruct changes in valuations and adjustments in the rates. The second measure is more easily adopted but less equitable.[16]

2. The real estate tax satisfies, at least in part, two requirements of equity in that the property is an irrefutable evidence of wealth and in that the owner receives benefits from the state for which he should pay. Even the failure of the tax to take into account the existence of mortgage debts often is not regarded as an inequity because of the almost universal tendency to reduce the amount of the mortgage debts with relation to the value of the property, which often rises rapidly while the indebtedness is materially decreasing.

Considerations of equity are strengthened if the tax does not apply to small holdings—in the sense of properties belonging to small proprietors—and are strengthened even more by the adoption of a progressive rate table applicable to the valuation of the aggregate real estate holdings of one person; in other words, if the tax is vested with personal characteristics.

3. The real estate tax, designed as suggested above, accentuates the progressivity of the tax system and promotes the redistribution of wealth.

4. As in the case of the wealth tax, the real estate tax should be regarded as an ineffective instrument for carrying out a stabilization policy.

[14]This is the evolution, recently confirmed in Argentina: the real estate tax in Buenos Aires Province comprises a basic proportional tax and an additional progressive tax on the sum of the appraised values of the properties of the same taxpayer.
[15]This has been tried in Argentina by a different progressive rate scale and by a lower exemption than that in effect for the individual.

[16]An effort in Argentina, Buenos Aires Province, to modify the valuations annually by use of coefficients calculated on the basis of statistics for each district provoked a strong political reaction and contributed to electoral reverses in the year 1960.

In periods of depression, especially in countries which produce foodstuffs for export exposed to the effects of price declines, the tax would constitute an added burden. In periods of prosperity, of rises in prices and income, the tax would not serve as an effective brake on expansion, especially in view of the collection machinery in which stability of valuations and rates prevails.

5. From the point of view of fiscal policy for economic development, special effectiveness is to be attributed to the real estate tax, particularly with respect to rural property, by reason of the system of automatic incentives which it provides if the tax is measured by a valuation computed as the capitalization of the land's potential production. In this connection, it is well to recall the importance which some authors attribute to the land tax as an instrument of economic progress.[17]

In particular, the rural land tax at progressive rates tends not only to promote utilization by the proprietor but in some cases the subdivision and sale to others able and willing to make use of it.

In countries in which tax administration has not reached a high enough degree of efficiency for application of personal taxes to aggregate property, the real estate tax, and especially that on rural land, can replace advantageously the net wealth tax. In federal states where the net wealth tax can meet with difficulties of a political order, the real estate tax is particularly advantageous.

Likewise the tax on urban property and suburban lots can be effective in promoting building or the subdivision and sale for construction purposes. In this respect the real estate tax can serve as a strong incentive for the conversion of unutilized property, or property held purely for purposes of luxury consumption, into building sites, especially for housing, in this way furthering the solution of this problem of a developing society in which housing shortages could otherwise impede industrial growth.

The tax on urban real estate has further the effect of hindering or stopping speculation and bringing about a fall in housing costs.

To achieve these objectives of fiscal policy in this case, as in the others, a necessary condition is that the tax be sufficiently flexible not to become ridiculous in periods of rapid price rises and runaway speculation in property.[18]

NET WEALTH TAX ON BUSINESS ENTERPRISES

Among property taxes, the tax on the net assets of business enterprises has become important, especially in some countries of Latin America. The reason for creating this tax was to provide a substitute for the tax on the transmission of property by death, which was the subject of widespread evasion, particularly in respect of corporate shares. Therefore an annual tax was created on the net assets of corporations, and, as good results in administration followed, it was an easy step to extend the tax to the assets of unincorporated enterprises organized as partnerships or sole proprietorships.[19]

If equal merit, or even an advantage, can be attributed to an annual tax on the net value of an enterprise's assets as compared with an inheritance tax insofar as concerns the production of public revenue, the same cannot be said of the effect in the fulfillment of the purposes of fiscal policy. I shall return later, when dealing with inheritance taxes, to these comparative aspects.

It is appropriate now, however, to appraise the net wealth tax as applied to a

[17] Einaudi, Carli, Cattaneo, with reference to the cadastral census of María Teresa in Lombardy.

[18] See, as a striking example, the deterioration of the real estate tax of Buenos Aires Province during the period 1948–57 in the work, "El Sistema Impositivo de la Provincia de Buenos Aires," prepared by the Economic Planning Board and published in the *Revista de Desarrollo Económico*, Vol. I, No. 1 (La Plata: 1958), pp. 154–56.

[19] A substitute tax has been in effect in Uruguay for many years. One was created in Argentina in 1951 for corporations and was extended in 1961 to sole proprietorships and partnerships.

business enterprise, comparing it with the net wealth tax as applied to the individual.

From the viewpoint of incidence, the net wealth tax on enterprises can be shifted as a general rule. This shift is possible even though the tax applies to all enterprises and not only to corporations; in fact, if limited to corporations, the shift could be hindered by the competition of enterprises otherwise organized.

While the individual net wealth tax, even when falling on the individually owned enterprise, is difficult to shift because the tax falling on the shareholders of large corporations is not shifted by the corporation to the prices of products, in the case of a tax that falls on the enterprise itself, the shift is to be regarded as normal.

Even if the possibility of shift is taken into account, the net wealth tax on the business enterprise would still constitute a factor discouraging investment, especially in periods of depression. The contrary would occur in periods of prosperity, in which the tax would not serve to check expansion because a shift of it would be made easy by the rising price movement and the increase in the stock of money.

The tax is particularly burdensome on marginal and newly founded enterprises. In this connection it is pertinent to emphasize that the valuation of assets, which is normally made by reference to the cost of acquisition or production of each asset, in periods of rising prices favors old enterprises and discriminates against new ones, although the possibility of shift tends to lessen this discrimination.

Imposition of the net wealth tax on business enterprises discourages productive investment and the acquisition of shares, inviting as a preferable alternative investment in real estate or tax free loans, because they bear no tax burden. In this aspect, the tax on the assets of an enterprise produces effects opposite to those produced by the individual net wealth tax.

In relation to the objectives of fiscal policy, the position of the net wealth tax on the business enterprise may be summarized as follows:

1. The net wealth tax on business enterprises can provide substantial revenue. This tax can be more flexible than the individual net wealth tax because the valuation of the net assets of an enterprise can be brought up to date better than the net wealth of the individual, as the annual balance will reflect changes that could not be shown for determining the value of capital interests or shares belonging to individuals in the absence of a complicated technical process. Nonetheless, the values of the assets reflect original cost, and hence the tax yield does not respond to rising prices.

2. From the equity point of view, the tax answers considerations of benefit rather than those of taxpayer capacity. However, its lack of evenness, especially when applied solely to corporations, and the possibility of shifting it can easily deprive it of any pretext of equity.

3. The shifting of this tax tends to accentuate the regressivity of the tax system. Hence it is not a suitable instrument for bringing about a redistribution of income.

4. The effects, above indicated, of discouragement of investment in periods of depression, of discrimination against new enterprises, and its slight influence in periods of rising prosperity because of the shift which is accentuated by the increase in price combine to render this tax less suitable than the individual net wealth tax for a fiscal policy of stabilization.

5. Finally, with reference to a fiscal policy for development, and aside from the revenue that the tax may provide, thus permitting the public sector to carry out a development policy, this tax, like the other types of property taxes mentioned, embodies an incentive factor in that it encourages enterprises to improve their returns and to rationalize and increase production.

However, this tax is not advisable as a fiscal instrument because it discourages investment and the acquisition of shares and discriminates against new enterprises.

TAXES ON TRANSFERS OF CAPITAL ASSETS FOR A VALUABLE CONSIDERATION

In spite of the numerous justifications and all the classifications advanced for these taxes, the only sure and well-founded one is its character as a form of tax on property.

Ever since the Dutch tried out the stamp tax long ago, these taxes have multiplied everywhere, and they are found in almost all countries of Latin America. Principally, they are in the form of a tax on real estate transfers, but they are also important levies on the transfers of commercial businesses and negotiable securities.

While it is true that the liability for the tax is generally on the seller and occasionally on the buyer, in either event it affects the property, in the sense that it absorbs accumulated savings and can reduce capital formation.

There is one exception. When the buyer is an enterprise and the tax is borne at least partially by it, the tax increases production costs and can be shifted to the products.

The tax, however, does not discourage savings, and, as has been clearly demonstrated, it gives rise to a process of financial illusion, in the sense that both contracting parties can imagine themselves so clever at negotiation as to unload the real tax burden on the other.

The following effects are to be noted as particularly interesting.

1. Taxes on transfers for a valuable consideration constitute a rudimentary form of taxing capital gains. Very often, genuine taxes on the increment in real estate value have resulted from taxes on transfers.

2. The tax can discourage the sale of property, thereby hindering the transfer of land from an owner who fails to utilize it to an owner prepared to utilize it.

3. The tax can serve as a check against speculation in urban real estate by making the purchase of this property for resale less attractive, especially during a period of inflation; thus the tax tends to channel savings into productive uses.

4. The tax on the transfer of commercial businesses absorbs savings which could otherwise be devoted to business expansion and capital formation.

For purposes of fiscal policy, the evaluation of these taxes can be summarized as follows:

1. The taxes produce a great amount of revenue. Especially in countries where, and periods when, real estate values are rising, the proceeds of these taxes, even when imposed at moderate rates, can be very substantial, but widespread evasion, through an understatement of the sale price, operates to reduce the proceeds. Evasion can be obviated by use of a presumed price, such as the appraised value assigned the property for real estate tax purposes. This method may not prove effective, however, in periods of rapid increase in prices if the real estate appraisals are not brought up to date. A presumptive price determination in each case would be a more adequate but laborious method; in practice it is little used.

In spite of this drawback, the tax proceeds automatically keep pace with the price rise inasmuch as there are naturally limits on concealment of the real price.

2. Principles of justice and equity are satisfied the least by taxes on transfers for a valuable consideration. The justifications advanced for this tax on the benefit principle—i.e., by the protection which the state provides in the legal process of transfer—or on the taxable capacity inherent in the implicit gains from these transactions are not acceptable, regardless of the repetition of them in the classical textbooks on finance. Expediency can explain these taxes but cannot justify them as based in equity. Besides, their failure to have an even impact is notorious. The use of a progressive rate table, which on occasion has been adopted, can be explained by reference to other objectives of fiscal policy but fails to meet the goal of justice.[20]

3. In spite of falling on property, it cannot be said that this tax discharges any function of redistribution because its application is

---

[20]A tax on real estate transfers has been adopted in Buenos Aires Province with a progressive scale and rates varying from 20 to 45 per thousand.

occasional and it affects, in an irregular manner, large and small properties in different measures and frequencies.

Sometimes the tax on a business can be shifted to the product's price, thereby contributing to the regressive character of the tax system.

4. From the viewpoint of a fiscal policy of stabilization, these taxes can constitute a check on real estate speculation and channel savings to other types of investment.

In addition, the opportune flexibility of these taxes allows them to be used for reducing the public's purchasing power in periods of inflation. Taxes on transfers of real estate and on transfers of negotiable securities have this effect in common.

5. In a fiscal development policy, the tax can be of significance for the tax potential of the public sector, especially in circumstances of rapid urban growth, accompanied by the consequent increase in real estate transactions. For this, it is not necessary to adopt progressive rates which clash with principles of equity, for the proceeds are substantial even at proportional rates. Moderate rates could even be rewarded by an increase in collections, for the incentive to conceal the true price disappears, and the considerations that lead the contracting parties to report the true price of real estate transactions may prevail.

As for the aspect of development by the private sector, this form of taxation is lacking in incentive and, as indicated above, can check any tendency to channel the property into young, enterprising hands. This effect is the opposite of that produced, as we have seen, by the real estate tax and also by the inheritance tax, as we shall see.

The effectiveness of this tax in checking real estate speculation and tending to favor productive investments should be favorably appraised. In this aspect, taxes which vary inversely with the time of tenure of the real estate can be profitably adopted.[21]

TAXES ON INHERITANCES AND GIFTS

The tax on inheritances and gifts can be regarded at first blush as an alternative to the individual net wealth tax. Statistically, the exact relation between the wealth tax and the inheritance tax can be found for any given yield or pressure that may be brought to bear on the taxpayers.

This statistical equivalence, however, does not mean an actual equivalence of the two taxes from the point of view of the taxpayers who pay them or of the taxes' effects on the economy. In individual cases, there is great variation in the number of years in which transmissions by death occur and an even greater variation in transfers by gifts. From the viewpoint of economic effects, under equal pressure, there can be a difference in the incidence, as well as in the source, from which the tax is finally paid.

The structure of inheritance and gift taxes can take two distinct forms: that of a global tax on the aggregate property of the estate transmitted by the decedent or donor or that of a tax on each inheritance, legacy, or gift, or as is sometimes said, on the share of each beneficiary. In different countries, one or the other of the systems prevails; there are also countries in which both forms of tax are combined.

Both taxes are generally progressive. The second is always so in relation to the amount and the kinship between beneficiary and decedent or donor. Considerations of equity, or basis for the two taxes, are different, but this difference has no substantial repercussion on the effects. We can, therefore, consider them together.

INCIDENCE

If the phenomenon of shift is regarded as a process carried out through the price mechanism, the conclusion seems plain that the tax

---

[21]See United Nations, *Tax Policy and Economic Development in Central America*, p. 77. In Argentina, Buenos Aires Province, there is an additional tax which falls on real estate transfers for a valuable consideration with rates varying inversely to the number of years of tenure. At present, the tax on the increment in value of land is a national tax (tax on capital gains) at a very moderate rate (5 per cent).

on inheritances and gifts is not shifted; in other words, the beneficiary actually pays it, whatever the forms of the tax. There is controversy, however, as to whether the tax falls on the beneficiary or the decedent. I do not think it possible to reach an unequivocal conclusion on this point.

The existence of this tax will serve to develop an urge to save in people who are foresighted and much attached to their families and who plan, not only for children, but also for grandchildren, a greater net inheritance after tax. On other people the tax can have the opposite effect, leading them to consume and squander their accumulated wealth rather than leave the government any sizable share of it. But leaving aside psychological considerations and taking into account that in modern society much saving and accumulation of wealth does not spring from the decisions of individuals, we can conclude that the existence of this tax will not have any substantial effect on the creation of savings.

As for the source of funds used to pay the inheritance tax, there can be little doubt that if the tax exceeds the amount of the income from the estate transmitted for the year or period in which the tax must be paid, the taxpayer will have to sacrifice a part of the corpus itself. Some authors contend that in such a case the individual's property is used, but the wealth of the nation is not diminished because the sale of these assets amounts merely to the transfer of them to others who must have savings available to acquire them. This theory leaves out of account the fact that those savings could create new capital instead of being utilized for the acquisition of existing capital.

Hence, the conclusion seems inescapable that collection of the tax in itself can have an effect on the national capital by hindering the replacement or increase of producer goods;[22] but the conclusion reached by the Colwyn Committee should also be retained as certain. This conclusion has been accepted in general by almost all authors. It is that, in the end, whether or not this effect of the tax is offset depends on the course followed for public expenditures.[23]

In this connection, Keynes's opinion is worth mentioning to the effect that in certain circumstances, even if no investments are made by the government, the inheritance tax and resulting public expenditure can promote new investment and capital formation in the end by encouraging consumption.

To a large extent, savings and capital formation in a modern economy are attributable to decisions of business enterprises, especially corporations. The fact that a large shareholder—even a majority shareholder—or his heirs may be subject to inheritance tax cannot materially alter these decisions, which are often entrusted to executive officers having none of the property interests of shareholders themselves.

Payment of the tax does not affect the enterprise itself, except in the case of small individual businesses and partnerships.

The incidence of the tax in the case of estates consisting of corporate shares or participating interests in business can mean the sale of a part of the decedent's investment. The practical possibility that there will be a sale is tied to the degree of salability of the shares or interests. In the case of shares listed in a stock exchange and for which there is substantial demand, payment of the inheritance tax will result in a share sale and a lessening of the concentration of the shares among few owners. If the shares are not listed or if partnerships or individual proprietorships are involved, disposition may be difficult, and even the liquidation of the business is conceivable unless the tax is not very high and the form of payments is adequately adjusted to the circumstances of the case.[24]

Likewise, in the case of real estate, payment of the tax can necessitate the sale of

[22]Cosciani, *Istituzioni*, Chap. IV, p. 225, and bibliography there cited.

[23]Report of the "Committee on National Debt and Taxation" (Colwyn Report), p. 198.
[24]See study on effects of the tax on sales and mergers of corporations in the United States by J. Keith Butters, J. Lintner, and W. Cary, *Effects of Taxation on Corporate Merger* (Boston: Harvard University Press, 1951).

urban or rural real estate. This possibility increases with the unproductive character of the property.

The effects of the inheritance tax incidence finally end in the breaking up of the dynastic ownership of businesses and of properties.[25] This can mean the transfer of business or properties from conservative hands to new aggressive and innovating owners. This consequence is of particular importance for wealth redistribution and economic growth in fully developed countries, in underdeveloped countries, and in developing countries.

In general, the political resistance of the dominant classes opposes an application of an inheritance tax of this kind on the pretext that the tax destroys capital and affects the productive structure of the country. The contrary should be accepted as the fact. The dynastic holding of real estate and business affects economic development adversely. What the tax can destroy in certain cases is the maintenance of family fortunes through the generations. It is really against this and not against the phantom of capital destruction that the opposition is directed. To conceal hostility to this tax, collection difficulties, annoyances caused to medium and small business, and resulting evasions are magnified.

Among the palliatives suggested by the dominant political forces to avoid the effects of the inheritance tax is the so-called substitute tax that falls on the net assets of business enterprises, especially corporations. By this substitute the shares and interests are exempted from the inheritance tax in the estates of shareholders in corporations and members of partnerships.

This substitute tax can be partially shifted and to that extent does not fall on the shareholder or partner. When it falls on the business enterprise, it acts as a check on the accumulation of savings and on expansion, and in periods of recession it makes the business situation worse. But more important still is the fact that this tax prevents a redistribution of wealth and the splitting up of great shareholdings and real estate holdings.[26] When the inheritance tax falls on small or medium business enterprises, the sale of the business to meet payment of the tax can have the effect of a concentration through consolidations and mergers that may take place as a consequence.

A long-range effect of the inheritance tax can be encouragement for keeping a substantial part of wealth in the most liquid form in order to provide the heirs with funds for paying the tax.

Among possible effects of the inheritance tax, the consequences of certain exemptions, customarily granted in most countries, should not be overlooked. For example, the exemption of government securities tends to favor this form of investment over investments that are more risky and subject to the inheritance tax, even though the latter investments may yield a greater return.

Likewise, exemption of the owner-occupied dwelling can stimulate a preference for the investment of savings in personal residences instead of in income-producing investments.

Finally, I emphasize the possibility that the exemption of life insurance and more comprehensive policies, the proceeds of which are not subjected to the inheritance tax in many countries, tends to channel savings to insurance companies or government agencies which are in charge of insurance. Because of the characteristic investments made by insurance companies in real estate, securities, or mortgage notes, the consequence of this channeling of savings, by means of exempting insurance, will result in the greatest volume of investment in the cited assets instead of in business enterprises.

---

[26]Separate consideration is due the creation of a substitute tax on wealth declared by the individual—almost a form of insurance of the inheritance tax tried recently in Argentina, the results of which cannot be quantitatively judged. In general, it can be affirmed that this tax is of a personal nature and nontransferable; in spite of its optional character and proportional rate, it accentuates the progressivity of the tax system as a whole. This tax allows the holders of great wealth, however, to avoid breaking it up at the time of transfer by death and constitutes, in a sense, a measure hindering the objective of redistribution of wealth and the breaking up of the dynastic continuity of its concentration.

[25]View expressed by H. M. Groves, *Postwar Taxation and Economic Progress* (New York: McGraw-Hill, 1946), pp. 248–49.

If we compare the inheritance tax with the income tax, keeping in mind the effects mentioned above, we must conclude that the inheritance tax affects productive activities, the accumulation of savings, and investments less than the income tax. While the inheritance tax can absorb accumulated savings, it has no substantial effect on new savings. That effect, too, can be compensated by the channeling of public expenditures and in periods of depression can serve as a greater stimulant for investment by increasing consumption.

Finally, the inheritance tax can constitute a method for reaching income and capital gains which have escaped tax because of exemptions or evasion when the income or gains were realized.

Specifically, if the exemption of income accumulated as savings, and of income invested, has been adopted as a well-advised incentive measure within the general fiscal policy, the inheritance tax recoups the avoided taxes for public use. The benefits of the exemptions, moreover, are neither neutralized nor annulled thereby.[27]

Let us now proceed to evaluate the inheritance taxes in the light of fiscal policy objectives.

1. Theoretically, the tax can completely fulfill the primary objective of fiscal policy by providing substantial revenue for the public treasury.

In practice, the technical complications of collection are frustrating for this objective because of the necessity of making appraisals of all elements constituting the estate and because of the good chances of evasion. In many countries with a federal form of government in which this tax is at the provincial level, these difficulties are increased by the absence of any co-ordination and technical assistance between the collecting agencies.

Evasion is particularly widespread with respect to movable property, jewels, cash, and, above all, securities. The technical difficulties of preventing fiscal evasion, however, have been greatly exaggerated, according to my own experience and to the information about different countries furnished by other authors. These difficulties have rather been seized upon as a pretext for undermining the inheritance tax and replacing it with other taxes, such as the so-called "substitutes," on the capital of a business enterprise. These are perhaps more productive of revenue but do not have the effects of the inheritance tax, especially the effects flowing from progressivity and redistribution.

2. The tax on the decedent's whole estate, as well as the taxes on the respective shares of the heirs, legatees, or donees, satisfies the principles of tax equity and justice, according to prevailing opinion.

The tax on the whole estate is justified by the benefit principle, by the protection which the state extends to the transmission of wealth, according to the doctrine especially favored by the North American courts of justice and often repeated by the Latin American tribunals. Considerations of taxable capacity also play a role if that tax is regarded as a final and posthumous levy on the net wealth of the decedent.

The taxes on inheritances, legacies, and gifts, with rate schedules progressive according to amount and relationship, take taxable capacity into account by reference to enrichment of the beneficiary. They can, however, be improved by adjustments in the rate progression, taking into account the beneficiary's own wealth.[28]

From the point of view of equity, consideration can be given to the famous proposal of Professor Rignano whereby a higher tax, approaching confiscation, would be imposed on the part of the inheritance which the decedent himself had inherited and a lesser tax would fall on the part representing the fruit of the decedent's own activity and accumulations.[29]

[27] See I. Fisher, "A Practical Schedule for an Income Tax," *Taxes, The Tax Magazine* (1937).

[28] This can be more easily realized if there is an individual net wealth tax without excessive technical complications. See also the proposals of W. Vickrey, *Agenda for Progressive Taxation* (New York: The Ronald Press Co., 1947), Chaps. 8 and 9.

[29] E. Rignano, *Di un socialismo in accordo colla dottrina economica liberale* (Turin: Bocca, 1901), Chap. III, translated into English under the title *The Social Significance of the Inheritance Tax* (New York: Alfred A. Knopf, 1924), p. 115.

Also, from the point of view of equity and taxable capacity, the possibility of integrating the inheritance and gift taxes with the income tax can be considered.[30] In my opinion, however, not only the weight of tradition but also serious technical difficulties in amalgamating income with wealth transmitted by death are insuperable obstacles to that possibility.

3. Statistical evidence on the distribution of estates is not needed to support the assertion that the inheritance taxes, in any of the forms that may be devised, are progressive and that they substantially contribute to the progressive character of the whole tax system, provided that administration is efficient and rates are substantial. However, the technical difficulties, the political resistance, and evasion greatly reduce the progressivity, inasmuch as the total proceeds of inheritance taxes is small relative to total tax collections.

The progression can be accentuated if small inheritances are made exempt and if the progressive rate table is extended to reach high marginal rates for the larger shares of an estate. As has been discussed in connection with the last point, the progression can be geared to the wealth of the beneficiary before getting his share.

It should be pointed out, however, that the rule of jurisprudence, accepted in Argentina, whereby an inheritance tax at rates exceeding 33 per cent is unconstitutional, largely neutralizes the progressivity for the larger estates.

The exemption from the inheritance tax of corporate shares and participating interests in business enterprises and their subjection to a periodic tax, termed "substitute tax," contributes to neutralize the progressivity of the tax itself and of the whole tax system, as it may be reasonably supposed that, particularly in slightly developed countries, share holdings are concentrated in the hands of men of great wealth.

The progressivity of the inheritance tax also runs into difficulties with the legal doctrine, long accepted in Argentina, which

brands as unconstitutional the progressive tax on the whole estate.

The redistributive character of the tax is evident if its progression is taken into account, but in this connection it must be borne in mind that the redistributive effect can be properly appraised only if account is taken of policy on public expenditures.[31]

I mentioned at first, as an effect of redistribution, the breaking up of concentrations of wealth through encouragement of subdividing estates and the disposal of blocks of shares or participating interests in businesses. From that point of view, as I have previously indicated, the effect of inheritance taxes is significant, this being precisely a fundamental reason why the tax is bitterly opposed in some countries by the dominant political elements who are against any break in the dynastic continuity of landlords, great businesses, and the very lucrative professions.

4. From the cyclical point of view, inheritance taxes can have negative effects in a depression period because of the forced sales of properties or interests in businesses on a falling market and the absence of investment incentives. It is possible, however, that in periods of depression there is a decrease in forced sales of properties and interests in businesses because uninvested liquid funds are available in large amounts in such circumstances. Anyhow, those considerations should be completed by comparison with the effects that other taxes would produce in the same circumstances; from this point of view the deflationary effects of inheritance taxes are much less than those of other taxes; for example, sales and consumption taxes.

5. Finally, let us evaluate the role of inheritance taxes on fiscal policy aimed at economic development.

At the outset, it should be repeated that inheritance taxes can be an efficient instrument of taxation for supplying the state with

[30]Henry C. Simmons, *Personal Income Taxation* (Chicago: The University of Chicago Press, 1938), Chap. VI.

[31]An example is the redistributive effect which the tax on transmission by death traditionally had in Argentina during the long period in which its proceeds were devoted to the maintenance of free and obligatory primary education.

means to finance economic development in the public sector. I cite again the case of Argentina, where for decades these taxes have been used to pay for primary education—a use which undoubtedly represents a good investment for development purposes.

Apparently the modest yield of inheritance taxes within the general picture of the tax system, and especially in underdeveloped countries, contradicts this possibility. Undoubtedly there are technical difficulties to be met in increasing the volume of revenue from inheritance taxes, and there is avoidance, especially by use of corporations and holding companies, which may be hard to overcome. As I have said, however, these difficulties cannot be solved when a political force exists which openly or clandestinely aims at the repeal of the inheritance taxes and their replacement by taxes with different incidence, solely for revenue purposes.

With respect to the evaluation of inheritance taxes in the framework of economic development by the private sector, it is merely necessary to assemble the elements of the prior analysis on the effects of the inheritance taxes with reference to saving, capital formation, and incentives, on the one hand, and the redistribution of wealth and breakup of dynastic concentrations of it on the other. Placing them beside other fiscal instruments, these taxes constitute less of a check on investment and capital formation than the income tax and other taxes which fall on business enterprises.

The redistribution of wealth brought about by the sale of participating interests in business and the sale of real estate tends to channel capital into new, enterprising hands and to reduce the cost of capital, goods, and land, both urban and rural, for those who acquire it for productive purposes.

It may be supposed that inheritance taxes do not have, of themselves, the "productivist" effect characteristic of the periodic tax on net wealth or of taxes on property, but it should not be overlooked that the mere existence of the tax constitutes a stimulus to the productive utilization of property, in view of the tax burden which, at a given time, the heirs must bear. This productivist effect can be exerted on the transmitter as well as on the heirs, especially if the latter benefit from facilities for tax payment.

By its mere existence, moreover, the inheritance tax stimulates productive activities of the presumptive heirs of large fortunes insofar as it diminishes their prospects of an increase in wealth through inheritance.[32] This particular effect, of importance for economic growth, could be increased by adopting Rignano's proposal.

The negative effect on small and medium business enterprises can be partially eliminated by making the tax moderate for small estates and granting facilities for its payment.

The effect, however, of favoring mergers and transfers of parts of enterprises to others than family members, as a result of the tax, should not be regarded as a negative effect for a policy of economic development. On the contrary, a tendency not to inject outside capital into a family enterprise can very often check expansion and hinder its attainment of economic stature. From this point of view, inheritance taxes can be positive factors in development by favoring the transfer of participating interests and the merger of enterprises. In many underdeveloped countries, and also in others at intermediate states of economic growth, there is a great propensity to consume, manifested especially in the ownership of luxury goods for use, such as automobiles, yachts, summerhouses with grounds, and swimming pools. The efficacy of subjecting these properties to progressive taxation has already been pointed out. In discussing the wealth tax in particular, I have indicated the beneficial effect for economic development of checking the propensity to consume and channeling savings to productive investments. The inheritance taxes can likewise contribute to the same ends.

[32] A. M. Dalton, *Principles of Public Finance* (London: Rutledge, 1954), p. 82.

Comment

CARLOS CASAS*

The objective of the interesting analysis of net wealth and property taxes in general made by Professor Dino Jarach is to explain how these kinds of taxes can be employed as instruments of fiscal policy.

To this end the author of the paper begins by listing the three most important objectives of the fiscal policy of a country, namely: (1) to influence the distribution or redistribution of the national income and to promote the splitting up of certain kinds of property that are concentrated in too few hands in order to make it more productive; (2) to influence stabilization policy in order to dampen cyclic fluctuations; and (3) to promote the economic development or growth of the country.

He then goes on to give a brief description of taxes on individuals and on business enterprises, real estate taxes, taxes on transfers of property, taxes on gifts and inheritances, and explains their different characteristics, what their incidence is, and what effects they have on the economy. Incidentally it seems necessary to me to clarify that, according to the analysis, by "incidence" is meant the distribution effect, that is, the change in the disposable income of different groups of persons before and after the tax, and by "economic effect" the change in the general level of production that takes place in the short, medium, or long run as a consequence of the tax. This can occur directly through the decrease or change in the volume of investment in business or indirectly through changes in supply induced by changes in demand resulting from a decrease or increase in consumption.

He then explains the relationship between net wealth and property taxes and the achievement of each of the three objectives mentioned above and finally expresses his opinion in regard to how taxes employed as sources of revenue for the government should fulfill the traditional characteristics of productivity and flexibility in order to make the achievement of the above-mentioned goals of fiscal policy possible within the changing situations of every economy.

The first part of the analysis refers to the net wealth tax on individuals and/or companies and the second part to some specific types of property taxes such as taxes on the transfer of property for a consideration and the taxes on inheritances and gifts.

PRINCIPAL CONCLUSIONS

Following an explanation of the nature and characteristics of taxes on net wealth, real estate, the net assets of business enterprises, the transfer of assets for a consideration, inheritances and gifts, the author of the study arrives at the following general conclusions.

1. The tax on the net wealth of individuals can be a suitable instrument for attaining the three basic objectives of fiscal policy, as long as it is administered and collected in an efficient manner.

2. Real estate taxes, both urban and rural, are capable as fiscal instruments of accomplishing a better redistribution of the wealth and can promote economic development, as long as their structure is flexible. However, they are inefficient from the point of view of stability, since they tend to make cyclical fluctuations more pronounced.

3. The tax on the net assets of business enterprises is not a proper instrument for either obtaining a redistribution of income or maintaining stability, or even as a factor in development, although, in regard to the latter, it can stimulate enterprises to increase their output and rationalize production—in the author's opinion.

*Economic Adviser to the Government, Bogotá, Colombia.

4. Taxes on transfers of property for a consideration do not have a redistributive function because they are not levied on a continuing basis and because they affect large and small assets irregularly. These taxes assist development by permitting the government to increase the volume of public expenditures, but, on the other hand, they retard it because they tend to discourage the breaking up of large accumulations of wealth. They can contribute to stability by acting as a brake on speculative investments in real estate and by reducing the purchasing power of the public in times of inflation.

5. The taxes on inheritances and gifts satisfy the principle of equity—at least in part, since they lend themselves to a great deal of evasion—inasmuch as they are a means of taxing income and capital gains that had escaped specific taxes at the time such yields and profits were produced and because, in addition, they introduce an element of progressivity in the tax system. These taxes have negative effects in times of depression, but they do not produce so strong deflationary effects as other taxes do, and they aid in economic development inasmuch as they permit the splitting of wealth and capital and a more advantageous use of them, without producing such an unfavorable impact on investment and capital accumulation as income taxes and taxes on the net wealth of individuals and/or business enterprises; but they can encourage the acquisition of superfluous consumer goods on the part of those who prefer this to turning over a portion of their assets to the government through taxation.

COMMENTS

The analysis on which these comments are based is of obvious theoretical interest and can lead to practical developments if the tools it furnishes are applied to the peculiar circumstances of our various countries.

Before making specific comments, it seems worth while for me to make some of a general nature. First of all, this kind of taxes has a supplementary role as a source of revenue. This is due to several things, but above all to the monetization of the economies, a phenomenon that gives greatest importance to income or profits as a measure of the financial standing of individuals and, hence, of their ability to pay taxes. For this reason the role of this kind of taxes as instruments of fiscal policy cannot and should not be exaggerated. However, one exception to this is the case of an economy characterized by very low levels of income. Such a situation is almost inevitably accompanied by wide disparities in the distribution of wealth and, more particularly, of the factors of wealth production, especially capital and natural resources (land). In this case, but only in exceptional circumstances—as pointed out by Ursula Hicks—taxes on property or other forms of capitalization of wealth acquire primary importance as a legal device for achieving a better combination of factors for a more accelerated, equitable, and stable growth.

In fact, taxes on capital are more clearly important in such economies than in the industrialized countries as instruments for achieving two aims:

1. Channeling available financial resources toward profitable investment, avoiding their concentration in the traditional and safer fields of investment.

2. Avoiding waste by the wealthy class, which takes the form of expenditures for greater personal pleasure.

Naturally, in thinking along these lines, consideration must be given to the danger of placing potential investors of a poor country in a position of seeking greater safeguards, liquidity, and profits in other countries, thus increasing the flight of capital.

In the second place, whatever the parameters and variables of a model of national income may be, the flexibility and elasticity permitted by taxes on property or the capitalization of wealth in its various forms are very relative, because such taxes may not be made highly progressive. In this case the progressivity of the tax has a natural limit in the lack of liquidity of the things taxed. For this reason they cannot be used as *principal* instruments of fiscal policy, but only as auxiliary taxes.

In the third and final place, property taxes, which in many countries constitute the most important means for taxing capital, are customarily the main source of revenue for all secondary governmental levels: provinces, departments, states, localities, and municipalities.

This is due partly to historic reasons and partly to the relation between wealth and revenue and the place where they are produced. However, that circumstance is precisely one of the reasons why taxes on capital may not be made an integral part of a tax system properly co-ordinated to achieve particular objectives of fiscal policy at the central government level.

With reference to the incidence and economic effects of this kind of taxes, a clear distinction should be established between the case of taxes on the net wealth of individuals or business enterprises, on the one hand, and taxes on property and the forms of transferring it, on the other. While both forms of tax are related to ability to pay, as represented by individual or corporate assets, the taxation criterion and the circumstances in which they operate differ in the two cases, both as to the way they affect the individual or entity taxed and as respects the national treasury.

Taxes on property or its transfer, for a valuable consideration or *mortis causa,* have as a tax base concrete facts that make their control easier. Moreover, they are facts related to material goods having a known value, or one easily ascertainable, at market prices. Finally, they are facts that occur from time to time (purchase or sale of a piece of real estate, transfer, gift, inheritance) and that require certain public formalities (deed, registration, etc.) providing an excellent opportunity for the levy. On the other hand, the tax on the net wealth of individuals rests on a broader and more general concept of ownership: on the value of the goods in the hands of an individual net of debts; this causes complicated problems of assessment. It is

also a periodic tax that, to a certain extent, is anticipated by the taxpayers. These kinds of differences, which appear trivial, make the management and treatment of taxes such as these quite different.

TAX ON THE NET WEALTH OF INDIVIDUALS

The real purpose of this tax should be to differentiate between income derived from capital and income derived from labor by taxing the former more heavily. But it serves two important social ends besides: on the one hand, taxing unexploited wealth, causing its owners to sell it or put it to work; and on the other, working as a second weapon against the tax evasion that results especially from occasional gains and from the rise in values of assets.

Incidence

This tax is not shifted. The persons from whom it is collected are those who pay it. The general application of the tax makes its shifting impossible. However, as Mr. Jarach points out, there may be exceptions. For the reason that it is not shifted and that it is not directly related to the actual income of the owner of the wealth, it affects savings.

Economic Effects

The effect on savings can bring about a decrease in production and in capital formation. Actually the tax falls on goods that have escaped the income tax and is paid out of accumulated savings when available income is insufficient.

However, it does not necessarily operate in this way, for there are two factors that render it less severe than the income tax; first, it does not discriminate against the more productive investments, and, second, by taxing unproductive assets it obliges owners to seek a way to make them productive or turn them over to persons who would make them productive, as Mr. Jarach points out.

Everything will therefore depend on the rate applied and its progressivity; and in no case should this rate be high enough to discourage the investor or the tax be applied at such a low level of wealth as to discourage persons who are beginning to accumulate savings.

In this sense I do not share the conclusion of Mr. Jarach that this tax discourages investment of modest assets, since there is understood to be a level of initial exemption and a mild treatment for small holdings. In any case, with moderate rates, the proportion that would go for the payment of taxes would not serve to discourage savings.

Regarding the impact on consumption, again I disagree with the writer when he states that taxation of wealth accentuates the preference for consumption in taxpayers of low income. If this does not occur in the case of taxpayers of medium or high income, it is less likely to occur with those of low income. What would happen is a change in the composition of consumption in the direction of the purchase of more nondurable goods, for the very reason that these would escape the tax. This can also be avoided through exemptions, such as that on one's own housing, when the social importance of the investment justifies this course.

In conclusion, the impact on productive savings of the tax on the net wealth of individuals will depend on the steps and progressivity of the rates, so that if the proportion of the income from the wealth used for payment of taxes is low there is no reason for the level of investment to be lowered. It should likewise be remembered that the expenditure of tax collections by the government should compensate for the reduction in investments by the private sector.

As an instrument of fiscal policy, the tax can be used only as a supplement to the income tax and should be graduated so as not to discourage investment.

As an instrument of redistribution, it is less effective than might be supposed, since it does not modify the present state of distribution but merely prevents, in part, the excessive concentration of property. And if it should be wished to convert it into a more active instrument, this might have an undesirable impact upon the general level of production.

The same thing occurs when it is used as the instrument of a policy of economic development: it is a good source of fiscal resources, but when used in excess it affects private investment. Incidentally, it should be mentioned that tax incentives (usually, exemptions) are not the effective manner that some have held them to be of promoting economic development and should be used only in exceptional cases. The real incentive that the government should furnish to private investors is the creation of basic conditions that are favorable to the development of economic activity.

TAX ON THE NET WEALTH OF BUSINESS ENTERPRISES

I agree with Mr. Jarach that this type of tax is unsuitable.

First of all, as stated before, the reason for levying a tax on wealth is, above all, to differentiate between income from capital and income from labor. Inasmuch as corporations do not receive income from labor, this tax is unjustified as an element of differentiation. Neither is it justified as encouragement to use unexploited assets, since the shareholders and partners in each enterprise are the best judges of the profitability of the investment, and even less as an instrument against tax evasion, since this is less likely in the case of enterprises than of individuals because of the government controls to which the former are subject.

It is likewise undeniable that this kind of tax on business enterprises has exerted a strong influence on productive investment, inducing capital to enter such speculative transactions as those involving land and securities.

The only advantage that can be credited to this type of tax is its relative simplicity of collection.

PROPERTY TAXES

This type of tax does not reflect capacity to pay, as Mr. Jarach points out, since it does not take into account the debts of the owner or other elements of his wealth.

Incidence

Property taxes are shifted or not according to the kind of good on which they fall. When it is a question of residential property not occupied by its owners, the shift is possible except under price control. There is also a partial shifting in the case in which the tax falls on the property of commercial firms, increasing costs.

In the most usual case of housing property, the tax is regressive, since the lower the income of a family, the larger the proportion of that income spent on housing and the greater the tax burden that cuts into that income.

Taxes of this type, which bear no relation to individual net income, hit owners particularly hard when income falls. This happens especially during times of extreme depression, which make it necessary to sell property in order to pay the taxes, in a manner that is clearly inequitable.

These taxes also work hardship on the owners when there are additional tax burdens on property and at the same time rigid price controls.

These taxes have, however, the merit of being historically accepted for the relation between property and benefit through community action as well as the characteristic of constituting an elementary form of levying taxes on an economically strong sector of the community.

Economic Effects

Because property taxes are not readily shifted in most cases, they do not alter the production level. But in no case should a progressive property tax system be established, since this would be self-defeating from the standpoint of incentives to produce and to accumulate capital, and particularly because it is important to avoid multiple tax burdens on the same object, a common characteristic of developing economies.

TAXES ON TRANSFERS OF WEALTH

These do not have sufficient justification except as stamp and registry taxes on deeds and the usual documents whereby these transfers are made, the revenue from which is used to organize the very offices where the public instruments are registered and secondarily to improve the cadaster.

In these cases their effect is either neutral or has no importance, not even on the volume of real estate transactions. On the other hand, a tax per se on transfers for a valuable consideration, such as that described by Mr. Jarach, is without justification and inadvisable, particularly when it is applied on the basis of a progressive scale, because it has an undesirable effect on the movement of real property and, indirectly, on capital formation.

This form of tax is justified only as a way of taxing capital gains. But in this case it should cover not the full amount of the transaction but the difference between the purchase and the selling price of the piece of real property sold. Furthermore, a credit or discount should be allowed for each year since the date of purchase so as to take into account monetary devaluation, the increase in value the property has undergone in the hands of the seller and through his action (improvements, etc.), and the right of the seller to obtain some gain from the transaction.

Some of the advantages and the importance of this kind of tax in countries such as those of Latin America are the following: (1) it slows down speculation; (2) it channels savings into productive investment; and (3) it forces the voluntary reassessment of real property and thereby improves the tax base of the other property taxes.

TAXES ON INHERITANCES AND GIFTS

Finally, I am in general agreement with Mr. Jarach's analysis of taxes on inheritances and gifts.

In summary, my main comments are:

1. There is no basis for wanting to give much importance to this kind of tax as an instrument of fiscal policy.

2. Neither do the property taxes themselves admit many changes or innovations. What needs to be improved is their administration and collection.

3. The tax on the net wealth of individuals is important, particularly where the income tax system is unitary instead of schedular.

4. The tax on the net wealth of business enterprises, where it exists, should be eliminated as being antieconomic.

Comment

Jaime E. Porras*

Mr. Dino Jarach, as an introduction to his paper on *Taxes on Net Wealth, Inheritances, and Gifts,* outlines the aims which, in accordance with present-day thinking, shape fiscal policy objectives. As this is a tax study, the necessary emphasis has been placed on the importance of taxation as an instrument of fiscal policy useful in achieving the goals of the state.

Fiscal policy has five aims:

1. To organize public finance as an economic system, different from that of the market or private sector, for the rendering of services that the political, economic, and social circumstances of a given country at a given time assign to the action of the state.

2. To obtain revenue through taxation adhering to the prevailing criteria of justice and equality.

3. To affect the distribution of national income.

4. To influence stabilization policies, i.e., to eliminate fluctuations in the economy.

5. To promote a country's development and economic growth.

The aims listed include, in one way or another, the objectives of obtaining a satis-

*Chief Adviser, Co-ordination Division Planning Board, Quito, Ecuador.

factory level of consumption and a desirable level of employment. Modern thinking stresses that the basic aims of fiscal policy are the distribution or redistribution of national income and the economic and social development of a country.

In order to achieve the objectives of fiscal policy, regardless of what these may be, the instruments that must be used are public expenditures, taxes, and public debt. One cannot be unaware of the importance of these instruments, due to the high level of financial activity on the part of the governments and the decisive impact they therefore have on the economy. The problem arises, then, as to how to employ these instruments in order to achieve the objectives established by the state; therefore, fiscal policy should be so shaped that it will avoid adverse effects on the economic and social well-being of the community. Public expenditures must be used as a compensating measure to private expenditures in an effort to counteract inflationary pressures. A series of arguments have been put forth against compensatory fiscal policy, but it is impossible to overlook the fact that it is in the interest of all governments to protect the private economic sector from the effects of instability.

Likewise, the economic and social development of a country depends on the accelerated formation of fixed social capital in which the governments themselves play a predominant role in view of their financing capability. Substantial investments in infrastructure projects, especially in the transportation field, cannot be undertaken by the private sector. The planning of expenditures and their direction toward development aims constitute one of the most important aspects of fiscal policy; taxation alone is not enough to achieve these goals. Expenditures and taxation should be correlated, since they constitute the antecedent and the result of the government's financial activities. They are two problems confronting fiscal policy and are closely interrelated.

The programing of economic and social development and its practical application as an objective of fiscal policy must be based on structural changes in the systems of administration, taxation, and land tenure; but this involves, at the same time, a fundamental change in the philosophy of government, in the thinking and attitude of those bearing the responsibility for the management of public affairs. The country itself, then, must give the required stimulus to progress; external financial aid, important in itself, nevertheless occupies a secondary position.

TAX ON THE NET WEALTH OF INDIVIDUALS

The tax on net wealth constitutes one of the large categories of direct taxation, although it no longer has major importance in modern finance; and the single, general tax on wealth has been practically eliminated from the tax legislation of the world.

The tax on wealth is levied on the monetary value of real and personal property after liabilities have been subtracted from the assets; in short, the tax is to be applied on the net value of the property owned by an individual. Some legislation also includes the value of intangible property in the form of securities, shares of stock, and bank accounts, although the last-named are seldom taxed.

It may be accepted as a general proposition that the value of property is an index for estimating the economic well-being of an individual; but the existence of certain assets that produce no income makes it impossible to evaluate the true earning capacity of a taxpayer and consequently his taxpaying ability.

The tax on wealth can hardly be considered as a substitute for the tax on actual income. Likewise wealth cannot serve as sufficient basis for the assessment of income tax, nor can income serve as the basis for taxing wealth. My personal opinion is that Benini's law cannot be applied in countries of insufficient development, precisely because of the lack of capital and of a spirit of enterprise. In fact, it is not pertinent to speak of correlation between income and wealth because of the existence of individuals of different incomes and wealth and because assets of equal value may yield different returns. The profitability of wealth depends on the form in which it is invested, whether in industry, trade, or agriculture, and, within these sectors of the national production, on the ability and initiative of the entrepreneur.

In fact, the tax on the net wealth of individuals should be considered as supplementary to the income tax, to cover what is not taxed by the latter; the existence of this tax as the sole instrument of taxation cannot be admitted, for in that way income from labor would be excluded from taxation.

Administration of the Net Wealth Tax

As is the case with administration of the income tax, the determination of the taxable base must be effected primarily on the basis of the statement of the taxpayer, with the necessary checking by the tax authorities later. If the tax is to fall on the net assets of an individual, the problem of applying the tax according to principles of justice and fairness begins here, for it cannot be made effective unless the tax administration has the necessary resources to carry out the assessments and inspection, particularly where personal and intangible property, which by its nature is easy to hide, is involved; otherwise, the incidence of the tax would be greatest upon those taxpayers having the highest standards of honesty.

One of the characteristics of underdeveloped countries is the lack of adequate administrative techniques. The application of the tax is the result of a long process: declaration of the taxpayer, verification by the tax authorities, assessment of property and administration of the tax, all of which require a series of complicated technical operations whose efficiency is difficult to ascertain even in highly developed countries and still more so in countries where administrative techniques have not yet reached the desired levels, especially in evaluation.

If due to the concealment of personal property and intangible assets the amount of taxable matter is easily reduced, the tax on wealth would become, for all practical purposes, a tax on real property; for this reason the tax on wealth in most countries, as a tax on net assets, either has not been established or has been dropped from the tax picture.

If the value of a good is given by the capitalized value of income, the evaluation of real property presents a series of obstacles that is difficult to overcome. It is well known that in the agricultural sector real property is overvalued and its market value is higher than that obtained from capitalizing income at the current rate of interest. On the other hand, it is difficult to estimate the commercial value of the property assets of a family partnership, owing to the fact that there are virtually no possibilities for comparison with other similar ones in the market. Also, certain assets that produce no income for their owners, but merely a sort of subjective satisfaction, present difficult problems of evaluation.

On the other hand, if, as happens under some laws, the deduction of liabilities is not accepted, double taxation automatically follows; this is one aspect of tax justice that is highly debatable. From the social point of view, the application of a tax on wealth carries with it a need to accept certain deductions, such as those for family exemptions, medical expenses, accidents, education of children, etc., as well as exemptions due to age limits. These important social aspects cannot be disregarded in tax legislation.

Shifting and Effects of the Tax

It is stated that the tax on individual net wealth cannot be shifted, as a general rule; as a result, the immediate effect, provided other factors remain constant, is that the tax is capitalized at the current interest rate.

There is, in fact, no possibility of shifting a tax on property devoted to the sole use of its owner; neither is shifting possible when applied to durable consumer goods, although there are cases when this might occur.

The lessor will try to shift the tax to the lessee and the creditor to the debtor, even though there are laws that prohibit this. It all depends on the scarcity of property to rent and of capital to loan.

On the premise that the tax is paid in fact by the owners of the wealth, it appears acceptable to state that consumption will be encouraged and saving discouraged in the case of low-income taxpayers and even those of medium income, in underdeveloped countries. But if the tax falls on high-income taxpayers, what would possibly be affected is the rate of capitalization but not the standard of living of economically powerful individuals.

From the social standpoint, there could be no objection if the tax should fall on property producing no income, since this would become an effective instrument for compelling owners to get rid of this property, thereby fulfilling one of the aims of fiscal policy, which makes use of taxation for redistribution of the national wealth.

The private ownership of large parks and gardens is socially unproductive; it brings subjective satisfaction to the owner but does not benefit the community; hence the net wealth tax on this kind of luxury property can serve to discourage it.

On the other hand, the principle that ownership should serve a social function is generally accepted. Hence the tax on net wealth should be an effective instrument for discouraging the holding of idle, but potentially productive, land. The owner would thus feel compelled to either work it or sell it, and this would benefit the community. The same may be said of the progressive tax on unoccupied urban lots to encourage the construction of city housing.

I agree on the uneconomic effects of the tax on net wealth when it is applied to business enterprises in their initial stages of development, when they have not yet become profitable. Hence it is preferable to levy the tax on actual income and not on what, in the final analysis, is potential income.

In order that the incidence of the tax on net wealth should not fall on small capitals, particularly in underdeveloped countries, certain exemptions should be made so as not to discourage the utilization of modest resources in productive enterprises. In this sense the tax becomes antieconomic, even though its purpose was to increase government revenue. On the other hand, I do not consider it wise to tax business capital even though the owner receives no income from his investment, for the deficit situation of enterprises would become more acute, thus discouraging the development of productive activity.

It is said that the annual control of net wealth makes it possible to assess the changes in value of property for the purpose of collecting taxes on capital gains due to price changes. It must be noted that this could be applied only if it is feasible for the taxing authorities to carry out the necessary periodic valuation. But in countries where there are technical gaps in tax administration, where even the periodic assessments that are made of real property leave much to be desired, it would be quite difficult to achieve the proposed objective through net wealth taxes. Also, it would be necessary to incur heavy administrative expenses of doubtful effectiveness.

The inflexibility that characterizes the tax on net wealth renders its use as an instrument of stabilization impossible, since it is extremely difficult to adapt it to changing price levels during periods of inflation and depreciation. The lack of flexibility is a result, among other things, of the difficulties of tax administration, which are much greater in countries where the control capacity of the taxing authority is weak due to the absence of the necessary human and financial resources.

Throughout this comment, I have been emphasizing a fact that characterizes the underdeveloped countries: the lack of administrative proficiency, which is a result, among other things, of the lack of stability of the officials having charge of tax administration in its various phases. Personally, I believe that if this is not overcome, at least to some degree, no thought should be given to the practical application of the tax on net wealth of individuals.

A good deal of the objectives sought through a tax on net wealth may be achieved with improvements in the administration of taxes on real property; for this reason it is unnecessary to give any further reasons why putting the tax under discussion into effect would be inadvisable.

REAL ESTATE TAX

Certainly real estate taxes do not reflect the taxpaying capacity of the subject, except in a very rudimentary fashion, since the property is taxed independently of debts that affect it and because this tax is levied irrespective of other forms of wealth of the taxpayer, as is quite properly stated in the study on which this comment is based. Nevertheless, in some countries, in order to avoid double taxation, the amount of mortgage debts on the real estate is deducted from the assessed value of the property.[33]

[33]Under the Rural Property Tax Law now in effect in Ecuador, debts used to guarantee mortgages on property are deducted from the assessed value; but the deduction in no case may exceed half of the difference remaining of the assessed value after all deductions allowed by the law have been made. Furthermore, in applying the tax on urban property the amounts owed in the form of mortgage loans on the property are deductible, but this deduction may not exceed 40 per cent of the amount of the mortgage.

It is impossible to shift the tax on urban property in the case of housing occupied by the owner; on the other hand, it is possible to shift it to the tenant either through an increase in the rental rate or through a contractual clause stating that the tenant is the *de facto* subject of the tax obligation.

With respect to rural property, shifting could take place in the form of a price rise during periods of scarcity of farm products. Note has been taken of the possibility of shifting the tax on rural property to the tenant, but this possibility exists also for other forms of landholding such as sharecroppers, etc. These cases are typical in certain countries where the colonial system of land tenure still prevails.

I have already noted that, in connection with real estate, the phenomenon of capitalization and amortization of the tax could take place whenever the other factors affecting price remained constant; this phenomenon can occur, of course, in other kinds of capital goods susceptible of producing periodic income.

I mentioned earlier as one of the basic objections to applying the tax on wealth the lack of proficiency and ability in the tax administration, particularly in underdeveloped countries. Administration of the tax on real estate in several countries presents considerable technical gaps: lack of uniformity in assessment standards available to the various local governments that are the beneficiaries of this kind of taxes; lack of proper periodicity of assessments and the lack of know-how in carrying them out, and especially when those making the assessments are not employees of the treasury department but individuals on temporary contract; the presence of partisan political interests or groups in the various local governments, who have quite often used the tax as a weapon of retaliation as well as to obtain a series of advantages in the application of the tax. The lack of financial resources of local governments has prevented the periodic carrying out of assessments, and this has resulted in the simple use of a coefficient to make an indiscriminate increase

in the value fixed at a previous time. While it is true that under certain legislations, in order to determine the taxable amount, the value of all real estate owned by one person must be added, it has often been impossible to apply due to the lack of the cross information between local governments that would make it possible to apply progressive tax rates when a single taxpayer owned property in different political jurisdictions in the country.

Because of the deficiencies noted and others that could be pointed out, it is advisable that at least rural property be taxed by the central government so as to make possible the application of technical standards and eliminate inequities in the administration of the tax. In this event, the central government might very well distribute the tax revenue among the various local governments.

It is known that the property tax lacks elasticity because it cannot be adjusted with due rapidity to price fluctuations. In periods of expansion, tax revenues do not increase proportionately, while in periods of depression there are unfavorable characteristics, since the owner is obliged to pay the same tax even though his relative economic position has deteriorated considerably. It is difficult to give the necessary flexibility to this kind of tax, which is levied generally and is based on assessments made at rather prolonged intervals.

The real estate tax is beneficial as an instrument of fiscal policy, including its social aspects, for a progressive tax on land that is idle but potentially suitable for farming, at rates that increase annually, is conducive to the redistribution of wealth and can be an effective means of land reform.

As is quite well pointed out in the paper on which I am commenting, taxation of urban property and of vacant lots can prove to be an incentive to change the use to which the property has been put; the results achieved will depend a great deal on the progressivity of the tax. On the other hand, if it is desired to discourage the building of luxury housing and to favor the channeling of investments toward low-cost housing, an increase in the base and greater progressivity in the rates could serve these purposes.

TAXES ON NET WEALTH OF BUSINESS ENTERPRISES

While it is true that there is widespread evasion in the payment of the inheritance tax on bearer shares of corporate stock, the tax authorities may have been able to find a substitute in the net wealth tax on business enterprises in their efforts to balance the public finances. But it is hardly equivalent with respect to redistributive effects of the national wealth, on account of the possibilities that exist for shifting the latter tax, a fact that completely changes its effects.

It is rightly noted in the paper that this tax accentuates the regressive characteristics that a tax system may have; in this sense it could be said that if the shift is forward, the tax on net wealth of business enterprises constitutes an excise tax and in no way a substitute for the inheritance tax, even though under certain circumstances marginal and new corporations may bear it, since the same phenomenon occurs with certain excise taxes.

It is natural that every taxpayer should try to avoid the tax, and thus, although the prospects for shifting the tax on net wealth of business enterprises are certain, the investor will prefer to employ his financial assets in lucrative activities on which the tax is lower or nonexistent, despite the fact that earnings are lower; hence the tax would in a certain way discourage the formation and growth of corporations, a factor that would have a negative impact on the development of the economy, particularly in countries where capital is scarce.

I find that the only advantage of this tax is that it makes larger tax collections possible and is easy to administer.

TAXES ON TRANSFERS OF CAPITAL ASSETS FOR A VALUABLE CONSIDERATION

It is known that the revenue from these taxes is affected by evasion carried out through false declarations of the sale value.

It has been said that evasion could be controlled by the establishment of a presumptive value of the sale, based upon the assessment of the real property. I wish to make it clear that this system of control can give good results only in countries where an acceptable technical level has been reached in the administration of taxes on real estate. But, as I stated earlier, the administration of this kind of taxes leaves much to be desired, since there are technical and administrative flaws that are hard to overcome in a short while and a series of factors that have a negative incidence on the reaching of accurate assessments, due mainly to the fact that real estate tax administration in some countries is in charge of local governments (municipalities). These and other facts make possible a good administration of the land tax as well as of taxes on transfers of capital assets. I believe that many present problems could be eliminated if land tax administration were placed in the hands of the central government, especially in countries having a unitary form of government.

Moreover, the taxes now under discussion have little flexibility, due to the impossibility of adapting them readily to price fluctuations, especially in countries whose laws have set fixed periods of time—and rather long ones—for the reassessment of real property.

These taxes can be employed as an instrument of stabilization in periods of boom, because it is precisely in those times that the greatest volume of transfers of property takes place; but since, as we have remarked, the legislation cannot be adapted promptly to the changing price situations, the weight of the tax no longer has major importance in the presence of speculative forces and the certainty of large profits.

TAXES ON INHERITANCES AND GIFTS

The justice of this kind of taxes can hardly be questioned now, since an inheritance, legacy, or gift constitutes an increment of wealth that enables the recipient to improve his standard of living. Under some circumstances this will not be absolutely true, as when the transmission is made in favor of the surviving minor children and the surviving spouse; but in modern legislations special exemptions and tax rates are provided for these cases.

The main stream of thought is that there is no shifting in this type of tax. Nor should thought be given to the negative effect of capital accumulation, considering the slight significance of these taxes in the total tax collections of a country.

The tax on gratuitous transfers of property should be paid by the one receiving an increase in his wealth that enables him to improve his economic well-being. For that reason, the tax on net wealth of business enterprises, because of its possibilities for being shifted, cannot be accepted as a substitute for the tax on gratuitous transfers.

The application of death taxes presents a major problem, namely, the evaluation of the assets involved. In this connection, the lack of administrative proficiency with respect to the land tax, whose appraisal often serves as the basis for figuring the amount of the estate, has an unfavorable incidence. Furthermore, fiscal experts of the government are not always employed, and for this reason the appraisals are not usually made on a technically acceptable basis. Likewise, certain assets such as jewels, cash, securities, and other items easily hidden pass on to the heirs without the knowledge of the tax authorities. Determination of the commercial value of certain assets, such as shares of family corporations that are not quoted on the market, is rather difficult, and this can mean injury to the treasury or to the taxpayers. In general it may be said that collection is easy, and it is unnecessary to maintain high administrative costs for the collection of taxes on gratuitous transfers of property.

The question of the inheritance tax being in agreement with the principles of equity, justice, and taxpaying capacity can no longer be discussed.

In order for the tax to be paid according to the real capacity of the taxpayer, it is necessary to introduce certain legal provisions to prevent evasion through fictitious sales of assets.

A progressive tax contributes to the redistribution of wealth both through the sale of assets and the utilization of the savings of the heir to pay the tax, all of which enables the treasury to turn over the revenue obtained, through public expenditures, to the community in the form of goods and services.

It must be recognized that the inheritance tax, due to its minor significance in the total volume of tax revenue, particularly in poor countries, is of little importance as a deflationary element.

Mr. Dino Jarach describes in his paper with ample documentation the various currents of thought that can throw light on the utilization in the tax system of taxes on wealth, inheritances, and gifts. In making marginal comments to the study, I have sought to bring out the deficiencies in the various countries, especially the underdeveloped, that slow down the application of such taxes, due to the lack of technical proficiency in tax administration; further, I have urged that laws be enacted in a manner conducive to the achievement of the basic objectives of fiscal policy, and at the same time I have called for a structural change of administrative organization on which the effective application of the principles of equity and generality in taxation rests.

Discussion

Mr. Jarach thought that before embarking upon an analysis of taxation on net wealth, inheritances, and gifts it would be well to stress that the objectives of fiscal policy should be constantly borne in mind, together with the advantages and disadvantages of taxes in relation to those objectives.

It had been argued that taxation of the value of property chronologically preceded taxation of income, which was no doubt true of certain partial aspects of the former but was not valid in the case of a global tax on net wealth, which presented all the administrative difficulties associated with income tax, as well as other problems. In his view, therefore, the net wealth tax could be applied only in countries which already had some income tax experience. Nor could a tax on net wealth be regarded as a substitute for income tax, but rather as supplementary to it. The replacement of one tax by another should be approached with the utmost caution and with due regard to its economic repercussions and its effects on the attainment of fiscal policy objectives.

There was no correlation between the distribution of property and income, although Benini had suggested that if the latter increased in the geometric proportion of two, the former increased at the geometric rate of three. Were this so, even the application of a proportional tax on net wealth would result in practice in a form of progressive taxation. The advantages of the tax on net wealth over income tax could be summed up under the following heads: (1) it was more equitable, because it was applied as a function of real tax capacity and could not be shifted; (2) it enabled a clear distinction to be drawn between earned and unearned income; (3) it was neutral with regard to its effect on decisions to invest in enterprises involving high degrees of risk; (4) it corrected distortions stemming from nonmonetary psychological causes, such as a predilection for specific types of investment which were not recommendable from the standpoint of their social usefulness; and (5), for the very reason that it fell upon potential rather than actual income, it implemented the principle termed "productivist" by the Italian school, whereby taxpayers who kept their capital productive were rewarded and those holding funds inactive or proper-

ties unproductive or underproductive were penalized.

As far as the practical difficulties of administering the tax in question were concerned, those of a technical nature were not excessive and should not be overestimated. It could be combined with a system of taxation on personal income based on yearly returns not only of income but of components of net wealth. As Mr. Rapoport had explained, tax returns of that type had been required in Argentina since 1947, although there was still plenty of room for improvement of the system. Returns of the type in question were also useful as controls in respect of the application of income tax.

The chief difficulty lay in valuation, since it was very difficult to keep market values up to date. There was consequently a strong element of presumption in the net wealth tax, as distinct from income tax, where presumed values were reduced to a minimum. A system of making accurate valuations and of keeping them up to date would therefore have to be instituted, especially for periods of inflation.

In his opinion, the net wealth tax ought also to reach all kinds of unproductive assets, such as automobiles, parks, gardens, etc. Clearly, the same problems would arise in that connection as in relation to the calculation of imputed income.

In countries where administrative technique had not yet reached a level high enough to permit of the introduction of the net wealth tax, taxes on real estate might still be levied. There, again, the problem of valuation arose, and in a more complicated form, because such taxes were generally applied by provincial or municipal authorities or others distinct from the central government. The real estate tax was less equitable than the tax on net wealth.

Referring to taxes on inheritances and gifts, he expressed the view that they affected neither incentives nor savings and could be considered as an alternative to the tax on the net wealth of natural persons. The main effect of the taxation in question was to secure the redistribution of wealth, and that was of great importance in Latin America, where wealth was overconcentrated. Payment of the tax did not affect enterprises, except in the case of small individual businesses or partnerships; and even there its effects might be considered beneficial, if it resulted in making foreign capital available to family enterprises short of capital and operating below the optimum dimension level.

The tax on inheritances and gifts often aroused political opposition among the ruling classes, which were anxious to maintain the permanent dynastic ownership of real estate or businesses. To conceal hostility to the tax, collection difficulties, annoyances caused to small- and medium-scale business enterprises, and the resulting evasions were magnified.

Among the palliatives suggested to avert the effects of the inheritance tax was the so-called substitute tax that fell on the net assets of business enterprises. The substitute tax could be partially shifted and was therefore not as equitable as the tax on the net wealth of natural persons or the inheritance tax, nor did it contribute in the same way to the redistribution of wealth or provide any incentive to economic development.

To sum up, in developing countries it would be desirable to apply income tax supplemented by the net wealth tax and other taxes on property which simultaneously fulfilled several objectives of fiscal policy and, last, by a progressive tax on inheritance and gifts.

MR. CASAS said that, broadly speaking, he was in full agreement with Mr. Jarach's views. With regard to the tax on the net wealth of individuals, he did not share the opinion that such a tax was discouraging to the investment of small assets because it was understood that there was an initial level of exemption and more lenient treatment was accorded. Nor did he agree that the tax in question increased the preference for consumer goods among low-income taxpayers; he considered that the composition of consumption would be modified in favor of nondurable goods which would escape taxation. That could be prevented by the establishment of certain exemptions.

He did not think there was sufficient justification for the tax on transfers. He considered that the transfer tax per se had no *raison d'être* and was justified only if used as a means of taxing occasional profits, in which case it should be applied, not to the value of the transfers, but to the difference between the purchase and sales price of the immovable item transferred. Moreover, an allowance or credit should be given in order to take into account the seller's right to a profit, the effects of monetary devaluation, and the improvements made by the seller in the item sold. Thus conceived, the tax on occasional profits in transactions had three advantages: (1) it curbed speculation; (2) it channeled savings into productive investment; (3) it compelled voluntary revaluation of real estate, thus improving the tax base for other property taxes.

MR. PORRAS said he was in entire agreement with the theoretical principles propounded by Mr. Jarach in his paper. He wished to stress one aspect of the subject, however, namely, the extent to which application of the net wealth tax would be feasible. The object of taxation in that instance would be the difference remaining after the subtraction of liabilities from assets, and it might be very difficult to compute that amount, especially as movable and intangible assets were easy to conceal. Moreover, the administration of the tax might imply such heavy expenditure that the financial results obtained would not be worthwhile. His emphasis on feasibility of application was based on his conviction that the role of an expert was not to formulate recommendations in a theoretical void. If the best was impracticable, the only thing to do was to accept the least unsatisfactory solution.

He attributed the difficulties of administering the real estate tax chiefly to its decentralized character. For example, in Ecuador the tax in question was in the hands of ninety-seven municipalities, not one of which had the slightest possibility of carrying out the land surveys required for accurate valuation. The same difficulty with respect to valuation would be encountered in estimating potential income from rural real estate, and while it was true that the system had been introduced in Chile, he did not think it could be adopted in Ecuador, where even the possibility of taking aerial photographs was limited by the poor light in some districts. Therefore he thought that more careful study should be given to Mr. Harberger's proposals for a system of voluntary returns on the part of the landowner, with the modifications suggested by Mr. Kaldor.

He agreed with Mr. Jarach that a tax on the net wealth of business enterprises was undesirable and that its only justification would be the ease with which the resultant revenue could be collected. He also disapproved of the tax on transfers for a valuable consideration because of the high degree of evasion to which it might lead.

Mr. PINTO considered that although in theory the same tax instruments were at the disposal of all countries, they should be assigned different weights. In Latin America, greater importance should be attached to the tax on property than in the more highly industrialized countries, for a number of reasons: the tax affected typical forms of hoarding which were not the most desirable from the standpoint of development; it was less difficult to administer than income tax; and it had more powerful repercussions on the inequitable distribution of wealth.

From the social standpoint, the population should be divided into three groups or brackets, and different tax instruments should be applied to each.

1. In the case of the highest social bracket, which consisted of 5 per cent of the total number of heads of households, absorbed 40 per cent of the national income, and was capable of carrying 60 per cent of the tax burden, income tax should be applied, because that tax should be concentrated in the groups which could provide a worthwhile yield; also a tax on assets in whatever form; and a tax on expenditure on luxury goods and services.

2. The middle bracket, which comprised 35 per cent of heads of households, absorbed 40 per cent of national income, and should contribute 30 per cent of tax revenue, would be subjected to a tax on expenditure on the so-called "nonwage goods," in Latin American terms, since that was a feasible way of collecting revenue and applying a form of income tax which would not have a heavy payroll incidence.

3. The low-income group, which was composed of 60 per cent of heads of households, absorbed 20 per cent of national income, and should not contribute more than 10 per cent to tax revenue, would have to be taxed through expenditure, but with the exemption of certain goods such as foodstuffs.

As the income of the last-named group increased, its members would move up into the middle-income bracket and would pay tax in accordance with the tax instruments applied to that group.

Mr. DESAI wondered whether, in the case of death duties, instead of taking into consideration the net wealth of the decedent, it would be preferable to apply the tax to the total net wealth of the beneficiary, including the inheritance. In India, the practice of gifts in the donor's lifetime had become widespread, since after two years death duties were not payable. An accessions tax levied on the beneficiary, if coupled with the net wealth tax, would make it possible to combine the inheritance and gift taxes into an easily administered single tax. One could even think in terms of a separate schedule for gifts and inheritance within the annual assessment and levy of tax on net wealth.

Mr. VIDAL considered that the main purpose of the substitute tax in Argentina and Uruguay was to prevent evasion in the case of bearer securities.

Mr. MATUS endorsed Mr. Pinto's suggestion and regretted that he had not been able to comment on Mr. Harberger's paper on tax reform, since the chief criticism he would level against it was precisely that it did not take into account total fiscal structure and the social distribution of taxation. Thus, in the case under discussion it was less important to consider the details of the net wealth tax than to know what other taxes were associated with it in the system as a whole for the purposes of achieving the desired objectives.

MR. COSCIANI, in reply to Mr. Desai, said that it was not always possible to determine on whom the burden of death duties fell. Among the wealthy groups, the transfer of savings was a residual item; in the middle brackets, there was some element of economic calculation. In any event, the tax might have two possible structures; it could either be progressively graduated according to the net wealth of the decedent or applied to the amount received by each heir.

MR. BACA expressed surprise at what Mr. Desai said of gifts made during the donor's lifetime, since in Latin America they were also taxable.

MR. HERSCHEL concurred with Mr. Pinto and Mr. Matus on the need for discussing the fiscal system as a whole, but in his view it was also useful to ascertain the effects and implications of each separate tax and the forms they assumed.

The CHAIRMAN said that the comments formulated by Mr. Pinto, Mr. Matus, and Mr. Herschel would be included in a document prepared for general discussion.

MR. JARACH, replying to the comments on his paper, thanked the participants, and particularly Mr. Casas and Mr. Porras, for their friendly judgments, though none of the very pertinent comments made had led him to change his views. He had never believed that the tax on net wealth played an outstanding role in relation to income tax, but at the same time we could not regard it as performing a secondary function. He believed that the two taxes complemented each other. He was also of the opinion that the tax on the net wealth of physical persons was a more perfect instrument even than schedular taxes and certainly than the unitary income tax to make an accurate and continuous distinction between earned and unearned income. Not only did it supplement them, but it could facilitate the administration of income tax, inasmuch as it enabled the latter to be based on the declaration of total wealth.

Nor did he agree with the view that great importance should be assigned to the tax on net wealth only in the case of a nonmonetized economy, since its role was not substitutive. It was precisely its complementary function that made it inevitably more important in those countries where income tax was in full development.

Actually, taxes on property were merely rather incomplete substitutes for the tax on net wealth, as was evident from the case of corporations. In some provinces of Argentina a tax on aggregate estate, which was a form of net wealth, was being introduced.

It was not for him to give his opinion on Mr. Pinto's interesting idea regarding the integration of tax systems, although it was certainly intriguing.

With regard to the tax on inheritances and gifts, he referred to the comments made by Mr. Desai and Mr. Cosciani during the course of the debate. He defended the global inheritance tax as a form of posthumous tax on net wealth which would make the progressivity of the tax more effective. As for the individual inheritance tax, it should be graduated according to the net wealth of each heir.

As Mr. Vidal had observed, the problem posed by bearer securities in connection with the taxes on net wealth and on inheritances and gifts was not without some importance. However, such problems were peculiar not so much to those taxes as to those types of securities.

With reference to the issue raised by Mr. Herschel as to the jurisdictional level at which the tax on net wealth should be levied, he felt that it would be advisable to establish such a tax only at the national level, to avoid fragmentation.

In conclusion, he summed up his views by saying that whatever technical or administrative difficulties the taxes on net wealth and on inheritance and gifts might raise, they should not be magnified to the point of discarding such taxes and replacing them by others which might distort the whole tax system.

NOTE

Commenting on the topic "Taxes on net wealth, inheritances, and gifts," Mr. Aníbal Pinto drew attention to the importance of examining the tax system, as a whole, with special reference to its composition or structure. Subsequently, Mr. Pinto handed to the secretariat the following table, which was circulated among the participants of the conference in view of its undoubted interest.

Scheme for Social Distribution of Tax Instruments *by* ANÍBAL PINTO

| Social group | Percentages | | | Tax instruments |
	Active population	Participation in national income	Reasonable contribution to fiscal revenue[a]	
1. High	5	40	60[b]	*a)* Income *b)* Property *c)* Expenditure
2. Medium	35	40	30[c]	*a)* Expenditure *b)* Income (payroll)
3. Low	60	20	10[d]	Expenditure

NOTE: In the example above (and as mentioned by Mr. Pinto in his comments) it is assumed that it is desirable to allocate tax instruments on a social basis, according to a classification, into large groups representing proportions of the active population and distributed income which are more or less characteristic of the average situation in Latin America. Personal income tax is concentrated in Group 1 (there is opposition to the "diffusion" of this tax), its progressive effect being reinforced by the taxes on property, which in Latin American tax structures would have decidedly greater weight than in industrialized countries. Taxes on expenditure, especially on the goods and services preferred at those levels of income, would complete the tax incidence. For Group 2, taxes on expenditure covering what might be called "nonwage goods" would be the main instrument, reinforced by a low rate of tax (e.g., between 3 and 4 per cent, perhaps with a slight progressivity), based on the payroll and deducted.

"Nonwage goods" should be understood in a very restricted sense, in keeping with the low average income, that is, covering nearly all consumption goods and services except the most essential, e.g., those consumed by the masses in rural areas and the urban periphery. Finally, the masses in Group 3, which would not make a net contribution to public finance in view of the effect of the expenditure, would be taxed to the extent that their consumption crossed the border line between "wage goods" and "nonwage goods."

[a]It is assumed that fiscal income represents 15 per cent of national income.
[b]In making this contribution, Group 1 retains for itself, after tax, 31 per cent of national income.
[c]After tax, Group 2 absorbs 35.5 per cent of national income.
[d]After tax, Group 3 retains 18.5 per cent plus the effect of public expenditure, probably progressive.

8

Corporate Income Taxation in Latin America

by Alan R. Prest*

It will be convenient to divide the subject matter of this paper into three sections. First, we shall have a little to say about the general principles of taxation in developing countries and the pros and cons of corporate income taxation. Second, we shall summarize the structure of corporate income taxation in Latin America at present. Third, we shall look at possible reforms and improvements. We shall be dealing throughout with income taxation at the central government level and shall ignore any corporate income taxation levied by states or provinces and any interrelationships between such taxes and those imposed at the central level. It must also be stated at the outset that the author is not an expert on Latin America and therefore there may be errors of fact or interpretation which a more experienced commentator could have avoided. Apologies are offered in advance if this is the case.

SECTION I

It is not necessary to say much here about the general principles of taxation in developing countries. For one thing, the subject is well covered by other papers at this conference. And in any case I have very recently set out my own views elsewhere on some aspects of this subject.[1] Perhaps the most salient points can be summarized as follows.

The typical structure of the public sector in many underdeveloped countries is that there is a constant, and sometimes increasing, pressure to raise government spending in many different fields. At the same time, many countries are liable to severe short-term balance of payments difficulties which in turn make for excesses of government expenditure over government revenue. When this combination of circumstances is taken along with the need to foster incentives on the part of owners to provide labor, capital, or other resources and the need to keep the tax system within the very limited administrative competence available, it is soon apparent there is no simple or single tax policy which will satisfy all these conflicting requirements. Therefore on these very general grounds one must expect to find that some use is made of a wide range of taxes, including corporate taxation.

In fact, there is a positive case for using corporate taxes, and one need not rely solely on these general and rather indirect arguments. First of all, it can be maintained on equity grounds that there is a case for taxing corporations even if dividends paid to shareholders are fully taxed as part of personal incomes.

*Christ's College, Cambridge, England.

[1]Alan R. Prest, *Public Finance in Underdeveloped Countries* (London: Weidenfeld and Nicolson, 1962).

234

If this were not done, undistributed profits would be free of tax at the time they were made,[2] and this is hardly compatible with general principles of income taxation. If for any reason (e.g., the likely case with bearer shares) dividends are not fully taxed in the hands of shareholders, the argument is so much stronger. These equity considerations are not so clear-cut if we think of corporation taxes as leading to changes in product prices rather than to changes in net profits. But evidence on this matter is not unequivocal, and insofar as one thinks that this result is the probable one, there are some far reaching implications for income taxation of other kinds, such as that on unincorporated businesses; and, even if the equity argument is weakened in this way, other arguments for corporate income taxation may, *per contra*, be strengthened.

Apart from equity matters, the ease of administering a corporate income tax is of no small importance in developing countries. The contrast between companies which have to comply with statutory accounting requirements and the category of small traders and farmers, who may well keep no accounts at all, is too well known to require elaboration. Even though corporations may account for a much smaller share of value added in the private sector than in advanced countries, they are nevertheless sitting targets for any tax administration, however backward and feeble it may be in other ways.

As far as political considerations go—and they may go a very long way, indeed, in some countries—there are strong pragmatic reasons for preferring to tax corporations, which do not have votes, to individuals, who do. And if one accepts the notion of corporate income taxes reacting on product prices rather than on profits, this argument is all the stronger. For, in this case, one cannot even point to the body of equity shareholders as a clearly defined category of losers from the imposition or raising of corporate income taxes.

[2]Insofar as they lead to capital appreciation or future income from additional capital investment, there may be, of course, a potential future liability to tax.

To the extent that dividends are paid abroad, there is the further argument that by virtue of tax credits corporate income taxation may be at the expense of foreign government revenue rather than net returns to foreign shareholders. The complications of this subject and the necessary qualifications are too great to cope with now, but the general proposition is clear enough.

All these arguments on equity, administration, politics, and foreign dividends have been developed so far in terms of a hypothetical situation where a government is trying to decide whether or not to impose a corporation income tax. In the case where a corporation income tax already exists, there is a further point to make: the inequity of allowing some individuals to make windfall gains as a consequence of removing the tax.

It may be possible to tax any such gain by means of a regular capital gains tax or by some special *ad hoc* device. Nevertheless, the fact remains that even if a particular corporation tax which is already in being cannot be justified as an ideal system, it may nevertheless be the lesser of two evils to retain it.

It may be noted that some of the arguments sometimes used to justify corporate taxation are not mentioned above. One is the benefit principle: that corporations should pay a tax in return for the benefit conferred by incorporation. Another is the proposition that corporation taxation is a means of taxing unearned income more heavily than earned and that such discrimination is desirable. We shall not go further into these propositions but simply state that we do not consider that corporate income taxation can be or needs to be justified on either of these bases. So it would weaken rather than strengthen the case to bring them into the picture.

So much for the general case in favor of levying corporate income taxes. We now have to look at the dangers facing us when formulating the details of such taxes. The first is that corporate income taxation may retard the development of the corporate sector, whether by discouraging existing corporations from growing or by deterring unincorporated businesses from adopting a corporate form or even by encouraging existing corporations to discard their corporate identity. One does not have to be a specialist in economic history to know how much Western economic development owes to the corporate form of enterprise. It is abundantly clear that without the pooling of funds and the limited liability associated with corporate enterprise, economic development as we have seen it in Western Europe or the United States could never have gone as far or as fast as it has done. It is especially important that at the time when new and more prosperous middle classes are emerging—as seems to be the case today in a number of Latin American countries—nothing should be done to deter them from making funds available to joint stock enterprises. There is also another aspect of this matter. Discouragement of new corporate enterprises may well place existing corporations in a more monopolistic position, with the usual results of distorting relative prices and outputs, stifling initiative, and so on.

A second danger in corporate income taxation is that any such revenue yield may be at the expense of private saving rather than consumption. One has to be careful here. First, it is not certain that this will happen, at any rate if one gives any credence to the proposition that high-income recipients in underdeveloped countries spend a very large fraction of their income. One cannot maintain that this latter proposition is valid and also say that any reduction in dividends due to a corporate income tax will cut deeply into private saving.[3]

But even if private saving, whether in the form of undistributed profits or personal saving, is cut down by corporate income taxation, that is not the end of the story. One also has to ask what use might have been made of such funds if they had remained in private hands and what happens in the public sector as a consequence of the higher tax yield. If

private domestic investment is reduced[4] and public spending on current goods and services increases, that is one thing. But if the result of diverting funds to the public sector is to allow more public domestic investment to go forward, whereas the private sector would have utilized these resources for investment abroad, that is rather different. We must be careful not to make too much of this contrast. Irrespective of whether the increase in public spending on goods and services is on current or capital account, we have a relative enlargement of the public sector; and this may be undesirable in itself. And one can argue endlessly about the relative merits of public and private investment projects. All that we are concerned to show is that in principle there can be a number of different results.

A further general point about corporate income taxation is that it has to be arranged in such a way as to constitute a minimum deterrent to the inflow of foreign capital. We have seen that quite frequently corporate income taxes are in effect paid by foreign governments rather than foreign investors. Nevertheless, there are clearly defined limits to this process. First, the domestic tax rate cannot exceed the foreign tax rate without cutting net returns to foreign investors. Second, insofar as foreign investors are not subject to their own governments' tax rates on the whole of their overseas income (e.g., foreign subsidiaries of United States corporations or Overseas Trade Corporations of United Kingdom companies) the maximum rate which developing countries can levy without cutting net returns to overseas investors is lowered further. Insofar as the aim is to give positive incentives to foreign investment, as distinct from avoiding deterrents, there are still further reasons for keeping down corporate tax rates, whether by making special allowances by, say, accelerated depreciation, temporary reductions or remission of tax, or one of the many other possible devices.

A major problem in formulating a corporate income tax system is the reconciliation

[3]In passing, one might ask why rich people in underdeveloped countries are usually alleged to spend a very large fraction of their incomes, while rich people in developed countries apparently do not.

[4]Whether due to a reduction in available funds or a reduction in the prospective net rate of return.

of taxation at the corporate level with that at the individual shareholder level. At one extreme, it can be argued that the correct principle is to tear aside the corporate veil and regard all profits, whether distributed or not, as belonging to shareholders and try to tax them at the appropriate marginal rate. From an equity standpoint, there is a great deal to be said for taxing corporations and their stockholders in the same way as partnerships—for that is what this procedure amounts to. But it does involve all sorts of problems, e.g., the imputation of undistributed profits to stockholders and the fact that undistributed profits may not have the same taxable capacity as distributions (e.g., the case of the upper tax rate bracket shareholder confronted with a larger tax bill than the dividend he receives). It is easy to exaggerate these difficulties, and especially those of allocating undistributed profits to individual shareholders, but at the same time the fact remains that most writers on this subject have not felt able to recommend the adoption of this principle other than for small, closely held corporations. It can also be argued that, in a sense, such a system really amounts to personal rather than corporate taxation. However, such an objection seems to be little more than a matter of semantics, especially if the corporation withholds part of the tax payable in each case.[5]

Another alternative is to levy a tax at the corporate level only and ignore distributions to shareholders. This is a simple administrative device but is hardly satisfactory from an equity viewpoint. Venezuela and Paraguay are two Latin American countries which essentially follow this practice.

Finally, we can have a mixed system, whereby taxes are levied both at the corporate and at the individual level. This can take many different forms, but the principal distinction relates to the differing treatments of undistributed profits. If one has the United States type of system, whereby corporations are taxed on the whole of their income and individuals are taxed on more or less the whole[6] of dividends received, we obviously have a greater degree of discrimination against distributed profits than if corporate income tax is restricted to undistributed profits (as in Uruguay). The United States system is also more favorable to undistributed profits than the United Kingdom system by which a substantial rate of income tax, as well as profits tax, is applied to them.

Any question of overlap between corporate and personal income taxes, and how much remission should be granted in the latter case to take care of it, is indissolubly bound up with the undistributed profits issue.

If one grants some sort of relief to the personal income taxpayer, whether by a "dividend paid credit," a "withholding," or a "dividend received credit" type of arrangement,[7] one is inevitably altering the relative tax burdens on undistributed and distributed profits. It is perfectly true that different types of relief are not all alike from an equity standpoint,[8] but the main issue, all the same, is the extent to which one wishes to favor undistributed profits.

The arguments on this are well known, and we shall not pursue them in detail. Essentially, it is a matter of balancing the merits of larger distributions and a greater possible flow of funds through the market with the danger that saving may consequentially be less than it would be with larger corporate retentions. Many considerations come into this: the possible reinforcement of monopolistic tendencies if a large proportion of profits is retained, the possible inadequacy of the capital market as a distributor of funds even if a large propor-

---

[5]The recent short-lived experiment in El Salvador is a specific example of the partnership principle.

It might be added that this general principle can be implemented in different ways; e.g., one might tax shareholders on their aliquot shares of total earnings but add the attributable portion of undistributed profits to the purchase price of the shares so that future liabilities to capital gains tax would be reduced pro tanto.

[6]Apart from the exclusion of the first fifty dollars of investment income and the 4 per cent dividend credit.

[7]See R. B. Goode, The Corporation Income Tax (New York: John Wiley and Sons, 1951), Chap. 10, for a detailed explanation of these terms.

[8]E.g., the Canadian system of a uniform 20 per cent tax credit to every dividend recipient resident in Canada means that low-income recipients of dividends are not able to take full advantage of this relief.

tion is distributed, and so on. The one certain thing is that big, bold generalizations are unlikely to mean a great deal,[9] and one must have some regard for institutional arrangements.

SECTION II

It may be helpful to start our survey of the structure of corporate income taxation in Latin America by considering the role of direct taxation in general. Table 8–1 shows data on central government revenue on a comparable basis for a number of countries; and Table 8–2 likewise, for revenue at all levels of government.

TABLE 8–1: Central Government Taxes on Income and Wealth As Per Cent of Central Government Revenue (*Average 1958–1960*)

Argentina	23.7
Bolivia	12.8
Brazil	31.6
Chile	34.4
Colombia	47.4
Costa Rica	17.2
Ecuador	15.1
El Salvador	15.3
Guatemala	9.5
Haiti	14.4
Honduras	17.5
Mexico	28.8
Panama	24.5
Peru	42.2
Venezuela	36.7

SOURCE: United Nations, *Statistical Yearbook, 1960* and *Statistical Yearbook, 1961.*

NOTES: 1. Data from budgets of respective countries.
2. In some cases, data for all these years (1958, 1959, 1960) are not available.

The first point to emphasize is that Table 8–1 should not be compared with Table 8–2, as the data are drawn from different sources

[9]E.g., the general proposition that fast growing firms retain a larger proportion of their profits than slow growers does not necessarily lead to the conclusion that a company tax confined to undistributed profits is more inimical to growth than a tax on all profits. First, a tax on total profits is likely to exact more tax from fast than slow growing firms insofar as they earn a greater return on capital; and second, fast growing firms will tend to benefit relatively more than stagnant ones from the greater supply of funds likely to be available in the market if undistributed profits taxation increases the proportion of profits distributed.

TABLE 8–2: Direct Taxes (*Average 1958–1959*)

	All direct taxes as per cent of total current revenue	Direct tax on corporations as per cent of total current revenue
Chile	52.1	18.9
Colombia	36.5	14.8
Costa Rica	21.0	1.0
Ecuador	21.7	7.4
Peru	55.3	31.6

SOURCE: United Nations, *Yearbook of National Accounts Statistics, 1960.*

NOTES: Data not available for both years in every case.

and relate to different concepts and different definitions of government. Ideally, one would have liked to have sufficient data from one source to rely on that alone, but in the absence of this it seemed best to extract what one could from both.

Obviously, the reliance on income and wealth taxes varies enormously from country to country, with Colombia raising more than 40 per cent of its central government revenue in this way and Guatemala less than 10 per cent. Similarly, direct taxes on corporations play considerably different roles in revenue structures, as Table 8–2 shows. So, even though the data are incomplete, we at least know that there is a great range of variation between Costa Rica at one end' and Peru at the other, whatever be the position of the countries not listed in the table.[10]

It may be helpful to set out the main characteristics of corporation income taxes in tabular form.

Needless to say, any attempt to compress the main characteristics of corporate income taxation in eighteen countries into one simple table is bound to skip over the finer points of detail even if these are all readily available. In fact, some difficulty was experienced in collecting the material, and so apologies are offered here and now for any inaccuracies in Table 8–3.

[10]One would expect the ratios of corporation taxes to total revenue to be greater than those shown in Table 8–2, if the central government component were taken on its own.

TABLE 8-3: Characteristics of Latin American Corporate Income Taxation

1	2	3	4	5		
	Corporate income tax separate from personal	World-wide income basis	Progressive rates	Withholding on dividends paid out		
Country				Resident registered shareholders	Bearer	Foreigners
Argentina	Yes	No	No	(No)	Yes	Yes
Bolivia	Yes	?	No	No	Yes	Yes
Brazil	Yes	(Yes)	Yes	No	Yes	Yes
Chile	Yes	Yes	No	Yes	Yes	Yes
Colombia	Yes	Yes	Yes	No	Yes	Yes
Costa Rica	No	No	Yes	No	No	No
Dominican Republic	No	No	Yes	No	No	Yes
Ecuador	Yes	No	No	Yes	Yes	Yes
El Salvador	Yes	No	Yes	No	No	Yes
Guatemala	No	Yes	Yes	No	No	No
Haiti	No	No	Yes	Yes	Yes	Yes
Honduras	No	Yes	Yes	No	No	No
Mexico	Yes	Yes	Yes	Yes	Yes	Yes
Nicaragua	No	No	Yes	No	No	No
Panama	Yes	No	Yes	Yes	Yes	Yes
Paraguay	Yes	No	Yes	No	No	No
Peru	Yes	No	Yes	No	Yes	Yes
Uruguay	Yes	Yes	No	Yes	Yes	Yes
Venezuela	Yes	No	Yes	No	No	No

TABLE 8-3: Characteristics of Latin American Corporate Income Taxation—(Continued)

	6		7			8	9		10
	Taxation of dividends received		Additional corporate taxes			Carry-forward of losses	Special incentives		Discrimination against foreigners
Country	Individual recipients	Corporate recipients	Excess profits	Capital	Other		Accelerated depreciation	Other	
Argentina	(Yes)	No	(No)	Yes	Yes	Yes	Yes	Yes	Yes
Bolivia	Yes	No	?	?	?	?	?	?	Yes
Brazil	(No)	No	Yes	(Yes)	Yes	Yes	No	Yes	Yes
Chile	No	No	No	No	Yes	No	Yes	Yes	Yes
Colombia	Yes	No	Yes	No	Yes	(No)	No	Yes	Yes
Costa Rica	No	No	No	No	No	Yes	No	Yes	No
Dominican Republic	Yes	Yes	No	No	Yes	Yes	Yes	Yes	No
Ecuador	Yes	Yes	No	No	Yes	Yes	Yes	Yes	Yes
El Salvador	Yes	No	No	No	No	No	No	Yes	No
Guatemala	No	No	No	Yes	No	No	No	Yes	No
Haiti	No	No	(Yes)	Yes	No	No	No	Yes	Yes
Honduras	No	No	No	No	No	No	No	Yes	No
Mexico	No	No	Yes	No	No	Yes	Yes	Yes	No
Nicaragua	No	No	No	Yes	No	Yes	No	No	No
Panama	No	No	No	No	No	No	No	Yes	No
Paraguay	No	No	No	No	No	No	No	No	No
Peru	Yes	(Yes)	No	No	(Yes)	Yes	Yes	Yes	No
Uruguay	Yes	Yes	Yes	Yes	Yes	Yes	No	Yes	Yes
Venezuela	No	No	No	No	Yes	Yes	No	Yes	No

SOURCES: Miscellaneous.
NOTE: Further explanations are given in the text.

It is hoped that the meaning of Table 8–3 is fairly clear, but perhaps one or two words of explanation are called for. First, when a "Yes" or "No" is bracketed, this means that the answer under that heading is a qualified one.[11] If a query mark is used, this simply means that information on that particular point is unavailable. The table relates to public corporations and not to the various species of private corporations to be found in Latin American countries.[12] The meaning of most of the column headings is fairly straight-

[11]In the case of Argentina, the meaning is that it is a very recent innovation of which full details are not available at the time of writing.

[12]In some cases these entities are treated more like public corporations, but in others more like partnerships.

forward, but it may be worth spelling out some of them explicitly. In Column 2 the separateness of corporate from personal income taxation is judged by differences in the rate structure rather than legal differences; e.g., if the same law embraces corporate and personal tax, but different rates are applicable (as in Paraguay, for instance), the answer is "Yes." Column 3 differentiates between those corporations which are taxable on their worldwide income and those whose liability is only in respect of income originating in the country concerned. In Column 7, an attempt has been made to bring taxes on corporations other than income taxes into the picture. The main type of excess profits tax is that which relates to profits in excess of a certain percentage of capital employed (e.g., Colombia and Mexico), but in Brazil there are alternative bases, such as profits in a preceding period and the profit margin on turnover. Examples of capital taxes are Argentina (1 per cent of capital and reserves, this tax being a deductible charge for income tax purposes) and Uruguay, where there is complex of taxes on different types of corporate property. "Other" additional taxes are of many kinds, such as those on the revaluation of capital or on capital increases (Brazil), the special housing tax in Chile, and the special taxes on oil companies in Venezuela. Column 8 (Carry-forward of losses) is to be interpreted liberally, in the sense that any provisions for carrying forward losses, for however short a period, are classified as "Yes." Under Column 9, "other" incentives are mainly of the tax holiday variety. Finally, Column 10 shows an answer "Yes" only where the element of discrimination is clearcut. For instance, if a withholding tax is imposed only on dividends paid abroad, but on the other hand dividends paid at home are subject to tax as part of personal incomes, this is not regarded as discriminatory.[13]

The main examples of discrimination are those where withholding is applied at a higher rate to dividends paid abroad than to those distributed at home (e.g., Chile) and where

branches of foreign companies are taxed more heavily than locally incorporated companies (e.g., Argentina, Brazil).

The outstanding impression from Table 8-3 is the diversity of corporate tax arrangements. Even when there is a good deal of similarity (e.g., between the tax laws of some of the Central American republics) we do not find identical arrangements. This impression of diversity becomes even stronger if one fills out the picture by looking at actual tax rates as well as the general structure. It is quite impossible to make any simple over-all comparison, but, to take one example, it is possible for a corporation in Colombia to pay tax at a marginal rate of 75 per cent of its world-wide income,[14] quite apart from the liability of stockholders to personal income tax on dividends received. This is no doubt an extreme case, but it may be noted all the same that in Chile foreign corporations pay income tax at a rate of 66.15 per cent together with a possible liability to 5 per cent housing tax. On the other hand, the maximum company tax rate in Paraguay is 25 per cent, and even this applies only to income originating in that country, with no further deductions in respect of dividends either at the paying or receiving end. And in Costa Rica we find the maximum rate to be 30 per cent of income originating without any additions of other kinds. If we look at the position inside any one country, we must again expect great diversity when the corporate tax rate is progressive in character (e.g., Guatemala, with a range from 1 per cent to 43 per cent).

Diversity does not extend to all characteristics of tax arrangements, however. In general, Latin American countries have been slow to enter into the world network of double taxation relief agreements. Apart from miscellaneous agreements on shipping and air transport profits, the only country known to have concluded a treaty covering the whole field is Honduras, with the United States.

---

[13] Provided the difference in tax rates is not enormous in the two cases.

[14] I.e., 36 per cent income tax, plus 56 per cent excess-profits tax (on profits less income tax paid) plus 6 per cent housing tax and 3 per cent electrical-power and steel tax (on profits less income tax and excess profits tax paid, in both cases).

Presumably, this situation can be explained by the exclusion of income from overseas from tax liability in about half of these countries. If it is unnecessary to think about mitigating double taxation of such incomes and if one can reasonably expect unilateral relief by foreign countries in respect of dividends reaching their nationals, the pressure for formal tax treaties is much reduced, and all the more so if domestic tax rates are low, too.

SECTION III

In discussing possible reforms and improvements, we shall first cover the technical aspects at some length and then consider the general political and social aspects more briefly. It will be convenient to divide the technical aspects into two: first, the most appropriate pattern of corporate tax legislation and, second, the administration of such legislation.

If we work on these lines, the first consideration is the most appropriate concept of income for corporate tax purposes. As we have seen, nearly half the countries adopt an income-originating rule rather than one based on both income-originating and income-received. This is a complicated subject which we cannot treat fully, but it is clear that the main problem is the differential effect of the choice of income base on the international flow of capital. It is usually argued that the optimum arrangement is for all countries to impose tax on an income-received basis; an originating basis is somewhat inferior; and a mixed system, whereby some countries operate on one basis and some on another, is the worst of all. Now, it can be argued that these considerations are not very important for Latin American countries taken as a group, in that the flow of capital between them is not thought to be large. But this proposition invites two comments: first, the development of common markets in South and in Central America will presumably lead to larger intercountry capital flows in the future, and so income tax harmonization (in

this respect) will become more important. Second, as a current and not just a future phenomenon, we have to consider the effects of corporate tax arrangements on capital movements between any one Latin American country and the outside world. If the basis of taxation in a Latin American country is income-originating, this means that in some circumstances (e.g., when foreign gross returns and home rates of tax are both relatively high [what one would normally expect]) capital flows may move the "wrong" way.[15] If, on the other hand, the tax base is income-originating plus income-received, the inducement for capital to flow out when domestic gross returns are higher will be removed; and if it is thought that one should not impede outward movements of capital aimed at taking advantage of higher gross returns elsewhere, a system of crediting foreign taxes against domestic taxes will take care of that.[16] Obviously, an extension of tax coverage from an originating to a world-wide basis carries with it the implication that the same rule should apply to deductible expenses, i.e., that corporations should not have expenses disallowed on the ground that they were received outside the taxing country. But this would probably be a desirable simplification anyway. Further complications arise with branches of foreign corporations if the tax base is changed from income-originating to a world-wide basis, but we shall not go further into these here.[17]

[15]E.g., if the gross rate of return on investment in the Latin American country is 20 per cent and that in, say, the United States 10 per cent, but tax rates are 75 per cent in the former and 40 per cent in the latter, the net rate of return to a Latin American corporation would be 5 per cent in its own country and 6 per cent in the United States, if the latter levied tax on an originating basis. If the United States tax base were limited to income received by its residents, the incentive to a Latin American corporation to invest there would be even greater; and correspondingly the incentive to an American resident to invest in Latin America would be less, unless additional domestic tax liability were fully offset by a credit for foreign taxation. If the United States tax base is taken (more realistically) as income-originating plus income-received, the Latin American investing corporation's position is the same as in the first case; the American's is the same as in the second case.

[16]Such a system is, of course, justifiable on equity grounds as well as those of resource allocation.

[17]On this point, and for that matter the whole of this issue, cf. Carl S. Shoup *et al., The Fiscal System of Venezuela* (Baltimore: The Johns Hopkins Press, 1959), Chap. iV and especially pp. 158–59.

Other matters of income definition arise with loss carry-overs and capital gains and losses. In about half the countries surveyed, there are no facilities for carrying forward losses and in some of the others the provisions are very restricted (e.g., in Chile and El Salvador losses cannot be carried forward at all, and in Nicaragua losses, except in the oil industry, can only be carried forward for two years subsequent to that in which the loss occurs). Whatever the origin of such provisions,[18] there seems to be no case for continuing in this way, and a regular system of allowing carry-forwards for a period of, say, five to six years seems essential if risk taking is not to be discriminated against. As far as capital gains are concerned, the picture is again mixed, but the general answer seems clear-cut: if capital gains and losses are taxed at the personal level, they should also be taxed at the corporate level. There are many complications of detail here, but this seems to be the essential general principle.

So much for the concept of income.[19] The next point to emphasize is the need for simplicity. The overwhelming impression one receives from looking at Latin American tax legislation is that it is overambitious. It seems quite unnecessary to have the variety of taxes on corporations which one finds in many countries. First, there may be more than one layer of corporate income tax, as with the schedular and complementary taxes in Venezuela. Second, corporations may be subject to a variety of taxes; e.g., Brazil has not only a corporate income tax but an excess profits tax (which itself has a number of alternative bases), a tax on the revaluation of capital assets, a tax on capitalization of profits, and a compulsory loan (based on income tax payable and on undistributed profits) to the Banco Nacional do Desenvolvimento Econo-

mico. Messrs. Surrey and Oldman have made similar observations in respect of Argentina.[20]

Nor is it that the individual taxes themselves are of the simplest. Quite apart from the progressive character of many corporate income taxes—to which we shall return shortly—there are many complicated provisions such as those distinguishing between different types of corporate enterprise, or those differentiating between dividends paid to residents (and frequently between different kinds of residents) and to foreigners, or those which tax undistributed profits at different rates, depending on whether they are reinvested or not.

As might be expected, even more complications occur in the other taxes, particularly those on excess profits and on capital. In some cases, complications come from attempts to tax according to recherché rather than straightforward accounting concepts; e.g., in Mexico the withholding tax on dividends relates not to actual dividends paid out but to those profits which could on certain assumptions be distributed.

No one can pretend for a second that corporate income taxation is simple. But the impression remains that many Latin American countries are trying to be overambitious in this section of their tax systems. No doubt it can be argued that these provisions are designed to increase tax yields, but it must be seriously doubted whether they really fulfill even this limited objective. It is commonplace in any country that the revenue authorities never remain ahead of the tax lawyers for long; and it has yet to be demonstrated that the gap between the two is greater, the more complicated the tax legislation. In fact, it may well be the reverse; and if so, the combination of additional administrative expenditure and loss of revenue due to evasion may defeat the original intentions of the legislators. In short,

---

[18]Often said to rest on the view that an income tax is an annual affair only.

[19]Many other problems also arise, such as the method of allocation of income to the country of origin (e.g., problems of "arm's length" pricing between related enterprises), but as these matters are dealt with in other papers at the conference, we shall not discuss them here.

[20]Cf. Stanley S. Surrey and Oliver Oldman, "Report of a Preliminary Survey of the Tax System of Argentina" (mimeographed), p. 11: "A corporation is subject to . . . income tax, excess profits tax and substitute tax on capital. . . . This situation produces a complicated structure whose complexity is not balanced by compensating advantages."

the end result is that countries are more taxed against than taxed.

There is a good deal to be said about the rate structure of corporate income taxes. As we have seen, there is no unique recipe for determining the height of profits taxation or the relative amounts which should be collected at the corporate and the personal levels. So bold generalizations about whether rates of tax are too high or deductions too low are unlikely to mean very much. At the same time, there are some points which do call for discussion. The first is that one clearly has to take the whole complex of corporate taxes into account, whatever they are called and however they work, to get a true picture. Collecting taxation in bits and pieces may deceive people in the short run but not in the long. Second, the most important criterion of all is probably the rate of development of the corporate form of enterprise. This calls for nice judgment in fixing tax rates: not so high as to have disincentive effects on investment and risk taking and not so low as to make unnecessary presents to companies or to foreign governments. Some of the evidence seems to suggest that, despite the untidiness of many tax systems, the worst excesses and deleterious effects of taxing corporate income have been avoided;[21] but on the other hand, there are some obviously bad examples, such as that of Colombia, referred to above. Obviously, judgments in this area must be inconclusive, but on one point we can be dogmatic: that it is much better to have lower nominal tax rates and effective enforcement than higher nominal rates and ineffective application.

The next point is the progressive nature of many of the corporate taxes found in Latin America. In some (e.g., Brazil) this is simply a two-rate structure which in effect amounts to small business relief. We shall postpone discussion of that point for the time being and consider the case of multirate structures such as those found in Central America. The

origin of this system is that if a corporation is family-owned and if the family is a single entity for personal tax purposes, then a rough degree of equity is achieved by taxing corporate income as if it were personal income. No doubt there are plenty of family-controlled corporations in Latin America; other arguments can be made for favoring small enterprises; and it is perfectly true that in both the United States and the United Kingdom there have been special provisions on the statute book for many years to ensure that closely controlled corporations are not treated too differently from individual persons. Even so, this does not add up to any argument for a progressive tax on corporate profits of every shape and kind. Rich men may be shareholders in small corporations and poor men in large corporations, so there is no case in equity. Incentives to growth are likely to be reduced. And the obvious results of any such system is that large companies are split into smaller components or that refuge is taken in some form of organization which escapes some of the tax liabilities. In some countries (e.g., the multiple majority holding tax in Colombia) efforts are made to check this by taxing "related" companies as if they were one single enterprise, but this is just one more complication to fit into an already unwieldy system. It would seem, in the light of these points, that this is one feature of Latin American taxation which has almost nothing to be said in its favor.

We saw in Table 8–3, that there is a withholding system in respect of bearer shares in most countries. This is not a very familiar issue to anyone accustomed to United States or United Kingdom practices, and so one must tread rather cautiously; but as far as can be seen, this problem may not be as great as is sometimes made out. If the identity of a dividend recipient is unknown, clearly there must be provision for withholding tax at a high rate; but if the bank or any other agent collecting dividends is prepared to identify the ultimate recipient, a low or even zero rate of withholding would suffice, provided, of

[21]Cf. J. Froomkin, "Some Problems of Tax Policy in Latin America," *National Tax Journal* (December, 1957), pp. 371–72.

course, that there is a thoroughgoing system of personal income tax.[22] It does not seem necessary to lay down elaborate regulations about the issue, control, and handling of bearer shares if these conditions can be fulfilled. In the case of anonymity, it will never be possible to match tax exactions precisely with tax liabilities, but the principle suggested above should secure a reasonable result, which is all that one should expect in the imperfect world we live in.

We now come to the thorny issue of integrating corporate and personal income taxes. Unless the partnership principle can be applied across the board—and this is unlikely, as we have seen—one must have some taxation of corporations over and above that on individuals. If the corporate tax takes the form of a tax on undistributed profits, there is no need to have any form of relief to avoid "double taxation." But if the corporate tax relates to all profits, there is clearly a case for relief of some sort on equity grounds and often on allocative grounds, too, consequential on the reduction in the tax burden on distributed, relatively to undistributed, profits.

Uruguay is the chief example of an undistributed profits tax in Latin America, but as this has been in operation for a short time only, one cannot expect to draw any firm conclusions from its operations. There are a number of ways of mitigating taxation over the whole range of company profits and dividends, as we have seen. The "dividend-received credit" approach, by which a shareholder includes dividends in his income and then is allowed to credit a certain percentage of such dividends against his liability to personal income tax, is usually rejected on the grounds that it is inequitable between poor and rich shareholders; i.e., for any given amount of dividend, the same tax credit is given, irrespective of the recipient's tax liability.[23] There is not a great deal to choose between the "dividend-paid credit"[24] approach and the withholding[25] approach. Both methods, if properly applied, will give the same total (i.e., corporate plus personal) burden at any given income level. Professor Shoup has discussed their relative merits at some length in the case of Venezuela,[26] and so it is unnecessary to go more fully into the arguments here. But we may note that, on balance, he seemed to think that the "withholding" approach might be slightly preferable, largely on the ground that in this case there would be less need for the tax authorities to extract additional taxation from individuals, once tax had been collected at the corporate level, and hence less risk of avoidance and evasion.

Whichever method one chooses, there is still the further question of the amount of the relief to be given; e.g., the corporation may be allowed a 50 per cent rather than 100 per cent dividend-paid credit. Obviously, no one can lay down a universal law on this question (who knows what is the optimum proportion of profits which should be distributed?), but it may be noted that some observers[27] have come out with the idea that a 33-1/3 to 50 per cent dividend-paid credit (or its equivalent in the form of a credit in the withholding approach) is the right kind of figure to balance the conflicting objectives of growth, equity, and so on.

Another major issue to be found in Latin

[22]Cf. Surrey and Oldman, "Report," p. 13, on Argentine experience. Clearly there has to be some control over the number and minimum qualifications of those entitled to receive these kinds of dividends.

[23]The Canadian adherence to this system (see above p. 237) seems to be due to an anxiety to confine tax relief to resident shareholders. If allowances were made at the corporate level, additional measures would then be needed to prevent foreign shareholders from benefiting.
[24]I.e., deduct dividends paid out from total profits to arrive at the tax base for corporation tax and then subject shareholders to tax at ordinary personal income tax rates on dividends received.
[25]I.e., apply corporate tax to total profits, gross up dividends paid out so as to include their share of corporate tax, and subject this total to personal income tax but allow a tax credit (equal to the difference between grossed-up dividends and dividends paid out) against this liability. This is the traditional method of operating income tax (though not profits tax) in the United Kingdom.
[26]Shoup, The Fiscal System of Venezuela, pp. 116–25.
[27]See Shoup, The Fiscal System of Venezuela, p. 122; and L. Shere, "A Tax Program for Colombia" (Organization of American States, mimeographed, 1959), Chap. 4.

America is that of discrimination in corporate taxes. Perhaps the most serious way in which this occurs is the imposition of excess profits taxes, whether related to some notion of standard earnings on capital or to profits of some preceding period. Excess profits taxes have always been recognized in public finance literature as desperate expedients which could be endured for short periods of time but so obviously discriminatory against successful and growing enterprises as to be undesirable permanent features of tax systems. If the imposition of excess profits tax is combined with absence of loss carry-over provisions (as in Colombia and Haiti), the position is worse still: heavy penalties are exacted if a risk taker is successful, and he cannot carry forward his losses if he is not.

Discrimination between small and large corporations is another common feature of the tax system, as even when the corporate income tax rate is formally separated from the personal tax rate, one frequently finds a gradation of rates depending on the size of the enterprise. Brazil and Colombia are leading examples, but a glance at Table 8–3 shows it is to be found in a number of other countries: roughly speaking, when the answer is "Yes" under both Column 2 and Column 4. There are, of course, arguments for differentiating in favor of small corporations—especially that of removing or offsetting obstacles to the adoption of the corporate form by small enterprises—and there are many examples of such legislation in many different countries. There are, however, two important points to put on the other side. Specially low tax rates for small enterprises may encourage the formation of new corporations, but the change from a low tax bracket to a higher one at some point in the income scale may be a deterrent to further growth. Second, it seems to be a common phenomenon that small enterprise standards of compliance with tax legislation are quite substantially below those of large firms. So it is very easy for tax treatment to be overgenerous in this case.

The differing treatment of corporate and noncorporate enterprises is another complex subject which we cannot explore fully. Experience seems to differ here: in some cases (e.g., Brazil) the public corporate form seems to be relatively badly treated[28] while in others (e.g., Argentina) there seems to have been tax encouragement to assume corporate forms.

Obviously, the right general principle is to steer between these two lines of policy, but one must make haste to admit that this is much more easily said than done.

The relative treatment of foreign and domestic enterprises or of foreign and domestic capital[29] raises many political as well as economic issues. One can appreciate the argument that taxation of dividends and interest going abroad is often at the expense of foreign governments rather than foreign private investors. But this is not always true, as we have seen.[30] And even when it is, we have to remember the role which foreign governments play in making loans and aid available to less developed countries. Overzealous or rapacious treatment of foreign capital may only too easily invite ripostes on these fronts. Nor do the sharp distinctions frequently drawn between branches and locally incorporated subsidiaries of foreign corporations have much merit. From an economic point of view, there is no case for arranging the tax system in such a way as to compel foreign corporations to adopt some particular legal form which they would not otherwise take. But, to repeat, economics is far from being the only relevant consideration in policy making in this field.

Tax discrimination between different kinds of activity—especially in the case of the oil and mining industries—is partly a matter of

[28]See *Memorandum on Setting Up of an Organisation in Brazil* (London: Bank of London and South America, Ltd., 1960), pp. 34–36, for a summary of the relative tax treatments of a *Sociedade por Quotas de Responsabilidade Limitada* and a *Sociedade Anonima*.
[29]E.g., in Chile the effective corporate income tax rates are 30.45 per cent (plus 18.9 per cent on distributions) for local enterprises, 30.45 per cent (plus 18.9 per cent on local distribution or 30.45 per cent on dividends going abroad) on foreign controlled companies, and in the case of a foreign company 66.15 per cent.
[30]It must be remembered that as far as the United States is concerned, the effective rate of tax is likely to be 38 per cent (i.e., the tax rate on Western Hemisphere trade corporations) and not the usual 52 per cent.

taxing foreign capital. But other issues, such as international practices in oil taxation and the generosity or otherwise of depletion allowances, enter this picture. On balance, the discrepancies in this respect do not seem as great as in others. One may hazard a guess that, if anything, manufacturing enterprises may suffer, as agricultural activity is likely to be undertaxed and the various allowances given to mining and similar activities seem reasonably generous. But this sort of conclusion is not much above the level of guesswork, and too much weight should not be put on it.

As a good deal is likely to be said by others about special concessions to new enterprises or to new capital formation, we can be brief about it in this paper. In general, the main relief so far seems to have been in the form of tax holidays or some analogous device rather than accelerated depreciation or investment subsidies, as in Table 8–3, Column 9. The relative merits of these various devices is a complicated subject,[31] but there is probably something to be said for redressing the balance by moving further toward depreciation or investment relief. If so, one or two further points might be added. Any attempt to differentiate between gross and net investment (e.g., by allowing net investment only for tax relief purposes) is likely to run into difficulties. The attempt to legislate on these lines in the United States in 1961 ran into such serious trouble that it had to be abandoned. And despite pleas for this kind of distinction, the authorities in the United Kingdom have never been persuaded that it would be workable. If, on the other hand, tax relief is given on all investment, we have the difficulty that this may lead to unnecessary gifts to business enterprises, in the sense that a large proportion of the investment actually made would have taken place even if there had not been any special tax relief. Finally, insofar as these devices are sprats to

catch foreign mackerel, there is a good deal to be said for taking action along common lines in different countries, as is envisaged in Central America.

We have now ranged widely over the various requirements of principle in tax reform: the concept of income, the need for simplicity and clarity in the relations between and the definitions of taxes, the appropriate rate structure, the discriminatory aspects of corporate taxation, and so on. Supposing tax laws were reformed to incorporate some or all of these points, what other technical problems would remain?

The first point seems to be the achievement of satisfactory accounting standards. It is not a bit of use having the most perfect tax ordinances in the world if accounting standards are such, either in the preparation or the auditing stages, that little reliance can be placed on statements of profit and loss, balance sheets, and so on. It is, of course, always the job of revenue agents to check such data, but they cannot do more than a certain amount. If the data presented to them fall below a minimum standard, it is impossible for them to discharge these functions in more than a perfunctory manner. Unfortunately, this seems to be the state of affairs in some Latin American countries, especially in respect of small businesses.

Unless and until improvements can be brought about in this field—and this can hardly be a speedy process—legislative action on tax reforms can hardly have its full effect.

The second point is another familiar one to any student of public finance in less developed countries: the quality of tax legislation and administration. Even when the general ideas in tax legislation are on the right lines, sloppy formulation of tax laws can be an endless source of trouble.[32] We have argued above in favor of simplicity, and certainly no one wants more complications in taxation than are necessary. But when one

[31]See Jack I. Heller and Kenneth M. Kauffman, "Tax Incentives for Industrial Growth in Developing Economies" (Cambridge, Mass.: Harvard Law School, International Program in Taxation—in process), for a definitive treatment.

[32]See J. P. Crockett, "Tax Pattern in Latin America," *National Tax Journal,* (March, 1962), p. 99. "There is a lack of precision and detail in legislation and regulations with the result that much must often be inferred."

compares the slim volumes giving the details of Uruguay profits taxation with the size of the Internal Revenue Code in the United States or the 1952 Income Tax Act in the United Kingdom, it seems clear that there is a major weakness at this level. As far as tax administration is concerned, the issues are well known and need not be rehearsed in detail. Without an honest and determined revenue authority, willing to fight its battles in the courts and sure of a fair hearing there, no amount of elaborate tax legislation will be of much consequence. In the nature of the case, not much information is available on the extent of tax evasion or avoidance, but the data cited by Surrey and Oldman seem to suggest that in Argentina tax losses on this amount are not only great but increasing.[33]

It would also seem that the corporate sector is heavily involved in this, with evasion being more common in small and medium corporations and avoidance in larger ones, as might be expected.[34] If this sort of experience is at all typical of other countries in Latin America —and one suspects that this is more than likely—there is an enormous improvement

[33]Surrey and Oldman, "Report," p. 20, state that unreported income was some 49 per cent of total income (as estimated from national income data) in 1952 and 59 per cent in 1957. For professional incomes only, the figures were 51 per cent and 54 per cent, respectively.
[34]Surrey and Oldman, "Report," p. 18.

job to be done, perhaps on international as well as national lines. At the same time, tax compliance is not independent of the tax structure. It seems reasonable to think that if some of the complexities and oddities of the structure were ironed out, there might be quite considerable improvements in revenue collection. And the same point no doubt applies to the necessity for honest and effective administration of government expenditure; the tendency to evade and avoid taxation is all the greater if that condition is not satisfied.

We have spent a great deal of time on the scope for technical improvements in taxation of different kinds. What must be stressed in conclusion, and stressed with the greatest possible emphasis, is that unless the necessary political conditions for reform are satisfied, details of this sort will be nothing more than academic musings. The aims of the Alliance for Progress in the taxation field are to release more resources for investment and to secure greater equity in the tax structure. Unless and until legislatures are willing to pass laws putting such aims down on paper and to provide the necessary machinery for implementing them in practice, irrespective of whether such measures operate against the interests of powerful sociopolitical groups, the best intentions in the world will not suffice to yield more than the most meager results.

Comment

BRAULIO JATAR-DOTTI*

In accordance with what I have considered to be the most direct procedure for dealing both with the complexities of corporate income taxation and with its application in Latin America and then for suggesting some avenues to possible change, I have divided this commentary into the following sections: one devoted to the paper by the distinguished

*Senator and President of the Congressional Bicameral Finance Commission, Caracas, Venezuela.

Professor A. R. Prest; another setting forth certain general principles of taxation; and, finally, a third dealing separately with various aspects of corporate income taxation in Latin America.

SUMMARY OF THE PAPER

In structuring this commentary on the paper "Corporate Income Taxation," I planned at first to follow the same outline as Mr. Prest; but since my material coincides only partially with his (in methodology, that is, for I share many of his arguments as to concept), I have decided against doing so. In addition, I shall perhaps enlarge upon various points of view appropriate to the study of a topic so important to the development of this hemisphere.

Broadly speaking, the three sections into which Mr. Prest has divided his paper are as follows: general principles of taxation, present tax structure, and possible reforms and improvements for the Latin American tax systems.

With respect to general tax principles, he upholds the idea that on equity grounds corporations should be taxed "even if dividends paid to shareholders are fully taxed as part of personal incomes," an idea that in my view admits of no question, as I shall later indicate more fully.

He emphasizes the ease with which a corporate income tax can be administered as important to developing countries, "even though corporations may account for a much smaller share of value added in the private sector."

Within these general principles, Mr. Prest also discusses the importance of political considerations; he believes that these also support the idea of taxing corporations, which "do not have votes," unlike "individuals, who do." This could well introduce an examination of the true abstract status of legal entities as against natural persons—a subject which, because of its breadth and nature, would put me off my charted course.

A further argument cited in support of taxing corporations is that if dividends are paid abroad, "taxation may be at the expense of foreign government revenue." This defense of national interests is a point in favor of taxing foreign corporations, though it should not be pushed too far.

Mr. Prest then passes, in the paper under discussion, to what he regards as the dangers of corporate taxation. The first is that it "may retard the development of the corporate sector"; the second is that the revenue it produces may come "at the expense of private saving rather than consumption." Fortunately, he recognizes the variety of circumstances that both enhance and diminish the likelihood that these possible dangers will become real, since the use made of its income by the private sector is debatable. Along these same lines would be discussion of the possible attitude of foreign capital toward investing in a nation that taxes corporations, since the motives that lead an investor to put capital into a particular country are not always clear and precise. Besides, these possible fears on the part of foreign investors could be suitably offset by a wide range of incentives through various deductions.

Mr. Prest properly stresses reconciliation of taxation at the corporate level with that at the individual shareholder level. The question arises here whether there should be a tax on all corporate profits, distributed or undistributed, or whether taxation should be applied only to the shareholders, regarded as members of a general or limited partnership. This is one of the fundamental aspects of Mr. Prest's paper, and I shall make special comments on some of its implications later on.

The second section of the paper on which I am commenting examines the structure of Latin American corporate income taxation, "considering the role of direct taxation in general." In this brief analysis of Latin American fiscal arrangements, the British professor sets forth the differing tax practices of the various hemisphere countries: what concept is employed in defining income (that originating in the country or that received from any source); whether or not the corporate rates are progressive; how dividends are taxed; whether or not additional taxes (such as excess profits or asset revaluation) are imposed; whether or not there is provision for carry-over of losses or for accelerated depreciation; and other characteristics of the Latin American tax systems. My subsequent comments will be based on this material.

The third and last section of Mr. Prest's monograph is the most varied in subject matter, dealing with the technical, political, and social aspects of the tax system that should be adopted in the event of any reform or improvement.

Under the technical aspects are described the two concepts of income—income-originating and income-received—which might be used as the basis for taxing corporate profits. Mr. Prest comes out in favor of income-received, and he sets forth the ill effects he sees resulting from the diversity of tax concepts employed.

Without embarking at this point on a more or less semantic justification of the term "income," I should like to mention my interest in this distinction between "income-originating" and "income-received," since I believe that the type of tax should depend on the country's economic structure and not merely on a desire for a tax system based on formal aspects alone.

One of the technical characteristics that Mr. Prest considers fundamental in tax administration is *simplicity*, which leads him to reiterate that "it seems quite unnecessary to have the variety of taxes on corporations" that exists in Latin America, both as regards the tax itself and as regards the tax distinctions based on type of corporation. Though I do not uphold such complexity, I consider it justified in certain specific cases—Venezuela, for example, with both *schedular* and *complementary* taxes on corporations—but this I shall go into more thoroughly in my commentary.

Another fundamental aspect of the general topic—perhaps the most "thorny," to use Mr. Prest's apt term—is that of integrating personal and corporate income taxes. I have given particular attention to this aspect, seeking to examine it from several standpoints: that of the opponents of double taxation, that of its advocates, and finally that of those who partially approve it.

After analyzing some of the technical details that must be considered in possible tax reform—including several that in my opinion partake of a high level of genuine legal-social philosophy, so that in my commentary I have devoted separate attention to it—Mr. Prest mentions the desirability of improving tax administration and making it more effective. This is an important consideration; in my opinion it points straight to a need for altering the statistical, accounting, inspection, and other procedures, the neglect of which by most Latin American countries has had the natural consequence of faulty tax imposition and collection.

ORIENTATION OF THE COMMENTARY

Having thus briefly summarized Mr. Prest's stimulating monograph, I can best begin my commentary by remarking, as he does, on the general importance of fiscal policy in the modern world, leaving for later the details specifically concerned with corporate taxation.

Mr. Prest mentions as typical of underdeveloped countries a growing pressure to increase public spending, the resources for which must be provided by means of tax policy. I should like to start out by saying that not only is a well-organized fiscal policy of basic importance to underdeveloped countries but the inherent requirements of economic dynamics have made increased spending in the public sector characteristic of all modern states. Hence one of the goals most eagerly sought nowadays by experts in political economy is the proper structuring of the wide variety of taxes within a government's legal-economic system.

I have closely followed my own country's experience in this field and had the satisfaction of contributing to Venezuelan tax reform with some modest suggestions I made in mid-1958. In my arguments at that time, several of the ideas I shall discuss below served as a common denominator. I pointed out then that the public sector's sphere of administrative activity was inexorably tending to expand and that, with the modern state thus increasingly responsible for meeting more and more needs, its resources must be increased accordingly. This leads almost automatically to thoughts of expanding or better controlling the tax systems.

Obviously, however, if the public sector exaggerates what will be forthcoming from this source and then overextends its spending, economically unfavorable situations ranging from inflationary pressures to reduced private investment can result.

I said then—and I consider this judgment equally valid today—that taxes should serve not only fiscal but also economic and social purposes, exerting influence in certain desired directions. This is a familiar distinction, clearly reflected in the case of tariffs: revenue producing tariffs on one hand and, on the other, protective tariffs that act as an indirect incentive to a country's economic development.

From the socioeconomic point of view, a well-known characteristic of all taxes, and of indirect taxes in particular, is that they can be used as a brake on the demand for relatively superfluous products and on certain more or less harmful habits of the population, such as the consumption of cigarettes and alcoholic beverages.

Some kinds of taxes, naturally, are better suited than others to the objectives of governments seeking a balanced increase in their resources. Prominent among these are such taxes as those on income, property, and imports.

Specifically, income taxation more than any other requires a formula that on one hand does not discourage saving and on the other exerts pressure on luxury and nonessential spending. This attention to consequences is all the more necessary in taxing the income of corporations, which periodically reinvest in the countries where they operate.

At the time I have cited, I also emphasized that taxes of any kind, and especially those on net corporate income, should be progressive and that preferential treatment should be considered for income reinvested in the country.

But since at this conference the infinite variety of details, consequences, and approaches pertaining to taxation in general will come under the scrutiny of internationally recognized authorities, I prefer not to expatiate further in this preface.

I should only like to add my firm conviction that in any planned tax reform, wherever and whenever it is to be carried out, attention should be given not only to the circumstances of the country in which it is taking place but also to the inner content of each form of taxation. By this I mean its moral and ethical implications as well as its economic and social purposes.

METHOD OF EXPOSITION

The Income Tax

Of the whole range of taxes, the income tax constitutes one of the most varied sources of revenue for modern states. And certainly for underdeveloped or developing countries—this may well be stressed—it is a means of meeting the constant need for increased public spending for their own development.

In Latin America, which makes up a large part of the *tiers monde,* this form of tax was first introduced in the 1920's. Although some countries had previously had certain taxes on income (El Salvador, for example, since 1915), the administrative methods employed to collect them were very defective. As their domestic economies evolved, the countries were spurred to create fiscal instruments more capable of mobilizing resources to increase government revenue, which in turn, reinvested in the country, would not merely increase effective demand but revitalize the economic structures generally.

When we now come to deal with the possibility of reform, modification, unification, and so on, we find ourselves with those Latin American fiscal systems that seem to various writers, among them Mr. Prest, to have been evolving rather anarchically and complicatedly.

Elsewhere in this paper I shall discuss why, in my view, some of these "complexities" are necessary in many countries. For the moment, conforming to my outline, I shall merely give in general terms what I think the basic aims of any projected change or reform of the income tax should be.

A relatively perfect tax system should take into account the following considerations, among others: (1) It should constitute the most equitable form of taxation, distributing the fiscal burden in accordance with individual and corporate ability to pay. (2) It should be based on manifest principles of social justice, distinguishing clearly between income from labor and income from capital. (3) It should be able not only to make up for budgetary deficits but also to reduce inflationary pressures at their source. (4) It should include high income tax rates for the upper income brackets, to reduce luxury consumption in the high-income sectors and permit, through public spending, a better distribution of the national product. (5) Finally, it should be capable of serving as an effective instrument of economic development, promoting both new investment where the economy needs it and reinvestment of profits in existing enterprises.

The foregoing is a broad general statement of principles. While some of these may be easily applicable everywhere, others must be varied in accordance with the specific individual patterns of underdeveloped countries, such as those of Latin America.

Concepts of Income for Tax Purposes

With respect to the taxation of income, the laws of the Latin American countries follow variously the principle of territoriality and that of residence or citizenship.

Under the territorial or income-originating concept, income received by resident citizens or domestic corporations is not liable to tax when it comes from sources outside the country. Under the citizenship or income-received concept, all profits or earnings of a resident are considered taxable income, whatever their place of origin. Each of these approaches, of course, has its defenders and its opponents.

Approximately half the Latin American countries follow the territorial principle. Some authors and critics—among them Mr. Prest—maintain that "the income-originating basis is somewhat inferior," while the income-received basis is considered "the optimum arrangement." The truth is, either may be beneficial or harmful to a given country, depending on its stage of development.

As is well known, one of the characteristics of capital importing countries is that their gross domestic product exceeds their national income because of the periodic remittance abroad of interest and dividends. The situation of industrialized or capital exporting countries is quite the opposite: their national income exceeds their gross domestic product because their residents receive interest and dividends from foreign investments.

It should be remembered, for example, that the amounts remitted abroad as interest, dividends, or royalties on foreign capital invested in Latin America exceed the net annual flow of foreign investment to the area. In 1947 these remittances abroad totaled $680,-000,000. With certain fluctuations caused by changes in the internal structures of the Latin American countries, this situation has continued, so that in 1959 such payments to the United States alone amounted to $1,096,000,000.

This characteristic must not be overlooked in determining which of the two concepts should be chosen by the developing countries, for it must be recognized that a majority of Latin American individuals and corporations receive no foreign income.

When the *income-originating* concept is used, rules are set up permitting taxpayers to deduct costs or expenses incurred within the country and certain *purposely limited* costs or expenses incurred abroad. These rules—particularly the latter—are intended to prevent foreign companies operating in the country from evading taxes for the benefit of their parent firms, their stockholders, or foreign treasuries. They also reduce the amount remitted abroad and thus lessen the unfavorable consequences to the country's balance of payments.

On the other hand, using the concept of *income-received* as the tax base entails the risk of the treasury's being cheated by means of fictitious expenditures abroad that reduce the net profits of corporations subject to tax. This is particularly likely in the case of companies with a parent firm located abroad (as with many firms in Latin America). To this must be added the negative effects of the residence concept on the balance of payments. Thus to these capital importing countries the income-received basis is harmful.

Unquestionably the economic and fiscal picture would be altered by greater integration of all the Latin American countries within the so-called common market or Montevideo Treaty. Not only would tariffs, postal rates, and so on be unified, but the flow of capital between countries would make it possible also to unify the policy on concept of income for tax purposes. The problem would still exist, of course, between the highly developed or capital exporting countries and those whose resources are meager.

So far as the flow of capital is concerned, complex situations can arise so long as capital exporting countries use one of these concepts and capital importing countries the other: when savings of an underdeveloped country taxing on the income-originating basis emigrate in search of profits that will not be taxed at home; or, conversely, when investors living in a capital exporting country that uses the income-received basis refrain from putting money into regions where the income-originating concept is used, since so doing would subject them to international double taxation.

International Double Taxation

One of the problems connected with the concepts of income-originating and income-received, as just outlined, is this one of international double taxation. It arises when countries that need resources adopt the territorial income basis while at the same time the capital exporting countries are taxing their residents' total income regardless of where it

originated. Unless something is done to prevent this situation, industrialized countries using the income-received concept will be imposing double taxation on the part of their taxpayers' income obtained from foreign investment.

Assuming that the dual practice continues to prevail, the only way of avoiding this anomaly would be for the capital exporting countries to deduct from their residents' tax liability the amounts they must pay in the foreign country. This solution could be achieved either unilaterally or by treaty. In this way the two systems could coexist without much risk of international double taxation, though neither relief granted by national law nor tax exclusions of foreign income under multilateral treaties would eliminate the danger altogether.[35]

Mitigating the likelihood of double taxation would have still another favorable effect: it would restore to capital its freedom of movement between markets, once the tax pressures that had been altering its normal direction of flow disappeared.

Obviously, if this matter of international double taxation is a problem when considered at the individual level, it is as much or more of a problem when applied to corporations.

It should be pointed out, finally, that if the countries using the territorial basis should switch to the residence or income-received basis, some link would have to be established between the present system and the new one.

Multiple and Unitary Taxes

In several hemisphere countries, income tax consists of a series of *schedular* taxes, with different fixed or proportional rates, and a *global* or *complementary* tax, with progressive rates. There are also excess profits taxes, as in Colombia and Mexico; taxes on capital revaluation or increase, as in Brazil; and, in Venezuela, an additional or special tax ap-

[35]Pertinent here is the fact that whereas Venezuela, by virtue of its concept of income, does not tax income from abroad, Mexico and Chile give the taxpayer a credit for the amount he has paid in the foreign country.

plicable to the production of hydrocarbons and minerals, including individual and corporate oil royalties.

If it is true that multiplicity in income taxes has sometimes been carried too far, leading to administrative difficulties in collecting them and even to infringements of the principle of equity that should govern such taxation, it is no less obvious that in some countries this variety results from fiscal requirements, internal economic patterns, and political circumstances arising out of a great many causes.

Such is the situation in Venezuela, for example, with its parallel systems of schedular and complementary taxes for all sorts of activities, whether carried on by individuals or by corporations. Not to trace the Venezuelan system—the same, incidentally, as the Brazilian and the Chilean—back to its theoretical origins, let it merely be noted that the idea of the proportional rates in schedular taxes is to distinguish clearly between earned, unearned, and mixed incomes. Thus preferential treatment (3 per cent) is given to salaries, wages, pensions, and similar income; higher rates (6 per cent) are set for income from investments and capital gains from real estate; while fortuitous gains such as lottery prizes or race winnings are taxed—penalized, we might say—at a 30 per cent rate.

An intermediate position is occupied by industrial, agricultural, and commercial profits and returns on fixed capital. The rate of only 2.5 per cent on profits from mining, hydrocarbons, and related activities was not modified in the latest partial income tax reform owing to the fact that the *additional* tax assures the Venezuelan government of receiving at least 50 per cent of the revenues of companies exploiting these natural resources. This is the reason for the *special* or *additional* tax in the Venezuelan income tax law.

As can be seen, this multiplicity of income tax arrangements—for all the administrative difficulties it may lead to—not only serves the inherent purposes of equity and social justice but also, as I noted above, corresponds to characteristics and needs of the Venezuelan economic structure.

The schedular tax, composed in general of various proportional taxes that facilitate the establishment of distinctions in liability between different types of income, could be used not only as between income from labor and income from capital but also in stimulating or discouraging particular activities in the over-all interests of economic development. Thus, for example, income from the industrial and agricultural sectors might well be given more favorable tax treatment than that derived from trade.

These important qualitative distinctions between various sources of income are reflected quantitatively in different tax rates. Insignificant though they may seem to some writers, without them there would certainly be the risk—in the case of Venezuela, specifically—that the adjustments necessary as the national economy evolves would not take place.

But all this should not be taken to mean that I declare myself categorically opposed to a *unitary structure* of tax rates applicable to income from all sources. What is necessary is that any such other arrangement must include the qualitative differences I have indicated, not just as a matter of theory but with attention to the aims of social justice and economic development, which the tax system can help to carry out.

As one of the regulatory features that should be included if the tax system is to be modified in the direction of a unitary structure, I recommend, in order to provide differential treatment to income derived from labor as against that derived from capital, the device of exempting from liability a percentage or a flat amount of the form of income to be favored. Alternatively, a tax credit could be granted on a flat amount of earned income.

More or less similar formulas could be used to provide differential treatment for various producing sectors in accordance with the development needs indicated by each country's economic structure, as I have pointed out.

Nevertheless, if a unitary structure is desired—which, of course, means eliminating schedular taxes wherever the laws now include them—the schedular and complementary rates would have to be combined in such a way that the new structure could perform the regulatory or orienting functions I consider fundamental.

Let me stress that in speaking of a possible unitary structure I refer solely to combining the schedular and the complementary taxes; by no means am I suggesting identical tax treatment, through a single schedule, for the incomes of individuals and corporations.

Separate Schedules for Personal and Corporate Taxation

In many Latin American countries the income tax systems do not provide for this differential treatment that I have just mentioned. In Venezuela, between the institution of this tax in 1942 and the reforms introduced in the middle of last year, individuals and corporations were subject to the same rates not only in the schedular tax but also in the complementary.

This situation is understandable in terms of the era in which it was created, when corporations belonged to and were administered by a single family or group of families. But it is wrong for the present day, when corporations have become truly anonymous (the members generally do not know each other and merely share in the ownership of the common capital) and have turned into large organizations with a managerial group that operates them independently of the mass of stockholders.

Because of this change, the Venezuelan tax authorities and experts decided to separate the complementary tax rates on personal income from those on corporate income, with the purpose of bringing in more revenue under conditions of equity and social justice.

A major consideration in the adoption of this distinction was that, though a broadly progressive scale with many steps was desirable for individual rates, neither similar progressivity nor a multiplicity of brackets was appropriate for taxing corporations. The

reform was therefore limited to the establishment of a new *progressive rate for corporations*—higher than the old one, which is still applicable to individuals—and reducing the number of brackets; the maximum rate remains at the previous level of 45 per cent, and the minimum is raised from 2 to 10 per cent.

To carry out this change of incidence in the lower and middle levels of net income required the regrouping of rates into only ten steps, instead of the thirty formerly applicable to individuals and corporations alike.

For the *personal complementary tax,* the same thirty-bracket scale as before was retained, the minimum rate being 2 per cent and the maximum 45 per cent.

The purpose of this separation was to make tax policy more flexible. And, limited though Venezuela's experience with it is as yet, there is already evidence of some increase in revenue from corporate income taxes, though this has perhaps come about through heavier taxation of medium-sized and small corporations than of large ones.

Taxation of Corporate Profits and Dividends

One of the most debated subjects in the field of tax theory concerns the profits of corporations and the dividends they distribute. Precisely because of its controversial nature, various positions are held on the subject.

First, there are those who hold that taxing a corporation's total net income and also its dividends constitutes double taxation and that therefore corporations should be exempt from all taxes and each stockholder be liable on his share of the profits, whether distributed or undistributed; or else that corporations should be subject to an income tax, but excluding dividends paid from taxable income.

Second, there are those who regard corporations as entities separate from their stockholders, to be taxed on their income, while the stockholders, treated as natural persons, should be taxed separately on their dividends.

Third, there are those who maintain an

intermediate position; they consider corporations to be groups of stockholders and not final taxable entities and therefore tend to favor some suitable means of diminishing the effect of double taxation. It is this last thesis—that of partial double taxation—that has been winning the widest acceptance not only in the sphere of theory but also in that of legislative action. The various methods that have been devised to apply this concept in practice are well known. They include, among others, the following:

The *dividends-received credit,* which consists in crediting part of the dividends received by the stockholder against his personal income tax liability. This method, as Mr. Prest cogently notes, "is usually rejected on the grounds that it is inequitable between poor and rich shareholders." In other words, it is a regressive formula.

The *dividends-paid credit* or *deduction of dividends,* which consists in deducting distributed dividends from total income in determining the corporation's taxable income. In my view, this has a doubly negative aspect: first, it indirectly stimulates the distribution of corporate profits, contrary to underdeveloped countries' need for increasing their domestic volume of savings; and, second, it facilitates tax evasion by accepting merely the stockholder's voluntary declaration of his personal income.

The *stockholder's credit* or *withholding method,* which consists in allowing the stockholder a tax credit equal to or less than the difference between the dividend he received and his actual share of the total profits, which he did not receive because the corporation paid tax on them before dividends were distributed.

Of all these methods, the last—withholding or stockholder's credit—has the most to recommend it, because (1) it levies the tax at the corporate level, thus making evasion difficult; (2) it promotes the collection of taxes by permitting their withholding at the source of income; (3) it maintains the principle of tax equity in its treatment of stockholders;

and (4) it discourages the distribution of profits.

If this last method were chosen, additional measures should be adopted to apply even more of a brake to the distribution of profits for consumption purposes. This could be done by exempting from tax the so-called stock dividends distributed to the members through the capitalization of profits.

If, finally, the corporate tax "takes the form of a tax on undistributed profits"—to quote Mr. Prest—there would certainly be no need for measures to avoid double taxation; but this, in my opinion, would be contrary to the interests of economic development because it would discourage saving. As against this risk, and if the object is *to avoid double taxation in principle,* even the taxing of all corporate profits and the exempting of dividends paid from personal tax would be preferable, whatever the ultimate effects of such a procedure.

Incentives to Save

The tax approach most generally followed to promote saving seems to be the use of more liberal depreciation methods.

Depreciation rates can be of particular significance to the developing countries, as can the carry-over of losses from one tax period to later ones. Yet many Latin American countries pay less attention than they should to increasing savings, specifically in the case of depreciation schedules. The systems they have adopted might be described as rigid, since in calculating depreciation the write-off may not exceed an even division of the price paid by the number of years of useful life. This is precisely the opposite of accelerated depreciation, under which shortening the useful life increases the allowable deduction.

This is why, in the past fifteen years, some countries have authorized higher depreciation rates. In Colombia, for example, the taxpayer may request a higher rate on property used for more than ten hours a day. The tax policy in this case is aimed at conserving the company's capital.

Venezuelan law authorizes deducting a "reasonable amount" for the depreciation of permanent assets and also permits the amortization of other costs necessary for initiating the income producing activity.

Though the Venezuelan system does not go so far as to provide for so-called *accelerated depreciation,* it is relatively flexible, permitting higher rates of deduction than rigid fiscal provisions do. These flexible depreciation systems are intended, of course, to force corporations to retain a higher percentage of profits.

Another form of stimulus to savings—in corporations, specifically—consists in excluding undistributed profits from taxes or setting a lower tax rate on them. This approach, which is gaining acceptance in Latin America, should be more carefully studied to measure the results obtained against the aims sought and the fiscal sacrifice entailed.

With respect to allowing the carry-over of losses from one tax period to subsequent ones, the countries vary considerably; some absolutely prohibit it and others fix time limits. Among the latter countries is Venezuela, where the law authorizes this carry-over for up to three years in the case of agriculture and stock raising and for only two years in the extractive, industrial, and commercial sectors.

Like Mr. Prest, I favor these deferments in principle. But I would specify that the term should not exceed three years and that it should serve the purposes of orientation, with a view to the dynamic function performed by certain sectors, such as manufacturing and agriculture, that should be stimulated.

Incentives to Capital Formation

While the political and social factors that enter an investor's calculations must not be underestimated, the influence that both a country's tax structure and its general economic policy can exert is obvious: they affect the security of his investments and his expectation of gain. This is why many experts and influential sectors are so anxious for the underdeveloped countries to adopt economic and financial policies that will attract foreign capital and will reward the reinvestment of profits, discouraging their distribution.

In this field of incentives to investment, the income tax can play an important role. Profits used for expanding or improving existing companies or for activities in sectors vital to economic development or for building up less developed regions can be granted total or partial exemptions.

For example, in the Venezuelan income tax law a partial exemption on complementary tax is now allowed, in accordance with a fixed scale, to taxpayers who make net investments in the country. This exemption applies to individual or corporate income during the tax year, when the investment is channeled into fixed assets of proven usefulness to the nation. Under the scale established by the law, the exemption depends on the relationship between the net investment and the taxpayer's total income: the reduction ranges from 10 per cent (when the investment amounts to between 10 and 20 per cent of income) to 25 per cent (when it is between 90 and 100 per cent of income). Because this provision was adopted so recently, there is not yet enough evidence to judge how well it succeeds in carrying out the purposes for which it was intended.

Besides this provision aimed at rewarding the reinvestment of profits, there are others intended to stimulate the employment of domestic and foreign capital in expanding and establishing industrial, agricultural, and stock-raising activities.

This is the purpose, for example, of a reform made early in 1961 to the corporate income tax law: a total or partial exemption on future profits may be granted when an industry considered especially important to economic development is set up within the country and also when capital is used for company expansion that will produce import substitutes. In each instance the total or partial exemption is granted only by means of an executive resolution, which fixes its term—

never longer than ten years. Both cases, and particularly the exemption so liberal in percentage and duration, not only stimulate sectoral investment but also promote the setting up of companies in less developed regions of the country.

Difficulties in Income Tax Collection

Among the difficulties encountered in trying to make Latin American tax legislation more systematic and effective, one of the most important has been the deficient statistics for carrying out economic valuations in most of the countries. In various tones and in various languages, a number of writers have lamented the obstacle created by the fact that until only a few years ago there was no way of finding out exactly what the demographic density and structure were, what the proportion of working population was within this structure, what the country's installed productive capacity amounted to, what the national income was and how it was distributed among the various social strata, what proportion of domestic savings was devoted to capital replacement, and so on.

The situation has been changing considerably in the past five years, however, and undeniably much of the credit must go to the specialized agencies of the United Nations and the Organization of American States. Working independently or together, they have striven for up-to-date population censuses, industrial and agricultural samples or censuses, and so on, the most recent data on which, until a short time ago, were for 1950 in many Latin American countries.

If to these shortcomings—now, as I say, being corrected—one adds the fact of chaotic accounting systems, sometimes aimed at falsifying the true situation and sometimes merely defective because incompetently drawn up, the likelihood of effectiveness in fiscal policy seems scant.

And among all the other impediments to flexibility in tax systems (the corporate income tax prominently included) is the paradox that, specialized as fiscal matters are, they are at the mercy of politics—both in formulation and in operation, both in the legislatures and in the public administration.

Prospects for Income Taxation in Latin America

Despite the difficulties mentioned above, the prospects for more effective income taxation in Latin America are rather favorable. As obstacles are overcome and imported standards are adapted to local actuality, more and more positive experience is being accumulated. Progress is also being made in molding a collective fiscal consciousness, which will produce greater vigilance in the conduct of public affairs and at the same time shape people's attitudes toward compliance with the tax laws and toward punishment of violators. Apart from this desirable evolution, there is also a need for accounting and administrative measures that will steadily reduce the total or partial evasion of taxes. Standards should be adopted requiring the use, especially by corporations, of precise accounting methods, including the determination of inventory costs.

It seems equally advisable to authorize the income tax administration to investigate transactions between taxpayers with common interests so as to prevent them from making improper transfers of income. Suppose, for example, that a corporation sells intermediate or final goods to a subsidiary and bills the sale at less than the current market price. The object of this seemingly inoffensive maneuver is to evade taxes by attributing relatively larger profits to the subsidiary (with its low volume of sales) and smaller profits to the parent company (with its high income). To prevent this kind of tax fraud, the income tax administration must have the power to calculate the actual value of the transaction and compute the true profit of each company on the basis of a fair price for the first sale.

Another means of preventing tax evasion, as Mr. Prest aptly points out, lies in convincing public opinion that government funds are honestly administered. Taxpayers must be able to recognize not only that fiscal resources are put to good use but that misappropriation is rigorously punished.

Outstanding among the reasons why the future seems promising for the development of the income tax is the corporation itself. Particularly in free enterprise economies, it is regarded as the chief source for the diversification of productive activities, for the carrying out of projects too large for any other form of organization, and for the generation of savings.

I am therefore pleased to have had the opportunity to make some contribution toward resolving the understandably great complexity that envelops this type of organization, on which the economic structure of the capitalist world so largely rests.

Comment

ALEXANDRE KAFKA*

The following comments refer only to the main points which appear to invite amplification.

PRINCIPAL PROS AND CONS OF CORPORATE INCOME TAXATION IN DEVELOPING COUNTRIES

Urban business income may be taxed without any basic distinction being made between corporations and unincorporated business. Again, the tax law may make no distinction between open and closely held corporations, including even personal holding companies. Both problems are closely linked to the existence of and—in many underdeveloped countries—the need for bearer shares. There are two main arguments in their favor. The most important one is the lack of confidence in the nondiscriminatory treatment of individual property rights. The alternative to bearer shares may often be capital flight. Moreover, it may be politically impracticable to rationalize the tax system to the extent necessary to achieve a given effective rate of taxation of certain classes of income, wealth, or transactions in the absence of bearer shares.

The other main argument, which is largely

*Getulio Vargas Foundation, Rio de Janeiro, Brazil.

technical, concerns the transferability of registered shares, which is often made difficult by the lack of institutions such as transfer agents or by the sheer problem of communications. The presence of bearer shares makes it partially impossible and therefore pointless to discriminate between open and closely held corporations. There is, on the other hand, from the economic and social point of view, very little to be said for tax discrimination between the income of closely held corporations and unincorporated businesses. Thus, there seems to be a good deal to be said, particularly in underdeveloped countries, for a general business income tax in preference over a corporation income tax.

In any case, the two problems just mentioned—no distinction between taxation of corporate and unincorporated business income, no distinction between open and closely held corporations—influence the effects of taxation decisively; so does the absence, in many underdeveloped countries, of a well-functioning stock exchange.

Few would question the practical grounds for corporation or general business income taxes in underdeveloped countries. In order to justify their maintenance, there is no advantage in appealing to the impossibility of taxing the resulting windfall gains nor even to the fact that the creation of substitute taxes would produce windfall losses, which are likely to affect quite different people than the beneficiaries of the windfall gains—for the same argument can be made against any tax change.

In underdeveloped countries, most of the circumstances under which shifting of business income tax can occur seem to be present to a considerable degree: the inclusion of cost elements in corporate profits as defined for tax purposes, e.g., insufficient allowance for top executives' salaries; oligopoly; and certain forms of profits sharing or the responsiveness of arbitral wage awards to the level of profits after tax. In addition to Mr. Prest's political arguments for corporation income taxes which can be shifted, there is perhaps another one. As long as statisticians are prepared to classify corporation income tax among direct taxes, collecting indirect taxes in this disguise will relieve the pressure for raising genuinely direct taxes which may cut into savings to an excessive extent.

That part of the corporation or business income tax which is shifted discriminates in favor of noncorporate sales, or, where the tax is a general business income tax, against non-business sales; in some countries a distinction is made between the taxation of urban business income and that of income derived from agricultural activities. The remainder of the tax, which is not shifted, discriminates in favor of income earned in the same activities. Discrimination in favor of agriculture may, justly or unjustly, command wide support. Such discrimination, as regards the shiftable portion, *may* be mainly the equivalent of a desired subsidy to the consumption of the poor or to rural wages; but discrimination, as regards the unshiftable portion, may be highly and undesiredly inequitable in addition.

Business income tax is far too crude an instrument for discrimination even between industries, which is better undertaken by commodity taxes. Income tax may, nevertheless, have its uses for other types of discrimination. This brings us to the crucial problem of savings. Mr. Prest reminds us that taxes need not reduce total savings; and tax receipts may finance private investments. Nevertheless,

many will wish to use the tax system to promote private savings. Granted that the corporation or business income tax is needed on practical grounds, how should it be used for this purpose? Corporate or even general business income is quite likely to be subject to a relatively high propensity to save. The correct procedure, of course, is not to discriminate in favor of income likely to have a high propensity to save, but rather to discriminate in favor of saving itself. At first sight, this may suggest discrimination in favor of undistributed earnings. This will be correct for the open corporation. The closely held corporation is just as much identified with its owners as the unincorporated business. Thus, discrimination in favor of retained corporate earnings is not necessarily an incentive to save the latter. Consumption expenditures of the owners (even if disallowed for purposes of corporation or business income tax) may (still) escape the personal income tax or the withholding tax on distributed earnings. An exemption in favor of actually invested retained earnings is more likely to be generally effective and should be extended to the unincorporated business where a general business income tax prevails. On the other hand, the argument that distribution is necessary to activate a capital market is less applicable to closely held than to open corporations. The former will be no less inclined to invest in new ventures than each of their few individual shareholders or partners.

Particularly where individual capital gains are not taxed, undistributed earnings may create an equity problem. In many underdeveloped countries, however, the market does not adequately register such gains unless evidenced by an increase in nominal capital. To this extent, the equity problem is avoided, provided increases in nominal capital through incorporation of reserves are taxed—accrued, rather than realized gains.

Discrimination in favor of undistributed earnings tends to discourage the small saver's access to equity investment. This is particularly important where inflation prevails. It is not necessary, however, for this purpose to abandon discrimination in favor of business savings. The appearance of open-end investment trusts has recently done much in many Latin American countries to encourage the medium- and even lower-income groups to invest in equities.

Where the personal income tax consists of a series of proportional schedular taxes plus a global progressive tax, business income taxation replaces the former. From the formal point of view, the integration of personal and business income taxation is then achieved automatically, without the need for tax credits. The remaining problems are the difference between the schedular rates on business and other income earning activities and taxing retained earnings. No endorsement of schedular discrimination is intended. In particular, there seems to be little to be said in favor of discriminating against unearned income, unless the different types of earned income are also subject to discrimination.

PRINCIPAL REFORMS

For many Latin American countries, the most important reform concerns the adaptation of corporate or business income taxes to protracted, and in some cases quite rapid, inflations. The problems are not in themselves of great theoretical interest, but they are of immense practical importance and extraordinarily hard to deal with.

Even slow but protracted inflation is likely to distort the intended pattern of taxation. The need for monetary correction applies to depreciable assets and, where corporate capital gains are taxable, to nondepreciable assets, including inventories. There is, in the first place, the pure index problem. There is also the problem of changes in technology which affect replacement costs of depreciable assets. An analogous problem has been much discussed in connection with the proper rate base for public utilities.

Where inflation is not only protracted but rapid, tax collections may be substantially and unforeseeably depreciated, and this may be true even where the corporate or business income tax is on a pay-as-you-earn basis. Under the latter, the least that will have to be done is to gear penalties for underestimation of tax to the rate of inflation.

This again raises the index problem mentioned earlier. After World War I it was solved in some cases by expressing tax liability in gold or foreign exchange. Today, with frequent interventions in the respective markets, no index may be available which commands confidence.

A second reform concerns the elimination of discrimination (where it exists) between the taxation of corporations and unincorporated businesses. Similarly business income taxation should, as far as possible, be extended to agricultural activities.

A third reform concerns the general treatment of business saving. Business savings actually invested might benefit from favors, without distinction between closed corporations and unincorporated businesses. These favors might go further than do those extended today to retained earnings as such. The investments entitled to benefit should not include every kind of asset, but government interference should be kept to a minimum. Investments in any local enterprise, and not only in the firm originating the savings, should certainly qualify. Firms, as distinct from individuals, can be controlled with sufficient ease to the extent necessary to ensure that the benefit is not abused.

A fourth reform concerns discrimination between open corporations, on the one hand, and closed corporations, as well as unincorporated businesses, on the other hand. There is much to be said for such discrimination, not only on economic but also on political grounds. The discrimination might include a lower tax rate on corporate income (where there is no adequate system of tax credits) or benefits regarding the taxation of business savings. To be effective, such discrimination will often have to be preceded by a series of reforms making registered shares easily transferable.

APPENDIX: SOME ASPECTS OF THE BRAZILIAN BUSINESS TAX

Brazilian law makes no distinction between the taxation of business income of corporations and unincorporated businesses. Agricultural activities, however, are taxed on a different basis, which is generally agreed, in practice, to amount to exemption. The Brazilian personal income tax is a combination of a series of proportional schedular taxes and a progressive global tax; business income tax is, however, a multiple of the highest schedular tax to which any other type of income is subject.

The following notes merely take up those aspects where Mr. Prest's paper suggests some amendment or explanation; the cases are very few.

The *basis* of Brazilian business income tax is income-originating.

Withholding on Dividends Paid Out. Mr. Prest is correct as to the present situation, but a withholding tax on dividends paid out to resident registered shareholders is now before Congress. Similarly, holders of bearer shares now pay a withholding tax corresponding to an intermediate rate of progressive global tax but are to become subject to a relatively high one, unless they identify themselves, in which case they will be treated, in a degree, like resident registered shareholders.

Income remitted to foreign residents at present pays a slightly lower rate than the withholding tax on bearer shares; it is now to pay the latter tax.

Taxation of Dividends Received. Dividends (to resident registered shareholders) are subject only to global progressive tax. Dividends (including those on registered shares) received by corporations are exempt from corporate income tax, and those on bearer shares are exempt also from tax when distributed by the recipient corporation. Since the law does not distinguish between personal holding and other corporations, it has, as it were, behind its back achieved the exemption from taxation of personal savings (and possibly even more than that). Because of this, a bill now before

Congress proposes a 15 per cent withholding tax on dividends (on registered shares) received by corporations and also limits the amount of expenses which a corporation, receiving profits paid out by other corporations, may charge against such income. The savings exemption is available, however, only to wealthy people, since others would be deterred by costs of establishing a personal holding company.

Additional Corporate Taxes. Firms may opt to establish investment deposits of 150 per cent of their excess profits tax liability. The deposits are available for approved investments within the firm or elsewhere.

The tax on capital revaluation (in accordance with inflation) and the excess profits tax are, in a sense, alternatives; one of the bases of the latter tax is registered capital.

While individual capital gains are tax free, this is not true of stock dividends which are considered income. However, the corporation may choose to pay the tax at a lower rate on the incorporations of surplus into capital. This is important because there is a high tax on surplus exceeding nominal capital.

Special Incentives. In addition to tax holidays available to businesses operating in underdeveloped regions of Brazil, the law authorizes the executive to establish coefficients of accelerated depreciation. No use has been made of this authority so far. More recently, profits invested in certain underdeveloped regions have been exempted from business income tax to the extent of 50 per cent of the investment.

Discrimination against Foreigners. The exemption just mentioned is available only to "purely Brazilian" firms. As discrimination between firms incorporated in Brazil, this provision may be challengeable on constitutional grounds.

The branches of nonresident corporations are taxed as if the entire profits, after corporate income tax, had been distributed to the mother company. The same rule, in respect of distribution to its owners, applies to Brazilian-owned unincorporated businesses.

No discrimination is intended, but the tax law cannot see a distinction between the owner and his unincorporated enterprise. Nevertheless, for some years the branches of non-resident corporations have been exempt from the tax on distributions in respect of profits reinvested in industrial activities in Brazil. Such an exemption is not available to Brazilian-owned unincorporated businesses.

Double Taxation. Brazil has no general double taxation agreements, and only a few regarding specific activities (air transportation). The problem so far has been of little practical importance to business, since tax rates have been lower than in most capital exporting countries. The rise in the tax on earnings distributed to foreign residents may change the picture.

Discussion

MR. PREST introduced his paper on corporate income taxation in Latin America and said that he had attempted to steer a middle course between attempting a textbook exposition of general principles and entering into the details of corporate income taxation in Latin America by indicating the main principles involved that provided scope for thought and possibly action. Section I dealt with the general arguments for a corporation tax, including the need to catch undistributed profits, the comparative administrative simplicity of taxing corporations, the fact that corporations had no votes, and the possibility that the tax would be at the expense of foreign government revenue. Where a corporation income tax already existed, the inequity of allowing some to make windfall gains argued against removing it. The arguments against the tax included the possibility that it might retard the development of the corporate sector, the danger of hampering development by reducing saving, and the need not to discourage the inflow of foreign capital. The reconciliation of the tax with personal taxation raised the question of differential treatment of distributed and undistributed profits, which involved both economic effects and equity issues.

Section II was a factual summary. Tables 8–1 and 8–2 gave data on income and wealth taxation in Latin America, and although full data were not available for all countries, the

tables showed that there was a wide variation in the ratio of income from corporate taxation to total government revenue. Table 8–3, which summarized characteristics of Latin American corporate income taxation, had been compiled from a large number of sources, since the information concerned was not available in standard reference books, and he hoped that any errors that had crept in would be corrected by participants from the countries concerned. The table showed some of the principal ways in which corporate income taxation could vary from country to country with respect to separation from personal income, withholding of dividends paid out, taxation of dividends received, additional taxes imposed, such as excess profits tax, and discrimination against foreigners (with respect to foreign and national resident shareholders or dividends paid abroad or in the country). It was clear that there was a great diversity in the arrangements for corporate income taxation in the various countries.

Section III considered the concept of income, the need for simplicity, the rate structure, the integration of corporate and personal income taxes, intended and unintended discrimination in present tax arrangements, and special concessions. Referring to the discussion at the seventh meeting, he said that the income basis chosen could be income-originating, income-received, or a world-wide concept, of which the first and third were relevant to the present discussion. The difficulty of measuring income-originating included arm's-length pricing and the overlapping of tax jurisdictions with respect to subsidiaries of foreign companies. A number of factors influenced the effect of corporate income taxation on the flow of international capital, including the income basis, i.e., whether originating or world-wide, the relative sizes of gross yields and tax rates in different countries, whether or not tax credits were allowed on income derived from other countries, and the relative treatment of resident and nonresident enterprises.

The great complexity of arrangements for corporate income taxation in Latin America seemed hard to justify. Corporations might be subject to more than one tax on income and to taxes on excess profits or business assets as well as on income; there were distinctions between resident and nonresident enterprises; rates of withholding tax depended on the types of recipient; and so forth. From the standpoint of administration and the preventions of evasion, such complexity was a serious disadvantage.

The rates of the tax should not be high enough to retard the growth of the corporate sector or low enough to make unnecessary presents to companies or foreign governments. A progressive corporate income tax did not appear justified on equity grounds, since a small corporation might have rich shareholders and a large one comparatively poor shareholders; in addition, a progressive tax would serve as a disincentive to growth and would encourage the splitting of corporations into small units, resulting in the need for preventive measures to enforce aggregation, which would be an unnecessary complication. As for bearer shares, unless some way was found of identifying the ultimate recipient, the only method was to subject dividends on such shares to a high rate of withholding tax.

Integration of personal and corporate income taxes could be achieved by making a tax credit to the individual shareholder in respect of his dividend or by affording relief at the corporation level on dividends paid out, so that the corporate income tax became a tax on undistributed profits. The same effect as that due to the latter course could be achieved by the withholding method, whereby dividends paid out were grossed up so as to allow for corporate tax paid and taxed as personal income, but with a credit for the corporate tax. Clearly the rate of tax on retained profits should be not less than that paid by the average shareholder if profits were distributed. The optimum balance between distributed and undistributed profits was a difficult question; retention of profits favored corporation savings, but it might be important to force out savings through the capital market, and there was always a danger that existing corporations would build up an entrenched monopoly position. Larger retained profits would be more likely to result in capital gains, which raised the question about the adequacy and comprehensiveness of the capital gains tax.

With respect to unintended discrimination, he pointed out that excess profits taxes were justifiable for short periods or emergencies only, and as a long-term measure were likely to impede growth. Discrimination between large and small corporations would be likely to hamper growth, although unincorporated enterprises might be encouraged to become incorporated. There was much scope for further study of the relative tax rates applying to unincorporated businesses and small corporations, which varied widely from country to country. There might also be differentiation between the rates of taxation applied to nonresident and resident subsidiaries of foreign companies and to oil and mining companies compared with companies engaged in other activities.

With respect to special concessions to encourage development and investment, a distinction might be made between net investment and the replacement of capital goods, but that was very difficult. It was not easy to determine how far tax relief for investment purposes was merely a gift to those who would invest in any case and thus simply represented a net reduction in the total tax revenue. It would be advisable for the countries concerned to take a common line on concessions to foreign corporations; otherwise the result might be free gifts to foreign governments or corporations. He concluded his review of the document by stressing the need for good accounting standards with respect to corporation balance sheets and profit-and-loss accounts and for clear and firm legislation and administration.

The value added tax and the possibility of using it to replace a corporate income tax constituted a third form of taxation, the first two being taxation of the income stream, in the form of wages and profits, and taxation on expenditure, in the form of excise and sales taxes on consumer or possibly capital goods. If the value added tax were substituted and the graduated personal income tax retained, the result would be a much more favorable treatment of undistributed than distributed profits, with no incentive to distribute. Moreover, rich shareholders would escape liability. Tax on capital gains resulting from retained profits was not satisfactory because it was not easy to operate and sometimes tax was collected only after the profit retention took place. The precise effect of substituting a value added tax for a corporate income tax would depend on whether the existing corporate tax favored distributed or undistributed profits. The effect of combining a value added tax with the personal income tax might or might not be desirable, but it should be recognized as not being neutral.

MR. JATAR-DOTTI, introducing his comments on Mr. Prest's paper, said that the concept of the income tax was relatively new in Latin America, having been introduced in most cases in the third decade of the present century. As far as the scope of the tax was concerned, both the principle of origin and that of residence were applied. In that connection, one of the features of capital importing countries was that their gross national product was greater than their national income, while the opposite was true of capital exporting countries. That feature had to be taken into consideration in determining which of the two concepts of tax applicability—income-originating or income-received—should be adopted for developing countries, where only a small minority received income from abroad. For the reasons outlined in his paper, he preferred the concept of income-originating.

One of the problems related to the two concepts above was that of international double taxation. It could be solved either through unilateral action, in which a government granted relief from taxation in respect of income already taxed in another country, or through agreements between the governments concerned.

On the question of multiple and unitary taxes, he observed that in many Latin American countries the income tax consisted of a series of schedular taxes at different fixed or proportional rates and of a progressive global or complementary tax. While the undue diversity of income taxes in some countries was to be deplored, it was unavoidable in some cases where schedular and complementary taxes were imposed on all types of activities, as was done in Venezuela. While a unitary tax structure would be desirable, it should be achieved only through a combining of schedular and complementary taxes and must not result in the same tax rate being applied to individuals and corporations. Unfortunately, in many Latin American countries no distinction between individuals and corporations was made for income tax purposes. Venezuela had done so by creating a new progressive tax on corporations at a somewhat higher rate than the personal income tax and by reducing the number of taxable categories, the complementary tax on personal income being left at its previous rates. The new system had produced increased revenue from the tax on corporate income.

On the question of the taxation of corporate profits and dividends and the need to avoid the double taxation which might result, he felt that the best method of granting the necessary relief would be the withholding tax approach, the merits of which were outlined in his paper.

With respect to incentives to savings, he supported the view that that could be done best through provisions for loss carry-overs, but he would limit such carry-overs to a period not exceeding three years.

With regard to incentives to capital formation, the income tax was a useful instrument in creating such incentives. In Venezuela, for instance, the income tax laws had been amended to allow a taxpayer who made net investments in the country to claim a partial rebate of the complementary tax. The new provision applied both to individuals and corporations.

In concluding, he referred to some of the difficulties which Latin American countries faced in collecting income taxes and to the prospects for a successful taxation of income in those countries, details of which were set out in the last two sections of his paper.

MR. LESSA said that high profits had been related to efficiency by some speakers and asked whether that concept was really in line with high social productivity of enterprises in the framework of economic development. Mr. Prest had seemed to imply the same view. But it was very doubtful whether in Latin America high profits were due to efficiency, in view of the various privileges and exemptions that were granted by governments. In the absence of organized capital markets in Latin America, the large financial resources called for by modern technology precluded the free entry of competitors to the market required by classical economic theory; hence there was more monopoly and less competition than in more developed countries. Moreover, high corporation profits were largely due to production functions that did not lead to the proper use of economic resources; the high capital intensity characteristic of industrialized countries was not well suited to an area where labor was plentiful and wages low. Consequently he thought the tax on corporate income should be progressive.

With respect to the stimulation of investment at the enterprise level through the treatment of distributed and nondistributed profits in corporate taxation schemes, he be-lieved that it was not defensible to allow exemptions solely to the enterprises and that the discrimination against personal income would accelerate the process of the concentration of wealth. If there were a progressive tax on corporation profits, either they could be distributed to shareholders or alternatively they could be added to capital by the distribution of bonus shares, but they should be taxed in both cases. It was more appropriate in the Latin American context to provide investment incentives at the shareholder level than at the enterprise level.

MR. KALDOR felt that the incidence of taxation on corporate profits had not been given sufficient attention in Mr. Prest's paper. That was a complicated question which depended to some extent on specific tax provisions such as the relative treatment of distributed and undistributed profits. He felt that the incidence of the tax had substantially shifted. Therefore the context should be clearly defined in order to determine whether it was considered as a substitute for other taxes or as an addition to the total revenue which would have been obtained otherwise. In the former context, the distribution of income between profits and wages was not very different from what it would have been if the same revenue had been obtained from indirect taxation. The shift in the incidence of taxation on corporate profits was a macroeconomic process which did not leave the distribution of net profits unaffected. If it was agreed that the role of the tax had shifted, it was a convenient revenue yielding device. If the view was that it had not shifted, then it had an important role in the equity of the tax system.

With respect to Mr. Prest's comments on the value added tax, he agreed that if it was Mr. Prest's view that the incidence of the tax on corporate profits had not shifted, it was correct to say that the value added tax should not be regarded as an alternative to the tax on corporate profits but as an alternative to a general tax on sales. Some European countries had considered the substitution of a value added tax for some parts of the corporate profits tax.

He agreed with Mr. Lessa on the relationship between the efficiency of a corporation and its profits. In comparing different branches of industry, the level of profits was not an indication of efficiency. However, if a comparison was made between enterprises engaged in the same branch of industry, the difference in profits would reflect their degree of efficiency.

Mr. Lessa had rightly observed that competition in industry occurred far less in developing countries than in the more industrialized states. There was, nevertheless, some competition, and a heavy tax on corporate profits would militate against more efficient firms which showed higher profits. He supported Mr. Lessa's suggestion that corporations might be required to issue bonus shares in respect of their undistributed profits and that such shares should form part of the income of shareholders. That was a most valuable recommendation, but unfortunately it had been rejected constantly by tax commissions and administrations because it would make the raising of capital by joint-stock enterprises more difficult. In connection with bonus shares, it should be borne in mind that undistributed income was not quite the same as distributed income. The shareholder did not derive the same advantage from bonus shares as from cash dividends since the market value of such shares would undoubtedly be lower if the owner wished to convert them into cash. They should therefore be taxed on their market value rather than on their nominal value. A possible alternative would be to tax income received in the form of bonus shares, and not as cash, at a lower rate than income received as cash.

Mr. Desai, referring to the treatment of domestic and foreign capital, said that there was some justification for a higher tax on income sent abroad. It was a matter of establishing equity between such income and investment income remaining in the country, since the former avoided future liability to taxes such as the inheritance tax.

Mr. Goode, on the question of the shifting of the incidence of the tax on corporate income, agreed with Mr. Kaldor that little statistical data were available. Not much weight should be given to statistics on the subject in the United States, which were suggestive rather than conclusive. His own view was that the greater part of the tax rested on the profits received by corporations.

With regard to the jurisdiction of the corporate income tax, or the place where the income was taxed, a country might take the position that in measuring the taxable capacity of its nationals or residents, total world-wide income would be the appropriate measure. In his opinion, that would not be an unreasonable standard for measuring taxable capacity. It was true that if every country adopted that standard, double taxation might well result. However, relief could be granted through unilateral action by the government concerned or through bilateral or international agreements. The unilateral method was applied in the United States and the United Kingdom, which recognized the priority of the country of origin. However, even if a country did not wish to grant relief from double taxation to corporate income, the financial implications were not likely to be very serious. It might discourage movement of capital to the more developed countries, which was not in fact an undesirable effect. Moreover, the flow of capital from developing countries was due not primarily to the tax system but rather to other factors.

Mr. Riofrío said that the dual personality of corporations was an invention of jurists applied by financial theorists for tax purposes through the taxation, on the one hand, of the profits of the corporations themselves and, on the other, of the income received by shareholders. Income was thus taxed twice. He also mentioned the omissions in Mr. Prest's paper to which the author himself had referred and pointed out that there were others as well. After describing the background and case history used in support of corporate income tax, he concluded that in spite of the reasons of equity which could have been adduced against that form of double taxation, the only arguments advanced had been based purely on expediency.

MR. DARDÓN said that, in his opinion, the great merit of Mr. Prest's paper lay in the fact that he suggested alternative methods for taxing corporate enterprises; that principle should be part of the general findings of the present conference in respect of all the topics. It was not possible to establish an over-all tax reform pattern which would be valid for all the Latin American countries, since each one had its own peculiar characteristics insofar as the historical background of its particular tax system was concerned, so that any reform would have to be firmly and harmoniously adapted to the particular economic development needs of each country. Nevertheless, the concentration of wealth, property, and income in the hands of a small percentage of the population was a common occurrence. That fact pointed to the advisability of a global progressive tax on personal income and on the income of corporate and noncorporate enterprises as well as a tax on wealth or, specifically, property.

In the case of corporations, a curious phenomenon had taken place in Guatemala, where enterprises formerly organized as partnerships made up of two or three partners, generally with various integrated activities and domestic capital of a family type, had been turned into two or three companies for the purpose of evading tax. The original partnership, with its assets compact and subject to a progressive tax on its profits, would undoubtedly have had to pay more tax.

The same thing had happened with the organization of corporations in which all or most of the shares were in the hands of a single person. In other words, the transformation or establishment of joint-stock companies had been due to motives far removed from the channeling of savings.

He therefore considered that the alternatives proposed by Mr. Prest were valuable criteria for each government to use in accordance with the particular conditions prevailing in the country concerned.

MR. HARBERGER said that corporate income taxation was really partial rather than global, applying not to all income from capital but only to the income from corporate equity capital. It was important to recognize this in judging the probable incidence of the corporation income tax. One extreme possibility was that the net rate of return on capital would not change as a consequence of the tax. In this case it could be said that the tax was borne by consumers, or, what is the same thing, that the tax was borne by capital and labor in proportion to their respective contributions to the national income. At the other extreme was the possibility that the net rate of return to capital would fall by the full amount of the tax. In this case capital would bear a burden greater than the tax collected by the government, since the fall in the net rate of return on capital would apply to corporate and noncorporate capital alike, while the tax would be collected only on the income from corporate capital. It was very important to realize that the case in which the full burden of the tax is borne by capital is not an extreme case but one which is intermediate between the extreme possibilities indicated above. For further explanation he referred to his article in the *Journal of Political Economy* for June, 1962. As regards incentive to invest, the exemption of corporations might direct investment to a number of different ends and could effect changes in the distribution of investment, but he was doubtful of the value of tax incentives as a stimulus to total investment. Savings and investment were equivalent, and the problem was how to increase savings in order to increase the volume of investment. He believed that the over-all effect of exemptions was a loss of revenue rather than an increase in total investment.

MR. NAHARRO said that the corporate tax benefited reinvestment in that it encouraged savings in the form of undistributed profits. The corporate tax also favored distinctions among undistributed profits, according to the type of enterprise concerned, for the purpose of directing reinvestment into channels most suitable to economic development. With respect to the progressivity of the corporate tax, it could be graduated in terms of the type of yield of the corporation itself. He wondered, in that connection, whether that formula could not be used for Latin American corporations. It was a question of fixing progressive rates as the percentage which represented the net profit in relation to capital and reserves increased.

MR. ABINADER, referring to Mr. Prest's comments on the income tax established in the Dominican Republic in May, 1962, described the structure of the tax and mentioned the additional advantages enjoyed by corporation executives. Those advantages fully justified the tax criterion adopted. The new income tax was expected to yield an amount equal to 25 per cent of the country's budget. The revenue would fill the gap left by the indirect taxes which had been abolished, since they had contributed another 25 per cent of the public sector's income.

MR. JARACH, referring to the relationship between the corporate tax and the personal income tax, recognized that the subject was controversial and that economists and tax experts were divided in their opinions. He suggested that dividends paid to shareholders and the value of the bonus shares distributed to them should not be included in corporate income tax; and he suggested, as a practical solution aimed at bringing the level of the corporation tax into line with that of the tax on natural persons, that corporations should be taxed on their whole profit, whether distributed or not, at a rate close to the highest average rate applied to personal income. Natural persons could thus claim partnership treatment for themselves; i.e., they could include in their declaration of total income the share of the corporation's profit corresponding to their shareholdings and to calculate as tax already paid on account the tax paid by the corporation on its share of the profit. The proposal avoided the difficulties inherent in dividends, the fluctuations in share values arising from capital profits and losses, and share dividends and allowed every taxpayer

selecting the system to have applied to him the rate corresponding to his total income, including his share of corporate profits.

MR. MATUS said he was in general agreement with the views expressed in Mr. Prest's paper but would like to refer to certain omissions therein. The Economic Commission for Latin America was concerned about the problems posed by tax manipulation as a method of changing the normal behavior of economic units with a view of bringing it into line with the behavior stipulated in development plans; the problem had not been mentioned by the author nor by the conference, which appeared to discuss tax problems in a manner entirely divorced from planning objectives.

In that connection he posed two problems: (a) the possible use of taxation on foreign enterprises, to mitigate in part the impact of foreign trade fluctuations, and (b) the use of taxation on corporations as a method of guiding the investment rate and structure along the lines of a development plan.

With regard to (a), it was a well-known fact that the Latin American countries were suffering the consequences of export fluctuations, although in some countries the effects tended to be the exact opposite of those felt in developed countries. In industrialized countries a decline in exports produced a depressive effect on the economy, whereas in certain countries of Latin America the same decline had an expanding effect. The reason for that lay in the fact that export fluctuations had a fundamental effect on remittances of profits abroad, the availability of foreign exchange, and fiscal revenues, because there were strong political pressures to maintain the employment of labor and, consequently, to reduce the effect on the volume of production. He believed that taxing of foreign enterprises in the countries that produced a very high percentage of total exports might be used to help to stabilize import capacity and fiscal revenue. If, instead of taxing real profits, a system of taxing minimum average profits were established—in the sense of the profits determined on the basis of average prices and volume of production over the past few years—the effect of fluctuations would be greatly mitigated. When export prices declined, import capacity and fiscal revenues would decline to a much lesser degree, and when prices rose, foreign enterprises would be taxed on real profits but would not be permitted to deduct the excess tax paid previously because of the effect of the average.

He recognized that such a system might discourage foreign investments; however, it could be graduated, since the stabilizing effect depended on the number of years covered by the average values. If the system of calculating the average covered a number of years in a full cycle, it would completely stabilize import capacity and fiscal revenue, thus transferring the fluctuations 100 per cent to the large foreign enterprises. Averages below the cycle, on the other hand, implied sharing the effects of fluctuations between enterprises and the public sector. Such a system would be useful only in countries where exports were in the hands of foreign enterprises.

He went on to refer to the orientation of private enterprises by taxing their profits. Non-Latin American economists seemingly had more faith in market forces and in sound business returns as a sign of efficiency than Latin Americans, as mentioned in a previous meeting of the conference. Mr. Kaldor's opinion was not the only exception, and he did not believe there could be any doubts in that respect. The very unsatisfactory distribution of income in Latin America was more than sufficient argument for such skepticism because it determined the structure of investments and of production. Just as in politics nobody would respect an election where a privileged few were entitled to ten votes while the rest of the population had only one, he saw no reason to respect an investment and business structure under which certain minorities had twenty or more votes because their incomes were twenty or more times as large as those of the majority. Moreover, it was an indisputable fact that there was a very high degree of monopoly in Latin America and distortion of price systems, etc.

Therefore, there was reason for concern, not about the neutral nature of the tax, but rather about the way of using the corporate tax to penalize certain activities and promote others. A development plan might contemplate very high rates of production growth and investment in sectors with low commercial returns, and vice versa. That posed an interesting problem of tax manipulation. The growth of certain enterprises had to be checked and the growth of others promoted. By penalizing the reinvestment of profits in certain sectors, it was possible to encourage the distribution of profits. In other cases, it was advisable to withhold profits at the expense of reserves for depreciation, without increasing total corporate savings. Therefore he would ask Mr. Prest what was the available experience in the matter or what ideas he had for making the transfer of savings from the sectors he wished to penalize to those he wished to promote. Thought might be given, perhaps, to putting a premium on the purchase of securities issued by enterprises included in the latter group or the purchase of government development securities.

MRS. DE NAVARRETE observed that a progressive tax on corporate income had, among its other advantages, that of reducing the difficulties arising from the difference in the size of corporations. With respect to the incidence of the tax, it would not have a direct effect on the profits received by shareholders. She supported both her arguments by giving examples based on actual legislative and administrative experience in Mexico.

MR. COSCIANI, referring to the total or partial substitution of the profits tax by the value added tax, as suggested during the debate, observed that the two taxes belonged to different tax groups. The value added tax, in the final analysis, taxed prices, which meant that it was levied on consumption. That might create major dislocations in the market. Therefore he advised careful study before any conclusion was reached in the matter.

MR. PIEDRABUENA observed that many Latin American corporations contributed to the economic development of their countries.

In general, however, intangible property was viewed with suspicion in Latin America, and an attempt should therefore be made to strengthen the structure of corporations. One way to do that was to grant them some measure of relief from double taxation and to tax them on their undistributed profits. While action to ease the tax burden of corporations might have an adverse short-term effect on economic development, it would be most useful to encourage small investors to contribute to that development, and that could be done only by ensuring a fair return on their dividends. Moreover, an unduly high rate of taxation on the distributed profits of corporations would cause corporations to refrain from distributing such profits. The best solution, in his view, and one referred to by Mr. Prest in his paper, would be to have the corporate tax take the form of a tax on undistributed profits.

MR. URQUIDI hoped that Mr. Prest would give his views on the question of the revaluation of assets, a particularly important problem in countries with inflation problems or where the currency was devaluated.

With regard to the rate structure of corporate income taxes, he felt that a progressive tax, particularly in countries with inflation problems, would ensure elasticity in the collection of revenue.

MR. VIDAL said that while he would like to stress the importance and thoroughness of Mr. Prest's paper, he must call attention to one or two errors into which the author had fallen in referring to the income tax in Peru. The excess profits tax had not existed since 1958. Neither was corporate capital taxed in Peru, nor the dividends of corporations registered in Peru, except when they were payable to foreign firms. Furthermore, accelerated depreciation was recognized in Peru.

Apart from the above reservations, he would only add, with regard to double taxation on the corporation and the shareholder—a matter appropriately pointed out by Mr. Riofrío—that it was mitigated by two provisions, i.e., incentives for investment, whereby it was possible to deduct from the tax base up to 40 per cent of profits, provided they were invested for improving production, and reduction of the tax on capitalization of earnings to one-third of the maximum rate. Neither of those measures prevented a shareholder from obtaining dividends, should he choose to sell the shares appreciated by investment or capitalization; and there again the profit was not taxed in Peru.

MR. GNAZZO said that his country, Uruguay, favored a single tax on corporate profits and had established a tax on the undistributed profits of corporations. He wondered whether Mr. Prest would express his views on the Uruguayan solution.

MR. PREST said that he would not reply to each individual speaker but would deal in a general way with the different points that had been raised.

The first question concerned the shifting of corporate income tax. As Mr. Kaldor had pointed out, he had not indicated the extent of the shifting precisely for the reason that he did not know the answer. The statements made with respect to the incidence of the tax by statisticians and businessmen were not convincing, in his opinion. The chief concern was to define the question, since much of the difficulty experienced in reaching a definite position was due to the multiplicity of factors involved. Therefore the first task was to decide what tax would be replaced by corporate income tax and the second to determine the real meaning of incidence. On the latter, the view generally held was that it signified the effects of the tax on income distribution, which again were many-sided. Three main variables were involved in tax substitution: (a) the effects on the relative prices paid for factors of production; (b) the effects on direct tax collection from individual taxpayers; and (c) the effects on relative prices. He pointed out that it was easy to become entangled with absolute prices, which were irrelevant. Generally speaking, any single tax could operate on one or all of the three variables.

In some circumstances, the main effect of corporate income tax on income distribution might be to alter the relative prices of goods.

But as an example of the opposite kind, he referred to enterprises that were mainly concerned with export trade. In their case, corporate income tax would be borne by shareholders or other factors of production.

He presumed that those speakers who upheld the taxation of corporations would agree that the same arguments applied to unincorporated enterprises. That immediately opened up the whole question of the justification for progressive taxation.

With reference to the interesting suggestions made by Mr. Harberger of a model for corporate income taxation, he doubted whether his ideas would be wholly applicable outside the United States.

His second main point related to the value added tax. He agreed with Mr. Lessa that there was no obvious reason why the substitution of that tax for a corporate income tax should conduce to raising efficiency. The ratio of profits to wages might increase because of one of three factors: greater efficiency, more inputs, or a more monopolistic position. The suggestion had been made that a value added tax operated in the same way as a multistage tax. He disagreed with that suggestion, since the great merit of the value added tax was precisely that it made allowance for capital outlays and was applicable to all types of business, incorporated or unincorporated.

In regard to the conflict between income-originating and a world-wide basis for assessment, he had little to add to Mr. Goode's statement. He would merely say that he did not advocate taxing income where received, as some speakers seemed to think, and, in regard to the point made by one speaker that income from foreign sources was not worth taxing because much of it would undoubtedly evade taxation for one reason or another, he maintained that it was better to obtain some revenue than none at all.

Some speakers had raised the question of the adjustment of the tax system to inflationary conditions, one possibility being the LIFO method and the other the revaluation of capital assets so that the money value of deprecia-

tion allowances was increased. The answer depended on the end that was pursued. If the intention was to use the tax system to check inflation, both these methods of applying it were wrong.

Another point concerned the progressive taxation of companies. Mrs. de Navarrete had doubted whether it was justifiable since it penalized small business firms with little access to the capital market. He agreed but reiterated his conviction that businesses should not be taxed on a progressive basis like individuals. Small firms could be helped through some kind of tax relief or easy credit facilities, as in the United States and the United Kingdom. The statement that progressive taxation of corporations would give more elastic yield was true theoretically as income levels rose in periods of inflation, but nevertheless the disadvantages outweighed the advantages.

With regard to investment, it had been asked whether accelerated depreciation was an effective stimulus. Did it add to the overall volume or simply conduce to the transfer of resources from one sector to another? In general, accelerated depreciation had two effects: it produced (a) a reduction of interest rates and (b) more funds for business firms. In one or both ways it could stimulate the level of investment. Experience with accelerated depreciation in the United Kingdom had clearly demonstrated that its effect was to raise the total level of investment.

His seventh point concerned tax concessions for investment. He agreed that they were liable to have an inflationary effect on the economy and that compensating revenue had to be collected at some other point.

In the same field, there was the question of exemptions for invested retained earnings of corporations. Two possibilities were involved: differentiation in the taxation of undistributed and distributed profits and tax relief for capital investment. But those two policies should not be confused, as was the danger with this device. An interesting suggestion had been put forward that companies making retentions should issue corresponding bonus shares which could then be taxed. That was tantamount to the partnership principle that undistributed profits should be allocated to shareholders and taxed accordingly. The case for that was a long-standing one and seemed to him to have a number of advantages in theory, but he thought it would be difficult to apply in practice.

His last point related to the appropriate rate of taxation for dividends paid abroad. He was not sure whether he agreed with the suggestion that foreign dividends should be taxed more heavily than domestic dividends because the latter might also be subject to inheritance or other taxes. The answer depended on the territorial jurisdiction of inheritance taxation and whether the principle was applied of taxing the estate of a resident in his home country or abroad or both.

9

Production and Consumption Taxes and Economic Development

by Jose Maria Naharro*

TERMINOLOGY AND DEFINITIONS

Tax terminology is so varied that it is not redundant, at the beginning of any paper on fiscal problems, to give the precise meaning and scope of the concepts to be employed.[1] Since this paper concerns taxes on consumption and production, it is important at the outset to define and locate these two types of levies within the over-all context of taxation.

Despite the ambiguities often imputed to an approach which divides taxes into direct and indirect categories, we shall utilize this general classification.[2] But simply to admit this distinction is not sufficient, since, as many authorities recognize, it rests upon quite diverse assumptions. Among these authorities, the ideas which seem best (or least objectionable) are those which divide direct and indirect taxes according to the point at which ability to pay is taxed. It is much more generally accepted that ability to pay is the natural basis of taxation and similarly that such ability is directly linked to the income or wealth of the taxpayer. Also, there seems to be a general consensus that income is the most important index of ability, while the taxpayer's assets or wealth are only auxiliary bases of taxation. Therefore, we shall concern ourselves only with income in this paper.

The economic process of the production and distribution of income may be divided, with relative clarity, between the point at which income is realized by the economic unit and the point at which this income is spent. Direct taxes, then, bear upon ability to pay at the time income is received by the taxpayer, while indirect taxes bear on this ability at the point where already realized income is spent.[3]

---

*Faculty of Law, University of Madrid, Spain.

[1] In the paper presented by John Due to the Conference on Tax Administration (Buenos Aires, October 11–19, 1961) on "Administrative Criteria in the Establishment of Sales and Excise Tax Structures," there are also a number of comments on terminology. In general, the definitions given of consumption and sales taxes are identical to those given here. However, it is likely that there may be some small differences.

[2] One criticism of this distinction appears in the well-known article of Ursula K. Hicks, "The Terminology of Tax Analysis," *Economic Journal*, XVI, 22 (March, 1946), which is reprinted in *Readings on the Economics of Taxation*, Vol. IX of the Series of Republished Articles on Economics by the American Economic Association, 1959, pp. 214–26. The distinction between direct and indirect taxes used in the English "Budget White Paper" is quite similar to ours. For a history of the problems of classification see "La Distinzione tra Imposte Dirette e Indirette," in *Quaderni dell' Associazione fra le Societá Italiane per Azione*, No. XXIII (Rome: 1957).

[3] I am not unaware of the many conflicts that this criterion fails to resolve. At times *income spent* has not yet been *realized;* in some cases *income spent* has not yet been appropriated to the final products of the process of production (consumer goods), etc. But what I consider important is the possibility of distributing the extensive and multiform taxes of the modern states into the two broad categories under discussion. Independent of the subsequent processes of the tax burden (and precisely in order to exclude them as a differentiating factor), it appears certain that in the various tax systems it is feasible always to distinguish between the tax, on the one hand, on the capacity to pay created in each period—that is, on the national product obtained, dividing it among the various participants therein (direct taxes, or taxation when income is realized)—and, on the other hand, taxes that fall on subsequent movements of that product or income (indirect taxes, or taxation when income is spent).

In this framework, taxes on consumption and on production are indirect, i.e., they are taxes on income when spent. For the latter, the tax liability is determined and the tax collected at the point where the goods or services are produced; for the former, the tax applies at the point, after the process of production is complete, when the goods or services are transferred to the consumer (or to distributional intermediaries).

Of course, in taxes on production the idea is implicit that the producer is merely a passive *de jure* taxpayer and that the actual *de facto* payer is the consumer, toward whom the tax law permits a forward shifting of the burden. This shifting occurs for all the various types of taxes arising at any of the many links in the distributional chain before goods reach the final consumer. At this point in the discussion, it is not necessary to consider the question of whether the tax is effectively shifted forward (either wholly or partially), as the law intends, for it does not depend on the law; it is a problem of differing market conditions and need not affect our definition of the essential nature of this tax.

A tax on the value of a kilo of cotton thread is normally a tax on production, intended definitely to fall on the final consumer of products made of this fiber (even though, in fact, the final consumer may not pay all or part of this tax); while a tax on the gross income of the manufacturer from the sale of thread (even though, in fact, the entire tax may be included in the price of cotton shirts, for example), is not a tax on production. The former tax is independent of the realization of income, while the latter (unless the contrary is clearly specified) is intended to fall on income.[4]

We indicated earlier that if the legally provided process of shifting the production tax does not occur, the purpose of the tax authorities is thwarted; nevertheless, we must consider the nature of this tax to be unchanged. This, of course, does not mean that we should ignore the repercussions of the tax. A system of production taxes whose burden systematically fell on the prices of productive factors and did not bear on income expenditures would be no more than a shadow of an indirect tax.[5] These important problems of tax policy, however, are not germane to the conceptual problems now under discussion.

We should now be able to ask whether indirect taxation consists exclusively of taxes on production and consumption. Where precise terminology has been worked out in great detail, as, for example, in Germany, attempts have been made to distinguish among three basic classes within the general category of indirect taxation (without taking customs taxes, discussed below, into account). On the one hand are sales taxes, the prototype of which is the tax on business volume (*Umsatzsteuer*); on the other hand are taxes on consumption and expenditures; and finally, there is an intermediate category of taxes on transactions (*Verkehrsteuern*). However, if it is difficult to distinguish a tax on business volume from a very complete system of specific taxes on consumption, since the first two categories overlap and mix and one or the other term may easily be applied to any specific tax one chooses, the confusion is compounded when the independent categories —probably first called "taxes on transactions" by Von Stein—are introduced. This category

[4]What in German terminology and that of other countries is called "taxes on the product" (*Ertragsteuern*) has nothing to do with our "production taxes." In fact, they are just the opposite, i.e., direct taxes, because they fall upon income as *realized* by the taxpayer (a subjective or personal tax), or simply because they are conceived of (independently of their personal distribution) by looking only at their functional distribution (as objective or *in re* taxes, or taxes in their own right on products). "Taxes on the product" often appear in the form of fixed payments for specific purposes (authorization to build or conduct a business, etc.) which also excludes them from our category of taxes on production (although perhaps they are in fact shifted to the final consumer). There are various authors who are in disagreement with this concept of fixed payments.

[5]In support of this, see a concluding paragraph in G. Schmölders, "The System of Consumption Taxes and Expenditures," in W. Gerloff and F. Neumark: *Handbuch der Finanzwissenschaft*, 2d ed. (1956). Spanish edition, *El Ateneo* (Buenos Aires: 1961), Vol. II, p. 628: "In this way, responsibility for the actual *shifting of the tax burden* is a matter of highest tax policy consideration; the will of the legislator is always to place the tax burden on the consumer, so that the attainment of shifting is a decisive factor in determining whether the tax achieves its purpose."

usually encompasses a diverse (and very heterogeneous) series of taxes, ranging from taxes on inheritances, stock exchange transactions, and the transfer of property titles to certain taxes on capital gains and taxes on corporate capital, etc.[6]

We shall not consider these taxes on transactions as taxes on production and consumption in the strictest sense, although taxes in this category are often simple levies on consumption. This obtains in particular where these taxes, unlike those on legal transactions, apply by extension to actual commerce (for example, taxes on transportation, communications, etc., and including customs levies). Normally, taxes on transportation are either direct—as, for example, taxes on the earnings of the transportation industry—or actually indirect taxes on the use or consumption of transportation (taxes on the use of public or private vehicles, etc.), in which case they fall at once into the group of taxes we are considering.

The final major category of indirect taxes, which are commonly grouped independently, consists of the customs taxes (which at times are not called taxes, but fees or duties). In addition to customs taxes, strictly speaking, there are other related payments, either as direct compensation for services (e.g., sanitary inspection, etc.), which are fees, or as certain levies additional to import duties or taxes, which in Latin American terminology are called "levies of equivalent effect" (*gravámenes de efectos equivalentes*).[7] Finally, there are nontax measures which are economically assimilable to taxes; e.g., manipulation of exchange rates, import quotas, etc.

Thus, import taxes (and the complementary

or supplementary measures just described, excluding fees, of course) may be grouped without difficulty with the indirect taxes which we are considering. Sometimes they are taxes on production, when they fall, for example, on raw materials, machinery, or semifinished or finished products, etc., which bear analogous internal production taxes; or they are consumption taxes when they are levied on specific imported consumer products which, when produced domestically, are subject to excise taxes.

For export taxes the case is not so clear (or nearly so important, despite their recent flourishing). In principle, some very special assumptions aside, these levies are not intended by the tax authorities to be shifted to the income expenditures of the foreign buyer. Nor is it possible, though the exporter may wish to do so, to shift the burden to the buyer. Viewed in this way, the export tax actually cuts into the income of the exporters (whether manufacturers or distributors) and falls outside our categories of production or consumption taxes. In a word, they are direct and not indirect taxes, a fact that is shown by their frequent use in developing countries as a substitute for the income tax, thereby eliminating the administrative difficulties of the income tax for the export sector. Notwithstanding this, and keeping in mind the customs parallel between export and import taxes, as well as their use for very important political and economic purposes in the underdeveloped countries (e.g., marketing boards for stabilizing the income of exporters),[8] we have decided to include them within the group of taxes with which we are concerned.

Since our interest in these taxes is only their special relationship to economic development and we are not concerned with their technical-administrative aspects, it is not necessary to differentiate and classify them further. Such refinements may be discussed in due course when the subject so requires.

[6]The most thorough attempt, perhaps, at an independent conception of "transactions taxes" was made by L. Mirre in the first edition of *Handbuch der Finanzwissenschaft* (1927), Book II, pp. 274-309. These taxes were defined as those falling upon the juridical changes in disposition or modification of a right. Most of the transactions taxes use assets as a measure of taxable capacity, but we have put that aside and taken only income into consideration.

[7]See United Nations, Economic and Social Council, *Customs and Other Burdens and Restrictions on Imports in the Latin American Countries and Their Levels of Incidence* (Caracas: 1961) (Memorandum presented in the 9th meeting of the sessions of the UN ECOSOC).

[8]See A. R. Prest, "The Fiscal Structure of Underdeveloped Countries," in *Colectânea de Estudos*, No. 12 (Lisbon: 1961), pp. 45 ff., which incidentally considers export taxes as indirect levies by including them in the broad grouping of customs taxes.

Nevertheless, looking forward to the technical and fiscal comments that may subsequently have to be made, it is appropriate to point out the more commonly used types of production and consumption taxes.[9]

In the first place, there is the general sales tax, which technically may take either of the following forms: (a) multiple stage or (b) single stage. In the first case, the tax (often called a "cascade tax") may reach all stages of manufacture and distribution, although most commonly it applies to only some of them. This is the turnover tax in English, or the *Umsatzsteur* in German terminology. Some hybrid forms of the multiple-stage tax, which attempt to eliminate its more undesirable effects, are the *double stage* (which taxes at only two levels) or those *on value added* (whose prototype is the French value added tax).

In respect to the single-stage tax, the point of its application may be either far removed from or close to the consumption stage. This tax is normally applied at the manufacturing level (the Canadian manufacturers' sales tax or the tax in Argentina), the wholesale level (Australia), or the retail sales level (the tax in some states in the United States).

The second large grouping of taxes on consumption consists of excise taxes, which, when generalized, can well form a system very similar to a general sales tax.

Consumption taxes may be established at the same three levels as the general sales tax; that is, at the manufacturer's (or importer's) level, as is the case in Uruguay and Mexico, the wholesale level, or the retail level.

The wide differences in proportional or variable rates in the types of taxes and the existence of specific taxes, along with ad valorem taxes, make further attempts at classification pointless.

TAXATION AND ECONOMIC DEVELOPMENT

According to the definitions given in the previous section, most indirect taxes in existing tax systems fall within the production and consumption tax categories. We have excluded only the more restricted of the transaction taxes.

Yet, even though we are considering so broad a range of taxation, it is only a partial picture, since we exclude direct taxes. Furthermore, taxation is only one of the instruments through which modern fiscal policy attains its ends. There are two others: public credit (which, together with the income from public assets and total tax collections, comprises the public revenue sector) and public expenditures. Neither of these lies within the purview of this paper. As a result of these limitations, any observations with respect to taxes on production and consumption are apt to suffer at times from the difficulties inherent in treating a subject in an isolated manner, when in reality it is but a part of a broader interrelated context.

Finally, fiscal policy in general and tax policy in particular are always subject to the contingencies of the national economic complex in which they operate. Structural and operational variations in each country are mirrored in its fiscal panorama. Consequently, it is impossible to think that assertions made in these matters are universally valid.[10]

[9]See John F. Due, "Administrative Criteria in the Establishment of Sales and Excise Tax Structures," as well as his *Government Finance, An Economic Analysis*, rev. ed. (Homewood, Ill.: Richard D. Irwin, 1959), especially Chaps. 18 and 19, and his *Sales Taxation* (Urbana: University of Illinois Press, 1957).

[10]This is a generally held opinion. See, for example, John H. Adler, *Recursos financieros y reales para el desarrollo* (Mexico: Center for Latin American Monetary Studies, 1961), p. 11. Differences between the developed and the developing countries have led many experts to design different fiscal policy aims and methods for growth, depending upon whether the country is underdeveloped or not. Among others, see Paul A. van Philips, *Public Finance and Less Developed Economy, with Special Reference to Latin America* (The Hague: 1957), who uses the term "activating finance" to designate the peculiar characteristics of an underdeveloped country, as compared to the term "functional finance" which is in vogue in the more advanced countries. Sharing this view is Raja J. Chelliah, *Fiscal Policy in Underdeveloped Countries, with Special Reference to India* (London: 1960), and very recently, Reuben E. Schlesinger, "Fiscal Policy Considerations for Underdeveloped Economies," *Kyklos*, No. 3 (1962), pp. 624–33. On the other side, not seeing any differences, are Walter Heller, "Fiscal Policy for Underdeveloped Economies," in *Taxes and*

With these warnings, and without the necessity of going into detail on the matter of economic development, it is evident that the general purpose of the tax system is to obtain as much revenue as is required for such development.

Confirming the famous Wagnerian law of the growth of state activities, the policy of development requires first of all that the means for carrying out its new functions be made available to the public sector. This raises two successive issues for the tax system: (a) to increase tax collection and (b) to ascertain the desirability of one tax compared to another for achieving this purpose.

But economic development is not the responsibility of public institutions alone, or at least not in the capitalistic economies to which our entire discussion is oriented. The private sector must also improve and grow in a process of development. In this respect, the role of taxation should be to remove the greatest possible number of barriers that block the way and at the same time positively to facilitate the growth of private production and consumption.[11]

We shall comment briefly on these two more general problems of taxation for economic development, with special reference to taxes on consumption and production.

The first problem is tied to another that has been the object of recent study. Especially since World War II, taxation has reached levels in some countries that had hitherto been considered unobtainable. The popular dictum of Colin Clark that the maximum limit for the total tax burden is 25 per cent of the national income, considering that figure to be the equilibrium point between the in-

flationary and deflationary effects of the tax pressures,[12] has merit less in establishing a fixed upper limit than in calling attention to the impossibility of indefinitely increasing the size of the tax burden.

It might be useful at this point to refer to the share of tax revenues in the national product from the standpoint of the Latin American countries. Table 9–1 contains estimates of the tax burden or fiscal pressure in a number of countries. Where possible, this figure has been divided by the net national product at market prices (although in some instances the data available required the use of other macroquantities). The total revenue figures used correspond to tax revenue of the central government exclusively. Local revenues and income from fees, services, and public assets have been excluded. The burden would be higher if items such as local taxes and the proceeds from the multiple exchange systems in various countries, which are not commonly included in the revenue budget, were taken into account. It would also be higher had data been available for including the income of certain state monopolies, whose income contains a high component of consumption taxes.[13]

In the light of these data, it does not seem risky to assume that there are no grave dan-

---

Fiscal Policy in Underdeveloped Countries (New York: United Nations, 1954), and S. and F. Andic, "Problems of Economic and Fiscal Policy in Underdeveloped Countries," in *Finanzarchiv*, Book 16, No. 3 (1956).

[11] These are the two basic points of view with respect to taxes and economic development as expressed today by most economists. What seems wrong to me, even admitting that sometimes the two purposes or policies—revenues and incentives—may clash, is to take a closed position in favor of one against the other. According to circumstances, they may have alternative importance, and almost always their joint utilization should be consistent with a more effective total result in development than the isolated use of one of them alone.

[12] Colin Clark, "The Danger Point in Taxes," *Harper's Magazine*, (December, 1950), pp. 67–69.

[13] Our figures do not differ much from those given for the same group of countries (except El Salvador) by J. H. Adler, *Recursos Financieros*, referring to practically the same period from 1953 to 1959. The singular position of Venezuela and the existence of two subgroups of countries, some with lower tax burdens (Argentina, Brazil, Colombia, and Mexico) and others with higher tax burdens (Chile, Costa Rica, Ecuador, El Salvador, Guatemala, Panama, Peru), remain the same with his data and ours. The greatest variation is in his average— 14.7 per cent—compared to the 10.7 per cent appearing in our table for 1959. However, he uses the gross national product, not the net as we do; he includes Venezuela; and his figures are very likely for total fiscal revenues and not just tax revenues.

The variability of the figures in this respect, depending on the sources used and the classes of revenues that actually enter into the computation, limit the validity of all of them and make comparisons practically impossible. By using domestic sources and including public revenues in the broad sense instead of only those yielded by taxes, R. Desai has prepared a table of tax burdens for Latin America, in which the figures differ from ours not only absolutely but in many cases relatively. It seemed useful to me to include this as Table 9–1 Bis.

TABLE 9–1: Tax Burdens

Countries and monetary units	1956	1957	1958	1959	1960	1961
Argentina (in millions of pesos)						
Net national product at market prices	161,473.00	206,415.00	285,462.00	535,565.00	701,006.00	—148,200.00—
Total tax revenues		13,359.20	19,884.30	41,632.70	50,605.90	
Tax burden (2:1)%		6.47	6.96	7.77	7.22	
Brazil (in thousands of millions of cruzeiros)						
Net national product at market prices	833.30	995.70	1,231.70	1,673.50	—153.34—	—232.19—
Total tax revenues		77.94	102.00	148.57		
Tax Burden (2:1)%		7.83	8.28	8.88		
Chile (in millions of escudos)						
Net national product at market prices	1,489.40	2,041.30	2,700.60	3,740.80	4,218.00	—764.10—
Total tax revenues		279.40	346.90	536.30	668.60	
Tax burden (2:1)%		13.69	12.84	14.34	15.85	
Colombia (in millions of pesos)						
Net national product at market prices	13,645.70	15,867.20	17,830.80	20,610.00	23,495.40	—2,204.10—
Total tax revenues			1,436.60	1,611.20	1,929.30	
Tax burden (2:1)%			8.06	7.82	8.21	
Costa Rica (in millions of colones)						
Net national product at market prices	1,996.30	2,156.30	2,309.20	2,406.30	2,570.00	—301.70—
Total tax revenues	233.20	271.60	290.90	304.70	307.20	
Tax burden (2:1)%	11.68	12.59	12.60	12.66	11.95	
Ecuador (in millions of sucres)						
Net national product at market prices	10,387.00	11,075.00	11,478.00	12,014.00	12,977.00	—1,426.00—
Total tax revenues		1,214.00	1,239.00	1,248.00	1,346.00	
Tax burden (2:1)%		10.96	10.79	10.39	10.37	
El Salvador (in millions of colones)						
Gross national product at market prices	1,142.80	1,218.20	1,249.90	1,226.70	148.20	
Total tax revenues	157.80	175.60	153.50	141.00		
Tax burden (2:1)%	13.81	14.41	12.28	11.49		
Guatemala (in millions of quetzales)						
Net national product at market prices	601.30	622.50	614.30	624.90	651.50	—80.40—
Total tax revenues		81.20	83.90	83.90	79.60	
Tax burden (2:1)%		13.04	13.66	13.43	12.22	
Honduras (in millions of lempiras)						
Net national product at market prices	605.50	647.30	675.80	—64.50—	—67.60—	
Total tax revenues	55.30	66.60				
Tax burden (2:1)%	9.13	10.29				
Mexico (in millions of pesos)						
Gross national product at market prices	94,000.00	103,000.00	114,000.00	122,000.00	134,400.00	—9,032.00—
Total tax revenues	7,546.70	7,417.90	8,502.20	9,093.00	8,427.00	
Tax burden (2:1)%	8.03	7.20	7.46	7.45	6.27	
Panama (in millions of balboas)						
Net national product at market prices	313.00	345.30	353.50	378.70	398.80	—47.10—
Total tax revenues	32.10	32.20	38.70	38.00	44.30	
Tax burden (2:1)%	10.26	9.32	10.95	10.03	11.11	
Peru (in millions of soles)						
Net national product at market prices	24,090.00	25,820.00	29,098.00	35,008.00		
Total tax revenues	3,868.20	4,134.60	3,986.90	4,775.70		
Tax burden (2:1)%	16.06	16.01	13.70	13.64		
Venezuela (in millions of bolivares)						
Net national product at market prices	16,237.00	18,582.00	20,333.00	21,915.00	21,445.00	—5,040.40—
Total tax revenues	3,100.00	5,428.20	4,765.30	5,156.10	4,906.80	
Tax burden (2:1)%	19.09	29.21	23.44	23.53	22.88	

SOURCES: United Nations, *Yearbook of National Accounts Statistics, 1961.* United Nations, *Statistical Yearbook, 1961.*

TABLE 9-1 Bis:* Latin American Countries: Government Revenues in Percentages of Estimated Net National Income, 1959[a]

Countries having a high level of fiscal collections		Countries having an average level of fiscal collections		Countries having a low level of fiscal collections	
Venezuela	27.0	Peru	19.5	Panama	15.0
Argentina	24.0	Chile	18.0	Mexico	14.0
Brazil	23.5	Costa Rica	16.0	Colombia	14.0
Ecuador	22.0	Guatemala	16.0	El Salvador	13.5
				Honduras	11.0
				Bolivia	7.0[b]

[a] Except Argentina (1960), Bolivia (1958), and Peru (1956).
[b] Percentage of the gross national product. Tax revenues in real terms increased around 50% between 1958 and 1961.

NOTES: Public revenues included all ordinary revenues—taxes, sales, charges, profits of public enterprises, etc.—of the national government and of local political subdivisions (except for Bolivia, Peru, and some Central American countries, where local revenues are of little importance). Some taxes collected by semi-official agencies and enterprises have not been included, to the extent that they do not appear in the available official statistics. The collections excluded for this reason may be of importance in some countries, Colombia, for example. Returns on capital have been excluded and so likewise have social security and retirement payments. The gross incomes from the social security systems are important in Chile (14% of national income) and Argentina (8%), and are only a little less in Brazil (6%), Ecuador (4%), and Mexico (3%). The net contribution of social security taxes, however, is much less than these gross levels, from which the Government's contributions and payments for the benefit of the private sector have been deducted.
*Table 2-1 of the paper by R. Desai, "Fiscal Capacity of Developing Economies," above. Included by courtesy of the author.

gers in making increased use of taxation in Latin America for collecting the resources necessary for economic development.

Increased tax revenues, however, are not as readily forthcoming in underdeveloped countries as in the more advanced ones. In the first place, there are the difficulties stemming from an administrative setup that is not always as efficient as could be desired. Also, in respect to direct taxes, one cannot ignore the possibility of political resistance to attempts to increase taxes by persons who would be affected by the changes. Similarly, it is not easy to increase indirect taxes because, as is generally recognized, for the majority of taxpayers per capita income is at a strict subsistence level or even lower. This observation, on which there is general agreement, should be kept in mind throughout this discussion. Whenever production and consumption taxes are endorsed as appropriate measures to raise revenue for development purposes, no increase is sought in the existing tax pressure that might further reduce income available for consumption; rather the purpose is to capture part of the increase in income due to development. This increase should permit an improvement in present living standards as well as (by forgoing the present enjoyment of part of it) a still greater improvement in the future.[14]

Finally—and we are not considering all the difficulties in increasing tax burdens in developing countries—a considerable part of the national product in many countries is not and cannot be easily monetized. Where this is the case, the treasury is powerless to act.

Despite the reservations just enumerated, the characteristically moderate significance of direct taxation in the majority of developing countries underlines the fact that indirect taxes must play an important role in producing the revenues needed for economic growth. This raises the second question: the desirability of using one tax or another for revenue purposes.

We shall not expound here the arguments

[14] It is felt, therefore, that growth in per capita income in an underdeveloped country also increases collections. This is consistent with H. C. Wallich and J. H. Adler, *Proyecciones económicas de las finanzas públicas; Un estudio experimental en El Salvador* (México: 1949), pp. 154–55, where they call this phenomenon the "organic flexibility" of the tax system. To the degree that these increases in income improve the standard of living and the tax yields, it is possible to obtain increases in collections through raising tax rates. The greater or lesser legal facility for varying these rates is called by the authors "administrative flexibility."

in favor of indirect taxes in general, and taxes on production and consumption in particular, as compared with direct taxes, because we shall have to review these arguments shortly when considering the various types of indirect taxes.

The fact is that there has been an accelerating growth in indirect taxation in recent years in nearly all countries. Thus, while collections under the postwar income tax in Great Britain are four times greater than prewar levels, the tax on tobacco has risen six or seven times, and the purchase tax, a type of single-stage general sales tax established in 1940, rapidly yielded as much as 50 per cent of the revenues from tobacco.[15] Similarly, in the underdeveloped countries of the Commonwealth, indirect taxes on exports, which had previously fallen into disuse because of free trade and the drop in world prices for raw materials, have been revived.[16] There are many similar Latin American illustrations, some of which we shall present subsequently.

Finally, it is curious to observe, as did William J. Fellner, that the industrial countries which are maintaining the highest growth rates during the current years (France, West Germany, and Japan) utilize tax systems based more heavily on indirect than direct taxes. Other countries, such as the United States and Sweden, which rely primarily on income taxes, have not enjoyed a comparable growth in recent years.[17]

As in our previous discussion about tax burdens in Latin America, it will be useful now to refer to the relative weight of direct and indirect taxes in the tax systems of these countries.

Using total collections of the central governments as a base, but excluding nontax revenues, fees, and proprietary income, the respective percentages of the two groups of indirect (export, customs, or internal) and direct taxes are shown in Table 9–2. As in Table 9–1, it is possible that some consumption taxes collected through state monopolies are not included in the figures. Also, revenues from the exchange rate differentials are, in general, not included. Finally, internal taxes may include not only specific taxes on production and consumption but also those which fall on wealth in the form of levies on transactions or transfers. With these imperfections, the data, of course, have value only as indexes, but they do serve to guide thinking.

The largest group of countries consists of those where the relative importance of indirect to direct taxes has tended to increase. A decline in the burden of indirect taxes is seen in only three countries—Peru, Guatemala, and El Salvador—but this decline is very slight.

Within these movements, indirect taxes occupy a more important position than direct taxes. The only exception is Colombia, where, with the singular development of the income tax, indirect taxes account for less than 50 per cent of total tax revenues.

To go on now to the relationships that exist within the framework of indirect taxes between production and consumption taxes on the one hand and customs taxes on the other, it is observed that in Mexico there is more or less a balance between these categories. Countries in which customs are more important than internal indirect taxes comprise the largest group.

To the earlier observations on increases in tax collections by indirect methods—and with due consideration for the problems of low consumption levels among large segments of the population in underdeveloped countries— certain other factors must be added, some of them technical in nature and others on which the possibility of strengthening this type of

---

[15]U. K. Hicks, "Les Impôts Indirects dans l'Economie Moderne," *Revue de Science et de Législation Financières* (October-December, 1952), p. 765.

[16]U. K. Hicks, "The Search for Revenue in Underdeveloped Countries," *Revue de Science et de Législation Financières* (January–April, 1952), p. 22; A. T. Prest, "The Fiscal Structure of Underdeveloped Countries," p. 43, indicates that Malaya obtained 35 per cent of its total revenues from export taxes, Ghana 33 per cent, and Ceylon 30 per cent.

[17]See Henry C. Wallich, "For Economic Growth— What Kind of Tax?" *New York Times*, September 6, 1962. Wallich observes, as is natural—and we completely agree—that this is inadequate proof: first, because the growth in these countries can be attributed to many causes; second, because among the underdeveloped countries whose growth is slower, there are tax systems strongly rooted in indirect taxes.

TABLE 9-2: Percentages of the Direct and Indirect Tax Burden (*Data in millions, of the monetary unit of each country*)

Country and taxes	1956	%	1957	%	1958	%	1959	%	1960	%	1961	%
Argentina												
Taxes on income and wealth	—	—	6,241.3	46.7	9,089.5	45.7	11,650.0	28.0	14,369.2	28.4	17,239.0	25.9
Customs taxes	—	—	1,042.7	7.8	1,422.7	7.2	2,400.0	5.8	21,400.0	42.3	24,500.0	36.8
Other indirect taxes	—	—	6,075.2	45.5	9,371.9	47.1	27,582.7	66.2	14,836.7	29.3	24,851.0	37.3
	—		13,359.2		19,884.3		41,632.7		50,605.9		66,590.0	
Brazil												
Taxes on income and wealth	—	—	32,023.8	41.1	37,351.4	36.6	54,773.2	36.9	51,871.0	33.8	88,166.2	38.0
Taxes on imports	—	—	2,763.6	3.5	12,925.5	12.7	19,113.8	12.9	24,943.0	16.3	24,300.0	10.5
Other indirect taxes	—	—	43,153.5	55.4	51,721.1	50.7	74,686.6	50.2	76,528.4	49.9	119,729.2	51.5
	—		77,940.9		101,998.0		148,573.6		153,342.4		232,195.4	
Chile												
Taxes on income	—	—	98.0	35.1	108.7	31.3	176.6	32.9	204.8	30.7	223.1	29.2
Taxes on wealth	—	—	12.9	4.6	24.3	7.0	28.9	5.4	37.0	5.5	43.0	5.6
Taxes on imports	—	—	53.4	19.1	52.9	15.3	89.5	16.7	137.5	20.6	154.0	20.2
Other indirect taxes	—	—	115.1	41.2	161.0	46.4	241.3	45.0	289.3	43.2	344.0	45.0
	—		279.4		346.9		536.3		668.6		764.1	
Colombia												
Taxes on income and wealth	—	—	—	—	762.3	53.1	947.1	58.8	1,111.9	57.6	1,178.7	53.5
Taxes on foreign trade	—	—	—	—	609.1	42.4	582.1	36.1	708.6	36.7	870.0	39.5
Other indirect taxes	—	—	—	—	65.2	4.5	82.0	5.1	108.8	5.7	155.4	7.0
	—		—		1,436.6		1,611.2		1,929.3		2,204.1	
Costa Rica												
Taxes on income and wealth	45.3	19.4	53.5	19.7	57.4	19.7	51.8	17.0	51.9	16.9	65.4	21.6
Taxes on exports	11.2	4.8	15.0	5.5	18.2	6.3	15.0	4.9	15.3	4.9	18.3	6.1
Taxes on imports	145.1	62.3	160.5	59.1	173.8	59.7	179.6	58.9	189.6	61.8	193.0	63.9
Other indirect taxes	31.6	13.5	42.6	15.7	41.5	14.3	58.3	19.2	50.4	16.4	25.0	8.4
	233.2		271.6		290.9		304.7		307.2		301.7	
Ecuador												
Taxes on income and wealth	—	—	182.0	15.0	218.0	17.6	200.0	16.0	220.0	16.3	240.0	16.8
Taxes on exports	—	—	98.0	8.0	87.0	7.0	90.0	7.2	108.0	8.0	151.0	10.6
Taxes on imports	—	—	478.0	39.4	492.0	39.7	498.0	39.9	549.0	40.8	524.0	36.7
Other indirect taxes	—	—	456.0	37.6	442.0	35.7	460.0	36.9	469.0	34.9	511.0	35.9
	—		1,214.0		1,239.0		1,248.0		1,346.0		1,426.0	
El Salvador												
Taxes on income and wealth	20.7	13.1	20.9	11.9	23.8	15.5	23.6	16.7	26.9	18.2	—	—
Taxes on imports	59.0	37.4	63.1	35.9	59.4	38.7	58.4	41.4	60.0	40.5	—	—
Taxes on exports	43.5	27.6	54.6	31.1	35.5	23.1	24.8	17.6	24.6	16.6	—	—
Other indirect taxes	34.6	21.9	37.0	21.1	34.8	22.7	34.2	24.3	36.7	24.7	—	—
	157.8		175.6		153.5		141.0		148.2		—	

TABLE 9–2: Percentages of the Direct and Indirect Tax Burden (Data in millions, of the monetary unit of each country)—Continued

Country and taxes	1956	%	1957	%	1958	%	1959	%	1960	%	1961	%
Guatemala												
Taxes on income and wealth	—	—	7.2	8.9	8.1	9.6	8.2	9.8	9.0	11.3	9.2	11.4
Taxes on imports	—	—	27.6	34.0	29.5	35.2	31.3	37.3	27.3	34.3	28.1	34.9
Taxes on exports	—	—	15.4	18.9	11.7	13.9	10.5	12.5	9.6	12.1	8.3	10.3
Other indirect taxes	—	—	31.0	38.2	34.6	41.3	33.9	40.4	33.7	42.3	34.8	43.4
	—		81.2		83.9		83.9		79.6		80.4	
Honduras												
Taxes on income and wealth	9.1	16.5	14.8	22.2	—	—	11.3	17.5	11.2	16.6	—	—
Taxes on imports	26.9	48.6	31.1	46.7	—	—	31.5	28.8	33.7	49.8	—	—
Taxes on exports	2.6	4.7	3.0	4.5	—	—	3.5	5.4	3.4	5.0	—	—
Other indirect taxes	16.7	30.2	17.7	26.6	—	—	18.2	28.3	19.3	28.6	—	—
	55.3		66.6		—		64.5		67.6		—	
Mexico												
Taxes on income and wealth	2,587.0	34.3	2,779.5	37.5	2,808.0	33.0	3,071.3	33.8	3,110.0	36.9	3,600.0	39.9
Taxes on imports	1,190.2	15.8	1,374.1	15.2	1,584.9	18.6	1,747.7	19.2	1,420.0	16.9	1,700.0	18.8
Taxes on exports	1,375.6	18.2	1,131.8	15.3	1,116.6	13.2	1,178.5	12.9	890.0	10.6	550.0	6.1
Taxes on the conduct of business	727.5	9.6	774.9	10.4	887.5	10.4	977.5	10.8	1,080.0	12.8	1,122.0	12.4
Other indirect taxes	1,666.4	22.1	1,600.0	21.6	2,105.2	24.8	2,117.9	23.3	1,927.0	22.8	2,060.0	22.8
	7,546.7		7,417.9		8,502.2		9,092.9		8,427.0		9,032.0	
Panama												
Taxes on income and wealth	12.2	38.0	10.1	31.4	14.5	37.5	10.6	27.9	13.7	30.9	47.1	100.0
Customs taxes	13.2	41.1	14.1	46.9	16.8	43.4	18.1	47.6	19.6	44.2	—	—
Other indirect taxes	6.7	20.9	7.0	21.7	7.4	19.1	9.3	24.5	11.0	24.9	—	—
	32.1		32.2		38.7		38.0		44.3		47.1	
Peru												
Personal income taxes	566.4	14.6	630.2	15.2	637.7	16.0	797.9	16.7	—	—	—	—
Corporate income taxes	1,301.1	33.6	1,374.1	33.2	1,412.7	35.4	1,759.6	36.8	—	—	—	—
Taxes on imports	744.7	19.3	841.4	20.3	655.4	16.4	575.2	12.1	—	—	—	—
Taxes on exports	443.4	11.5	477.8	11.6	306.0	7.8	23.5	0.5	—	—	—	—
Other indirect taxes	812.5	21.0	811.1	19.7	975.1	24.4	1,619.5	33.9	—	—	—	—
	3,868.1		4,134.6		3,986.9		4,775.7		—		—	
Venezuela												
Direct taxes on petroleum and mining corporations	687.5	22.2	883.1	16.3	1,045.8	21.9	1,604.6	31.1	1,385.3	28.2	1,349.0	26.8
Other direct taxes on income and wealth	226.7	7.3	234.2	4.3	264.1	5.5	426.4	8.3	434.9	8.9	637.0	12.6
Petroleum royalties	1,103.6	35.6	3,104.2	57.2	1,870.0	39.2	1,565.9	30.4	1,519.6	31.0	1,433.2	28.4
Taxes on imports	598.8	19.3	641.8	11.8	779.7	16.4	750.1	14.5	721.1	14.7	762.0	15.1
Taxes on exports	159.3	5.1	170.4	3.2	360.4	7.6	379.1	7.2	418.6	8.5	362.0	7.2
Other indirect taxes	324.1	10.5	394.5	7.2	445.2	9.4	440.2	8.5	427.3	8.7	497.0	9.9
	3,100.0		5,428.2		4,765.2		5,166.3		4,906.8		5,040.4	

SOURCE: United Nations, *Statistical Yearbook, 1961*.

tax depends to an important extent. Since indirect taxes in general fall upon items consumed by the taxpayer, the elasticity of demand for the taxed products is a basic factor. Other circumstances being equal, the greater the inelasticity of the demand, the greater the "income effect" of the tax—to use a term that is currently finding wide acceptance. The opposite is true of the income elasticity: the greater the elasticity, the more tax revenues will increase as the capacity to pay increases. Both of these factors clearly point to taxes on luxury consumption items which, along with other factors relating to the redistribution of income, stand out as cardinal elements of efficient and rational indirect taxation. We cannot overlook, however, that the tax yield also depends on the total amount spent on the taxed commodity. In this respect, however, taxes on luxury consumption cannot be as effective as taxes on mass consumption, which in turn may be objectionable for other reasons.

We shall now take up the second of the problems referred to above, that is, the role of taxation in the growth of the private sector.

This involves the question of tax incentives. As stated above, in a broad sense incentives have two aspects, the first of which is usually overlooked. From the *negative* side, certain taxes may cause burdens of an indirect nature (visits, inspections, presentation of documents, accounting data, etc.), which constitute an additional difficulty in the way of the progress of private production and one that a tax policy designed for development purposes should seek to avoid. However, the *positive* aspect of the incentives, that is, differentiating the tax burden in order to favor sectors or industries that are of special significance to development, or in some other way decreasing costs, is the more important feature and the one that can yield greater results.

With respect to taxes on production and consumption, the *negative* aspects are usually missing, and this is one of their advantages. As for the *positive* incentives, their immediate action in the direction of orienting or facilitating or otherwise helping the productive

processes is not ordinarily so intense as the impact that could be exercised by direct taxation. But there are forms of incentives— especially customs taxes—which provide adequate instruments for policies of this sort. In connection with the level of consumption, and consequently the level of savings as well, the impact of taxes of this kind may be much more substantial.

Therefore, it is necessary to examine the principal characteristics of the taxes on production and consumption, insofar as these are reflected in and have an influence on the entire body of private business. As already indicated, the advantages and disadvantages of indirect taxes, as compared to direct taxes, will be discussed. Consideration will be given to matters of both an economic and administrative nature as well as to the specific influence of these taxes on important problems of the national economy, such as the distribution of resources and income, incentives to work and to save, etc.

In presenting the subject, it has been considered best to separate the internal from the external taxes on production and consumption, although this may require a certain amount of repetition. Organization of the material by taxes, rather than by problems, has seemed simplest.

INTERNAL TAXES ON PRODUCTION AND CONSUMPTION AND ECONOMIC DEVELOPMENT

A detailed examination of these taxes can be made within the framework indicated, separating the administrative and the fiscal-economic aspects.

While the problems of tax administration are outside the scope of our discussion, it is nevertheless important to mention some of the essential points in passing.

There is practically general agreement that there are fewer difficulties in the administration of production and consumption taxes than in that of direct taxes. When the technical or administrative proficiency is low, as it is in the majority of less developed nations, without doubt an increased volume of revenues can be obtained at a lower cost by increasing indirect taxes rather than by tightening up on direct taxes.

Without going into great detail,[18] the operational simplicity of taxes on production and sales is one reason for preferring them as a means of obtaining revenues to finance the costs of development.

From the development standpoint, the first and most fundamental economic-financial issue regarding production and consumption taxes is their impact on the allocation of productive resources.

Because of the different effects on the allocation of resources resulting from a tax on income or a tax on consumption, under classical fiscal theories the latter was considered anathema, a view which remained in force until the modern discussion and re-examination of the problem. We shall not summarize this discussion here,[19] but instead shall simply examine its conclusions.

The well-known classical argument is that since consumption taxes do, and direct taxes do not, alter the system of relative prices, different results will flow from the collection of *an equal amount of revenue* by either. It is argued that indirect taxes will result in a loss of consumer welfare, because of a harmful alteration in the allocation of resources, a situation that will not occur with the income tax.

It is also well known that this line of reasoning rests upon a number of accepted implicit and explicit conditions. In the first place, the argument is undone if it can be shown that direct taxes also alter relative prices. As U. K. Hicks observes,[20] Today's direct tax rates reach such heights that they must necessarily influence the supply of labor and thus may alter the relative prices of the

final products through this avenue. This, of course, does not prove that the effects of consumption taxes on the allocation of resources are better than those of direct taxes, which may also alter prices, but the a priori condemnation of the former is no longer so cogent.

In the second place, the classical theory assumes that the distribution of resources prior to taxes is optimum. However, in the world of today, where marginal costs and prices are not always equal, an optimum allocation cannot be taken for granted. As shown by M. Friedman, consumption taxes can be utilized to discriminate against products where allocation is optimum (production under the competitive system), as opposed to situations where it is not optimum (the monopoly or oligopoly situation), thus forcing, via transfer of factors from the former to the latter, a more approximately optimum redistribution of resources. In such circumstances, a direct tax which does not have a reallocative effect is worse than an excise tax. Further, if there is an optimum allocation to begin with, analysis of the impact of the income tax would necessarily have to be based not simply on the general proportional levy often utilized in theoretical models but upon the actual manner of applying the tax in the various countries (progressive scale, incomplete incidence for all types of goods, etc.). Such an analysis might eliminate the presumption in favor of the direct tax.[21]

In the third place, as is commonly the case in discussions of welfare problems, the arguments both for and against the classical theory assume a fixed level of resources upon which the production possibility curve is constructed; that is, one begins with a position of full employment of the country's resources, and all equilibrium positions must move along this curve, because all points outside it are technically ruled out, while all inside imply less than full utilization of resources. The more realistic assumption for the underdeveloped

[18]For this, reference is made especially to John F. Due, "Administrative Criteria."

[19]The well-known article of David Walter, "The Direct-Indirect Tax Problem: Fifteen Years of Controversy," *Public Finance*, X, 2 (1955), 153–76, provides an excellent synthesis.

[20]U. K. Hicks, "Les Impôts Indirects," p. 767.

[21]M. Friedman, "Welfare Effects of an Income Tax and an Excise Tax," reprinted in *Essays on Positive Economics* (Chicago: 1953), pp. 112–13.

countries is that not all factors are being utilized. Where this is the case, it is necessary to take into account the fact that any allocative changes may not only imply a movement along the original curve but also, assuming better utilization of existing resources, a possible shift of this curve to the right. Of course, the possibility of a shift of the curve to the left cannot be excluded, as a result of a decreased utilization of resources. Because of the many changing circumstances, such as the complementarity of resources, it appears that this point of view does not permit general conclusions either in favor of or against the use of consumption taxes in underdeveloped countries.[22]

Other things being equal, reallocation effects depend, as is known, upon the elasticities of supply and demand, decreasing or increasing in direct ratio thereto. This leads us to offer an example of some possible conflicting effects of a tax according to the varying purposes sought. Thus, admitting the possible desirability of a consumption tax which might induce approximately optimum resource distribution, it is no less certain that such a tax would fall upon goods which are competitively produced. Now from the standpoint of higher revenue collections, and also in order to attain a better distribution of income and to reduce tax regressivity, it is desirable to tax luxury articles, considering the generally high inelasticity of the demand for them. But, since to a great extent this type of goods is produced under other than freely competitive conditions, a tax levy on them would not be conducive to improving the allocation of resources. In other words, some goals are incompatible with others.

The principles thus far established for consumption taxes extend to a general sales tax

as well. If this tax is really general, if it is applied without discrimination to all final products, and if it is entirely shifted to consumers, its impact on resource allocation will be nil. This conclusion is generally accepted today.

However, this conclusion might be invalidated both theoretically and empirically when tested against the inclusiveness of the actual base of the tax. If it is admitted that indirect taxes always exclude a final important product —that is, leisure—then the general sales tax is not complete, and there is a discrimination in favor of certain goods that will lead to a reallocation of resources. It is difficult to conceive of a genuinely general sales tax. That is to say, these taxes will always induce some changes in the structure of the utilization of the factors of production.

Accepting this view, it is clear that there are inherent difficulties in the scope of the tax burden in any efforts to utilize a general or selective tax on consumption for attaining an approximately optimum allocation of resources where this does not already exist. There is always room for discrimination, by doing away with uniform rates, against those productive sectors from which resources ought to flow; but, apart from the practical difficulties of selection in a world where competition or its absence can mix in quite varied proportions, it must be taken into account that when independent discriminations occur, deriving from the tax on productive factors or from the multiple nature of the tax, there may be a combination of effects making it impossible to develop a coherent policy.

Problems arise more commonly with a general than with a selective consumption tax. Among these is the question of a tax on productive goods, which only with difficulty can be excluded from a tax of a general nature. Their inclusion implies discrimination against goods in whose production process there is a higher ratio of capital investment per unit cost, and the resulting alteration of relative prices will create new possibilities for the inadequate reallocation of productive resources.

[22]To the extent that the usual lack of full employment of resources in a developing economy is attributable to a lack of complementarity of resources, and there is no reason to believe that the existing utilization of resources will improve this complementarity, it is not irrational to lean toward neutral consequences in the growth of resource utilization owing to redistribution. Nonetheless, I do not believe that it is easy to offer conclusive proof for excluding an eventual improvement in resource utilization.

Moreover, if finding a relationship between capital intensive methods of production and noncompetitive markets is plausible, and indeed this does not seem difficult, there is also an additional argument—for reasons of improving the allocation of resources—for not burdening productive goods with special consumption taxes. In fact, in view of this relationship, reliance on a tax on capital goods would never solve a problem of nonoptimum allocation, because it would discriminate precisely against noncompetitive production processes.

Passing now to the principal impact of production and consumption taxes on the economic variables, other than resource allocation, that influence development, it is important to stress at the beginning that the conclusions which can be reasonably established with some generality are not very relevant.

The problems concerned here of the possible alternative uses of indirect instead of direct taxes have been more than fully discussed elsewhere. But, except for situations presupposing a high level of abstraction, unrelated to the real situation of these taxes, the results of these discussions have been meager.

The most important point about production and consumption taxes as they affect final products is that their burdens are distributed according to income expenditures and that savings are therefore exempt. A privilege (or right) of this type, depending on the position taken in respect to the well-known discussion of the multiple taxation of savings, does not require detailed argument in principle or fact in support of its usefulness for development. Anything that increases the potential productive means of a society is desirable for that society's economic growth. Together with the immediate exemption of savings and the favorable effects on increased accumulation of savings, there is the negative effect of the tax as it falls on consumption of these accumulated savings. Thus, indirect taxes do not so much provide an incentive to saving as a barrier to its disappearance.

To the degree that indirect taxes fall with comparatively more force on lower incomes, for which the marginal propensity to consume is higher than for larger incomes, the result is a greater reduction in real consumption.[23] This presents one of the inconsistencies of taxation to which we have frequently alluded. While the tax on mass consumption may be useful for the formation of savings, it is inadvisable when the matter of equity is considered.

The stimulation of savings through indirect taxation is, of course, only one aspect of the entire process of capitalization upon which development ultimately depends. It is as important as generating savings to see that investment flows into goods that will advance this purpose. That is, it is important that the funds released from consumption be directed to investment of genuine interest to economic growth and away from irrelevant investment such as land speculation or exportation to other countries.

Seen in this perspective, the effects of production and consumption taxes are only relative. Their influence may be much greater in respect to their neutrality for investments than in the positive inducements they offer. Once again it is important to mention the tax on capital goods—this time, however, not in terms of allocative effects, but in terms of its direct influence in increasing prices for these goods. Such increases lead in varying degrees to changes in the structure of production in favor of the more direct processes at the expense of capital intensive methods. This necessarily means a decline in the productivity of the resources and therefore a real obstacle to development. As already indicated, this signifies only that there will be harmful effects if capital goods are not exempted from the tax on production and consumption, although exemption itself is not a positive inducement to capitalization.

In general, the tax discrimination that can be achieved through direct taxation for stimulating investment is not unfeasible through

[23]See Challis A. Hall, Jr., *Fiscal Policy for Stable Growth* (New York: Holt, Rinehart & Winston, 1960), p. 184.

production and consumption taxes. Yet, while the tax on entrepreneurial investments, either individual or corporate, can be directly reduced in sectors capable of promoting growth, here the most that can be achieved is to establish differences in costs for certain productive factors which, not being specific, may be generally utilized in the productive processes. Nonetheless, customs taxes, to which we shall refer later, offer certain advantages in this respect.

After these observations about savings and investment, some comments are necessary about the effect of these production and consumption taxes on the supply of labor, which is an important factor in economic development. Of course, it is impossible here to go into a complete discussion of this question or to establish rules of indisputable value.

It is generally agreed today, as pointed out by Nicholas Kaldor,[24] that the impact of a tax on the labor supply depends upon two types of reactions: one is the "income effect" of the tax through which a new tax creates an incentive toward increased work effort by the taxpayer to recoup his pretax level of income; the second is the "substitution effect" through which it becomes less attractive for the taxpayer to forgo leisure for additional work, given the diminished after-tax rewards from the latter.

While the direct tax, which falls upon increments of the taxpayer's income, alters the relationship for the taxpayer between leisure and work effort which would prevail in a tax free world, by discriminating against the latter, the consumption tax changes this relationship only if the increase in income is spent, but not if it is saved. Thus, the indirect tax can stimulate work effort (where its purpose is savings) by not imposing a penalty, which is inescapable under the income tax, whatever the taxpayer's purpose, upon increased effort. In short, if the income effect is strong and the taxpayer's rate of substitution between work and leisure is not inclined too

much toward the latter, the consumption tax will be neutral and the work effort will increase. The final outcome, it is clear, will depend upon the combination of these two effects.

It is interesting to note the case observed in Guatemala—whose experience can probably be generalized to other countries in Latin America—where the Indian population shows a strong preference for leisure, once the minimum subsistence level is reached. When this level is reduced, the income effect is so strong that the Indian will work to regain his former position, but scarcely has this been done when the tendency toward leisure again prevails. Thus, it is currently believed that if human and fiscal equity considerations could be ignored, it might be desirable to levy indirect taxes on the basic consumption items of this group, thus compelling people to work more and then providing certain important but neglected consumption (education, hygiene, etc.) free of charge through public services.[25]

The absence of discrimination against saving, which we have noted as an estimable aspect of indirect taxes, can induce increases in work effort in other ways. For example, suppose that tax levels will decline in the future (a hypothesis which is not very realistic but necessary for the sake of argument). This would result in an inducement to substitute future for present consumption, since the latter is more expensive in terms of work effort. With an income tax, which falls as much on consumption as on savings, the only way of effecting this substitution is working less at present and more in the future. With a consumption tax, however, under which savings are tax free, there is no reason to diminish work effort.

[24]Nicholas Kaldor, *An Expenditure Tax* (London: Macmillan, 1955), p. 130.

[25]See J. H. Adler, R. E. Schlesinger, and E. C. Olson, *Las finanzas públicas y el desarrollo económico de Guatemala* (México: 1952), p. 253. Analogous verbal reference to this has been made with respect to Bolivia to the author of this paper. For a statement of this principle with respect to the African countries, see Nicholas Kaldor, "The Role of Taxation in Economic Development" (Santiago, Chile: December, 1962) (a paper presented at the Conference on Fiscal Policy and Economic Development), pp. 4, 5.

On the other hand, if we discriminate in favor of work through measures designed to fall directly on leisure, we may bring about an increase in work effort. That is, if we tax products highly complementary to leisure through selective taxes on consumption, while exempting (or even subsidizing) rival products, it is possible to obtain favorable effects on work.[26]

The point of view adopted concerning the repercussions of the indirect tax can significantly alter the modest conclusions which have thus far been put forward. If, as Rolph, Break,[27] and others maintain, the consumption tax results in a reduction of factor income, the differences with direct taxes are much less, and both types of tax will affect labor supply in approximately the same way, so that the disincentive effects on labor will generally prevail, except in very special cases.

Let us now pass to some other effects of production and consumption taxes which, although taking us somewhat far afield from problems of development, should be noted.

The question here is the distribution of the tax burden. Consistent with the traditional view of the impact of indirect taxes, the tax —as we have acknowledged from the beginning of this paper—is shifted forward toward the consumer, with a consequent increase in the price of the taxed commodities. The burden, then, is proportional to the income spent on each good, or if a general sales tax is assumed, to total consumption.

The part of the tax which is not eventually shifted forward falls on productive factors or profits, and it is impossible to provide universal principles as to their ultimate distribution, since this depends upon the structure of the markets of those factors, etc.

This conclusion about the lack of uniformity between the distribution of the burden and the level of the taxpayers' income is, of course, imperative when the backward shift-ing of the tax is viewed as the general rule instead of the exception.[28]

When one considers the multiple effects of a tax on changes in prices and income, it is clear that the whole story of the distribution of the tax burden cannot be told by reference to its forward or backward shifting. A complete theory of tax incidence would also require that the compensatory effects of government expenditures for public services be taken into account as well as the additional influence exerted through the price system by public sector demand.

Since we cannot look into these complex issues, it will suffice here merely to give some conclusions, whose validity is limited by the simplicity of the assumptions on which they rest.

In the first place, the possible heterogeneity of tax rates, the effects of pyramiding, and the certainty that the shifting forward can be neither universal nor identical for all the various consumption taxes, etc., make the principle that indirect tax burdens are proportional to consumption expenditures merely approximate. Even excluding, for one reason or another, all the disturbing incidence effects that can be assumed, the discriminatory aspects inherent in the varying relative weight of consumption at different income levels always remains.

Leaving this side of the problem for the moment, several others, which are in many ways related to it and which raise other discriminatory aspects of these taxes, must be mentioned. To illustrate these, it is sufficient to cite differences in family size, the preferences and the ability of certain population sectors to consume articles that can be included only with difficulty in even the most general taxes (as in the case of services), the

---

[26] See R. A. Musgrave, *The Theory of Public Finance* (New York: McGraw-Hill, Inc., 1959), p. 152.

[27] Earl R. Rolph and G. F. Break, *Public Finance* (New York: Ronald Press, 1961).

[28] Taking this position that we would call dissenting, already mentioned in the text and the preceding note, are the following, among others: Earl R. Rolph, *The Theory of Fiscal Economics* (Berkeley: 1954), and G. F. Break, "Excise Tax Burdens and Benefits," *American Economic Review*, Vol. XLIV, (September, 1954), pp. 577–94. The original idea was expressed by H. G. Brown in "The Incidence of a General Output or a General Sales Tax," *Journal of Political Economy*, Vol. XLII (April, 1939), pp. 254–62.

TABLE 9–3: Tax Burden, by Quartiles* (*Taxes as a percentage of income*)[1]

Quartiles	Argentina	Bolivia	Brazil	Chile	Colombia	Ecuador	Paraguay	Peru	Venezuela
0–25	11.1	5.2	11.5	13.4	4.5	13.6	7.3	5.4	7.0
25–50	20.3	12.1	22.0	29.5	12.0	29.5	15.3	12.3	16.5
50–75	8.8	6.2	9.7	14.3	7.7	14.4	7.1	6.6	8.9
75–100	10.9	4.0	8.3	9.6	9.1	8.2	11.3	9.2	35.0
Total	11.9	5.1	9.7	11.9	8.8	12.2	10.5	8.7	26.8

*R. A. Musgrave, *The Distribution of Tax Burdens in South America* (Buenos Aires: 1961), p. 9.

[1]Assuming a distribution of income similar to that in Venezuela.

existence of persons who have fixed minimum incomes (annuities or pensions), etc.

The classic argument about the inequitable distribution of indirect tax burdens rests on their regressivity—without excluding other reasons—because of the variations in the propensity to consume according to the income level. This regressivity is especially reinforced when food and other basic consumption goods are also taxed. This is the reason why these commodities are commonly exempted from tax, and certain corrective measures are sought to make the system more progressive by discriminating against luxury items.

Without going into further detail in respect to these issues, which are very well known, attention must be called, nevertheless, to the substantial empirical uncertainties which generally underlie almost all judgments on regressivity. Thus, it is worth while to mention some studies on this subject conducted in respect to the general sales tax in various states in the United States, from which more refined conclusions than those generally accepted can be drawn.[29] According to the study by D. G. Davies, the tax is regressive whether or not food products are included and whether gross or net income is considered. The elimination of taxes on food eliminates regressivity for the middle income levels but not for the lower incomes. When the concept of "disposable income" (see the preceding

footnote) is used and food items are excluded, the tax is progressive for all income levels except one (between $7,500 and $10,000 per year), and progressivity still holds for incomes in excess of $6,000, even when food items are included. Whatever the absolute value of these results, they are mentioned here as an indication of the caution required in considering conclusions in this area which do not rest upon a sound statistical test.

To complete our consideration of this point, we should also mention R. A. Musgrave's study on the distribution of tax burdens in ten Latin American countries.[30] The results (upon the technical bases of which we shall not comment) are as interesting as they are probably little known. Thus it seemed useful to us to reproduce one of his tables in this paper, demonstrating the regressivity of taxes in various countries. An examination of the figures in Table 9–3, as Musgrave points out, "partially confirm[s] the belief that the incidence of taxation in South America is regressive in the lower income groups. . . . All the countries show progression from the first to the second quartile, and—this being a rather unexpected characteristic—regression from the second to the third quartile. In most cases, regression continues from the third to the fourth quartile, but in some cases there is progression."

In the following section of this paper we shall see that the unexpected regressivity found by Musgrave in going from the second

[29]See David G. Davies, "An Empirical Text of Sales Tax Regressivity," *Journal of Political Economy*, Vol. LXVII (February–December, 1959), pp. 72–78. The concept of "disposable income" used by this author is equal to net income in money, plus other types of money revenues, plus (assets sold and liabilities acquired), minus (assets acquired plus liabilities canceled); that is to say, the consumption of the taxpayer.

[30]See R. A. Musgrave, "The Distribution of Tax Burdens in South America," in OAS/IDB/ECLA Joint Tax Program, *Problems of Tax Administration in Latin America*, The Johns Hopkins Press (forthcoming).

to the third quartile coincides with conclusions reached by economists in special studies of the burden of customs taxes in El Salvador and Guatemala. Although the data do not indicate whether the income brackets used correspond precisely in each of these studies, the middle income levels, which, according to the latter studies, bear the greatest burden of customs taxes, must coincide within certain limits with those covered by the quartiles used by Musgrave.

CUSTOMS TAXES AND ECONOMIC DEVELOPMENT

It is now necessary to turn to customs taxes and their likely favorable or unfavorable impact on the economic development process. As was indicated at the beginning of this paper, from the fiscal standpoint an import tax is very different from an export tax. They have, however, a common dual nature: they are connected, on the one hand, with the national treasury as tax instruments and, on the other, with international trade as protective measures. These twin or double components of taxes on external production or consumption can combine in very different proportions and can even oppose or exclude each other. Furthermore, in directly affecting the exchange of goods and services between countries, they end up by bearing upon the functioning, if they continue long enough, of the internal structure of the national economy. Without overlooking their revenue or fiscal aspects, when these taxes are placed in the context of the problems of economic development, the importance of their impact on the external and internal aspect of the economy is manifest; and thus it is necessary to delve into their consequences, with special reference to the theory of international trade. Comment will be made first on import taxes, and then there will be a brief reference to export taxes.

There are two lines of thinking that serve as a basis for making judgments on the possible effects on development of import taxes

or duties, or for that matter of any other type of policy to restrict commerce.

The first, resting upon the classical or neo-classical doctrine of foreign trade—the theory of comparative costs—advocates the desirability, both static and dynamic, of free trade and rejects protectionism. Protection, through tariffs or other types of restrictions, generates a twofold welfare cost from the standpoint of the distribution of resources. On the one hand, it reduces total consumption and consumer satisfaction. On the other, it increases national production at the expense of imports, which substitution creates additional costs.

In a welfare economics context, a restrictive commercial policy would make sense only in the situation where the country had monopoly power of demand or supply in the international market. In those cases, since the economic units do not have monopoly power individually, the equilibrium point reached in the international market would not be the same as when a country exercised its monopoly power or made all the decisions.

This classical theory is static and is therefore considered inadequate for dealing with dynamic problems of development. Specialization implies only a movement along the production possibility curve, where resources and techniques are held constant.

In meeting this objection, the present-day adherents to this approach underline that Adam Smith already saw that foreign trade could be a dynamic force when widened markets increased the level of national production.[31] This idea was further developed by John Stuart Mill,[32] who distinguished between the direct and indirect benefits of foreign commerce. With these precedents, what Myint[33] calls the "theory of productivity" of foreign commerce contributes to development, as Gottfried Haberler[34] points out, not only through the advantages of a better realloca-

[31] Adam Smith, *The Wealth of Nations*, Vol. I, Cannan ed., p. 413.
[32] John Stuart Mill, *Principles*, Ashley ed., p. 581.
[33] H. Myint, "The 'Classical Theory' of International Trade and the Underdeveloped Countries," *Economic Journal* (June, 1958), p. 317.
[34] G. Haberler, *International Trade and Economic Development* (Cairo: National Bank of Egypt, 1959).

tion of resources but also through increasing the productive capacity in the underdeveloped countries. In addition to the static benefits of displacement along the production possibility curve, there is a dynamic improvement through a shift of the curve to the right. Thus a possibility reappears, which we pointed out above when discussing the problems of resource redistribution in internal taxes on production and consumption.

Thus, free trade becomes the most desirable commercial policy for all countries, although this general proposition is advanced by modern authors with more reservations than the classic, after having carefully examined possible exceptions to the general rule, perhaps in order to take into account the strong protectionist trend that has arisen, especially in the economic thinking of the underdeveloped countries.

Protectionism can be justified from the point of view of the industrial sector in the following cases.

First, for industries with possibilities of future expansion and reduction of costs, since in these cases the customs tax permits the developing country to engage in a production where it can enjoy comparative advantages. There is a sacrifice over the short run which, however, can be offset by long-run gains.

This is the question of the old "infant industry" protectionist argument, which Sir James Stewart developed after it was first formulated by Friedrich List. In order for a policy of customs protection for incipient or "infant industries" to be successful, it must be limited, transitory, and at an optimum level.[35]

Because it is based upon differential effects,

protection will be most effective when it is limited to a few products. Frequently protection tends to become a permanent feature instead of being terminated when an industry no longer requires it or when the industry has demonstrated its inability to survive without this artificial help. Finally, while it is difficult to determine the optimum level of protection in a situation of equilibrium in which prices are adjusted to marginal costs and production factors are remunerated according to their productivity, it is even more difficult in the underdeveloped countries because of the absence of competitive markets, the lack of mobility of the factors of production, and the complexity of the measures for controlling foreign trade.

In any case, the hoped-for advantages depend on the size of the market, and while protection assures this market to domestic industry, the market may be too small to stimulate the desired effects. From the point of view of the Latin American countries as a whole, this raises the problem of overcoming the limited size of their markets. The co-ordination of their industrial policies and their ultimate economic integration, which have already been initiated, are important steps in the solution of this problem.

Protection may be justified for a second class of industries, namely, those which cannot compete internationally but which nevertheless can stimulate development in other sectors. A modern theory of development has been devised along these lines,[36] according to which protection should be given to productive activities which have a substantial backward and forward linkage in the industrial process. Thus, they act to stimulate investment in other interdependent sectors through the backward linkage effects of the purchase of raw materials and the forward linkage effects of sales of final products.

According to the studies of Chenery and Watanabe on the degree of interdependence

---

[35]Two fundamental themes on the limitation and temporary aspect of protection are found in List. These are consistent with recommendations of previous authors such as Yarronton and Arthur Dobbs, who leave no doubt about the "infant" or incipient nature of the industries to protect. The former, in fact, limits protection to a period of seven years; the latter believes that these advantages should be given only for the purpose of stimulating infant manufacturing industries and should not be continued if, in spite of these advantages, they do not grow. A. Yarronton, *England's Improvement by Sea and Land, to Outdo the Dutch without Fighting, to Pay Debts without Money, to Set at Work all the Poor of England* (1677, 1681). A. Dobbs, *An Essay on the*

Trade and Improvement of Ireland (1739), cited by J. A. Schumpeter in *History of Economic Analysis* (New York: Oxford University Press, 1955), p. 349.

[36]A. Hirschman, *The Strategy of Economic Development* (New York: Yale University Press, 1958).

of the various economic sectors in Italy, Japan, and the United States, the final production of primary products and the manufacture of intermediate products are at the opposite and extreme ends of the scale. For the former, the index of forward and backward linkage is very low, while for the latter the index is very high in both directions, being highest in the case of iron and steel. In the center of the scale is the intermediate production of primary goods, with a high degree of forward linkage and a low index of backward linkage, and the manufacture of final products, in which the reverse is the case.[37]

These results can explain why the expansion in specific sectors—mining, oil exploitation, and planting—have scarcely left an impression on the rest of the economy in certain underdeveloped countries, and they make it very clear that protective policies should be concentrated fundamentally on the intermediate stage of manufacture. In this respect, it is interesting to underline, as Hirschman points out, that since the iron and steel industries have the highest combined linkage score, the underdeveloped countries may perhaps have reasons, other than exclusively prestige motives, for attributing prime importance to these industries.

All the points made in favor of certain forms of protection also require comparison between the harm done by the tariff to the allocation of resources over the short run and the benefits that will be obtained from protection over the long run. Although they have certain limits of a statistical nature, the empirical studies of the cost of protection have made clear that this cost is only a small percentage of the national income or product of each country.[38] Even though in certain cases,

as mentioned, these estimates may be open to criticism regarding their underlying conceptual and statistical bases, they are important from the point of view of protectionism, as Johnson has pointed out,[39] since all of them seem to confirm the fact that the welfare cost associated with protection is small. Under this assumption, then, it is not wholly accurate to say that the long-run gains from protection must be very large in order to justify protectionist measures.

The observations made thus far provide some guidelines for understanding the effects that import taxes may have on economic development. The possible desirability of using these taxes (or other measures that restrict free trade) to increase resources or improve their allocation and the sectors where this procedure would be most appropriate have been pointed out. Side by side with this type of effect, which was also examined in the preceding section for internal production and consumption taxes, it is appropriate here to refer, as was done before, to other consequences of customs protection for development.

The immediate risk of growth is inflation, if growth is forced without the necessary volume of resources for maintaining the economy in a situation of equilibrium. Consequently, import taxes should contribute to domestic savings.

We already know that the *income effect* of a tax has some results which reinforce

---

[37]Chenery's classification distinguishes primary production from manufacturing. Either can be final or intermediate. In the primary final group are fishing, transportation, services, and trade. In the primary intermediate group are mining of metals, petroleum, coal, agriculture, lumber, electricity, etc. In the final manufacturing category are machinery, shipbuilding, milling, wool manufacture, tanning, etc. Finally, in the intermediate manufacturing category are iron and steel, paper, and articles transformed from the primary intermediate stage (coal, petroleum), textiles, chemicals, etc.

[38]Thus, the Brigden Committee calculated it as some 6 per cent of the Australian national income in the period 1927–29. Young established it for Canada as 3.4 to 4.0 per cent of private gross spending, excluding indirect taxes. Harberger estimated that the cost of protection in Chile is not greater than 2.5 per cent of the national income. Wemelsfelder concludes that a reduction of 10 per cent in the customs taxes in Germany would result in only a 0.18 per cent increase in national income; and two estimates made respecting the economic effects of European integration also seem to confirm that the costs of protection tend to be small. Scitovsky estimates that the gains which integration would produce would be less than 0.05 per cent of the gross social product of the integrated countries; and Johnson believes that, for England, gains from the formation of a free trade zone would, at a maximum, be less than 1 per cent of national income.

[39]H. G. Johnson, "The Cost of Protection and the Scientific Tariff," *Journal of Political Economy* (August, 1960).

public sector savings. But customs taxes may also influence the savings of enterprises through redistribution effects which create additional benefits for the protected industries.

In the case of infant industries, which it is assumed must be developed with decreasing costs, the creation of savings will increase and can bring about a cumulative process of re-investment in the same enterprises.

Savings may also be increased through the use of import taxes as a selective control on the consumption of specific goods, particularly luxury items. But since such measures depend on the elasticity of the demand for those goods and on the degree of substitution of domestic products for imports, their effects can be quite varied.

Finally, as in the case of internal taxes on production and consumption, tariffs make it possible to have a policy of incentives through rate differentials. This has been the case in the Latin American countries where total or partial exemptions from customs and other taxes have been considered a major policy instrument in promoting development.

In contrast to the essentially free trade position that has been discussed to this point is the protectionist theory of the use of tariffs, supported by Latin American economists and echoed in the United Nations (in the reports and studies of the Economic Commission for Latin America).[40]

The classical model, according to their opinion, is theoretically unobjectionable insofar as its assumptions are concerned, but there is no reason to think that it can be universally applied to all types of economies and under all historical circumstances. Latin American experience, as Prebisch points out,[41] is clear proof of this, since international free trade has not resulted in these countries in the benefits promised by the classical doctrine. Along with a secular tendency toward a

worsening in the terms of trade, the advantages of technological progress have been concentrated chiefly in the industrial countries, and in some instances inequalities among countries have not only failed to disappear but have increased.

Specialization and the division of labor have made the Latin American economies predominantly agricultural, with exports concentrated on a very few—at times only one or two—primary products, and as a consequence there is a dangerous vulnerability to cyclical fluctuations. In this way, a dual structure has been forged in these economies, so that they have one developed export sector while the other sectors fail to rise above subsistence conditions and inferior production methods. Exports have not been a sufficient factor to stimulate economic development in Latin America. In spite of their growth, market imperfections have prevented this expansion from exerting a substantial impact on the remainder of the economy.

Foreign investment has also been primarily directed to these exports, and the profits obtained, on leaving the country as earnings and interest, have diminished savings in the underdeveloped countries.

The above-mentioned authors conclude that industrialization is the only avenue open to the Latin American countries for sharing in the advantages of technological progress, for achieving diversification of their economies, for absorbing their excess labor supplies, and for attaining an adequate pace of development.

Industrialization presupposes a process of replacing imports by domestically produced goods, and since industry in the underdeveloped countries is incipient, the "infant industries" argument can be generalized to the entire economy. The replacement of imports by means of protectionism, if one assumes a surplus labor supply, will not result in a decline in the volume of trade or create a welfare cost associated with the allocation of resources.

Thus, what was an exception under free trade is elevated to the status of a general

---

[40]It would be unfair to assume that ECLA upholds unlimited protectionism; this is plain without any need to refer to its many efforts on behalf of Latin American economic integration to prove it.

[41]R. Prebisch, "El desarrollo económico de la América Latina y algunos de sus principales problems," *Boletín económico de América Latina*, Vol. III, No. 1 (February, 1962).

rule, and customs taxes are not an ancillary tool but an essential instrument for development.

Without ignoring the realistic side of the theory, some of these arguments are currently undergoing harsh criticism. A case in point is disguised unemployment. The absorption of such labor very likely could not take place without a decrease in agricultural production. "I know of no evidence," Schultz points out, "for any poor country anywhere that would even suggest that a transfer of some small fraction, say, 5 per cent, of the existing labor force out of agriculture, with other things equal, could be made without reducing its production."[42]

Similarly there has been discussion of the supposition that in the long run the terms of trade move against countries that are producers of primary commodities. Against the Prebisch-Singer theory of the worsening of the terms of trade for the countries of Latin America, some authors—Haberler, for one—

[42]T. W. Schultz, "The Role of Government in Promoting Economic Growth," in L. D. White, ed. *The State of the Social Sciences* (Chicago: The University of Chicago Press, 1956), p. 375.

dispute the very concept of the relationship, and others, such as Atallah, point to the possibility that agriculture may suffer impairment as well as improvement.[43]

We can now make some observations on these problems of tariff protection and development in Latin American countries. In none of them is there actually a trade policy prompted by the needs of economic development, or at least so it seems to us. Policies followed are rather the result of measures adopted to solve balance of payment difficulties and to obtain revenues.

The dominant principle is to prevent competition, real or potential, by foreign producers. The levels of protection are high and almost always exceed what would have been necessary to restrict imports effectively.[44]

Tables 9–4 through 9–13 show the theoretical and actual incidence of customs and similar taxes on different classes of goods.

[43]Some very interesting comments on the concepts referring to terms of trade in general and their behavior in Ecuador may be seen in Néstor Vega's comments on this paper, below.
[44]This is the conclusion reached in United Nations, ECLA, *Derechos aduaneros y otros gravámenes*, p. 26.

TABLE 9–4: Average Incidence of Customs Duties, Argentina* *(percentages)*

		Weighted averages			Arithmetical averages		
Category and group	Value of imports[a]	Customs duties	Burdens of equivalent effects[b]	Total	Customs duties	Burdens of equivalent effects	Total
Category I. Primary goods	26.1	2.9	15.6	18.5	8.3	45.9	54.2
Group 1. Unprocessed food products	3.5	1.0	39.6	40.6	3.3	37.1	40.4
Group 2. Raw materials	7.6	8.1	34.6	42.7	10.9	54.1	65.0
Group 3. Unrefined combustibles	14.9	0.8	0.2	1.0	0.3	6.6	6.9
Category II. Intermediate products, capital goods, and consumer durables	70.2	7.4	58.4	65.8	10.5	86.4	96.9
Group 1. Intermediate products	34.2	8.2	43.5	51.7	12.3	49.8	62.1
Group 2. Refined combustibles	7.7	0.7	0.5	1.2	1.2	2.8	4.0
Group 3. Capital goods	27.2	8.3	69.9	78.2	9.9	74.8	84.7
Group 4. Durable consumer goods	1.0	5.8	693.9	699.7	12.1	600.1	612.2
Category III. Current consumption goods	3.7	6.9	59.6	66.5	16.4	93.6	110.0
Group 1. Processed food products	0.1	13.8	128.6	142.4	11.4	125.0	136.4
Group 2. Chemical and pharmaceutical products	0.5	6.4	56.5	62.9	7.7	95.0	102.7
Group 3. Other manufactured products	3.1	6.7	56.9	63.6	19.2	89.4	108.6
Theoretical incidence		6.2	47.3	53.4	10.8	80.7	91.5
Effective incidence		2.8[c]	16.6	19.4			
Effective incidence Theoretical incidence		61.0[c]	35.0	37.0			

*Taxes in effect from April 30, 1960.
[a]Percentages calculated on a sample representing 93.9 per cent of the total imports in 1959.
[b]Including exchange charges.
[c]Excluding the charges applied to imports of woods and iron materials and products allocated to special development funds.

SOURCE: United Nations, Economic and Social Council, *Derechos aduaneros y otros gravámenes y restricciones a la importación en países latinoamericanos y sus niveles promedios de incidencia* (Caracas: 9th Sess. of ECOSOC, 1961), Annexes Nos. I–XI.

TABLE 9–5: Average Incidence of Customs Duties, Bolivia* (*percentages*)

Category and group	Value of imports[a]	Weighted averages			Arithmetical averages		
		Customs duties	Burdens of equivalent effects[b]	Total	Customs duties	Burdens of equivalent effects	Total
Category I. Primary goods	8.7	4.3	5.6	9.9	13.4	7.7	21.1
Group 1. Unprocessed food products	7.3	3.6	5.1	8.7	10.4	7.4	17.8
Group 2. Raw materials	1.2	8.6	8.0	16.6	19.0	8.0	27.0
Group 3. Unrefined combustibles	0.3	4.1	8.0	12.1	4.0	8.0	12.0
Category II. Intermediate products, capital goods, and consumer durables	56.4	6.1	7.3	13.4	9.9	7.7	17.6
Group 1. Intermediate products	14.9	2.0	5.6	7.6	4.6	7.5	12.1
Group 2. Refined combustibles	3.2	6.1	8.0	14.1	6.8	8.0	14.8
Group 3. Capital goods	33.1	5.4	7.9	13.3	9.6	7.8	17.4
Group 4. Durable consumer goods	5.3	21.4	8.0	29.4	29.1	8.0	37.1
Category III. Current consumption goods	34.8	26.3	7.9	34.2	44.7	7.8	52.5
Group 1. Processed food products	19.2	11.1	8.0	19.1	27.9	8.0	35.9
Group 2. Chemical and pharmaceutical products	3.6	12.8	8.0	20.8	29.8	8.0	37.8
Group 3. Other manufactured products	12.0	54.8	7.8	62.6	50.9	7.8	58.7
Theoretical incidence		13.0	7.4	20.4	22.6	7.7	30.3
Effective incidence		—					
Effective incidence Theoretical incidence							

*Taxes in effect as of December 31, 1959.
[a]Percentages calculated on the basis of a sample which includes 91.9 per cent of the total value of imports (averages 1957–58).

[b]Includes consular fees and the sale shares.
SOURCE: Same as Table 9–4.

TABLE 9–6: Average Incidence of Customs Duties, Brazil* (*percentages*)

Category and group	Value of imports[a]	Weighted averages			Arithmetical averages		
		Customs duties	Burdens of equivalent effects[b]	Total	Customs duties	Burdens of equivalent effects	Total
Category I. Primary goods	24.4	2.5	0.4	2.9	11.5	1.9	13.4
Group 1. Unprocessed food products	11.3	1.0	0.1	1.1	8.3	1.2	9.5
Group 2. Raw materials	2.2	18.6	3.4	22.0	16.2	3.5	19.7
Group 3. Unrefined combustibles	10.9	0.8	—	0.8	10.2	—	10.2
Category II. Intermediate products, capital goods, and consumer durables	70.1	33.2	3.7	36.9	36.1	4.7	40.8
Group 1. Intermediate products	21.2	22.2	3.9	26.1	26.4	4.6	31.0
Group 2. Refined combustibles	10.8	22.6	0.2	22.8	27.6	1.7	29.3
Group 3. Capital goods	36.8	41.0	4.6	45.6	41.2	4.9	46.1
Group 4. Durable consumer goods	1.4	74.1	5.0	79.1	55.0	5.0	60.0
Category III. Current consumption goods	5.4	36.6	3.8	40.4	45.9	4.5	50.4
Group 1. Processed food products	1.4	46.4	4.1	50.5	52.3	4.0	56.3
Group 2. Chemical and pharmaceutical products	0.8	30.4	5.0	35.4	20.0	5.0	25.0
Group 3. Other manufactured products	3.3	33.9	3.4	37.3	47.5	4.5	52.0
Theoretical incidence		25.9	2.9	28.8	35.6	4.5	40.1
Effective incidence		12–12.5					
Effective incidence Theoretical incidence		46–48					

*Taxes in force as of August 31, 1960.
[a]Percentages calculated on the basis of a sample representing 92.9 per cent of the total value of imports (averages 1957–59).

[b]Including the fee on customs commissions.
SOURCE: Same as Table 9–4.

TABLE 9-7: Average Incidence of Customs Duties, Chile*

Category and group	Value of imports %[a]	Weighted average of customs incidence			Simple arithmetical average of customs incidence	
		Including the ad valorem tax of 3 and 30%[b]	Excluding the ad valorem tax of 3 and 30%	Including the ad valorem tax and consular fees	Including the ad valorem tax of 3 and 30%	Including the ad valorem tax and consular fees
Category I. Primary goods	20.1	20.4	10.9	22.6	39.2	41.4
Group 1. Unprocessed food products	8.9	15.0	5.1	17.2	33.7	35.9
Group 2. Raw materials	5.7	15.7	4.7	17.9	41.8	44.9
Group 3. Unrefined combustibles	5.5	34.1	27.0	36.3	53.5	55.7
Category II. Intermediate products, capital goods, and consumer durables	65.4	39.6	9.7	41.8	45.8	48.0
Group 1. Intermediate products	16.3	40.6	13.6	42.8	45.3	47.5
Group 2. Refined combustibles	5.5	40.1	13.8	42.3	45.5	47.7
Group 3. Capital goods	41.8	37.3	6.0	39.5	40.3	42.5
Group 4. Durable consumer goods	1.7	86.5	49.8	88.7	87.0	89.2
Category III. Current consumption goods	14.5	56.8	42.8	59.0	66.2	68.4
Group 1. Processed food products	8.6	62.8	57.6	65.0	126.4	128.6
Group 2. Chemical and pharmaceutical products	1.0	14.7	8.8	16.9	16.5	18.7
Group 3. Other manufactured products	4.9	55.1	23.9	57.3	64.5	66.7
Theoretical incidence		38.3	14.8	40.5	48.1	50.3
Effective incidence		15.0				
Effective incidence / Theoretical incidence		39.0				

*Taxes in effect as of March 15, 1960.
[a]Percentages calculated on the basis of a sample which includes 93.2 per cent of the total value of imports, excluding those from Arica and Punta Arenas (averages 1957–58).

[b]The sources used calculate only the effective incidence taking internal ad valorem taxes into account, which inflates the results of the strictly customs taxes.
SOURCE: Same as Table 9–4.

TABLE 9-8: Average Incidence of Customs Duties, Colombia* (*percentages*)

Category and group	Value of imports[a]	Weighted averages			Arithmetical averages		
		Customs duties	Burdens of equivalent effects[b]	Total	Customs duties	Burdens of equivalent effects	Total
Category I. Primary goods	10.9	26.5	1.8	28.3	39.8	3.5	43.3
Group 1. Unprocessed food products	3.7	43.9	1.7	45.6	65.0	3.0	68.0
Group 2. Raw materials	7.2	17.5	1.8	19.3	27.2	3.7	30.9
Group 3. Unrefined combustibles	—	—	—	—	—	—	—
Category II. Intermediate products, capital goods, and consumer durables	70.5	24.7	3.6	28.3	29.9	4.0	33.9
Group 1. Intermediate products	31.2	28.4	4.5	32.9	31.3	4.6	35.9
Group 2. Refined combustibles	4.5	6.7	5.4	12.1	6.0	5.4	11.4
Group 3. Capital goods	33.3	19.7	2.5	22.2	23.5	3.0	26.5
Group 4. Durable consumer goods	1.6	108.7	5.0	113.7	96.2	4.7	100.9
Category III. Current consumption goods	18.6	45.0	3.2	48.2	54.9	4.0	58.9
Group 1. Processed food products	1.6	156.3	4.2	160.5	133.6	4.0	137.6
Group 2. Chemical and pharmaceutical products	3.7	22.2	2.4	24.6	27.6	3.2	30.8
Group 3. Other manufactured products	13.3	37.8	3.3	41.1	52.9	4.2	57.1
Theoretical incidence		28.7	3.4	32.1	37.3	4.0	41.3
Effective incidence		13.7					
Effective incidence / Theoretical incidence		48.0					

*Taxes in effect as of September 30, 1959.
[a]Percentages calculated on the basis of a sample which includes 94.3 per cent of the total value of imports (averages 1956–58).

[b]Includes the advance deposit on customs duties and consular fees.
SOURCE: Same as Table 9–4.

TABLE 9–9: Average Incidence of Customs Duties, Ecuador* (*percentages*)

Category and group	Value of imports[a]	Weighted averages			Arithmetical averages		
		Customs duties	Burdens of equivalent effects	Total	Customs duties	Burdens of equivalent effects	Total
Category I. Primary goods	5.6	9.1	15.6	24.7	17.0	17.0	34.0
Group 1. Unprocessed food products	5.2	8.4	15.5	23.9	16.2	16.7	32.9
Group 2. Raw materials	0.4	19.0	17.2	36.2	18.2	17.6	35.8
Group 3. Unrefined combustibles	—						
Category II. Intermediate products, capital goods, and consumer durables	62.7	24.1	16.6	40.7	27.4	16.9	44.3
Group 1. Intermediate products	21.4	21.2	16.8	38.0	27.0	16.7	43.7
Group 2. Refined combustibles	6.8	54.3	15.9	70.2	44.6	16.6	61.0
Group 3. Capital goods	28.9	13.0	16.2	29.2	16.2	16.5	32.7
Group 4. Durable consumer goods	5.6	56.1	19.1	75.2	87.0	19.5	106.5
Category III. Current consumption goods	31.7	44.4	17.9	62.3	55.0	18.1	73.1
Group 1. Processed food products	4.2	93.5	20.5	114.0	104.4	20.4	124.8
Group 2. Chemical and pharmaceutical products	7.5	25.4	16.6	42.0	41.4	17.9	59.3
Group 3. Other manufactured products	20.0	41.3	17.8	59.1	49.9	17.7	67.6
Theoretical incidence		29.7	17.0	46.7	37.6	17.3	54.9
Effective incidence		26.8					
Effective incidence Theoretical incidence		90.0					

*Taxes in effect as of September 1, 1959.
[a]Percentages calculated on the basis of a sample which includes 87.5 per cent of the total value of imports (average 1957–58).

SOURCE: Same as Table 9–4.

TABLE 9–10: Average Incidence of Customs Duties, Mexico* (*percentages*)

Category and group	Value of imports[a]	Weighted averages			Arithmetical averages		
		Customs duties	Burdens of equivalent effects	Total	Customs duties	Burdens of equivalent effects	Total
Category I. Primary goods	13.6	4.7			7.8		
Group 1. Unprocessed food products	7.6	4.1			12.8		
Group 2. Raw materials	4.8	6.5			7.0		
Group 3. Unrefined combustibles	1.2	1.4			2.0		
Category II. Intermediate products, capital goods, and consumer durables	80.6	14.1			16.8		
Group 1. Intermediate products	22.3	19.2			17.2		
Group 2. Refined combustibles	5.2	6.9			7.1		
Group 3. Capital goods	51.9	11.7			14.9		
Group 4. Durable consumer goods	1.2	56.2			46.7		
Category III. Current consumption goods	5.8	30.8			33.9		
Group 1. Processed food products	0.7	132.8			121.6		
Group 2. Chemical and pharmaceutical products	2.5	9.8			10.9		
Group 3. Other manufactured products	2.6	24.0			28.3		
Theoretical incidence		13.8			18.1		
Effective incidence		10.0					
Effective incidence Theoretical incidence		72.0					

*Taxes in effect as of December 31, 1959.
[a]Percentages calculated on the basis of a sample which includes 83.75 per cent of the total imports, excluding imports from the free perimeters (averages 1957–58).

SOURCE: Same as Table 9–4.

TABLE 9–11: Average Incidence of Customs Duties, Peru* (*percentages*)

Category and group	Value of imports[a]	Weighted averages			Arithmetical averages		
		Customs duties	Burdens of equivalent effects	Total	Customs duties	Burdens of equivalent effects	Total
Category I. Primary goods	11.6	14.5			18.1		
Group 1. Unprocessed food products	9.7	12.9			15.1		
Group 2. Raw materials	1.9	22.7			22.5		
Group 3. Unrefined combustibles	—	—			—		
Category II. Intermediate products, capital goods, and consumer durables	66.5	18.3			22.0		
Group 1. Intermediate products	18.2	18.6			23.6		
Group 2. Refined combustibles	4.5	15.4			15.9		
Group 3. Capital goods	34.6	15.0			17.6		
Group 4. Durable consumer goods.	9.2	31.5			35.2		
Category III. Current consumption goods	21.9	33.9			40.9		
Group 1. Processed food products	6.5	25.2			29.1		
Group 2. Chemical and pharmaceutical products	2.9	20.4			20.6		
Group 3. Other manufactured products	12.5	41.3			47.9		
Theoretical incidence		21.2			28.3		
Effective incidence		10–11					
Effective incidence / Theoretical incidence		47–52					

*Taxes in effect as of September 15, 1959.
[a]Percentages calculated on the basis of a sample which includes 85.1 per cent of the total value of imports (averages 1957–58).

SOURCE: Same as Table 9–4.

TABLE 9–12: Average Incidence of Customs Duties, Uruguay* (*percentages*)

Category and group	Value of imports[a]	Weighted averages			Arithmetical averages		
		Customs duties	Burdens of equivalent effects[b]	Total	Customs duties	Burdens of equivalent effects	Total
Category I. Primary goods	34.3	7.2	2.2	9.4	6.8	5.5	12.3
Group 1. Unprocessed food products	19.0	10.2	0.8	11.0	9.7	4.1	13.8
Group 2. Raw materials	9.3	6.0	6.4	12.4	5.6	6.8	12.4
Group 3. Unrefined combustibles	6.0	—	0.1	0.1	—	0.1	0.1
Category II. Intermediate products, capital goods, and consumer durables	54.3	10.9	8.4	19.3	15.7	8.3	24.0
Group 1. Intermediate products	22.4	9.1	6.7	15.8	15.0	7.7	22.7
Group 2. Refined combustibles	2.1	15.8	0.1	15.9	21.1	0.1	21.2
Group 3. Capital goods	26.2	11.8	10.5	22.3	16.5	10.0	26.5
Group 4. Durable consumer goods	3.6	12.3	8.0	20.3	14.4	9.7	24.1
Category III. Current consumption goods	11.4	13.9	5.3	19.2	15.8	6.9	22.7
Group 1. Processed food products	3.0	19.9	3.4	23.3	14.7	3.7	18.4
Group 2. Chemical and pharmaceutical products	0.6	3.7	5.8	9.5	2.5	7.6	10.1
Group 3. Other manufactured products	7.8	12.4	6.0	18.4	18.5	7.5	26.0
Theoretical incidence		10.0	5.9	15.9	13.7	7.4	21.1
Effective incidence		—					
Effective incidence / Theoretical incidence		—					

*Taxes in effect as of August 15, 1960.
[a]Percentages calculated on the basis of a sample which includes 87.3 per cent of the total value of imports in 1957.

[b]Includes the advance deposit on customs duties and the transfer tax.
SOURCE: Same as Table 9–4.

TABLE 9–13: Average Incidence of Customs Duties, Venezuela* *(percentages)*

Category and group	Value of imports[a]	Weighted averages			Arithmetical averages		
		Customs duties	Burdens of equivalent effects[b]	Total	Customs duties	Burdens of equivalent effects	Total
Category I. Primary goods	6.5	32.9	2.7	35.6	49.5	2.7	52.2
Group 1. Unprocessed food products	4.4	17.6	2.7	20.3	35.3	2.7	38.0
Group 2. Raw materials	2.1	65.4	2.7	68.1	73.0	2.7	75.7
Group 3. Unrefined combustibles	—	—	—	—	—	—	—
Category II. Intermediate products, capital goods, and consumer durables	67.6	9.9	2.7	12.6	19.6	2.7	22.3
Group 1. Intermediate products	21.4	20.5	2.7	23.2	37.7	2.7	40.4
Group 2. Refined combustibles	0.9	29.3	2.7	32.0	37.6	2.7	40.3
Group 3. Capital goods	34.9	2.5	2.7	5.2	8.2	2.7	10.9
Group 4. Durable consumer goods	10.5	11.6	2.7	14.3	12.0	2.7	14.7
Category III. Current consumption goods	25.9	63.6	2.7	66.3	108.9	2.7	111.6
Group 1. Processed food products	7.7	84.6	2.7	87.3	284.3	2.7	287.0
Group 2. Chemical and pharmaceutical products	3.1	34.8	2.7	37.5	118.4	2.7	121.1
Group 3. Other manufactured products	15.1	58.6	2.7	61.3	71.3	2.7	74.0
Theoretical incidence		25.3	2.7	28.0	53.3	2.7	56.0
Effective incidence				11–12[c]			
Effective incidence / Theoretical incidence				39–43			

*Taxes in force as of February 23, 1960.
[a]Percentages calculated on the basis of a sample which includes 86.6 per cent of the total value of imports in 1959.

[b]Includes consular fees.
[c]This figure is understated since calculated on the basis of duties in force before September 1, 1959.
SOURCE: Same as Table 9–4.

Examination of these tables indicates that the average burden on raw materials is less than that on intermediate products, although in some instances the relationship is inverse to what would be a rational structure. Thus, in Bolivia the burden on raw materials is 16.6 per cent and for intermediate products 7.6 per cent. In Venezuela, the figures are 68.1 per cent and 23.2 per cent, respectively. An analogous relationship also prevails in Peru. In other cases, even though the relationship is normal, the difference in burdens for these types of products is very small (Argentina, Brazil, Ecuador, and Uruguay). This points out the high level of protection afforded domestic products in the first group (raw materials), a situation which is difficult to justify, given the situation of primary goods producers in these Latin American countries. The result of this burden is to increase the cost of the productive processes by taxing them heavily from the beginning. Customs taxes on raw materials reach 43 per cent in Argentina and, as we have already pointed out, 68 per cent in Venezuela.

It could be inferred from these tables that in view of the high burdens on the importa-

tion of capital goods—45 per cent in Brazil, 53 per cent in Paraguay, and 78 per cent in Argentina—there is in general no policy of stimulating investments in the Latin American countries. But these figures, which reflect theoretical burdens, do not faithfully accord with reality since they omit the great number of existing partial or total exemptions. Thus, there are partial or total exemptions from import duties for machinery and equipment for agricultural purposes or for new or expanding industries or for these goods if imported by foreign investors. The exemption policy is general in some cases and tied into the use of the imported goods in others.

The impact of the exemption policies within the Latin American systems can be discerned —always within the limitations of available data—by comparing actual with theoretical levels of incidence. In the majority of countries, the proportion between these two varies between 40 and 60 per cent; in only two countries, Mexico and Ecuador, is the ratio higher. In those cases in which exemptions are not automatic, this policy works through a licensing or quota system.

A policy of heavy taxation on luxury imports, not always accompanied by an internal

tax of the same amount on similar, domestically produced items, is common in Latin
America. In these cases, it is a true protectionist tariff. Because of the inelasticity of
demand for such goods in these countries,
luxury taxes are a revenue producing measure
rather than a means of restricting consumption and increasing savings. However, they do
introduce an element of progressivity into the
tax systems of these countries.

Because of the complexity of the Latin
American systems, in which all types of trade
policy measures are intermixed, it is desirable
to look into the relative role played by customs taxes, strictly speaking, within the over-
all framework of trade policy instruments.

From this point of view, three groups of
countries can be distinguished. The first,
consisting of Bolivia and Peru, is characterized by the fact that there are no quantitative
or exchange controls and that tariffs are
utilized either preponderantly or exclusively
as trade policy instruments. The second group,
consisting of Argentina, Chile, Paraguay, and
Uruguay, is also characterized by the absence
of exchange or quantitative controls, while
customs tariffs play only a secondary role
and import controls are applied through taxes
known as "levies of equivalent effect." In the
third group, consisting of Colombia, Ecuador,
Venezuela, and Brazil, there are quantitative
(prohibitions, licenses, or quotas) and exchange controls, although only Brazil has
transformed the exchange controls into a multiple exchange system.

Nevertheless, it is necessary to underline
the fact that there is a marked tendency in
Latin America toward simplification by eliminating exchange and quantitative controls and
replacing them with customs duties, so that
these taxes will again take their place as a
fundamental instrument of import policy, a
role which they had lost during the crisis of
the 1930's. The process of transition has been
carried out by replacing controls with levies
which are not actually customs tariffs on
imports but taxes of similar or equivalent
effect. This is a necessary intermediate step,
since in the majority of countries the old

customs have been or will be gradually replaced by new taxes whose structure is better
adapted to the demands of economic development. This, however, requires a series of administrative adjustments that cannot be quickly
realized. Colombia provides an example of
the extent to which effective protection based
on old tariffs had been reduced; when a new
tariff was enacted in 1951, it was observed
that the average rate of protection had fallen
from 30 per cent in 1933 to 8.6 per cent in
1950.[45]

This paper should end with a reference to
export taxes, the last to be considered according to the outline given at the beginning. As
was indicated there, these can be regarded as
indirect taxes only under special circumstances.

The principal situation in which they fall
on the foreign consumer is where demand is
inelastic, but there may be other situations
where this occurs, even though demand is
elastic. This happens, for example, when a
specific exporter's cost price is lower than the
world price for the exported product. (As is
well known, the bulk of taxable exports are
raw materials or food products for which
there is a very wide regional if not world-
wide market.) As U. K. Hicks points out,[46] it
may also happen that the widespread general-
ization of these taxes by countries that produce primary products, increasing the difficulty of acquiring substitutes for the taxed
goods, may result in their forward shifting
(the tax on jute in India benefits Tanganyika,
Haiti, and other producers of sisal). Even in
cases of high inelasticity of demand, it is
often impossible for the exporter to maintain
a privileged position. In fact, the purchasers,
which are generally countries more developed
than the supplier countries, have means to
join forces against a monopolistic policy,
especially by building up reserves during the
recurrent—and thus far unavoidable—periods
of decline in the prices of the exported goods.

[45]United Nations, *El desarrollo económico de Colombia*
(Mexico: 1957), p. 101.
[46]U. K. Hicks, "The Search for Revenue in Underdeveloped Countries."

Of course, when the tax falls on the consumer, the effects can be highly beneficial to the exporting countries. The same occurs in the normal situation, where it is impossible to shift the tax forward, if the exporter is a foreign enterprise—a common occurrence—by blocking the partial outflow of profits. The use of the revenue yields of these taxes for investments which compensate for the export outflows of certain reserves of raw materials, such as minerals, precious metals, petroleum, etc., has been justified on the basis of this type of reasoning.

For other reasons, these same principles have been used as the basis for establishing public institutions or syndicates for centralizing exports and supporting the price of various products and at times for building up reserves, with the proceeds of a tax or with the profits, for the purpose of maintaining an average level of income for exporters during periods of depressed export volume or prices. Insofar as they also help to maintain production and avoid ruinous catastrophes, the export taxes are useful for development and stability. However, price stabilization policies through marketing boards (or other analogous bodies) are very difficult to sustain through prolonged periods of crisis. Since the accumulation of reserves is an essential negotiating instrument in periods of commercial inactivity, a policy of expanding productivity can hardly be favored if it constantly creates additional problems of price support. Nevertheless, as an alternative to policies which aim at similar results (exchange rate differentials, variable withholding of foreign exchange, duty free reimport privileges, procedures for compensatory imports, etc.), the marketing boards seem preferable.

Finally, export taxes can serve as an intermediate step toward the income tax itself (or as an inexpensive substitute therefor, for the export sector, when the tax administration is not equipped to implement an income tax). There are operating advantages here whose value should not be overlooked.

In contrast to these and other advantages that could be pointed out, export taxes offer a number of disadvantages. These are important and likewise should not be overlooked. In the first place, as revenue devices they are even more susceptible than import duties to fluctuations in price and the volume of the taxed goods. High tax rates may become a vehicle for a shift in the structure of production in the direction of untaxed (or less heavily taxed) internal consumption items. In any case, even when burdens are moderate, these taxes will produce discrimination between taxed and tax free products, with the consequent resource allocation effects. Added to this, except where a delicate balance is maintained with direct internal tax burdens, is the fact that the surcharge on the exporters' incomes has regressive effects which are not justifiable simply because they deal with foreigners instead of nationals.

As stated in the second section of this paper, export taxes present the most marked illustration of the postwar resurgence of indirect taxes. The vigorous flowering of those taxes has coincided with increased prices in certain typical exports of the underdeveloped countries. Examples are to be found everywhere in Latin America.

The yield of the export tax on tin is one of Bolivia's major sources of tax revenue. El Salvador introduced a coffee export tax in 1943, which also has been one of its major revenue sources, even though there have been fluctuations over the years, with the progressive rates changing according to the New York City market price. Gold and silver exports, as well as all goods which are not packaged in sacks manufactured from domestically produced sisal or cotton, are also taxed. This latter tax exemplifies the use of export taxes for protectionist purposes.[47] Also, in Guatemala, export taxes on coffee, bananas, and chicle are important sources of revenues which are being used in part in the promotion of development. A similar tax on coffee was established in Nicaragua in 1950–51, and additional examples could be cited at length.

[47]H. C. Wallich and J. H. Adler, *Proyecciones económicas*, pp. 294 ff.

CONCLUSIONS

It is not simple to draw conclusions when, as has been apparent throughout this paper, there are so many variables that affect a judgment on production and consumption taxes.

In the first place, with respect to the essential function of the tax—that is, to obtain public funds for financing the processes of development—it seems possible to conclude (exercising the caution mentioned elsewhere in this study) that the aforesaid taxes can be a very important instrument for the desired purpose. The average burden of taxes on production and consumption in the developing countries, and especially in Latin America, still leaves a margin (and so likewise does the total tax burden) for obtaining additional public funds. The possibility for the greater or lesser use of this instrument depends, of course, on the situation of each country in particular. But in general, and in view of the modest real (and even prospective) returns which direct taxes offer in these countries, the importance of indirect taxation is reaffirmed.

The administrative procedures to be selected to strengthen collections of taxes on production and consumption present an independent (and important) problem that has not been taken up in this paper. It was stated at the beginning of this study that there are two kinds of formulas to be utilized, either singly or jointly: general taxes on sales and special taxes on consumption. Taking into account the fact that, granted the kind of tax administration existing in underdeveloped countries, it is usually more effective not to attempt large-scale reforms but rather to improve and make moderate changes in the existing system, it is suggested that reorganization—and, in almost all cases, simplification—of present tax structures will produce the most profitable and most immediate effects. Therefore, the reforms should evaluate the yields of the various taxes and eliminate many which, either because of their low yield or their positively disturbing economic effects,

ought to be eliminated. Attention should be directed toward the integration and, as we said, the simplification of the remaining taxes,[48] adding such new ones as may be desirable or in due course widening the tax base of the existing ones. Special attention should be given to the tax on the consumption of luxury items and also—pursuant to what I judge to be the wise proposal of the economist Aníbal Pinto—the consumption of durable goods which constitute a very important item in the budget of the middle classes and the higher levels of the low-income groups in the Americas in their desire to participate in the advantages of an "affluent society."

If one considers the different structure, stage of development, and idiosyncracies of each tax system and the hundred other differences existing from country to country, it does not seem to me to be advisable to advocate any one general formula, applicable in stereotyped fashion to all countries. Furthermore, uniformity would be a costly proposition, because, as noted in the previous paragraph, it would require of the tax administration an effort that is not possible everywhere.[49]

---

[48]Without any desire to point out any one country in particular, and only because it is impossible to refer to all of them separately, the case of Bolivia may be taken as an example. By merely looking over the Budget of Revenues for 1961, Chap. I, par. C, Direct and Indirect Taxes, one discovers 111 different items. The majority of these—at least judging by the brief references to the budget laws—could be classified as indirect taxes. Setting aside those of an external nature (customs), which include only five items, the taxes on internal production and consumption approximate 100.

[49]At the Conference on Fiscal Policy, for which this paper was prepared, Mr. Kaldor and a number of others present, spoke in favor of the value added tax as the best solution to this problem. Without denying the merits that this tax may have, but likewise without ignoring the criticism due its application in a tax system as superior to that of a developing country as the French system is, it seems to us that it does not offer a good solution.

General taxes on sales—at levels as close as possible to the manufacturer, which is the way to ensure their functioning in the less developed countries—together with a few selected taxes on luxury items constitute a tax mechanism that is cheaper, more efficient, and less difficult to introduce—being already established in most countries—than a value added tax. This undoubtedly sacrifices theoretical and financial principles for the sake of results in collections, but fiscal policy, insofar as it is a policy, and even more under these conditions, is more the art of *the possible* than of *the best*.

In relation to the second general purpose of taxation for economic development—that is, its effects on the principal economic variables that stimulate such development—which includes the special problem of incentives, the analysis made in this study does not appear to lead to rules that point to taxes on production and consumption as a panacea for development. Referring first to internal taxes, they offer, as does probably any other kind of levy, both advantages and disadvantages which can scarcely be estimated outside the concrete circumstances of place and time, in order to arrive at a positive or negative judgment.

Perhaps the truth is to be found in the much-abused middle course. In the light of the theoretical inexactitude of many long-standing appraisals of indirect taxes, one cannot today support the derogatory opinion of the classics, nor is it possible to swing to the other extreme and exaggerate their fiscal virtues. With these strident notes on both counts eliminated, positive values remain that will not allow us to ignore the possible favorable influences of taxes on consumption on the process of development.

One particular problem that merits attention is the matter of the regressivity of these taxes. Aside from the warnings expressed concerning a tax on food—which to me seem very important—it is difficult to arrive at a precise judgment on the regressivity of the distribution of the tax burden in general and of its possible strengthening through indirect taxation in its relationship with development. If one regards the problem as essentially one of equity, it can scarcely be reduced to the more technical categories of economic growth. But leaving aside value judgment which, without doubt, would be negative, the important thing that remains is the pressure on the lower levels of consumption, thus freeing resources for productive purposes—resources that it would be difficult to obtain by other means. It is certain, in principle, that any redistribution of income from the powerful to the humble, coming up against the latter's greater inclination to consume, cannot be defended as the best means for increasing the resources needed for development. While this may perhaps point to the fact that the problems of income redistribution must wait, at least until it becomes possible to redistribute something more than an extremely low per capita welfare,[50] in no way does it prove that the grave social traumas of tax regressivity can be offset by the meager additional accumulations coming from a reduction in consumption that is already at the very edge of the minimum level.

With respect to external taxes on production and consumption, there can be no doubt of their effective contribution to the process of development. From the standpoint of collections, in certain circumstances they present the most basic part of the entire indirect tax picture. In relation to the principal variables that influence development, the conclusions must be eclectic and colored, as stated, by the internal taxes; but, as we see it, emphasis should be placed on the positive idea that they can be used as an incentive producing instrument.

One last aspect to be considered pertains to the relative value of customs taxes in comparison with other instruments of trade policy. It seems to us that from the economic development standpoint, a system based essentially or exclusively on customs taxes makes the trade policy the most suitable instrument for attaining the objectives pursued. In the first place, any and all simplification must be looked upon as desirable, because with some

[50]In examining the influences of the taxes under discussion on the variables more closely related to economic development, the problems of income redistribution have not been discussed. Some believe that this is a decisive question and that it is impossible, in view of the levels of consumption existing in the majority of the developing countries, to promote economic growth without a redistribution of income. Not by oversight, but because I disagree entirely with that position, I have not touched upon this topic. I do not think it possible to establish efficient processes of redistribution in the developing countries, or at least it could be done only through bloodless revolutions of the political type. But even accepting this latter premise, I believe, as stated in the text, that we should merely be distributing poverty. Another thing is to take care *pari passu,* with the growth of global income, that its distribution tends to be more equal, functionally as well as personally, than it is today in most of the developing countries. Fiscal policy can help to do this, but I think that the more important role devolves upon the social policy in this respect.

mixed systems, such as those that exist at the present time, it is very difficult to isolate the effects of each of the various types of measures adopted, and it is difficult even to ascertain the total results of all those different impacts on the structure of production, investments, prices, and profits. In the second place, customs taxes may be regarded as a suitable form of control, as compared to direct restrictions and multiple rates of exchange.

Although in principle multiple exchange rates have the advantage over customs taxes of being more flexible and more adaptable to the needs of a changing economy, it is also true that in practice they involve such complexities that they add largely to the difficulties of entrepreneurial planning and matters are left in the hands of the administrative authorities, with all the dangers that this implies. Few countries that have suffered the consequences of a system of multiple exchange rates would advocate its adoption. Schlesinger himself—a writer who has given

most careful attention to pointing out the advantages of multiple rates of exchange, considering them especially adaptable to the economic structures and problems of countries having low per capita income—ends by stating that their chief advantage, flexibility, is lessened by the extreme complications to which the system leads. A simple system of multiple exchange rates, he concludes, may, under specific conditions, contribute to a country's economic development, but a complicated system will probably never do so.[51] To this we must add that while theoretically both measures are similar in their effects on prices and the consequent repercussions on production, customs taxes offer the advantage, when compared with multiple exchange rates, of not interfering with the monetary mechanism of the economic system.

[51] R. E. Schlesinger, *Multiple Exchange Rates and Economic Development* (Princeton: Princeton University Press, 1952), pp. 18 and 19.

Comment

NÉSTOR VEGA-MORENO*

The study made by José María Naharro entitled "Production and Consumption Taxes and Economic Development" is divided into four sections:

1. Terminology and definitions.
2. Taxation and economic development.
3. Internal taxes on production and consumption and economic development.
4. Customs taxes and economic development.

Annexed to the study are thirteen tables referring to various tax aspects of ten Latin American countries, to wit: Argentina, Bolivia, Brazil, Chile, Colombia, Ecuador, Mexico,

*Adviser to the National Council for Economic Planning and Co-ordination, Office of the President of the Republic, Quito, Ecuador.

Peru, Uruguay, and Venezuela. The first three tables are general and refer, respectively, to tax burdens, the percentages of the direct and indirect tax burden in the aforesaid countries, and the tax burden by quartiles. The remaining ten tables deal separately for each of the above-mentioned countries with the incidence of customs taxes on the following three categories of products: (1) primary goods; (2) intermediate products, capital goods, and durable consumer goods; and (3) current consumption goods.

I shall offer my comments on Mr. Naharro's paper in two basic parts, first making some brief observations on economic development, which the author thought it unnecessary to dwell upon, and then taking up one by one the various chapters of the study. My only purpose in doing this is to make my own modest contribution to the work of this conference, the success of which stems from the excellent studies presented by all the other delegates or other persons present.

GENERAL CONSIDERATIONS ON ECONOMIC DEVELOPMENT

Despite the fact that economic development has been a matter of constant concern to all countries at all times, it can properly be said that this concern has been increasing in recent years among governments, international organizations, and private citizens themselves. Economists and sociologists have made profound studies of the problems of development, and at the present time abundant and excellent literature on the subject is available. It can be affirmed without reservation that this is the era of the economics of development.

The purpose of this conference on fiscal policy, sponsored by the Joint OAS/IDB/ECLA Committee, is not only to discuss the best means of financing government expenses and administering taxes but also to discuss and search for the best possible policies of taxation for development, to provide governments with the resources they need to accomplish their specific purposes and to make their investments without withdrawing incentives from private industry and private activity in general, but rather broadening opportunities and incentives so that this sector may properly carry out its function.

In Article 4 (e), the Charter of the Organization of American States specifies that one of the Organization's purposes is "to promote, by cooperative action, their economic, social, and cultural development."

To meet this objective, there is the Inter-American Economic and Social Council, and within the new structure of the Pan American Union there is an Assistant Secretary for Economic and Social Affairs.

In the Agreement establishing the Inter-American Development Bank, it is stipulated that the purpose of the bank is "to contribute to the acceleration of the process of economic development of the member countries, individually and collectively."

Finally, the Charter of the United Nations begins with this declaration of faith: "We, the peoples of the United Nations, [are] determined . . . to promote social progress and better standards of life in larger freedom, and for these ends . . . to employ international machinery for the promotion of the economic and social advancement of all people. . . ." To implement this declaration, Chapter X of the Charter provides for the establishment of the Economic and Social Council, and in addition the United Nations has created Economic Commissions for Europe, Asia, Africa, and Latin America. The latter, known by the abbreviation ECLA, is cosponsoring this meeting.

It is understandable, then, why the question of taxation in relation to development must be dealt with and why Mr. Naharro has entitled his paper "Production and Consumption Taxes and Economic Development."

In line with that title, the author might have offered some basic observations on the economic development of the countries and on the question of how taxation in general, and taxes on consumption and production in particular, help or impede that development. However, he begins, first, by establishing certain concepts of terminology; and then, in the second part, he discusses the relationship between taxation and development. But the analysis is confined essentially to measuring the tax burden borne by certain Latin American countries and breaking down those taxes between direct and indirect on the one hand, and internal and external on the other hand, without, however, establishing the relationship between the degree of development of those countries and their prevailing tax systems. The policy of development seeks resources to attain harmonious growth in both the public and private economy; the criterion of the financing purist, of looking for resources for the government even at the cost of private interests, is disappearing from the present-day world, even though some instances may still be found.

According to the theories of economic development, such development "consists in a process by which the real income of an economy is increased over a long period of time."[52] But if there is to be genuine growth, there must be an increase in the real per capita income; that is, the rate of growth of real income must be greater than the rate of growth of the population.

Economic development is characterized by an increase in per capita production and the attainment of higher standards of living, which are obtained by more efficient activity in agriculture as well as industry and commerce.

"Finally, economic development is but a part of social progress, which is expressed in terms of broader human values—health, education, individual liberty, security, the creative spirit, and other attributes that enhance human dignity, including a democratic government and a free country that will not be looked upon by the others as second-rate."[53]

Economic development is attained, therefore, by a better utilization of the human, natural, and financial resources which a country possesses. More education and technical facilities for the training of professionals and skilled workers who will serve industry are part of a development program. The establishment of an inventory of natural resources and adequate planning for their use are also part of a development program; so too is the provision of basic services that will help such utilization, such as the construction of highways, electric power plants, telecommunications systems, water supply systems for both domestic use and agriculture, etc.

But, in addition, the government's economic policy must make itself felt by influencing the attitudes that shape the economic institutions and the use of the resources; by seeking a better distribution of income; by controlling the amount of money and cyclical fluctuations; by striving for full employment of the factors of production; and by influencing the level of investments.

The foregoing makes it evident that the government has double functions: direct and indirect. I believe that the success of a government in the field of economic development depends more on its indirect than on its direct functions, and the failure of many of them is due to their neglect of their indirect duties and obligations.

It is easy for everyone to understand the first functions of a government, which pertain to the maintenance of public services—order and peace at the national level and security at the international level; protection for the citizens in their safety and liberty, their education and health; the construction of highways and schools; the maintenance of research and statistical services, etc.

But, through legislative and administrative action, the government must also adopt a firm attitude with respect to private enterprise, markets and contracts, land tenure and ownership, protectionism or free trade, taxation and money. According to the needs of the country, it may favor one or another type of industry—large or small, competitive or monopolistic, public or private.

The government must also exert its influence on the attitudes of the private sector in respect of the use of resources, the distribution of income, and the level of investment. These are difficult functions, because they depend upon the response of the private sector, where reactions are not always logical. But the government must act in such a manner as to attain the desired ends.

"No country has made economic progress without positive stimulus from intelligent governments," states W. Arthur Lewis, offering the cases of England and the United States as examples. "On the other hand," he says, "there are so many examples of the mischief done to economic life by governments that it is easy to fill one's pages with warnings

[52]Gerald M. Meier and Robert E. Baldwin, *Economic Development* (New York: John Wiley and Sons, 1957), p. 2.
[53]Néstor Vega-Moreno, *Industrias e industrialización en el Ecuador* (Quito: Junta Nacional de Planificación y Coordinación Económica, 1959); *Manual of Industrial Development* (Washington, D. C.: Foreign Operations Administration, 1955).

against government participation in economic life."[54]

But the provision of these services, the professional and technical training, and the exploitation of natural resources can be accomplished solely on the basis of an accumulation of financial resources. Herein lies the fundamental role of the monetary and fiscal policy.

There are only two ways of increasing investments that will lead to the formation of capital and hence to an increase in production and economic development. These are an increase in internal or domestic savings and external credit. Of course, external credit is in the last analysis merely an advance on domestic savings, since there must necessarily be savings in order to service the contracted debt. So, the one means of development is savings.

These internal or domestic savings may be, and in fact are, distributed among the business sector, the individual sector, and the government. Adequate participation by each of these sectors will make harmonious development possible; otherwise, there will be an imbalance in favor of one sector and against the other two.

It is appropriate to make an analysis of the particular tasks of the government. In addition to providing for the services that are indispensable to itself and the public order, the government must carry out certain works and services that are outside the purview of the private sector, either because they are incompatible with it or beyond its capacity. Thus, the government is obligated to provide ways of communication, ports and airports, irrigation, school buildings, and, in most of the underdeveloped countries, such services as electrification, telecommunications, and certain types of transport (railroads), the very magnitude of which prevents the private sector from undertaking them, even though they might be in the hands of private enterprise. This leads to the conclusion that, although

there is no standardized participation between the private and public sectors, the latter must have sufficient resources to cover its ordinary services and to enable it to make rational plans for the capital projects that devolve upon it. On the other hand, government participation, through taxes or other means, should not exceed the limits of the pressures and friction that are felt in the private sector when the tax burden is very great, because it is highly dangerous to wipe out all incentive for the private sector which, because of its own nature, holds the key to the major part of economic activity.

The way to obtain financial resources for the government, without divesting the private sector of incentives but rather giving it greater opportunities for employment, is the principal topic and purpose of the paper under discussion. There are many ways for the state to obtain revenues through taxes. These taxes may be levied on assets or wealth; on urban and rural real property; on income, whether it be salaries and wages, interest, business profits, or earnings on capital; on international trade, through customs duties, consular fees, or foreign exchange taxes; on transportation and communications; on production of the extractive and manufacturing industries; on sales and consumption, etc. The study on which we are commenting refers to the last-mentioned of these categories, that is, taxes on production and consumption as related to economic development. We shall follow the author's division of his paper and shall comment on the different sections in turn.

SPECIFIC COMMENTS ON THE STUDY BY JOSE MARIA NAHARRO

Terminology and Definitions

The author begins by giving a definition of taxes on production and consumption, going into a long discussion in order to classify them as direct and indirect, stating that the direct tax falls upon income when the latter is received by the natural or juristic person, while

[54] W. Arthur Lewis, *The Theory of Economic Growth* (Homewood, Ill.: Richard D. Irwin, 1955), Chap. VII, p. 376.

indirect taxes fall upon income at the time it leaves the assets of the taxpayer through expenditure. Furthermore, the author accepts ability to pay as a principle of taxation, ignoring the criterion of benefit received and social desirability. Of course, the principle of capacity to pay is more widely accepted by all experts in public finance and fiscal policy, and for that reason taxes at the time of expenditure, which include all indirect taxes, are opposed as being unjust since, by not taking account of the taxpayer's capacity to pay, they are regressive as far as low incomes are concerned. On the other hand, the capacity to pay adjusts better to the direct tax, although in this case, too, some economists offer objections, because the direct tax affects the savings of the more active enterprises, and these are precisely the ones which, through successive reinvestments, can give employment and help toward a better distribution of income a posteriori. This is more serious, because the direct tax gives the taxpayer no opportunity for avoidance; while the indirect tax is collected only under certain circumstances and according to the volume of consumption of certain goods.

Another characteristic of the indirect tax is the shifting of the tax burden—which does not mean that this aspect applies only to indirect taxes; there are cases where direct taxes are also shifted, but it happens more rarely. The volume of shifting to third persons and the final picture of the tax incidence depend upon the structure of the markets: that is, whether the supply comes from monopolistic or fully competitive sources; whether the economy is in a phase of expansion or of depression; whether there is elasticity of demand and prices; and whether substitutes are or are not available. Thus, the incidence of the tax is quite beyond the will of the lawmaker, who can neither control nor direct it.

The author states that taxes on production and taxes on consumption, being indirect—that is, on income spent—are of the same nature, the difference between them being found rather in the technique used to apply them. This concept seems to us to be in error,

since taxes on production are collected at the producer level, even though the burden on costs may be shifted to the consumer. Basically the difference is that these taxes are collected not only on sales but also on stocks. The consumption tax, on the other hand, is collected only on sales; and it may be collected at the producer level, but also at the wholesale or final retail level. The tax may be paid in its totality by either the consumer or the producer, but in most cases it is absorbed in more or less proportional parts by the producer and the consumer, depending on the price elasticity of demand and on the specific economic situation. A tax on a completely inelastic article will have to be paid in full by the consumer, while a tax on an article for which the demand is highly elastic will have to be absorbed in full by the producer. The majority of cases fall between these two extremes. Likewise, a depressed economic situation will place the producer at a disadvantage, because he will have to absorb the tax if he does not wish to have his sales curtailed even more; conversely, boom conditions put the producer on the strong side and the tax will be transferred to the consumer. That is why an economy in the process of inflation benefits producers to the detriment of consumers.

By treating production and consumption taxes as indirect levies, the author quite rightly asks whether these two categories cover the entire field of indirect taxation, and he answers this question with the division made in Germany, which classifies indirect taxes in three principal categories: (1) taxes on sales, (2) taxes on consumption and expenditures, and (3) taxes on transactions.

He does not indicate which of these categories includes the tax on production; possibly it is among the taxes on consumption and expenditures. The truth is that there is no difference between sales taxes and taxes on consumption. The differentiation should be made rather between taxes on production on the one hand and taxes on sales, consumption, and expenditures on the other.

Since the tax on transactions is somewhat

vague, the author himself states that it encompasses a very diverse and heterogeneous series of taxes, among them being taxes on inheritances, stock exchange operations, the transfer of real estate titles, unearned increment, corporate capital, etc. This list indicates that these taxes on transactions—to borrow the term from the German terminology—should not be classified as indirect taxes; taxes on capital are direct, unless they are levied at the time of a transfer of ownership. The reason for this is that the owner of the capital cannot himself get rid of the obligation to pay the tax. On the other hand, taxes on transport and communication can very well be integrated with the tax on expenditures and consumption.

As for customs taxes, the author acknowledges that taxes on imports are indirect and that taxes on exports do not belong in the category of production and consumption taxes because they are direct. Nonetheless, he discusses them, although somewhat summarily, in the final part of his study. The truth is that a tax on exports is a substitute for or an addition to the tax on the profits of exporters. No country taxes exports that do not produce sufficient profits. There are also cases where the tax on exports is a substitute for the rural real property tax, which in turn is a substitute for a tax on farm income. Consequently, the fact that foreign trade is taxed in both cases is not sufficient reason to consider them jointly.

The author states in his paper that he does not intend to take up the administrative and technical side of the taxes, since he is interested only in their special relationship to economic development. It must be said, however, that technical and administrative questions are very often genuine measures of the fiscal policy which favorably or unfavorably affect economic development, considering that one of the foundation stones or pillars of such development is the efficiency and flexibility of the administration. The frequency and time of the tax are also questions of policy; both depend not only on the theory of public finance and fiscal policy but also—and essentially—on the administrative efficiency of tax collection.

The author refrains from commenting on the desirability of specific or ad valorem taxes and uniform or multiple tariffs, although precisely this discrimination can clothe indirect taxes with a modicum of justice, because, since they fall more heavily on low incomes when they are based on uniform or specific tariffs, they are unjust. Excise taxes, which modify the incidence of general levies on consumption or sales, likewise tend toward a better distribution of the tax burden.

Taxation and Economic Development

The author begins by stating that he will not discuss public expenditure policies or methods of financing such expenditures other than taxes, since his paper refers only to these. He begins by affirming that "the policy of development requires first of all that the means for carrying out its new functions be made available to the public sector." This being so, this section of the study deals with (a) methods of increasing tax collections and (b) the desirability of using this or that type of tax to achieve that purpose.

Since development is based on savings, and since savings are very low in underdeveloped countries, the author insists on the compulsive action of taxation as a means of achieving forced savings. The tax burden cannot logically increase indefinitely, and it is necessary to apply the brakes when the red light of danger appears. He mentions the limit of 25 per cent of the national income set by Colin Clark, a limit which has been considerably exceeded in developed countries such as England, for example, where the tax burden went beyond 35 per cent ten years ago. But this exception says nothing with respect to underdeveloped countries where the red light may flash at very low levels of the tax burden, when the per capita income is also so low that it barely covers the subsistence level. This is the case with most of the population in the underdeveloped countries.

If savings constitute the country's only means of forming capital and therefore of achieving its economic development, and if the government must undertake some of the tasks of that development—a matter we shall discuss later—it is acceptable to resort to the compulsion of taxes in order to accumulate the savings that are to serve the government for its capital projects. But one must not forget the objections raised against taxation as a means of compulsory savings on the grounds that taxes are a counterincentive to voluntary savings.[55]

An excessive decrease in voluntary savings may seriously damage the private economy, which will hold the view that all incentives for investment are limited and will reduce the sources of employment it could offer; the government will be unable to offset this decline with its own investments and will have to adopt measures that are quite the reverse of taxation, that is, exemptions and subsidies, which it would otherwise not be compelled to take.

Since economic growth depends on investments, investments depend on savings, and savings depend on earnings, these latter should be favored and not penalized. That is why Arthur Lewis, in his book cited in this study, mentions the desirability of decreasing rather than increasing the wages of the non-skilled class.

The author of the study under discussion then makes an analysis of the tax burden in ten Latin American countries. He relates central government tax collections with national income. But this raises two serious

[55]Ver Ragnar Nurkse, *Problems of Capital Formation in Underdeveloped Countries*, 5th ed. (Oxford: Basil Blackwell, 1957), p. 145.

problems in the analysis. First, he takes up only those taxes that accrue to the central government and excludes those whose proceeds accrue to other levels of government; yet at times these are considerable, and therefore to disregard them is to give a completely erroneous idea of the true tax burden. Furthermore, it seems to be a serious mistake to take the net national product—or in other words, the national income—as the counterpart of the taxes in order to measure the tax burden, for the reason that indirect taxes, which account for the major part of government revenues in the Latin American countries, as the author himself admits, do not form part of the national income but rather of the gross national product. Finally, there seems to be another error in making the analysis on the basis of current figures without due consideration of deflation, although it is indeed true that the relationships are not altered. (In Table 9–14 the real situation in Ecuador may be noted, this being the only case I have been able to verify.)

The author also observes that the tax system in the underdeveloped countries does not have the same elasticity it has in the more advanced countries; that is, an increase in the tax does not necessarily increase actual collections. There are many explanations for this situation. If a direct tax on income is concerned, the cause may be that the rate is not sufficiently progressive in the upper brackets, or it may be that there was a change in income distribution. If an indirect tax on sales and consumption is concerned, the explanation may be that collection of the tax depends on the elasticity of demand. Finally, as the author very properly notes, the administration of the tax may not respond efficiently

TABLE 9–14: Tax Burden in Ecuador (*Millions of sucres*)

	1956	1957	1958	1959	1960	1961
1. Gross national product	10,987	11,631	12,053	12,624	13,662	14,624
2. Total tax revenues (excluding fees)	1,578	1,803	1,884	1,989	2,127	2,292
3. Tax burden (2:1) (percentage)	14.5	15.5	15.6	15.7	15.6	15.7

SOURCE: Ecuador, Central Bank, *Memoria*, 1961.

to a legal increase in the taxes, and it may be actually unable to collect them.

On the other hand, we agree that it is impossible to increase the tax burden when the per capita income of the vast majority is strictly at the subsistence level; we agree that when a great part of the population is not monetized it cannot easily be burdened with taxes. These are the types of people who neither produce nor consume, and they constitute one of the greatest problems in the economic development of a country.

In regard to the second point of this chapter, on the choice of one or another type of tax to obtain revenues for the government, the discussion centers on the preference for either direct or indirect taxes for such purposes. Various arguments can be offered in theoretical proof that direct taxes are more desirable because they are more fair and equitable, inasmuch as the burden falls on each according to his capacity to pay and because they do not distort commodity prices. On the other hand, indirect taxes, which are included in the price of the goods, simultaneously decrease real income, distort prices, and take on all the characteristics of regressivity, since in terms of percentages they represent a heavier burden on the lower incomes than on the higher ones.

But a tax system cannot be based solely on these considerations of equity. It must also look toward a sufficiency of resources to cover the services vested in the government, and no underdeveloped country could take in enough funds solely on the basis of direct taxation, for in such a country the taxed population would amount to scarcely 10 per cent, and in many it would be less than 5 per cent. It is obvious that to collect sufficient budget revenues merely through taxing a very limited group of the population, the rates would have to be so high that they would remove every incentive for investment, and the people would complain, with good reason, that a heavy penalty was being laid on industriousness and hard work, while inactivity was being rewarded. And since the high-income group is the one that also provides jobs and wages for the working people, to tax the management class too heavily would be to kill the goose that lays the golden egg.

On the other hand, as the author very well mentions, indirect taxes have the advantage of being easier to administer. This circumstance, however, should not be the determining factor in preferring them. If from the standpoint of equity they are less fair, there should be sufficient economic justification for their adoption. If direct taxes do not provide enough revenues to cover the government's budget, indirect levies should be adopted; furthermore, it is necessary that all citizens of a country, even the poorest, contribute something to the support of the state. Thus, a combination of various kinds of taxes may be useful, so that a person who does not contribute in one way will do so in another. But above and beyond all these financial considerations is one basic economic consideration, and that is that the low-income class should be forced to save in some manner, even at the sacrifice of their present consumption, in order that the financial institutions and the government may accumulate funds which, upon being invested, will soon yield benefits for the low-income groups, who will then have greater opportunities for employment and consequently larger incomes for their consumption needs. In simple terms, it is a matter of a temporary sacrifice for an expanding future benefit.

This has been the tax pattern followed by England, Russia, and Japan in their industrial revolutions; it does not involve an increase at the start in the incomes of farm people and wage earners with a strong inclination toward consumption, but rather an increase in private profits and public resources in order to form capital.

At the present time, however, all countries must base their tax system on a combined structure of direct and indirect taxes, to be selected according to the purpose and the circumstances. It is fair that general services should be based on taxes on income and wealth, but it seems logical that certain projects should be financed by their users.

This applies to the construction of highways, which represent one of government's largest investments; they should be financed by those who use them. The gasoline tax, which is an indirect tax on the consumption of that article, is best suited to that purpose. It can be supplemented by taxes on unearned increment and vehicles. On the other hand, electrification and water systems should be financed exclusively through the rates charged for the service. To finance them with general taxes would lead to waste and would constitute a subsidy that should be avoided.

In commenting on Table 9–2, which compares indirect and direct taxation as components of a tax system, it must be said that the author again falls into the error of comparing only the taxes accruing to the central government, while in many countries assets such as urban and rural property are taxed at other levels of government, which would cause great variations in the proportions. His analysis, therefore, could be radically changed. (See the case of Ecuador in Table 9–15.)

To close this chapter, the author briefly mentions "the role of taxation in the growth of the private sector," pointing out that the government may favor the private sector in two ways: (a) by returning part of the resources collected by the government to the private sector, not in the form of general public services but in the form of subsidies and credits directed toward stimulating the

improvement of the country; and (b) by the impact of taxes on the economy.

It is understood that subsidies and credits may directly favor production, but is there any direct or indirect tax that can completely favor production? Every tax either decreases earnings or increases costs, but it is difficult to see that the tax impact or burden can favor production.

Internal Taxes on Production and Consumption and Economic Development. In this chapter the analysis concentrates principally on the following points:

1. The tax and production.
2. The tax and consumption.
3. The tax and savings.
4. The tax and investment.
5. The tax and wages.
6. The tax and labor supply.

Logically, the analysis necessarily becomes perplexing when it deals with production and consumption, saving and investment, wages and labor. The incidence of the tax on consumption is very diverse. If the tax falls on production, it represents a displacement of the cost curve toward the left. Higher costs will cause industry to fix a new point of equilibrium according to the demand curve. Except in the case of absolutely inelastic goods, this leads to a reduction in consumption, often despite increased expenditures. A general tax on production would decrease

TABLE 9–15: Direct and Indirect Taxes in Ecuador

	1956	1957	1958	1959	1960	1961
	(Millions of sucres)					
1. Taxes on income and wealth	528	585	633	695	702	753
2. Taxes on exports	110	136	134	144	175	188
3. Taxes on imports	447	544	571	579	642	682
4. Other indirect taxes	493	538	546	571	608	669
	1,578	1,803	1,884	1,989	2,127	2,292
	(Percentages)					
1. Taxes on income and wealth	34	32	28	35	33	33
2. Taxes on exports	7	8	7	7	8	8
3. Taxes on imports	28	30	30	29	30	30
4. Other indirect taxes	31	30	30	29	29	29
	100	100	100	100	100	100

SOURCE: Ecuador, Central Bank, *Memoria,* 1961.

effective demand, and, by decreasing profits of the producers, a reduction in sales will curtail incentives for investment.

A tax on consumption would have exactly the same incidence, since in the case of taxes on both production and consumption it cannot be ensured that they will be paid only by the consumer or only by the producer; more frequently they must be absorbed by both parties.

With reference to a reduction in effective demand, we cannot agree with the statement that the demand for luxury goods is highly inelastic. This may be the case with a very small group of the population with very high incomes, for whom an increase in price does not reduce consumption. But there is a large percentage of the population that could be catalogued as middle- and upper-middle-class who, as their incomes rise, increase their consumption of goods normally regarded as luxury items. Actually, the classification of goods as luxury items is very inexact, since it may vary according to the standards of the various countries. But in general it may be stated that aside from jewelry, fine furs, etc., which are exclusively luxury goods, there are many articles that make for comfort in the home and that are being bought more and more by the middle- and upper-middle-classes to whom we referred above, who would halt their demand if the costs were to increase. So, luxury items are in general very elastic, and if the demand for them is not reduced, contraband will increase. In any event, a scale of excise or specific taxes on specific products, according to whether they are essential or nonessential, is adequate, since the injustice of the indirect tax is thus eliminated in part. Of course, the final incidence of a tax of this kind depends not so much on the elasticity of demand as on the structure of the market, that is, whether the latter is fully competitive, fully monopolistic, or monopolistically competitive.

With respect to savings and investment, it must be noted that the indirect tax first affects the savings of the private sector and, when this is insufficient, the income intended for consumption. When savings are reduced, investment by private enterprise is also reduced, because private companies see that the possibility for them to obtain credit from financial institutions is reduced. On the other hand, government savings may be increased by this system, which helps the government to make investments in infrastructure and to lay the ground for a subsequent industrial economy. From this point of view, taxes on consumption are desirable in developing countries, because they obligate all the inhabitants of a territory determined to help to a greater or lesser extent to achieve the basic structure demanded by a more developed economy. Of course, this is true only when a good budget policy is followed, one that does not employ all of the government's resources in consumption expenditures but invests a good part of them. An adequate policy of this type is in line with the statement made above, to the effect that today's sacrifice is made for tomorrow's good; if this relationship between the tax policy and the expenditure policy is not present, taxes on consumption will only lead to increasing poverty.

If it is not desired to reduce private investment—which necessarily follows decreased sales with the consequent decrease in total income and smaller profits for business—and if it is desired to concentrate financial resources in the hands of investors, the negative effects of a tax on consumption can be offset by a reduction or elimination of the income tax on undistributed profits. In this case, larger state investment could be co-ordinated with larger private investment, thereby developing an industrial economy. One can go even farther, if the policy suggested by the author, of allocating part of the state's resources to the financing of credit agencies for industry and agriculture, is followed.

In respect of wages and labor, it must be said that if consumption taxes reduce real family income, wage earners will be put in a highly disadvantageous position with regard to consumption. The action of labor unions could lead to a demand for higher wages, with the demands backed by force and strikes.

Thus, producers not only would have their income reduced by decreased sales but would have to face political situations caused by the pressure of the labor unions, and they would have to cut down their production and employment, to the greater detriment of the wage-earning classes, whose job opportunities would be lessened.

This problem can be solved if, along with the consumption taxes that affect all classes, incentives are offered to businessmen through the reduction or elimination of the tax on undistributed profits destined for reinvestment. With an incentive of this kind, firms would continue to invest and produce despite the increased salaries and wages, which process, by extending to all economic sectors, would also increase sales, thus leading to a new point of equilibrium. Consequently, assuming these conditions, in the long run the state could in turn take in greater revenues from the increased consumption, and these revenues would enable it to finance not only normal services but also capital investments and credit organizations. All of the foregoing leads to the conclusion that a tax on sales and consumption should be levied on the final product and not on raw materials and the means of production, in order not to put a double tax burden on final products and not to increase their cost. This danger can be resolved, of course, on the basis of the system of sales taxation and the value added tax, even though this is not very popular; few countries use it, among them France and Japan and, in the United States, only the State of Michigan.[56]

Following the idea of taxing consumption but not savings, the latter could be channeled either toward government or industry by exempting public bonds and rated industrial securities from taxation. This would be a good way to introduce frugality and to develop savings which, on being invested, would contribute toward the objectives of economic development. In any event, care must be exercised with respect to the flight of capital, because if that occurs the economy of the country will reap no benefit whatever.

The author remarks that taxes on consumption constitute discrimination in favor of a final product, namely leisure. By taxing consumption, which is made possible by income which in turn is derived from work, and not taxing leisure, which is also a final product, people might be persuaded to work less in order to pay less taxes and have more hours for rest. If this were to happen, logically consumption taxes would be playing a role completely at odds with economic development, this being the product of work, not of idleness. This seems to us to be splitting hairs about the behavior of the people. Actually, idleness is one of the most valued items among the more primitive peoples, but the normal reaction is that rest is taken after the minimum requirements of life have been met. Consequently, the more normal reaction is that when the people who live at the minimum level see their income reduced by taxes, they will work longer hours in order not to cut down that minimum, and this may turn out to be beneficial to economic development.

The author mentions an interesting case observed in Guatemala, "where the Indian population shows a strong preference for leisure, once the minimum subsistence level is reached. When this level is reduced, the income effect is so strong that the Indian will work to regain his former position, but scarcely has this been done when the tendency toward leisure again prevails."

Before finishing with this subject, I should like to state that it is really impossible to make a table showing the incidence of taxes at different levels of income. It has been said that the indirect tax is essentially regressive and unfair, but it is impossible to measure to what extent this is so. Musgrave's analysis, reproduced in Table 9–3 of the study under

---

[56]On the question of the sales tax and the value added tax, the following may be consulted:

a) *Value Added Taxation* (Cambridge, Mass.: Harvard Law School, International Tax Research Seminar, 1959).

b) "Sales Taxation in France and Value Added Tax," in John Due, *Sales Taxation* (Urbana: University of Illinois Press, 1957).

c) Clarence W. Lock, Donovan J. Rau, and Howard D. Hamilton, "The Michigan Value Added Tax," *National Tax Journal*, VIII, 4 (1955).

discussion, showing the tax burden by quartiles, should be very interesting, but the author should have offered some comments, making a minimum of analysis of the real situation and not simply presenting without comment a somewhat incomprehensible and completely theoretical table.

In this connection, the author states that while "the problems of income redistribution must wait, at least until it becomes possible to redistribute something more than an extremely low per capita welfare, in no way does it prove that the grave social traumas of tax regressivity can be offset by the meager additional accumulations coming from a reduction in consumption that is already at the very edge of the minimum level." In this respect it may be stated that since the low-income social group is the most numerous, a small contribution from this group can accumulate fairly appreciable sums to help development; this thought has prevailed in many countries, for example, in Japan, where industrial development has been paid for by the poorest class: the farmers. It is all the more important to consider this, since the sacrifice of a few years can be more than compensated for by future benefits, as already stated in these comments. Therefore, I believe that indirect taxes on consumption, aided by other measures favoring savings and investment, can be a good fiscal policy for the purpose of development. By this I do not mean to say that only the poor classes should pay for development; the wealthy classes should pay, and with even more reason; and for that purpose the consumption taxes on luxury goods should be high, so that the high-income groups, who spend a large part of their income on this type of goods, also pay their share in the development. The purpose behind a general sales tax is simply that all the inhabitants of a country should share in financing its development.

Customs Taxes and Economic Development. This section of the taxation study for the most part consists of comments on import taxes, followed by some points of view on export taxes. Basically it is a discussion of the advantages and disadvantages of the doctrines of free trade and protectionism. The advantages are measured from both the economic and the tax revenue standpoint in each case, but on the other hand there is insistence on the price of protectionism.

Free trade was strongly supported by the classical and neoclassical doctrine of foreign trade, as the author very well notes in his study. The points in favor of free trade, according to Gottfried Haberler in his book *International Trade and Economic Development,* are:

1. It makes it possible to obtain material goods (machinery, raw materials, and semi-finished products) required for economic development.

2. It favors the transmission of ideas, technical know-how, etc.

3. It serves as a vehicle for the international movement of capital.

4. It increases the degree of free competition within the country, since free trade is the best antimonopoly policy.

These conditions make free trade one of the most useful policies for all countries, because it permits economic specialization and complementation, although it still involves certain reservations and undesirable features, as acknowledged by modern authors with classical tendencies. Against these general principles, the author makes the following affirmation: "This classical theory is static and is therefore considered inadequate for dealing with dynamic problems of development. Specialization implies only a movement along the production possibility curve, where resources and techniques are held constant."

Actually, the classical pattern was essentially dynamic, and that is how it was conceived by Adam Smith, John Stuart Mill, and Ricardo. Thus, the modern tendencies toward common markets and customs unions are directed essentially to the elimination of customs barriers as a means of increasing production and consumption and of accelerating development. We shall return to this point later. Protectionism is basically useful to strengthen industries that have potentials for expansion and those industries that can promote the development of other sectors, as the author notes. Logically, protectionism must be temporary, and it would be a mistake to maintain it permanently, because such a practice would lead to stagnation in the systems of production and would fill the pockets of producers to the detriment of consumers, if the latter did not resort to contraband goods to satisfy their needs. In this latter case, protectionism would favor neither industry nor the state, because the former would find their sales decreased instead of increased and the latter would lose fiscal revenues.

The author states that protectionist tariffs have been favored by economists in the Latin American countries and supported by United Nations officials, especially ECLA. As a matter of fact, Prebisch is an indefatigable advocate of industrialization and is constantly pointing out the undesirability of keeping the Latin American countries as mere producers of raw materials and primary articles, which, because of the low price elasticity of demand and supply, are susceptible to great price alterations which upset the calculations of producers and seriously damage their economies. Furthermore, because of the low income elasticity of the demand, the saturation point for such products is soon reached in international markets and, because of new areas incorporated into the production of the same commodities (as in the case of Africa, which is competing with Latin America in the production of raw materials), the increased supply causes a price deterioration, which makes it difficult for this kind of country to achieve development, for in addition they have to pay more for industrial goods. So, although it may seem paradoxical, the underdeveloped countries subsidize the high income of the developed countries, where production costs are consistently on the rise because of the wage increases exacted by well-organized labor unions.

As an example of this situation, I should like to refer to Ecuador. An examination of the indexes of volume shows that the country's total exports increased 94 per cent from 1950 to 1960; that is, they almost doubled. However, foreign exchange receipts do not depend solely on the volume of exports; they also depend on the price of the products in the foreign market. Prices for Ecuador's principal export products—bananas, cacao, coffee, and rice—increased strongly up to 1954. In fact, the prices of the food exports increased 48.4 per cent from 1950 to 1954; but from this latter year to 1960 they dropped 35.12 per cent. The prices for other products which Ecuador exports, such as industrial goods, chemicals, pharmaceutical products, minerals, and so on, were incapable of neutralizing the effects of the prices of the food products, which are so important that they determine the direction of the price curve as a whole. The general index of export prices rose 13 per cent from 1950 to 1954 and then dropped 18 per cent from 1954 to 1960. The final result for the period is a decrease of 4.65 per cent.

In contrast to this behavior of export prices, the prices of the country's imports rose 45.3 per cent in the period 1950–60, and the products which the country needs for development are those that have increased most in price. As a matter of fact, the prices of industrial and mining machinery have risen 108 per cent, the prices of farm machinery 95 per cent, those for construction machinery and equipment and permanent fittings for buildings 41 per cent, transportation and communications equipment 89 per cent, spare parts and accessories for machinery and equipment 82 per cent, tools and implements for farmers and skilled workers 100 per cent, nonspecialized machinery and implements 74 per cent, and other equipment and machinery, including laboratory and office equipment, 156 per cent.

The result of this price trend is that the terms of trade index deteriorated 39 per cent in the period reviewed. This unfavorable situation is going to make development increasingly difficult, because it means that the effort to save and to make capital investments must be much greater.

This is the real situation as understood by Prebisch, and that is why he insists that the countries on the periphery, as he calls them, meaning the underdeveloped countries, must not be eternally condemned to their under-development, and that is why he may seem to be protectionist in his views.

But the author of the paper under discussion questions the supposition that in the long run the terms of trade move against the countries that are producers of raw materials, and he even questions the concept of terms of trade, which ought to be re-examined because, he states, decisive factors relating to the earnings from international trade, or the country's income, are not taken into account.[57] The truth is that the concept of terms of trade is not a supposition but a genuine economic phenomenon, because of the enormous supply of primary products of low income elasticity of demand on the one side and the high income elasticity of demand for industrial products on the other side, which, considering the steady increase in their sales, permit higher wages for industrial workers and thereby increase costs. Furthermore, the terms of trade are a price relationship, aside from the gains from international trade and the income of the country. In any event, deterioration in the terms of trade leads to less and less gain from international trade for the underdeveloped countries, and the rate of growth of their income is very low.

Mr. Naharro believes that the concepts which M. K. Atallah has set down as "double factoral terms of trade," "single factoral terms of trade," and "index of total gain" would be more significant than the concept of commodity terms of trade.

But Haberler himself,[58] in discussing terms of trade, compares "commodity terms of trade" with "factoral terms of trade" and concludes that simple commodity terms of trade still offer the most useful yardstick in international trade. The purpose of "factoral terms of trade" is to weigh the simple export and import price indexes according to the indexes of national and foreign productivity, respectively.

When the weighing is for both export and import indexes, we have the "double factoral terms of trade"; if it refers only to the export indexes, we have the "single factoral terms of trade."

Thus, the difference between the commodity terms of trade and the two concepts just mentioned can be expressed by the following formulas:

$$CTT = \frac{\text{export price index}}{\text{import price index}}$$

$$S.F.TT = \frac{\text{export price index} \times \text{national productivity index}}{\text{import price index}}$$

$$D.F.TT = \frac{\text{export price index} \times \text{national productivity index}}{\text{import price index} \times \text{foreign productivity index}}$$

Theoretically, the "double factoral terms of trade" concept is the fairer, because it relates not only prices but also productivity, which, combined, indicate what is lost or gained in international trade. However, because of the great difficulties of calculation Taussig has suggested

$$\text{"gross barter terms of trade"} = \frac{Qi}{Qe}$$

and Dorrance and Staehle refer to the

$$\text{"income terms of trade"} = \frac{Qe\ Pe}{Pi}[59]$$

Imlah calls this last formula the "export gain from trade index," that is, the index of the total gain mentioned by Mr. Naharro.

[57] Part of the discussion that follows refers to statements that do not appear in the revised version of Mr. Naharro's paper.

[58] Gottfried Haberler, A Survey of International Trade Theory (Princeton: Princeton University Press, 1955).

[59] The symbols have the following meanings: Qi is the import quantity index; Qe, the export quantity index; Pi, the import price index; and Pe, the export price index.

"Neither an increase in the index of the gross barter terms of trade nor of that of the income terms of trade can be regarded as an indication that a country's position has improved or that its gains from trade have increased," says Haberler. "In fact," he continues, "both of these measures are inferior to, and a less reliable guide than, the simple commodity terms of trade, because each of them treats as equivalent cases that have to be judged differently, even if other things have remained unchanged."

To continue with reference to Latin America's foreign trade policy, it must be said that in the face of the apparently protectionist theories of the Latin American countries and of ECLA, those same countries have formed two substantially broad regional common markets: the Central American Free Trade Zone, which comprises five countries—Costa Rica, El Salvador, Guatemala, Honduras, and Nicaragua (of which three—Guatemala, Honduras, and El Salvador—form a genuine common market, and they are inclining toward integration with Nicaragua), and the Latin American Free Trade Association, established by the Treaty of Montevideo in February, 1960, signed by Argentina, Bolivia, Brazil, Chile, Mexico, Paraguay, Peru, and Uruguay, and to which Colombia and Ecuador adhered later.

It is to be noted that ECLA has been the foremost promoter of the formation of these markets, with a view to achieving more rapid growth by means of regional economic integration.

Multilateralism in the matter of trade agreements stems from a new philosophy that is extending throughout the world—a philosophy of mutual co-operation and reciprocal technical assistance to solve economic, social, and cultural problems, both individual and collective, of all countries of the world, as set forth in the Charter of the United Nations and, in regional terms, in the Charter of the Organization of American States. To this end, all technical advances must be used to satisfy the growing requirements of the population if the latter is not to remain outside the margin of modern civilization. And if there is no country in the world that is economically self-sufficient, the proper thing to do is to establish multilateral relations to supplement its economy. Needs have increased considerably over the course of time, and to meet those needs, nations become parties to bilateral treaties; but even these are not sufficient, not adequate, and therefore broader international integration becomes necessary. Furthermore, international trade and the exportation and importation of capital are made difficult by customs barriers and very burdensome tax legislation which, by increasing the cost of goods, obstruct the sharing of the progress obtained through modern technology by all countries in the world, and especially by the more needy sectors.

Thus, common markets mean free trade within the region concerned and protectionism with respect to the rest of the world. Their basic objective is economic development, to be attained through expanded markets, more factors of production, and mobility of raw materials, capital, finished products, and technical know-how.

As may be understood from the foregoing, customs duties on imports will have to be eliminated step by step from the regions of economic complementarity, and substitute fiscal resources will have to be sought in fields other than international trade. This is a point that was not touched upon by the author; it deserves special attention, for it deals with the factual situation in which we are living and it cannot be disregarded by the signatory countries. Furthermore, Europe is giving us an example; it is showing us that in addition to the industriousness of the European peoples and their accumulation of techniques and capital, the prime factors in their economic development have been the elimination of customs barriers and the formation of the common market. In the near future, customs duties and similar taxes will have to be forgotten as means of obtaining public revenues and protecting industry, at least in regional terms, because the trends of development are diametrically opposed to that type of tax and that type of protection.

With respect to export taxes which, despite their being direct levies, the author does discuss—and, I believe, with some reason, because in a certain manner they are taxes on production, paid in the last instance by the producer or by the foreign consumer, according to the volume of supply and the international demand—they also will have to disappear in order to come to competitive terms. Of course, this is the world tendency, because taxes on exports are collected only when there is evidence that the exporters are making large profits; in reality, they are either substitutes for or supplementary to the income tax. The extent to which exports are able to bear a tax is governed more by prices on the international market than by domestic conditions. A country where costs are very low in comparison with other countries is better able to sustain taxes on its exports. If exports are the only means of obtaining foreign exchange to increase the capacity to import, and if the country's economic development depends largely upon the importation of capital goods and raw materials, it will be good policy to eliminate obstacles to and burdens on exports, which are the source for the acquisition of foreign exchange. A country might even possibly use a policy of export subsidies, but customs unions and common markets prohibit this practice because it would constitute a policy of dumping, against the interests of the other countries. For example, Article 52 of the Treaty of Montevideo expressly prohibits export subsidies because this would result in unfair competition with the other members of the zone.

The author states that the underdeveloped countries do not have a trade policy that meets the needs of economic development. In general this is true, because policy is directed to circumstantial balance of payments problems rather than being steered on a steady course toward economic development, and the tariffs themselves have served more for obtaining fiscal revenues than for orienting production one way or another. In any event,

it may be noted from the tables presented by the author on the average incidence of customs on various types of products (which he has divided into three groups, i.e., primary goods; intermediate products, capital goods, and durable consumer goods; and current consumption goods) that these countries have designed their foreign trade policy with the intention of favoring the importation of products required to meet basic needs and to provide the raw materials and fuel needed by industry. Except for Venezuela, all of them have lower duties for what they classify as primary products than for the semifinished and finished goods, that is, if weighted averages are considered, since simple arithmetical averages are not adequate for the purposes of the analysis.

The taxation differences in the subgroups under the three basic categories may be due more to a false estimate of the theoretical duties than to the direction of the policy. Furthermore, many countries manipulate their foreign trade policy not so much through the tariffs as through other measures of direct control, including full exemptions for agricultural and industrial products or the absolute prohibition of the importation of goods regarded as luxury items. From this point of view, the customs tariff is a measure for obtaining fiscal revenues, but it does not represent a development policy which, in the case of Ecuador, for example, is governed by the regulations of the Monetary Board, the Law on Industrial Development, and special contracts with specific companies.

I agree with the author that a foreign trade policy essentially based on tariffs might be the best, but only if the country's economic trends are more or less stable and permanent, because the tariff does not have sufficient mobility to control changes in the composition of the imports. That is why many countries have resorted to multiple rates of exchange, as in the case of Brazil, and others have utilized direct controls, as in the case of Colombia with its Foreign Trade Control Agency. In any event, the thinking on foreign trade has changed remarkably, and the world has witnessed the spread of multilateral trade treaties which, in addition to regulating trade in commodities as such, also look toward an easier movement of capital and multilateral industrial integration. For these reasons it may well be assumed that in the not distant future taxes on international trade will disappear completely and governments will have to look for revenues to taxes on income and the domestic consumption of goods without discriminating between imported and domestic products. Of course, this will be the best means of attaining economic and social development, since all countries will be able to enjoy the advantages of technology, wherever it may be found. The Latin American countries have embraced this philosophy, and in twelve years we shall see them forming a single market under the terms of the Treaty of Montevideo, intensifying regional production and consumption and raising the standard of living of the people of all the member states. This, of course, is the desire of all citizens of the hemisphere.

To summarize, it may be said that internal taxes on production and consumption—provided they do not exceed bearable limits, which differ from country to country—are just as adequate as direct taxes, or more so, in the effort to achieve economic development, because they signify a large contribution on the part of all citizens to the requirements of the state. Naturally, in order to obtain optimum results, there must be a proper relationship between the expenditure and investment policy and the positive effect on the private sector. As for customs taxes, which are useful for achieving both industrial development and fiscal revenues, they will become less and less important with the establishment and expansion of regional common markets. They will have to be replaced by other kinds of taxes in order to cover government budgets.

Discussion

Mr. Naharro explained that in his paper he had begun by locating production and consumption taxes within the framework of public finance as a whole. To that end he had used the old classification of direct and indirect taxes.

Like Mr. Kaldor, he held that two aspects of such taxation had to be taken into consideration in any analysis of the subject, namely, its revenue producing effect and its implications for the economy, particularly the possibility of providing an incentive to activities. With regard to the former, he thought that taxation of the type in question, although already widely applied in Latin America, could be extended still further. With respect to the second aspect, various reservations would have to be taken into account, such as the possibility that such taxes, by affecting levels of consumption, might reduce consumption below minimum subsistence levels, plus the difficulties inherent in its application because some sectors of the Latin American economies were not monetized. The region also showed a preference for indirect taxes falling on the external sector, as against those applied to the internal economy.

The effect of indirect taxes as incentives could not be defined with the same precision nor, in general, as effectively as that of direct taxes.

Although import duties, for example, unquestionably exerted an encouraging influence on certain productive activities, he had in general been more concerned with studying the effect of indirect taxes on some of the variables of economic development, such as distribution of resources, savings and investment, and the labor supply. He was less concerned with their probable effect on income redistribution, since to him that had only a relative incidence on economic development.

In connection with production and consumption taxes applied to the external sector, he drew a distinction between export duties, which were direct taxes, and import duties. He realized that in Latin America there was a trend toward protectionism, and he realized the danger of waving a flag of opposition at ECLA, but he confessed that he was in favor of a moderate degree of protectionism or—if that term was preferred—a moderate policy of free exchange rates. There were undoubtedly instances in which customs protection contributed to economic development, as in the case of incipient industries or other activities producing beneficial repercussions on the rest of the economy. He considered that in Latin America the system of external indirect taxes should be overhauled and remodeled, since in the past a lack of logic had been observable in their administration.

Broadly speaking, he believed that indirect taxes constituted the main source of the additional funds required by Latin America for its economic development. Nevertheless, the proliferation of indirect taxes of every kind in Latin America was inconsistent with sound principles of tax administration. To reform the system, a widespread sales tax, for instance, might be levied, to be applied either at the level of the producer, the wholesaler, or the retailer, although he would have it applied to the producer. Alternatively, consideration might be given to a reorganization of the excise tax on more progressive bases for some assets. To eliminate risks of multiple taxation, it had been suggested that an overall sales tax should be replaced by a tax on value added. That idea failed to convince him, since he did not believe that, in its application, such a tax would be as neutral as was claimed, and, in addition, it presented much greater administrative difficulties.

MR. VEGA noted that there had been a consensus among the participants to the effect that direct taxes needed strengthening, but in underdeveloped countries the budget could not be financed solely on the basis of such taxation, even though it was more equitable.

Indirect taxes were applied because direct taxes could not suffice to finance development and because it was desirable that all the inhabitants of a country should contribute to its economic improvement.

He pointed out that Mr. Naharro had not touched upon certain infrastructure projects, such as highways, etc., for which the users had to pay through indirect taxation.

Although Mr. Naharro had said that the nature of production and consumption taxes was the same and that the difference between them lay in the tax technique adopted, he personally held that they differed essentially inasmuch as the former taxes fell on inventories and the latter did not.

He suggested that the technical and administrative issues which Mr. Naharro had not dealt with in his paper were often of decisive importance for economic development since one of its basic prerequisites was the efficiency and flexibility of tax administration.

He agreed with Mr. Naharro that development was based on saving, and as the latter was very limited in underdeveloped countries, recourse to the compulsive action of taxation was essential in order to enforce saving. It should not be forgotten, however, that objections might be raised to taxation as an instrument of compulsory saving on the grounds that it discouraged voluntary saving.

In analyzing the tax burden in ten Latin American countries, Mr. Naharro related the tax revenue collected by the central government to national income but took no account of the taxes levied at other governmental levels, which were sometimes considerable; so much so that if they were ignored a completely false impression of the tax burden might be formed. It also seemed to him illogical to measure tax pressure by taking national income as a counterpart to taxes, since in the Latin American countries indirect taxation accounted for a major proportion of government revenue, and the taxes in question formed a part, not of national income, but of the gross national product.

In relation to internal production and consumption taxes, he said that to prevent a decline in savings and investment and, consequently, in production employment and wages, it was necessary to establish incentives to voluntary saving within the system of direct taxes.

Referring to customs duties, he dissented from Mr. Naharro's view that the Latin American countries were preponderantly protectionist. Protection had not been established arbitrarily, but in order to prevent the countries from remaining peripheral. ECLA had advocated the establishment of common markets with a view to fuller liberalization of intraregional trade, and although protectionism might be said to exist in Latin America vis-à-vis countries outside the region, within it a free trade policy prevailed.

MR. FERNÁNDEZ maintained that tax policy should be analyzed strictly as a function of economic development. Mr. Naharro had expressed the view that production and consumption taxes were one and the same thing, although there was a marked difference between their effects on economic development. The former pushed up production costs and consequently increased capital requirements, which was a very serious drawback in countries where there was a shortage of capital. On the other hand, a tax on consumer goods, whether specific or generic, was applied at the time of purchase for final consumption, and its only effect consisted in restricting the purchasing power of the individual for the benefit of the state, which would use it for development purposes either directly or through redistribution of the income obtained.

Furthermore, taxes on consumption should be applied, within the framework of an overall policy, in conjunction with income tax, and the balance between the two systems should vary according to the country concerned and to its gross national product. It should not be forgotten that one of the major problems of the Latin American countries was the size of the market, and therefore consumption could not be unduly restricted. In his view, a perfect balance between the two types of taxes might be achieved if 50 per cent of tax revenue came from indirect taxes, especially those on luxury consumption, and the rest from taxes on income and capital.

MR. HERSCHEL endorsed Mr. Lessa's view that the tax system served as a means of influencing the direction of aggregate demand. The possibility of using sanctions or disincentives instead of incentives to channel such demand in the best interests of development should be analyzed, as well as the question of whether indirect taxes could be used to steer aggregate demand along new lines and influence the structure of production. Customs duties might be applied as a disincentive to industrial inputs or purchases of capital goods for industries which it was not deemed desirable to encourage. A good deal of caution would have to be used in interpreting the conclusions shown in the table in Mr. Naharro's paper on the distribution of the tax burden, which in Argentina amounted to approximately 19 per cent of national income (federal government taxes).

With reference to the tax on value added, he said that the sales tax applied in Argentina was of a similar type, since it allowed deduction of inputs forming a constituent part of the goods produced (principle of physical integration). Moreover, it only reached the manufacturer's level. Argentina's experience suggested that such a tax could be established in Latin America.

MR. PINTO considered that the views and arguments put forward by Mr. Naharro represented an old-fashioned approach and were out of touch with the real situation in Latin America. It was not the idea of self-sufficiency that had prompted the Latin American countries to adopt a protectionist policy. They were anxious to achieve structural reforms which would enable them to develop along other than the traditional lines and were using any tool that came to hand. In essence, their aim was to alter the pattern of the international division of labor. The key point lay in the fact that the development of Latin America's traditional exports, on account of the terms of trade effect, no longer sufficed to mobilize the resources required by the region for its economic growth. The obvious solution was industrialization, which did not imply any suggestion of self-sufficiency or isolation but merely the desire to compete in the world market on less unfavorable terms.

Again, while taxes on luxury consumption might be one of the components of the tax system, another type of consumption—that of manufactured durable consumer goods—would have to be taxed. In Latin America a prematurely wealthy society, formed by the new well-to-do middle classes, had arisen, and the goods and services consumed by those strata should be taxed, especially as from 60 to 70 per cent of the Latin American population were still living at the merest subsistence levels. The process of industrialization in Latin America had been directed toward production of the goods and services required by the well-to-do classes in question, to the detriment of the interests of the community as a whole. The problem might be solved through the tax mechanism.

MR. URQUIDI fully concurred with Mr. Pinto's remarks on protectionism and considered that the general conception of taxation expounded by Mr. Naharro was influenced by an economic liberalism that would seem to be out of date in Latin America.

He did not share Mr. Naharro's view that the purpose of indirect taxation was to facilitate the private sector's activity. If such taxes were not used for purely revenue producing ends, they constituted a powerful weapon with which to exert a negative influence on production and/or imports of certain goods. In a planned economy, the state had to watch over the interests of the country as a whole and restrain specific types of production while allowing others to develop.

The paragraph quoted in Mr. Naharro's paper with reference to the application of indirect taxes as a cure for the predilection of idleness displayed by the indigenous population of Guatemala seemed to him absurd. A predilection for idleness was surely not exclusively characteristic of the indigenous populations of Latin America but pertained

to a certain cultural level which might also be found elsewhere.

Mr. Naharro ought to have taken into account the incidence of indirect taxes, especially when they were shifted backward until they reached the rural wage earner. In considering this incidence, allowance should be made for the level at which the taxes were established, since at 2 or 3 per cent their influence was nil. The criterion governing a development plan should be whether or not such taxes constituted an obstacle to a specific branch of activity.

He endorsed Mr. Fernández' opinion that such taxes should be applied at the stage of final consumption and removed as far as possible from earnings in productive or agricultural activities. It was also important that a sales tax should not be identified with particular industries. It was better to tax consumption of beverages than to apply taxation only to certain producer enterprises. Again, the conference should recommend the simplification of the system of consumption taxes. The ideal solution seemed to be that of a global tax at a rate of, say, 5 per cent, plus taxes on specific branches of consumption by groups or categories of items which would be multiples of the over-all rate.

MR. LESSA explained that indirect taxes were the basis of tax revenue in Latin America. He did not think they would alter investment patterns, since Latin America's experience had shown that relative prices, too, had proved ineffectual in that respect. Nevertheless, indirect taxes might be very useful for economic development purposes when they were applied to goods with a high consumption elasticity and substitution possibilities. They might result in a saving of foreign exchange if import duties made it possible to purchase lower-cost goods abroad; where they fell on domestic consumption, goods which had a sale on the world market might be released; and the same instrument might be used to reduce domestic consumption of goods in short supply within the country and needed for development.

The tax-by-tax method of analysis was unsatisfactory, since what mattered was that the various fiscal measures should be mutually complementary. Thus, for example, a high duty on imported whisky might encourage domestic production of beverages unless other steps were taken to discourage it.

MR. BACA said he could not agree that indirect taxes were inequitable and that in the context of the discussion the term did not refer to the classic taxes of that type but to those indirect taxes whereby discrimination could be practiced in respect of the middle class.

Indirect taxes accounted for 90 per cent of tax revenue in some Latin American countries. Moreover, they responded more readily to administrative measures, which should be improved by the introduction of order and method.

With reference to Mr. Naharro's contention that exemptions from direct taxation were more effective as an incentive than exemptions from indirect taxes, he said that would not be true in Central America, where the best incentive was provided by exemptions in respect of raw material imports. In fact, under the terms of the agreement on standard tax incentives to industrial development, exemption from taxation on raw materials was granted in favor of those industries which enjoyed priority in industrial development planning.

MR. LEWIS stressed that the basic consideration before the meeting, with which he hoped Mr. Naharro would deal fully in his summing up, was the question of indirect taxes, which produced from 30 to 90 per cent of total revenue in the different countries. The meeting should concentrate its future discussions on that question, with particular reference to practical aspects of application in a given country. Since the problems were quantitative, the answers should be quantitative as well. His suggestion for a new approach should be linked up with Mr. Porras' statement on the previous day regarding the context of the net wealth tax. The property tax might be less efficacious than the net wealth tax, but from the practical point of view he supported Mr. Porras' contention that for the Latin American countries in the immediate future the property tax was best suited to deal with their revenue problems.

He also thought it would be helpful to hear about Chile's experience in introducing the recent reform in the field of excise taxes.

MR. DESAI referred to the question of the terms of trade of the underdeveloped countries, and Latin America in particular, which had been raised by a previous speaker. The concept of "terms of trade" was open to misinterpretation, since their value at any given time depended on the year that had been taken as a base year. The general tendency was to choose years following World War II or during the Korean War when the prices for raw materials had been abnormally high, which falsified the present picture of the terms of trade. Moreover, commodity prices were only one element in the income received by the underdeveloped countries. He suggested that, instead of linking questions of aid from the industrialized countries to the fall in their terms of trade, it would be best for them to concentrate on the basic trade problems, such as supply factors and the difficulty of changing from one type of commodity to another in response to demand.

MR. NAHARRO congratulated Mr. Vega on his excellent paper, which expanded and elucidated many of the ideas in the background document. He acknowledged that, for the sake of brevity, he had devoted little attention to development problems and that he had shelved the benefit principle, since he thought it was more properly applicable in relation to prices and tariffs for public utilities not paid for by taxation.

He dissented from Mr. Vega's opinion that production taxes fell on inventories and taxes on consumption did not. As an example, he cited the tax on tobacco consumption in Spain, collected through a monopoly. The tax was already included in every packet placed on sale. He admitted that the opposite might be true in other cases. In his paper he had not gone into technical and administrative details on the application of such taxes because he thought that aspect had been sufficiently discussed at the previous conference in Buenos Aires. As far as using national income instead of the gross national product for purposes of comparison was concerned, he regarded that as an error of terminology and not a substantive issue. Mr. Vega held the same views but had used different names. He pointed out that in his paper he had not used the national income but the net national product, i.e., NNP less depreciation. If indirect taxes were subtracted from the net national product, the cost of factors would be estimated, but not at market prices. It was clear that the author had not done that. He agreed that he had not taken tax collection by local authorities into account, but he did not think the omission affected the validity of his conclusions in every case. That, of course, had been a mistake, but he had been unable to obtain the data needed for the calculations. He hoped to correct his figures, particularly in view of Mr. Desai's estimate. Nor did he consider that taxes on consumption could reduce the level of savings; on the contrary, they were reflected in compulsory savings which passed into the hands of the government.

He agreed with Mr. Desai that the terms of trade argument was a fallacy.

He did not understand why Mr. Fernández advocated a perfect "fifty-fifty" balance between direct and indirect taxes, and in his opinion there would be no grounds for so exact a division.

He had unfortunately not clearly followed the points raised by Mr. Lessa and had therefore been unable to give them the attention they deserved in his comments, although in general he accepted them by sharing Mr. Herschel's ideas on the possibilities of channeling aggregate demand by means of indirect taxation. He explained that he had included Musgrave's table in his paper as background information, but its validity was no doubt limited, and he was aware of that.

In reply to the comments formulated by Mr. Pinto and Mr. Urquidi, he confessed that he was a conservative liberal—a very rare species destined to disappear—but he also thought that however old-fashioned the terminology he employed, it expressed his ideas clearly enough. After all, everyone knew what protectionism and free exchange meant. They were old terms which might harbor new concepts. He fully understood the situation of Latin America and the need for developing the region beyond the traditional patterns, and he assured Mr. Pinto that he understood his position and agreed with him.

He could not accept Mr. Urquidi's views on the private sector, since without its cooperation economic development would be impossible. He was surprised that Mr. Urquidi dismissed as absurd the paragraph he had quoted on the pressure which indirect taxation might exert on the labor supply, especially as Mr. Kaldor, without using exactly the same words, had expressed identical ideas, and Mr. Urquidi had raised no objection. The paragraph had no value other than as an example of theoretical hairsplitting which, perhaps, it was. More particularly, it was inhuman, but in his paper he had avoided value judgments as far as possible. He thought Mr. Urquidi's suggestion of a combined system of general and specific taxes on consumption was greatly preferable to the proposal of a tax on value added which had been discussed at other meetings. While agreeing with Mr. Lewis, he referred him to Mr. Jarach, who was an expert in the questions raised.

10

Reform of Agricultural Taxation to Promote Economic Development in Latin America

by Haskell P. Wald*

The essence of development planning is the setting of realistic targets for transfers of resources to the most productive uses. Similarly, the essence of fiscal planning, if it is to serve the development plan, is the determination of the most efficient ways of absorbing each sector's taxpaying capacity in order to release the resources required by the development plan. Indeed, because the underdeveloped countries can place so little reliance on private capital markets, the needed mobilization of resources in each domestic sector to accelerate over-all economic growth must be accomplished primarily through appropriately selected fiscal instruments. That is the only sure way for these countries to avoid disruptive inflation.

The need of a sectoral approach to fiscal planning is clearest in the case of the agricultural sector. That sector, with its distinctive economic, institutional, cultural, and even demographic features, is at the same time the mainstay of the economies of almost all underdeveloped countries and the area where economic and social reforms are most urgently needed. More importantly, it is doubtful whether the development process can proceed very far in these countries without substantial

* Mr. Wald is with the U.S. Treasury Department.
The views expressed are the author's personal views and are not necessarily those of the Treasury Department.

increases in output and per-worker productivity in the agricultural sector. A casual attitude toward the impact of taxation on agriculture is certain to have seriously adverse consequences; even a policy of holding agricultural taxes to a minimum may handicap the sector's own development as well as the development of the country as a whole.

Except in a few countries which seem to have been moderately successful with export taxes on agricultural products, the prevailing taxes on Latin American agriculture are generally primitive in form, poorly administered, and productive of almost negligible amounts of revenue. From every viewpoint—equity, revenue need, and economic effects—this is an unmistakably damaging state of affairs. The tax shelter enjoyed by wealthy landlords in most Latin American countries, paradoxically enough, actually impedes agricultural development and, more generally, exerts a drag on over-all economic progress in the region. This is a problem that has not gone unnoticed; in fact, a few countries have been trying to deal with it for many years, and others have started to do so within the past year or two, but the progress to date has not been appreciable.

It is widely recognized that the new drive toward tax reform and agrarian reform in Latin America must necessarily assign a high priority to possible improvements in the methods of taxing the agricultural sector. It is notable, for example, that the Act of Bogotá relates agrarian reform to tax reform and specifically recommends the provision of "increased incentives in the land tax structure."

The purpose of this paper is to examine the experiences of Latin American countries with taxes on agriculture and to suggest various ways of strengthening these taxes so that they will best serve these countries' immediate and long-run development needs. The equity arguments for reform of agricultural taxation will not be emphasized, although most observers would probably attach as much importance to them as to the economic arguments which are the main concern of this paper.

A GLIMPSE AT PRESENT TAX PRACTICES

In the ordinary course of economic development, the agricultural sector will decline in relative size. Even countries whose resource endowment makes them major agricultural exporters will experience a reduction in the proportion of total income arising in agriculture. Such countries cannot rely on expanded international trade to provide all the non-agricultural goods needed as the composition of consumption changes with increases in per capita incomes. Approximately 70 per cent of the labor force in Latin America is employed in agriculture today.[1] Ten years from now, if economic development proceeds at a good rate, the percentage will be 60 per cent or perhaps 50 per cent.

This prospect of a secular decline of agriculture relative to other economic sectors must not be permitted to obscure the fact that the policies of the Latin American countries with respect to agriculture will be a crucial determinant of the pace of their economic development for many years ahead.[2] These countries must employ every policy

instrument at their disposal in order to assure larger agricultural production and maximum increases in agricultural productivity. They will need more food for sale to the growing city and industrial population and more agricultural exports to meet rising foreign exchange requirements. At the same time, they will want to facilitate the release of man power from agriculture, because no other source of labor supply will be available to the more rapidly expanding economic sectors. In addition, more farm purchasing power will be needed to provide wider markets for domestically manufactured goods. It will be shown below that decisions on agricultural taxation intrude in each of these phases of agriculture's needed support of the development process in Latin America.

Anyone who surveys the present methods of taxing agriculture in Latin America cannot escape the conclusion that the tax instrument is not being used as effectively as it might be to promote more intensive and extensive land cultivation. Moreover, it is plain that agriculture is not contributing as much as it should to the expanding capital requirements of economic development and that these weaknesses of Latin American tax systems are aggravating the problems of agrarian reform. In some countries the absence of adequate taxation of agriculture, and particularly of large landholdings, is also tending to undermine the public's confidence in the equitableness of the tax system as a whole. The following short descriptions of the tax practices in a few countries illustrate the main problems the Latin American countries face in reforming their taxes on agriculture.

Like almost all countries in the area, Guatemala has had a tax on the capital value of land for many years. But the tax produces only 1.5 per cent of total central government revenue; moreover, possibly as much as half the amount collected is absorbed by the high cost of administering the tax.[3] Three-fourths

[1] The percentage is above 50 per cent in all countries except Argentina, Chile, and Uruguay.

[2] See Bruce F. Johnston and John W. Mellor, "The Role of Agriculture in Economic Development," *American Economic Review* (September, 1961), pp. 566–93.

[3] Twenty per cent of the amount collected is generally retained by nonsalaried tax collectors. Direct and indirect administrative costs absorb an even bigger share of the comparatively small amount collected.

of the Guatemalan population live in rural areas and are only lightly touched by the customs duties and sales taxes that provide the bulk of the government's income. Guatemala is handicapped in land taxation because its cadastral maps are seriously incomplete, so that there is no way of checking the accuracy of the assessment rolls. The tax base is the taxpayer's own declaration of value, and while the government has the authority to have properties revalued by expert appraisers, it has not had the funds to make systematic and current assessments throughout the country.[4]

Since 1956 Guatemala has had a special tax on idle lands, with the aim of forcing owners of large estates to bring such lands into production. The tax rate is adjusted to the quality of the land and is supposed to be increased by 25 per cent per year until it is twice the initial rate. The landowners, however, have discovered ways to avoid this tax, mainly because the definition of idle land is difficult to administer. Many other countries have encountered similar difficulties in enforcing penalty taxes on idle land.

The main impact of taxation on Guatemalan agriculture is associated with the export taxes on coffee, chicle, bananas, and certain lumber products. The possibilities for increasing the yield of these taxes are limited by the ever-present danger that the export sector's competitive strength will be weakened.

Land taxation is somewhat more productive of revenue in Costa Rica, where it accounts for about 4.5 per cent of total national government revenue. The Costa Rican law exempts properties below a minimum value, which is high enough to exclude about four-fifths of all property owners from taxation. The tax rates are graduated according to the value of each taxpayer's total holdings. As in Guatemala, the owner's declaration of the value of his property is the basis of his tax and is not

open to public inspection. The authorities adjust the assessment, however, when they have reason to believe that the owner has understated or overstated the value. Records of mortgages and land transfers are used to keep values current, although many properties remain on the tax rolls indefinitely at the owner's declared value. Moreover, there seems to be no effective control over the listing of properties, because the system is not supported by cadastral or tax maps.

An additional low-rate tax on real estate, assessed simply according to each field's area, became effective in Costa Rica at the end of 1961. The tax is to be paid by landowners who do not pay the ad valorem property tax. One of its purposes is to discourage large nonproductive holdings which were not adequately taxed under the old law.

Costa Rica's income tax has little impact on agriculture because it provides comparatively high exemptions and low tax rates. The coffee tax, which is applicable when the export price of coffee is above a specified figure, is much more important and, in fact, exceeded the yield of the land tax in 1961.

An example of a different approach to agricultural taxation is provided by Colombia, which has one of the more advanced tax systems in Latin America. With the help of tax missions sent by international agencies, the Colombians have given much thought to the ways and means of using taxes on agriculture to induce a better utilization of the large estates. Nevertheless, the special taxes that have been applied to agriculture, although highly popular, have not worked well, mainly because the country's cadastral survey has not been completed and because the many exemption and penalty provisions introduced into the net wealth tax and the property tax have proved beyond the government's capacity to administer.

With the agricultural population being pushed more and more onto poorer land on the hillsides, while many large estates on the rich land continue to be used for extensive livestock raising, Colombia has recently intensified its efforts to improve landownership

---

[4]According to a statement in the *First Annual Report on the Social Progress Trust Fund,* Guatemala has requested external assistance to finance a four-year cadastral survey. The government is accelerating its property reappraisals and hopes, with the aid of such a survey, to achieve a tenfold increase in real estate tax collections.

and use. A comprehensive soil survey now under way will aid in establishing realistic cadastral values for tax assessment purposes and also in planning changes in land use. In the future, Colombia is planning to rely less on tax incentives and more on direct programs to redistribute land.

In Chile, where agricultural production is a much smaller share of gross national product (about 13 per cent) than in most other Latin American countries, tax receipts from agriculture are estimated at approximately 2 per cent of national revenues in 1958.[5] The old method of assessing the land tax on the basis of market value was recently changed. Instead, each plot of land is now taxed on the basis of its potential (as opposed to actual) share in the country's total net agricultural production. The tax base is revalued each year in line with the over-all change in net agricultural production. The first results of a scientific valuation of farm lands based on an aerial photographic survey of Chile are now becoming available for use in revising the land tax assessments and in aiding land reform and regional development.

Little revenue in Chile is provided by the income tax on agriculture, notwithstanding the requirement that individuals owning land valued at more than fifty times the minimum wage must declare their income on the basis of actual accounting records. The yield of the tax on land transfers is also small. On the other hand, the special taxes on new wine plantations and wine production yield substantial revenue.

Venezuela appears to be the only Latin American country where agricultural land is not taxed at all. However, the Shoup report, noting that the absence of a land tax has encouraged many property owners to keep their lands idle, recommends that land surveys and appraisals be made as soon as possible, so that at least the larger holdings can

be taxed.[6] The report emphasizes the country's growing requirements for more agricultural production to meet the needs of the rapidly expanding population and the demand for more food per capita as income rises. The agrarian reform law enacted in Venezuela in 1960 empowers the government to tax uncultivated or idle lands with the intent of compelling the owners to transfer them or place them under cultivation.

THE FIRST REQUIREMENT: A HIGHER LEVEL OF TAXATION

There is a temptation, when agricultural taxation is being discussed, to focus too much attention on the intriguing possibilities of special incentive tax provisions designed to penalize large landowners, absentee landlords, or lands that are not being cultivated or perhaps to induce changes in land use by granting exemptions. Such provisions have a place in many Latin American tax systems, provided the conditions exist for effective administration and there is full appreciation of the cost of incentive tax concessions. But the more immediate need is to establish a comparatively broad-based and fiscally productive tax on the agricultural sector. This can be done without imposing hardships on low-income farmers. In most of Latin America there is a heavy concentration of agricultural income—and even more so of tangible wealth—in a relatively small segment of the population. Furthermore, paying higher taxes need not be burdensome on the taxpayers if the added revenues are used to finance expanded social services and public investments which stimulate larger agricultural output.

Experience shows that the penalties of too light taxation of agriculture are a stagnating farm sector, a financially starved public sector, and a retarded rate of economic growth in the country as a whole. These results are in evidence almost everywhere in Latin America

[5]See José L. Pistono, *La tributación agrícola en Chile, 1940–1958* (Santiago: University of Chile, Economic Institute, 1960). The percentage was substantially higher in the early 1950's.

[6]Carl S. Shoup *et al., The Fiscal System of Venezuela* (Baltimore: The Johns Hopkins Press, 1959).

today, although it should be added that tax policy is not the only explanation. Thanks to the prevailing tax system, Latin American capitalists generally find idle land—even land that is rich in soil qualities and favorably located—an inexpensive and relatively riskless form of investment, while they largely shy away from equity investments in manufacturing. These capitalists often become complacent about inflation, and therefore they resist tax increases because they can protect themselves by investing in properties which rise in value with inflation (or they can accumulate deposits abroad).[7] The favored tax position of investment in land, compared with that of alternative investments in commerce or manufacturing, inevitably leads to land speculation and unrealistically high land values, both of which are conducive to a landownership pattern dominated by large holdings, often by individuals having no intention of cultivating the land up to its true productive potential.[8] Because capital gains arising out of land speculation largely escape taxation, the distribution of income is made more unequal.

The absence of adequate taxation of large landholdings not only promotes landownership concentration—which has been carried to extremes in many Latin American countries—but also deprives the governments of a powerful policy tool to enforce land redistribution and better land use. Taxation can be used to induce landlords either to cultivate their fields up to optimum efficiency or else rent or sell them to others who would do so.

A generally higher level of agricultural taxation, therefore, would automatically create incentive pressures of the desired sort on agricultural production. The "income effect" of heavier taxation would tend to spur additional productive efforts and larger marketings of agricultural output. One way to reap the full advantage of the favorable "income effects," while avoiding adverse "substitution effects," is to assess the taxes on the land's potential economic income, as is now being done in Chile, instead of its actual value in its present use. Landowners deriving less than the full potential value would then be penalized by the tax, while those exceeding the rated income of their properties would not be taxed on the excess.

The prime requirement, nevertheless, is to satisfy the basic fiscal and economic need for more revenue from the agricultural sector. Some countries may decide that the best way to start is simply by correcting the obvious defects of their present land taxes: incomplete, unequal, and unrealistically low assessments, poor collection results, and too low tax rates. But other countries, perhaps a majority, will probably conclude that a fundamental overhauling of the structure and administration of their taxes is needed.

SUGGESTIONS FOR SIMPLER METHODS OF TAXATION

A considerable additional investment in land mapping and soil classification surveys, and also in the registration of land titles, will be necessary almost everywhere in Latin America if land taxation is to become a more substantial revenue source. Much more than the cost of that investment could certainly be recovered, and probably without much delay,

---

[7] See Adolf A. Berle, *Latin America—Diplomacy and Reality* (Council on Foreign Relations, 1962), Chap. III.

[8] See United Nations, Economic and Social Council, *Progress in Land Reform, Third Report* (April 5, 1962—mimeographed) (E/3603), p. 167: "One of the most important aspects of the interrelationship between land taxation and land reform is the impact which taxation, or the absence of taxation, has on the evolution of land values. Unrealistically low assessments of agricultural land, comparatively low levels of land taxes and negligence in tax collection have frequently been the main reasons for the high market values which agricultural land enjoys in many underdeveloped countries, particularly in those with high population pressure on the land. In addition to many other personal advantages gained from large land ownership, such as social prestige and political influence, the possession of land guarantees in some countries of Latin America, the Near and the Far East comparative freedom from tax burdens, or at least a favored tax position as compared with that of alternative investments in commerce or industry. In the absence of adequate assessments and of progressive land taxation, therefore, land speculation, social prestige and other irrational factors continue to fix land values at an unrealistically high level and to maintain a rigid land distribution pattern, dominated by large estates; this fact presents one of the most effective obstacles to the implementation of land reform programmes."

through increased tax collections, because land valuations could then be updated, tax rates could be raised, and lands that have hitherto escaped taxation could be added to the assessment roll. An even more important consideration favoring such an investment is that accurate land maps and surveys of soil productivity and land use comprise the foundation on which sound planning of agrarian reforms should be built.[9] Chile's land classification program, for example, is a multipurpose project, only a small portion of whose cost should properly be allocated to tax administration per se. Bolivia has encountered major difficulties in implementing its land-reform law because of the absence of a cadastral survey and land records. The delay in certifying ownership titles has also deprived many beneficiaries of land reform from receiving agricultural credit.[10]

A recommendation for a country-wide cadastral survey is not easily implemented, however. Apart from the high initial cost, there may be a shortage of personnel who are trained for such work; moreover, such surveys are extremely time consuming, notwithstanding the appreciable time savings made possible by the new developments in aerial photographic mapping.

The question arises, therefore, as to how the structure of land taxation might be accommodated to situations where large land areas have not been surveyed and property descriptions are not recorded. It is abundantly clear from the experience in Latin America that taxes based on capital value are poorly suited to such situations. Because land sales each year are relatively few in comparison with the number of fields to be appraised and because reported selling prices often do not reflect true market valuations, correct assessments must be made by trained assessors on the basis of information on all factors which account for differences in property values. Even many of the more advanced countries have not been able to accomplish equitable assessments of property values for tax purposes.

Countries relying mainly on owners' declarations of property values cannot expect to obtain large revenues from their land taxes unless they adopt some new techniques. It is often suggested that self-assessments might be tied to the taxpayer's self-interest; for example, by giving the government (or any other bidder) the option to purchase the land at the declared value (or at a multiple of that value). Similarly, legislation could be enacted which stated that an underdeclaration of the size of one's holdings would jeopardize his title to the land in the event of a transfer by sale, gift, or inheritance. Such suggestions for a self-enforcing system would place a heavy strain on the administrative machinery —for example, declarations of land value would need to be adjusted continually in line with changes in current market value—but it is conceivable that they could be made effective in some countries.

Governments that are determined to raise increased revenues from the agricultural sector, but have not yet progressed far with land and soil surveys to support capital value assessments, should probably consider replacing their capital value taxes with a simpler form of land tax as an interim step. One such form used successfully in some countries is a tax assessed according to land area, with graduated tax rates and an exemption for small holdings. That type of tax was imposed in Panama in 1961. The rates of an area tax need not be uniform for all classes of land in all locations; instead, they could vary with the economic classification of the land—perhaps as few as four broad classifications would be sufficient at the start—so that the tax would make at least rough allowances for differences in basic soil qualities, topographi-

[9]See United Nations, Food and Agriculture Organization, *Report of the FAO Regional Land Reform Team for Latin America* (July, 1960—draft subject to revision), p. 46: "A basic and common handicap in the implementation of agrarian reform programs is the partial or complete absence of accurate knowledge of the facts on which the programs must rest. Cadastral surveys, large scale maps, soil studies, land records and agricultural census data are necessary to the success of any measure of agrarian reform such as those involving the fundamental reorganization of the land ownership pattern, the settlement of new areas and the design of an efficient taxation system."
[10]*Ibid.*, pp. 46–49.

cal features, irrigation, and location. The rates could also be graduated according to each taxpayer's aggregate holdings, to make the tax broadly progressive with respect to income. This form of classified-rate area tax is proposed because it is believed that the size of holdings is more easily determined and verified than is capital value and because broad economic classifications of land according to readily observable criteria can be done reasonably well, even in the absence of scientific soil classifications and productivity studies.

Several countries of Asia have had considerable experience with another form of land tax, one that is assessed according to the "normal" gross yield of each field. These countries find that type convenient to assess because gross yield is often recorded in land registers and may also be used as the basis for rental arrangements and the allocation of fertilizer and seed. Some Latin American countries may already have usable records of gross yield, particularly for the major export crops; even if they do not, they may still see administrative advantages in using gross yield (potential as opposed to actual) as the tax base instead of outdated and unevenly assessed capital values. To be successful with a gross yield tax, however, they would still require land records of field areas and at least a rudimentary land classification system which could be used in conjunction with unit-yield tables. If the assessments were made according to fractions of rated gross yield which varied with the classification of the land—in order to allow for estimated differences in its income-earning potential after production and marketing costs—they would give rough approximations to presumptive net income.

THE LONG-RUN GOAL IN LAND TAXATION

In view of the far-reaching differences among the Latin American countries as regards types of agriculture, systems of landownership and occupancy, and the administrative burdens the countries are equipped to carry, no single approach to land taxation can be recommended for general use. The suggestions made above, which might serve immediate revenue needs, should also be judged on the basis of their usefulness as possible steppingstones toward a more appropriate long-run plan of taxation. The long-run plan should aim to integrate the land tax, except for a small share that might be assigned to local governments, with the personal income tax. Before the two taxes can be integrated, however, not only must the basic tools of land tax assessment be improved, but also the land tax base must be reformed in concept to make it conform as closely as possible to individual taxpaying capacity. The ideal concept is that based on each landowner's or cultivator's presumptive net income in excess of a subsistence minimum.[11]

The requirements of successful implementation of this ideal plan are undeniably burdensome and perhaps even prohibitive for many countries at their present stage; but it would nevertheless be advantageous for all countries to set their sights on the goal they would like to reach eventually and then to lay plans to move toward it as rapidly as feasible, with due allowance for the practical obstacles that must be overcome.

To implement the ideal plan, two types of soil classifications would be required: (1) in terms of inherent soil characteristics, often described as the "soil profile," and (2) in terms of economic use capabilities, as determined by climate, exposure to sunshine and rainfall, potential irrigation, topography, availability of productive requisites (e.g., fertilizer, farm implements), marketing and milling facilities, etc. Each delineated land area, as identified in the cadastral maps, should be assigned a rating in accordance with its potential net income under average growing conditions and prudent management, with appropriate allowances for storage facilities

[11] A fuller description of the proposals for more effective land taxation is presented in Haskell P. Wald, *Taxation of Agricultural Land in Underdeveloped Economies* (Cambridge, Mass.: Harvard Law School International Program in Taxation, 1959), Chaps. x, xi.

and distances to trading centers. The use of yardstick farms, patterned after the successful experience with such farms in Northern and Central Europe, can be a valuable aid in such a rating process. Such farms can also serve as agricultural experiment stations.

As already noted, a comprehensive program of agrarian reform will require land mapping and productivity studies of the identical sort needed to put the land tax on a modern basis. Furthermore, an agrarian reform program will bring improvements in land administration, such as the registration of property rights and new farm credit programs, which can be helpful for the identification of potential taxpayers and facilitate the co-ordination of tax assessments with valuations approved for farm loans. In the long run, agrarian reform programs will provide more taxable capacity and a larger cash flow for tax payments. It will be unfortunate if countries that have embarked on such reform programs suddenly find themselves fiscally handicapped because they have failed to adjust their tax structures to take full advantage of the more favorable circumstances for tax collection.

SPECIAL INCENTIVE TAX MEASURES TO ASSIST AGRARIAN REFORMS

Taxes are versatile policy instruments, and land taxes, in particular, lend themselves to various regulatory and incentive applications in furtherance of specific land redistribution and production goals, provided the conditions exist for efficient administration. One example of an incentive usage is the surcharge on absentee owners of agricultural land which is levied in several Latin American countries, though apparently with much less success than in Australia and New Zealand, where the surcharge has been in force for many years. Other examples are the penalty taxes on idle land, tax exemptions on newly reclaimed land or land that is shifted to new crops in accordance with a development plan, and favorable tax treatment of small landowners who acquire land under land redistribution programs.

There is virtually no limit to the variety of incentive schemes that can be devised, but it must be admitted that, with few exceptions, the results of most schemes tried in Latin America have been disappointing.

One such instance is the 1957 legislation in Colombia, already mentioned above as not having worked well, presumably because it was beyond the administrative capacity of the public agencies.[12] That legislation provided a variety of tax incentives and deterrents designed to improve land use. Among the "carrots" were an exemption of agricultural machinery from the net wealth tax and customs duties, a substantial cut in income and net wealth taxes for those who converted unfit into useful land or shifted land out of coffee, bananas, and sugar cane, and expensing instead of capitalizing various investments in farming. The "sticks" of the legislation included an extra land tax (based on assessed cadastral value) on owners and tenants with more than 50 hectares who did not cultivate a specified portion of their land at least once a year. The law stipulated a tax rate that increased year by year for five years. The cultivation requirement varied with the classification of the land; on the best land it was a minimum of 25 per cent. The taxpayer's declaration that his property was under cultivation was accepted as proof of that fact, subject to penalties for false declarations; but the required land classification was never completed, except for some lands that were already being cultivated well above the minimum requirement. Thus, the government has been without the necessary information for the effective administration of penalties in the law. However, the tax exemptions are operative.[13]

---

[12] See Robert R. Nathan Associates, *Program of Economic Development of the Magdalena Valley and North of Colombia* (Washington, D.C.: November 7, 1959), chap. 4. See also Thomas F. Carroll, "The Land Reform Issue in Latin America," in A. O. Hirschman (ed.), *Latin American Issues* (New York: The Twentieth Century Fund, 1961), pp. 191–94.

[13] Louis Shere, in his "Tax Programme for Colombia" (Organization of American States, mimeographed, 1959), recommended that the system of agricultural tax inducements and penalties be greatly simplified.

The Colombian government's inability to enforce the 1957 tax on underutilized agricultural land repeated its experience with a 1936 law which provided that lands which remained uncultivated for a ten-year term would revert to state ownership for land settlement. That law, too, was virtually disregarded, owing to procedural difficulties in declaring the lapse of ownership. In 1961 a new Agrarian Social Reform Law was enacted that sought to remedy that problem. In addition, a detailed soil survey is under way which goes far beyond the survey of cultivation practices required by the 1957 law and will aid in establishing more realistic cadastral values.

A somewhat similar attempt at incentive taxation of agricultural land is being made in the State of São Paulo, Brazil, which passed an Agrarian Revision law at the end of 1960. The law imposed a graduated land tax of from 2 per cent to 6 per cent per annum. The tax is doubled if at least 70 per cent of a particular property is not being used productively or if more than half of it is leased, but it is reduced if a farm is being cultivated up to a reasonable standard, if soil-conservation practices are being employed, and if farm workers are furnished adequate housing. The effectiveness of this law remains to be tested. Indeed, there is already concern that the operation of the law may be undermined by a constitutional amendment transferring the rural land tax from the states to the municipalities.

Numerous other examples can be cited of land tax provisions motivated by incentive objectives. Guatemala recently adopted provisions to strengthen its per-hectare tax on idle land. Many provinces in Argentina add a land tax surcharge on absentee owners. Furthermore, as noted at several points above, tax rates that are graduated by capital value or land area, in order to fall more heavily on owners of large estates, are prevalent among the Latin American countries.

What is lacking, however, is clear-cut evidence that these incentive tax features are being effectively administered and producing the desired results. In all probability, many of them are not, because the essential cadastral information is generally lacking and because the level of land taxation is too low for the taxes to exert the intended incentive pressures. Yet the existence of incentive tax provisions on the statute books may give semblance of action toward solving a problem and thus may delay more direct measures to redistribute land holdings and encourage better cultivation.

A particularly bad fiscal practice is the liberal granting of tax exemptions to encourage changes in land use. Exemptions for limited time periods are probably necessary to encourage land reclamation or to relieve the tax burden on settlers who must pay annual installments for land acquired under redistribution programs. But when exemptions are made available to a wide range of activities, their effectiveness as pinpointed incentive devices is blunted and their over-all result is to shift more of the tax load onto persons who may not have the capacity to carry it. Moreover, the state can never know how much subsidy it is paying to secure the desired result.

Preferably, the Latin American countries should assign the first priority to a basic reform of the structure and administration of their land taxes, leaving incentive applications as possible appendages to these taxes after they have been made substantially more productive of revenue than at present. Furthermore, the governments should always satisfy themselves that the tax instrument is the best one to use to achieve the desired non-fiscal end. In pursuing the revenue goal, moreover, the countries must constantly be on guard against tax effects that are damaging to development objectives, perhaps because some segments of the population or some agricultural activities that should be encouraged are overburdened. Taxes frequently have hidden incentive effects that do not become significant until the taxes are raised. Although none of the Latin American countries have emulated the Near East countries in imposing marketing taxes—which inhibit the growth of commercial crops and tend to perpetuate outmoded forms of land tenure—some of them may be risking similarly adverse economic effects by their resort to heavy taxes on exports in periods when their export markets are weak.

DYNAMIC ASPECTS OF AGRICULTURAL TAXATION

Very few countries of Latin America have provided for the systematic adjustment of their agricultural tax policies to the evolving needs of an expanding agricultural sector in the context of their agrarian reform and overall development programs. Nor have they faced up to the problem of the depreciation of land tax collections under inflationary conditions.

The revenue provided by most land taxes is extremely inelastic. Both the tax rate and the tax base tend to be kept stable for long periods, even in the face of substantial price and production changes. Thus, the land taxes cannot serve the important function of diverting part of the increase in agricultural income, as a country's agrarian reform program brings results, to the financing of new development projects. Furthermore, the fiscal havoc created by inflation is particularly acute where land taxes are concerned.

The practice of local governments in the United States of setting the property tax rate each year in accordance with budget requirements cannot be applied in Latin America until the methods of land tax assessment are improved and properties are rated on a uniform and realistic basis. After the latter steps have been taken, consideration might be given to devising a formula for tying the assessments to current price and production indexes, or perhaps to an index of current property values in the principal regions. Across-the-board adjustments, as opposed to individual adjustments for each taxpayer, are comparatively simple to administer, and they would still leave taxpayers the maximum incentive to adopt more productive farming techniques. It is interesting to note that Chile recently instituted annual revaluation of the land tax base in proportion to the annual change in the net value of agricultural production.

The progress of agricultural development, if it generates some highly localized benefits, may provide opportunities for the imposition of betterment levies or special assessments to cover the cost of specific public improvements. On the whole, however, the successful use of betterment levies requires specialized administrative skills that are not often found in the land tax assessment offices of Latin American countries. It would be more practical for these countries simply to impose a surcharge in regions that have benefited from a major resource development project, without attempting to apportion the aggregate benefit in a scientific way among individual properties. This was done, for example, in the Cauca Valley of Colombia, where the development project included flood control, drainage, control of water use, and hydroelectric power.

Another desirable component of a tax plan that is designed to meet the needs of a developing agricultural sector is a method of taxing increases in land values. This might be done through an incremental value tax at the time land is sold or through a capital gains tax as part of the income tax. To buttress the enforcement of such taxes, the official valuation of the property might be used as the minimum value for the determination of a taxable gain. This type of provision is contained in the tax on land transfers in Chile. The official valuation cannot be used for that purpose, however, unless it is kept up to date, probably by applying an adjustment formula. To require reassessments at the time of each sale would be impractical.

CONCLUSIONS

Land taxes offer strategic advantages over other methods of raising large revenue in the agricultural sectors of underdeveloped countries. Sales taxes are blocked from wide usage there because of the importance of nonmonetary transactions in the typical rural setting. A broadly based income tax is impractical because of that obstacle and because low-income farmers do not keep income and expense records and the withholding method of tax collection cannot be adapted to agricultural incomes.

Not all of the farm sector's characteristics, however, are inimical to tax collection. Some characteristics actually facilitate collection, although it would appear that most governments have not been appreciative of that fact. Because the bulk of the sector's income is derived from working the land, extensive use of presumptive tax assessments is possible. In addition, the valuation of farm output is often aided by the concentration of production in staple crops, while the fact that land (or its produce) stands as security for the tax can be a valuable help to tax enforcement.

A program for more effective agricultural taxation in Latin America should not overlook opportunities to improve the application of income taxes—presumptively assessed, if necessary—on the wealthier recipients of agricul-

tural incomes and on the owners of large tracts of cultivable land that is not being farmed. Nor should the countries neglect the taxation of windfall incomes and capital gains arising out of economic development or price fluctuations. But the most feasible means of broad-based taxation in the agricultural sector is through land taxation. Land taxes can become a positive instrument of agrarian reform, and they can be accommodated to the size of the administrative burden a country can successfully manage.

The major defects of the present land taxes as instruments of development financing are that they produce little revenue, are not assessed in an equitable manner, and do not absorb a significant portion of increases in agricultural income to permit noninflationary financing of a growing public investment budget. To find solutions to these critical problems of land taxation is probably the hardest task of tax reform in Latin America today, but it is one that must be accomplished to remove some major fiscal obstacles to economic progress there.

Comment

WADE F. GREGORY*

Present conditions in the agricultural sector and the role that agriculture is expected to play in economic development should influence and help to determine the kind of tax policy developed for the agricultural sector. At an early stage in the formulation of tax policy, a decision must be made concerning which of three types of resource transfers is to take place: (1) a transfer from the agricultural sector to the government for reinvestment in the agricultural sector, (2) a transfer from the agricultural sector to the government

for investment in urban and industrial sectors, or (3) a transfer from other sectors to the government for investment in the agricultural sector. In addition to these, regardless of which is selected, there will also probably be some resources transferred from agriculture to government for the financing of general governmental expenses.

The question of whether the agricultural sector is to (help) finance economic development in the rest of the country (choice 2) or whether agriculture is in fact a stumbling block, a bottleneck, holding back economic development and therefore needs capital transferred into it (choice 3) must be decided, and tax policy will depend upon the decision reached. There is, however, no generally ac-

*The views here expressed are the author's own and do not necessarily reflect those of the Department of Economic Affairs of the Pan American Union, with which Mr. Gregory is affiliated.

cepted description of the agricultural situation in Latin America, for conditions vary from country to country and, in some cases, within agricultural regions of given countries. Furthermore, these generalizations result in contradictory conclusions regarding the direction sectoral transfers should take. One can marshal arguments and find qualified supporters for each point of view: that agriculture should be treated as a source of development capital for the nonagricultural sectors of the economy and also that, if economic development is to take place in the economy, and particularly in the agricultural sector, additional resources need to be transferred into that sector.[14]

Concurrent with, or perhaps prior to, the question of the sectoral transfer of resources is the problem of the quantity of resources the government wishes to have direct control over or, stated another way, the amount of revenue that is to be raised through taxation. The answer to this problem must concern itself with the transfer of resources from consumption to investment, from the private to the government sector, and from one sector to another—with the final solution depending upon development priorities established by the decision-making authority.

This paper does not concern itself with questions such as the size of the government budget, the portion to be raised through taxation, or the appropriate sectoral shares; these are taken as given. Rather, the main focus is directed toward a consideration of agricultural taxation as a development tool. Attention is directed toward the merits of different taxation schemes with reference to the extent to which they can expedite programs of land and income redistribution and induce farmers to adopt improved practices. Specific atten-

tion is devoted to land taxes, since these are usually the taxes thought of in connection with agricultural taxation and also since they probably offer the greatest possibilities for achieving the desired ends. Also, most suggestions related to incentives, distributive effects, and other nonrevenue producing features of tax programs generally refer to land taxes.

Historically, land has been the principal base for taxation, and in Latin America it has represented, and in many cases still represents, the chief capital stock of many countries and has been a major source of national income. The concentration of landownership has also led to the belief that a land tax will fall primarily on the rich, and recently the theory has been advanced that land redistribution and more intensive land use can be achieved or encouraged through appropriate taxes on land. These two latter beliefs often appear to have become the main reasons advanced by many people for land taxes, with the consequence that the amount of revenue raised or to be raised receives only secondary consideration. It follows, therefore, that tax rates would be set, not to produce a given amount of revenue, but rather to achieve other nonfiscal objectives.

In a discussion of land taxes, it becomes apparent that programs of land reform and tax reform can reinforce each other if they are tied together, for the proper tax policy can greatly encourage a redistribution of land which would result in less concentration of ownership. Land taxes can act as a lubricant to the entire process without any resultant loss in income, since present land tax revenues are now so low that there need be no loss in land tax revenues resulting from a program of land redistribution. Many tax variations have been suggested for bringing about land redistribution, from proposals for high tax rates on idle and extensively worked land (the idea being that such land is found primarily on large estates) to a highly graduated land tax on the basis of size of holding.

There can be no doubt that very progressive rates, based on size of holding and en-

[14]See, for example: Delbert A. Fitchett, "Land Taxation and Land Reform in Underdeveloped Countries: A Comment," *Economic Development and Cultural Change*, Vol. X, No. 2, Part 1 (January, 1962); Address by Orville L. Freeman at the National Conference on International Economic and Social Development, Chicago, Illinois, July 19, 1962; A. W. Lewis, *The Theory of Economic Growth* (London: G. Allen & Unwin, Ltd., 1956); Alfredo Saco, "Farm Productivity and Income as Related to Economic Growth," *Series of Lectures on Economic Growth* (OEEC, 1961).

forced by an agency *having the power and the desire to collect taxes,* can and will encourage owners to decrease the size of their holdings. However, at this point the problem of equity in assessments is often introduced. For it is argued that since cadastral surveys stating exact property limits do not usually exist and also, since information is insufficient about soil characteristics, extent of erosion, slopes, etc., fair assessments cannot be made, and therefore there is no good base against which a tax can be levied. The usual remedy suggested to overcome this situation is the preparation of a three- to four-year plan for a comprehensive, detailed cadastral survey, with the implication that present tax programs are to remain unchanged in the interim. But, because of the shortage of technicians qualified to make cadastral surveys and the lack of funds to pay technicians, the initial three- to four-year plan also has to be delayed, with the result that no change is made in tax assessments or collections. To resolve this problem, a commonly suggested solution is that in lieu of using land values, the potential earning value of the land should be imputed and used as the basis for assessments. But this proposal also requires the services of many well-trained technicians to determine the potential earning value of the land. As an alternative, the following proposal is suggested: that the owner himself assess the value of his holdings and that this value be used by both the taxing authority and land reform authority.[15] It is at this point that these two agencies working together can be much more effective than each one working alone.[16]

What happens under this system if an owner undervalues his property in order to keep his tax liability low? The land reform agency, having the authority to buy any and all property at say 10 or 20 per cent above the assessed property value, can now acquire land at a low price.[17] If owners do not wish to run the risk of having to sell their land at less than its real value, they must pay taxes on what they consider to be the real value of their property. The system should permit annual adjustments in assessments to reflect changing land values which might result from inflation, improved technology, and changed market conditions. Therefore, if inflation becomes a significant factor, a mechanism is provided to ensure that land assessments will keep pace with it. This method of determining property values does not lessen the need for progressive rates, which should be based on assessed values rather than on the number of hectares owned.

It is important that measures be taken to ensure that the progressive-rate feature is not circumvented through a figurative subdivision of property among members of the same family. To avoid this, tax rates should be calculated on the basis of the total land

[15]This should not be interpreted as suggesting that cadastral surveys are not needed; rather the intention is to show that initial land tax reforms can be carried out in the absence of cadastral surveys. The argument for accurate cadastres should be made on grounds other than that they are an essential precondition for land tax reform.

[16]If the plan for self-assessment of land is not adopted, an alternative plan, based on the amount of water from nonfarm sources a farm unit controls as an index of potential earning value of the land, is suggested as a provisional solution for those regions having inadequate rainfall until adequate cadastral surveys become available. While this plan is considered inferior to that of self-assessment, it is suggested primarily to illustrate that

some immediate improvements can be made in collecting land taxes even though detailed cadastral surveys are lacking.

The quantity of water a farm has rights to is a fairly good index of production potential and in most cases is already known—at least in rough measure—either in terms of volume of water or as a proportion of the total water in a river or irrigation canal. Specific details for this plan have not been worked out, but from the limited attention it has already received, it appears that no difficulties would arise. For example, progressive rates can be built into the plan, but they should be based on the property value of the farm as estimated by the quantity of water the farm has rights to rather than on farm size as measured by number of hectares. Also, since not all land in any one area is suitable for irrigation and the proportion of irrigable to nonirrigable land varies from farm to farm, there should probably be a flat per-hectare land tax in addition to a progressive tax based on the potential income-earning ability of the farm.

[17]It can be argued that if one is forced to sell, he should receive more than the market price, for there are costs of moving, etc.; but more important, any given property is unique in terms of location, and therefore the present owner may value his land above the market for sentimental or other reasons, and it is only fair to reimburse him for these values if he is forced to sell.

owned by all family members, regardless of whether titles are held by husband, wife, or children. Likewise, rates should also apply to operating units regardless of whether titles are held by one or several related or unrelated owners. Possibly, as time goes on and effective land redistribution has taken place, it may be desirable to relax this last provision, but it would seem doubtful that the provision regarding the taxing of family land as a unit should ever be relaxed.

For this proposal to be effective, the land reform agency must have sufficient funds and authority to be able to buy undervalued land, for it is only the threat of loss of capital through sale at a low price that will motivate correct assessments. However, the amount of land which the land reform agency can acquire will be determined by the size of the budget available for this purpose and the price that is paid for the land.[18] Therefore, it is recognized that high assessments may limit the amount of land which can be acquired for redistribution. However, while the Charter of Punta del Este urges that land redistribution take place so that the land belongs to the man who works it, it also contains the philosophy that just compensation be paid for expropriated properties. If just compensation is

to be paid, it is doubtful that land acquisition costs would be higher under a program in which owners received an amount equal to the value they themselves placed on their property for tax purposes compared to other methods of valuation attempting to pay just compensation. For the land reform agency should be free to purchase only that land deemed desirable, and therefore overvalued land would not be purchased; and since owners must pay taxes on the basis of their declared valuation, probably they would not be inclined to overassess their land. However, as a safeguard, the price paid for land purchased by the land reform agency should be an average of the assessments for, say, the last three years for which taxes have been paid.[19]

Assuming that both the tax collecting agency and the land reform agency perform their functions well, the revenues collected from this system should be considerably more than the amount now being collected.[20] In fact, the increase in revenues may be great enough to provide for the establishment of adequate credit systems, extension services, experiment stations, general education systems, etc., and thereby help to reduce the need for forced land sales.

Land taxes are also often suggested as a way to improve land use and resource efficiency. Here it is argued that large landholders are not concerned about low rates of re-

---

[18]Problems related to methods of payment for expropriated property should be dealt with independently of the method of assessment used. However, assessments and the amount paid can be closely related, as has been suggested. While forms of payment and the ability of governments to finance land redistribution programs are outside the scope of this paper, a few related comments may be in order.

The acquisition of property for redistribution need not put serious financial strain on government budgets if payments for land purchases are delayed from three to five years, for by that time, if the objectives of land redistribution and agrarian reform programs are achieved, the new owners should be in a position to start paying for their land, and these payments can then be used to pay the former owners. The extent to which the program will be self-financing will depend upon the extent to which income redistribution is to be achieved along with land redistribution. If former owners are to receive the full real value of their properties, the program probably cannot be completely self-financing. However, those proposals which suggest that owners receive less than the real value of their property (either through a progressive scaling down of property values based on size or present land use and/or through monetary depreciation of bonds issued in payment for the land) may closely approximate self-financing depending upon (1) how well the new owners operate their farms and (2) the amount of income redistribution that is to take place.

[19]A more effective but drastic system of determining the price to be paid for expropriated land would be to base purchase price on the average value of assessments for *the last three calendar years*, where nonpayment of taxes for any one year would imply zero assessment for that year. Therefore, if taxes were not paid for three consecutive years, the purchase price would be zero; if not paid for two of the last three years, the price would be one-third of the assessed value for the year in which taxes were paid; and if not paid for one of the last three years, two-thirds of the average value for the two-year period. Such a system would greatly encourage full payment of taxes.

[20]In comparing tax proposals, the same level of enforcement should be assumed when evaluating the consequences of suggested and actual tax programs. However, part of the reason for suggesting changes is that evasions are more difficult under some schemes than others. The belief held by the author is that evasions would be more difficult and enforcement easier under a system of self-assessment whereby the value set by owners would determine the amount of taxes paid and at the same time determine the price they would receive for their property if it were purchased by the land reform agency.

turn per unit of land because, with the large number of hectares owned, their income is still sufficient to allow them to live at a fairly high level. Therefore, they have no incentive to put forth more effort and change from traditional, inefficient farming practices to improved methods of production. As a solution to this problem, high land taxes, usually with provisions for higher rates on idle or poorly used land, are suggested as a good way to provide an incentive for better land use. The position advanced in this paper is that a tax on land is not the best way to achieve these ends and furthermore that it is questionable whether, in fact, such a tax can be administered sufficiently well to reach the desired goals.

At heart, this is a not too subtle roundabout way to attack the problem of latifundia, where control of lands is concentrated in the hands of a few who are not interested in the general welfare. Because of the resistance encountered to direct measures (such as land redistribution schemes) to remedy this situation, the indirect approach of specialized land taxes is gaining favor. However, the question needs to be raised, if land redistribution programs cannot be instigated because of the opposition of large landholders, is there any reason to believe that a selective land tax proposal, designed to accomplish the same end, would not meet with equal opposition from these same landholders?[21]

Conceptually, a land tax affects the level of fixed costs and thereby determines whether or not a firm stays in business. But, aside from affecting the entry and exit of firms into and out of an industry, fixed costs are not a good tool to use to modify production techniques. This paper advances the argument that changes in the number of firms in an industry are caused by a different set of factors than those responsible for bringing about changes in methods of production and that different, though related, action needs to be taken to produce each kind of change. Modifying the level of fixed costs is an appropriate way to

[21]See footnote 7.

affect entry and exit of firms, but it is not an appropriate tool to use in modifying production techniques; for this, marginal costs must be altered through changes in the relative prices of factor inputs.

The level of fixed costs, which reflect the amount of land taxes paid, determines whether or not an individual will continue to farm but does not affect decisions such as what and how much to produce. These decisions are determined by relative factor and product prices. However, if the situation with regard to latifundia is as static and resistant to change as often pictured, some modifications are needed to complete the suggested analysis. For, so the characterization goes, "latifundistas" prefer maintaining the *status quo* to earning higher incomes; therefore, they continue to use outmoded methods in the production of the traditional crops usually grown on latifundia rather than earn higher incomes by producing other crops with modern methods of production.

To analyze the effect of land taxes in the setting of latifundia, the concept of industry must be modified from including all of agriculture as one industry to the concept of many industries within agriculture (such as the extensive cattle industry, the dairy industry, the wheat or grain industry, the vegetable industry, etc.). Within this framework, an increase in land taxes could raise fixed costs to the point where income from certain types of farming (e.g., cattle raised on native pasture) would not be sufficient to cover costs, and the firm would then leave the industry. This exit could be by either of two routes: (1) sell the farm or (2) change to producing higher-value products (change to another industry). However, once either of these changes is made, unless there is the assumption of complete nonresponsiveness to price, the decision of how much to produce and the kind and amount of factors to use in the production process would be determined by relative factor and product prices.

Conceptually, it has been argued that in a price-responsive economy a land tax is not the best tool to use to induce more intensive land use and, in fact, may be somewhat inoperative. However, these arguments are not valid if the oft-pictured stereotype of latifundia and "latifundistas" correctly characterizes Latin American agriculture. If, however, the latifundia description is representative of an important segment of the agricultural sector, proposals for improving land use through higher land taxes must be questioned from still another point of view. This refers to the possibility of really enforcing such tax laws to the point where they become operative: that is, by reducing incomes to the point where owners are forced either to sell land or to reject the traditional way of farming and adopt new methods in order to earn enough to pay the land tax. This paper presents the thought that, if governments cannot marshal sufficient authority to carry out direct programs of land redistribution, it is highly unlikely that they can get the authority needed to achieve the same ends through a tax program.

This leads to the question, what ends can be achieved by agricultural taxation, apart from raising revenue? As mentioned in the beginning, taxes are usually considered primarily as a fiscal tool, with the kind of taxes and rates set so as to yield a given amount of income to the government with the least disruptive effect possible. But in discussing agricultural taxation, this concept is changed, with the disruptive (beneficial) effect the important facet of tax policy and revenues raised more or less a by-product. So we return to the question, to what extent can taxation be a proper allocative device in the agricultural sector?

An excellent example of how tax policy can improve resource allocation is the case of water. Water is an essential factor of all agricultural production, but in many parts of Latin America it is in very short supply, with the result that its availability is often a more limiting factor of production than is land. Under these conditions, one would expect to find water being used only on high-value crops which were quite yield-responsive to irrigation. However, there is much evidence

to indicate that criteria of economic efficiency are not the guiding principles now used in determining water use. Rather, one can conclude that historical patterns of rights to water determine the quantity controlled by any one farm and tradition determines the methods used and the crops irrigated, with the result that this scarce resource is used in a very inefficient manner. This point is often illustrated by the fact that native pasture is irrigated, while other higher-value crops are not grown for lack of water.[22]

On many farms, water is used as if it were a free good, which in fact may be a fair approximation of the general situation, for the only out-of-pocket cost to the operator is the cost of applying the water. However, there is another much more important cost apparently not recognized or appreciated by those who irrigate low-value crops such as native pasture. This is the opportunity cost or the income forgone by irrigating low-value rather than high-value crops. While some owners may choose to ignore such a cost, most of the countries of Latin America can ill afford to lose this potential income. A use tax on water would change the situation and would achieve the dual purpose of raising revenue and at the same time making for a more efficient allocation of water use. For while native pasture will be irrigated when water is a relatively free good, probably it will not be irrigated if there is a cost involved, for yield increases resulting from irrigation will not be great enough to cancel out any costs; therefore, water would be available for other, higher-value crops.

The equitableness of a water tax need present no problem, for the tax would be levied on the amount of water bargained (contracted) for at the start of the year, and since water is

[22]Usually there is a much better use for water than to apply it to native pasture, but not all instances of irrigated native pasture should be condemned. It is quite possible that due to the fact that production decisions must be made in advance in the face of many uncertainties, situations such as failure of irrigated crops, the availability of more water than expected, or the uneven seasonal crop demand for water may result in a "surplus" of water which for that particular time period has no alternative (higher) use than being applied to native pasture.

water (at least in the same river or canal), no assessment problems would arise from the existence of different kinds and grades of water. Likewise, progressiveness, reflecting size of farm, could also be built into the rate structure on the basis of the quantity of water one has control over. A progressive rate structure would also make for a more equitable distribution of water rights; not only would rates increase as more water was controlled by any one operator, but after some point less productive lands would be irrigated. These two factors reinforce each other and would tend to reduce the demand for water on the part of any one operator.[23]

The problem of the inability of small farmers to pay such a tax, which would preclude them from having rights to water, is certainly a matter for concern, but it is not a sufficient reason to eliminate consideration of adopting a tax on water use, for the taxpaying ability of this group of farmers is always doubtful, regardless of the kind of tax. The solution usually suggested is to exempt small farmers from paying taxes, but exemptions to a water use tax should not be permitted or the allocative feature of the tax will be weakened. Rather the solution is to enforce the tax, but at the same time provide subsidies to small farmers (such as credit facilities, time payments, etc.), to enable them to pay the tax. Financing these subsidies should present no more of a problem than tax exemptions, for the tax revenues paid by small farmers could be the principal source of funds for the subsidy.[24] Subsidies, however, appear to be preferable to exemptions for at least two reasons:

(1) The principle is firmly established that everyone who uses water pays a tax on the quantity of water used. This principle, if enforced, would help to eliminate tax evasion. (2) The allocative features of the tax would be kept intact, thereby ensuring maximum, or at least higher, productivity from the scarce quantities of water available.

Even though major attention has usually been directed toward property (land) taxes in Latin America, the focus is now quite often broadened to include income taxation as an integral part of tax programs, for the experience of countries having rigorously enforced income tax laws indicates that income taxation can be a powerful tool to raise government revenues and to redistribute income. However, the experience also indicates that because of the nature of the agricultural industry, income from this sector has been difficult to tax, not only in Latin America but in all parts of the world.

In addition to raising revenue and redistributing income, taxing of agricultural income in Latin America is often suggested as a means to another end: that of providing an incentive to encourage the adoption of improved farming practices and more intensive land use. This is to be achieved by means of a tax on presumptive or potential income as contrasted to a tax on income actually received, the reasoning being that farm incomes are now much lower than they would be if all land were used in an efficient manner. Therefore, a tax levied on presumed income would achieve two ends: (1) tax rates would be set high enough so that farmers would have to adopt improved methods of production and farm intensively *all* land in order to have sufficient income to pay the tax and maintain present standards of living[25] and (2), since in

[23]The possibility exists, of course, that if land distribution is such that the land best suited for irrigation is controlled by large owners and the poorer land by small owners, then progressive tax rates might result in water being misallocated to lands less adapted for irrigation. This possibility seems remote, but if true (and the proposition is easily tested), it certainly deserves immediate and direct measures to bring about a different pattern of land distribution.

[24]This, of course, ignores the costs of administering the tax and subsidy program, which costs usually come out of general government (overhead costs), but water taxes paid by small farmers should certainly equal or exceed the amount of money needed, say, for a credit system designed to lend money for payment of water taxes—that is, a production-type credit limited perhaps to water.

[25]In considering income resulting from higher productivity or from employing idle resources as a source of tax revenue, the counterargument is often made that the incentive to earn additional income will be removed if it is subject to tax, and therefore new practices will not be adopted. If this is in fact the case, the solution is to so structure taxes that they will be imposed as if the practice had been adopted and the income received. Therefore, tax revenues will be increased, and owners of resources have the choice of either not adopting the new practice and having their consumption level reduced

most cases presumed incomes exceed actual incomes, more revenue would be produced.

In taking a hard look at the proposal for a presumptive income tax, it appears that the concepts of a property tax and an income tax have been merged into one; hence the actual consequences of the tax may be somewhat difficult to predict. As mentioned earlier, a property tax is a fixed cost which influences both the exit and entry of firms in an industry and the minimum level of earnings needed for a firm to stay in business. It can therefore force the adoption of new production techniques, as well as the intensification of land use.[26] A presumptive income tax is also a fixed tax and might be called a property tax (the presumed income being capitalized to determine property values) or a franchise tax, i.e., a tax which must be paid in order to farm a given piece of land; and being fixed, the presumptive tax does not vary with or depend upon the actions taken by operators.

On the other hand, an income tax is a variable tax the liability of which depends upon and varies with the amount of income received. If more income is received, tax liability increases; if less income is received, less taxes are paid. Therefore, equal tax liability under an income tax would produce the same jolt to farmers in inducing them to adopt new practices as tax liability under a presumptive income tax, for in both cases incomes available for consumption would be reduced unless additional income were

earned.[27] Furthermore, in the case of the conventional progressive income tax, only part of each additional dollar earned would go for consumption, as contrasted to the presumptive income tax, where all of additional income is available for consumption; therefore, more effort would be needed to be put forth to maintain former consumption levels under a progressive income tax than under a tax on presumptive income.

Income taxes should not be sectoral taxes, but rather the tax should be levied on total income received, regardless of its source. Therefore, if a landowner is, for example, also a merchant, there should be a tax on his total income, not a tax on his agricultural income and another on his business income. Presumed income can, of course, be added to other forms of income to arrive at total income, but fluctuations in agricultural income are thereby prevented from influencing the final tax rates paid. If a partial objective of the tax is to turn investment opportunities in favor of agriculture (at the expense of non-agricultural investments), a presumptive income tax is a more powerful tool to achieve this end than a regular income tax,[28] but this is just another way of saying that agricultural incomes over a certain amount are exempt from taxation.

Having made this brief analysis of the presumptive income tax, some parts of which imply dissatisfaction with it, its use is recommended largely because of the idea contained in the saying that "the best should not be the enemy of the good." The experience from many countries indicates that even under the most favorable conditions, actual income from agriculture is very difficult to estimate and that considerable amounts of farm income are not reported for tax purposes. At the present time in most of Latin America, it would be very difficult and costly to make an accurate determination of actual farm income, and,

---

by the amount of the tax or adopting the practice, thereby earning additional income to pay the tax. The argument might also be made that the incentive to adopt practices would be stronger if their adoption prevented a decrease in income rather than resulting in an income increase, for the marginal utility of money for big landowners is reputed to be declining at a very rapid rate.

[26] In a price-responsive economy, this process is continually going on as a consequence of profit motivation. An extreme example of this is illustrated by a statement made by the Dean of Agriculture of Rutgers University in which he commented that New Jersey farm land is both the most expensive farm land as well as the most heavily taxed land in the United States and that New Jersey farmers produce by far the highest value of crops per acre, but that unless property taxes can be held at present levels, the complexion of New Jersey agriculture will be drastically changed and many areas will inevitably go out of farming. Statement in *New Jersey Agriculture*, Vol. 44, No. 4 (July–August, 1962).

[27] This, of course, assumes fairly high incomes, which is the assumption usually made concerning consumption levels of big landowners.
[28] Evidence in the United States indicates that some agricultural investments are made because of the difficulty of taxing income earned by these investments.

in addition, such a determination would require a corps of trained people that does not exist. Therefore, a realistic program of taxing farm income needs to be based on something other than actual income. The alternative suggested is that the tax be levied on presumed income, which should be calculated by applying some rate of interest to property values as set by owners under the system of self-assessments, advocated in an earlier part of this paper. The same value would then be used for three purposes: determination of property tax liability, income tax liability, and the price to be paid if the property were acquired by the land reform agency. This system would not only economize on the number of people needed to administer these three programs but also go far toward preventing underpayment or nonpayment of taxes. In addition, it should go a long way toward eliminating complaints of unfairness, for property values would be determined by owners themselves.

Tying these three together, however, may create the need for one modification in the proposal. For, if both property and income tax rates are quite progressive, owners may choose to keep their tax liability low by greatly undervaluing their properties in the hope that the land reform agency will not be able to acquire all undervalued property in the immediate future. They may, therefore, prefer to run the risk that their property would not be one of the first to be expropriated, rather than pay high property and income taxes. This situation can be easily prevented by declaring that anyone, not just the land reform agency, can purchase any property for, say, 25 per cent above the assessed value placed on the property by the owner and that the purchase price must be the minimum value at which the property can be assessed by the new owner. This would ensure not only that assessments were more in line with real values but also that properties would be transferred from less efficient to more efficient operators.

In any consideration of income taxes, it should be realized that the incomes received by a large segment of the agricultural population are so low that they would be exempt from taxation under most income tax schemes; therefore, a substantial part of total agricultural income is eliminated from the tax base. However, because of the very skewed distribution of agricultural income, it is quite probable that the present distribution, in which much of present income is exempt from taxation, may result in more revenue being collected than would result from an income distribution in which fewer incomes were exempt from taxation. This by no means argues in favor of the present patterns of income distribution. Quite the contrary, for it indicates the need for a rapid leveling of incomes, which can be done by means of a progressive income tax.

However, the fact that much of the agricultural population does not have sufficient income to pay income taxes should not relieve them completely from their responsibility to help support government activities.[29] While a money tax may be undesirable, a labor tax would be both feasible and desirable, for it could go a long way toward making possible the development of much-needed infrastructure, such as roads, irrigation works, and schools, without creating the need for financial resources. Such a tax was common in rural areas in the United States and provided the means for the construction of many rural roads. The tax could be fairly simple, such as requiring each male over eighteen to work a given number of days on public works projects during periods of the year when there is little farm employment. Since the major cost of many of these projects is primarily labor, such a tax would not only provide the means of accomplishing these projects but also provide communities the opportunity to take part in actually planning projects and in this way help in developing community leaders.

[29] In those places where sales taxes exist, these people pay a proportionally greater part of their income in taxes than do many segments of the population.

SUMMARY AND CONCLUSIONS

One of the major difficulties faced in administering a land tax in Latin America is that of determining farm values with the inadequate information presently available. As a solution to this problem, the proposal is made that owners themselves assess their properties and pay taxes on the basis of this assessment. In addition, this value should also be the price paid by the land reform agency for properties acquired by it under a land reform program. Owners would then be faced with the choice of either paying taxes on the full value of their properties or running the risk of having to sell their farms for less than their actual value. If there is also to be an income tax, farm income should be calculated as a given percentage of the self-declared property value. This method of estimating farm income is suggested because of the difficulties that would be encountered in trying to determine actual farm income.

From a discussion of the extent to which fixed taxes can influence farmers to adopt new and improved practices, it was concluded that high fixed taxes, if high enough, can in fact drive out inefficient methods as well as producers but that similar ends could be better achieved through policies aimed at modifying variable factor and product prices. A tax on irrigation water as a means of improving the allocation of this very scarce resource in areas of inadequate rainfall was suggested as illustrative of the way in which selective taxes could improve resource use.

The highly unequal distribution of agricultural incomes creates the need for progressive rate structures for both property and income taxes and at the same time suggests that a large part of the agricultural population does not have sufficient income to pay either property or income taxes. However, this fact should not mean that this group becomes completely tax exempt, for in many instances a labor tax of a specified number of days of work from every able-bodied male over eighteen would go a long way toward providing badly needed infrastructure, such as roads, schools, health centers, etc., while at the same time helping to develop a sense of pride and feeling of responsibility toward the community.

Permeating the entire discussion was the need for sufficient authority and means on the part of tax administrators to enforce tax laws vigorously, for there are many examples where existing laws call for the payment of more taxes than administrators have either been willing or able to collect. Therefore, taxes levied against the agricultural sector can be effective only if tax administrators have the desire and authority to collect these taxes. One way of expediting this is to tie together those parts of tax and land reform programs which reinforce each other.

Comment

SOL DESCARTES*

The urgency of improving taxes on land in Latin America is fully recognized by all who are familiar with the subject. Mr. Wald summarizes the limitations of this type of tax in Latin America in his paper, pointing out that (1) they produce inadequate revenue, (2)

*Economic Consultant, San Juan, Puerto Rico.

property is not taxed on a uniform equitable basis, and (3) they do not absorb a significant proportion of the increase in agricultural income and thus they do not contribute to the financing of public investment in such a way as to prevent inflation. For purposes of emphasis, I should like to summarize some of the main points made by Mr. Wald with which I am in complete agreement.

He recognizes the relative backwardness or, as he calls it, the primitive or rudimentary character of this class of tax in Latin America and maintains that there is no escaping the conclusion that taxes on agricultural land are very low and proportionally extremely light. He repeatedly emphasizes the discouraging results of attempts to use taxes levied on land to further objectives connected with agrarian reform.

Mr. Wald explains the general lack of adequate basic information, such as maps, property registers, etc., which are indispensable requirements for the development and administration of agricultural land tax systems such as are found in the technologically more advanced countries.

He points to a very common defect in Latin America, namely, the fact that the complexity of the tax laws frequently hampers their administration and militates against their usefulness as instruments for economic and social reform and for furthering economic development.

He points out very wisely that the primary purpose of taxes on land, that is, their revenue producing function, should not be underestimated and that undue weight should not be given to the goals of economic and agrarian reform. He performs a valuable service in underlining the self-defeating effects of excessive liberality in granting tax exemptions in respect of agricultural holdings.

He also wisely points out the limitations of betterment levies or special assessments because of the administrative problems to which they give rise in the few cases where they could apply.

Discussing the problem in general terms, he underlines the marked differences among the Latin American countries with respect to their physical environment, their land tenure systems, and the capabilities of their administrations to impose and to collect taxes. This leads him to one of his most useful and pertinent conclusions: that it is impossible to recommend a system of land taxation which is generally applicable to all or even to most of the countries. Although this may seem obvious, the fact that it should be borne in mind at all times cannot be overemphasized.

Mr. Wald's basic recommendation on the kind of tax he would propose is that underdeveloped countries should begin with a tax related to the size of agricultural holdings. This tax would be applied on the basis of rates which would vary in accordance with the approximate productivity of the land. Small holdings would be tax exempt.

Mr. Wald indicates that the rates of taxation could be graduated in accordance with each taxpayer's total holdings so that the tax would be progressive in relation to income. I have some reservations about this suggestion. I take it that before that provision is put into effect, the country's whole tax system would be studied in order to avoid a self-defeating degree of progressivity where adequate legislation on personal income is in effect.

He wisely suggests that the proposed system should be considered as the initial stage of a long-range plan leading to more advanced land-tax systems.

It must also be kept in mind, as Mr. Wald says, that the existence of legal penalties and incentives aimed at remedying defects in land tenure systems may result in unwarranted postponement of direct agrarian reform measures. Experience shows that to achieve agrarian reform, direct measures are far more effective than the indirect effects of income laws.

I also agree with the recommendation that Latin American countries should be alert to the need to adjust their agricultural tax systems to changes which take place in its agricultural sectors and economic structure. Only in this way could the country concerned set aside a reasonable proportion of its total product for public purposes which, in turn, would facilitate the financing of its economic expansion programs.

Mr. Wald's paper ends by stressing that action to overcome the difficulties and principal deficiencies in the agricultural tax systems in Latin America, as a prerequisite to their achieving a more rapid rate of economic progress, is both important and urgent.

It is a fundamental premise that a program to improve agricultural taxation must be developed specifically for each country. This is imperative in view of the many major differences among the countries concerned. Another equally important principle—and one which Mr. Wald does not emphasize—is that each phase of an agricultural tax reform program should be formulated in the light of its relationship to the country's over-all tax system. To do otherwise would be self-defeating.

Another of Mr. Wald's principal recommendations is: "The ideal arrangement (in the imposition of taxes on agricultural land) is that it be based on the presumed [gross or] net income of each holding or cultivation over and above minimum subsistence needs." While this is a worthy objective, I do not believe that it must necessarily be achieved through a tax on the presumed net income from agricultural holdings.

In my view, a combination of a land tax calculated on the value of the holding, but not progressive in respect to income, and an adequate income tax would be a more feasible and perhaps a more equitable arrangement. In the area in which I have been working, this combination has led to a satisfactory achievement of these objectives, although not without the unavoidable minor defects produced by these complicated forms of fiscal legislation. Besides, I have a basic doubt as to the desirability of imposing taxes on presumed income or agricultural production. The theoretical and practical limitations of taxes on income, even in the more advanced countries where they are based on income actually received, are well known. Administrative difficulties and the possibility of inequities in the determination of presumed income or productivity present greater problems than determining income already earned.

In Puerto Rico, which has been influenced by United States concepts and practices, there is a general tax on property, including buildings, which is computed by applying to the assessed value of the property rates that vary only slightly among the different municipalities. The criterion for assessment in accordance with the law is the market value of the property. The rates of taxation on property consist of a uniform share which goes to the treasury of the state government and a varying share imposed by and intended for the municipalities. There is also an income tax law—similarly patterned on the United States model—which applies to all income regardless of its origin: agriculture, industry, salaries, wages, etc. From my own experience, I naturally lean toward this solution, which might be called co-ordination of land and income taxes rather than integration.

Mr. Wald's exposition provides a useful summary of the chief practices in respect of taxes on agriculture in Latin America, with particular reference to taxes on agricultural land. His recommendations for improving these taxes are quite pertinent. With a high degree of practical sense, he emphasizes that the primary function of these taxes—more so than their role as instruments for economic expansion—is to provide revenue. Finally, he makes specific practical recommendations as to the program which should be undertaken with a view to improving taxation on agricultural land in Latin America and on the final objectives to which the progressive evolution of these taxes should lead.

The work is useful and, if attention is paid to his observations, will accelerate the introduction of improvements in the property tax which will contribute to economic development.

In the preceding pages, I have summarized and supported the most useful main concepts in Mr. Wald's paper in the light of my own practical experience in similar matters. What can I add to Mr. Wald's presentation? Very little, if anything, with regard to general principles or to the principles or theory underlying his recommendations, except for a few reservations on specific points.

In my view, the most important thing to do now is to start introducing tax reforms. In connection with this task, which should be given first priority, I might mention some practices which we found useful in improving the property tax in Puerto Rico.

We did not find it easy to initiate the property tax reform. There had not been a general revaluation of property in the period 1917 to 1949. There was strong opposition, not only from the taxpayers affected but also from some government officials and some members of the legislative branch. The reform could get under way only because the highest political and executive leaders were determined that it should.

The conviction at high political and executive levels that reform is necessary, the enthusiasm of the treasury officials who are to carry out the reform, and persistence and determination on the part of all concerned are essential requisites to the successful outcome of this type of undertaking. Dedication to the proposition that the property tax should be reformed must, however, be accompanied by flexibility in the detailed application of the reform. It should be understood that adjustments may have to be made in order to secure broad political backing for the carrying out of the reform. Appreciation of this fact at the very outset will prevent the executives and technicians in charge of the reform from being discouraged when confronted with realities.

It is most desirable to have someone with a broad understanding of the significance, urgency, and benefits of the reform as well as of the theoretical and practical implications of the proposed changes who could serve as an intermediary between the technicians and the executive branch, on the one hand, and the political sector and community at large on the other. Preferably—and ideally—this intermediary ought to have authority to make decisions, or, failing this, he should have a close official relationship with, and enjoy the confidence of, the government official responsible for decisions.

In Puerto Rico, political conditions were stable, there was relative experience in these matters, and the political parties in power had a decisive majority; yet even there the

basic plan had to be adjusted in order to carry out successfully the general property revaluation of 1949–51. Property was taxed for the first time on the basis of a scientific system of cadastral maps, soil studies, classification of land, changes resulting from other natural characteristics, and adjustments due to economic factors such as location in respect to populated areas or processing industries and assessment of buildings on the basis of replacement cost and depreciation. It should be noted that in our case all that was attempted was an improvement of assessment and tax collection procedures and not the even more difficult task, confronted by the Latin American countries, of adopting new tax concepts or drastically modifying the concepts already being applied.

The tax to be paid by a taxpayer cannot be increased disproportionately from one year to the next, lest there should be strong adverse public reaction which in one way or another would vitiate the effects of the reform. In Puerto Rico, following the property revaluation the taxable value of property almost doubled, and the rates of taxation had to be adjusted to avoid exaggerated increases in the actual tax payable by a large number of taxpayers. The main effect of the revaluation was thus, at the beginning, to make the tax more equitable. Over the long term, however, it produced a considerable increase in the property tax collected. It is interesting to note that in our case the revenue collected from the agricultural sector as a whole was reduced, while the revenue from the urban areas increased.

The desirability of ensuring public support for the assessment and collection of taxes is generally recognized by tax experts. I therefore deem it essential with respect to tax reform measures in Latin America that every reform program should be provided, as an integral part of the program itself, with an informational section to educate and persuade the public concerning the need and benefits of tax changes.

A decisive contribution to public good will can be made by having the public participate in the institution of reforms. In my country, we sought to achieve this through advisory committees of private citizens, who considered the evaluation factors to be used for the new assessments.

When the collection of the tax on the basis of the revised valuations was begun, a very liberal system of administrative review was established, easily accessible without charge to any citizen who had a grievance concerning the amount of his tax. We found this to be a very useful procedure, both for correcting inevitable errors and for reducing protests and gaining public confidence. In this way, a large number of complaints regarding excessive assessments were resolved without the necessity of adjusting valuations or reducing the tax simply by explaining to the complaining taxpayer how his property was valued and the amounts which his neighbors were paying. Also, it drastically reduced the number of legal proceedings challenging the new assessments.

I think that two or three concepts might also be useful for international or private organizations or for tax reform consultants. The firm conviction that the recommendations made are the right ones, loyalty to the principles, postulates, and the political, social, and economic philosophy on which the recommendations are based—these do not exclude the respect which the consultants should have for local judgment or for the wisdom which is the result of years of experience in each region. This is particularly true in respect of agriculture and the introduction of agricultural programs.

The consultant should understand the difficulties and problems facing political leaders in attempting to make any changes in institutions that have been in existence for many years. As in everything, moderation and balance are indispensable for performing this difficult advisory function. Inflexibility is fatal to the effectiveness of the consultant's advice, but, on the other hand, ready submission to political demagoguery or to ignorance is equally disastrous.

Above all, the function of a consultant is to educate, to persuade, to understand, and to gain the confidence of those whom he advises. Of great relevance is a comment by the eminent English novelist and thinker, C. P. Snow, in his Godkin Lectures at Harvard University in 1960 on Science and Government: "The lesson for the scientists (who advised the armed forces before and during the Second World War) is that the prerequisite to sound military advice was that he who gives it must be convinced that if he had the responsibility to act, he himself would act in that way. This is a difficult lesson to learn. If it were learnt, the number of theoretical treatises on the future conduct of war would be considerably reduced."[30] This lesson is equally pertinent to advice on fiscal matters.

In order to facilitate action—to begin to take action, which, as I said earlier, is where we must now concentrate our energies—I must again emphasize the importance of beginning with relatively simple objectives which are both easy to explain to the public and easy to manage, under conditions where administrative expertise and experience are scarce. Simplicity—the elimination of all complexity to the greatest possible extent compatible with the complicated nature of the economic processes themselves—is desirable in every field of endeavor. It is even more important where economic development is in an initial or intermediate stage.

Lastly, an encouraging note to all, to the political leaders, to executives, and to consultants: it is a truism—obvious but nonetheless worth mentioning—that tax reform is something being undertaken by every community, from the most technically advanced to those which are just taking their first steps toward economic and social progress. Everywhere, changes and reforms are, in the final analysis, the result of compromise between ideal models and the social, economic, and political realities of each area.

[30]Translated from Spanish.

Discussion

MR. GREGORY, introducing Mr. Wald's paper, said that agricultural taxation should be discussed in relation to the general aim and objectives it was to achieve. These ranged from the usual fiscal objectives of raising revenue to proposals aimed primarily at providing incentives to the agricultural sector. The revenue and incentive aspects of agricultural taxation were at some point bound to conflict, and the kind of tax policy suggested would depend upon the views held on the role the agricultural sector should play in the over-all economic development—whether it should be a source of capital for the rest of the economy or whether it needed capital to be brought into it. It was unfortunate that the terms "agricultural taxation" and "land taxation" were often used synonymously, for there were other taxes in addition to a tax on property which should be levied on the agricultural sector, even though a tax on land was probably the most important from the standpoint of revenue potential, distribution effects, and, to some extent, incentive effects. A tax on land could serve as an excellent lubricant for land reform, and the two programs should therefore be developed together.

His remarks were based on the following assumptions: (a) that at present the amount of tax revenue paid by the agricultural sector was not only far less than its legal tax liability but also much less than it was capable of paying; (b) that the reason for underpayment of taxes was the manner in which tax laws were written and administered and the nature of the agricultural industry which made tax evasion relatively simple; (c) that underpayment of taxes tended to perpetuate the existing pattern of very unequal income distribution as well as to encourage inefficient use of resources, particularly of land and capital; and (d) that the objective was therefore to find some way of levying taxes which would greatly increase the amount of taxes paid by the agricultural sector and, at the same time,

redistribute incomes and provide some incentives for improved use of resources.

With respect to his proposal that the best way to ensure a fair assessment of land for taxation purposes would be for the owner himself to assess the value of his holdings, he realized that the proposal had some limitations but felt that the disadvantages did not offset the benefits to be derived from that method. The problem of correct property assessment was particularly acute in Latin America, and its solution required a corps of well-trained technicians who would need much time to get the necessary data on which a fair assessment could be based. Self-assessment, therefore, seemed to be the only method susceptible of immediate application. Underevaluation could be guarded against by providing that land reform agencies could acquire the property at the value placed on it by the owner. The latter could then either pay taxes on the full value of his property or run the risk of capital loss through having his property bought at his own assessed value. Carrying the proposal somewhat further, some fraction of the property value declared by the owner could be used as the presumed income of his property for the purposes of a tax on farm income.

With respect to incentive taxation as a means of improving the use of land, he thought that the same objective could be achieved better through a progressive tax on land. Incentives to improved farming practices should be determined through variable rather than fixed costs. In view of present conditions in Latin America, a combination of a progressive land tax and a tax on presumed agricultural income, applied equally regardless of land used, would be more effective than a program of discriminatory incentive taxes.

Another useful tax on the agricultural sector would be a specific tax on water, which was one of the most critical inputs in the area and was often used inefficiently. A progressive tax on water would improve its allocation and use, help to redistribute water rights, and increase revenue. Such a tax would ensure that the use cost of water could be paid only if it was used on highly responsive crops. The progressive feature of the tax would discourage farmers from bidding for large quantities of water, thus ensuring its availability to small farmers. The latter would not be exempted from the tax, but a system of subsidies or credits could be devised to help them pay the tax if they were unable to do so.

Mr. DESCARTES agreed with the objectives sought by Mr. Wald in his proposals but had some reservations on the feasibility and effectiveness of the methods suggested.

With regard to the self-assessment of property by the owner, he had no objection, provided that all that was intended was a mere declaration of the value of a piece of property. Mr. Gregory, however, had gone further in suggesting that a government should be able to purchase the property on the basis of the value assessed by the owner. He opposed that suggestion because it might be at variance with the constitutional position in some countries. Moreover, land reform should not be based on purchase of property merely because an owner had understated its value. Land reform was an instrument of economic development, and it would be wrong to complicate its implementation. Land could be more properly acquired by other methods. The method proposed might well be considered an undesirable form of expropriation. The right of expropriation was undeniable, provided that adequate compensation was paid to the owner.

Even more objectionable would be a proposal to allow individuals to purchase property by paying 25 per cent more than the value set by the owner. Such a scheme would affect the stability and productivity of the agricultural sector, even if it were applied as a provisional measure. A better system would be to tax land on the size of the property concerned and its productive capacity and to use the revenue for the purchase of land

by the state. At the same time, an attempt should be made to obtain more data on which to assess land values.

The suggestion that a tax might be imposed on the imputed income of agricultural property was less objectionable than self-assessment of its value. Such a tax could be used as an expedient to facilitate taxation of the agricultural sector, although the rate of taxation should not be based on the value set by property owners.

Emphasizing the need for an efficient tax administration, particularly in the Latin American countries, he said that much depended upon public good will, which could be ensured only through the participation of the public at large. He stressed that specific tax policies with respect to agriculture should be adapted to the conditions prevailing in each country and should be in harmony with the other taxes. Changes in agricultural taxes should be made in the light of the tax system as a whole.

Mr. MOISÉS BEATRIZ congratulated the organizers of the conference for including in the agenda the study of agricultural taxation, a subject of fundamental importance, since the Latin American economy was primarily agricultural; agricultural taxation afforded the least possibilities for effective application of income tax while calling for the greatest economic and social reforms. For those reasons, the tax could contribute to higher productivity of the land and a better distribution of holdings.

Although the ingenious methods proposed in the papers by Mr. Wald and Mr. Gregory to obtain the economic and social effects sought were most intriguing, he believed that before complicated methods could be applied it would first be necessary to establish a sound land register. He would be interested, therefore, in knowing the results obtained in the application of the new agricultural tax laws in Colombia and Chile.

The tax on exports was one way of taxing agricultural income. In El Salvador, in view of the problems which had arisen in the application of income tax on income derived from coffee growing, it had been replaced by an export tax on the product with progressive rates adjusted to international prices. The result had been satisfactory from the standpoint of tax yield, since it was easily and cheaply administered and almost perfect fiscal control was possible. To make the tax on coffee exports more equitable, it would be advisable to integrate it with income tax so that the taxpayer could apply all or part of the pertinent export tax against income tax.

As to extending income tax to capital gains, he said that such a measure would be valuable in obtaining fair distribution in the agricultural sector.

MR. CASAS observed that in the Latin American countries agricultural production was often cyclical, with all that that implied. Hence he did not consider it possible to apply in Latin America the same systems as were in use in other countries whose agricultural economy was more highly developed and where price supports and other measures contributed to its stability. Since agriculture was a very sensitive sector of the economy, care should be taken that any measures adopted did not discourage it still further. As to the revaluation system and the presumptive income tax suggested by Mr. Gregory as possibilities for agriculture, he entirely agreed with the idea and disagreed with Mr. Descartes on the subject. Optional assessment of property by agricultural landowners for purposes of the tax on occasional profits was provided for by the 1960 tax law in Colombia, failing which the state made the assessment on cadastral or commercial bases. Both the self-assessment and the tax—fixed at a rate of 6 per cent per annum—had been placed at the service of the 1960 agrarian reform in Colombia. He explained the rural tax and the tax on net wealth as applied in Colombia and referred to the decline in the value of land in that country, which could be attributed to the prevailing insecurity in certain areas and the shortage of cash, which had reduced demand in relation to supply. As to the progressive water tax, he disagreed with Mr. Gregory's views.

MR. DARDÓN, referring to certain comments made by Mr. Wald with regard to land tax in Guatemala, pointed out that actually the tax on the capital value of land was integrated with other taxes which likewise affected land, such as the tax on free conveyances (tax on inheritances, legacies, and gifts, which taxed land at an equal rate in each case) or transfers against payment (tax on purchases and sales and on exchanges of land).

Recently, as a result of the enactment of the progressive personal income tax law, the agricultural sector was included in it with a 10 per cent reduction on the net income tax rate. In his opinion, such taxes represented the maximum taxpaying possibilities of the agricultural sector. With them it was to be hoped that Guatemala would be able to implement its economic development programs in the next few years.

With reference to revaluation of rural property for the purpose of increasing fiscal income, an obstacle had been the lack of cadastral survey maps, although some progress had now been made in that respect. To solve the problem temporarily in accordance with the laws of Guatemala, the system of personal returns had been adopted. To supplement it, banking institutions had been required to send to the tax collectors' offices the property revaluations which served as a basis for granting loans. Furthermore, before filing their returns, the owners themselves usually requested the services of professional appraisers authorized by the ministry of finance and properly trained for the purpose.

MR. BACA said that in Latin American countries there were two problems connected with agrarian reform which aroused tremendous interest because of the difficulty of solving them, namely, the problem of determining what land was subject to expropriation and that of fixing its value. Both had political overtones, and adequate solutions to them had been suggested by Mr. Gregory. Experience in Colombia had shown that the suggestions were feasible.

MR. DESAI observed that land taxation involved social and political objectives and was therefore difficult to implement in practice, although it was possible to do so in theory. It gave rise to diverse questions such as the social redistribution of land (land reform proper) where the tax machinery was used to break up large estates into small holdings; taxation of land in relation to inflationary conditions where the value of the land increased as a result of inflation, the backward sloping supply curve, the breakdown of traditional farming methods in order to improve efficiency, and the need for cadastral maps.

He agreed with Mr. Gregory's view on land redistribution. If land reform measures were defeated by the opposition of the landowners, land taxation measures would be defeated as well. If land reform was important it should be tackled directly; taxation of land was not the most effective means to achieve it.

His own country, India, had had considerable experience with cadastral maps, but experience with land taxation had been rather unsatisfactory. The government had been unable to take effective action in that field because of the political value attaching to land and the strong opposition from large and small landowners alike.

Land redistribution did not necessarily contribute to efficiency in the agricultural sector. While large landowners were mainly responsible for the problem of idle land, a small landowner might not be able to increase productivity because of such factors as lack of capital and credit.

While more revenue might be obtained by taxing the small landowner, such a tax might defeat the other aspects of rural reform, such as community development programs. A better method of increasing revenue from the small farmer might be through excise taxation, which was less objectionable from the political point of view.

MR. GNAZZO agreed that a distinction should be made between land distribution and productivity. However, he could not support Mr. Desai's view that a land tax could not make a useful contribution to land redistribution.

On the question of the assessment of agri-cultural property, he pointed out that in Uruguay authority to tax land was vested in the local governments which, for constitutional reasons, chose to raise the rates without touching the assessments.

With respect to the over-all tax on income, he pointed out that in Uruguay a system had been established for determining income on the basis of an average potential yield according to property assessments mathematically brought up to date.

A major problem in Latin America was the concentration of wealth in the agricultural sector, usually in the hands of corporations belonging to the same family. The danger of tax evasion by such corporations could be overcome if they were not permitted to issue bearer shares.

MR. PREST said that although he was in sympathy with the idea of a proportional land tax, he did not believe that a progressive land tax would be practicable. If land owned by one family was split up among the various members to reduce the incidence of a progressive tax, it would not be easy in practice to take countermeasures to aggregate family holdings for tax purposes, and forms of evasion might develop, such as the formation of corporations with bearer shares. If family holdings were in different parts of the country, the tax administration would have to be centralized, although land taxation would be easier to administer on a regional basis. In establishing the relative capacity of different land, the annual tax liability would have to be adjusted in accordance with some measure of output or price or income changes. The relative prices of the crops grown on different land units would change from year to year; hence it could not be assumed that the relative capacity to pay of such units would remain the same. He could not agree that a land tax affected the level of fixed costs and that action should therefore be based on what would be a suitable course if fixed costs changed. A graduated land tax would affect the capitalization of the existing landowner; if he sold the land immediately, its value would be reduced, and there was no way in which he could avoid the tax by changing his occupation, as an industrialist could if his product were taxed. He asked if Mr. Gregory's belief that a land tax would not lead to better utilization of land would still apply if he accepted the proposition that the tax was not in fact reflected in the level of fixed costs.

With respect to the use of water, it would be reasonable to levy a tax, but he could not agree that it should be progressive in accordance with the amount used, which would be analogous to levying a progressive tax on such inputs as electricity or transport.

MR. GOODE said that he could not accept as a long-term goal Mr. Wald's proposal that the land tax should be integrated with the personal income tax; both equity and economic policy demanded that both forms of tax should be imposed in the agricultural sector. Referring to what Mr. Prest had said about capitalization, he said that if the land tax was reflected in land values it amounted to a once-and-for-all tax and if subsequently revoked would bestow windfall gains on any landowner who had bought the land after imposition of the tax. Second, personal income tax was levied in view of the total income of an individual in the light of his personal circumstances, at graduated rates according to the income received, whereas a land tax was an impersonal tax that had no regard to the total situation of the landowner; consequently one form of tax could not replace the other. Third, a land tax was at least partly a benefit tax, reflecting the landowner's payment toward the cost of public improvements, such as irrigation or road building, that benefited landowners and consequently could not be replaced by the income tax. In any case, he did not believe that Mr. Wald would argue that it would be possible in the near future to apply personal income tax to agriculture effectively enough to make it possible to do without a land tax.

He agreed with Mr. Prest that a land tax could not be regarded as a fixed charge that did not affect farming operations, and in fact Mr. Gregory had withdrawn somewhat from that position by referring in his paper to the possibility that effort would be diverted from one agricultural sector to another.

He did not believe that progressive tax charges on water use would increase allocative efficiency, and he supported what Mr. Prest had said on that point. If the aim was the social one of redistributing water rights, there were more effective means of doing so. On the other hand, there should be adequate charges for irrigation water from public projects.

He shared Mr. Descartes' doubts about land valuation by self-assessment, which might prove arbitrary and erratic in application. The method would be more acceptable if used in connection with government acquisition of land under a land reform scheme than if third parties were allowed to force a sale on that basis; but although the present system was not very good, it would be better to try to improve it than to resort to self-assessment.

Although Mr. Desai was correct in saying that a good cadastral survey was not a guarantee of a good land tax, it was an indispensable condition, and if supplemented by technical capacity and political determination, it could result in a good land tax. Land tax arrangements in India might not be very good but were better than in Latin America as a whole. At one time the Indian land tax was an efficient means of mobilizing resources; but pressure from landowners, especially small landowners, had prevented assessments from being kept in line with prices, because political leaders were afraid of losing the support of the small landowner, who had expected to find himself much better off when India became independent. Once a good cadastral survey had been made, it must be kept up to date, otherwise adjustment to real values after a lapse of time would result in a large increase in the tax which would be strongly resisted.

Excise taxes were not a good means of reaching the agricultural sector, because in many countries small farmers depended largely on a nonmonetary economy, so that much consumption would escape the tax; nor were they a good method of reaching the large landowner.

MRS. DE NAVARRETE brought up the question of the relationships between the redistribution of land and the increase in productivity in the agricultural sector, expressing skepticism on the subject. In support of her views she cited the case of Mexico, where there were wide differences in productivity between modern industrial-type farms using advanced technology, established in areas that had recently been opened up to cultivation and highly productive, and others where farmers cultivated the land for their own consumption and not for markets, using rudimentary techniques. In the latter case, it was possible that structural improvements, revaluation, and land taxation might have some influence in increasing productivity. Furthermore, drift from the land and migration of the population toward the cities were phenomena which undoubtedly militated against the productivity of the land; notwithstanding, it was possible that in certain cases they should be encouraged. It should also be taken into account that the tax on landownership was usually a local matter, while taxation of income was under national jurisdiction.

MR. KALDOR said that he and Mr. Wald seemed to have arrived independently at very similar views on agricultural taxation. Agricultural taxation was very important in Latin America for three reasons. First, the agricultural sector tended to be heavily undertaxed in underdeveloped countries, apart from the large plantations producing cash crops for export, which were sometimes overtaxed because they were also subject to heavy export duties or corporation taxes. But undertaxation was the rule, especially as regards the production of food for domestic consumption. Second, agricultural taxation could improve land productivity and help to secure a freer land market. One reason for backward agriculture was the ownership of land by those who had so much that they were not interested in making good use of it. On the fixed charge aspect of the land tax, he agreed with Mr. Goode, and not with Mr. Gregory. Incentives to improved management should be in the form of pressure rather than concessions. The effect of the land tax was greater turnover of ownership, which would result in the average farmer's being more efficient than he was at present. The third point was that where landownership was as concentrated as it was in most of Latin America and in the Middle East, the resulting income, if untaxed, represented a dead burden carried by the community. Luxury consumption based on large corporate incomes could to some extent be regarded as a reward for getting the economy to produce through the market mechanism, but the landowner was supported by the community even if he failed to produce. He believed that the social burden of supporting the large landowners in Chile, for example, was larger in terms of the total gross national product than the whole military expenditure of the United States in terms of the United States gross national product. A progressive land tax seemed to be the only way to tap those resources, and he agreed with Mr. Goode that an agricultural income tax was not the ultimate goal and could not be an alternative to an efficient land tax.

He did not agree with Mr. Prest that land taxes should not or could not be progressive; in the early days the same had been said of the income tax. The problem of dividing up family holdings could arise equally well in relation to income tax and could be countered by aggregation of the property of husbands and wives and minor children. In general, the danger of evasion was less than with income tax, because marginal rates were lower.

He agreed with Mr. Goode that Mr. Harberger's self-assessment proposal was open to objections as it stood, but if it was combined with a method under which the owner was free to retain his property if he raised his valuation, as he himself had suggested, it would be a valuable means of ensuring that the owner would be forced to increase the valuation to the full market value. Even so, the market value was not such a satisfactory basis for a land tax as the potential annual yield determined by objective criteria. Consequently he favored a cadastral survey in conjunction with a points system to establish potential fertility and potential yield in relation to the average yield in the region or in the country as a whole. The valuation could be kept up to date on the basis of the current value (or five-year moving average value) of net agricultural output per hectare. However, he was certainly in favor of self-assessment on the lines indicated until such time (which might be a long one) as the necessary classification of lands could be completed; he was also in favor of making land taxations the responsibility of the central government and not of the local authorities.

He agreed with Mr. Goode that excise taxes could not be an alternative to land taxation. Referring to what Mr. Desai had said, he pointed out that India had once had a good land revenue system, but unfortunately the five-year revaluations had not been kept up after the nineteenth century. Under the new constitution, land taxes had been assigned to the states, where the political pressure of landowning interests was very strong.

He agreed with Mr. Goode and Mr. Prest that there was no point in a progressive water use tax apart from a progressive tax on the value of landholdings. A progressive land tax on potential yield would have income effects but no substitution effects, and there would be a strong incentive to additional effort to make more money. Land values would be reduced, and large landowners would sell part of their land in order to get into a lower tax bracket. There would be a free land market, making possible an improved relationship between the supply of efficient users of land and the distribution in the ownership or control of land.

MR. MONTERROSO, although in general agreement with the views set forth by the various speakers, said he would like to make some reservations. Thus, in his opinion, excessive use should not be made of agricultural taxes through taxes on exports in underdeveloped countries. To support his statement, he mentioned the case of coffee exporters in Guatemala, who had exerted such pressure

that the tax on exports had had to be reduced when the international prices of coffee dropped. He also believed that in the less developed countries the tax on value added might give good yields and contribute to the prevention of unequal ownership of land, as the experience in Colombia suggested. Taxes on inheritances, legacies, and gifts were also important and easy to apply indirectly in relation to agriculture because of the concentration of real property, and he felt that it might even be advisable to increase them. Taxes on production were being applied in Guatemala at the municipal level, which could give rise to arbitrary action. However, the system would prevent evasion if properly established.

MR. DESCARTES, replying to the comments made by different speakers in the course of the discussion, said he agreed with them as to the importance of making good use of taxation on real estate. He emphasized that it should be extended to urban property. Like Mr. Moisés Beatriz and Mr. Monterroso, he believed that taxes on imports should not be overdone. The same applied to taxes on production, and he stressed the danger of applying them at the local level. He agreed with Mr. Casas' comments regarding the cyclical effects of agriculture and with his objections to the progressive water tax and his recognition of the undoubted influence of assessment on nonagricultural taxes.

He believed with Mr. Desai that a land register did not in itself improve the yield of land taxes unless it was kept up to date. Nevertheless, he considered it very important. Credit was due to Mr. Desai for having raised the problem of agricultural productivity, in relation to agrarian reform, a subject also referred to by Mrs. de Navarrete. He agreed with them both that certain areas were better suited to cultivation on large estates; however, pertinent measures would have to be adopted to destroy the social power to which the concentration of property gave rise.

In his opinion, the stimulating effect of the tax level on productivity, as mentioned by

Mr. Gnazzo, Mr. Kaldor, and Mr. Goode, could not be gainsaid; referring to Mr. Prest's preference for a tax system based on a proportional land tax, supplemented by personal income tax, it appeared to him that it would be best if such a system were used according to the conditions prevailing in the country where it was applied.

Despite the views set forth by Mr. Casas and Mr. Baca, he was still opposed to self-assessment. He did not believe it could facilitate implementation of agrarian reform or reduce the political opposition which any change in a land tenure system brought about. Rather, self-assessment could lend itself to manipulations that would make it still more objectionable and create strong opposition.

He concurred with Mrs. de Navarrete in believing that there was not necessarily a correlation between productivity and agrarian reform. He stressed the importance for taxation of the difference between commercial and subsistence agriculture. Commercial agriculture could be taxed in the same way as in the more developed countries. Probably the contribution of the modern agricultural sector to the gross product was larger and could be taxed effectively, but he felt that the sector should not be abused. He also agreed with Mrs. de Navarrete as to the importance of jurisdictional differences, as he believed that local autonomy should be encouraged.

Lastly, he agreed with most of Mr. Kaldor's comments and, in view of his training and experience, with Mr. Goode's statement.

MR. GREGORY said that he had confined himself in his paper to attempting to indicate where fiscal reform in agriculture and agricultural reform would complement each other. Where a small number of farmers produced the bulk of income in agriculture, the tax must be aimed at the large landowners and agricultural producers. The details of the tax program must fit the needs of each country, but certain basic principles of agricultural taxation applied to all countries. His proposal for self-assessment of land values had been criticized on the grounds that the redistribution of land under agricultural reform programs should not concentrate on land undervalued by the owners. But acquisition should not be confined to undervalued land; it must be objective and not exclude land with a high valuation. The difference between his own viewpoint and that of some other speakers related mainly to the time factor. How soon could a start be made on taxing away the excess accruing to large agricultural producers? If assessment was based on cadastral surveys and appraisals of productive capacity, it was hard to see how any tax action could be taken within the next two or three years. The only answer was self-assessment combined with safeguards against undervaluation and possible substantial capital losses.

He agreed that excise taxes could not provide a large source of agricultural taxation. With respect to a tax on presumed income, he thought there were reasons for relying on the self-assessments under property taxation rather than on production calculated on the basis of average practice and yields. The latter method would require trained staff and data that were not available, whereas with the use of a multiple or factor of an assessed value an early start could be made with the tax. The possibility that tax liability might be higher than farm income was not a reason for not imposing a tax on presumed income, since it would have the desired effect of increasing productive effort. He added that the self-assessment system would have the virtue of relying less on the tax administration and its officials, compared with other systems.

The main reason for differentiating between fixed and variable costs was that high fixed costs were known to act as an incentive in determining the exit and entry of firms. He recognized the need for more than a mere choice of enterprises; there must also be a choice of practices and quality and quantity of inputs. Such marginal choices of good or poor managements were not affected by fixed costs.

He agreed that the progressive feature of a water tax might hamper the allocative effect, but water distribution in Latin America tended to follow landholdings, and in the absence of a good water tax, redistribution could not be effected. He did not believe that the social principle would conflict with the criterion of efficiency, since the small farmer, who would have no access to water use if the tax were not progressive, would not use it less efficiently than the large farmer. Water, being a scarce resource, was not in the same category as fertilizer or electricity; moreover the allocative criterion should be used with respect not only to use but also to the owners who controlled water.

His position with respect to a progressive land tax was that the highest rates should apply to the largest units, either ownership units or operating units, whichever were the larger. He concluded by saying that many of the practical difficulties attending land valuation with respect to cadastral surveys, references to price indexes, and so forth would be solved automatically by the self-assessment system. In addition, it was suited to tax policies for different kinds of farming in different countries and the relationship of output to land values in different areas. It would avoid tax pressure on farming areas with poor resources and low production levels.

11

Fiscal Problems of a Common Market

*by Cesare Cosciani**

PROBLEMS OF DEFINITION

The requirements of mass production techniques, of economic development, of ambitions to obtain lasting economic stability, and not least, the needs of a political order have prompted the various countries in the direction of a steadily increasing liberalization of their international trade and to effect a more or less complete integration of their economies with those of other countries with a view to expanding the market.

To this end a number of treaties have been concluded since the war in the socialist countries, in Western Europe, and in Latin America: hence the various customs unions, common markets, free trade zones, and areas of preferential treatment that have been created. The vast range in the pattern of such treaties is reflected in a variety of terminologies, though these do not always reflect different economic conditions, since political emphasis frequently distorts and exacerbates the provisions of such treaties. Often, too, in economic writings such terminology becomes confused; the same term is at times applied to different economic groupings, and different names are used to define one and the same type of economic structure established by an agreement.

To avoid confusion, it would therefore seem useful to define the specific problem under consideration. And since treaties define economic problems in political and financial terms, using not only a very approximate

*Faculty of Law, University of Rome, Italy.

terminology but also one with many shades of meaning, so that it is not always possible to ascertain whether the economic grouping created is a customs union, common market, or other device, for purposes of clarity and simplicity, at least in this general section, it may be well to distinguish two antithetical categories, two extreme cases or hypotheses to which the arguments will be referred. These are the customs union and the common market. The first reflects a very moderate urge toward the economic unification of the various markets, whereas the second seeks the utmost degree of integration, to the point of fusing the individual markets as though they were a single domestic market. In the former, we still recognize the characteristics of international trade; whereas in the second, the economic relations between the countries concerned develop as though they had come about within the framework of a domestic or national market.

Once these two extreme cases are cited, the study of individual regional agreements, which may be somewhere in between, perhaps tending toward the one extreme or the other, and calling for a rather more subtle handling than the extreme cases, becomes easier insofar as all that need be done is to fill in the background of the extreme hypothesis with factual data.

The term "customs union" may be taken to mean a commercial union between two or more countries whereby these countries remain sovereign and independent in respect of their internal economic policy but endeavor to eliminate all customs duties or similar charges, as well as all other quantitative or qualitative restrictions, upon the exchange of goods and services between the countries forming part of the union. Tariffs in respect of third parties are unified so that external commercial policy is harmonized. Nevertheless, since currency controls may subsist and there may not be complete freedom for one country in the union to set up enterprises or employ labor in the others, the factors of production of all the countries remain immobilized.

Monetary and credit policies, the economic policy, and the budget in each country remain independent. It may be said that a customs union unifies market competition only with respect to goods and services but not to the factors of production, for which the theory of international trade evolved by Ricardo with subsequent adjustments and additions remains substantially valid.

A "common market" may be defined as an economic grouping of two or more countries on a decidedly more intensive basis: not only are there no qualitative and quantitative hindrances or charges resulting from the exchange of goods and products within the orbit of the group, but full and effective freedom of internal movement also extends to the factors of production (labor, capital, and enterprises). In view of the ties that bind the countries together, if a common market as such is to function efficiently, there must be unification of monetary and credit policies, of the economic and social policies of the various countries, and of the aspects of the legal structure most likely to affect production and trade. From the point of view of public finance, a common market in the proper sense implies, at least theoretically, the elimination of internal fiscal barriers designed to even out different levels of taxation and hence a very slight shift in the financial structure from the level of the individual state to the federal level. Once all these conditions are forthcoming—with the high degree of "political harmonization" they imply, even though it cannot be considered "political

integration" in the strict sense—the common market takes on all the characteristics of a domestic market. This does not mean that differences may not exist—especially at the beginning, but also subsequently on a lasting basis—between one country and another, just as within a single nation, especially one with a dualistic economy, we find regional differences.[1] Such differences may also exist in the field of finance: tax regulations may be drawn up on a different basis from one locality to another, as decided by a central or local authority. However, such differences must be relatively slight in order to avoid obstacles to the movement of goods or the factors of production or an artificial stimulus to such movements.

Having thus defined the two extreme concepts which are the subject of this analysis, it may now be useful to define another fundamental factor, namely "distortion." The opening up of further markets, regardless of the manner in which it is done, can give rise to distortion, i.e., to movements in trade exchanges or in the investment of factors of production harmful to one or another of the countries or to the union or community as a whole. The opening up of such markets gives rise, in the natural course of events, to new economic phenomena and to new sectoral or regional stimuli or the contrary. There is no doubt that every new trend, every variation that occurs following the opening of a market, brings about a distortion in relation to the situation that existed previously. But the important thing for the countries comprising the economic or customs union is to avoid distortions attributable to the decisions of the public authorities or calculated, whether intentionally or not, to secure some particular advantage at the expense of the other member countries.

The only distortions of interest to us at the moment are those attributable to the fiscal factor, which can mean advantages or draw-

---

[1]For a simple illustration of the differences between regional and international economy see R. Bachi, *Principii di scienza economica* (Turin: Einaudi, 1940), Vol. 2, No. 4, pp. 3–104.

backs for this or that country, once interstate trade has been liberalized.

The concept of distortion can be defined as that movement in the factors of economic equilibrium that can be attributed to any legislative provision, whether statutory or administrative, of a given country, which implies directly or indirectly, knowingly or otherwise —as far as competition between the countries belonging to the union is concerned—an appreciable degree of discrimination in respect of the goods, services, or factors of production of another country of the community, calculated to bring about modifications in the normal flow of goods, services, or factors of production between the countries, or to eliminate or hamper competition within an industry or on the market relative to a factor of production.

In other words, distortion can be said to be the result of voluntary or involuntary discrimination.

TAX PROBLEMS OF A CUSTOMS UNION: GENERAL PRINCIPLES

As has been said, the customs union does not infringe upon the political sovereignty of the individual countries which are parties to the agreement; the limitations imposed upon the economic and financial freedom of the countries are reduced to the absolute acceptable minimum, being circumscribed by the needs that arise out of the existence of a common tariff imposed against third parties and the necessity for avoiding economic distortions unduly detrimental to one country while benefiting the others. In order to avoid undesirable distortions, certain fundamental principles must be observed.

Prohibition of Fiscal Discrimination

In the first place, it is essential that all factors of production and all goods and services in any part of the market be placed and treated on an equal competitive footing, regardless of their origin within the customs union or the nationality of their owner. This principle, though in a less drastic form, is also found in many commercial agreements between countries with or without most-favored-nation clauses.

This means that no internal tax can be imposed under the same tax heading and for the same tax reasons but at a different rate, depending on whether the case refers to a citizen of the country concerned or a domestic product, as opposed to a citizen or products of other countries of the customs union. In other words, if domestic product A pays tax X, the same product produced outside the country cannot pay more than X.

The prohibition must extend in the same way to indirect discrimination that exists when goods and services which are not produced internally but which can be produced within the area of the customs union are taxed at rates higher than the average, or (a similar case, though on a more moderate scale) when goods produced in other countries of the customs union are taxed also in the internal market of the country concerned, though such goods can compete with other products obtained in the internal market and hence are of greater economic significance. The following would be an example of the former case: Product A is produced in country X but not Y. Country Y may not impose a special tax on product A produced outside the country. As an example of the second case, products A and B are obtained in both countries X and Y; but in country Y the production and consumption of product A predominates, while product B, which is a substitute for product A, is produced mainly in country X. In order to avoid indirect protection for product A from the competition of product B, country Y may not impose a special tax on product B which does not apply to product A as well.

Ban on the Formation of Tax Havens

Second, it is necessary to avoid having the statutory tax system of a country organized in such a way that a particular norm, or the fiscal or legal structure as a whole, makes it an extremely easy matter to conceal taxable goods, thus providing an incentive to the factors of production of other countries to seek a haven in the country in question for the purpose of tax avoidance. It is not a question here of movements attributable to the desire to invest the factors of production (capital) in the country under discussion, but simply of using them temporarily, and ordinarily in monetary form, to avoid taxation in a given country; or of cases where capital seeks a haven in a country in order to return to its country of origin in the form of foreign investment, thus avoiding the payment of taxes. A typical example of the first case is where bank secrecy exists in a country, along with the *de jure* and *de facto* possibility of making securities payable to bearer, while in the other countries of the customs union there is no such safeguard of secrecy in favor of the taxpayer. If the taxes in the other countries are very high or if it is feared that they will be increased or that a special tax is likely to be levied on net wealth, a transfer of capital is likely, possibly on a large scale, to the country that guarantees secrecy of banking vis-à-vis the treasury, even though it cannot be considered as investment in the true sense but simply a cash deposit.

Therefore, in the second of the two cases cited, the hypothesis may be taken of two countries A and B; in the first, direct taxes are applied according to the principle of the domicile of the creditor and in the second according to the principle of the territory where the revenue is produced. A person owning capital who resides in the second country may find it convenient to invest his capital in the first country, where, not being a resident, he is not taxable (unless there are regulations to the contrary applicable to aliens, though these might constitute a discriminatory measure in the case of a customs union), while the earnings are likewise not taxable in his own country either, because they were not produced there.

The fundamental problem consists in abol-ishing the regulations whereby a country is transformed into a haven exclusively from the tax point of view. The problem is not always one of legislation: it may also be one of determining what taxable income is. The names of certain countries, usually small ones, that offer this type of opportunity for tax evasion, both in Europe and in Latin America, are well known to everyone. If such countries are a distinct stumbling block to international relations, it can be easily understood how much worse this is if the countries form part of a customs union and exist side by side with other countries where tax controls are stricter. Concretely, this implies the need above all to unify the regulations governing bank secrecy and personal ownership of transferable securities (that is to say, the legal instrument for identifying possession of such securities in order to determine the revenue for purposes of the progressive personal tax).

Co-ordination of Fiscal Policy for Development

Every modern state has as one of its aims the development of national revenue as part either of an economic program or of an economic policy designed to provide the stimulus necessary for furthering this development. Such a policy must be followed even more resolutely by a customs union, which is normally created to meet this very need. Within the framework of this policy, the fiscal instrument is an efficient device, and the policy of exemptions or reductions in taxes for certain productive investments can now be said to be generally followed. Fiscal facilities are justified not so much by the way in which they stimulate and increase the absolute volume of savings or the volume of investments or consumption of goods as by their effect on the movement of investments. That is to say, they are a very effective device for inducing investors to invest in sector A rather than in sector B and in zone X rather than in zone Y, i.e., for creating deliberate distortions in the free choice of markets according to individual interest. On this premise, it is clear that if the fiscal facilities granted by one country are more substantial than those of another, an artificial movement of the factors of production will be brought about, thus inhibiting a co-ordinated and harmonious development in the economy of the countries forming part of the customs union which would seem desirable.

Co-ordination of Fiscal Policy for Stabilizing Income

Along with the development of the national income, which is the ultimate goal of every modern state, there is also the question of its stability over a period of time. That is, the state attempts as far as possible to bring about a countercyclical policy (fiscal policy and public expenditure). It is a well-known fact that the more restricted a market, the more it is exposed to the influence of the cyclical movement of the rest of the world and particularly of the countries with which it has close economic ties, in view of the high percentage of international trade in the national income. The customs union, while increasing the volume of trade within the union itself, makes the economies of the various participating countries more closely dependent on one another and frees them, in a greater or lesser measure, from the economies of third countries. On the one hand, this means that a countercyclical policy is distinctly more efficient and has a greater chance of success; on the other hand, it implies the need for pursuing anticyclical policies in a co-ordinated manner in order to prevent an active and positive policy by one country from being nullified by the passive policy of other countries.

Problem of Double Taxation within the Customs Union

There is no question that simultaneous taxation of the same items (either the income or the net wealth of either a company or an individual) by more than one country, because the activities of the company or individual concerned are conducted not merely within a single country but in several others at the same time, constitutes a brake on international economic activities or at any rate obliges the operator to misrepresent his own affairs in order to avoid such excessive taxation. The strengthening of economic ties within the customs union naturally increases the number of such instances of multiple taxation, at least within the area where the union is producing positive results. Moreover, the economic integration of the member countries is impeded by this tax anomaly. Since unilateral measures do not always prove to be the best means of circumventing these difficulties, an essential requisite would seem to be a multilateral covenant within the customs union area, designed to prevent such double taxation and to ensure administrative co-operation among the countries with regard to both accurate assessments and the collection of taxes.

The ideal solution would consist not only in a multilateral agreement among the individual participants to forgo dual taxation within the framework of the customs union but also in the replacement of bilateral conventions between the members of the union and third countries by bilateral pacts between third countries and the customs union collectively, which would be binding on and valid for all member states. It would thus be possible to secure greater uniformity in internal tax treatment of the factors of production, whether they came from third countries or not.

A basis for the establishment of such a multilateral convention might be found in the Mexico City and London standard agreements or in those currently being perfected by the Organization for European Economic Co-operation and Development (formerly OEEC, now OECD). Such models, however, should be adapted to the particular requirements of a customs union. In order to prevent the income of a company operating in more than one country of the customs union from being simultaneously assessed by each of the individual countries in question, for the purpose of determining the percentage of the income produced therein, in the light of all the different criteria involved in this apportionment, it is imperative that a taxpayer's income or net wealth be assessed once and for all, on behalf of all the countries in the customs union, and with the collaboration of all the parties concerned. In other words, all taxable income, wherever generated, should be taxed in the place of domicile of the taxpayer. The more the principle of imposing taxes in the place of legal domicile is shelved in favor of the principle of taxation in the place where the income is produced, the greater the risk (through the multiplicity and variety of taxes existing within the customs union) of hampering the normal development of business and creating inequities in relation to a progressive tax. If any problem arises in connection with apportioning the taxes among the several countries, it must be settled directly among the various countries concerned, without the taxpayer's intervention.

LIMITATIONS ON FREEDOM TO LEGISLATE ON TAX MATTERS WITHIN THE CUSTOMS UNION

It has been said that the customs union presupposes a maximum of autonomy in the economic and financial policy of the individual countries. This autonomy should be understood as extending also to the field of taxation, the only limits being those absolutely necessary for avoiding economic distortions.

What conditions must be observed in order to maintain this autonomy within the broadest limits possible?

Principle of Taxation in the Country of Destination

The first, the broadest, and the most essential condition is undoubtedly acceptance of the principle of taxation in the country of destination. Application of this principle means assigning the right of taxation to the country of destination of the product or income; in other words, to the country in which the product is consumed or the income is received.

From the standpoint of the product, where the principle is applied consistently from the raw material to the finished product, through an appropriate policy of exemptions and rebates at the time of exportation and of normal taxation in addition to the application of compensatory or equalizing duties to imports, the product will be taxed in the consumer market at the rates appropriate to the market in question.

As regards income, observance of the principle implies taxation in the country of domicile of the recipient. Thus, income received in a given country is taxed equally, irrespective of its place of origin, just as the taxes incorporated in the price of products circulating in the same country are equal, whatever the country of origin of the goods.

A few distinctions may be usefully drawn to prevent misunderstandings.

"Export exemption" simply means that no taxation is imposed on the act of exportation, without reference to any prior transactions.

By "tax rebate" is meant restitution to the exporter, subsequent to the time of departure of the exported goods from the national territory, of a sum equivalent to the tax paid by the exporter or by other entrepreneurs on earlier transactions before the product acquired the form it had at the time of export.

By "taxation on entry" is meant the levying of duty on goods at the time of importation at the normal rate.

"Compensatory duty" means the additional or equalizing tax imposed at the time of importation to compensate for the higher tax that would have been paid on the merchandise had it been produced domestically.

Where the principle of the country of destination is applied, it is necessary, as stated before, to exempt sales made abroad from all taxation and to refund all taxes paid within the country at the various stages of production and on the different transfers to which the product is subject prior to exportation, and then to impose supplementary taxes in the importing country, comprising the taxes on the final transaction and a compensatory duty equivalent to the various taxes paid on similar domestic products at previous stages.

This system is a means of ensuring uniform taxation in the consumer market and, if applied *in toto,* a guarantee that the consumer in a given country can buy a commodity at the same price (or, more accurately, at a sales price incorporating the same tax), whatever its market of origin and whatever the amount of taxation included in its value. There is, of course, no guarantee of uniform treatment as among consumers in the various member countries of the common market, since their individual tax burdens must ultimately depend on the taxation imposed by each country on the domestic consumer.

Accordingly, viewed strictly from the standpoint of the consumer market, this procedure permits a leveling off of the taxes included in prices and guarantees uniform taxation for consumers in the same market. Wherever they buy the product, the tax incorporated is always the same and therefore cannot be said to exert any distorting influence on competition.

If, instead of indirect taxation or the taxes levied on goods and services, direct taxation on the remuneration of the factors of production is considered, the principle of taxation in the country of destination is implemented by taxing all income and all net wealth in the country in which the recipient of the income or owner of the net wealth is domiciled rather than in the place where the income is produced. Within a customs union, this principle of taxation in the country of destination is the only one that is practicable if the countries participating in the union are to be allowed the necessary fiscal autonomy.

Goods and services cannot compete with those from other customs union countries if varying amounts of taxation are incorporated in their production costs and consequently in their sales price. And since the very meaning of financial autonomy is freedom of action as regards types and levels of taxation, such

a divergence of taxes can be counterbalanced precisely through application of the principle in question.

This means that establishment of a customs union will eventually result in the abolition of *economic frontiers*—that is, of the barriers set up for purposes of economic protection—and, at the same time, in the retention of *fiscal frontiers*—that is, of those caused by the movement of goods through the borders of a country and whose only aim is to level off the varying incidence of taxes on costs and prices. The fiscal frontier is therefore conceived as an instrument of equalization used to eliminate economic distortions.

First Limitation on the Principle Relating to Indirect Taxes

As shown above, application of the principle of taxation in the country of destination entails not only exempting exports and taxing imports but also resorting to rebates and compensatory duties in order to take into account the taxes paid in the stages prior to importation or exportation.

In computing these rebates and compensatory duties, highly refined techniques of calculation must be employed, inasmuch as it is necessary to analyze the legal incidence of the tax on the commodity exported, bearing in mind the various prior stages of production, the importance of the taxable commodity incorporated in the production process during processing or manufacture, etc. These technical computations normally have to be made on the basis of broad averages, for two reasons: first, the importance of the commodity taxed may vary from one instance to another (for example, the quantity of cacao on which an indirect tax was paid, the said tax being incorporated in the cost of the chocolate exported, may vary according to the type of product, and the discrepancy becomes more marked if instead of volume we consider value); or, second, the production process may be concentrated in a few enterprises or in only one or may, in respect of one and the same product, involve a number of establishments, thus giving rise to a series of taxable transactions. The rebates and compensatory duties must therefore be determined on the basis of averages for each product; and these averages imply differences in one direction or another which are impossible to eliminate in most cases and often difficult to identify.

Within the limits of such discrepancies between the tax actually included in the price and the tax computed, tax rebates may really represent a disguised form of export subsidy, while compensatory duties may give rise to protectionist measures.

These effects may be produced not only as a result of the authorities' express desire to extend protection to national production, under the disguise of a tax device, but also because it is always possible for omission or evasion of tax payments to occur in the course of the production process, so that the actual tax burden may turn out to be less than the legal or formally established amount. This criticism may become still more valid in a case where the tax assessment is not based directly on the value of the final product or on specific components thereof but on certain factors of production or on the raw materials used, or, again, when the tax is levied at stages of manufacture prior to exportation and is separated from this by other commercial transactions (for instance, the cumulative multiple-stage turnover tax).

Consequently, the foregoing practice never provides complete assurance that the tax will be impartial with regard to international trade.

This is all the more true inasmuch as the shortcoming noted above stems not only from the difficulty of computing the formal incidence of the tax but also from more substantive causes of an economic nature. In other words, the argument advanced is based on the assumption that the tax is passed on and increases the sale price. While this assumption may be considered valid where it relates to special taxes (such as the single-stage tax on manufacture) on production of particular goods that are exported without later processing, it leaves room for doubt where other indirect taxes are concerned.

The problem becomes particularly difficult with respect to a general sales tax. Here it is not certain that, as is commonly affirmed, the process of shifting the tax paid at the manufacturing level is invariably and completely carried out. The most recent theory on the subject admits that where there is a general and uniform tax on all sales, it may well be shifted backward rather than forward, at least in part, so that it reaches the factors of production. Therefore it cannot be ascertained how far these taxes are incorporated in the cost of the product at the various stages of manufacture and thus go to swell the final production cost at the time of exportation. Consequently, to a formal (estimated) incidence of 100 may correspond an actual incidence of less than 100, although in practice it is impossible to say how much less. If the process of passing on the tax is only partial, complete reimbursement of the tax actually constitutes an export subsidy, just as a total compensatory duty results in protectionist tariffs. This argument is particularly relevant with respect to general and uniform sales taxes, in relation to which current theory is tending more and more to acknowledge, within certain limits at least, the possibility of a backward shift to the various factors of production.

To carry the foregoing general considerations into the realm of practical discussion, it may be said that if the indirect taxes in respect of which export rebates and compensatory import duties are applied amount to very little because of the low rate, no real objection can be raised to the system of rebates and duties in question.

If the rate of the said taxes and, accordingly, the rebates to be granted and the compensatory duties to be levied are comparatively high, then the possible discrepancies between the average scale applied and the tax actually incorporated in the price and cost take on more substantial proportions, and the concealed subsidies and customs duties become operative and effective.

This being so, it is advisable, in order to avoid economic distortions, to declare incompatible with the customs union all taxation systems that entail accrued rebates or compensatory duties, i.e., the cumulative multiple-stage or cascade tax on the entire volume.

Conversely, both taxation on the basis of value added (the noncumulative multiple-stage tax) and the single-stage tax levied on the last producer or at any subsequent commercial stage may be regarded as entirely compatible with the customs union. These are forms of taxation in which the tax levied on the product can be computed accurately. From the theoretical viewpoint, the single-stage tax on the last producer or at the marketing level may be said to constitute a better safeguard than mere exemption. In actual fact, it is only on the assumption that it will be passed on in its entirety that the value added tax can be relied upon not to give rise to distortions. But there is no guarantee that this will occur and that the tax on value added will not be shifted backward, at any rate to some extent, at the various stages subject to taxation. In such an event, the export subsidy would reappear. In any case, the choice is between the tax on value added or the single-stage tax levied on the last producer or at a subsequent level, according to the preference of each individual country, with different rates if necessary, and equalization at the frontier.

Second Limitation on the Principle
Relating to Direct Taxes

According to the latest economic theory, taxation on corporations, at any rate where long periods of time and markets in highly developed economies are concerned, is included in the cost of production and the tax in question is incorporated in the price of the product.

If this premise is accepted, the inference is that export rebates and compensatory import duties should be extended from indirect to direct taxation. Otherwise, a distortion would be produced at the expense of the country in which the tax on corporations was heavier. An extreme case would be afforded by a customs union between country A, in which the tax system was based on indirect reimbursable export taxes, and country B, in which, in contrast, it was based on a tax on corporations and could not grant tax rebates in respect of goods exported.

In principle, these considerations are quite convincing and should be given serious thought. Their practical implications, however, are limited in two directions.

First, it must be borne in mind that the percentage relation between direct and indirect taxes depends chiefly, as is common knowledge, upon a country's economic development. Countries at less advanced stages of economic development make greater use of indirect taxes, which are thus reimbursable in the form of export rebates. In all likelihood, the structure of production costs in these countries is also less developed, and therefore cost levels are higher. Consequently, the advantage deriving from this higher incidence of reimbursable indirect taxes as against non-reimbursable direct taxation may be said to offset the disadvantage in respect of costs. Nor can a tax system conceived on these lines be regarded as an artificial instrument of distortion, since the structure of the economy and the fiscal structure are closely related.

Second, it is virtually impossible to calculate the incidence of direct taxes on income and net wealth in relation to the sales price, for the same volume of production may give rise to widely varying amounts of taxable income and, therefore, of taxation.

Again, even when direct taxes on the profits of corporations exert their full effect on prices, their repercussions are not as significant as those of indirect taxes. To put this point more clearly, let it be assumed that in one country the rate of tax on corporate income is 40 per cent and in another 50 per cent. The incidence on costs of the 10 per cent difference in the rate is 0.5 per cent if the relation between the volume of sales and profits is 5 per cent (sales 200, profits 10, and tax 1) and 1 per cent if the relation between sales and profits is 10 per cent (sales 200, profits 20, and tax 2).

However, to prevent any risk of distortion

—especially when the members of the customs union include countries at less advanced stages of economic development, where no tax on corporations exists, and others in which it not only exists but has a high rate—some degree of equalization of the over-all tax burden on corporations would seem highly desirable. That is, when it is impossible to resort to rebates and compensatory duties, even if the type of taxation levied on corporations cannot be standardized, steps should be taken to ensure that the percentage of the tax burden on total profits should be roughly the same in the various countries of the union.

TAX PROBLEMS IN CONNECTION WITH THE ESTABLISHMENT OF A COMMON MARKET

As pointed out above, the common market may be defined as one which fulfills the conditions of an internal market; there will no longer be as many different markets as there are countries but a single one similar to a domestic market. It must be characterized by complete freedom of movement not only of goods and services but also of the factors of production. Nor is this all; a further requisite is a single monetary and credit policy, to safeguard a market so unified, and hence sensitive to structural divergencies, against distortions likely to jeopardize the equilibrium of the individual economies. This implies a minimum of unification of the economic authorities responsible for the policy of a given country and a marked restriction of freedom of action in the economic sector on the part of the national authorities.

To confine the discussion of the relevant problems to those of public finance, it has been stressed in many circles that such an internal market can be successfully established only if the principle of taxation in the country of origin is introduced.

Some attention may now be given to the essential features of this principle and the conditions in which it could be applied.

Principle of Taxation in the Country of Origin

In contradistinction to the principle of taxation in the country of destination, that of taxation in the country of origin implies taxation of the product or service in the place where it is obtained and of income in the countries where it originates; and when the said product, service, or income is transferred abroad, it is understood that the tax burden is already incorporated either as an increase in prices (as is generally the case with indirect taxation) or as a decrease in income (as may happen in the case of direct taxation) and that no further payment of tax will be made in the country of destination.

If the principle of taxation in the country of origin of goods or services is applied, goods are taxed in the country where they are transformed or manufactured, whatever the country to which they are shipped or in which they are consumed.

The widespread introduction of this principle implies the elimination of frontiers from an economic point of view; the various markets are no longer differentiated from one another but are converted from "international" to "internal" markets, for all purposes, including those of taxation, inasmuch as the transfer of goods or services from one country to another is of no account. If this approach is adopted, it is meaningless to speak of export exemptions and rebates, on the one hand, or of the assessment and imposition of compensatory import duties, on the other.

The Problem of the Abolition of Fiscal Frontiers

Acceptance of the principle of taxation in the country of origin would seem to be indispensable for the abolition of fiscal frontiers. The maintenance of tax frontiers between countries constituting an economic community is regarded in many circles as a contradiction in terms in relation to the economic features characteristic of an internal market.

It has been urged that if a single market is really the desired goal, elimination of customs duties and the other qualitative and quantitative restrictions imposed on international trade is not enough but must be accompanied by the abolition of all frontier barriers where goods are held up, inspected, and subjected to strict scrutiny for assessment purposes and to tax charges or compensatory payments. The maintenance of tax barriers, it is asserted, is contrary to the intrinsic nature of a common market, which must, to the fullest possible extent, identify the internal market with that of the member countries. To maintain a boundary line for purely tax purposes, i.e., to subject goods crossing the frontier to a compensatory duty to equalize the differences in the taxes to which a product is liable in each of the two countries concerned, would be tantamount to setting aside the cost involved, to keeping the individual country markets separate as before. The existence of a tax barrier is bound to encourage or at least facilitate the re-erection, at the first opportunity or as soon as the first disequilibrium is registered in the economy or in the balance of payments, of the customs barriers laboriously broken down by the treaty establishing the economic union.

This is a matter of paramount importance because of the underlying principles at stake and the practical implications of those principles if they are adopted. In concrete terms, the problem consists not so much in determining whether the principles in question are good or bad, admissible or inadmissible, but in investigating whether they can or cannot be put into practice, given the factual situation in the various economic unions, and if so, under what conditions.

As has been pointed out, a tax frontier is said to exist between two countries when the fact that a product is exported or imported gives rise to tax implications, such as a rebate on the tax paid in the country of origin granted at the time of exportation, or an import duty to compensate the taxes not paid on the product concerned but payable on other similar goods produced in the importing country.

These exemptions and duties can be divided into two categories. Those in what may be called category A have a distorting effect and are applied when the intention is to lay a heavier tax burden on imported goods than on those produced in the domestic market and to make the goods exported cheaper than those obtainable in the foreign market; while those in category B are of a compensatory nature and are found where the purpose of the duties and exemptions is to eliminate disparities in costs and prices deriving from tax factors, following the so-called principle of taxation in the country of destination. Tax frontiers under category A are designed to create a distortion or, in other words, to protect domestic industry; those in category B, on the other hand, are aimed at the prevention of all distortions, all forms of discrimination between the domestic product and its counterpart from the other countries. The former type of fiscal boundary is in complete conflict with the existence of an economic community; the latter type, on the other hand, is compatible with it, although its elimination seems desirable and perhaps even necessary if distortions are to be avoided.

A more thorough study of the problem suggests that in theory the existence of tax controls, with the resultant financial implications in relation to the crossing of a given territorial frontier, is not at variance with the principle of the common market. Such controls may exist even within an internal market without warranting the assertion that the market itself lacks unity.

A case in point, though not the only one, is that of Italy, where for the purposes of municipal excise taxes some degree of control over the movement of goods is exercised. The fact that the goods in question are imported in a particular municipality may render them liable to an excise tax, whereas in another they would be exempted or taxed at a lower rate. In some instances, there is an actual physical line of demarcation along the road; in others, it exists in the form of various technical devices. But no one would dream of declaring on this account that Italy does not have, economically speaking, a single domestic market.

It must be acknowledged that the existence of tax controls at the border increases the risk of encouraging any possible protectionist trends that may become apparent at a given moment in this or that common market country. This problem is of particular importance during the first phase of the existence of a common market, when relations are not yet definitively consolidated on the economic or political plane.

It is time, however, to dismiss these questions of principle and consider the problem in more concrete terms in order to determine the conditions that must be fulfilled if tax frontiers are to be successfully abolished.

If every commodity exported incorporates in its cost the taxes paid in the country of origin, and if these vary from one country to another to any marked extent, a factor of distortion with respect to competition is clearly created. In other words, tax frontiers can be eliminated without the creation of distortions only on the hypothesis that divergencies in rates of taxation are kept within very narrow limits.

It should be borne in mind, however, that not every disparity in tax structure necessarily gives rise to economic distortion. Very slight divergencies produce distortions only on the purely theoretical and abstract hypothesis of an ideally competitive market, in which consumers and producers are extremely sensitive economically and the prevailing system is such that the link between the different areas belonging to the market are always closely maintained and the equilibrium of the various factors involved is stable. But a "single market" is a rarity, found in practice only within fairly narrow territorial boundaries.

Even a domestic market is broken down into regional markets within which production conditions (such as rates of interest, wage levels, supply of skilled personnel, availability of credit, existence of transport facilities, and other internal factors) differ, sometimes only slightly, sometimes considerably. And just as these production conditions may differ without much harm being done, the same is true of certain tax factors whose divergency is attributable either to variations in the practical application of taxes in the individual countries or to the local financial situation, which may lead to differing degrees of severity and different procedures in the taxation of both income and production. This last factor may assume particular importance in states where the local financial authorities exert a decisive influence or enjoy a special degree of autonomy. Consequently, if these divergencies are kept within very modest limits, they do not give rise to any considerable economic distortions, tax barriers can be removed without cause for concern, and the principle of taxation in the country of origin applies in its entirety.

Significance of Different Levels of Tax Pressure

The problem of a distortion in world trade when the frontiers of the various countries that are members of the common market are thrown open must be studied in the light of over-all tax pressure. If this pressure, conceived in terms of a ratio between a country's whole system of taxes and the volume of national income, is higher in one member country than in another, since taxes always represent an addition to costs or a reduction of income, the former country will apparently be at a disadvantage in relation to the latter where conditions of production are concerned, and distortion may therefore arise.

This problem has been discussed by scholars and technical experts, and some authorities (Professor Tinbergen, for example) have contended that (1) despite divergencies in over-all tax pressures, distortion would not take place, since the exchange rate, at least in some situations, is capable of automatically compensating the varying incidence of tax pressure on the goods traded, and (2) there is no need to adopt deliberate corrective measures.

In essence, the argument is as follows. Let us postulate a system of flexible exchange rates and the absence of barriers to international trade, as should be the case in relations between the various members of a common market. On such a hypothesis, if the balance of international trade is disturbed by the introduction of an indirect tax, equilibrium is restored automatically. It is true that the new tax does push up the over-all level of internal prices; but by virtue of a principle which can be traced back to Ricardo and Mill and was later developed and disseminated mainly by Cassel under the name of the principle of "purchasing power parity," after a period of adjustment the evolution of exchange rates adapts itself to the new relationship between price levels in the countries with reciprocal contracts, and the original equilibrium is restored.

Cassel starts from the assumption that the purchaser who agrees to pay a given price for foreign currency does so with the idea of obtaining a given amount of purchasing power possessed by that currency in relation to goods in the internal market. Consequently, if the foreign currency loses value in the market because of a rise in over-all price levels attributable to an aggravation of tax pressure, the foreign purchaser who wants to secure the same purchasing power in the currency of the other market will have to buy foreign exchange at a higher nominal value. But since the real value he wants to buy has not altered, he will be prepared to pay the same sum as before in his own national currency. That is, he will expect to purchase the same amount of foreign currency as before against a proportionally smaller amount of national currency. In other words, the rate of exchange pursuant to the intensification of tax pressure adjusts itself to the change in price levels, with the result that the former equilibrium is restored.

Let us assume that the exchange rate between two members of the community (country A and country B) is 100 to 100. When a resident in country A seeks to obtain foreign exchange from country B, his aim is to purchase the indispensable means of obtaining a given quantity of goods in B's market; let us suppose that these are contained in an imaginary basket. In order to buy this basket, he is prepared to concede a given amount of purchasing power, a given sum in his own national currency, i.e., another equivalent basket from his own market. If the two baskets have exactly the same value for him, the price will also be the same. In the present hypothetical case, the two baskets will be worth 100 units of national currency in A and 100 units of national currency in B.

If A now introduces a 10 per cent tax, so that the price of A's basket rises to 110, since the intrinsic value of the two baskets remains the same, the resident in country B, who wishes to buy a basket from A, will be prepared to hand over 100 units of his own national currency only if he can thereby obtain 110 of A's currency units. In other words, the exchange rate will tend to establish itself at 110 to 100.

As can be seen, at least in this rough approximation, the rate of exchange has automatically offset the disadvantage suffered by the country whose own prices have risen as a result of the new tax, since the alteration in the exchange rate has allowed its citizen to increase his own monetary income in the same proportion in which the tax has raised costs and prices. Therefore, it seems strictly unnecessary, at least after a period of adjustment, for the country which has increased its tax rates to apply the principle of taxation in the consumer country with a policy of export rebates and compensatory import duties, since no harm will have been done to trade in the long run.

Moreover, it is important to take into account the fact that if the state increasing tax pressure introduces export rebates, this does not improve its own export situation; it merely corrects the exchange rate through the mechanism of rebates and compensatory duties. On the hypothesis under discussion, this rate will in nominal terms remain fixed in the original relationship. In short, the two systems, as has already been pointed out, amount to exactly the same thing.

But the theory of the compensation of differing levels of tax incidence through the automatic exchange rate mechanism has met with so much criticism as to give rise to grave doubts as to its theoretical validity and, certainly, the extent to which it can be considered realistic.

In recent times, such severe criticisms have been leveled against the theory of purchasing power parity as the basis of the foregoing argument that its conceptual validity and its practical usefulness have both been called in question—even taking at their face value the basic premises of the theory, which are totally at variance with the real situation in the present period of history, since they imply (a) completely uninhibited freedom of international trade (a hypothetical situation which might be forthcoming within a common market), (b) transport of goods from one state to another free of charge (without transport or customs expenses), and (c) the existence of completely free and flexible exchange rates (without customs and exchange manipulations on the part of public agencies). Even those who have upheld the theory, like Haberler, have noted that the principle of purchasing power parity is not valid if applied to absolute price levels but only if applied to variations in prices.

The weakest point in the theory is undoubtedly that of the relative prices of goods which, according to it, are calculated to influence the exchange rate. The problem would not arise if the two countries produced the same goods and if all these goods were included in their reciprocal trade. Only in that case would the internal purchasing power of currency be identical with its external purchasing power. But this is an entirely unrealistic hypothesis.

It is a proven fact that in all countries there are many kinds of goods which are produced and consumed solely in the domestic market. In these circumstances, if the theory is to be tenable—that is, if the purchasing power of the currency is to be the same at home as abroad—it will have to be assumed that any and every variation in the price of goods circulating only in the domestic market affects the over-all level of internal prices to the same extent that variations in the prices of the same

goods in the other market affect its own over-all price levels. The fact that this parallelism of price variations does not prevail is clear from the mere fact that the structure of prices in any given country is never the same as it was just previously or will be shortly, since the factors bearing upon each individual price are different.

The over-all level of prices in a particular country depends upon the price of all the goods traded in it. Only a portion of these goods are significant from the point of view of international trade; and only these, in the form of imports and exports, play a part in determining supply and demand in respect of foreign exchange, i.e., have a direct repercussion on exchange rates. All the others may undergo price variations and thus influence the general price level without affecting the exchange rate. On the other hand, to confine the theory to goods for which there is an international market is to reduce it to a mere truism, since obviously such goods, if transport costs and tariff duties, etc., are excluded, can only have a single price.

The Achilles' heel of the theory of purchasing power parity is the very premise on which it is based: namely, that no fundamental changes take place in the basic conditions of trade between the two countries. Supposing that a country, as the result of a balance of payments disequilibrium, has to restrict imports of certain goods from another country; in such a case, domestic consumers will be compelled to turn to home production, and consumer tastes may become accustomed to the domestic substitutes thus brought into circulation and even prefer them to their imported counterparts. In this way, once the temporary crisis is past, the foreign country, in order to achieve a new equilibrium, will have to lower the prices of the goods it exports to the other market in order to meet the new situation. This is a case where price variations are not reflected in the exchange rate.

The balance of payments, or, in other words, the supply and demand situation in respect of foreign exchange, is affected by many factors which are not sensitive or hardly sensitive to variations in domestic prices, e.g., remittances on the part of emigrants, interest on capital invested, freight charges and insurance premiums, bank commissions or brokerage fees, etc.

Disequilibriums in exchange rates may be remedied in various ways, of which price variations represent one of the many possibilities. Alternative factors of adjustments are changes in the level of employment or in taxation relating to movements of capital, foreign exchange controls, qualitative and quantitative import restrictions, etc.

The literature of economics and actual experience, both in recent times and in the more distant past, have clearly shown how persistent balance of payments deficits can be remedied by contracting external debts rather than by altering the rate of exchange. This situation is particularly common among countries in those earlier stages of development during which they need foreign capital. On the other hand, unilateral transfers of means of payment, whether in the shape of movements of capital, war reparations, or mere grants, alter the exchange rate but may leave prices unchanged.

The theory of purchasing power parity makes the balance of trade between two countries dependent entirely upon price levels. It regards foreign exchange as purely a function of the price of goods, and since it is based on the effect of prices, it tends to ignore that of income. Evidence has been adduced, for example, to show that import and export fluctuations lead to expansions or contractions of national income, processes which in turn—given a certain marginal propensity to import and some degree of elasticity in demand for foreign products—produce fresh repercussions on the balance of payments and once again restore equilibrium without the intervention of price and exchange mechanisms.

The theory under discussion has its origin in essentially static hypotheses, taking no account of cyclical and structural disequilibriums and assuming the permanency of full employment.

Furthermore, its supporters admit that its validity is always conditional upon two requisites: (a) that exchange rates are flexible, not rigid; (b) that the theory of automatic compensation formulated can be taken as meaningful only in relation to average tax pressure and is invalid in all cases where the sum of taxes on a commodity included in foreign trade is above or below that average.

It must be pointed out that this second requisite limits the scope of the theory much more than would appear at first sight. Even if it is assumed, merely as a hypothesis, that the theory of purchasing power parity is valid, and on the equally hypothetical assumption that there is no time lag in the adjustment of the exchange rate to the changes in price levels, automatic compensation would in any event come about only through taxes' affecting all goods and services at the same rates and at the time of exportation. Only thus would a specific percentage increase in the prices of all exported goods be followed by an equivalent increase in external rates of exchange. But if an average weighted tax rate of, say, 10 per cent derives from taxation on some goods at a rate of 25 per cent and on others at a rate of 5 per cent, exchange rates will rise, according to the hypothesis set forth, at a rate of 10 per cent. This adjustment, however, implies an insufficient degree of equilization for goods taxed at the rate of 25 per cent, which, despite the partial compensation afforded by the exchange rate, will be at a disadvantage in respect of costs vis-à-vis similar goods on which a 10 per cent tax is payable; whereas goods on which the tax amounts only to 5 per cent will enjoy a veritable export subsidy, since their earning capacity on the external market will be increased by the 5 per cent difference in the tax chargeable.

In short, even if the theory under discussion were accepted, the conclusion would have to be reached that in relation to goods taxed at rates different from the average (as happens in the case of indirect taxes affecting specific production or consumption), it is necessary either to apply the principle of the country of destination and maintain tax frontiers or to level out still farther the selection of the goods to be taxed and the pertinent rates.

The Problem of Tax Harmonization

If the theory that the exchange rate constitutes an automatic means of regulating the various levels of tax pressure either in the over-all sense or within a given sector is set aside, it is clear that the principle of taxation in the country of origin can be applied only if taxation is standardized or "harmonized" beforehand, at least in those sectors where divergencies in tax incidence most easily give rise to economic distortions.

This harmonization must be extended at least to all indirect taxes, with respect not only to taxed goods but also to the system of taxation and the rate. But in the direct tax sector, too, some degree of leveling out of tax systems should be introduced, even though actual standardization may not be required.

It should be clearly established that a really strict degree of harmonization is possible only if the economic characteristics and structures involved, viewed not only from the static but also from the dynamic standpoint, are fairly homogeneous.

Only a tiny fraction of a country's tax system springs from the imagination of the legislator. Its structure depends essentially on the environment in which it operates and to which it must be adapted. Per capita national income, the over-all economic situation, structures of production, consumer preferences (which up to a point are impossible to change because they are bound up with environmental conditions), historical traditions, and social trends are all factors which produce specific repercussions on the qualitative composition of customs tariffs. And the historical development of the economy also determines the development of the structure of the tax system.

If there is not a minimum of uniformity as regards these factors in the various member countries of the community, harmonization of the tariff system is impossible. In such circumstances, applying the same tax system to all the common market countries would have the same effect as compelling all individuals, whether tall or short, fat or thin, to wear one and the same type of garment in one and the same size. The concept of fair taxation would be seriously undermined, and equity would suffer severely everywhere, in a greater or lesser degree.

However, the possibility cannot be excluded that after a careful study of the structure of consumption and income and of the concentration of the latter in each of the individual countries concerned, a tax system might be discovered which could be standardized in all the member states of the common market and could yield in each of them exactly the same revenues as had been obtained under the old tax system. But it is highly doubtful whether this harmonized system would conform as closely as its predecessors to a common norm of equity, because the parameters taken as the basis of taxation would have a different significance in the different individual economies.

Dismissing considerations of equity, it should be stressed that fiscal yields—and this is the most serious financial shortcoming— would become a *de facto* entry in each state's balance sheet, in the sense that, given different volumes of output in each of the member countries, an equal rate of taxation throughout the community would mean that some of the states would have more revenue than they needed, while others would register an incurable deficit. The problem becomes still more complicated if it is considered from the dynamic standpoint; if at a given juncture a country's financial requirements were to induce it to modify its tariff system, in order to maintain harmonization the other states would have to introduce changes accordingly in theirs, without feeling the need to do so. That is, in each country's balance sheet, tax revenues would be a function not only of its own requirements but of the requirements of the other states, so that confusion and imbalances would appear in government budgets, as can be readily understood.

The only way of preventing such disequilibriums would be to raise a proportion of the finances of the individual countries to the community level by means of a federal type of financial system or equalization funds in the various public balance sheets. Such a federal type of financial system may be described as a prerequisite for harmonization. To gain a clearer conviction of the validity of this conclusion—namely, that a very high degree of tax harmonization is conditional upon the creation of a federal financial system or an international system of financial compensation—suffice it to reflect on the consequences that would result if in any given country state finances were abolished and the same tax system as was currently in force for the country as a whole were applied in the various smaller localities. There would certainly be local authorities with substantial credit balances and others showing structural deficits.

Furthermore, harmonization would mean fettering all subsequent freedom of action of a country with respect to the fiscal system; a change in any given country's tariff system, either for budgetary reasons or on grounds of equity, would be a serious obstacle not only in the internal field but also as regards the prior international agreements required.

In other words, tax harmonization presupposes not only the beginnings of economic integration but also a unitary policy among the states, since it is incompatible—as has been amply demonstrated—with the sovereign autonomy of the national treasury of each of the individual states. And it is therefore to be expected that the common market will evolve from the unitary economic system of the various member countries toward a form of federalism, having a single budget, but always remaining compatible with the full and rational decentralization of activities.

To sum up, even if steps are taken to standardize indirect taxes, since these are in the nature of excise taxes, the revenue from the various manufacturing taxes affecting products should accrue not to the producer country but to the consumer country. In that case, the country receiving a tax paid by the manufacturer on a commodity which is exported and consumed in another country should make the corresponding payments in favor of the treasury of the consumer country. This can be done (the problem of distortion does not arise here) only through a statistical record of imports and exports; that is, preserving tax frontiers, even if only for statistical purposes, so that the compensation in question can be arranged.

Conclusions Relating to Common Market Tax Policy

Accordingly, if the individual economies are to be converted into a true domestic market with no tariff barriers to obstruct the movement of goods, indirect taxes must be completely harmonized and some of the direct taxes most likely to give rise to distortions in movements of capital must be brought closer together.

In the normal course of events, such harmonization is feasible only if part of each individual country's financial organization is transferred onto a federal basis or if a system of financial equalization among the various members of the community is established. This procedure gives rise to certain inevitable consequences of a noneconomic nature.

However, if so extreme a solution cannot be put into practice, an intermediary position might be advocated. If the existence of tax frontiers is admitted to be necessary for equalization purposes, the question is whether this requirement can be met, not by controls at the political frontier, but by an alternative method less at variance with the idea of an internal market: for example, by the application of controls to goods at the manufacturing level. This proposal has the laudable aim of eliminating all frontier controls and replacing them by other procedures based on administrative controls over tax collection and tax drawbacks or exemptions in respect of enterprises exporting to or importing from other members of the community. The accounts of the establishments concerned would have to constitute the basis of the new system.

Thus, when a commodity exported from one country to another was taxed in the two countries at a rate differing from that of the turnover tax or the tax at manufacturing level, the exporter would declare the operation to the tax office of his place of residence, applying for the stipulated export drawback. This declaration would be checked, not by a customs certificate testifying to the passage of the goods across the frontier, but against his own ledgers. And the importing enterprise would have to declare the compensatory duties payable, without the treasury consulting the customs documents. Clearly, the importing state would need to have at its disposal all the requisite information from the exporting country.

As can be seen, the tax frontier is thus not abolished but shifted from the political frontier to the whole of the national territory, wherever an enterprise engaging in external trade is to be found. For a developed economy, in which indirect taxes are highly differentiated, the system is somewhat cumbersome because of the exchange of information required between one country and another and the ample opportunities for evasion, especially in the case of importers, who have to pay compensatory duties to counterbalance the taxes not paid in the external market. In less developed countries, with a limited number of industries, the problem is perhaps simpler.

For the public administration, such a system would mean replacing the customhouses established at a few frontier points by a control network spread over the whole of the national territory, while the taxpayer would be subject to further supervision, harassed by the unavoidable inspections on the part of the public administration, with endless claims and counterclaims. Moreover, an establishment conducting even sporadic business with another country and encountering no special difficulties under the existing system, partly because customs formalities are handled by an experienced intermediary (a customs broker), would suddenly find its books subjected to thorough auditing on account of some minor transaction, and perhaps even in respect of periods during which it had conducted no external operations at all, as a precaution against fraud.

In a word, the fiscal controls which today are concentrated at a few points along the national frontiers would be multiplied and scattered over the entire territory, and practically all enterprises would be trammeled by the inevitable inspections.

From the psychological standpoint, the effect would certainly be bad, if only because nowadays, as stated above, a number of enterprises are hardly aware of the existence of customs formalities, since these are actually dealt with in conjunction with the shipment of the goods customs clear, once left in the hands of a broker, so that for many establishments acquaintance with the customs is limited to the duty they pay. By contrast, in the future the burden of formalities and controls would fall on the taxpayers' shoulders. And matters would be complicated by the fact that in any event trade operations within the common market would have to be differentiated from all the others, which would continue to be subject to frontier controls.

TAX PROBLEMS RELATING TO THE TREATY ON EUROPEAN ECONOMIC INTEGRATION

European efforts to bring about the economic integration of a number of countries did not begin in our generation: aside from economic unions arising out of political mergers, such as the Austro-Hungarian Empire, suffice it to recall the famous German *Zollverein* which in 1834 brought together eighteen states with a population of 23 million people within the German Customs Union—a prelude to political union. However, in all these economic unions the tax problem did not arise, save where the customs union made its effects felt on budget income; furthermore, the pressure of taxation was relatively moderate and caused no distortion.

However, it was primarily in the economic mergers of the period following World War II that the fiscal aspect of the problem arose. In the treaty establishing the European Coal and Steel Community, the first example of sectoral economic integration, taxation is not regulated directly and explicitly. This notwithstanding, during the early years of the Community the responsible authorities showed concern over the tax problem, particularly in connection with the turnover tax, so that in 1953 the High Authority appointed a commission of independent experts, headed by Professor Tinbergen, to study the problem. This commission, on the conclusion of its work, produced a detailed study which served as a basis in reaching a preliminary decision. The High Authority subsequently appointed a small committee to study the effect on the coal and steel industry of the provisions governing the turnover tax. This committee found that the present structure of the turnover tax caused no disturbing effects and therefore proposed that no action be taken on the matter.

Benelux is the first example of postwar regional integration. The effects upon taxation of the economic union between Belgium, the Netherlands, and Luxembourg were felt exclusively in the sector of indirect taxes. A series of agreements, in fact, unified a number of indirect taxes (1947: taxes on wine and sparkling fermented beverages other than beer; 1948: a number of manufacturing taxes of minor importance were suppressed and taxes on beer and tobacco consumption unified). In 1950, provision was made for the consolidation of all manufacturing taxes, and a number of these were suppressed, establishing a new principle: products on which the tax rate has been unified are allowed to cross the borders freely but are taxed by the country where they are consumed. If the tax is collected in the country of origin, the country collecting the tax must turn it over to the country where the product is consumed. However, even now the problem is far from being wholly solved.

The treaty establishing the European Eco-nomic Community (EEC) among the six countries of Western Europe (Belgium, France, Germany, Italy, Luxembourg, and the Netherlands) is the sole example of a treaty by which the tax problem is organically and satisfactorily regulated. Indeed, in Part III (Policy of the Community), Chapter II (Fiscal Provisions), Articles 95 to 99 introduce the following principles.

1. *Elimination of discrimination.* A member state shall not impose, directly or indirectly, on the products of other member states any internal charges of any kind in excess of those applied directly or indirectly to like domestic products.

Furthermore, a member state shall not impose on the products of other member states any internal charges of such a nature as to afford indirect protection to other productions.

2. *Elimination of excessive drawbacks.* Products exported to the territory of any member state may not benefit from any drawback of internal charges in excess of those charges imposed directly or indirectly on them.

3. *Average rates for drawbacks.* Any member states which levy a turnover tax calculated by a cumulative multistage system may, in the case of internal charges imposed by them on imported products or of drawbacks granted by them on exported products, establish average rates for specific products or groups of products.

4. *Observance of the principle of taxation in the country of origin for direct taxes.* With regard to charges other than turnover taxes, excise duties, and other forms of indirect taxation, exemptions and drawbacks in respect of exports to other member states may not be effected and compensatory charges in respect of imports coming from member states may not be imposed, save to the extent that the measures contemplated have been previously approved for a limited period by the council acting on a proposal of the commission.

5. *Harmonization of direct taxes.* The commission shall consider in what way the law of the various member states concerning turnover taxes, excise duties, and other forms of

indirect taxation can be harmonized in the interest of the common market.

With regard to direct taxes, it is always possible to invoke Articles 100 and 101, whereby, should a disparity between the legislative or administrative provisions of the member states distort the conditions of competition in the common market, causing an undesirable state of affairs, the commission may take any appropriate measures.

6. *Elimination of double taxation.* Article 220 provides for negotiations with a view to a multilateral convention within the framework of the Economic Community to eliminate double taxation.

Article 53 of the agreement establishing the association between the European Economic Community and Greece, signed at Athens on July 9, 1961, repeats, though in a very attenuated form, the principles embodied in the Rome Treaty. The problem of uniform taxation is not specifically dealt with.

In view of the seriousness of the tax problems which, in the judgment of some members, were causing distortions at variance with the treaty, the EEC commission appointed a first working group, composed of the chiefs of the ministries of finance of the six countries, to study the various problems relating to the turnover tax. After lengthy and very thorough study, the working group reached the following conclusions.

1. For the time being, it is not feasible to eliminate tax frontiers since, in the opinion of the majority, it would mean adopting uniform tax systems, rates, exemptions, and fields of application.

2. The cumulative multistage turnover tax is incompatible with the common market treaty and should accordingly be abolished.

3. The turnover tax should be systematically unified and the tax on retail trade should be discontinued in view of the difficulty of enforcing it in many countries; as to the tax on the final producer, the working group proposed a tax on value added, extending as far as the dealer stage, the power to levy a tax on the gross profits of retailers remaining unchanged.

The commission subsequently appointed a tax and finance committee composed of professors from the various countries, to be responsible for examining the whole problem of public finance within the framework of the community. The report issued on completion of the work (it is still in the form of a provisional text of 135 pages) reaches the following conclusions.

1. *Income tax.* It recommends a single personal tax, having the same structure in the various countries, although with differing rates, together with a tax on net wealth to be levied on natural persons, and a corporation tax. Harmonization is suggested in the following areas: a system of fixed deductions, allowances for husband or wife, suppression of the system of global assessment, uniformity in the assessment of income on personal property, including 15 to 25 per cent withholding at source.

Harmonization of the over-all burden of taxes levied on companies is recommended and leveling out of the treatment of increases in net wealth. It calls for harmonization of the corporation tax on the basis of a uniform rate for all income produced.

2. *Inheritance tax.* It recommends the formal harmonization of the tax system.

3. *Business taxes.* Harmonization of the taxes on the establishment of corporations, capital increases, stock and bond issues, exchange operations.

4. *Sales tax.* Suppression of the "cascade" tax and replacement by a tax on the value added at each stage up to but excluding the retailer, at a flat rate, and retail sales tax at a free rate.

5. *Special consumption taxes.* It recognizes the impossibility of rapid harmonization.

FISCAL PROBLEMS ARISING OUT OF LATIN AMERICAN TREATIES

In Latin America today we can observe two very interesting experiments in the expansion of the economic market, decidedly different from each other either because of the size of the markets or because of the intensity of economic integration. The one is the Latin American Free Trade Association established by the Montevideo Treaty of February 18, 1960, which became effective at the beginning of 1962, and the other, the General Treaty on Central American Economic Integration of 1960.

The Latin American Free Trade Association

The principal objective of this association is to establish, within a period of twelve years, a free trade zone among the participating countries. The Montevideo Treaty contains the following provisions which have fiscal implications.

Article 3 contains the obligation, similar to that contained in other treaties of the same kind, gradually to eliminate, in respect of reciprocal trade, customs duties and any other charges of equivalent effect, whether fiscal, monetary, or exchange.

Articles 21 and 22 of Chapter V (treatment in respect of internal taxation) stipulate that (*a*) products originating in the territory of a contracting party shall enjoy treatment no less favorable than that accorded to similar national products with respect to taxes, assessments, and other internal duties and charges. (*b*) each contracting party shall endeavor to ensure that the charges or other domestic measures applied to products included in the liberalization program which are not produced, or are produced only in small quantities, in its territory do not nullify or reduce any concession or advantage obtained by any contracting party during the negotiations.

Article 52 stipulates that an export shall not be deemed to have been subsidized if it is exempted from duties and charges levied on the product or its components when destined for internal consumption or if it is subject to drawback, and therefore the article does not prohibit this.

As we see, these fiscal standards are not substantially different from those frequently included in commercial treaties. This is understandable when we consider that the treaty

proposes to create only a relatively loose free trade area. In fact, the complete elimination of every duty or restriction in international trade is applied only to products in the common list, while for other products included on the national list such restrictions are eliminated in a considerable measure. On the other hand, Article 49 does not establish a common tariff with third-party countries but only a uniform tariff nomenclature.

However, the distance between many countries of the free trade area is such that in order for fiscal divergences to have a distortive effect, they would have to be of substantial magnitude.

Fiscal problems therefore will not be likely to constitute obstacles to the functioning of this free trade area.

Central American Economic Integration

Central American economic integration is somewhat complex, since it is governed by a large number of treaties.

The basic treaty is, undoubtedly, the General Treaty on Central American Economic Integration signed in Managua on December 13, 1960, and brought into force on June 4, 1961, in respect of Guatemala, El Salvador, Honduras, and Nicaragua, with Costa Rica acceding on July 23, 1962.

As the preamble of the treaty states, "to unify the economies of the four [now five] countries and jointly to promote the development of Central America in order to improve the living conditions of their peoples," the treaty establishes (Articles I and II) a common market which shall be brought into full operation within a period of not more than five years (by June 4, 1966) and a customs union as well. For such purposes, the contracting states undertake to establish a Central American free trade zone and a standard Central American tariff. As regards the customs union, the Central American Agreement on the Equalization of Import Duties is applicable, by virtue of which the principle of the common tariff was established as well as the prohibition on imposing duties on the importation of goods freed from duty by the other countries of the community.

Article XXV of the General Treaty stipulates that the contracting states "agree not to sign unilaterally with non-Central American countries, any new treaties that may affect the principles of Central American economic integration."

It must be borne in mind that according to information received, 25 per cent of goods now enjoy the benefit of the standard tariff, and by 1963 this percentage will be increased to 90 per cent.

As far as the fiscal consequences are concerned, the following can be pointed out:

1. Under Article III of the General Treaty the signatory states "shall grant each other free trade treatment in respect of all products originating in their respective territories, save only for the limitations contained in the special regimes referred to in . . . the present Treaty."

Later on, defining the origin of goods, the treaty says that goods shall not be considered as originating in one of the contracting states if they originate or are manufactured in a third country and are simply assembled, wrapped, packed, cut, or diluted in the exporting country.

Likewise in Article III we read: "Consequently, the natural products of the Contracting States and the products manufactured therein shall be exempt from import and export duties, including consular fees, and all other taxes, dues and charges levied on imports and exports or charged in respect thereof, whether they be of a national, municipal or any other nature. . . . Goods originating in the territory of any of the Signatory States shall be accorded national treatment in all of them."

This series of regulations is designed to guarantee a freedom of movement for goods within the common market without charges of any kind.

2. Article VI lays down certain rather drastic general principles regarding the prohibition of tax discriminations calculated to aggravate even indirectly the competitive situation of products coming from the other states.

If the goods traded are liable to internal taxes, charges, or duties of any kind levied on production, sale, distribution or consumption in any of the Signatory Countries, the country concerned may levy an equivalent amount on similar goods imported from the other Contracting State, in which case it must also levy at least an equivalent amount for the same respective purposes on similar imports from third countries.

The Contracting Parties agree that the following conditions shall apply to the establishment of internal taxes on consumption:

(i) Such duties may be established in the amount deemed necessary when there is domestic production of the article in question, or when the article is not produced in any of the Signatory States;

(ii) When the article is not produced in one Signatory State but is produced in any of the others, the former State may not establish taxes on consumption of the article concerned unless the Executive Council so authorizes;

(iii) If a Contracting Party has established a domestic tax on consumption, and production of the article so taxed is subsequently begun in any of the other Signatory States, but the article is not produced in the State that established the tax, the Executive Council shall, if the State concerned so requests, deal with the case and decide whether the tax is compatible with free trade. The States undertake to abolish these taxes on consumption in accordance with their legal procedures, on receipt of notification to this effect from the Executive Council.

Thus the individual states retain full freedom to establish or modify taxes on consumption only where there is domestic production of the goods taxed or when such goods are not produced in the other member states. In other instances, the amount chargeable is subject to the limitations shown.

3. In order to avoid distortions, under Article IX, "The Contracting States shall not grant customs exemptions or reductions in respect of imports from outside Central America of articles adequately produced in the Contracting States."

4. Finally, under Article XI, "No Signatory State shall grant any direct or indirect subsidy favouring the export of goods intended for the territory of the other States, or establish or maintain any system resulting in the sale of such goods for export to another Contracting State at a price lower than that established for the sale of similar goods on the domestic market, due allowance being made for differences in the conditions and terms of sale and taxation and for any other factors affecting price comparability."

However, "Tax exemptions of a general nature granted by a Signatory State with a view to encouraging production shall not be deemed to constitute export subsidies. Similarly, any exemption from internal taxes levied in the exporting State on the production, sale or consumption of goods exported to the territory of another State shall not be deemed to constitute an export subsidy."

Article XI of the Multilateral Treaty of Tegucigalpa is substantially the same, with minor shades of difference.

5. In order to avoid distortion within the factors of production, under Article XIX a Central American agreement on tax incentives was drawn up creating a system of uniform tax exemptions applicable to the establishment or development of the manufacturing industries which contribute effectively to the economic development of Central America.

6. It is well to keep in mind Article XIX of the Multilateral Treaty on Free Trade and Central American Economic Integration through which the Central American Trade Subcommittee was entrusted with the task of studying and drawing up adequate measures for establishing a uniform tax system for the national products of a state or for goods subject to tax on their production, sale, and consumption, as well as the drawing up of a multilateral agreement to avoid double taxation in the direct tax sector.

7. Last, some significance must be attached to the report received from the Central American Economic Co-operation Committee (note of May 11, 1962) in which it was pointed out that the committee had convened a meeting on the cartography of the Isthmus in Guatemala from May 3 to 5, 1962, for the purpose of instituting a cadastral survey in Central America as a regional project.

There was unanimous agreement that the cadastral survey of Central America was not to be regarded as an individual operation by each state of the Isthmus but rather as a joint and co-ordinated effort. For that purpose, a study was made of the current situation relating to cadastral surveys in each one of the countries of the area, and consideration was then given to the integration of a Central American program in that field—unity of aims, proper delimitation, methods, necessity for maintenance, estimate of technical resources required, cost of the project and time involved, preparations for the project, obtaining of funds, etc.—and the basic outline of every one of these aspects was sketched out.

Thus the initial steps toward the Central American cadastral survey have been taken; this, in addition to performing important economic, fiscal, and civil functions in each state, will constitute an efficient instrument for the economic development of the Isthmus.

If conclusions were to be drawn from this review, they could be as follows:

1. The substitution of a Central American standard tariff for the national customs tariffs will, in the first place, have immediate budgetary repercussions. Advantages will accrue to some states, since the new tariff is more protectionist than the former and the shift in the movement of goods from third countries to the Central American customs free zone will not cancel out the increased returns. Other countries may find themselves in a different situation. In the second place, it poses the problem of allocating the proceeds of customs duties on transient traffic within the common market area. This problem does not arise if fiscal frontiers are maintained, since they enable the final destination of products to be ascertained. However, if it were decided to abolish the fiscal frontiers and, after careful study, the states were convinced of the feasibility of doing so, customs revenue might form the nucleus of a federal financing

system which sooner or later, as economic integration developed, would become inevitable.

2. The institution of a standard tariff vis-à-vis third countries is a factor making for inflexibility in the accounts of the member states. Actually, if at a given moment state budgetary demands increase, national governments can no longer have recourse to this revenue since the tariff can be modified only by the Central American common market authority in accordance with the trade agreements entered into with third countries and the trade policy followed by the Community. This means that for some countries a good 50 per cent of the fiscal revenue will be kept out of the hands of the various national authorities, thus increasing the inflexibility of the tax system, which will have to seek new sources of revenue.

This inflexibility makes itself felt even more if we remember Article VI, mentioned above, which fixes the taxation of consumer goods extremely strictly. This is a particularly serious problem because of the fact that such taxes on consumer goods, relatively strictly fixed in this way, represent very high percentages (as much as 35 per cent of the total) so that the percentage of state revenue over which government authorities exercise full control is reduced to a very modest figure.

3. The fact that the principal nonessential consumer items are imported, except for certain special items (beer, alcoholic beverages), has led the countries of Central America to consider such taxation not so much as protectionist measures (and in any case a protection for the balance of payments as a whole rather than for certain products not available domestically) but rather as a method of taxing consumer products and a means of financing the budget. With the establishment of the customs union, these duties will assume their characteristic function as a protective measure for an economy in the process of integration which aims at development. To this end, the fiscal function that the state had assigned to such duties must be separated from them and take the form of a tax on consumption, even though it is collected in the customs on imported goods. This is a need which must inevitably arise under the guise of development of special taxation and also, perhaps, of general taxation on consumption.

CONCLUSIONS

The problem of the fiscal consequences of standardizing the markets in Latin America cannot be underestimated.

While in the case of the Latin American Free Trade Association, which is essentially a zone for the liberalization of trade of a very moderate kind, the fiscal factor cannot play a very important role (especially in view of the distance that separates the various markets), the same cannot be said of Central America, where a movement toward economic integration in a very intense form is under way.

The more general problems have been dealt with in the course of this paper, but comparative statistical and legislative data from which more concrete conclusions may be drawn are unfortunately lacking.

It would be a good thing, therefore, if a recommendation emerged from this conference to set up a committee of experts representing five countries of Central America with instructions to collect and study (a) the statistical and legislative material needed in order to determine what type of taxation in present circumstances produces or is likely to produce effects of distortion and (b) what measures can be devised to eliminate them and to restore to the state finances something of the elasticity that the treaty has taken away from them.

Comment

MAURICIO BACA MUÑOZ*

PROBLEMS OF DEFINITION

In the first section of his study, "Fiscal Problems of a Common Market," Professor Cesare Cosciani, on whose paper I have the great honor of commenting, offers us the opportunity to take up the definition of our movement of Central American economic integration.

According to Mr. Cosciani, a customs union consists basically in free trade in goods and services among member countries and a unified customs tariff on imports from third countries.

He conceives of a common market as "an economic grouping of two or more countries on a decidedly more intensive basis," the free movement of goods and services being complemented by the free movement of the factors of production among the member countries, and likewise requiring the unification of monetary and credit policies, economic and social policies, and the legal structure most directly liable to exert an influence on production and trade. In short, the common market assumes the form and characteristics of an internal market.

The Central American integration movement is based on two fundamental treaties: The General Treaty on Central American Economic Integration, signed in December, 1960, by Guatemala, El Salvador, Honduras, and Nicaragua, and to which Costa Rica adhered in July, 1962, and the Multilateral Treaty on Free Trade and Central American Economic Integration, signed by the same five countries in June, 1958. The General Treaty takes precedence among the contracting parties over the Multilateral Treaty, but the latter remains in force with respect to certain matters not dealt with by the former. Further-

more, the Multilateral Treaty would enter into full force—to regulate trade relations among the parties—if for any circumstance the General Treaty should cease to be applicable between one or more of them and the rest. This could occur in case of a denunciation of the General Treaty by any of the parties; in such an event the trade relations of that country or countries with the others would be governed by the Multilateral Treaty.

In Article I of the General Treaty, the contracting states agree to establish among themselves a common market which is to be brought into full operation in a period of not more than five years. However, in the terminology used in that treaty, the concept of "common market" was taken in a less broad scope than that found in the definition in the paper under discussion. This may be understood from a reading of Article II of the treaty, which provides that for the purposes of the common market, the contracting parties undertake to bring a Central American free trade area into full operation within a period of five years and to adopt a standard Central American tariff within the same period. Furthermore, in the aforesaid Article I, the contracting parties agree to create a customs union, but without fixing a time limit therefor, which clearly indicates that to those who drafted the General Treaty, "common market" meant an earlier and less complete stage of economic integration than "customs union."

From the foregoing it may be inferred that in the present stage of development of Central American economic integration, what is commonly called a "free trade area" has been reached. However, both the General and the Multilateral Treaties establish the bases for achieving, in a relatively short period of time, what we might call an "economic union," which corresponds to the concept of "common market" according to Mr. Cosciani's definition.

*Chief of the Legal and Fiscal Section, Permanent Secretariat of the General Treaty on Central American Integration (SIECA), Guatemala.

Under the General Treaty, there is unrestricted free trade among the countries of Central America for all natural products of those countries and products manufactured therein, except for a small number of products, chiefly natural ones, which are subject to special regimes such as preferential or reduced tariffs, trade quotas, or controls. These special regimes are temporary, however, and must terminate by the end of five years, by which time free trade will be absolutely unrestricted for products of Central American origin.

Furthermore, since September, 1959, when the Central American Agreement on the Equalization of Import Duties was signed, going on to the Managua Protocol and up to the signing of the latest protocol in San José, Costa Rica, in July, 1962, the contracting parties have agreed to equalize more than 95 per cent of the duties in the Central American Standard Tariff. This equalization was immediate in 90 per cent of the items and progressive in the others, and it is expected that within the next five years Central America will have a common tariff vis-à-vis the outside world.

However, this does not necessarily imply that the free trade also extends to products not originating in the member states. The geographic situation of some of the countries of Central America could result in detours of the traffic of goods imported from third countries. For example, El Salvador, because it has no access to the Atlantic Ocean, might receive goods imported through Guatemalan ports without collecting taxes. Or the capital of Honduras, which has the problem of difficult communications with Honduran ports, might receive its imports through Salvadoran ports on the Pacific. Both of these cases would represent a real transfer of fiscal revenues from one country to another.[2] Consequently,

we should then find ourselves in the situation, not of a customs union, but of a customs community, or common market, to use the language of the treaty, which is a more highly developed step than a simple free trade area.

But this situation will have to be the subject of special treatment, agreed upon prior to reaching it, since Central America is working to bring the free trade area into full operation just as soon as the tariff schedule is unified.

This special treatment will be accorded when the states of Central America fulfill their commitment to adopt a common customs administration and negotiate the bases for an equitable division of the revenues produced by the customs tariff. Then, beyond any doubt, it will be possible to have absolute free trade among them; that is, not only for products originating in Central America but also for those originating elsewhere, since the reasons for restricting free trade only to the former will have disappeared. The customs union then will have been accomplished. The Central American treaties give to this concept the same meaning attributed to it by Mr. Cosciani and adopted by the GATT.

THE CENTRAL AMERICAN PROCESS TOWARD INTEGRATION (COMMON MARKET)

But the process initiated by the Central American countries goes further still toward economic integration or union (or common market, as Mr. Cosciani has it). In fact, in the treaties mentioned before there are provisions that necessarily lead to this goal.

Provisions of the Multilateral Treaty

The Multilateral Treaty on Free Trade and Central American Economic Integration, which—as we pointed out—is in force in all matters not considered in the General Treaty, includes the following provisions of this nature.

---

[2]It is interesting to note that in the Benelux countries, even if they do not yet have a common customs administration, it is possible to have free movement of all goods, including those coming from third countries, because the geographic position of Belgium and the Netherlands would not permit a detour of customary commercial traffic.

Internal Free Flow of Capitals

Article XVII provides that each Central American country shall grant equal treatment to capital investments made by nationals of the other states, and shall permit without discrimination transfers of funds accruing from these investments, either as profits or as capital repatriation; this means that there is full and effective intra-Central American circulation for this factor of production.

Free Movement of Persons

Article XXIII provides that all Central Americans shall be granted national treatment in commercial and civil matters in the territory of all other member states.

International Unity

Article XXIV declares that the member states agree that before negotiating any international agreement or acceding to any international organization, they shall consult each other with a view to agreeing, if possible, on a common and united policy. To such prior consultations shall have to be submitted, before signing, any new treaties, even those among member states, which may affect free trade, in accordance with Article XXVIII of the General Treaty.

Provisions of the General Treaty

Likewise, some of the situations that might possibly cause the distortions of which Mr. Cosciani speaks—which must be corrected only in an economic union or common market system—are envisaged in the General Treaty.

Uniform Tax Incentives for Industrial Development

In Article XIX, the contracting states agreed to sign, within a period of six months, an agreement on the equalization of tax incentives applicable in each country to the establishment and operation of industries. This agreement was signed by the five countries in July, 1962. This agreement specifies that the tax benefits may be granted only for the establishment of industrial enterprises or for the expansion of existing ones, in the amount and for the period of time designated for the various groups into which the industries are classified. Three basic criteria are followed in making the classification, to wit: the economic importance of the product to be manufactured; the origin of the materials to be used in the manufacture; and the novelty or innovation of the product or the process of manufacture. The agreement also provides for correcting temporary situations of possible distortion in the trade in products of industries established in the various countries under the provisions of national legislation prior to the agreement's conclusion.

It is appropriate to mention that for the benefit of the countries that are generally and relatively less developed, and for the purpose of applying the principle of balanced development in the region, such countries are permitted to grant broader exemptions from the taxes on income and wealth. The primary purpose of the agreement is to prevent the creation, through governmental action, of artificial advantages designed to influence the location of industrial undertakings. In order to ensure uniform compliance with the agreement in all of the countries, an attempt was made, in selecting the factors on which to base the classification of the industries, to choose factors that could be easily weighted. Furthermore, the co-ordination and supervision of the agreement's proper implementation was vested in a supranational organization, the Executive Council.

Industrial Integration

In the field of industries to which the entire Central American market is a necessity if they are to operate under economic conditions, a still broader step has been taken, for not only have possible situations of artificial distortion been corrected, but it is provided that the location of industries in the member states should be agreed on multilaterally. The purpose of this unusual system is to promote the development of industries that will have genuine economic impact and that in turn will serve for the operation of other industries and the soundest use of investment resources in order to prevent duplication.

This system of Central American industrial integration is based on the treaty on this subject signed by the contracting parties in June, 1958, which establishes the bases and procedures for distributing these industries among the countries of the region. It had its origin in the relative differences existing among the countries of Central America in respect to their industrial development, development of the infrastructure, number of inhabitants and their distribution, etc., all of which could exert a decisive influence on the location of this type of industries, to the probable detriment of the countries having a relatively lesser degree of development.

This represents an application of the principle of balanced development—a principle that was also taken into account, as stated before, in the drafting of the agreement on tax incentives.

Although no list of priorities for integration industries has been prepared, a list has been made of the qualifications to be met by those to which the system will apply and of the studies and procedures that will have to precede such classification. In the near future, the contracting parties will sign the first protocol to this treaty, which will set forth an equitable distribution of the first group of industries considered to fall in this category.

Of course, in industries that use natural resources, the location of the raw materials as a factor for establishing or locating the business (regional specialization) must not be neutralized by unilateral or multilateral governmental action.

Unfair Trade Practices

Article XI of the General Treaty makes provision to prevent unfair trade practices (dumping) in the inter-Central American market, be they encouraged by governmental

decision or by the action of private individuals. We shall come back to this matter later on.

Trade Discrimination

Article VII of the General Treaty prohibits national regulations on the distribution or retailing of goods originating in Central America that would place or tend to place such goods in an unfavorable position in relation to similar goods of domestic origin or imported from any other country; that is, the free and unrestricted circulation of such goods is ordered.

Organizations

The integration movement is also provided with its own organs, which fact gives it a firmer sense of unity. The Economic Council, composed of the Ministers of Economy, directs the integration and co-ordinates the economic policies of the member states and is the maximum authority for deciding any problems that arise among them. The Executive Council, composed of government officials, has the more specific duty of administering the General Treaty and putting it into practice, that is, carrying out the measures and studies necessary to bring the economic union into being. Finally, there is the Permanent Secretariat, serving both councils, whose function is to see that the treaties in force and the decisions of the Economic Council and Executive Council are implemented.

TAX PROBLEMS IN CENTRAL AMERICAN ECONOMIC INTEGRATION

The distortions that the tax havens pointed out by Mr. Cosciani may cause within a customs union are not especially envisaged in the Central American economic integration treaties. It is probable that the negotiators of these agreements did not deal with this subject for the reason that the legislation of the countries of Central America that might affect the movement of capital within the region has traditionally been similar and offers no differences that could constitute sufficient encouragement to make any of these countries a haven for capital coming from their neighbors.

Tax Havens. Even though in some countries of Central America the commercial legislation provides for the existence of bearer shares in companies legally organized as corporations, there is no secrecy for tax purposes with respect to the identification by name of the owner of such securities. Neither is the system of numbered bank accounts known in Central America, and therefore these situations would not arise in the framework of Central American commercial legislation.

Furthermore, in Central America corporate income is not subject to a special tax; the same type of tax applies to it as to the income of natural persons, and the tax on dividends is not collected from shareholders, since it is not included in personal income. Under these conditions the existence of bearer shares or securities could not constitute a factor in tax evasion.

Aside from these comments, it is appropriate to observe from the standpoint of doctrine that systems such as that followed in Central America—of a single tax on the income of corporations without consideration of the persons who receive the profits in the form of dividends—are open to criticism from the point of view of equity and can be looked upon as not being conducive to the promotion of the investment of savings in companies of an economic size that goes beyond the requirements of the internal markets.

From the standpoint of tax equity, this scheme is not in line with the principle of levying more tax on those who have more (which is the definite purpose of direct taxes), because the burden falls with equal intensity on the small saver who has invested his funds in a corporation and on the capitalist of great resources who has invested in the same company. The injustice becomes even more glaring when the large investor, by dividing his resources among a number of companies,

succeeds in dividing up his taxable income into partial nonintegrated amounts which are subject separately to a lower tax scale than would apply to the same profits if they were all totaled as the taxpayer's personal income.

This same structural characteristic of the tax gives rise to the second consequence of this system that we have pointed out; that is, it is a serious obstacle to the formation of genuine corporations, meaning those that bring together, by means of the sum total of small investments, the considerable amount of resources needed by medium- and large-sized enterprises. By subjecting the profits of the corporation, distributed or not, to a progressive tax equal to the rate applied to natural persons, encouragement is given to the splitting up of productive activity into many small companies or the breaking up into a number of companies activities that had already been integrated. It is obvious that when confronted by a tax system of this kind, a person who has some savings, let us say five thousand dollars, as his only capital, will find it more desirable and more attractive from every standpoint to put his money out at interest than to buy shares in a corporation with a capital in the neighborhood of a million dollars. By doing the former, his net income would be higher than if he followed the second procedure, since income he received in the form of interest would be subject —if it were taxed at all—to the minimum rate of tax or to a very low tax. On the other hand, the tax on the dividends to which he would be entitled in a corporation would have to be paid while those dividends were still in possession of the corporation, and the tax thereon would be high up in the progressive scale because the total income of the corporation, in absolute terms, would also be high. This, in turn, gives rise to two economic situations worthy of mention: (a) the lack of incentive for small savings and the investment of such savings in industrial corporations and (b) failure to make use of the advantages of the larger market that economic integration would favor. In other words, this means the bogging down of industrialization and balanced economic development.

If one takes into account the fact that in the countries of Central America a very high percentage of the total yield of the income tax is paid by a very small number of corporations, it may be affirmed that in all likelihood this situation is maintained for the benefit of administrative simplicity and, of course, to the detriment of equity and economic development.

As for the system followed to determine the tax jurisdiction to which assets located in each of the countries of Central America and the income derived therefrom are subject, there is complete uniformity. The legislation in all of the countries taxes the property located in their own territories and the income obtained therein, that is, the income produced by domestic companies or assets or as the product of activities carried out within their own territorial limits, with no consideration in any case of the domicile or nationality of the owner of the property or income. It is impossible, then, to conceive of a taxpayer subject to the tax on income or assets who could evade payment on these grounds.[3] The case might arise if some of the countries followed exclusively the system of the taxpayer's domicile and the others the system of location of the source. Theoretically speaking, the Central American system of determining tax jurisdiction might rather be an encouragement for the distribution of investments in the various countries, because in this case each country would tax the amount of income derived from the investment in its own territory, and in none of the countries would these partial incomes be added into the total of the taxpayer's income.

While it must be admitted that a system of determining tax jurisdiction based on place of production instead of the taxpayer's domicile may cause some obstacles to the development of business because of the several systems to which the taxpayer finds himself

subject, it can be affirmed that technically the system eliminates the possibility of double taxation. Furthermore, it is to be hoped that by means of uniform progressive rates and a similar system of determining taxable income in all the Central American states, the difficulties the taxpayer has to face will be less marked than those that would stem from an equitable distribution among the states of a single tax collected at the domicile of the taxpayer, not to mention the problems that the collecting state would have in enforcing tax collections and checking returns of companies located outside its territory.

TAXATION IN COUNTRY OF ORIGIN OR COUNTRY OF DESTINATION

In relation to the two tax systems (in country of origin or in country of destination) expounded by Mr. Cosciani, insofar as their advantages or disadvantages within a system of free trade relations among countries are concerned, we must admit that thus far Central America has made no definite plans about the problem, and consequently it has not adopted any over-all solution; it has not, so to speak, set a course for either of the two systems.

Nonetheless, the economic integration authorities are convinced—and this must necessarily be stated—that the rigidity accompanying the adoption of a common tariff, which does not permit the mobilization of customs taxes for increasing fiscal revenues, will have to be faced from the regional standpoint, and quickly, too. Otherwise the countries may in all probability adopt individual remedies that could cause artificial distortions, to the detriment of the normal functioning of the common market.

In this respect, I am happy to inform this conference that the Permanent Secretariat has been authorized by the governments of Central America to undertake negotiations with the OAS/IDB/ECLA Joint Tax Committee for technical assistance in the form of a group of experts to work out new structures for the

---

[3] It is noted that Honduras also taxes the incomes of persons domiciled in its territory, even though the source of the income may be foreign.

tax systems of Central America in order to achieve the greatest degree possible of harmonization.

Furthermore, the countries of Central America have made progress in their joint work for taking the Central American real property census, of which one of the principal purposes is to provide an instrument that may serve for more efficient taxation in the field of direct taxes.

As we have already said, Central America has not systematically adopted a line of conduct with respect to the principle to be followed on direct or indirect taxes under the system of free movement of goods and factors of production in the Central American Common Market.

This is so, notwithstanding the fact that in the treaties on integration we find certain provisions that would appear to coincide with the principle of taxation in the country of origin in respect of the indirect taxes or consumption taxes to which the freely traded goods are subject. There are, on the other hand, some legal provisions that might seem to adhere to the principle of taxation in the country of destination or consumption of the goods, although even in this case we do not find systematic repetition. Therefore, we propose to make a more thorough analysis of both types of provisions in order to explain the position adopted at this stage by the Central American Common Market.

The first paragraph of Article VI of the General Treaty provides:

If the goods traded are liable to internal taxes, charges, or duties of any kind levied on production, sale, distribution, or consumption in any of the signatory countries, the country concerned may levy an equivalent amount on similar goods imported from the other contracting State, in which case it must also levy at least an equivalent amount for the same respective purposes on similar imports from third countries.

This means that when a product imported from other Central American states is also produced domestically, the principle of coun-

try of destination is applied, since when the importing country makes the imported article liable to the taxes it levies on the production, sale, distribution, or consumption of the national product, it is logical to think that the exporting state will agree to reimburse or exempt from its own taxes the article that is exported, because in this case it must put itself in a position to compete with the domestic product in the market of the country of destination. Thus, in this situation one sees the complete cycle of the principle of taxation in the country of destination, since on the one hand there is reimbursement or exemption in the exporting country for the exported article, and on the other that same article is made subject to the internal taxes of the importing country.

Article XI of the General Treaty prohibits export subsidies or the maintenance of any other system that would result in unfair trade, but it expressly excepts from this classification reimbursements of taxes on exports. This article reads, in part, as follows:

No signatory State shall grant any direct or indirect subsidy favoring the export of goods intended for the territory of the other States, or establish or maintain any system resulting in the sale of such goods for export to any other contracting State at a price lower than that established for the sale of similar goods on the domestic market, due allowance being made for differences in the conditions and terms of sale and taxation and for any other factors affecting price comparability.

·　·　·　·　·

However, tax exemptions of a general nature granted by a signatory State with a view to encouraging production shall not be deemed to constitute export subsidies.

Similarly, any exemption from internal taxes levied in the exporting State on the production, sale or consumption of goods exported to the territory of another State shall not be deemed to constitute an export subsidy. The differentials resulting from the sale of foreign currency on the free market at a rate of exchange higher than the official rate shall not normally be deemed to be an export subsidy; if one of the contracting States is in doubt, however, the matter shall be submitted to the Executive Council for its consideration and opinion.

This type of provision supplements Article VI, already commented upon, because by permitting tax reimbursements or exemptions in favor of the experted goods, it makes it possible to comply with the principle of taxation in the country of destination.

However, it should be noted that reimbursements or exemptions are not granted automatically, nor do they constitute a right of the exporter, and therefore he cannot compel their implementation; this is a prerogative of the country of origin.

It is likewise pertinent to call attention to the fact that the reimbursements permitted under the aforementioned provisions of the General Treaty include only taxes on the production, consumption, or sale of manufactured goods and not taxes levied on the various earlier phases of production, such as the indirect taxes (on importation, sale, consumption) that may have been paid on raw materials and other components of the manufactured product, on invested capital, licenses, social security, etc., all of which are incorporated into the cost of the product. This is the interpretation given to the provisions mentioned above, and it represents the practice of Central American business. The concept of "tax on production" has been used in its more restricted meaning as a tax paid because of the very act of manufacture and not in its broader sense which would encompass all fiscal charges paid throughout the entire process of production.

In support of this theory, we should cite Article 10 of the Central American Agreement on Tax Incentives for Industrial Development, which provides as follows:

ARTICLE 10. The return made by any of the member States of the amount of tax paid on the importation of raw materials, semifinished products, or containers used for products exported to countries outside Central America shall be considered as being adjusted to the terms of this Agreement.

Making a legal interpretation of this precept, *a contrario sensu,* it must be understood that these refunds of import taxes cannot occur when the export of the manufactured product is destined to another country of Central America.

This opinion was expressly stated in the report of the group of experts who drafted the agreement, when doubts were expressed about whether the refund could be applied to inter-Central American exports.

However, Article VI (b) of the General Treaty provides as follows: "When the article is not produced in one signatory State but is produced in any of the others, the former State may not establish taxes on consumption of the article concerned unless the Executive Council so authorizes."

No great effort of interpretation is required to conclude that this provision will be incompatible with the principle of taxation in the country of destination or consumption of the product. It might even be interpreted as an application of the contrary principle, that is, taxation in the country of origin or production, because the fiscal authorities of the latter are free to decide whether to reimburse the exporting manufacturer for the domestic taxes on production, sale, or consumption, according to Article XI of the aforementioned treaty.

Thought must also be given to the fact that it is very improbable that the fiscal authorities of the exporting state will feel inclined under these circumstances to grant drawbacks or exemptions in favor of the exported product, in view of the fact that there is no real competition in the market that is to receive the exported goods. Since there is no local production in that market, the only remaining competition, if we can call it so, would be from a product imported from third countries under a protective tariff schedule. However, this type of provision is necessary in a free trade system in order to prevent discrimination against products imported from member states.

To summarize the points covered in this section, we can state that in Central America at the present time there is no meeting of minds in regard to the types of taxes, direct and indirect, in order to determine the tax jurisdiction between country of origin and country of destination. On the contrary, both systems coexist, the system of taxation at the source being followed for direct taxes (on capital and income) and both systems being followed for indirect taxes on goods in free trade; that is, the system of the country of origin when there is no similar production in the country of consumption, and the system of the country of consumption when there is domestic production and when, at the same time, the domestic product is taxed. But even in the latter case, taxes on the earlier phases of production, which are incorporated into the cost of the final product, are not included.

CRITICAL ANALYSIS AND CONCLUSIONS

We shall now proceed to make a critical analysis of the tax structure of Central America in relation to the common market, on the basis of Mr. Cosciani's paper and our own judgment.

Direct Tax on Wealth

In all the countries of Central America there are taxes on the source of income, that is, wealth; these taxes are more extensive in some countries than in others, and they are subject to various classifications. In some, real property is taxed; in others, all assets, both real and personal.

The desirability of this tax is no longer questioned from the standpoint of doctrine, since fundamentally it is a tax on economic capacity represented by the holding of property. Furthermore, it is supplemental to the income tax, especially in countries which, because they do not have a schedular income tax system, find it impossible to discriminate in favor of taxpayers whose only source of income is their personal effort. Through the application of a tax on capital or assets, an extra levy is imposed on persons whose in-

come is obtained through the ownership of some source of wealth.

On the other hand, some authors hold that the income tax may become a disincentive to investment in industrial or business enterprises whose income is easily subject to checking, which leads to a channeling of resources toward the purchase of houses and land on the outskirts of cities, which produce little or no taxable income. Here, again, the tax on capital may be an important factor in directing resources toward productive investments.[4]

When the tax rates on capital are substantial, they may provoke a considerable mobilization of wealth, at relatively low prices, from the hands of nonproductive holders toward those capable of producing. The more optimistic supporters of this tax point to it as being an important instrument for achieving a new structure of land tenure and a redistribution of wealth. We share that opinion, and we believe, furthermore, that it is a fair tax capable of channeling resources into industry; and because of its greater ease of administration, it can well be an important source of fiscal revenues in a shorter time than the income tax.

We stated earlier that in Central America the system of territorial jurisdiction is applied to this tax; that is, it is collected by the country in whose territory the investment is made, without consideration of the domicile of the owner. This seems fair to us, because the taxes which the state collects are the counterpart of the services which it gives, and among these latter, the services rendered through the police, the courts of justice, transportation, communications, etc., benefit the citizen insofar as he is the owner of properties. Thus, it would be unjust from any standpoint to have proportional amounts of the sums which the state spends for the protection of the properties and the development of businesses belonging to foreigners find their way, not into its own treasury, but to the treasury of the country where the owner has his residence.

---

[4]These investments in unoccupied lands, which acquire considerable added value, generally escape taxation unless the income tax is levied on capital gains.

Furthermore, as long as the system is uniform throughout Central America, it will not be a factor in the creation of tax havens, because tax evasion through the movement of capital is technically impossible. Of course, measures must be adopted to attain maximum harmonization in the five countries in such fundamental matters as the tax base, rates, assessment methods, etc.

Income Tax. We stated above that the tax on income in the countries of Central America is collected in the state where the investment is located or where the personal activity that produces the income is carried on, without consideration of the domicile of the income recipient. We pointed out the desirability of this system on account of the practical advantages to the state in being able to check on business concerns in its own territory, as compared with having to do it in the territory of another state. Tax evasion is considerably more unlikely when the authorities have access to the books of companies than when they must depend on information supplied to them by the authorities of a neighboring country.

As for the justice of the position that the country where the source of the income is located is also creditor of the tax, this is implicitly recognized in Mr. Cosciani's paper; he tells us that the tax should be divided among the states of the customs union after the collection has been made in the country of the taxpayer's domicile. However, it is appropriate to point out that such a distribution might present problems, in view of the progressivity of the tax.

Actually, the problems of possible double taxation or the possibility of a person's being able to evade all taxation in a customs union would indeed be great. But such problems do not arise so long as the system, whatever it may be, is uniform. On the other hand, the problem does arise—and it is extremely important that it be solved—with respect to countries that export capital. Such countries generally apply the income tax not only to profits derived from assets located in their

own territories, regardless of the residence of the taxpayer, but also to the income of their residents which is produced abroad. It is true that in this latter case credits are allowed for the amounts paid in the country of production. However, these countries have lower rates in general than the capital exporting countries, and almost always the latter receive an appreciable share of the resources generated in the countries that have received the exported capital. This policy nullifies the tax exemptions that the underdeveloped countries can offer foreign capital for their industrial development.[5]

Indirect Taxes

The distortions that indirect taxes may cause with respect to goods traded in Central America were considered in the integration treaties, although not in a uniform manner, as we stated earlier.

We must say here that the system of taxation in the country of destination, which Mr. Cosciani supports, in essence completely meets our concept of the principle of balanced development and equity, which is the cornerstone of modern economic integration movements,[6] because these movements stem from the voluntary determination of sovereign states which are seeking a better standard of living without ulterior motives—and in some cases the goal is political integration.

We consider it acceptable in theory that all tax charges, both those levied in the stages prior to production and general sales taxes, should be refunded by the exporting states, so that in the last instance they would find their way to the consuming country in the form of compensatory levies.

However, it must be admitted, along with Mr. Cosciani, that in regard to taxes on the

[5] Actually, if the country of the investor's residence collects the total income tax, the exemption becomes a gift of the country that grants the exemption in favor of the former country. This situation is covered in Article 8 of the Agreement on Tax Incentives for Industrial Development.

[6] If the tax is collected by the country of origin, a situation of chronic disadvantage is created for the countries in a lesser stage of industrial development.

various factors of production, the shifting is done in a backward direction, and therefore the formal tax incidence at the time of exportation is generally greater than the real incidence. Consequently, a full rebate may become an export subsidy, and, as a counterpart, a compensatory duty may become a customs duty.

The practical consequences of this theory increase in proportion to the number of taxes prior to production. Now, considering the fact that in Central America taxes of this type are generally reduced to those on imports of raw materials and other components of manufactures, we must agree that the problem is less when there is customs standardization,

However, the system brings us to another kind of problem of the greatest importance, i.e., the problem created for free trade by border inspections.

So, a perfect system of taxation in the country of destination, with its procedures for the total refund of taxes and payment of compensatory duties, could be adopted in Central America by adapting it to the principle of elimination of customs controls.

FINAL CONCLUSIONS

As a result of the rigidities created by the standardized tariff schedule, as noted above, and in view of the fact that customs duties are of major importance in Central American budgets,[7] it is not difficult to anticipate that in order to collect additional revenues for economic development, the governments may turn to taxes on consumption and, in general, on the cost factors of industry with even greater intensity than at present. It is not difficult to imagine that the income tax may also undergo revisions that might possibly give rise to double taxation or tax havens in Central America. These situations could well lead to problems of artificial distortion in the common market.

These lines of reasoning lead us to the conclusion that steps should be taken as promptly as possible to study the problem jointly, in order to find regional solutions, or, in other words, the greatest degree of uniformity that can be reached—solutions that will not only meet the needs for public funds to cut down budget deficits and to provide impetus for economic development but also simultaneously make possible the uninterrupted progress of the integration movement.

The final solutions adopted to take care of the pressure on budgets that will occur during the next few years will depend to some extent on the studies made and, in the last instance, on the decision of the governments themselves.

[7] The proportion varies from 38 to 60 per cent from one country to another.

Comment

José María Cazal*

Definition of the Problem

The thoughtful paper presented by the distinguished Professor Cesare Cosciani takes up the fiscal problems of a common market, and with great skill he approaches the first difficulty of the topic: the definition of the problem under consideration.

In fact, as he very well suggests in his paper, the attempts in Europe to achieve the economic unification of diverse countries are not a new product of our time. The many efforts toward unification and the solution of problems common to groups of countries have led to a great variety of systems and,

*Latin American Free Trade Association.

even within some systems, to a wide range of nuances.

Consequently, if one is to attempt to systematize the problems and solutions of this subject, it is most necessary to bring the question within certain limits, either by defining the structure under discussion with the greatest possible precision or by specifying the problem in such a way as to eliminate all possible confusion. In this sense Mr. Cosciani, displaying admirable competence, has defined the question in his paper, offering us two structures for attaining economic unification among groups of countries, to wit, the customs union and the common market.

It is our understanding that in using this approach Mr. Cosciani is not attempting to exhaust the field of joint solutions for economic problems common to two or more countries but rather analyzing in his paper the two forms which, on the basis of experience, he judges to be more productive of useful results. It is possible that this may be the reason why he has not touched at all in his study upon an analysis of the fiscal problems of a free trade area such as the one envisaged in the Treaty of Montevideo, which establishes the Latin American Free Trade Association (LAFTA).

Nonetheless, as we shall see later on, Mr. Cosciani's observations represent an extremely worth-while contribution of suggestions to LAFTA.

Free Trade Area

Following Mr. Cosciani's example, we, for our part, shall attempt to describe the free trade area as it is conceived in the Treaty of Montevideo, in order to make the necessary comparisons between the problems of the area and both the observations and the conclusions contained in the paper under discussion.

In the first place, it is appropriate to emphasize that LAFTA cannot be characterized solely by what it is accomplishing at this moment; one must also, and very particularly, take into account what it proposes to accomplish.

The Treaty of Montevideo begins by establishing in its Chapter II a program for trade liberalization which calls for the gradual elimination, by the countries concerned, in respect of substantially all of their reciprocal trade, such duties, charges, and restrictions of all kinds as may be applied to imports of products originating in the territory of any contracting party.

Possibly, with respect to the liberalization program covered by that chapter, Mr. Cosciani can in all truth say that these fiscal standards are not substantially different from those frequently included in commercial treaties. But the Treaty of Montevideo goes far beyond the current patterns of commercial treaties and sets up an entire system that we might describe as a "converging process."

It is not limited to a program for the liberalization of present trade; it also contains a series of measures for promoting an "expansion of trade and economic complementarity" (Chapter III), and in this connection it may be pointed out that Article 15 of the Treaty of Montevideo, indicating the course the system is taking, provides:

In order to ensure fair competitive conditions among the contracting parties and to facilitate the increasing integration and complementarity of their economies, particularly with regard to industrial production, the contracting parties shall make every effort—in keeping with the liberalization objectives of this Treaty—to reconcile their import and export systems, as well as the treatment they accord to capital, goods, and services from outside the Area.

Furthermore, Article 54 of the same treaty also provides, "The contracting parties shall make every effort to direct their policies with a view to creating conditions favorable to the establishment of a Latin American Common Market. . . ."

When we say that the Treaty of Montevideo is an agreement calling for gradual convergence, we mean to point out that it is designed to bring about a progressive process of rapprochement of the economies of the countries that make up the free trade area. As stated, this process involves a program for the liberalization of present trade; it envisages the expansion of that trade; and it proposes the gradual reconciliation of their import and export systems, as well as the treatment they accord to capital, goods, and services from outside the area, and a gradual and increasing co-ordination of their industrialization policies.

Now, in theory, this agreement for gradual convergence comprises two types of problems: (a) those matters which the contracting parties have already agreed to carry out, such as those, for example, covered by the liberalization program stipulated in Chapter II of the treaty, and (b) those matters on which the contracting parties are authorized to come to an agreement later, even assuming the obligation in some cases to make every effort to do so.

This special feature of the Treaty of Montevideo is the logical and necessary answer to the situation as it exists in Latin America, where customs barriers, jealously preserved for so many decades, have helped the development of divergent economic structures. So much is this so that the economic integration of the countries of the area faces difficulties, not so much in the matter of geographic distances as in the distances that separate degrees of development and economic structures. This situation has made it necessary to exercise not only great prudence but particular wisdom in selecting the ways and determining the rate of integration of the economies of the LAFTA countries. This is why, with respect to present, immediate accomplishments, agreements were concluded on those operations which, while not requiring fundamental changes in existing setups, could result in real progress in the trade and integration of the contracting parties. As for the future, the treaty sets goals, spells out purposes, and establishes preparatory measures for gradual integration and complementarity, and it does this in a way that does not prematurely bind any country to a definitive future structure. Under the Treaty of Montevideo, if the contracting parties so agree—

and they themselves will be the ones to decide—a customs union may be worked out and the common market may be established. The contracting parties reserve the right to make the final decision in this respect in due course. In this way integration, complementarity, the customs union, and the common market may be achieved under the Treaty of Montevideo when and as the contracting parties deem it desirable. Meanwhile, the treaty offers a number of measures that will be clearing the way, so to speak, constantly bringing economic, tax, financial, and monetary policies more into line with each other. Thus, not only is the gradual economic integration of the countries of the area being prepared and facilitated, but in addition the best possibilities and the proper occasions for determining opportunities and concretely accomplishing the integration of Latin America are being evaluated.

Applications of Mr. Cosciani's Conclusions

As we have just noted, the nature of the Montevideo Treaty makes it possible to select step by step the most desirable procedure for the integration of Latin America and to make progress in eliminating the difficulties, sometimes even before they appear. In this sense it is extraordinarily useful to learn about the difficulties which, as Mr. Cosciani points out, have been involved in customs union and common market experiences and, very especially, the solutions to those difficulties.

It is possible that this is where the advantage of the Montevideo Treaty lies. Compared to other experiences, it is something of a reverse process. Others have established customs unions or common markets and then have gone about clearing away the problems. The Treaty of Montevideo provides for gradual progress toward the final structure, advancing stage by stage as the contracting parties consider it possible and as they succeed in solving the major problems of the changes necessary for integration.

In this connection, the fiscal problems of the free trade area should be studied from two standpoints: (a) problems related to the liberalization program, that is, the process currently under way, and (b) problems related to the processes of integration and complementarity which the contracting parties propose to undertake. We agree with Mr. Cosciani that the fiscal factor cannot play a very important role in the first group of problems mentioned above, but it is unquestionably of capital importance for the second group.

This is what we had in mind when we said that Mr. Cosciani's study contains an extremely worth-while contribution of suggestions for LAFTA.

From the analysis that Mr. Cosciani makes of the difficulties of a customs union and their solutions, he appears to conclude that most of those difficulties disappear in the common market.

The difficulties of the common market, in their turn, lie chiefly in achieving an adequate measure of tax harmonization that will produce the greatest possible leveling of the tax burden without neglecting the static and dynamic financial requirements of each state.

According to Mr. Cosciani, the best solution for this problem seems to indicate that "tax harmonization presupposes not only the beginnings of economic integration but also a unitary policy among the states." In short, the magnitude of the problems appears to be in inverse ratio to the degree of unification of the states.

Indeed, if we are correct in our appraisal of the final conclusions of the paper by the distinguished professor from the University of Rome, it must perforce be acknowledged that one task to which LAFTA must continue to pay special heed embraces precisely the two matters of concern that pervade the whole treaty: "progressive harmonization of their diverse systems and elimination of situations characterized by relatively less advanced stages of economic development."

Discussion

MR. COSCIANI explained that his paper had been based mainly on European experience in the field of economic integration and that possibly, therefore, some of the lines of approach adopted might not be applicable to the Latin American situation. He would have liked to expand the part relating to Latin America but had not had at his disposal sufficient statistical and legislative documentation on the fiscal systems of the region. He was therefore glad that Mr. Baca and Mr. Cazal would be giving additional information on the Latin American Free Trade Area and the Central American integration system.

He suggested that it would be a mistake to attach too much importance to fiscal problems bearing on the establishment of a common market and especially to take for granted that they might be a cause of distortions without sufficient evidence that the latter really existed.

In his paper he had defined two extreme cases of economic integration, namely, the customs union and the common market. The former was essentially a commercial union among several countries which retained their sovereign independence with respect to their economic policy. A common market, on the other hand, implied closer economic ties and the unification of the monetary, credit, economic, and social policies of the member countries as well as the establishment of a juridical structure capable of exerting a more direct influence on production and trade. The basic principles of a customs union could be summed up as follows: (a) the prohibition of fiscal discrimination, (b) a ban on the formation of tax havens, (c) the co-ordination of fiscal policy for development, and (*d*) the problem of double taxation. In the last connection, he indicated the desirability of multilateral conventions like those formulated in Mexico City and London or the treaty currently being perfected by the Organization for European Economic Co-operation and Development.

The limitations affecting fiscal legislation within a customs union related to the principle of taxation in the country of destination, in which context various methods had to be considered, such as exemption at the time of export, export drawbacks, and compensatory import duties. A customs union implied the abolition of economic frontiers—those whose purpose was economic protection—and the maintenance of tax frontiers. The first of the limiting factors to be noted in connection with the principle of taxation in the country of destination was the question of indirect taxes. The usual method of calculating the drawbacks and compensatory duties corresponding to the legal incidence of taxation on imported goods was based on approximate averages implying discrepancies that were often impossible to eliminate and difficult to identify. The simplest solution would be to convert all multiple-stage taxes into a single tax on final consumption; or a tax on value added might even be introduced. The greatest difficulty lay in the dissimilarities between the fiscal systems concerned.

In its final form, a common market was analogous to an internal market and should therefore be characterized by complete freedom of movement not only of goods and services but also of the factors of production. In that case, the principle of taxation in the country of origin was applied, since the tendency was to do away with tax frontiers. To that end, some degree of harmonization of the fiscal systems of the various countries was essential, and its ultimate expression would be the establishment of a federal fund.

He thought that the fiscal problem was not yet very important for the Latin American Free Trade Area but that it was so in relation to Central American economic integration,

owing to the fact that integration was being rapidly intensified. It would be desirable to set up a group of experts to study the problem.

The CHAIRMAN explained that Mr. Cazal and Mr. Baca, who were commenting on Mr. Cosciani's paper, had been chosen not in their personal capacity but as representatives of the Latin American Free Trade Area and the General Treaty on Central American Economic Integration, respectively.

MR. CAZAL said he did not oppose Mr. Cosciani's view that a customs union and a common market constituted extreme cases, but in his opinion Mr. Cosciani's definitions of a customs union and a common market were relevant to Europe and differed from those applicable to other parts of the world.

Although it might very well be that in other regions problems of fiscal policy did not arise, they did so in Latin America because there were many countries whose revenue depended, for example, upon customs duties, and when the various countries agreed to include a revenue producing good in the common schedule of exemptions, the countries affected had to replace that source of revenue by another. Consequently, in Latin America a genuine problem of fiscal policy came to the fore even in the initial stage of product-by-product negotiations.

The basic objectives of the Montevideo Treaty establishing the Free Trade Area were the progressive liberalization of existing trade through the gradual elimination of tax barriers and an increase in the number of goods in which intra-area trade was carried on.

As Latin America had no previous experience in the field of integration, study had been devoted to the problems that might arise, and solutions had been sought before any measure was adopted. In that connection, he thought Mr. Cosciani's remarks on some of the fiscal problems that had presented themselves in Europe, where considerable previous experience of integration had existed, were of great interest, inasmuch as Latin America could profit by such object lessons and avoid stumbling into the same pitfalls. With reference to Mr. Cosciani's suggestions as to the establishment of a federal fund, he concluded that political integration would be needed to solve most of the difficulties, and that would lead to the definition of a principle which should be stated to the effect that the intensity of the problems was in inverse ratio to the intensity of integration.

Since all the Latin American countries were currently overhauling their fiscal policy and in addition were striving after economic integration, it would be highly advisable to take future fiscal problems into consideration —especially as many of them stemmed from the diversity of fiscal structures—and solve them in advance by endeavoring to introduce uniformity into the structures in question.

MR. BACA described the events leading up to the General Treaty on Central American Economic Integration and the principles by which it was inspired.

With reference to tax havens, he said that for the present there was no such problem in Central America, nor one of dual taxation, because the systems of direct taxation were very similar and because the tax on bearer securities, which offered most opportunities for evasion, was collected at the corporate level and at the same rate as personal income tax. The solution was not altogether satisfactory, since it discriminated against the large-scale business enterprise, which was precisely the type that should be encouraged.

In Central America the principle of taxation in the country of destination was always applied, since it was considered to be more equitable, especially as there were countries at a less advanced level of development than others, and it would not be fair for a less developed country to derive no revenue from the services rendered by the state for the protection of property and the development of enterprises belonging to foreigners.

Broadly speaking, fiscal problems did not seem very difficult to solve in Central America because the systems of the countries concerned closely resembled one another.

In reply to Mr. Cosciani's concluding remarks, he said that it had already been decided in Central America to set up a group of experts to study the problems in question, and the assistance of the Joint Tax Program would undoubtedly be requested.

MR. PIEDRABUENA drew the attention of the meeting to the Montevideo Treaty. From the Preamble it appeared that integration would soon be approached, but the articles themselves were often too unspecific in their phraseology and made no provision for some aspects of fiscal policy that were liable to cause difficulties in the future and which, as Mr. Cazal had pointed out, were extremely important.

One of the first gaps in the treaty was the lack of measures to rationalize or limit the use of incentives in Latin American countries to entice foreign capital. No mention had been made of the problems of double taxation, nor was there an explicit statement as to whether countries had a unilateral right to exempt exports from payment of duty. The question of fiscal subsidies had been left unclear, and no attempt had been made to solve problems of monetary devaluation. Last, insufficient attention had been paid to the burden that social security contributions represented for enterprises and individual taxpayers, which was a high proportion of the gross national product.

MR. JARACH considered that the matter of tax havens was highly important in relation to a customs union or common market. The achievement of economic integration at the cost of fiscal disintegration would defeat its own ends. Mr. Baca's view was that in Latin America the repercussions of the problem on corporations were inconsiderable. Clearly, however, even if dividends were taxed at the corporate level, there was still a loophole for evasion, as holdings might be falsified and a shareholder might thus evade personal income tax. Systems of corporate income tax would have to be brought into line with those applied to natural persons. A possible solution would be to maintain a relatively high level of taxation on corporations but to give the shareholder the option of having his share of the profits taxed as personal income, a corresponding credit being allowed for the tax paid by the corporation.

MR. MÉNDEZ supported Mr. Cazal's points of view with respect to the gaps in the treatment of fiscal problems in the Montevideo Treaty which had just been pointed out by Mr. Piedrabuena.

The free trade area created by the Montevideo Treaty should be regarded as the first step toward a more complete type of integration. Since it was about to advance toward that goal, the problems that might arise should be studied promptly in order not to delay the subsequent stages of integration. Unless immediate consideration were given to those problems and their solution, the results would be as serious as those of failing to devise a system of payments which would ensure rational multilateral equilibrium in the free trade area.

Since the free trade area was already being beset by fiscal problems at its present stage of development, it was clearly necessary for the signatory states to take steps to remedy the lacunae in the Montevideo Treaty either through a standing committee or by means of resolutions taken at the annual conferences which could subsequently be incorporated into the treaty. Otherwise there was a danger that discriminatory practices or exchange, fiscal, and monetary manipulations would invalidate the concessions negotiated under the treaty.

MR. MATUS considered that there were two major aspects of the analysis of fiscal problems in relation to the common market, and although it was true that one of them—the question of how to perfect fiscal mechanisms for economic integration—had been sufficiently elucidated, it was equally undeniable that the other, which concerned the reconciliation of the use of fiscal mechanisms for economic integration purposes with their application in favor of planning aims, had not received enough attention. The operation of a common market or customs union entailed the rejection of certain instruments that had been applied by planners because they might have discriminatory effects on trade.

Moreover, there was good reason to fear that in the early stages the free trade area might aggravate the inequity of income distribution, since there would be a tendency to invest in the introduction of technological improvements in existing industries; and at the same time, a price policy designed to create better competitive conditions would be pursued. If political and social structures were taken into account, such competition in Latin America would probably not be reflected in a reduction of entrepreneurs' profits but would affect wage policies. Such a situation would be counteracted if the common market encouraged the establishment of new industries, but that would not happen during the early years.

He agreed with Mr. Piedrabuena that social security contributions raised a serious problem in that context; a common market might possibly restrict the scope of such systems, and that would also help to perpetuate the existing inequitable distribution of income.

MR. CAZAL explained that the reason why he had not touched upon the points raised by Mr. Piedrabuena and Mr. Matus was that he had wished to confine himself strictly to the agenda item under discussion, and he felt that the topics in question could not properly be regarded as fiscal matters. He concurred with Mr. Piedrabuena's opinion that though the Preamble to the Montevideo Treaty spoke of final objectives, the operative part was much more cautious without providing clearly defined rules. It should not be forgotten that the Montevideo Treaty was not only describing a *fait accompli* but also sketching a program of future achievements. As its objectives were gradually attained, solutions would be found for the different problems. Thus, for example, the Montevideo Treaty took no decision on the maintenance of concessions and the problems of discrimination that might arise therefrom. But at the most recent meeting of the Latin American Free Trade Association, a specific decision had already been adopted in that connection. By degrees, all the aspects arising from the implementation of the treaty would be covered.

With reference to Mr. Matus' comments,

he did not see what limitations on the use of fiscal instruments for planning purposes were implicit in the establishment of a free trade area. On the contrary, LAFTA was also concerned with planning, and a meeting of planning experts to discuss such matters had already been convened for the first quarter of 1963. In Latin America the problem was not so much lack of co-ordination in the use of fiscal instruments for economic integration and planning as the lack of planning itself, even in countries which carried great weight in the region.

MR. MOISÉS BEATRIZ asked Mr. Cosciani how the Treaty of the European Economic Community had dealt with the difficulties that might be caused by the existence of state monopolies. For instance, a state monopoly in a given country might try to eliminate competition by levying an indirect tax on the item produced at home or abroad or by charging lower prices than its competitors.

MR. NAHARRO referred to the harmonization of indirect taxation for purposes of economic integration, which he regarded as a serious problem that was likely to cause great difficulties in Europe in the near future and should be given immediate consideration by the Latin American countries. The theoretical drawbacks and advantages of harmonization had been fully dealt with by Mr. Cosciani, but he was anxious for him to give the participants his personal opinion on the practical problems faced by the European Economic Community in that respect and their possibilities of solving them in the future, because he was aware that Mr. Cosciani had followed the question closely.

MR. MONTERROSO referred to the question of monetary planning in the Central American market. One institution set up for that purpose was the Central American Integration Bank, of which the five countries, parties to the treaty, were members. The bank took an active part in the work of planning since, before granting credit for new industries, roads, etc., it determined whether the use to which the funds were to be put would aid the process of integration.

Another institution was the Cámara de Compensación Centroamericana at Tegucigalpa, which had created an accounting currency, the "Central American peso," that was equivalent to the value of the dollar at a given date, thus averting the dangers of monetary devaluation in any of the member states.

The Central American system was therefore more advanced than LAFTA in that it was already making specific provision for the future.

MR. COSCIANI, referring to Mr. Cazal's remark that the definitions of a common market and a customs union applied in Europe were different from those current in Latin America, said that he had put two extreme cases merely for simplicity's sake and that each treaty adopted brought into being unions which might resemble others in greater or in lesser degree.

With regard to the problem of the reform of fiscal structure, he thought that both short-term and long-term reforms would have to be applied. The former related to changes conducive to the creation of a customs union. With respect to the latter, which would pave the way for the establishment of a common market, it was advisable to proceed with caution to avert the risk of failure.

He agreed with Mr. Cazal that when a higher degree of integration was attained, it became easier to solve the fiscal problem and that it would ultimately be possible to move from economic to political integration.

He then referred to Mr. Baca's remarks to the effect that it was more equitable to tax goods in the country of origin than in the country of destination because the taxes concerned could be regarded as payment for the public services by which an enterprise benefited and ought therefore to be collected by the state providing the services in question. In his opinion, the tax ought to be applied in the country of origin of the good, as he had pointed out in his paper, subject to the necessary compensation, because in that way uniform taxation on the consumer market could be achieved. The principle was not valid, however, in the case of trade between industrial and agricultural countries.

With regard to what Mr. Piedrabuena had said of the gaps in the Montevideo Treaty, he expressed the view that it was a trade treaty rather than anything else. He also agreed that there should be a high-level regulating agency.

He did not think that drawbacks could be established in respect of social security contributions, which were a form of taxation impossible to compute. In Europe no such drawbacks were made, but it was a problem that would have to be taken into consideration if the United Kingdom joined the Common Market, since social security costs were charged to the national budget.

In his opinion, the problem of specific taxes on consumption was insoluble, because the economic structure of the various countries differed, and if an attempt were made to tax similar goods and apply similar rates in all of them the financing of their budgets would be jeopardized.

With regard to the difficulties indicated by Mr. Naharro in the context of the harmonization of indirect taxes, he thought that the so-called "cascade" or multiple-stage taxes could be abolished and that each country might establish whatever over-all tax it deemed most appropriate (a tax on value added or any other), with a system of exemptions.

In reply to Mr. Monterroso's question as to how the problem of monopolies might be tackled within a common market, he said that once such a market was established, the creation of new monopolies would be prohibited, and that as far as fiscal monopolies were concerned, a distinction was drawn between fiscal revenue and business income.

12

Report of the Conference

PRELIMINARY REPORT*

1. The participants at the Conference on Fiscal Policy, which met in Santiago, Chile, under the auspices of the Organization of American States, the Inter-American Development Bank, and the Economic Commission for Latin America of the United Nations, were in agreement that the fiscal policy of the Latin American countries must be closely integrated with the economic development plans which these countries are preparing or implementing. Such integration must encompass the financial plans which will make economic development a realizable goal.

In this connection, fiscal policy must be broadly defined to include all state action which influences the amount and composition of public revenue and expenditures and private investment and consumption, including internal and external debt policy and the operations of autonomous state agencies.

2. The participants of the conference were in agreement that the overriding problem of Latin American countries is to increase public revenue both by means of taxation and through an increase in the income of public enterprises.

Increased revenue is essential to enable the countries of Latin America to spend more on purposes essential for development, both of a current and a capital nature. It is essential, also, in order to improve the relationship between the level of expenditures and the level of revenue. At the present time, most Latin American countries have sizable deficits in

*The drafting committee for this report was chosen at a meeting of the authors of papers and the Secretariat staff and consisted of Messrs. Arnold C. Harberger, Nicholas Kaldor, Victor L. Urquidi, and Marto Ballesteros, as representative of the Secretariat.

their public accounts which are a major cause of their continued inflationary tendencies and which, by swelling profits artificially, also aggravate the inequality in the distribution of income and wealth. Increased public revenue is thus seen as the most effective instrument both for the acceleration of economic growth and for the mitigation of social and economic inequality.

3. The participants of the conference are agreed that there is ample capacity in most Latin American countries to increase public revenues and that the single most important cause for the insufficiency of public revenue is the failure of the tax system to impose effective levies on the propertied classes. While the great masses of the population bear considerable fiscal burdens through indirect taxes of various kinds and also through personal taxes deducted at source, the benefits derived from the ownership of capital—whether in the form of income, capital gains, or the spending power derived from the ownership of wealth as such—largely escape taxation. Considerations of equity and of expediency alike require that any major reform of the tax system should ensure that the propertied classes, as well as the working classes, should pay their due share in the common burden.

4. The members of the conference are agreed that a comprehensive reorganization of the existing fiscal system is urgently called for and that this must encompass both a reform of existing taxes, so as to improve their yield, and the introduction of new taxes.

The participants recognize that the social, political, legal, and administrative characteristics of the various Latin American countries differ and that fiscal reform, to be effectively put into practice, must be conscnant with

402

local characteristics. However, recognition of such considerations does not imply a modification of the objectives or a reduction of the required pace or pervasiveness of tax reform. It is essential, if the goals of accelerated development and improved distribution are to be achieved, that countries overcome, by special efforts, such barriers as may in the past have prevented a comprehensive fiscal reform.

5. There was agreement that simultaneously with the reorganization of the tax systems there must be a rationalization and coordination of expenditure policy to assume efficient use of increased revenue to achieve accelerated economic growth and desirable social objectives. In this context, program and performance budgeting are essential tools.

6. The majority of the conferees are agreed that the most important objectives of a reorganization of the fiscal systems of Latin America relate to the following:

a) The reform of the system of indirect taxation.

b) The creation of a comprehensive unitary system of progressive personal income tax, which includes the taxation of capital gains both on mobile and immobile property.

c) The separation and harmonization of corporation and personal income taxes.

d) The imposition of heavier taxation on real property, both urban and rural.

e) The strengthening of the system of inheritance and gift taxation.

f) The placing of public enterprises on a self-sustaining basis through the adoption of adequate rates for services rendered.

g) The harmonization of the tax treatment of the income of foreign enterprises and of the income of residents received from abroad as well as of the taxation of income derived from capital in its various domestic uses.

Though these measures are discussed separately below, the conference recognized the high importance of considering the merits of any tax system, not on the basis of the effects of individual taxes, but on the basis of the total impact on the economy of the system as a whole.

7. As regards *the reorganization of indirect taxation,* it was generally felt that such taxation as at present administered is unnecessarily complicated, has undesirable economic effects in distorting the price system, and is also inefficient in terms of yield. It was felt that the reform of the existing systems could be so designed as to produce significant increases in yield and substantial improvements in progressivity while mitigating the economic distortions which such taxation involves.

Substantial increases in yield, together with important administrative simplifications, can be achieved by removing the multiplicity of specific taxes that now exist on articles of mass consumption and by substituting in their place a single sales tax with a low rate and a broad tax base. Improvement in progressivity, as well as further augmentation of yield, can be achieved by the special taxation of articles of luxury consumption such as automobiles, electrical appliances, jewelry, luxury clothing items, etc. Luxury items imported from abroad already bear substantial import duties in most cases, but there is no substantial indirect taxation of home-produced luxury articles, which now account for the greater part of luxury consumption.

Some of the members of the conference felt that there was a strong case for substituting a uniform and comprehensive *value added tax* in replacement of the existing sales and excise taxes. Such a tax would be payable by all enterprises on the difference between their total sales and their purchases from other enterprises—a difference which is approximately equal to the net income generated (in the form of profits, wages, salaries, interest, and rent) by each enterprise. It was also thought that since under this system enterprises would have to list their purchases from other enterprises in order to claim relief, the administration of this tax would enable the tax authorities to build up independent sources of information on the sales of each enterprise which in turn would be of inestimable value both in the proper enforcement of indirect taxation and in the efficient administration of direct taxation. A universal value added tax could thus provide the basic framework for the effective administration of the whole tax system.

8. With regard to *income tax*, the participants agreed that the Latin American countries should aim at the introduction of a unitary system which encompasses all forms of income, including capital gains on the sale of mobile or immobile property, and that it should avoid exemptions such as interest on government bonds or on mortgages which are ostensibly introduced for incentive reasons but which in fact weaken the effectiveness of the tax.

9. It was agreed that an essential requirement for the efficient operation of a *personal income tax* system is that the rate schedule should be both simple and moderate. While it was thought that the exemption levels should be higher, in relation to average income per head, than those obtaining in the developed countries, it was felt that the existing exemption levels are too high in many cases. The participants agreed that there was no point in starting to levy tax at a very small rate, as is the custom in many Latin American countries, and that there are too many separate tax brackets. Ten per cent may be regarded as a reasonable minimum chargeable rate for income in excess of the exempted amount, and the rate of tax on successive brackets of income should rise by steps of no less than 5 per cent. It is an essential precondition of an effective system that the maximum rate of tax should not be an immoderate one.

The present high nominal rates (exceeding 70 per cent in some cases) make it in practice impossible to extend the tax to all forms of income (for example, capital gains) or to get rid of numerous exemptions. They also make it impossible to secure the willing cooperation of the taxpayer; they are the cause of much waste of time and talent in the search for tax loopholes; and they induce too high a temptation to corruption and bribery.

It must also be remembered that the revenue obtained at present from the excess of marginal tax rates over 50 per cent is exceed-

ingly small in all countries. With more moderate ceiling rates—say, of the order of 50 to 60 per cent—the extension of income tax to cover capital gains presents no insuperable difficulty, though in conditions of substantial inflation it may be advisable to make some allowance for the increase in the price level in calculating the net gain on capital assets. It is essential, on the other hand, that capital should be recognized and brought into charge whenever there is a change of ownership of capital assets, irrespective of whether it is by way of sale, gift, or inheritance.

10. The participants of the conference were agreed that when a person owns disposable property, the ownership of such property confers advantages which are distinct from and additional to the income which is derived from such property. It was suggested, therefore, that in addition to a progressive income tax there should also be a *progressive tax on net wealth* of individuals or families. For this purpose "wealth" should include property in the form of real estate and financial assets, as well as valuable personal possessions, and "net wealth" is the excess of the value of such property over liabilities. Such a net wealth tax should be levied at relatively low rates, rising from, say, 0.5 to 2 per cent per annum on the wealth in excess of, say, twenty times the per capita income so as to bear a proper relationship to the additional taxable capacity derived from the ownership of wealth. It was recognized that the net wealth tax requires a high degree of efficiency of tax administration, and therefore its introduction in the near future may be advisable only for countries which possess these administrative prerequisites.

11. The participants agreed that the administration of the income tax could be greatly improved if the individual taxpayer were required to make a regular and full disclosure of all the real property, stocks, shares, etc. owned by him and that the tax authorities should be in a position to verify the completeness and accuracy of the taxpayer's returns.

Legal and administrative procedures need

to be established, therefore, which enable the identification of the beneficial ownership of immobile property and of financial assets. This requires the compulsory registration of all real property in the name of the beneficial owner and the adoption of means whereby the ownership and transfer of securities (including bearer shares) are comprehensively registered with the tax authorities.

An efficient administration of the income and real property taxes also requires the establishment of suitable procedures for the valuation of capital assets at their approximate market value. Under present conditions in Latin America this necessitates a significant strengthening of both the technical and administrative capacity of tax enforcement administrations. Other techniques for achieving efficient assessment of property require further detailed consideration.

12. The participants were agreed that corporation income tax rates should not be fixed so high as to deter new investment and risk taking nor so low as to favor foreign governments unduly. While some progression in rates may be justified to favor small businesses, progressive rate schedules are not appropriate to corporations in general. Moreover, undue progression invites corporate split-ups and evasion and impedes the exploitation of the economies of scale.

13. The participants of the conference felt that an effort should be made to rationalize and harmonize existing and possible new taxes on the income from different classes of property. Traditional taxes in this area include the corporation income tax, the tax on urban real estate, and the tax on agricultural property. It was felt that, in the interests of equity and also of an efficient allocation of resources, the different forms of capital should bear an approximately equal weight of tax, when income and capital taxes are considered together. This consideration suggests the possibility of imposing additional taxes on those forms of income from capital—such as the profits of unincorporated enterprises and the interest paid by business firms—which now

do not bear any tax corresponding to the corporation income tax.

14. The conference felt that taxation of urban real estate and agricultural property is based in most countries on completely out-of-date valuations and is in urgent need of reform, both to provide an important source of revenue and also to serve major economic and social objectives.

In countries where the ownership of land is highly concentrated and where the prevalence of absentee ownership militates against the introduction of progressive techniques in agriculture, a progressive agricultural property tax is a potent instrument for increasing the efficiency of land use, for creating a freer market in land, and for promoting the objectives of agrarian reform. Especially for this last purpose, the conference felt that methods of agricultural property taxation based on potential rather than actual yield, or on the self-assessment method to be discussed below, were worthy of consideration.

15. The participants felt that rather than relying on direct estimation of agricultural income for personal income tax purposes, it was advisable that the assessment of such income should be based on the value of the properties from which the income was derived. It was emphasized that the taxation of personal income arising out of agricultural activities, even when based on the value of properties, was to be considered as distinct from and additional to the taxation of property as such.

A number of participants felt that in arriving at the value of agricultural properties, the method of self-assessment should be introduced. Under this method the owner would himself set the value of his property, but these values could be placed on public record, and any individual or enterprise would be free to make a bona fide bid to purchase the property. In the event that such a bid exceeded the owner's declared value by a significant amount (say, by 20 per cent), the owner, if he chose not to sell, would be required to revalue his property up to the amount which was bid. In this case the maker of the frustrated bid would be entitled to a premium, which might be in the amount of the extra tax obtained in the first year following the revaluation of the property. Where inflationary problems are of serious dimensions, provision would have to be made for the automatic readjustment of assessed values during the period between successive declarations required of the owner. As a possible alternative to this proposal, some participants suggested that owners be required to sell their properties at their declared values if the government, at its own initiative, chose to acquire them.

16. In order to counteract the tendency toward a growing concentration in the ownership of wealth, the conference felt that there should be progressive taxes on inheritance complemented by similar taxes on *inter vivos* gifts. These serve the purpose of reducing the importance of inherited wealth in the distribution of wealth and income, an objective which is distinct from the general goal of progressive taxation of reducing economic inequalities. If the recommendations made above concerning the full disclosure of property in connection with income tax are adopted, the administration of inheritance and gift taxes will no longer present special difficulties.

17. The conference felt that in the countries of Latin America the provisions of the law relating to foreign enterprises are relatively better administered than other provisions. However, attention was drawn to the fact that in a number of countries excessive concessions may have been granted to attract foreign investment. This is particularly true when this problem is considered from the point of view of the group of undeveloped countries as a whole. Concessions made by any one country, if successful, are more likely to divert the flow of funds from other countries than to increase significantly the total flow of such funds.

In addition, attention was drawn to the fact that it was possible in some cases for international companies to understate the value of their exports or to overstate the value of their imports and thereby show a smaller profit on their local accounts than the true profit arising from their local operations. The conference felt that both for the purpose of limiting undue concessions to foreign companies and for the purpose of ascertaining the true profit of such companies to be taxed, there is need for international consultations aiming at the adoption of uniform principles in the tax treatment of foreign enterprises.

18. The conference also felt that there is a strong case on equity grounds for extending the liability for income taxation to income received from abroad, as is already the case in most European and North American countries, particularly since the residents of many Latin American countries own very substantial amounts of capital abroad. The conference felt that in order to enforce such provisions the co-operation of foreign countries should be enlisted to provide information on incomes received by residents of Latin America. It is known that some countries already provide such information on a mutual basis under international tax treaties.

19. Finally, the conference felt that many Latin American countries fix the prices of services provided by public enterprises at unjustifiably low levels, thus depriving their governments of an important source of revenue. It is not often realized that the greater part of these services is sold, not to the final consumer, but to private enterprises, with the effect that the profits of private enterprises are artificially raised at the same time as the profits of public enterprises are kept at low or even negative levels. The participants felt that a reasonable goal of price policy for most public sector enterprises would be to obtain profit rates comparable to the gross-of-tax profit rates achieved in the private sector. This is especially important in Latin American countries where the profits earned in public enterprises can provide a significant source of financing for the needed expansion of their operations.

Discussion

The CHAIRMAN read a statement by Mr. Victor Urquidi, one of the participants at the conference, whose pressing duties had compelled him to leave Santiago the previous day. Mr. Urquidi felt that the task of the experts at the conference had not been to speculate on new forms of taxation, ingenious and interesting though they might be, but to deal with fiscal policy within the framework of existing political and social institutions and to guide it into areas which would, above all, increase the resources a government needed in order to give greater impetus to economic development programs as soon as possible. A critical examination of Latin American tax systems disclosed major defects, and as a result the countries concerned might be tempted to experiment with fiscal techniques which had been proposed in many parts of the world. He felt that while new possibilities should be studied, the basic course to follow was to improve existing systems, create better fiscal structures, and ensure a more efficient administration in order to overcome the many obstacles to reform through public acceptance and a full understanding of the objectives sought.

In his view, the conference had made it clear that most of Latin America was not lacking the factors needed for a good tax policy directed toward economic development. There was growing awareness of the fact that fiscal policy as a whole—of which tax policy was a part—was but one feature of economic planning. Taxes were conceived in terms of their function in development plans, and that meant that the structure of demand and of supply had to be modified continually without necessarily following the indications provided by the free play of the market. Thus, many of the criteria which had so far prevailed in the more developed countries with respect to fiscal policy, and especially as regards the best way of combining the different taxes, would have to be revised and continually adapted.

Discussions such as those held at the conference should therefore continue, with the participation of experts from all over the world and of Latin American government officials and experts. At some future stage a joint meeting should be arranged between fiscal experts and tax administration experts and officials. Moreover, strong encouragement should be given to empirical research in fiscal questions, both in the Latin American countries themselves and in regional agencies such as the OAS, ECLA, the Latin American Institute for Economic and Social Planning, and the IDB.

Last, Mr. Urquidi pointed out that while tax reform was a very powerful instrument contributing to the economic and social changes to which the Latin American countries had committed themselves under the Punta del Este agreements, there must be a clear definition of the scope of fiscal policy. It was not a question of either instituting forthwith a drastic tax reform or else suffering a major economic and social catastrophe. There were many other elements militating in favor of the structural changes implied in economic development that were essential to an improvement in social conditions. Once the objectives were fixed, fiscal policy, in conjunction with other measures, could gradually and firmly be directed toward their attainment without having to bear the full responsibility for it. Moreover, it would be irresponsible to construe the delay required in the adoption and practical application of particular reforms as a weakening of the resolute aim of progress and social justice which the Latin American governments had set for themselves and which were fully supported by the experts at the present conference.

Speaking in his official capacity, the Chairman explained that the draft report before the conference was an attempt to capture the sense of the participants with respect to questions discussed, in the hope that the recommendations would prove useful to Latin American countries. The comments made during the general discussion would no doubt require revision of some of the statements in the provisional report, which would be amended accordingly. The participants should bear in mind that the conference was being held within the framework of the conclusions reached at the Punta del Este Conference regarding the economic and social objectives of the Latin American countries. The emphasis placed in the report on certain recommendations reflected the guidelines laid down at the Montevideo Conference.

MR. PAZOS attached importance to Mr. Pinto's table on the social distribution of tax instruments. He suggested that Mr. Pinto's percentage breakdown of the active population (5 per cent for the upper-income level, 35 per cent for the middle-income level, and 60 per cent for the lower-income level) should be changed to, say, 15 or 20 per cent for the middle-income groups and 75 per cent for the lower-income groups. He felt that would better reflect the true situation. He also suggested that the tax burden as given for the respective income groups was the desirable objective. The upper-income group at present carried only 33 per cent of the tax burden, and the lower-income group was carrying 60 per cent.

MR. WEISSMAN stressed the need to relate fiscal reform to over-all economic and social development and agreed that there was no dividing line between the legal structure and administrative techniques in the field of taxation. The report should emphasize the dedication of the countries concerned to move ahead in the field of fiscal policy within the framework of their legal structure.

MR. NAHARRO said that while he realized the work which had been involved in preparing the draft report, recourse should be had to what was known in parliamentary circles as a "drafting committee" not only in order to correct a few drafting errors but also to make some changes relating to concepts.

Thus, with respect to the second paragraph of Point 1, private investment and consumption was influenced by state action as a whole, particularly by certain types of action related to well-defined and accepted areas such as monetary, labor, and industrial policy and so forth. Even if Mr. Urquidi's broad conception of fiscal policy were accepted, some limits must be set, since the scope of the concept was somewhat vague. The danger of the text in the draft report was that it was less the exposition of a concept than the drawing up of a list. The solution might be to relate the fiscal instruments proper (revenue and expenditures) to the others by inserting the words "through them" before the reference to private investment and consumption.

In the first sentence of Point 3, it was stated that the single most important cause for the insufficiency of public revenue was the failure of the tax system to impose effective levies on the propertied classes. That was but partly true, since the insufficiency should also be attributed to deficiencies in tax administration. However, even if the statement were correct, it would seem impolitic to single out a segment of society which, after all, was part of the nation, with the same rights as all other citizens. He suggested, therefore, that the administrative deficiences should also be mentioned, and that such clauses as "one cause" or "another cause," etc., should be used.

With respect to the last paragraph of Point 7, he thought that a more suitable place should be found for it in the draft report since it dealt with a thorny subject—the value added tax—on which the views of participants had not been sufficiently aired. It would be wise, in any event, to delete whatever the paragraph included in the way of a potential threat to taxpayers in describing the possible use which the tax authorities could make of the data presented.

At the end of Point 12, he suggested the addition of the words "and sometimes put a premium of inefficiency" on the part of enterprises with low yields resulting from poor organization, etc., in other words, the exact opposite of the economies of scale.

Last, he deplored the fact that, save for an inadequate reference in Point 12, nothing was said in the draft report about the important function of tax incentives.

MR. PREST said that an economist should not compromise his technical expertise because of political or allied considerations. There were three levels at which an economist could operate: he could analyze the effects of different taxes on prices, output, capital formation, etc.; he could advise a government that if it wished to follow a given policy, it should apply a particular tax or taxes; or he could tell a government that income distribution should be changed and indicate how that could be done by taxation. For the last two courses of action, detailed statistical data were required, and the third involved political preconceptions. He believed that the lack of substantial statistical data before the present conference precluded any expression of precise views as to what should be done. Tracing the effects of a tax was something very different from recommending that governments should adopt it, particularly with reference to twenty different governments.

With respect to the draft report itself, he was strongly opposed to the first six paragraphs. The first sentence in Point 2 seemed to imply that increasing public revenue should take priority over all other political and social changes, and in the light of the declared aims of the conference, this appeared sweeping and even somewhat arrogant. The next sentence stated that increased revenue would enable Latin American countries to spend more on development, whereas in fact it would enable governments to spend more for such purposes; that implied a judgment of a political character which would be out of place in a report issued by the present conference. The draft report went on to suggest that sizable deficits in the public accounts in Latin America aggravated the unequal distribution of income and wealth, although no evidence had been produced at the conference in support of that view. There were other statements not thus far supported by any evidence, with respect to the low revenue obtained from high marginal rates (Point 9), the tendency toward a growing concentration in the ownership of wealth (Point 16), excessive concessions to foreign enterprises (Point 17), and the proportion of sales from public enterprises going to private enterprises (Point 19). In addition, there seemed to be possible inconsistencies in the arguments set forth; for example, was agricultural income to be taxed both under personal income tax and under the land tax? And how was it proposed to combine a system of high excise taxes on locally produced goods with the protection of developing local industries? Last, he doubted whether it was advisable to go into the degree of detail included in the draft report with respect to certain taxes, such as the specific rates of taxes on income and net wealth.

Having dealt with the faults of the draft report in its present form, he turned to the question of the form it should take and suggested that it should be confined to a summary of the different views expressed by the participants, including as many shades of opinion as possible, such as the opposing views on whether land taxation should be proportional or progressive, the relative merits of the corporate income tax and the value added tax, and so forth. It would not be advisable to state that the conference as a whole agreed on particular points or to include detailed recommendations about policy, and the report should go no further than to draw the general attention of the governments concerned to the issues raised in the papers and discussions. It would be quite inappropriate for a conference organized by respected international organizations to express views that were essentially political rather than economic. If it appeared that other participants did not share his views and if the document retained its present form, he must ask to be disassociated from it.

MR. MONTERROSO congratulated the sponsors of the conference and expressed his general agreement with the draft report. However, there were some points on which he disagreed. First, he thought the definition of fiscal policy was too broad and should be amended as suggested by Mr. Naharro. Second, the report did not seem to attach much significance to the redistributive aim that fiscal policy should have or to give sufficient emphasis to the importance of the role that public expenditure should play both in redistributing income and in economic development in the various countries. Nor was there much recognition of the importance for underdeveloped countries of increasing their expenditure on education and on transfer payments or on the economic effects of public expenditure and of the national debt. Third, he could not agree with the statement in Point 8 that there should not be exemptions of income tax on such income as the interest on government bonds; if such exemptions were appropriate in highly industrialized countries such as the United Kingdom, the same type of tax incentives must be regarded as necessary in much less developed countries where there was only a rudimentary form of stock market. Fourth, he suggested that the second paragraph of Point 7, stating that there was no substantial indirect taxation of home-produced luxury articles which now accounted for "the greater part of luxury consumption," should be amended so that the reference was to "a large part of luxury consumption," since even the most developed Latin American countries did not produce a substantial proportion of such goods.

MR. ABINADER thought that it would not be appropriate to suggest specific rates of taxation in the report and that the section on the taxation of agricultural property should be drafted very carefully since it was a controversial subject. He agreed with Mr. Pazo's remarks on Mr. Pinto's table.

MR. GOODE said that he could not agree with the Chairman as to the relative importance of the report of the conference and thought that the papers presented and the record of the discussions should overshadow the report. It would be imprudent for the conference to adopt such a specific and detailed document as the present draft.

He did not believe that the statement in Point 3 (that the failure to tax the propertied classes was the single most important cause of the insufficiency of public revenue) was based on confirming evidence, and he would not endorse it as a general proposition applying to all countries. The last sentence in Point 7 referred to a universal value added tax, which presumably meant one applying to agriculture and self-employed professionals as well as industrial and commercial enterprises, but the conference had never discussed a value added tax of that nature. Nor could he accept the general pronouncement against exemptions such as interest on government bonds or mortgages, in Point 8, which though usually inefficient might sometimes be useful. The specific rates mentioned in Point 9, though useful as illustrations in the discussions, were out of place in a final report that would be widely read; rates must depend on conditions in the country concerned. The statement in the next paragraph that all change of ownership of capital assets should be recognized and taxed as capital gains was too sweeping. In Point 10, the suggestion that there should be a progressive tax on net wealth in addition to a progressive income tax should be represented as advocated by some, or a few, of the participants rather than a general suggestion emanating from the conference as a whole. The implication in Point 12 that low rates of corporate income tax would favor foreign governments needed further clarification. Although he himself supported the idea of taxing income on a world-wide basis, as suggested in Point 18, he was not sure that that view was widely supported by other participants.

His criticisms were based on the fact that he took a different view of what was the appropriate nature of the final report of the conference, which should be more modest in scope than the present draft.

MR. VEGA congratulated the Chairman and his colleagues on the draft report now being discussed. He proposed the following amendments.

The last paragraph of Point 1 should read as follows: "In this connection, it should be pointed out that fiscal policy includes all state action which influences the amount and composition of public expenditure, including the problems posed by the external and internal debt, international treaties and common markets, and the operations of state agencies. Fiscal policy should, moreover, influence private consumption and investment, in order that these economic factors should contribute to the economic growth of the countries."

The following subclauses should be added to Point 6: "*h*) The provision of suitable incentives to private investment with a view to securing a harmonious growth of the economies. *i*) Fiscal reform should include both the legal and administrative aspects."

The following sentence should be added to Point 15: "This recommendation is, of course, valid only in those countries where it does not conflict with legal or constitutional provisions."

The following new point should be added to the report: "20. Since capacity to pay is the chief factor in taxation, the conference believes that some government works and services should be self-financed, either on the basis of well-calculated rates or of taxes related to the principle of the benefit received."

As a general recommendation based on orderly arrangement, he proposed that all the points dealing with the same subject or the same tax should be brought together.

MR. DESAI agreed with other speakers that the report should include some reference to incentives. There should also be a reference to Mr. Herschel's suggestion that more fiscal research was required. In Point 7, a single sales tax with a broad tax base was recommended in place of excise taxes, but Indian experience suggested that a sales tax was very difficult to administer compared with an excise tax; if the tax was to be broad-based, a value added tax would be preferable. He agreed with Mr. Goode that the reference at the end of Point 7 to a universal value added tax was incorrect. In any case, the conference should be cautious in recommending a tax which was comparatively new in practice. He also agreed with Mr. Goode about the in-

advisability of including specific rates and suggested that the reference in Point 10 should be to a multiple of the per capita income rather than to the specific multiple of twenty. He would like to see in Point 16 a reference to his suggestion that gift and inheritance taxes should be combined in a single accession tax. He would also like to see special emphasis on the fact that whatever the fiscal capacity of the Latin American countries might be, it far exceeded the present revenue collected. There should also be more emphasis on the obligation of governments to spend wisely. The second paragraph of Point 1 seemed irrelevant, and if included in the final report it should be redrafted to read: "In this connection, fiscal policy must be broadly related to all state action which influences. . . ."

MR. HARBERGER said there appeared to be a difference of views as to the degree of strength appropriate to such a report. He thought that it was generally agreed that governments needed to spend more on development. That did not imply any conclusion as to what should be the scope of the public sector, since it was recognized that even in accordance with any minimum concept of that scope, not enough was being achieved in Latin America, and he cited educational services as an outstanding example. With respect to the criticism that not enough data had been presented at the present conference to warrant certain types of conclusions, he said that if statements made in the presence of acknowledged experts in the field from the countries concerned were not disputed, they could be regarded as accurate. As for the general tone of the report, he pointed out that the same tone had already been adopted in official agreements signed by all the governments concerned, with the exception of Cuba, and that the Act of Bogotá and the Charter of Punta del Este implied acceptance of the facts on which the draft report was based. It did not appear amiss to maintain a tradition already embodied in the official policies of the countries of the hemisphere.

MR. HERSCHEL considered that the task of experts, far from being confined to an analysis of developments and of institutions, should also include making practical recommendations that governments could use in working toward their economic development objectives. He explained the reasoning underlying certain parts of the report. He agreed with what Mr. Naharro had said about the last part of Point 1, but not with what Mr. Naharro and Mr. Vega had said about incentives, since he himself considered that there had been general agreement at the conference in condemning the abuses to which a policy of tax incentives could lead. He agreed with Mr. Pinto's suggestion for a systematic integration of the various taxes.

MR. COSCIANI said that he agreed with the criticisms leveled by other speakers at the second paragraph of Point 1, and he proposed that the very broad expression "all state action" should be replaced by the more precise expression "all action relating to the national budget." He did not consider that the reorganization of fiscal systems proposed in Point 4 need be "comprehensive"; it would be sufficient if the reorganization were described as extensive. He asked what was meant by "heavier taxation" in subsection d) of Point 6. He doubted that the list of purchases compiled as a basis for calculating the value added tax could be used as suggested in the third paragraph of Point 7 and said that the system of records employed for that tax in France and Italy did not lend itself to such a use of the tax. He did not think that capital gains should be liable to income tax, as stated in Point 8. He also thought the reference to suggested rates of personal income tax in Point 9 inappropriate and that a more general formula based on parameters would be preferable to listing percentages. He was also opposed to a register of transfers of assets, as proposed in the second paragraph of Point 11, on the grounds that the system would be incomplete and should not be recommended for underdeveloped countries. Nor did he agree that personal income from agriculture should be imputed on the basis of the value of the properties concerned, as maintained in Point 15.

He concluded by saying that he was not in complete agreement with the draft report as a whole and consequently reserved the right to disassociate himself from it and to make public comments on the work of the conference.

MR. PINTO was generally in agreement with the character of the draft report, which contained recommendations and was not merely descriptive. While he intended to submit a number of suggestions to the executive officers which, in his view, would improve the report, he wished to make a general comment on certain taxes.

With respect to the personal income tax, dealt with in Point 9, he asked whether the tax base was to be narrow or broad. That was an important consideration in taking a decision regarding the proposals contained in that point. The intention of the drafters was not clear from the present wording.

MR. BACA agreed with the general tone of the report, particularly with the emphasis placed on the yield both from the income tax and from indirect taxes insofar as they were levied on the middle- and high-income groups.

In his view, the wording of Point 6 of the draft report could be improved by amending subclauses a) and c) and rearranging the order of subclauses d) and g).

He was opposed to the special taxation of articles of luxury consumption which was suggested in the second paragraph of Point 7 as a means of augmenting yield.

With respect to Points 17 and 18, he was skeptical as to the possibility of obtaining practical results from the information which foreign countries were expected to provide under the recommendation in the draft report.

MR. DARDÓN said that he wished to refer only to two items in the draft report. The first was the definition of fiscal policy. He did not believe that it was or should be an essential aim of the experts participating in the conference to seek a definition, in the strict sense, since that would seem to imply that they did not already have a full understanding of that concept, which was completely untrue. The problem was to analyze what was the scope and content of the concept of fiscal policy that would help in attaining the aims and objectives of the conference. Consequently he considered that the second part of Point 1 of the draft report should be so redrafted as to take account of that view.

The second item related to the alternative set forth in Point 15 of the draft report. As he had stated when the self-assessment procedure had been discussed earlier, it was already used in Guatemala but not in the form of forced sale of properties recommended in Point 15. That alternative method conflicted with the right to dispose freely of private property, which was enshrined in most of the constitutions of the Latin American countries. To include it in the report might therefore give rise to harsh criticism by the sectors concerned, not only of that particular point, but of the whole philosophy of the report. Consequently he suggested that the paragraph in question be deleted altogether in order to obviate criticism that might prejudice the aims of the conference.

Mr. DESCARTES agreed with those who had suggested that emphasis be placed in the report on the operating machinery of fiscal policy, in other words, the application and administration of fiscal measures. He also supported those who favored the inclusion of a paragraph on tax incentives and shared the view of the participants who were opposed to the inclusion of specific rates of taxation. He felt that the reference to the value added tax in Point 7 should be toned down somewhat, since no agreement had been reached as to the applicability of such a tax.

On Point 8, he agreed with Mr. Goode that the objection to exemptions on interest on government bonds or mortgages was not valid.

On Point 10, the word "agreed" was too strong. Something like "the view was expressed" was better.

The first sentence in Point 15 was more applicable to the least developed countries than to Latin America as a whole. The references to self-assessment gave the wrong im-

pression, since it was at best a short-term measure. That should be pointed out in the report.

With respect to taxation of agricultural land, the support expressed at the conference for the proposals made in Mr. Wald's paper was not reflected in the report.

He agreed with the views expressed in Point 18, but with respect to Point 19 he felt that the report should point out that the price of public services in Latin America should not only cover costs but also provide social benefits.

Mr. KALDOR said it was for the Latin American countries to decide whether or not they agreed with the basic message of the report as drafted and were willing to face its implications. That message was that the weakness of the Latin American tax systems lay in their inability to get at the income from property, which represented such a large share of the national income. If the system was to be changed so that the propertied classes bore their fair share of the tax burden, radical action was required; capital gains must be treated as income, and there must be a full disclosure of individual wealth to enable the tax authorities to verify individual returns in relation to income from real property or shares and the possession of capital assets. He did not agree with Mr. Cosciani that bearer shares were an essential requirement in underdeveloped countries. Either they should be abolished or information about their ownership should be made available through a system of deposit with registered banks that kept a record of owners that would be accessible to the tax authorities. The basic proposition before the conference was that it was wrong for the capitalist classes to escape taxation. The technical question followed of whether it was possible to introduce a system to tax those classes effectively, and if so, what the implications would be. Experience in India and Ceylon showed that it was not impossible to establish a net wealth tax in underdeveloped countries. The difficulties were political, not technical. Some Latin American participants had said that not enough stress had been placed on income redistribution, which amounted to the same as forcing the propertied classes to surrender to the state their due share of tax.

He agreed that the reference in the draft report to the value added tax should make it clear that the subject was merely aired, without any conclusions being reached. The fact that in France it was not used to provide a framework for the administration of other taxes did not mean that it could not be so used; there was no reason not to take advantage of the potential self-reinforcing features of that tax. He agreed with other speakers that the second paragraph of Point 1 was not useful and thought it could well be deleted.

MR. RODRÍGUEZ MOLINA felt that great care should be taken in the drafting of the report before it was published in order to avoid criticism which might deform and even vitiate it. While there might be agreement on the basic points, he felt that the final report should be limited to the necessary general appreciations and considerations. Several alternatives should be provided so that a choice could be made, depending upon the different cases involved and the individual characteristics of each country.

With respect to Point 2, he felt that emphasis should be placed on the need not only to increase revenue but also to program public expenditure and to control it properly so that it might contribute effectively to the desired economic development. A recommendation should be made that state agencies must be efficient.

In connection with Point 3, the general comments made were not quite suitable. Each Latin American country had its own peculiar conditions, and it should therefore be left to each state to make use of tax incentives in the way best suited to its needs.

MR. HART said that the value of a report from the conference lay largely in that it gave the economist participating in a tax reform discussion an insight into the opinions of his colleagues in other countries. From that standpoint, the authors of the provisional report were right to discuss many types of taxes.

It would be desirable to recommend that a strong and well-integrated combination of the suggestions made in the report should be adopted and to point out that each suggestion had its economic merits and deserved serious consideration in every country where it would be administratively feasible.

In view of those two suggestions, an effort should be made to keep intact the list of objectives in Point 6, since if the items were quoted separately they might be misinterpreted. For instance, it might be assumed that to *enact* a tax was *to put it into effect*. Defects in administration could so distort a good tax that its application might do more harm than good.

He wished to make a specific suggestion that the following subparagraph be added to Point 6: "*b*) Establishment of an objective and co-ordinated system of administration, using each tax to give more solidity to others, so as to guarantee that the benefits of substantive reforms will not be lost in administration."

MR. JARACH suggested that a preface should be added to the report in which it would be clearly stated that, although the conclusions reached by the conference were based on a general consensus of opinion, reservations had been expressed by some of the participants.

With respect to Point 2 of the provisional report, the words "the overriding problem" in lines 1 and 2 should be replaced by "one of the overriding problems."

The list of points in Point 6 did not include any mention of the co-ordination of personal income tax with the net wealth tax. In Part *d*) of the same paragraph, the words "the imposition of heavier taxation" should be replaced by "the imposition of taxes with particular incidence on real property." Some indication should also be given that the tax on rural property ought to be applied as an alternative when such co-ordination could not be achieved.

With respect to Point 10, he considered that a progressive tax on net wealth would be a little too severe and that a proportional tax would be enough to serve its purpose. With further reference to the same paragraph, he thought that it was dangerous to give examples of low rates. It would be more desirable to define a moderate rate.

Point 15 contained a conceptual error, since it was the value of capital that was determined on the basis of potential income instead of vice versa.

MR. MÉNDEZ said that it was necessary to amplify Point 5, bearing in mind the view put forward by various participants that stress should be laid on the need to rationalize and co-ordinate fiscal expenditure in order to ensure that it played a useful part in economic and social development and provided an effective instrument for redistributing income.

It had been suggested that the systematic application of integrated development programing and the adoption of public investment plans would be particularly effective for achieving those aims, since they would enable a proper assessment to be made of how far public expenditure could and should be in co-ordination with the interests and requirements of the private sector in the process of development and allow such expenditure to be distributed in the way that would most conduce to a progressive solution of social and economic problems. For the satisfactory implementation of public investment plans, he specifically stressed the value of the technique of program budgeting, which was already being applied in some Latin American countries.

He also pointed out that, as part of the movement toward economic integration which was already under way in Latin America, studies should be undertaken on the problems of fiscal co-ordination that might arise in the course of integration, in order to prevent certain fiscal practices from distorting trade transactions among the countries concerned.

MR. MOISÉS BEATRIZ suggested a new schema for the presentation of the report. going from the general to the particular and from points on which there was unanimous agreement to those with which only a minority

concurred, since he had observed during the discussion on the report that the participants agreed on theoretical aspects but differed considerably when they came to deal with specific taxes.

The CHAIRMAN thanked Mr. Moisés Beatriz for his suggestion but thought that it would be possible to take into account all the views expressed by the participants without changing the presentation of the report.

MR. PORRAS said that successful achievement of the aims of fiscal policy depended on the instruments used. That was why it was important to improve financial techniques. Changes could be made in the legal structure at any time, but they should be accompanied by a reform of the financial administration. Such a reform would not be easy, but it was essential to break down administrative apathy, and time was needed to perfect the technique and even the hierarchy of administration.

With respect to Point 3, he pointed out that equity could be achieved not only through a revision of the tax laws but also through financial administration. It was essential for the tax laws to be codified.

He suggested that the following sentence be added at the end of Point 4, in order to make it quite clear that the purpose sought was redistribution of income: "in such a way as to enable highly regressive taxes to be abolished or at least substantially reduced in favor of the lower-income groups that form the bulk of the population."

In relation to Point 8, he pointed out that in countries where capital was scarce, incentives had to be created for the purchase of government bonds by private persons. Accordingly, he thought that the interest on bonds or mortgages created for economic development purposes should be tax free.

He also considered that the rent of owner-occupied property should be assessed and taxed.

The net wealth tax referred to in Point 10 would, in his opinion, be difficult to apply in the absence of an efficient tax administration.

In connection with Point 14, it seemed to him that if the objectives of land reform were to be achieved, tax administration should be in the hands of the central government.

He was not in agreement with the view put forward in Point 14 that the author of a bid that had been rejected should share in the tax increment, because it would be difficult in such circumstances to ensure that the bids made for properties were bona fide.

MR. RAPOPORT agreed that greater significance should be attached in the report to the management of public funds, particularly since the only way to enlist the co-operation of the private sector was to convince it that the government authorities were making effective use of their funds for constructive ends and were not wasting them through superfluous expenses such as adding unnecessarily to the number of civil servants.

The guidelines laid down by Mr. Pinto regarding the distribution of national and fiscal income served a useful purpose, although he did not think that specific figures should be included. In Argentina, the structure was similar to the one presented, although it might be different in other countries.

With respect to the description of rates, he thought that the term "moderate" was inadequate and should be replaced by "equitable," "reasonable," or "fair."

He felt that the tax on net wealth would have a progressive effect even though the rates might be proportional. There was no need to mention specific rates.

MR. MATUS said that he knew a great many people who were skeptical of the objectives of the Alliance for Progress because they considered them to represent a long overdue reaction, but until the present conference he had not encountered conservatives who looked upon the principles of the Alliance as too progressive and opposed income redistribution and planning.

The statement made by Mr. Prest at the previous meeting had led him to doubt the interpretation, since Mr. Prest had seemed to him to be asking for proof of things that were self-evident to everyone. No one present could doubt that the propertied classes were practicing tax evasion or that they should

make a fundamental contribution to economic development. He fully agreed with Mr. Harberger's replies to Mr. Prest during the same meeting.

There were several gaps in the provisional report that should be filled. No criticism of market forces had been made, nor had any definite statement been made with respect to the general framework of a tax system. In that connection, Mr. Pinto's comments should be taken into account and an analysis included of the intercontrol mechanisms that operated among the different taxes. Lastly, the use of taxes to promote development had not been explored. In Point 2, reference was made to fiscal deficits in relation to stability. He assumed that the authors of the report were not attempting to suggest that if deficits were eliminated stability would be achieved. If so, the paragraph should be redrafted. Moreover, frequent references were made to the distorting effects of indirect taxes, which was absurd since a great deal of distortion already existed. Arguments of that kind should be suppressed, or the report would have an old-fashioned flavor. He regretted that more attention had not been paid to the taxation of foreign enterprises.

With respect to public expenditure, he fully supported the remarks made by Mr. Méndez and added that greater details should be given on the budget as a short-term plan of action. The examination of incentives in the report was sketchy. The fact that their importance had been exaggerated in the past did not mean that they should be entirely overlooked in the present.

He also pointed out that the report failed to deal with the fiscal aspects of a common market.

He fully agreed with the political tone of the draft report, which was in line with contemporary thought.

MR. CASAS agreed with Mr. Jarach that a paragraph should be introduced into the report explaining that the ideas included did not necessarily represent unanimous views. He suggested that the first sentence of Point 2 should read, "The participants of the conference were in agreement that from the standpoint of the aims of fiscal policy the overriding problem of Latin American countries is to increase public revenue both by means of taxation and through an increase in the income of private enterprises." In Point 3 he thought that the phrase after "the tax system" should be replaced by the phrase "impose effective levies lower than the capacity to pay." He considered the idea of compulsory registration of transfers of assets to be naïve. Lastly, he suggested that the report should include a reference to the need for every country to make a careful study of the distribution of the tax burden and of the methods resorted to by taxpayers to evade income tax.

Mr. Gnazzo thought that the draft report adopted the correct approach, but he agreed with Mr. Jarach as to the desirability of indicating that in some cases there might be basic objections by certain participants. He agreed with Mr. Méndez on the need to expand the reference to public expenditure. He thought that the scheme suggested by Mr. Pinto might be included as an item of general economic policy but that it would not be useful to include his figures, since those would have to vary according to circumstances. He suggested that a subitem g) should be added to Point 6, referring to incentives, the co-ordination of taxes on wealth and income, the ideas on tax administration put forward by Mr. Hart, and the need to codify and simplify tax legislation.

Mr. Vidal supported the idea of including a paragraph explaining that there were differences of opinion to be found in the summary records and in other conference documents. He also pointed out that there was no reference whatever to tax incentives. Referring to Point 4, he said that there should not be any reference to the introduction of new taxes, since the question was rather that of reorganizing the taxation system.

Mr. Jatar-Dotti agreed that the paragraph on public expenditure should be expanded and thought it was important to distinguish between incentives, more liberal depreciation allowances, and deferred compensation for losses.

Mr. Fernández considered that the report should have referred more directly to the aims and methods of economic development.

Mr. Lessa agreed with Mr. Matus' remarks on price distortion, since the purpose of indirect taxation was precisely to change relative prices. As regards taxes on luxury goods, he thought that the meaning of the term should be clarified. It should be explained that it referred to superfluous consumption over and above that of the mass of the population. With reference to Point 12, taxes on corporate income should be based on the rate of return, irrespective of the amount involved.

Mr. Piedrabuena said that a special paragraph on inflation should be included. He believed that the net wealth tax should not be a special tax but a complement to income tax. The references to corporations should include some mention of the incorporation of the masses into the capital formation process as being one of the aims sought. With respect to Point 15, he did not agree with the idea of self-assessment or the punitive measures suggested. Other omissions in the report that should be repaired concerned tax policy in relation to LAFTA and the question of planning.

Mr. Martínez was of the opinion that the second paragraph of Point 2 should not refer to the expansion of revenue to provide more funds for current expenditure, since the phrase was open to misinterpretation. Point 6 should outline a general framework for tax reform, with due regard for the suggestions made by Mr. Matus and Mr. Pinto.

With respect to the mention made in Point 3 of the need to tax the propertied classes, some indication should be given that, apart from reasons of equity, such taxes represented the price they should pay for maintaining their privileged position.

Mr. Harberger remarked that Mr. Lessa's statement was not incompatible with his own views. The important thing was simply not to lose too much fiscal revenue through the application of the systems in question.

With reference to Point 6 *c*) of the preliminary report, he suggested that it be recast as follows: "The collection of more revenue from taxes on urban and rural property, which are additional to personal income taxes on the income derived from such property and which should also be co-ordinated with other forms of special taxation of income from property."

He further suggested that subparagraphs *d*) and *g*) be combined and replaced by the following: "Tax incentives are a powerful instrument for channeling the resources of an economy toward the desired ends and preventing their diversion to less important uses. They should nevertheless be carefully studied with a view to ascertaining whether they can obtain results without unduly reducing fiscal revenue. It should also be pointed out that tax incentives are more effective in changing the distribution of investment than in increasing its total amount, owing to the fact that an increment in the said amount can be obtained only if a country's total savings increase."

MR. KALDOR had two comments to make. First, he agreed with Mr. Harberger's remarks on incentives but thought they should be rephrased so as to stress the point that true incentives did not imply a loss of revenue but were actually a stimulus to production.

Second, he thought that if the report was to be prefaced by an introduction of the kind proposed by Mr. Jarach, he did not think that the inclusion of the net wealth tax would commit its opponents too deeply. It should not be included as a kind of tax on real property, however, since it was a new idea which, as some speakers had emphasized, should be integrated with a progressive income tax if introduced at all. The need for integration, which would considerably increase the efficacy of the income tax, should be underlined in the relevant paragraph of the report.

MR. GOODE thought that a strong case could be made for the net wealth tax on grounds of economic expediency and justice but wondered whether it would be possible to apply it in Latin America at the present

stage of its tax administration. The tax was not widely used, being most successfully applied in Sweden and the Netherlands, where the tax administration was particularly good.

MR. KALDOR stated, with reference to Mr. Goode's remarks, that he knew of eighteen countries where the tax was being applied in a progressive way and always at a low rate of about 2 per cent. He agreed that it was not an easy tax to apply, since it required a full disclosure of property on the part of the taxpayer, but he did not consider that it was any more difficult than either income tax or the tax on capital gains. It was necessary to draw attention to the difficulties of application in the report, but no distinction should be made between one tax and another.

FINAL REPORT

1. The participants were in agreement that the fiscal policy of the Latin American countries must be closely integrated with the economic development programs which these countries are preparing or implementing. This integration must encompass the financial plans for such economic development programs.

2. The participants at the conference likewise agreed that an overriding problem in the fiscal field in Latin American countries is that of increasing public revenue both by means of taxation and through an increase in the income of public enterprises.

3. Increased revenue is essential to enable the countries of Latin America to spend more on purposes essential for development and on the mitigation of social and economic inequality. It is essential also in order to improve the relationship between the level of expenditure and the level of revenue. At the present time, most Latin American countries have sizable deficits in their public accounts which are a major cause of their continued inflationary tendencies and which, by swelling profits artificially, also aggravate the inequality in the distribution of income and wealth.

4. The participants were agreed that there is ample capacity in most Latin American

countries to increase public revenue and that among the most important causes for the insufficiency of such revenue is the failure of the tax system to impose effective levies on the wealthy classes and to collect existing ones. While the great masses of the population bear considerable fiscal burdens through indirect taxes of various kinds and also through personal taxes deducted at source, those who possess capital and derive ordinary income and capital gains, or otherwise have taxpaying ability, largely escape taxation. Considerations of equity and of expediency alike require that any major reform of the tax system should ensure that the wealthy classes, as well as the working classes, pay their due share of the common burden.[1]

5. There was agreement that a comprehensive reorganization of the existing fiscal systems is urgently called for and that this must encompass a reform of the structure and administration of existing taxes so as to improve their yield, as well as the introduction of new taxes.

6. The participants recognized that the social, political, legal, and administrative characteristics of the various Latin American countries differ and that fiscal reform, to be effectively put into practice, must be consonant with local characteristics. However, recognition of such considerations does not imply a modification of the objectives or a reduction of the required pace or pervasiveness of tax reform. It is essential, if the goals of the accelerated development and improved distribution are to be achieved, that countries overcome, by special efforts, such barriers as may in the past have prevented a comprehensive fiscal reform.

7. The participants, while overwhelmingly supporting the need for augmented public revenue and expenditure, were equally emphatic in insisting on the improvement of expenditure policy. Even in the face of today's inadequate revenues, it was recognized that

much wasteful expenditure is undertaken in the Latin American countries. Greatly improved methods of over-all investment planning, of project evaluation, of checking the performance of public sector operations, and of control over current expenditures of governments are all essential if the burdens of increased taxation are to bear the fruits to which the conference aspires.

8. It was agreed that the most important aspects of a reorganization of the fiscal systems of Latin America relate to the following:

a) The reform, simplification, and updating of the system of indirect taxation.

b) The creation of a comprehensive unitary system of progressive personal income tax, which includes the taxation of capital gains both on real and personal property, complemented by a net wealth tax where feasible.

c) The collection of more revenue from taxes on urban and rural property, additional to personal income taxes on the income derived from such property, and co-ordinated with other forms of special taxation of income from property.

d) The strengthening of the system of inheritance and gift taxation.

e) The placing of public enterprises on a self-sustaining basis through the adoption of adequate rates for services rendered.

f) The harmonization of the tax treatment of the income of international enterprises and the imposition of taxes on the income which residents receive from abroad.

g) The creation of a fiscal climate which, with the cautious use of incentives, will be attractive to the formation of private capital and its investment in productive enterprise.

h) The reform of budgetary practices and the inclusion in budgets of the operating results of autonomous agencies.

i) The establishment of an objective and co-ordinated system of tax administration, using each tax to give more solidity to the others, so as to guarantee that the benefits of substantial reform will not be lost in administration.

---

[1] The problems of tax administration were considered during the conference held at Buenos Aires in October, 1961. While the Santiago Conference dealt with the problems of fiscal policy, it was recognized that in practice neither subject can be separated from the other.

9. Though these measures are discussed separately, the conference recognized the high importance of considering the merits of any tax system, not on the basis of the effects of individual taxes, but on the basis of the total impact on the economy of the system as a whole.

10. As regards the reorganization of indirect taxation, it was generally felt that such taxation, as at present administered, is unnecessarily complicated, has undesirable economic effects in distorting the price system, and is also inefficient in terms of yield. It was felt that the reform of the existing systems could be so designed as to produce significant increases in yield and substantial improvements in progressivity while mitigating the economic distortions which such taxation involves.

11. Substantial increases in yield, together with important administrative simplifications, can be achieved by removing the multiplicity of specific taxes that now exists on articles of mass consumption and by substituting in their place a single sales tax with a low rate and a broad tax base. Improvement in progressivity, as well as further augmentation of yield, can also be achieved by levying more severe excise taxes on luxury goods consumed predominantly by the middle- and higher-income groups. Luxury items imported from abroad already bear substantial import duties in most cases, but there is no similarly heavy indirect taxation of home-produced luxury articles, which now, in some countries, account for the greater part of luxury consumption.

12. Some of the participants considered that there is a case for substituting a uniform value added tax in replacement of the existing sales and excise taxes. Such a tax would be payable by enterprises on the difference between their total sales and their purchases from other enterprises—a difference which is approximately equal to the sum of the net incomes generated (in the form of profits, wages, salaries, interest, and rent) by each enterprise. A value added tax, by yielding independent information on the sales of enterprises, would also provide the basic framework for a more effective administration of the whole tax system.

13. With regard to the personal income tax, most of the participants believed that the Latin American countries should aim at the introduction of a unitary system which encompasses all forms of income. It is desirable that a capital gain should be recognized and taxed whenever there is a change in the ownership of either real or personal property, irrespective of whether it is by way of sale, gift, or inheritance. In conditions of substantial inflation, it may be advisable to make some allowance for the increase in the price level in calculating the net gain on capital assets. There is also justification in principle for taxing the imputed rent of owner-occupied dwellings in order to provide equal treatment between owners and renters.

14. It was agreed that an essential requirement for the efficient operation of a personal income tax system is that the rate schedule should be both simple and not immoderate. While it was thought that the exemption levels should be higher in relation to average per capita income than those obtaining in the developed countries, it was felt that the existing exemption levels are too high in many cases. The participants agreed that there was no point in starting to levy tax at a very low rate, as is the custom in many Latin American countries, and that there were too many separate tax brackets. It is also an essential precondition of an effective system that the maximum marginal rate of the tax be moderate. Excessively high marginal rates make it impossible to extend the tax to all forms of income (for example, capital gains) or to eliminate numerous exemptions. They also make it impossible to secure the willing co-operation of the taxpayer; they are the cause of much waste of time and talent in the search for tax loopholes; and they create too great a temptation to corruption and bribery. Hence they are not productive of revenue.[2]

[2]Social and economic conditions in each Latin American country will dictate the appropriate minimum and maximum rates, but for illustrative purposes, it is sug-

15. The conference gave special attention to the administrative problem of calculating agricultural income for purposes of income taxation. While there was almost universal agreement that some form of presumed income rather than actual income had to be used, there was a difference of opinion with respect to the best way to determine such income. One group suggested that presumed income should be calculated on the basis of average yield of lands with similar characteristics. Others questioned this method, as requiring information and technicians not at present available, and suggested that some fraction of self-assessed valuation of property be used as a measure of presumed farm income.

16. The participants were agreed that the ownership of property confers advantages which are distinct from and additional to the income derived from such property. It was suggested, therefore, that in addition to a progressive income tax there should also be a tax on net wealth of individuals or families. For this purpose "wealth" should include property in the form of real estate and financial assets as well as valuable personal possessions and "net wealth" should be the excess of the value of such property over liabilities. Such a net wealth tax should be levied at relatively low rates on the wealth in excess of some reasonable multiple of the per capita national income. It was recognized that the net wealth tax requires a high degree of efficiency of tax administration, and therefore its introduction in the near future may be advisable only for countries possessing this administrative prerequisite.

17. While the majority of the participants felt that this tax should be progressive, with low rates (rising, say, from 0.5 per cent to no more than 2 per cent on the excess of wealth over the exempted amount), a substantial minority felt that the tax should be proportional.

18. The participants agreed that the administration of the income and net wealth taxes could be greatly improved if the individual taxpayer were legally required to make a regular and full disclosure of all the real property, stocks, shares, etc. owned by him and if the tax authorities had legal powers to verify the completeness and accuracy of the taxpayer's returns.

19. Legal and administrative procedures need to be established, therefore, which enable the beneficial ownership of real property and of financial assets to be identified. This requires the compulsory registration of all real property in the name of the beneficial owner and the adoption of means whereby the ownership and transfer of securities (including bearer shares) are comprehensively registered with the tax authorities.

20. An efficient administration of the income and real property taxes also requires the establishment of suitable procedures for the valuation of capital assets at their approximate market value. Under present conditions in Latin America, this necessitates a significant strengthening of both the technical and administrative capacity of tax enforcement authorities.

21. The participants were agreed that, in the setting of corporation income tax rates, countries should balance the following considerations: the rates should not be set so high as to discourage domestic investment and risk taking; on the other hand, the rates should not be set so low as to forgo substantial amounts of tax on the income of foreign enterprises where, as is typically the case, a reduction of the tax paid by such enterprises to the particular Latin American government would only be offset by a corresponding increase in the tax payable by these same enterprises to the governments of their home countries. While some progression in rates may be justified to favor small businesses, continuous progression through all income levels, similar to that applying in personal income tax systems, should be avoided. Such continuous progression invites corporate split-ups and evasion, impedes the exploitation of

---

gested that the minimum chargeable rate for income in excess of the exempted amount should be about 10 per cent, and the ceiling marginal rates should not exceed 50 or 60 per cent.

economies of scale, and rewards inefficient firms by taxing them at lower rates precisely because their profits are lower than would be the case if they were efficient.

22. The participants felt that an effort should be made to rationalize the taxation of income from different classes of property. Traditional taxes in this area include the corporation income tax, the tax on urban real estate, and the tax on agricultural property. It was felt that, in the interests of equity and also of an efficient allocation of resources, the different forms of capital should bear an approximately equal weight of tax, when income and capital taxes are considered together. This consideration suggests the possibility of imposing, where they do not already exist, additional special taxes on those forms of income from capital which now do not bear any tax comparable to the corporation income tax, such as the profits of unincorporated enterprises and the interest paid by business firms.

23. Taxation of urban real estate and agricultural property is based in most countries on completely out-of-date valuations and is in urgent need of reform, both to provide an important source of revenue and also to serve major economic and social objectives.

24. In countries where the ownership of land is highly concentrated and where the prevalence of absentee ownership militates against the introduction of progressive techniques in agriculture, a progressive agricultural property tax is a potent instrument for inducing efficient use of land, for creating a freer market in land, and for promoting the objectives of agrarian reform.

25. The basic problem in the taxation of urban and agricultural properties is to obtain adequate assessments, i.e., to determine the tax base. The participants considered two methods as possible substitutes for, or supplements to, the traditional one of direct valuation by fiscal officers.

26. The first was the method of self-assessment: the declaration by the owner himself of the value of his property. This declaration would be placed on public record, and any individual or enterprise would be free to make a bona fide bid to purchase the property. In the event that such a bid exceeded the owner's declared value by a significant amount (say, 20 per cent), the owner, if he chose not to sell, would be required to revalue his property up to the amount which was bid. In this case, the maker of the frustrated bid would be entitled to a premium, which might be in the amount of the extra tax obtained in the first year following the revaluation of the property. Where inflationary problems are of serious dimensions, provision would have to be made for the automatic readjustment of assessed values during the period between successive declarations required of the owner.

27. Some participants thought that the self-assessment system was likely to be superior to the traditional system, even where this latter system was well administered; others considered self-assessment to be desirable over a transitional period during which the administrative means would be developed for an adequate assessment by fiscal officers. A further group felt that the principle of self-assessment was a good one but that the mechanism for enforcing proper declaration should be legislation authorizing the proper governmental authorities, on their own initiative, to acquire properties at the values declared by their owners. This variant has in fact been applied by a number of countries in the implementation of their agrarian reform programs.

28. The second method, considered in the case of agricultural but not urban property, was the assessment of land on the basis of its potential yield, taking into account the data provided by cadastral surveys.

29. The conference felt that there should be progressive taxes on inheritance complemented by similar taxes on *inter vivos* gifts. These serve the purpose of reducing the importance of inherited wealth in the distribution of wealth and income—an objective which is distinct from the general goal of progressive taxation, namely, that of reducing economic inequalities. If the recommendations made above concerning the full disclosure of property in connection with the

income tax are adopted, the administration of inheritance and gift taxes will no longer present special difficulties.

30. It was felt that many Latin American republics fix the prices of services provided by public enterprises at unjustifiably low levels, thus depriving their governments of an important source of revenue. It is not often realized that the greater part of these services is sold, not to the final consumer, but to private enterprises, with the effect that the profits of private enterprises are artificially raised at the same time as the profits of public enterprises are kept at low or even negative levels. The participants felt that a reasonable goal of price policy for most public sector enterprises would be to obtain profit rates comparable to the gross-of-tax profit rates achieved in the private sector. This is especially important in Latin American countries where the profits earned in public enterprises can provide a significant source of financing for the needed expansion of their operations.

31. It was felt that in the countries of Latin America the provisions of the law relating to foreign enterprises are relatively better administered than other provisions. Attention, however, was drawn to the fact that in a number of countries substantial concessions have been granted to attract foreign investment. When the problem is considered from the point of view of the group of underdeveloped countries as a whole, concessions made by any one country, if successful, are more likely to divert the flow of funds from other countries than to increase significantly the total flow of such funds. In addition, attention was drawn to the fact that it was possible in some cases for companies to understate the value of their exports or to overstate the value of their imports and thereby show a smaller profit on their local accounts than the true profit arising from their local operations. The conference felt that both for the purpose of limiting undue concessions to foreign companies and for the purpose of ascertaining the true profit of such companies to be taxed, there was need for international consultations, aimed at the adoption of uniform principles in the tax treatment of foreign enterprises.

32. The conference felt that there was a strong case on equity grounds for extending the liability for income taxation to income received from abroad, as is already the case in most European and North American countries, particularly since the residents of many Latin American countries own very substantial amounts of capital abroad. It was felt that, in order to enforce such provisions, the co-operation of foreign countries should be enlisted to provide information on income received by residents of Latin America. It is known that some countries already provide such information on a mutual basis under international tax treaties.

33. The participants recognized that tax incentives can be a potent instrument of economic policy, both to induce resources into desired uses and to impede their use in less desired areas. These incentives, however, have in the past had the effect of producing substantial revenue losses in most cases, while producing limited or even negligible positive economic effects. It is essential, therefore, that extreme caution be exercised so that there will be a high expectation that the tax incentives will produce the desired effect with minimum loss of revenue; and it is a reasonable goal of policy, when incentives in a particular direction are contemplated, to contrive methods which accomplish this aim without any revenue loss. In the particular case of investment incentives, it was noted that it is not easy to devise and administer an efficient system and that the use of these incentives is more powerful in influencing the character of investment than in increasing total investment.

34. The conference was in agreement in applauding the recent trend toward the development of common markets among the Latin American countries. It was noted, however, that as successive reductions of trade restrictions occurred, they might create transitory fiscal difficulties for some of the participant countries. The conference also emphasized the need for preventing differences in fiscal

provisions among the countries involved from producing undue distortions in the patterns of production and trade and stressed the importance of further research in this area.

35. The participants indicated that for the implementation of reforms, the administration of the tax system, and the analysis of the effects of taxation, there is an urgent need for improvement in the quantity and quality of statistical data and for a substantial augmentation of the supply of technical experts of the highest professional capacity. They urged that governments and international agencies continue their present efforts and undertake new and additional measures to accommodate these needs so as to make the fiscal reforms which have been the subject of the present conference as effective as possible.

APPENDIX A

Tax Policy Recommendations of Technical Assistance Missions: Evolution, Pattern, and Interpretation

by Eugene R. Schlesinger*

1. The Fiscal Policy Conference sponsored by the Joint ECLA/OAS/IDB Tax Program for Latin America offers a timely occasion for a review and analysis of the tax policy recommendations of technical assistance missions. More than a decade has now passed since the last comprehensive examination was made of technical assistance recommendations in this field,[1] and at that time there existed only three to five years of technical assistance experience in the area of taxation. The considerably greater body of reports now available provides a much broader basis for analyzing the general *pattern* of recommendations with respect to a much larger number of economically less developed countries, and the experience of an additional eleven years offers an opportunity for studying any *evolution* in thinking that may have taken place among technical assistance experts working in this field.

2. In reviewing the reports submitted by various missions, special emphasis has been placed on policy issues and recommendations which are of particular interest to the Latin

American countries.[2] In this connection, however, it must be kept in mind that no two technical assistance reports can ever be completely comparable. This is because the recommendations of any given mission necessarily evolve from the mutual interaction of three variables: (a) *The formal terms of reference specified by the host government* (e.g., investigation of the impact or administration of an individual tax or group of taxes, or qualitative review of the tax system as a whole, or analysis of the optimum method for raising a specified amount of government revenue, or determination of the level of taxable capacity with a view to discovering the optimum level of government expenditures, or the relative priority assigned to economic development, social reform, and other objectives of govern-

*The author wishes to express his sincere appreciation to Mr. Martin R. Blyn for his excellent summaries of a considerable number of technical assistance mission reports.

[1] The Technical Assistance Conference on Comparative Fiscal Administration, Geneva, July 16–25, 1951[54]. The numbers in brackets [ ] in both the main text and the footnotes refer to the "List of Cited Technical Assistance Reports and Other References," which is appended to this report.

[2] With the exception of one or two very recent missions, the coverage of the present paper is limited to the technical assistance reports included in the list compiled and published by the United Nations Technical Assistance Administration [54] [55]. Since obvious limitations preclude complete coverage of this lengthy list, priority was given to those missions which served Western Hemisphere countries and dependencies, and what is considered to be a reasonably representative selection was made from the reports of missions to other areas.

All references, moreover, are to be interpreted as illustrations of particular points of view and not as an exhaustive catalogue of recommendations; no attempt has been made either to refer to every report which was examined or to include the viewpoint of each mission on every policy issue. Furthermore, whenever direct reference has been made to a report which has not yet been released for general distribution, care has been taken to ensure that the observations are of a general nature so as to respect the "restricted" character of the report.

ment, etc); *(b) The analytical frame of reference implicitly or explicitly adopted by the particular expert or experts involved* (e.g., the nature of economic growth and of the relative roles of the government, industrial, and agricultural sectors; the comparative importance of the effects of taxation on equity, incentives, and resource mobilization; the degree to which tax policy is believed to be influenced by the stage of economic development or underdevelopment; etc.); and *(c) the economic and political characteristics of an individual country at a particular moment of time* (e.g., receptivity of social blocs to tax reform, size and distribution of the national income, degree of industrialization and urbanization, importance of foreign trade, rate of inflation, etc.).

3. In the light of the large number of individual possibilities inherent in each of these underlying variables, and given the vastly greater number of combinations and permutations that can exist among the three, the chances are exceedingly small that any two technical assistance reports will ever deal with precisely the same issues either explicitly or implicitly. Any comparative analysis of the kind undertaken here must, as a consequence, inevitably involve a considerable amount of personal *interpretation* on the part of the writer with respect to *(a)* selection of and emphasis upon those issues which are considered most important and *(b)* judgment as to what answers are implicit in the analysis of individual reports in cases where the experts do not themselves raise particular questions explicitly. The present writer assigns the highest priority to the views of the missions on broad issues of tax policy. Not only is this the only way in which the various reports can be placed in common perspective and on a broadly commensurate basis, but an understanding of the differences which arise on the subject of over-all tax policy also provides a useful explanation of most conflicts which may exist in the case of more specific policy issues. At the other extreme, in view of the special concern with tax policy of this year's conference, comparatively little

weight is given to purely administrative considerations—except, of course when these exercise a direct influence on tax policy recommendations.[3]

I. THE VIEWS OF THE MISSIONS ON OVER-ALL TAX POLICY

4. The different viewpoints on the subject of over-all tax policy to be found in the mission reports can be explained to some extent by the conflicts that have always existed among public finance specialists concerning the relative priority which should be assigned to the four principal criteria for evaluating taxes: (1) economic effects, (2) social justice, (3) administrative suitability and convenience, and (4) provision of revenue for the government. But the problem of defining the most rational tax system for an underdeveloped country is, in fact, far more subtle and complex than this. What is involved is not merely conflicts in priority taken in some abstract or generalized sense. The really basic questions entail *(a)* judgment as to the degree, if any, to which the interaction of these four criteria *does* change with the stages of economic development and *(b)* appraisal of the extent to which such differences in interaction *should* actually be taken into account in formulating tax policies.

5. There is, upon a superficial first reading, considerable disagreement to be found in the reports with respect to the subject of taxation and the stages of economic development. This is largely because there is a definite tendency on the part of the technical assistance experts to treat one or more of the four tax criteria in an implicit fashion.[4] The only criterion

[3]See, in this connection, the report of the Joint Tax Program's Conference on Tax Administration (Buenos Aires, October 11–19, 1961) [53].
[4]In this connection, it is interesting to note that only one of the reports reviewed clearly and explicitly spelled out the implications of all four criteria [36]. However, the technical assistance expert involved carefully refrained from taking any stand on the central problem, namely, the relative priority to be assigned to each. Presumably his justification for not making any recommendations on this subject was the belief that the decision was so vital that only the government itself could make it.

which appears to be handled explicitly in almost every instance is that of social justice, for virtually all the reports pay homage to the notion of progressiveness embodied in the familiar ability-to-pay principle. Even here, however, there is a complete gamut of treatment, ranging from a simple classification of taxes in accordance with their progressiveness or regressiveness [14] [35] to a forthright statement that the criterion of social justice should be abandoned [11] in the short run because of the requirements of economic development.[5]

6. For the most part, the reports have treated the problem of taxation and the stages of economic development almost exclusively in terms of the potential role of income taxation. This tendency has been unfortunate from one standpoint, for most of the discussion has been inevitably concerned primarily with the criterion of administration. From another point of view, however, this concentration on the role of the income tax is quite understandable, since the technical assistance experts all agree that its functions are unique. A definite consensus exists that only this type of tax offers progression over the complete range of the income distribution, provides (if so desired) that similar persons will be treated similarly, and ensures a high degree of yield elasticity in the revenue system, particularly under conditions of inflation.[6]

7. Agreement on the ultimate desirability of income taxation is, nevertheless, entirely consistent with different views on how fast such taxation can and should be introduced. The majority of the reports under review do, of course, favor rapid introduction of a global individual income tax, but there are a few reports which recommend that comprehensive modern income taxation should either be approached gradually after considerable experience with separate schedular taxes [31] or evolve through the slow adaptation of export and production taxes [34]. It is important, however, not to underestimate the significance of this minority view, for to the extent that the ability of a country to absorb an income tax system is a function of its stage of development, it should be recognized that the presently existing body of technical assistance reports covers for the most part the more economically advanced of the underdeveloped countries and, as such, may be unrepresentative of the world (and Latin American) group as a whole. In order to avoid any possibility of such a bias, therefore, the reports of the missions must also be examined with regard to (a) attitudes on the degree to which alternatives for the income tax are available, (b) the nature of the evidence put forth in support of the "majority" view, and (c) judgment as to whether the income tax or any viable alternatives to it are likely, either singly or in combination, to produce sufficient revenues to meet the basic requirements of a government in a rapidly developing country.

8. In view of the comparatively low level of the average standard of living and the relatively undiversified nature of the structure of production that are characteristics of underdeveloped countries, it is not surprising that almost all the experts appear to believe that consumption taxes, import duties, and (with a somewhat smaller degree of agreement) export taxes are likely to be more progressive over a significant range of the income distribu-

[5]It is now almost universally recognized that the ability-to-pay principle should be applied, not to individual taxes, but to the tax system as a whole, and the established techniques for statistically allocating the overall burden of the tax system among different income groups were clearly demonstrated at the Buenos Aires Conference on Tax Administration [50]. Furthermore, since what is really important, from a social welfare standpoint, is the redistribution of income through the fiscal system as a whole, the distribution of the benefits of government expenditures among different income groups should, to the extent that they can be measured, also be taken into account. This is particularly important in countries where social reform is given high priority. Although techniques for allocating expenditure benefits are not nearly so clearly defined as in the case of the tax burden, several of the mission reports did attempt to quantify the distribution of such benefits [17] [19].

[6]A considerable number of the reports call attention to the distortions introduced into the individual income tax by *past inflation* (i.e., the lowering of the real value of exemptions and the change in the degree of progression), but suggestions that automatic provision for *future inflation* be introduced by linking the level of exemptions

to some cost-of-living index are relatively rare [31]. The impact of inflation on other types of taxation (including business income taxation) is discussed in various places below.

tion than they are in more developed and diversified economies. A considerable number of the reports recommend that the progressiveness and yield elasticity of import duties and consumption taxes be increased by placing all such imports on an ad valorem rather than specific basis, and a good number also support increasing the selectivity of the consumption and import tax bases. Nevertheless, the majority of the experts treat such improved methods of indirect taxation as a useful *complement* to income taxation rather than as a *substitute* for it. Selective taxation of consumption and imports is viewed as a way of reinforcing the income tax while, at the same time, perhaps inducing favorable or preventing unfavorable changes in the structure of production.

9. The relatively few experts who seem to believe that there are really effective short-run substitutes available for income taxation in underdeveloped countries apparently base their case on the revenue potentialities of export taxation. In interpreting these views, however, it should be remembered that the reports concerned were largely written in the early nineteen-fifties when the relatively high level of primary commodity prices on world markets made the conflict between substantial export tax revenues and the balance of payments far less serious than it is under present conditions.

10. The principal evidence in support of the rapid introduction of a global income tax is the well-documented fact that the only effective method of improving administration of and compliance with this tax is through actual experience; if an income tax is not introduced because of an existing lack of administrative capabilities, the majority of the reports imply, the capacity to administer the tax will always appear inadequate, thereby creating a vicious circle. However, the mere existence of an income tax does not by itself mean that its revenue yield will be reasonable. For this reason, it should be recognized that the evidence in the reports on the relationship between income tax administrative capability and revenue yield is conflicting and points, to

say the least, to the existence of a considerable range of differences among the underdeveloped countries. One factor which emerges, for example, is the importance for income tax administration of the presence in a country of relatively large-scale economic or industrial units [45], which would indicate that significant yields can be obtained only in economies that are already semideveloped or semi-industrialized [48]. Moreover, there is also evidence that some technical assistance experts may tend to exaggerate tax administrative capabilities in all underdeveloped countries in the sense that they recommend reforms (e.g., treatment of all corporations as partnerships [40], introduction of a graduated tax on global expenditures [6] [22]) which the majority of technical opinion believes would be difficult even under the best administrative practices possible in the highly developed countries.[7] Finally, one should bear in mind that experts in public finance have traditionally been influenced by the adage that "old taxes are good taxes"; in this connection, it is interesting to note (*a*) that reports dealing with countries where income taxes do not exist are far less optimistic about their potentialities [20] [34] than reports on countries which already have such taxes and (*b*) that the one report [31] which recommends any significant change from the *status quo* definitely favors drastic simplification of the existing income tax.[8]

11. The effective yield of the income tax, it has long been recognized [47], depends only in part on such largely subjective factors as the ability of administrative personnel and the "tax consciousness" of the citizenry. It is also a function of the basic structural characteristics of a country. Many of the technical assistance reports, for example, recommend a lowering of personal exemptions under the

---

[7]In the light of this, it is interesting to note that India has already abandoned her expenditure tax. However, the technical assistance expert who originally proposed the tax has himself criticized the Indian version [23].

[8]There are conflicting interpretations of the experience of countries which have introduced income taxes in recent years. Compare, for example, the cases of Malaya [32] and Afghanistan [1].

income tax. However, there is no way of appraising from most of these reports how much additional revenue is to be expected in the absence of quantitative estimates of the impact of such factors as the degree of monetization of the economy and the proportion of the population living at or close to the subsistence level.

12. One strategically important structural characteristic that is analyzed in some of the reports is, on the other hand, quite susceptible of measurement, namely, the relative importance of the profit, dividend, interest, and rent components of the total share of the national product accruing to property. Because the share of profits and dividends in total property income is relatively small, as compared to developed countries, in even the most industrialized among the underdeveloped nations,[9] and since actual and imputed rental income is everywhere far less susceptible to effective taxation than is profit income, there is a definite tendency for a given amount of income taxation to fall more heavily on the industrial sector in underdeveloped countries. As a result, such nations are faced with a dilemma unless they can find efficient alternative direct or indirect ways of reaching *rentier* income. Under these conditions, a government can either, as some reports recommend, accept the existence of a lower level of taxable capacity and thereby hope to encourage the growth or emergence of the industrial sector [4] or, as other technical assistance experts suggest [48], give priority to the revenue needs of the government and accept thereby the attendant risks involved in terms of unfavorable effects on the private sector.

13. There is a definite problem in measuring the effects of alternative tax policies on private capital formation, which has resulted from the way in which the study of public finance has evolved over time. Formal microeconomic tax theory placed its emphasis solely

on the effects of taxation on incentives, and this tradition has continued strong even though macroeconomic theory, with its emphasis on resource mobilization, has been increasingly applied to other fiscal policy problems. No matter what view one takes of the quantitative importance of incentives, however, the fact remains that they are inherently unmeasurable. Moreover, there is a mounting volume of evidence that, when the problems of incentives and disincentives are translated to a particular institutional or social setting, they become infinitely more complex than is envisioned in pure economic theory. In the light of these difficulties, several technical assistance experts have come out firmly in favor of the use of macroeconomic techniques by making resource mobilization, rather than incentives, the central criterion of tax policy [48], and significant support for this point of view can be found in the general literature on development economics and in informal discussions among tax economists. However, nearly all the technical assistance reports under review continue to lay principal, if not exclusive, stress on incentives. This general reticence about using the criterion of resource mobilization may have some justification in the case of the vast majority of underdeveloped countries where there is no significant industrialized private sector, for under these conditions the neglect of incentives means the virtual abandonment of the traditional central problem of public finance (namely, the allocation of resources between the government and private sectors of the economy). However, in modern empirical work in the United States and other highly developed countries, this difficulty has been minimized by placing both analysis and quantification on the useful middle ground of the *financial capacity* (rather than incentives) of the industrial sector to save and invest. The same type of analysis would appear to have definite relevance for those underdeveloped countries that are semi-industrialized.

14. The government of a developing country can also raise revenues through the use of the income tax complements described above,

[9]Those countries in which all components of property income account for only a small proportion of national product constitute a special, although important, case [31]. However, this economic characteristic does not have particular relevance for the Latin American nations.

through taxes on the mass of the population, and through a combination of both of these.[10] However, the consensus of opinion in the mission reports is that selective indirect taxes and mass taxes should be treated as alternatives rather than as compatible supplementary devices; not only, as has already been noted, does the majority view favor the former but it also tends to oppose mass taxation on the grounds of social justice.[11] It must be recognized, nevertheless, that estimates of prospective revenue yield from the pattern of selective indirect taxes recommended in the mission reports are, for a number of reasons, somewhat hazy. First, given the limited analysis of the price elasticity of demand for luxury items to be found in the reports, one cannot be certain to what extent highly selective consumption taxes would work to improve progressiveness of the system and to what extent they would tend to reduce consumption of the taxed items; although many of the experts, naturally enough, point to the benefits from a development standpoint that could stem from the resulting changes in the existing or potential structure of production and especially imports, the fact remains that government revenues would be correspondingly smaller. Second, most of the reports do not appear to pay much attention to the fact that a considerable proportion of luxury consumption in underdeveloped countries is for personal services of a kind that is not particularly susceptible to selective forms of indirect taxation; the interesting suggestion has, however, been made that some study be given to the possibility of imposing old-fashioned types of direct taxes on some key items of luxury personal services [46]. Third, the understandable policy, not uncommon in a large number of developing countries, of attempting to alleviate chronic balance of payments difficulties by favoring capital imports at the expense of luxury items would, given the policy of tariff exemption for such equipment imports that is frequently recommended

in the mission reports, aggravate greatly the loss of revenue from import duties.

15. A policy of mass taxation would, on the other hand, tend to inhibit the growth of investment in industry by limiting the size of the existing or potential market [4] [45]. However, in comparing the quantitative impact of this kind of disincentive with the disincentives created for industry by high taxes on net business income, other mission reports emphasize the fact that, all other things remaining the same, the industrial sector is usually better off with heavy indirect taxes than with heavy direct taxes [19]. For a rapidly developing country, moreover, all other things do not usually remain the same. For instance, one cannot speak of the incentive and disincentive effects of taxation without taking into account whether the exchange rate is undervalued or overvalued relative to what it would be in a foreign exchange market in which the rate were permitted to fluctuate freely. Given the critical relationship which exists in an underdeveloped country among the capacity to import investment goods, so-called protective effects, and the potential rate of economic growth, there is a delicate interaction between the balance of payments and the fiscal system [51]. In an economy characterized by an overvalued currency, the disincentive effects of high taxes on private investment would be correspondingly smaller.

16. Furthermore, the existence of inflationary pressures which are usually taken as an index of an adequate development effort tends to alleviate the effective impact of any decline in potential market demand that may result from the imposition of indirect taxes [46]. In the case of direct taxes on net business income, on the other hand, inflation tends to have a different sort of effect and, in the absence of incentive depreciation policies, intensifies significantly the burden of taxation in the industrial sector. As a number of mission reports point out, this has been the actual experience in a number of Latin American countries where heavy rates of inflation have turned net business income taxes par-

---

[10] The taxation of land, property, and agricultural income is discussed in Section III, below.
[11] See, however, footnote 5 above.

tially or wholly into taxes on capital [2] [9] [36].

17. Irrespective, therefore, of any superficial lack of consensus which the technical assistance reports may initially appear to exhibit on the subject of taxation and the stages of economic development, several conclusions definitely do emerge from the reports when they are read and collated as a group. First, proper perspective on the general problem cannot be obtained unless full and commensurate weight is assigned to each of the four traditional criteria for evaluating taxes; in the particular case of income taxation, extreme care must be exercised in some instances not to confuse the normative goal of continuously improving administration and compliance with the positive reality of limited administrative absorptive capacity, while the proven fact of administrative capability should not, in other instances, be permitted to camouflage the equally important reality of low yield potential. Second, as the preceding conclusion already implies, the structural and institutional differences which exist *among* the various underdeveloped countries themselves are probably more significant, from the standpoint of tax policy, than those which exist *between* the most economically advanced and industrialized of these nations and the so-called developed countries. Finally, the not inconsiderable differences which also exist between these semideveloped countries and the developed nations involve some quantitatively minor, but economically critical, variation in the limits of taxable capacity that should not be ignored.

18. No matter what attitude one takes toward the validity of some of the schemes which have been elaborated for classifying countries with respect to stages of *general* economic development, it seems clear that a highly *specialized* system of country classification based on the constraints which comparative economic structure and institutions place on the tax policy mix would have real significance and relevance. Even if there were to be unanimous agreement that there is one unique kind of efficient modern tax system

which is the ultimate long-run goal of all countries, the fact remains that, for the vast majority of the underdeveloped countries of the world (including a good number in the Western Hemisphere), the effective time dimension of the particular "long run" involved in this case is, for reasons which vary for groups of countries, far too lengthy to have very much significance for government decision making based on any reasonable planning horizon. Moreover, even for those countries where the potential realization of a comparatively modern tax system does not fall outside the limits of a reasonable planning horizon, the reconciliation of the conflicts which always exist among the major tax criteria point to a somewhat different policy mix than would be found in highly industrialized countries. Given the delicate gradations of influence which the degree of industrialization, monetization, literacy, and level of average living standards exercise on the determinants of taxable capacity, it would appear—on the basis of the reports of technical assistance missions interpreted as a group—that the most rational tax system for countries at several different stages of underdevelopment and several different phases of development can and should vary significantly.

II. THE VIEWS OF THE MISSIONS ON SELECTED PROBLEMS IN INCOME TAXATION

19. Turning from the ideas of the missions on over-all tax policy to a consideration of their views on problems of a more limited scope, it seems appropriate to begin with individual issues in the area of income taxation where the treatment in the reports has been quite exhaustive. The particular problems to be analyzed are grouped under five topics: (a) tax treatment of foreign capital, (b) specific methods of stimulating business investment, (c) miscellaneous problems of individual income taxation, (d) the relationship between individual income taxation and corporate income taxation, (e) the taxation of capital gains.

Tax Treatment of Foreign Capital

20. With respect to the taxation of foreign capital, the mission reports are in virtually complete agreement on one essential point: favorable tax treatment is considered to be only a marginal factor in the decisions of foreign investors because the prospective tax burden is only one (and by no means the most important) of the factors influencing such investment decisions. Despite the near unanimity which exists on this point, however, there is a considerable difference of opinion in the area of actual policy recommendations. Much of the explanation for this seeming paradox lies in the fact that, while some experts treat tax considerations in a direct narrow sense, others lay stress on the possibility that tax policy can exert a broad indirect influence on attitudes toward the other factors which enter into investment decisions.[12] Indeed, of the missions favoring low rates of taxation for foreign investment, only one appears to emphasize the particular value, in money terms, of the tax savings or deferral [18]. The others lay stress on such broad qualitative factors as (*a*) the publicity[13] involved in directing attention to the investment opportunities available in the country [4] [37], (*b*) the sense of security against expropriation that such action may create on the part of foreign investors [21] [34], and (*c*) a clear demonstration, in the case of prospective investors interested in the local market, of the government's desire to create an environment favorable to private economic growth [4].

21. All the technical assistance missions recognize either implicitly or explicitly that, for very obvious political reasons, it is unsound policy to grant foreign capital pref-

erential tax treatment over domestic capital.[14] For this reason, the really critical factor in shaping a mission's attitude concerning the level of taxation to be levied on foreign investment is its judgment as to the relative extent to which the domestic level of business income taxation should be based on the expectation of attracting additional foreign investment or be determined by purely domestic considerations and requirements. Such judgment is, in turn, influenced largely by a mission's general views on the relative importance that should be assigned in over-all tax policy to the criteria of revenue requirements and economic effects.

22. Some of the reports also stress the primary importance of taking into account the tax policies of other countries. There is, for example, the necessity, in the short run, of adjusting tax policies to take full advantage of the tax laws in the countries of legal domicile of foreign firms which have already established operations [18] [20] and the desirability, in the longer run, of entering into treaties to avoid double taxation with countries which are likely to provide potential sources of investment capital [18]. At the same time, a country should not ignore the tax policies of neighboring countries which may offer similar investment opportunities for the location of foreign capital [18] and should in appropriate cases try to sign treaties with such countries standardizing the tax treatment of foreign capital, thereby avoiding mutually harmful tax competition [4].

*Specific Methods of Stimulating
Business Investment*

23. A useful way of approaching the technical assistance experts' recommendations on specific methods of stimulating business investment is to compare their attitudes toward tax exemption with their views on such other techniques as accelerated amortization, loss carry-forwards, and special investment credits

---

[12]There is considerably less controversy about granting favorable income tax treatment to *foreign technicians;* the few reports which raise this issue strongly endorse such a policy.

[13]In view of the location of Puerto Rico in the Caribbean area and the considerable interest that has been aroused by "Operation Bootstrap," it is important to note that expert opinion attributes the "success" of this program to such publicity effects [41] and to the island's unique position in having free access to the North American market [37].

[14]Naturally enough, a number of reports point out the economic dangers inherent in overdiscriminating against foreign capital. See, for example, [10].

or development bonuses.[15] Specific criticisms which the reports make of tax exemption programs may be grouped in three broad categories, which are interrelated rather than mutually exclusive. First, there is a group of problems which are associated with the loss of government revenues that such policies usually entail when considered from the point of view of the resulting tax favor shown to what is commonly the most prosperous sector of the economy and when compared to some of the other types of tax incentive that can be utilized to stimulate industrial investment. Second, there is a set of problems which is created by differences in the degree of profitability or lack of profitability among the firms receiving the benefits. And finally, there are the difficulties which arise in connection with the possibilities of discriminating, on the one hand, between new enterprises and existing firms and, on the other, between expanding business and stagnant enterprises; among the chief problems here is the competitive advantage which firms obtaining tax exemption may gain over other firms in the same industry.

24. In interpreting the attitude of individual reports toward these three categories of problems, it should be recognized that they are not always present to the same degree. Their comparative severity depends not only on the specific type of exemption program involved but also on the characteristics of a particular country's structural and institutional economic environment. Moreover, care should be exercised not to distinguish too sharply, as some of the reports do, between tax exemptions and other methods of stimulating investment; the policy choice for a country need not be of the "all or nothing" variety since several devices can be combined into a package that can work to mitigate the disadvantages of tax exemption alone.

25. An excellent example of the kind of

benefit that can be obtained from a tax package of this sort emerges in connection with the problem of revenue loss. One of the major reasons for the inferiority of tax exemptions as compared to accelerated depreciation is that the former entails a permanent loss of revenues for the government, while a policy of rapid tax write-offs involves only a temporary postponement or deferral of taxes (unless the firm continues to expand indefinitely). However, a policy recommendation originally made in the case of Ghana [18] and subsequently suggested as a device for joint adoption by the Central American countries [4] consists essentially of a combination of tax exemptions and accelerated depreciation. Under this plan, profits would be exempted from taxes for an indeterminate period sufficiently long in duration for a firm to recoup its entire original investment out of net income. Presumably the temporary exemption from taxes would apply to all investments and not merely to investments in depreciable capital assets, but since capital allowances on the *initial* capital investment would not be permitted after the termination of the initial "holiday" period, the treatment of depreciable assets would be virtually identical to that envisioned under accelerated amortization. As a consequence, the largest part of the impact on government receipts under this type of arrangement would take the form of tax deferrals rather than of a permanent loss of revenue.

26. A policy which combines the advantages of tax exemption and accelerated amortization does appear to offer more benefits than simple tax exemption. But the question also arises as to whether these benefits are sufficiently greater than those of simple accelerated depreciation to justify the additional administrative complexities involved. An announced policy of deferring taxes until the initial investment is recovered would seem to be more effective from the standpoint of publicity since it would be more likely to capture the attention of prospective investors than would the staid and prosaic device of accelerated depreciation schedules. Moreover,

[15]Favorable tax treatment for reinvested profits and unfavorable treatment for distributed profits are best treated in connection with the relationship between individual income taxation and corporate income taxation. See paragraphs 38 ff., below.

such a policy (a) reduces somewhat further the risk inherent even in accelerated amortization that the distribution of a firm's profits over time may be such that the enterprise may not be able to utilize the tax benefits in any given year and (b) also enables the taxing authority to avoid the problems involved in determining what rate of acceleration is the proper one.

27. On the other hand, the original proponent [18] of the policy of allowing recoupment of investment out of profits over an indefinite time span based his recommendation on an extremely narrow view of the nature of investment decisions by arguing that the most effective tax incentive that can be offered is a reduction in the period of time in which investment capital is exposed to risk.[16] This view of the investment decision making process appears, from a strictly a priori standpoint, to have far more relevance for foreign investors than for domestic investors, but the technical assistance expert in question apparently also believes it to be a key factor for domestic investors since he advocates very strongly that the dividends paid out of such tax-holiday profits be made exempt from the individual income tax. In either event, it seems evident that the rationale behind the policy of tax free recoupment of initial investment is more likely to lead to the establishment of new firms or the one-time expansion of existing firms than to encourage the continuous expansion of firms. For this reason, it is particularly appropriate for countries where the decisive problem is that of getting the industrialization process started initially.

28. Another kind of revenue loss under a tax exemption program arises because many of the firms which avail themselves of the benefits would have commenced or expanded operations even in the absence of the tax incentives. The number of companies in this category tends to be greater if the general level of tax rates is low [10] [33], but in those cases where a high level of business income taxation prevails, the unnecessary revenue loss to the government may actually be greater [49]. Closely related to this weakness of tax exemptions is the fact that a tax-holiday period tends to favor the more profitable companies when business income taxes are graduated and always discriminates against companies which obtain losses, even under proportional rates [42].

29. Any discrimination against firms which make losses, it has been occasionally argued, is consistent with a sound development policy since such companies are obviously inefficient [39]. But, as a number of the technical assistance reports point out, this argument does not take into account the tendency for most companies to lose money in their early years. Adequate provision for the carry-forward of losses [37] [40] actually offers greater incentives than tax exemptions,[17] and, if combined with a loss carry-back, would provide some means of averaging business income over time and introduce an additional element of fairness into the tax treatment of all companies [45]. One technical assistance expert, moreover, carries the argument one step further. Contending that even a loss carry-forward would not be enough to neutralize the effects of a business income tax (since the government still shares in net gains but not in net losses), his report makes the interesting recommendation that, in a list of designated industries, those firms showing no profits be entitled to a full 50 per cent return of any net loss.[18]

---

[16]The other report which advocates this policy [4] bases its recommendation, instead, on the argument that one of the strongest tax incentives which can be offered is that of assuring the investor that the government will share in profits only after the basic investment risk has been amortized.

[17]As one of the reports notes, however, the loss carry-forward and the tax exemption need not be treated as mutually exclusive alternatives since a tax exemption program can provide that losses be carried forward to the period beyond the initial tax holiday [18].

[18]The government's potential liability in this case would, in view of the prevailing level of tax rates, have been greater than its potential gains; however, the expert argued that the subsidy inherent in such excessive sharing of losses would be justified by the need to provide adequate incentives for investing in particularly risky industries and by the fact that the subsidy, under these circumstances, would not enrich the beneficiary. There is, on the other hand, the danger that this policy would also encourage uneconomic ventures.

30. Problems involved in the comparative treatment to be given to different kinds of firms within an industry constitute the third type of criticism which, as mentioned above, the technical assistance reports make of temporary tax exemption policies. Special issues arise in this connection with respect to, first, the differential tax burden on growing and stagnant firms and, second, the relative treatment of new and old firms. If, on the one hand, the exemption privilege is not granted to all firms in an industry, some companies are placed at a competitive disadvantage; on the other hand, if the program is extended to all firms, regardless of whether they are expanding, the revenue losses to the government are considerable and the program degenerates into a general subsidy instead of a method of encouraging new investment [33]. At the same time, however, it would appear unwise, on the one hand, to limit the program to new firms because the objective should be to stimulate all new investment in the designated industries [18], and in some underdeveloped countries the scarcity of managerial talent [42] might actually make it sounder policy to favor the expansion of existing successful firms;[19] yet, on the other hand, there are serious difficulties, from an administrative point of view, in allocating profits between the old and new parts of a business [42].

31. It is interesting to note, in the light of all this, that those few technical assistance experts who recommend some form of a tax-holiday period are dealing with countries where very little industrialization has already taken place [4] [18]. There are, moreover, other reports which advise that if a tax exemption policy is adopted at all, its use should be limited to new industries (as distinguished from new firms in existing industries) [37]. Nevertheless, the opinion expressed in the majority of the reports is that accelerated amortization of productive facilities, with its emphasis on new investment, is su-

perior to tax exemption. Liberal depreciation allowances can provide many of the advantages of tax exemption without that policy's economic and fiscal disadvantages and administrative complexities. In the limiting case of a very rapidly growing firm, such allowances may offset taxable income entirely, and the benefits of rapid write-offs are automatically canceled if a firm ceases to expand.

32. The reports under review tend to treat the subject of accelerated depreciation in a general fashion and do not, with very few exceptions, give detailed recommendations on such technical issues as (a) the degree of acceleration to be granted, (b) schedules for various individual industries, and (c) whether the benefits should be provided by rapid write-offs, special investment credits, or a combination of both. What is stressed primarily is the general suitability of the device and its flexibility in the face of conditions which may vary from country to country and period to period. Naturally enough, the strongest support for rapid amortization comes in the case of reports dealing with countries which are experiencing or have experienced substantial inflation. Many reports, however, mention the incentives that are provided in the form of "interest-free loans" even in the absence of inflation,[20] and some emphasize that, where an industrial sector is already established, a policy of rapid write-offs can exert as much (or more) influence through its impact on financial capacity as through its effects on incentives.

33. A system recently introduced in Ceylon [8] which seems to merit study by other underdeveloped countries consists of (a) lump-sum depreciation of an asset in the year of acquisition equal to the discounted value of the total depreciation that would be allowed under the declining-balance method over the life of the asset; (b) carry-forward over an indefinite number of years of the amount of

---

[19]The same sort of consideration could, of course, apply to the question of whether the reinvestment of profits should be encouraged by the tax system. See Section paragraphs 38 ff., below.

[20]One mission intimates that these incentives are likely to be more pronounced in a country with very high interest rates [37], but the existence of high interest rates also implies that the attractiveness of alternative investment opportunities is commensurately greater.

any unabsorbed depreciation, increased by 5 per cent each year to reverse the effects of the initial discounting; and (c) a system of development rebates (or special investment credits) equal to 20 per cent in the case of a new business or the expansion of an old business and equal to 40 per cent in the case of an *approved project*. The first two features go a long way toward eliminating the deterrent effect of an income tax on investment by "reducing the risk that the firm may not be able to take account of all allowable deductions for depreciation" and by "wholly avoiding the risk that allowances will become inadequate in the future because of rising prices" [5]. Moreover, since the third feature offers positive incentives (rather than the mere neutralization of disincentives), investment in the industrial sector is made more attractive relative to other investment possibilities.

Miscellaneous Problems in Individual Income Taxation

34. The views of the tax missions on the optimum degree of progression in individual income taxation (including the interrelationships among exemption levels, bracket sizes, and maximum rates) are difficult to discuss systematically. For one thing, meaningful quantitative comparison of the reports is made all but impossible by differences in income distributions among countries, by inflation, and by the numerous other difficulties involved in placing different income tax rate structures on a comparable basis. Furthermore, the range of recommendations on rate structure is quite wide; as is to be expected, the differences in viewpoint reflect the different basic attitudes toward over-all tax policy discussed above.[21]

35. The reports of more recent missions tend to confirm the conclusions reached at the 1951 Geneva Conference with respect to the comparative merits of schedular and unitary income taxes [54]. Differentiation between earned and unearned income, it is generally believed, can be obtained under either system. Moreover, there has been an increasing concern with the irrational forms of differentiation among various sources of income under some patterns of schedular taxes [45] and a growing awareness of the psychological and administrative advantages inherent in building a global income tax on the basis of some adaptation of the existing schedular pattern [31]. The tendency has been, however, to recommend that the number of schedules be reduced to the bare minimum consistent with the essential requirements of effective administration. For example, one report [10] suggests that the six categories in the Chilean income tax be reduced to three: income from personal services (including wages, salaries, professional fees, etc.); income from business operations (resulting from the combination of capital and personal services); and income from capital (including real property).[22]

36. The comparative income tax treatment of earned and unearned income is discussed in a large number of reports. From the standpoint of the criterion of social justice alone, most of the missions would appear to favor some tax differentiation in favor of earned income and argue that income from property (or the past accumulation of income) provides an additional basis for the ability to pay.[23] However, the fact that so few of these missions actually recommend such income tax differentiation reflects, in part, their belief that selective benefits to earned income run counter to an over-all policy of furthering economic development [37]. Moreover, many missions seem to feel that discrimination in

---

[21]The taxation of income from land is discussed in conjunction with real estate taxation. See paragraphs 53 and 54, below.

[22]The relationship between individual income schedules and business income schedules is discussed in the next section.

[23]Tax differentiation may sometimes involve a consideration of both *de facto* and *de jure* factors. For example, one report dealing with Peru argued that the fact that there was *de facto* discrimination against earned income through the more effective collection of taxes on wages and salaries (by withholding) was not a reason for introducing *de jure* discrimination in its favor. It pointed, instead, to the need for improved income tax administration [37].

favor of earned income can be more suitably achieved through the introduction of effective property taxation [3] or a net worth tax [25].

37. Only a very small number of reports suggest that individual income tax differentiation be used to encourage private savings,[24] and those which do, limit any favorable treatment to highly selective forms of savings such as government bonds [27] or the securities of a development institute [34]. There are serious political difficulties involved in almost all countries in introducing differentiation which favors personal savings into the individual income tax structure directly. Most missions apparently prefer to achieve such effects indirectly by favorable treatment under the business income tax (as discussed above) or through the preferential treatment of capital gains.

The Relationship between Individual Income Taxation and Corporate Income Taxation

38. Some reports approach the question of the relationship between individual income taxation and corporate income taxation purely from the standpoint of social justice and equity. There are pronounced differences in viewpoint between those who feel [40] that the individual is the only ultimate basis for all taxation and those who believe [3] that the special privileges and powers granted to the corporation by the government and the separation in economic and administrative reality between company and stockholder (at least in the widely owned corporation) justify reliance on a separate and distinct basis for legitimate taxation. Even where missions take the latter point of view, however, they do not favor graduated tax rates for the corporate income tax; such progression, it is argued, tends to penalize the more efficient and larger firms and has no real ethical justification.[25]

[24]Those reports which favor replacement of the individual income tax by a graduated expenditure tax constitute, of course, a special case [6] [22].

[25]See, however, the discussion of granting favorable tax treatment to small corporations in paragraph 42, below.

39. In many instances the discussion of whether corporations have a legitimate taxable capacity which is separate and distinct from that of their shareholders is handled in an abstract manner equally applicable to either developed or underdeveloped countries. Sometimes, however, it is argued that the substantial benefits provided to business enterprises in developing countries by government expenditures actually make the case for separate taxation of business firms far stronger there than in an industrialized nation [30]. Above all, it must be recognized that in many underdeveloped countries the business sector is foreign owned so that for the country it is the company that is the ultimate taxpayer.

40. The attitudes expressed in the reports as to an *equitable relationship* between individual and corporate taxation thus range all the way from the virtual disregarding of "double taxation" of dividends to favoring complete integration of the individual income and corporate income taxes by treating all corporations like partnerships [38]. Some missions recommend partial integration in the form of either permitting a corporation to deduct dividend distributions from its tax base or allowing the individual taxpayer a credit for income taxes paid by the corporation [45]; others, however, point to the danger that a crude method of integration, given limitations on administrative capabilities, may have unfortunate economic and equity consequences [3].

41. There is significantly more agreement on the subject of the effects of "double taxation" on capital formation. Although a few technical assistance experts argue that such taxation is in itself a serious deterrent to investment [40], the majority of the reports appear to believe, either implicitly or explicitly, that the full taxation of dividends tends to promote the retention and reinvestment of dividends. In fact, some reports recommend that specific tax measures be introduced to encourage such reinvestment even further by placing a special tax on distributed earnings [3] or nonreinvested profits [25] or granting special allowances to reinvested

profits[26] [4]. It has been pointed out, however, that the use of selective taxation of this nature assumes either that dividend distributions will be devoted largely to consumption expenditures or that the reinvestment of earnings within an individual enterprise is preferable to their investment in other areas [37]. Moreover, when the basis of differential treatment is the reinvestment or nonreinvestment of profits, there exists the thorny administrative problem of distinguishing between genuine reinvestment and unnecessary additions to reserves [3]. Nevertheless, under the economic and institutional conditions prevailing in most underdeveloped countries, most experts feel that tax discrimination in the form of undistributed profits is a rough, but reasonable, incentive in the right direction.

42. Concern about the impact of the tax system on the form of business organization is sometimes expressed in those reports dealing with countries which tax corporations under the same rate schedule as individuals. The practice of taxing individuals and corporations under identical schedules may be thought justified in a society where virtually all corporations are family owned and managed, but it is not considered appropriate in a more economically developed country where a considerable number of large nonfamily corporations exist [45] and it may even act as a potential deterrent to the development of *large-scale* corporations which are so essential for bringing together the capital of a great number of individuals [4].

43. Where separate rate schedules already exist, concern is sometimes expressed about the possibility that the tax system may prevent the emergence and development of *small* corporations. For this reason, it is sometimes recommended that reduced rates be levied on corporations below a certain size so that the corporate rate is definitely below the rates which are likely to apply to the stockholders

as individuals [18], or it is suggested that corporations with fewer than a given number of stockholders be granted the option of being taxed as either a corporation or a partnership [10]. Under either form of recommendation, the advantages of the corporate form of organization as a device for promoting progressive practices are retained and the emergence of new corporations is not impeded by unduly severe taxation.[27]

The Taxation of Capital Gains

44. The views of the missions on the taxation of capital gains, like their attitudes on the integration of individual income taxation and corporate income taxation, reflect a difference of opinion between those who believe that the proper treatment of such gains is independent of the stage of economic development and those who argue that capital gains taxation should be adapted to the particular characteristics of underdeveloped economies. The missions which take the first view are in a minority. Moreover, they are concerned with what are essentially semi-industrialized and semideveloped economies; emphasis in these cases is given either to the role of capital gains taxation in achieving partial integration of individual income taxation and corporate income taxation [45] or to the fact that capital gains are like any other kind of income, differing only in that they are obtained over a period of years and should therefore be handled by some method of averaging [25].

45. The majority view is that capital gains taxation has an especially vital role to play in underdeveloped countries. Most frequently the emphasis is given to the *disincentive* possi-

[26]For the most part, the reports which favor differential treatment for reinvested profits appear to recommend that the granting of benefits be limited to investment in physical capital; occasionally, however, a report may recommend the inclusion of intangible investment in research and development [13].

[27]Where the corporate form of organization is already widespread, the principal problem with closely held corporations is avoidance of the individual income tax; when stockholders have effective control over both salaries and dividend policy, they can, of course, allocate profits in such a way as to minimize over-all taxes. The one technical assistance report which goes into this problem extensively recommends that closely held corporations be taxed as partnerships on a mandatory basis [25].

bilities inherent in this kind of taxation, and particularly heavy taxation is recommended for some sources of capital gains (e.g., land, real estate, luxury construction). The imposition of a schedule of rates which varies inversely with the period of time the asset is held will (a) act to discourage the frequent speculative buying and selling of land and real estate that is characteristic of so many underdeveloped countries and, at the same time, (b) give the government, in the case of land, a reasonable share in the social values created by population growth, public improvements, and other factors which are not the result of individual foresight and initiative [9]. However, the really essential consideration is to set the rates high enough so that they are effective in discouraging speculation. One report, for example, recommends that the maximum rates be imposed after five years [10].

46. Some missions also stress the *incentive* features of favorable tax treatment or exemption of other sources of capital gains. There are, for example, reports which favor relatively low rates on the sale of industrial plant [12] [13], while others strongly recommend that gains originating in the sale of securities be exempt in order to promote the creation and development of a local capital market [16]. One technical assistance expert goes so far as to suggest that all gains except those arising from the sale of land be granted tax-free status so as to promote industrialization, capital formation, and general development [10], and there is even a rather ingenious device recommended for achieving differential treatment within the industrial sector itself: capital losses realized in a list of designated preferred industries would be permitted to be deducted in full from total income, while losses realized in other industries could be offset only against capital gains [40].

47. A problem sometimes arises in the case of gains realized through the sale of the capital assets of a business. During an inflationary period, frequently it may become more profitable to sell such assets than to continue to employ them in business operations.[28] It has been suggested, however, that waiver of the capital gains tax in cases where the asset is replaced within a given period of time is an excellent way of avoiding excessive taxation of the normal turnover of capital assets and, at the same time, of discouraging purely speculative transactions [25].

III. THE VIEWS OF THE MISSIONS ON SELECTED PROBLEMS IN OTHER KINDS OF TAXATION

48. The views of the technical assistance missions on selected problems in other kinds of taxation can be usefully analyzed under six headings: (a) the taxation of agricultural income and rural land, (b) urban and general property taxation, (c) the taxation of consumption and domestic trade, (d) the taxation of foreign trade, (e) inheritance and gift taxation, and (f) municipal and departmental taxation. However, the treatment which the reports give to these topics is far less exhaustive than in the case of income taxation and tends, at the same time, to show a significantly greater consensus of agreement. Moreover, much of the discussion deals with problems which are essentially administrative in character and which fall, as such, outside the scope of the present report. All the missions, for example, recognize the extremely vital role of land and property taxation in underdeveloped economies, but only a very small part of their analysis is concerned with purely policy issues. The emphasis is for the most part on such factors as better trained assessors and improved assessment procedures, adequate land surveys and property censuses, and the need for periodic reassessments to take account of higher values resulting from economic expansion, population growth, and (most especially) inflation.

[28]There is, with few exceptions [37], very little discussion to be found in the reports of the impact of inflation on capital gains taxation in general. Presumably this is because the missions are, in this particular instance, more concerned with curbing speculation than with abstract questions of equity.

The Taxation of Agricultural
Income and Rural Land

49. Collation of the policy recommendations of the reports on the subject of agricultural taxation is also made difficult by the
additional complexities created by different
patterns of land use, different systems of land
tenure and ownership, and different distribution of landholdings. Nevertheless, the great
majority of the missions stress, in one way or
another, the importance of employing the tax
system to improve the economic utilization
of agricultural land. The particular recommendations made to implement this objective
vary in terms of both the special conditions
of individual countries and the degree of
"imagination" of individual experts.

50. Some reports, for example, believe that
a combination of a realistic level of assessments and a reasonable scale of proportional
rates would in itself be sufficient to discourage
the holding of idle farm land [3] [34]. Others
argue that this result could be achieved more
effectively through progressive rates levied on
either individual parcels [40] or cumulative
holdings [28]. Frequently, moreover, a report
will go further and recommend either a flat
percentage penalty tax on unused cultivable
land [7] [10] [13] or the introduction of a
more complicated system in which there is a
progressive increase in the basic tax rate to
the extent that net income falls below a certain percentage return on market value [12].

51. Favorable income tax treatment for
land development expenditures is sometimes
suggested [18] [34], and the imposition of
special assessments or benefit taxes is occasionally recommended on land that is improved through state irrigation [43] or other
kinds of government expenditures [4]. One
mission to Libya [31] even makes the novel
suggestion that an elaborate system of land tax
exemptions be introduced for farmers who
agree to a specified list of land improvements.
There is some question, however, as to just
how applicable this procedure would be to
other underdeveloped countries; the major
incentive in the case of Libya was not so

much a lower tax burden as the possibility of
obtaining full legal title to the land.

52. Another question which is frequently
raised by the missions is the exemption from
property taxation of small rural landholdings.
This is, in part, a purely administrative consideration. The costs of assessment and collection may easily exceed revenue yields in
the case of parcels below a certain size [14].
On the other hand, even if such parcels are
exempted, they should be included in the
registration rolls so as to prevent fragmentation of individual holdings [28].

53. Basic economic and social issues are
also involved in the exemption of small rural
holdings. Some missions, for example, recommend that such parcels be excluded from
taxation to prevent hardships to subsistence
farmers [45]. Others, on the other hand, contend that mere poverty does not justify exemption because taxes are levied for the benefit of all the people [31], or believe that if a
piece of land cannot bear a minimum tax, it
is probably not suitable for private ownership [3]. In general, however, many of the
more recent reports tend to agree with the
conclusion reached at the Geneva Conference
on Comparative Fiscal Administration [54]
with respect to the taxation of the small
farmer: if he is to be taxed at all, it should
be through the medium of land taxation since
this method will tend to capture some of the
"unearned increment" to his land resulting
from public improvements. There also appears
to be some agreement that selective excise
taxes (e.g., on salt) are superior to marketing
taxes since the latter act to prevent the emergence of the much-to-be-desired market economy. Production taxes are considered to have
notoriously perverse effects, the precise nature
of which varies with the type of base (e.g.,
livestock, trees, or cereals) and with the individual conditions of the country [31] [42].

54. Occasionally an individual report will
argue that only the nonmonetary income of
middle-size farmers need be exempted from
the income tax [44]. However, the broad
consensus seems to be that such farmers
should not be made subject to this tax and

that land taxation is the most suitable method of reaching them. On the other hand, the majority of the reports definitely believe that large farmers should be included under the income tax; there is, however (as noted above in paragraph 7), a minority view that land taxation should be used as a short-run substitute for income taxation [9] [31].

Urban and General Property Taxation

55. The treatment in the reports of urban real estate taxation is much more sporadic than that of real estate taxation. The only issue which is discussed several times is the degree of comparative severity that should be applied in the taxation of urban land and capital improvements. A mission to Bolivia [3], for example, noted the inability of special taxes on vacant urban sites to curb speculation during a period of inflation because of the low rates on improved property. In the case of Venezuela, on the other hand, where the problem was one of a shortage of buildings rather than excessive speculation, a mission argued [45] that buildings should be taxed at higher rates than land; a tax on buildings would increase costs and thereby lead to a decline in supply, while a tax on land could have no effect whatsoever on supply.[29]

56. This same mission to Venezuela undertook a comprehensive analysis of the comparative merits of capital value and rental value as the basis for urban real estate taxation. The ratio of rents to capital value will vary among different types of property, and compared with a capital value tax, a tax on gross rents would be relatively higher on inferior properties and lower on high-grade properties. The report favored *rental value* as the preferential basis for three reasons. First, the tax base is determined by market forces. Second, it is easier to estimate rental values than capital values in the case of owner-occupied property because data on

rentals of similar spaces are more plentiful than sales data. Finally, the rental-value system had the advantage of familiarity in Venezuela.

57. A number of reports strongly favor the use of general property or net worth taxes for developing countries. The ones which have received the greatest publicity deal with India [22] and Ceylon [6], where net worth taxation was considered by the expert to be a necessary administrative concomitant of a graduated expenditures tax. However, a powerful and far more general argument for the introduction of a net worth tax is made in a report to the Government of Israel [25]; the chief argument advanced there is that a tax of this kind is the most effective way of taxing those important sources of income which are obtained on an accrual rather than a cash basis.

58. There is also some discussion of the most desirable degree of comprehensiveness in the property tax base. Some reports recommend the inclusion of "movables" [10] [16], while others favor their exclusion [3]. Similarly, there are reports which favor the deduction of such business assets as inventories, office furniture, and good will from the base, while others recommend that assets of this nature be included [25].

The Taxation of Consumption and Domestic Trade

59. The views of the missions on the taxation of consumption and domestic trade exhibit a very high degree of agreement. In all probability the consensus to be found in the reports on this subject is greater than in any other major area of taxation. Most of the discussion is concerned primarily with *administrative matters,* and the recommendations made in this connection have been put forth with such frequency that they need only be summarized briefly here: (*a*) the preferability, because of the greater certainty of their effects, of sales and excise taxes to turnover taxes, gross receipt taxes, and stamp taxes; (*b*) the need to avoid imposing indirect taxes

[29]The interesting program of comprehensive land taxation recommended for Jamaica proposed that both urban and rural land be taxed at progressive rates and improvements at proportional rates [28].

on the manufacturer's level so as to prevent excessive pyramiding; (c) the desirability, in economically less developed countries, of levying sales and excise taxes on the wholesale (rather than retail) level so as to facilitate collection and administration; (d) the necessity of eliminating the practice of earmarking in order to reduce inflationary pressures and improve budgetary decision making; (e) the need to consolidate the many individual taxes which are frequently imposed on the same item as a result of historical accident; and (f) the desirability of eliminating the very large number of *patentes*, licenses, and nuisance taxes which raise little, if any, revenue and merely interfere with the efficient conduct of business operations.

60. Virtually unanimous agreement is also found with respect to the *economic policy effects* of consumption taxation. One report does, indeed, criticize the use of this kind of taxation because of the distortion which indirect taxes produce in comparative price relationships [45]. However, the vast majority of the missions tend to emphasize the positive role which consumption taxes can and should play in underdeveloped countries. As has already been mentioned (paragraph 8), there are frequent recommendations as to (a) the need for increasing the selectivity of the consumption tax base and (b) the desirability of substituting ad valorem for specific taxes. The interesting suggestion has also been made that consideration be given to the introduction of a graduated purchase tax [26].

61. For the most part, the mission reports appear to accept implicitly the assumption of national income accounting that there is complete forward shifting of indirect taxes in the *ex post* sense of measuring the tax burden in terms of actual collections.[30] This is, of course, entirely consistent with some of the *ex ante* burden falling on the seller in the form of a reduced physical volume of sales. One report that questions the validity of this

assumption deals with Venezuela [45]. Differences in the degree of shiftability among various firms in an industry is cited as one of the reasons for the inferiority of indirect taxes to direct taxes.

62. Comparatively little attention has been paid in the technical assistance reports to the implications of possible differences in the degree of shiftability in developed and underdeveloped countries. Such differences are to be expected in the light of the high markup and low-volume pricing policies which are so characteristic of economies with small mass purchasing power. One report on Guatemala does, however, comment on the fact that even the substantial differentials in tax burdens associated with a *graduated* business tax do not appear to inhibit competing firms from raising prices to an extent determined by their individual tax rates [19]. This is in marked contrast to the United States, where the much smaller differentials in tax burden associated with what is essentially a *proportional* business tax do seem to reduce the degree of shiftability [52].

The Taxation of Foreign Trade

63. The views of the missions on import taxes tend to exhibit almost as much consensus as in the case of taxes on consumption and domestic trade. A majority of the reports, as has already been pointed out in the discussion of over-all tax policy, make three major recommendations in this area: (a) exemption or low rates of duty on imports of equipment, (b) a high degree of selectivity in the duty schedules for imports of consumption goods, and (c) the substitution of ad valorem for specific duties.

64. There is widespread recognition that the ease of collecting export taxes gives this form of taxation a certain attractiveness. At the same time, however, many reports emphasize that export duties discriminate (a) against the export sector as a whole and (b) among high-cost and low-cost producers within that sector. Moreover, although the desirability of imposing sliding-scale rates based on world

---

[30]The analysis of shifting tends to be more elaborate in the case of export taxes and includes such considerations as the relative share of the world market [21] and the possibility of backward shifting to wage earners [17].

market prices is also frequently recommended, the effects of such sliding-scale taxes on the export sector can be expected to vary considerably with the direction and degree of departure from the true equilibrium rate of exchange [51]; this may not be too much of a problem in the case of cyclical departures from the normal rate of exchange, but it is of considerable significance when there are secular inflationary trends.

65. Given the growing disenchantment with the possibilities of utilizing export taxes as a major long-run source of government revenues (see paragraph 9), the modern tendency among technical assistance experts is to view the usefulness of export taxes in one of two ways: either they are considered as a stand-by supplementary device for curbing inflation and taxing excessive profits during periods of cyclically high export prices or they are treated as an evolutionary method, involving both credits and refunds, for effectively bringing the net profits of the export industries under the scope of general income taxation. In this second case, however, it should be recognized that, even if there is full or partial integration of export taxation and income taxation, there will still be some discrimination against export industries as compared to other industries because of time lags in payments and refunds [36].

Inheritance and Gift Taxation

66. The missions for the most part favor fairly heavy death taxes. The experts believe that such duties have far less detrimental effects on savings and investment than do taxes which are more closely related to the production of income [9]. Only one of the reports surveyed advocates introducing specific incentives in connection with death taxation; it recommends that private corporate securities of all types and the value of partnership interests in certain designated areas be included at only 50 per cent of full value [40].

67. Some missions show no relative preference for inheritance or estate taxation, believing that either type can be made to serve the purposes of raising revenue and checking the undue accumulation of wealth [45]. Others definitely favor the use of an estate tax because of administrative convenience, greater yield, and the fact that progressive rates can be more easily applied [34] [40]. A third group appears to favor, for reasons of social justice, the inclusion of both types of death duties in the tax system [9].

68. The introduction of gift taxes is strongly advocated in cases where they do not already exist [43]. Almost without exception, moreover, the recommendation is made that gift taxes and death taxes be levied on a common cumulative base.

Municipal and Departmental Taxation

69. Quite a few of the reports are keenly aware of the critical responsibilities which fall on lower levels of government in developing countries. Missions emphasize the need for such governments to provide a satisfactory amount of social and educational services and to carry out such economic activities as the construction and maintenance of secondary and feeder roads. The desirability of greater independent taxing powers for local governments is thus frequently stressed.[31] However, while some reports seem unclear on the question of whether the taxable capacity of municipalities would be sufficient to meet local needs adequately [44], others appear definitely convinced that for the countries with which they are dealing, the answer to this question is either affirmative [40] or negative [24].

70. Sometimes the emphasis in a report is placed on the need for more elastic revenue sources [33], and occasionally missions recommend the use of income taxation either

---

[31]There is not very much discussion of whether there should be two or three levels of taxation within a country. Of those missions which go into this subject, reports dealing with Venezuela and Mexico strongly advocate giving the states independent taxing power [45] or more elastic revenue sources [33], while another report covering Bolivia recommends that the departments be deprived of their existing powers because the three-tier system is too elaborate for a country of her size [3].

through the direct implementation of local income taxes [7] or the introduction of a supplementary nationally administered tax, the proceeds of which would be returned to the state governments [45]. Attitudes on the relative suitability of grants-in-aid and shared taxes differ in the reports which raise this issue at all. Some missions apparently favor the latter [24] [45], but one report definitely prefers grants-in-aid because of their greater flexibility and sensitivity to varying local needs [40].

IV. TAXATION AND TECHNICAL ASSISTANCE: THE "STATE OF THE ART" AS REFLECTED IN THE MISSION REPORTS

71. A comparative study of the recommendations of past technical assistance missions on individual policy issues reveals a number of interesting ideas and suggestions which merit consideration by tax experts, host governments, and sponsoring organizations. Indeed, the kind of review undertaken here points also to the existence of a large number of *potential* laboratories in various underdeveloped countries throughout the world for studying the effects of certain tax policy alternatives. Although limitations of time and resources preclude examination of this phase of technical assistance work in this paper, a comprehensive empirical investigation of the *actual* economic and fiscal effects experienced by countries where major recommendations have been implemented could prove to be an extremely desirable follow-up to what should be considered only a preliminary exploration.[32]

72. The major value of analyzing previous technical assistance reports, however, probably lies less in the realm of specific policies

[32]As an intermediate step, of course, a detailed study would have to be made of the degree to which the suggestions contained in individual reports have actually been implemented. Analysis of the comparative failure or success of various missions in terms of implementation would also serve an additional useful purpose in the organization of future technical assistance work. See, in this connection, paragraph 87, below.

and ideas than in the broad terms of learning more about the fundamental nature of technical assistance in relationship to tax policy. From the standpoint of any future work in the area, it is very useful to obtain insight into (a) comparative economic structure and the pattern of tax policy recommendations, (b) changing approaches to tax policy analyses, (c) the relationship of tax policy to other government policies, (d) the optimum nature of technical assistance missions and personnel, and (e) problems of implementing the reports.

Comparative Economic Structure and the Pattern of Tax Policy Recommendations

73. The main justification given at the beginning of this paper for making a comprehensive survey of the recommendations of past tax missions was to obtain useful perspective on the *pattern* and *evolution* of thinking in the area of tax policy as reflected in some sixteen years of technical assistance experience. Unfortunately, however, our review and interpretation of the existing body of reports has not yielded a completely unambiguous answer to the first of these questions. On the one hand, when the reports are read and collated as a group, there emerges a very definite consensus of opinion that the optimum over-all tax policy can and should vary with the stage of economic development or underdevelopment (paragraph 17). At the same time, however, it is extremely sobering to recognize that very often the recommendations of the individual expert writing about different developed, semideveloped, and underdeveloped countries tend to bear much closer resemblance to one another than do the views of different experts dealing with the same country.[33]

74. This contrast in viewpoint is, to some degree, unavoidable in that it reflects the basic differences which have always existed in public finance with respect to the relative priorities to be assigned in tax policy to financial

[33]See, for example, paragraphs 7, 10, 13, 15, 16, 40, and 44.

capacity, incentives, and revenue yields. Nevertheless, to an important extent the ambiguities in the pattern of tax policy recommendations reflect the comparatively narrow range of geographical experience of many technical assistance experts. The principal reason why there is a major need for developing a systematic classification of the relationships between comparative economic structure and taxation (paragraph 18) is that this would offer such technicians a useful basis for relating their knowledge of one economy to conditions in another and, at the same time, enable them to make modifications and adaptations in their thinking where these were required.

75. From the standpoint of tax policy, the differences in economic structure which exist *within* the underdeveloped countries as a group appear, from careful reading of the technical assistance reports, to be as important as the similarities. Such differences, moreover, may frequently be of greater significance than the similarities, particularly when comparing completely unindustrialized countries with semi-industrialized economies. In the case of the former, the gap between optimum tax policies for the short run and for the long run seems to be extremely large—so vast, in fact, that one may question whether these policies are consistent with one another. If, for example, the short-run taxable capacity of a country is fully exploited, the pattern of future development may be such that the longer-run tax policies which presently appear optimum may never become the appropriate ones. On the other hand, failure to exploit short-run taxable capacity may result in continued economic stagnation.

76. For the vast majority of underdeveloped countries (including many in Latin America), the relationship between short-run and long-run policies also creates some doubts as to the relevancy of the pattern of the tax policy recommendations found in the technical assistance reports to the realities of conditions in these countries. This survey of past reports has faithfully attempted to reflect the relative weights assigned by the technical assistance experts to individual policy issues. For this reason, it is quite possible that a disproportionate amount of attention may have been paid to the long-run normative goal of effective taxation of income and wealth. This would imply a correspondingly dangerous lack of emphasis on short-run taxable capacity.

Changing Approaches to Tax Policy Analysis

77. The most pronounced trends exhibited by the body of technical assistance reports reviewed here are, first, an increasing tendency to frame the analysis and recommendations in terms of the tax system as a whole and, second, a growing recognition of the interdependence of recommendations affecting groups of individual issues. These evolutionary changes, in turn, reflect both a deepened awareness of the critical importance of adequate taxable capacity for development programing and a heightened realization of the need, in the face of the structural imbalances characteristic of underdevelopment, to utilize the tax system to produce a delicate combination of incentive and disincentive effects.

78. To an increasing extent, furthermore, the technical assistance missions have with the passage of years made it standard practice to include in their reports comprehensive estimates of the revenue yields to be anticipated from their recommendations. This has been a salutary and useful change. With very few exceptions, however, the missions have not carried the development of revenue estimates to their logical conclusion: there has been in recent years a growing world-wide consensus among experts in public finance that the most effective way of making meaningful and commensurate comparisons of different packages of interrelated tax recommendations is by estimating the revenue yields of the *alternative* policy combinations. In this way, one can be certain that all the tax policy criteria have been implicitly taken into account.

79. Quantitative estimates of the effects of tax policies should also, from a logical point

of view, form an integral part of any comprehensive technical assistance report. But apart from the revenue yield estimates mentioned above, actual attempts at measurement are found only rarely. The failure of most missions to make quantitative estimates, even in the critical case of the effects of taxation on private investment, can be explained by a lack of the availability of data or even the ability to obtain data. Those few reports (for example [19]) which have made ample use of quantification have even been criticized for placing too great a burden on the existing statistical data of a country, but the technicians concerned justify their statistical methods by contending that even the roughest quantitative estimates of the economic effects of taxation are better than none. In any event, statistical methods and sources are in themselves subject to flux and development, and as more and more underdeveloped countries benefit from large-scale technical assistance programs in the area of statistics and data collection, it is to be hoped that future tax missions will make full use of the new and improved statistical data.

*The Relationship of Tax Policy
to Other Government Policies*

80. Ideally, moreover, a package of tax policy recommendations cannot be meaningfully framed unless government expenditure policies are also fully taken into account. According to the formal theory of public finance, intelligent over-all tax policy must involve not only a balancing off and reconciliation of the marginal social costs of alternative lines of taxation but also an assessment of these costs against the marginal social benefits of expenditures. For this reason, governments requesting and receiving technical assistance in the area of taxation must be made sufficiently aware that their expenditure policies have as much critical significance for the economic development of their countries as their tax policies and that the latter cannot be realistically formulated independ-

ently. The impact of the tax system on the development of the private sector of the economy must be appraised in the light of its effects on the government sector.

81. Tax experts serving on technical assistance missions must, in turn, take care to include government expenditures as part of their analytical frames of reference. To some degree this entails, as in the case of governments, normative consideration of the optimum types of expenditure policy for developmental purposes. But to a considerably greater extent the problem for the technical assistance experts involves a positive and realistic appraisal of the most likely course of future expenditures. The inexorable tendency of ordinary (or nondevelopment) government functions to expand up to the limits set by available funds creates a special dilemma and responsibility for the tax policy adviser. Unless he is firmly convinced that a significant portion of an increase in government revenues will be devoted to developmentally beneficial purposes, he may, in the short run, be wise to refrain from making recommendations that fully exploit the country's taxable capacity. There is a considerable danger, under these circumstances, that when the country later becomes willing and able to pursue an aggressive development policy, the reserve of taxable capacity (which constitutes an immensely valuable resource in most underdeveloped countries) may have been largely dissipated.

82. There is also an important question concerning the extent to which missions should consider money, credit, balance of payments, and other types of government policies in framing their tax recommendations. In part, what is involved here is differences in individual taste and judgment as to the desirability of using taxation as a substitute for other types of government policies. One finds in the mission reports, for example, disagreement on such matters as the suitability of employing taxes as a balance of payments corrective [29] [30] and the question of whether the tax system should be utilized to counteract basic inflationary pressures [9] [27]

or merely be adapted to minimize the distortions which inflation creates in the tax system itself [31] [37].

83. Of far more fundamental significance, however, is the need for tax missions to bring the effects of other kinds of government policies into their over-all analytical frames of reference. Unless such critical factors as the degree of overvaluation of the exchange rate and the existence of inflationary pressures are taken into account, it is impossible, as discussed in Section I, to make quantitatively meaningful appraisals of the effects of alternate tax policies.[34]

The Optimum Nature of Technical Assistance Missions and Personnel

84. From the standpoint of strict logic alone, therefore, it might appear desirable to give very broad and comprehensive formal terms of reference to future technical assistance missions in the area of tax policy.[35] In an idealized analytical sense, no tax policy issue can be studied in isolation, and some treatment must be given to other taxes, to the pattern of government expenditures, and to the effects of other types of government expenditures. In practice, however, considerations of financial costs, time priorities, and the unavailability of personnel come into play. It would be quite unrealistic, for example, to expect all missions concerned with broad tax policy to undertake comprehensive analyses of the pattern of government expenditures and to make detailed recommendations in this area; the most that can be reasonably asked of most such missions would be to make rough implicit estimates of the probable amount and direction of future government spending. Furthermore, not every country is in need of over-all tax reform; this is particularly the case when the recommendations of earlier missions have been implemented to a reasonable extent.

85. For the organizations which sponsor technical assistance, a review of the reports of past tax missions raises important questions with regard to both the kind of expert to be employed and the kind of mission to be sent. From the standpoint of the consistency and long-run validity of tax policy recommendations, the reports prepared by economists seem, on balance, to exhibit a better over-all perspective than those written by experts with other functional specialties. This is to be expected in the light of the multitude of subtle economic interrelationships which are involved in creating a meaningful package of tax policy recommendations for a developing country. Not unsurprisingly, moreover, among the economists who have served on past missions, those who possess broad general economic backgrounds appear to do a more effective job in bringing in the co-ordination of tax policies with other kinds of government policies than do men who are exclusively specialists in taxation and public finance.

86. Too much reliance on economic generalists, on the other hand, also appears to produce less than optimum results. To make useful and meaningful recommendations, the policy generalist must have, in addition to broad economic training and understanding, a reasonable amount of knowledge of the specilized field of tax economics. Otherwise, he will be unable to make even rough evaluations of the constraints which administrative factors place on both the revenue yields and the economic effects of various tax policy alternatives. Nevertheless, a full and complete tax policy program may sometimes require more than the rough evaluations of administrative complexities that can be made by tax economists. Ultimately, therefore, a specialist in tax administration may also be required, even when the frame of reference of a mission is policy recommendation rather than implementation. Effective technical assistance in the area of *tax policy* frequently involves some division of labor because the particular

---

[34]See, in particular, paragraphs 14–16.
[35]An interesting example of the activities of a comprehensive mission with very broad terms of reference and involving a variety of experts in different functional fields is to be found in the report of a special mission appointed by the Government of Ecuador [15]. The work of this group resulted in proposals for a major redrafting of the country's revenue code.

combination of skills required is unlikely to be found in any one individual.

87. Even the best policy recommendations, however, can have little or no effectiveness unless they can be implemented technically through practical legislation or reasonably efficient administrative procedures. As a consequence, what is needed in the area of technical assistance in *taxation* (as contrasted with tax policy) is much greater co-ordination of the efforts of administrative specialists and policy generalists than is possible within the confines of a formal one-visit mission. From the standpoint of formulating tax policy recommendations, the activities of these two types of technical assistance experts are co-existent in time, but from that of implementing the recommendations, they are sequential. The work of the specialist in tax administration necessarily continues long after that of the policy generalist has been completed.

Problems of Implementing the Reports

88. The field of taxation and public finance has, furthermore, always embraced more than purely technical problems in economics and public administration. The policy-minded tax technician faces a definite challenge if he wishes to see his basic ideas translated into effective tax legislation; compromise on numerous minor issues may become necessary in order to achieve essential objectives, and recommendations have to be modified and adapted to political realities. Acquaintance with the field of political economy is thus vital even in cases where an expert is dealing with his own government. Such knowledge becomes considerably more crucial in the sensitive area of technical assistance to a developing country where the relationship of the visiting foreign technician to the government is an especially delicate one. Inevitably the work of technical assistance missions has to be viewed as an art as much as (or more than) a science.

89. The art of technical assistance can be formally incorporated into the reports of missions in three ways. In the first place, a mis-

sion's actual recommendations can be made dependent on its appraisal of the chances that individual parts of its program will be adopted by the host government. One interesting example of how a mission can take a "second-best" stand on a policy issue, rather than an "optimum" one,[36] is illustrated by the case of Israel, where the same expert visited the country on three separate missions over a period of several years. In his first two reports [25] [26] the expert repeatedly argued that the high level of income tax rates, when coupled with a very steep scale of progression, seriously hampered personal savings and incentives to undertake overtime work, and he strongly urged that both the average and marginal rates of income tax be lowered substantially. In his final report, however, the expert, recognizing that rate reduction would probably never be forthcoming to the degree he desired, endorsed the special tax treatment already introduced for overtime bonuses and recommended that selective tax incentives be offered to some forms of personal savings [27].

90. Second, for any given country, there may be a considerable contrast between the benefits that can be obtained from a tax policy in *theoretical* and *actual* terms. For example, none of the mission reports that were reviewed opposed tax concessions to individual economic sectors on the purely formal grounds that such specialized treatment conflicted with the "neutrality" canon of the modern economic theory of public finance. There is a general consensus among the technical assistance experts that the low or stagnant rates of economic growth associated with underdevelopment are in themselves a result of existing structures of production and patterns of relative prices. However, once the reports move away from a theoretical framework and consider more practical matters, the recommendations of the experts on this

[36]Even when a technician is convinced that an "optimum" tax system may initially result from his recommendations, it may be encumbent upon him to evaluate the risks of subsequent changes that would bring a drastic move away from optimality. Many practicing tax attorneys and certified public accountants justify the retention of what might be considered unjustified "loopholes" on the basis of such risks.

subject run the complete gamut of possibilities; they range from a point of view that favors tax concessions in all fields where they can reasonably be expected to encourage higher output and productivity [7] to one which appears to be against all forms of special concessions [45].

91. Much of this wide diversity of viewpoint can be explained by differences in judgment as to whether the benefits that can be theoretically obtained from special tax concessions would be realized in practice or whether such a policy would be more likely, in fact, to produce a decline rather than improvement in economic well-being. The strongest views of the improbability of any of the theoretical benefits being obtained were expressed in a report of a mission to Venezuela [45]: the introduction of a small number of special exclusions or exemptions to accomplish rational objectives, it was argued, would open the door to similar demands by all types of pressure groups; as a result, there would be an inevitable tendency for the income tax base to shrink slowly and for the pattern of tax discrimination to take on an increasingly nonrational basis that would ultimately create undesired distortions in the economy.[37]

92. The third method of incorporating the art of political economy into formal technical assistance reports has been through the use of alternative policy recommendations. Some reports, for instance, have not only made recommendations aimed at immediate adoption but have also established standards for future reform, while others have distinguished between short-run and long-run recommendations [3]. Nevertheless, valuable as these typical devices can be, they may not be

[37]That a prediction of this kind can be fairly realistic is borne out by the experience of a number of Latin American countries, among them Chile and Mexico. Interestingly, however, missions to these two countries gave diametrically opposed remedies for the existing situation. A report on Chile, for example, argued that temporary special tax treatment is, in effect, merely a disguised form of subsidy and that direct subsidies are always preferable to such hidden subsidies [9]. On the other hand, the mission to Mexico simply urged considerably greater selectivity in the granting of tax relief with a view to avoiding what had become a system of general subsidies for extended periods of time [33].

sufficient to overcome political difficulties in view of the growing tendency of technical assistance reports to recommend complete packages of closely interrelated recommendations (paragraph 77). Given political realities, it is quite visionary to expect any government to accept a complete package of recommendations, and under these circumstances the chances are considerable that partial adoption of a package may actually produce detrimental rather than beneficial results [23].

93. The governments of countries receiving technical assistance should, of course, become much more aware of the closely interrelated nature of many groups of specific recommendations and of the potential dangers involved in adopting only part of a recommended program. However, a considerable amount of responsibility for reducing risks of this kind also falls on the technical assistance expert and the sponsoring organization. The former should make every effort to break down his over-all list of recommendations into clearly defined subpackages and to develop, if possible, flexible alternatives for each of those. On its part, the sponsoring organization should see that the technician is given sufficient time to work with the government concerned to ensure that the essential elements of each such subpackage are handled in an integrated manner.

94. In view of the critical need for developing flexible and clearly defined subpackages of alternative recommendations, the usefulness of missions which merely submit formal reports and then depart would appear even more limited than when viewed from the standpoint of the work requirements of the administrative specialist alone (paragraph 87). The same sort of considerations apply to the activities of the policy generalist. As a consequence, it is reassuring indeed to see the degree to which the various organizations sponsoring technical assistance programs in taxation are moving increasingly in the direction of stationing continuous advisory missions (which include both policy generalists and administrative specialists) in countries for extended periods of time.

95. Technical assistance in the field of taxation is just emerging from its infancy after sixteen years of experience in the field. Pragmatism and experimentation in both approach and policy recommendations are still very much needed. But if there is one major lesson to be learned from a review of the work of past missions, it is the desirability for flexibility in both method and thinking. Such flexibility is required not only in terms of the functions and make-up of the missions themselves but also in terms of adapting the general principles of taxation to the different economic structures and political realities characteristic of individual developing countries.

LIST OF CITED TECHNICAL ASSISTANCE REPORTS AND OTHER REFERENCES

1. *Afghanistan:* H. H. HINRICHS. "Certainty as Criterion: Taxation of Foreign Investment in Afghanistan." *National Tax Journal,* XV, 2 (June, 1962).

2. *Argentina:* S. S. SURREY and O. S. OLDMAN. *Report of a Preliminary Survey of the Tax System of Argentina.* (English edition: Cambridge: Harvard Law School, 1960.) (Spanish edition: Buenos Aires: Ministerio de Hacienda, 1960.)

3. *Bolivia: Report of the United Nations Mission of Technical Assistance to Bolivia.* (New York: 1951. United Nations Sales No. 1951.II.B.5) (Experts in Taxation and Public Finance: R. Goode and A. Lepawsky.)

4. *Central America:* K. E. LACHMANN. *Leyes de Fomento Industrial en Centroamérica.* (Comisión Económica para América Latina, Comité de Cooperación Económica del Istmo Centroamericano. E/CN.12/CCE/235, 1961.)

5. *Ceylon:* R. GOODE. "New System of Direct Taxation in Ceylon." *National Tax Journal.* XIII, 4 (December, 1960).

6. *Ceylon:* N. KALDOR. *Suggestions for a Comprehensive Reform of Direct Taxation.* Sessional Paper IV. (Colombo: Government Press, Ceylon, April, 1960.)

7. *Ceylon: The Economic Development of Ceylon.* Report of a Mission of the International Bank for Reconstruction and Development. (Baltimore: The Johns Hopkins Press, 1953.) (Expert in Taxation and Public Finance: L. Baranyai.)

8. *Ceylon: Personal Tax Act. No. 14 of 1959,* Parliament of Ceylon, 3rd Session, 1958–1959, 15 May 1959; Department of Inland Revenue. *The New Tax System.* (Colombo: Government Press, Ceylon, 1959.)

9. *Chile: Report of the United Nations Economic Mission to Chile, 1949–1950.* (New York: 1951. United Nations Sales No. 1951.II.B.6.) (Experts in Taxation and Public Finance: C. Iversen, S. E. Leland, and E. Lindahl.)

10. *Chile:* H. K. LIDSTONE. *Legislación y Administración de Impuestos en Chile.* Report of an expert designated by the United Nations Technical Assistance Administration. (New York: 1956. Restricted United Nations document TAA/CHI/1.)

11. *Chile: El Programa de Estabilización de la Economía Chilena y el Trabajo de la Misión Klein and Saks.* (Santiago: Universidad de Chile, 1958.)

12. *Colombia: The Basis of a Development Programme for Colombia.* Report of a Mission of the International Bank for Reconstruction and Development. (Washington: 1950: IBRD Special Publication Sales No. IBRD.1950.2.) (Expert in Taxation and Public Finance: R. A. Musgrave.)

13. *Cuba: Report on Cuba.* Findings and Recommendations of an Economic and Technical Mission of the International Bank for Reconstruction and Development. (Washington: 1951. IBRD Special Publication Sales No. IBRD.1951.3.)

14. *Ecuador:* J. S. COSTA. *Taxes in Ecuador: A Review of Some of the Ecuadorian Tax Laws and their Administration and Proposals for Reform Thereof.* (Washington: International Cooperation Administration, 1956.) (Mimeographed.)

15. *Ecuador: Informe de los Trabajos de la Misión Económica Especial en Ecuador.* (Quito: 1959.)

16. *El Salvador:* L. A. EHRHARDT. *La Hacienda Pública en El Salvador.* Report of an expert designated by the United Nations Technical Assistance Administration. (New York: 1954. United Nations document ST/TAA/K/El Salvador/6.)

17. *El Salvador:* H. C. WALLICH and J. H. ADLER, with the collaboration of E. R. SCHLESINGER, P. J. W. GLAESSNER, and F. NIXON. *Public Finance in a Developing Country, El Salvador—A Case Study.* (English edition: Cambridge: Harvard University Press, 1951.) (Spanish edition: Mexico: Fondo de Cultura Económica, 1949.)

18. *Ghana:* J. H. PERRY. *Taxation and Economic Development in Ghana.* Report of an expert designated by the United Nations Technical Assistance Administration. (New York: 1959. United Nations Document TAO/GHA/4.)

19. *Guatemala:* J. H. ADLER, E. R. SCHLESINGER, and E. C. OLSON, with the collaboration of the Research Department of the Central Bank of Guatemala. *Public Finance and Economic Development in Guatemala.* (English edition: Stanford: Stanford University Press, 1952.) (Spanish edition: Mexico: Fondo de Cultura Económica, 1951.)

20. *Guatemala: The Economic Development of Guatemala.* Report of a Mission of the International Bank for Reconstruction and Development. (Washington: 1951. IBRD Special Publication Sales No. IBRD.1951.2.)

21. *Haiti: Report of the United Nations Mission of Technical Assistance to the Republic of Haiti.* (Lake Success: 1949. United Nations Sales No. 1949.II.B.2.) (Expert in Taxation and Public Finance: E. Gomez del Rey.)

22. *India:* N. KALDOR. *Indian Tax Reform, Report of a Survey.* (New Delhi: Department of Economic Affairs, Ministry of Finance, Government of India, 1959.)

23. *India:* N. KALDOR. "Inadequacy of Recent Tax Measures." *Economic Weekly Annual* (Bombay: January, 1959.)

24. *Iran:* J. CERTEUX. *La Fiscalité et les Finances Iraniennes.* Report of an expert designated by the United Nations Technical Assistance Administration. (New York: 1951. United Nations document No. TAA/NS/Iran/6.)

25. *Israel:* H. S. BLOCH. *Revenue Administration and Policy in Israel.* Report of a United Nations Technical Assistance Expert. (New York: 1953. United Nations Sales No. 1953.II.H.5.)

26. *Israel:* H. S. BLOCH. *Revenue Administration and Policy in Israel (Second Report).* Report of a United Nations Technical Assistance expert. (New York: 1954. United Nations Sales No. 1955.II.H.3.)

27. *Israel:* H. S. BLOCH. *Revenue Administration and Policy in Israel (Third Report).* Report of a United Nations Technical Assistance expert. (New York: 1958. United Nations Sales No. 1958.II.H.2.)

28. *Jamaica:* J. F. N. MURRAY. Report to the Government of Jamaica on *Valuation, Land Taxation and Rating.* Report of an expert designated by the United Nations Technical Assistance Administration. (Kingston: Government Printing Office, 1956.)

29. *Laos:* N. H. JACOBY. "Taxation in Laos: Policies for a New Country with an Undeveloped Economy." *National Tax Journal,* XIV, 2 (June, 1961).

30. *Laos:* R. W. LINDHOLM. "Taxation in Laos: Policies for a New Country with an Undeveloped Economy—a Comment." *National Tax Journal,* XV, 1 (March, 1962).

31. *Libya:* S. H. AHMED. *Problems and Recommendations on Taxation in Libya.* Report of an expert designated by the United Nations Technical Assistance Administration. (New York: 1957. Restricted United Nations document TAA/LIB/4.)

32. *Malaya:* M. C. TAYLOR. "Income Taxation in the Federation of Malaya." *National Tax Journal,* XIV, 2 (June, 1961).

33. *Mexico: The Economic Development of Mexico.* Report of the Combined Working Party of the International Bank for Reconstruction and Development and the Government of Mexico. (Baltimore: The Johns Hopkins Press, 1953.) (Expert on Taxation and Public Finance: V. Urquidi.)

34. *Nicaragua: The Economic Development of Nicaragua.* Report of a Mission of the International Bank for Reconstruction and Development. (Baltimore: The Johns Hopkins Press, 1953.) (Expert on Taxation and Public Finance: G. Garvy.)

35. *Paraguay:* J. S. COSTA. *Proposals for Legislative and Administrative Reforms with Respect to Tax Collection in Paraguay.* (Washington: Institute of Inter-American Affairs, 1953.) (Mimeographed.)

36. *Peru:* R. BLOUGH. *Informe sobre la Política Tributaria en Perú.* Report of an expert designated by the United Nations Technical Assistance Administration. (New York: 1959. Restricted United Nations document TAA/PER/9.)

37. *Peru:* R. BLOUGH. *Informe Suplementario sobre la Política Tributaria en Perú.* Report of an expert designated by the United Nations Technical Assistance Administration. (New York: 1960. Restricted United Nations document TAA/PER/9/Add.1.)

38. *Philippines:* United States Economic Survey Mission to the Philippines. *A Report on a Tax Program for the Philippines.* (Washington: 1950.) (Mimeographed.) (Expert in Taxation and Public Finance: L. Shere.)

39. *Puerto Rico:* M. S. BHATIA. "Tax Exemption in a Developing Economy: A Case Study of Puerto Rico." *National Tax Journal,* XIII, 4 (December, 1960).

40. *Puerto Rico:* L. SHERE. *A Tax Program for Puerto Rico.* Report by a Consultant to the Treasurer of Puerto Rico. (San Juan: 1951.) (Mimeographed.)

41. *Puerto Rico:* M. C. TAYLOR. *Industrial Tax Exemption in Puerto Rico.* (Madison: University of Wisconsin Press, 1957.)

42. *Syria: The Economic Development of Syria.* Report of a Mission of the International Bank for Research and Development. (Baltimore: The Johns Hopkins Press, 1955.) (Expert in Taxation and Public Finance: R. Goode.)

43. *Thailand: A Public Development Program for Thailand.* Report of a Mission of the International Bank for Reconstruction and Development. (Baltimore: The Johns Hopkins Press, 1959.) (Expert in Taxation and Public Finance: F. Neumark.)

44. *Turkey: The Economy of Turkey: An Analysis and Recommendations for a Development Program.* Report of a Mission of the International Bank for Reconstruction and Development. (Washington: 1951. IBRD Sales No. IBRD.1951.1.) (Expert in Taxation and Public Finance: R. A. Rennie.)

45. *Venezuela:* C. S. SHOUP, J. F. DUE, L. C. FITCH, D. MACDOUGALL, O. S. OLDMAN, and S. S. SURREY. *The Fiscal System of Venezuela.* Report by the Commission to Study the Fiscal System of Venezuela appointed by the Government of Venezuela. (English edition: Baltimore: The Johns Hopkins Press, 1959.) (Spanish edition: Caracas: Ministerio de Hacienda, 1959.)

46. R. GOODE. "Taxation of Savings and Consumption in Underdeveloped Countries." *National Tax Journal,* XIV, 4 (December, 1961).

47. R. GOODE. "Reconstruction of Foreign Tax Systems." *Proceedings of the National Tax Association* (1951).

48. N. KALDOR. "The Role of Taxation in Economic Development." Paper presented to the *Conference on Latin American Fiscal Policies.* (Santiago, Chile: 1962.)

49. K. M. KAUFFMAN. "Income Tax Exemption and Economic Development." *National Tax Journal.* XIII, 2 and 3 (June and September, 1961).

50. R. A. MUSGRAVE. "Calculo de la Distribución de la Carga Tributaria, Y Distribución de la Carga Tributaria en América del Sur." Paper presented to the *Conference on Latin American Tax Administration.* (Buenos Aires, Argentina: 1961.)

51. E. R. SCHLESINGER. *Multiple Exchange Rates and Economic Development.* (Princeton: Princeton University Press, 1952.)

52. E. R. SCHLESINGER. "Corporate Income Tax Shifting and Fiscal Policy." *National Tax Journal.* XIII, 1 (March, 1960).

53. United Nations Economic Commission for Latin America. *Informe Provisional de la Conferencia sobre Administración de Impuestos.* (Buenos Aires: 11 to 19 October 1961. E/CN.12/AC.50/6.)

54. United Nations Technical Assistance Administration. *Taxes and Fiscal Policy in Under-Developed Countries.* (New York: 1954. United Nations Sales No. 1955.II.H.1.)

55. United Nations Technical Assistance Administration. *Supplementary List of Reports of Technical Assistance Missions to Under-Developed Countries in the Field of Public Finance.* (New York: 1961. United Nations document ST/TAA/M/8/Add.1.)

APPENDIX B

Participants, Observers, and Secretariat of the Conference

PARTICIPANTS

José Rafael Abinader, Under-Secretary for Finance, Secretariat of State for Finance, Santo Domingo, Dominican Republic

*John H. Adler, Director, Economic Development Institute, IBRD, Washington, D.C., U.S.A.[1]

Mauricio Baca Muñoz, Chief of the Legal and Fiscal Section, Permanent Secretariat of the General Treaty on Central American Integration (SIECA), Guatemala

Carlos Casas, Economic Adviser to the Government, Bogota, Colombia

José María Cazal, Representative of the Latin American Free Trade Association (LAFTA or ALALC), Montevideo, Uruguay

*Cesare Cosciani, Faculty of Law, University of Rome, Italy

Félix Dardón, Under-Secretary, Ministry of Finance and Public Credit, Guatemala

*Rajanikant Desai, Fiscal and Financial Branch, Department of Economic and Social Affairs, United Nations, New York, U.S.A.

Sol Descartes, Economic Consultant, San Juan, Puerto Rico

Mario Fernández Provoste, Adviser to the Ministry of Finance, Santiago, Chile

Ulises Flores, Doctor of Jurisprudence and Social Sciences, San Salvador, El Salvador

Edison Gnazzo, Director of the Income Tax Office, Ministry of Finance, Montevideo, Uruguay

*Richard Goode, Brookings Institution, Washington, D.C., U.S.A.

*Arnold C. Harberger, University of Chicago, Chicago, Illinois, U.S.A.

Albert Hart, Columbia University, New York, U.S.A.

Alvaro Hernández, Faculty of Economic Sciences, University of Costa Rica, San Jose, Costa Rica

Federico Herschel, Faculty of Economic Sciences, University of Buenos Aires, Buenos Aires, Argentina

*Dino Jarach, Doctor of Law and Professor of Finance, Faculty of Economic Sciences, University of Buenos Aires, Buenos Aires, Argentina

Braulio Jatar-Dotti, Senator and President of the Congressional Bicameral Finance Commission, Caracas, Venezuela

*Author of paper.
[1]Mr. Adler was unable to attend the conference. His paper was presented by Mr. Marinus van der Mel.

*NICHOLAS KALDOR, King's College, Cambridge, England

CARLOS FRANCISCO LESSA, Joint ECLA/BNDE Economic Development Centre, Rio de Janeiro, Brazil

MACKENZIE LEWIS, AID, Washington, D.C., U.S.A.

PEDRO MAÚRTUA, Central Reserve Bank, Lima, Peru

MANLIO MARTÍNEZ, National Economic Council, Tegucigalpa, Honduras

CARLOS MATUS, Latin American Institute for Economic and Social Planning, Santiago, Chile

JORGE MÉNDEZ, National Council for Economic Policy and Planning, Bogota, Colombia

ALFONSO MOISÉS BEATRIZ, Salvadorian Association of Industrialists, San Salvador, El Salvador

SERGIO MOLINA, Director of the Budget, Ministry of Finance, Santiago, Chile

HÉCTOR MONTERROSO, Director of the Department of Economic Studies, Bank of Guatemala, Guatemala

HAROLD MOSS, Director, Foreign Tax Assistance Staff, Internal Revenue, Washington, D.C., U.S.A.

*JOSÉ MARÍA NAHARRO, Central University, Madrid, Spain

IFIGENIA M. DE NAVARRETE, National School of Economics, University of Mexico, Mexico City, Mexico

RODRIGO NÚÑEZ A., General Planning and Administration Authority, Panama

FELIPE PAZOS, Member of the Panel of Nine (Alliance for Progress), Washington, D.C., U.S.A.

ENRIQUE PIEDRABUENA, Professor of Financial Law, Catholic University of Chile, Santiago, Chile

ANÍBAL PINTO, Director of the ECLA/BNDE Economic Development Centre, Rio de Janeiro, Brazil

JAIME PORRAS, Chief Adviser, Co-ordination Division, Planning Board, Quito, Ecuador

*ALAN R. PREST, Christ's College, Cambridge, England

MANUEL RAPOPORT, President of the Council of the Internal Revenue Administration, Buenos Aires, Argentina

EDUARDO RIOFRÍO, President of the Fiscal Tribunal, Quito, Ecuador

MIGUEL RODRÍGUEZ MOLINA, General Administrator of Income Tax, Ministry of Finance, Caracas, Venezuela

RAÚL SÁEZ, Acting Co-ordinator of the Panal of Nine (Alliance for Progress), Washington, D.C., U.S.A.

ALVARO SANCHO, Supervisor of the Department of Economic Studies, Central Bank of Costa Rica, San Jose, Costa Rica

EDGARD TABOADA, Under-Secretary for Finance, Ministry of Finance, Asuncion, Paraguay

*VÍCTOR L. URQUIDI, Adviser to the Ministry of Finance and Public Credit, Mexico City, Mexico

EDUARDO URZÚA, Director of Internal Revenue, Ministry of Finance, Santiago, Chile

NÉSTOR VEGA-MORENO, Adviser to the National Council for Economic Planning and Co-ordination, Office of the President of the Republic, Quito, Ecuador

ENRIQUE VIDAL CÁRDENAS, President of the Peruvian Institute for Tax Law, Lima, Peru

*HASKELL P. WALD, United States Treasury Department, Washington, D.C., U.S.A.[2]

MARVIN WEISSMAN, Director of Technical Assistance for Latin America, AID, Washington, D.C., U.S.A.

OBSERVERS

HÉCTOR ASSAEL, Institute of Economics, University of Chile, Santiago, Chile

RODOLFO BALBI, Chief Adviser, Department of Technical Supervision, Internal Revenue Administration, Buenos Aires, Argentina

PABLO BARAONA, Catholic University, Santiago, Chile

MAXWELL E. BECKER, United States Economic Mission, Santiago, Chile

ANGEL BOCCIA, Faculty of Economic Sciences, National University of Cuyo, Mendoza, Argentina

JOSÉ BORDÓN, Chief of the Department of Tax Studies and Research, Finance Secretariat, Buenos Aires, Argentina

RAMÓN DONIS, Income Tax Administration, Caracas, Venezuela

ERNESTO FONTAINE, National University of Cuyo, Mendoza, Argentina

MARION H. GILLIM, Barnard College, Columbia University, New York, U.S.A.

RAÚL GRIEN, Venezuelan Development Corporation, Caracas, Venezuela

AUGUSTO GRIVOT, Internal Revenue Administration, Buenos Aires, Argentina

JORGE MACÓN, National Investment Council, Buenos Aires, Argentina

CARLOS MARTÍNEZ MOLTENI, Secretariat for Finance, Buenos Aires, Argentina

NORMAN D. NOWAK, Regional Commission, Internal Revenue, New York, U.S.A.

OLIVER OLDMAN, International Tax Program, Harvard Law School, Cambridge, Massachusetts, U.S.A.

YAMANDÚ S. PATRÓN, General Inspector of Taxes, Ministry of Finance, Montevideo, Uruguay

NOEL RAMÍREZ, General Revenue Authority, Ministry of Economic Affairs, Managua, Nicaragua

GUSTAVO SERRANO, President of the Chilean Tax Law Institute, Santiago, Chile

JOHN D. STRASMA, Institute of Economics, University of Chile, Santiago, Chile

DAN THROOP SMITH, Harvard University, Cambridge, Massachusetts, U.S.A.

DAVID SANTIAGO TOBÍO, Internal Revenue Authority, Buenos Aires, Argentina

OSVALDO TORRES AHUMADA, Tax Auditor, Santiago, Chile

[2]Mr. Wald was unable to attend the conference. His paper was presented by Mr. Wade F. Gregory.

MARINUS VAN DER MEL, International Bank for Reconstruction and Development, Washington, D.C., U.S.A.

GEORGE W. YOUNG, COMAP, Santiago, Chile

SECRETARIAT

Directors
ALVARO MAGAÑA (OAS)
JAMES LYNN (IDB)
PEDRO MENDIVE (ECLA)

Technical Advisers
MARTO BALLESTEROS
WADE F. GREGORY
GEORGE E. LENT
MILTON C. TAYLOR

Conference Officer
JUANA EYZAGUIRRE OVALLE

INDEX

A

Act of Bogotá, 95, 411

Agriculture: and institutes for the regulation of supplies of foodstuffs, 17; and economic objections to personal income taxes, 176; equipment exempt from customs duties, 299; and sectoral transfer of resources, 336, 337
———reform and development, 33, 115, 326–58; and distribution of income, 21; and productivity, 357
———taxation, 66, 74–77, 91, 92, 97–98, 99, 101, 103–6 *passim;* and indirect tax policy, 12, 13; of land, 59, 60, 337–41, 440–41; of capital gains, 118; reform of, 326–58; dynamic aspects of, 335; present practices, 327–29; methods of, 330–32; special incentives by, 333–35; of water usage, 341, 342, 350, 351, 356; and stability of the sector, 352; discussed in Final Report of the Conference, 405, 421–22

Argentina, 98; inflation in, 97; growth of output, capital formation, and public expenditures in, 1950–59, t141; financing capital formation in, 1950–59, t142; subsidies for railways, 144; public expenditures on education, literacy, health, and defense, t145, 146
———taxation: sales taxes on exports, 52; of income, t56, 58, t238, t239, 240, 242; of individuals, 57; survey of incentives, t89, t90, 334; of agriculture, 92; tax burden on provinces, t92; of customs, t92, t294, 300; incidence of indirect, t93; of net wealth, 206; of inheritances, 215; burdens of, t278, t281, t289
———government revenues: ratios to net national income, 49; sources of, t50; from import sector, 53; from commodity taxation, t54; percentages of net national income, 1959, t279

Automobile taxation, 112, 113, 122, 124

Autonomous and semi-autonomous agencies, 4; role in budget preparation, 138

B

Balance of payments, 8, 19, 51, 53, 234, 372, 373

Basic industries, 24

Benini, R., 199, 202

Bolivia: sources of government revenues, t50; public expenditures on education, t145
———taxation: of exports, 52; of commodities, t54; coverage of income, t56; revenues from income, t238; of corporation income, t239; burdens of, t289; incidence of customs duties, t295; and foreign trade, 300; of tin exports, 301

Brazil: current expenditure, 50; compulsory savings, 85; inflation, 97; exchange profits, 121; per capita income, 137; capital formation, 1950–59, t141, t142; subsidies for railways, 144; public expenditures on education, literacy, health, and defense, t145
———taxation: of exports and imports, 52, t92, t295, 300; of commodities, t54; of income, 56, 61, t238, t239, 242, 243; and exemption coefficient, 57; of agriculture, 60; of capital gains, 164, 252; of business enterprises, 261–62; burdens of, t278, t281, t289; and special-incentive measures, 334
———government revenues: ratios to net national income, t49; from import sector, 53; from commodity taxation, t54; in percentages of net national income, 1959, t279

British Guiana: compulsory savings, 85; progressive taxation, 107

Budget preparation, 138–39

Business enterprises: net wealth taxation of, 208–10, 220; taxation of net assets of, 217

C

Capital, 18; and public expenditure and financing, 1950–59, t141–t142; movements between Latin American countries of, 241; incentives to formation of, 256–57
———taxation, 43–46, 57, 79–82, 95, 106, 113–20, 121, 124–27, 130–34 *passim,* 184–85, 196, 432, 438–39; and personal income taxation, 164–65; and net wealth taxation, 203; of transfers of assets, 210–11, 227

Central American Agreement on the Equalization of Import Duties, 379, 384

Tax policy, 9–14 *passim,* 62, 110–11, 122; and objectives of fiscal policy, 7; and reform, 32, 80–81, 127–29, 403; and objectives of economic development, 276–83, 309–12, 326–58, 426–27; and other government policies, 446–47

Taxation: investment and progressive scale of, 23, 24; differentiation of, 36; and pre-existing structures, 41; revenues versus incentives in, 44–45; equity in, 45–46; and fiscal capacity, 47–48, 57, 58, 60; problem of evasion, 58, 59, 61, 68, 111, 214; distribution of burdens of, 67, t94, 129, t278, t281–82, t289; determination of potentials of, 71, 72; and the subsistence sector, 74; schedular system of, 79; and public expenditures, 88; and inflation, 90–91; flexibility of the Chilean system, 91; regional problems of, 94; of pure economic rent, 98–99; planning of, 111; purpose of contended, 122; and fluctuations of foreign trade, 127–28; to maximize the restrictive effect on demand per peso of tax collected, 128; global versus schedular, 162–64; scheme for social distribution of tax instruments, 231, t233; and national product, 277; direct versus indirect, 280, 311; and the problem of havens, 361–62, 387; double within a customs union, 363–64; and the common market, 368–78; recommendations of technical assistance missions on, 425–50 *passim;* municipal and departmental, 443–44; and technical assistance, 444–50; changing approaches to analysis, 445–46. *For taxes see specific citations.*

————exemptions and other incentive measures, 10, 11, 66, 70, 89–90, 96, 99, 100, 104, 108, 435; revenue yields versus, 43–45, 62; and fiscal policy, 64, 65; survey of, t89–t90; and capital gains taxation, 117; and personal income taxation, 158, 167–68, 170, 174; and agricultural development, 333–35; and industrial development, 385; Final Report of Conference on, 427

Tegucigalpa, Treaty of, 381

Transactions taxation, 12, 32, 54–56, 71–79, 221–22, 227, 274, 275, 441, 442

Transportation services, 16, 143, 144

U

United Nations Charter: provisions for economic and social development, 305

Uruguay: corporate income taxation, t239; undistributed profits taxation, 244; average incidence of customs duties, t298, 300

V

Value added taxation, 101–9 *passim,* 410; Final Report of the Conference on, 403, 420

Venezuela: distribution of income, 22, 34; government revenues and net national income, t49, t279; current expenditure, 50; royalties from petroleum exports, 52; revenues from the import sector, 53; growth of output, capital formation, and public expenditures, 1950–59, t141; financing capital formation, 1950–59, t142; public expenditures on education, literacy, health, and defense, t145

————taxation: of imports and exports, t92, t299, 300; of income, t56, 237, 238, t239, 254, 256; burdens of, t278, 282, t289; agricultural, 329; of hydrocarbon production, 252, 253

W

Wages: and policies for redistribution of income, 21, 33, 183, 313, 314